Acclamation for *Modern Orth*

This book is destined for success, a success based on three merits: expertise, critique, and compassion. The author's knowledge of Orthodox theology and its history is encyclopedic. He successfully navigates the reader between the Scylla of naive eulogy and the Charybdis of damning criticism. He loves the tradition that he describes so well, yet he does not hesitate to offer balanced judgement and critique. A book for those seeking an informed and serious conversation about modern Orthodox Christianity.

Cyril Hovorun (Professor of Theology, Loyola Marymount University, Los Angeles)

This is a veritable guidebook of contemporary Orthodox thought, revealing the dynamism, richness, and diversity of modern Orthodoxy. Highly recommended.

Paul Meyendorff (Professor Emeritus, St Vladimir's Orthodox Theological Seminary, New York)

With the rare ability to combine encyclopedic attention to historical detail with incisive theological analysis, Paul Ladouceur has produced the most comprehensive account of modern Orthodox theology. Reaching as far back as the Council of Ferrara-Florence, he provides a thorough account of the most important theologians and themes that have shape the development of Orthodox theology. Given that books on modern Christian theology often simply ignore Orthodoxy, he fills a much needed gap that will be useful to both students and scholars of theology, while also disabusing the notion that Orthodoxy never encountered modernity.

Aristotle Papanikolaou (Co-founding Director and Professor, Orthodox Christian Studies Center, Fordham University, New York)

Paul Ladouceur's *Modern Orthodox Theology* is a magnificent book on the theological achievements of Orthodox theologians of the last two centuries. The author has mastered an enormous bibliography, carefully presenting and analyzing complex material both chronologically and thematically, with superb concluding remarks. In its titanic effort to contextualize the rich tradition of the Eastern Christian thought and to meet the challenges of modernity, this is the best in-depth study of modern Orthodox theology that we will have for a very long time.

Petros Vassiliadis (Professor Emeritus, Department of Theology, Aristotle University of Thessaloniki)

Modern Orthodox Theology

Modern Orthodox Theology

Behold, I Make All Things New (Rev 21:5)

Paul Ladouceur

Preface by Andrew Louth

t&tclark
LONDON • NEW YORK • OXFORD • NEW DELHI • SYDNEY

T&T CLARK
Bloomsbury Publishing Plc
50 Bedford Square, London, WC1B 3DP, UK
1385 Broadway, New York, NY 10018, USA

BLOOMSBURY, T&T CLARK and the T&T Clark logo are trademarks of
Bloomsbury Publishing Plc

First published in Great Britain 2019

Cover design: Nick Evans
Cover image: St John the Theologian and St Prochorus at Patmos (Novgorod, Russia, 17th c.) /
Nizhny Novgorod State Art Museum

A catalogue record for this book is available from the British Library.

A catalog record for this book is available from the Library of Congress.

ISBN: HB: 978-0-5676-6481-5
PB: 978-0-5676-6482-2
ePDF: 978-0-5676-6483-9
ePUB: 978-0-5676-6484-6

Typeset by Deanta Global Publishing Services, Chennai, India
Printed and bound in Great Britain

For my loving parents,
Jacqueline Cloutier and Léopold Ladouceur
Memory eternal!

Contents

Preface

Interest in Orthodoxy shows little sign of decreasing: but what is Orthodoxy? There is (now, at least) no lack of introductions, the most durable being the two books by Metropolitan Kallistos (Ware), *The Orthodox Church* (1963; new editions 1993 and 2015) and *The Orthodox Way* (1979, revised 1993), the former more historical and doctrinal, the latter introducing Orthodoxy as a way of life (as the title suggests). There are more recent (and indeed many older) books on Orthodoxy, both single-authored monographs and multi-authored works (encyclopaedias, companions, handbooks, symposia, etc.). There is even a massive work, *Orthodox Christianity* (2011–16), by Metropolitan Hilarion Alfeyev, the four volumes of the English translation running to well over 2,000 pages.

Where does Dr Paul Ladouceur's book fit amongst this abundance of works? It is unique in several ways. First of all, it is concerned with modern Orthodox theology and, though well aware of the historical background, Dr Ladouceur does not let himself, or his reader, get lost in the myriad detail of historical events. Secondly, he is conscious that Orthodoxy does not just come from the East, but regions in the East with different histories and traditions. Thirdly – and this is the concern of more than half of the book – he explores the theological themes that have dominated Orthodox theology in the last century and a half, and advancing into the present. So we have, to begin with, a concise account, not however lacking in detail, of engagement between Orthodoxy and the West up to the mid-nineteenth century. Dr Ladouceur's account of Orthodox theology itself, as encountered in the West, begins by recognizing it as the convergence of various traditions of theology, mostly national, which, though confessing a common Orthodoxy, developed in different historical circumstances.

Russia, inevitably, given the immense influence of the Russian emigration of the twentieth century in the wake of the Bolshevik revolution, takes pride of place, but Greece and Romania are well covered, too (not, however, Serbia, with its own distinctive tradition, that has strong links both with Russia and with Greece). Paul Ladouceur then turns to discuss the various themes that have dominated modern Orthodox theology: God and Creation; Christ and Godmanhood; the Church; Ecumenism (both Christian, and also globally); what he calls, following St Maria of Paris, on whom he has written much, and illuminatingly, the 'Christification of Life'; its entailment, social and political theology; the 'Name of God' controversy; the question of the ministry of women and their ordination. He ends with a panorama of modern Orthodox theology, singling out threads that run through all the tapestries that constitute his theological themes.

What is distinctive about Dr Ladouceur's approach? First, his extensive and even-handed learning. Too many discussions of themes in modern Orthodox theology are concerned to argue a case, to be themselves part of the on-going intellectual adventure that modern Orthodox theology is. Dr Ladouceur seems to have read everything in English and French (or available in translation into these languages), but his concern is to present the various voices of these conversations/arguments/(often alas) noisy confrontations, not to advance his own point of view. Indeed, often enough, Dr Ladouceur is so self-effacing that one would be hard put to say what his own view is. He is a supreme and supremely successful interpreter, happy to leave the conclusion to the intelligence of his reader. This is, it seems to me, quite rare in Orthodox theology (or indeed, in theology in general).

So much in general terms. Any study of modern Orthodox theology is bound to be concerned by (if not haunted by) the fundamental division among the inheritors of the Russian nineteenth-century theological and philosophical tradition: the division between those who saw themselves as continuing, in a new context and with fresh insights, the religious and philosophical concerns that dominated much Russian Orthodox thought in the nineteenth century, stemming from the Slavophiles and culminating in Vladimir Solov'ev and his successors, helpfully dubbed by Nicolas Zernov the 'Russian religious renaissance', and those critical of this heritage (though, often enough, still deeply in hock to many of its fundamental perceptions), who proposed a new approach, more directly based on the Fathers of the Church, sometimes called the 'neopatristic synthesis' – a division exemplified by Pavel Florensky and Sergii Bulgakov, on the one hand, and Georges Florovsky and Vladimir Lossky, on the other. This division runs through Dr Ladouceur's treatment of theological themes in the second part of the book. Dr Ladouceur's treatment of this division is nuanced, without actually calling the division in question (as some would want to). He is well aware of the extent to which representatives of these traditions often shared more than they were prepared to acknowledge, and indeed he makes clear that the basis for a neopatristic synthesis, namely, ready access to the patristic texts, was already well advanced by the end of the nineteenth century in Russia, and that furtherance of this access in the twentieth century owed far more to developments in Roman Catholic theology than to Orthodox scholars themselves. The notion of the neopatristic synthesis as the future for Orthodox theology was very much the fruit of Florovsky's analysis of the history of Russian theology. Dr Ladouceur's book benefits from the work he has done, together with Dr Brandon Gallaher, in providing greater access to Florovsky's most important writings, including fresh translations of works already known and publication of works hitherto unavailable in English.[1]

Furthermore, Dr Ladouceur explores the history and ramifications of this fundamental divide much more deeply than anyone else. He discusses, too, those who are critical of any talk of the 'neopatristic' as being backward-looking and constituting a hindrance to the Orthodox Church's ability to face the problems posed by the challenges of the modern world: challenges both from twentieth-century intellectual developments in philosophy and other disciplines and from the way modern Western society has evolved, which cannot be brushed off as alien influences from the West. He also draws into the discussion those critical of any attempt to abandon (as they see it) the

[1]Brandon Gallaher and Paul Ladouceur, eds., *The Patristic Witness of Georges Florovsky: Essential Theological Writings* (London: T&T Clark, 2019).

tradition of the Fathers, many of whom have found the opportunity to articulate their concerns after the collapse of the Communist yoke in Eastern Europe (Russia, Romania, not to mention Greece and Serbia). This tension has only intensified in the twenty-first century. Dr Ladouceur's attempt to give voice to all these different views, with their potential for deepening already damaging divisions, and draw them into some kind of dialogue is important both for understanding the state of modern Orthodox theology and also (more fundamentally) for the future of Orthodox theology itself (which sometimes seems in danger of being consumed in self-destructive controversy).

One conviction that comes through with rare power is Dr Ladouceur's unwavering certitude that we are beholding in modern Orthodox theology, not the dying whimpers of an outdated tradition, but the movement of the Holy Spirit, who 'makes all things new'. For this, as well as for his learning and insight, we owe Paul Ladouceur an enormous debt.

Andrew Louth
Commemoration of the Fathers
of the Fourth Ecumenical Council, 2018

Foreword and Acknowledgements

Charting Modern Orthodox Theology

Orthodox theology since the mid-nineteenth century has witnessed a flowering such as had not been seen in many centuries previously, certainly not since the era of St Gregory Palamas in the fourteenth century. This study is a guidebook to the principal features of Orthodox theology in modern times, with an emphasis on broad movements or approaches to theology and on the principal issues which have preoccupied Orthodox theologians over the last century and half.

Although the focus of this study is the period from the mid-nineteenth century to the early twenty-first century, the first chapter is an overview of the main themes of Christian theology to the fall of Constantinople to the Turks in 1453. Chapter 2 sets the scene more particularly by examining Orthodox theology in the long centuries following the fall of Constantinople, a major crossroads in Christian history. The subsequent four centuries were a difficult period in Orthodox theology. Like the early Middle Ages of Western European history (fifth to tenth centuries, previously often called the 'Dark Ages'), intellectual pursuits during these centuries, while not entirely absent, were decidedly muted and often lacking in originality. Mere survival in often hostile circumstances, whether under the Arab and Ottoman yokes in the Middle East, or in a Russia emerging from Mogul domination, was the order of the day for fragile Orthodox communities. Orthodox theology consisted in large part of preserving the past, mostly in the absence of printing and of institutions of higher learning, and defending Orthodoxy not only against non-Christian invaders and rulers, but also against ecclesial, philosophical, theological and political influences from Christian Western Europe. In the process, important elements of Orthodox thought faded from memory or took on Western flavours, under what is sometimes characterized as the 'Western captivity' and even the 'Babylonian captivity' of Orthodox thought.[1]

Modern Orthodox theology may be studied from three broad perspectives, with corresponding objectives. A historical perspective seeks to establish a chronological framework within which

[1]These expressions are associated in particular with Georges Florovsky, Christos Yannaras and John Zizioulas. Florovsky more typically referred to the *pseudomorphosis* of Orthodox theology under Western influence (see Ch. 1, 17 and 26; and Ch. 5, 96–7). Florovsky writes of the ecclesial reforms of Peter the Great as inaugurating a 'Protestant pseudomorphosis in the life of the church', thus inaugurating a 'Babylonian captivity' of the Russian Church (Georges Florovsky, *The Ways of Russian Theology*, vol. I (Belmont, MA: Nordland, 1979), 121). See also his 'Western Influences in Russian Theology' (1937) in Brandon Gallaher and Paul Ladouceur, eds., *The Patristic Witness of Georges Florovsky: Essential Theological Writings* (London: T&T Clark, 2019), 129–51. Also Christos Yannaras, *Against Religion: The Alienation of the Ecclesial Event* (Brookline, MA: Holy Cross Orthodox Press, 2013), 197; and John Zizioulas, *Being as Communion: Studies in Priesthood and the Church* (Crestwood, NY: St Vladimir's Seminary Press, 1987), 20.

modern Orthodox theology evolved – a study of the principal moments or events in modern Orthodox theology, their causes, linkages, interactions and consequences. A biographical approach highlights the role of leading personalities and authors, their lives, writings and thinking. Finally, a thematic perspective focuses on the study of the principal issues or themes in modern Orthodox theology, especially those which have been addressed by a number of authors, seeking to identify commonalities and differences among various theologians and to trace the evolution of thinking on key issues.

In practice, these three perspectives intermingle and indeed, while each is valuable in its own right, together they constitute a powerful instrument to examine complex historical, personal and intellectual movements. In this study, we employ all three approaches: the first part is predominantly historical, to some extent biographical, while the second part is eminently thematic, constituting case studies in modern Orthodox theology. While each part could stand on its own, they are complementary. Part I provides a historical and conceptual framework examining the ebb and flow of modern Orthodox thought, highlighting especially different approaches to the great Christian mysteries in the context of the immense challenges facing Orthodoxy in the modern era: wars and revolutions; the rise of secular modes of thought, especially the Enlightenment and its aftermath; the development of modern science and technology; the appeal of atheistic and revolutionary philosophies; the migrations of peoples; the emergence of nationalism and the nation-state; and the establishment of modern social, economic and political systems. Part II examines in more detail key issues or themes which have dominated modern Orthodox thought. While the selection of the themes is necessarily personal, we have sought to emphasize those which are marked both by conflicting ideas and by continuity and evolution – 'breaks and links', to adopt Georges Florovsky's expression.[2] In fact, throughout the book we emphasize the 'links' among different approaches and periods in modern Orthodox thought, where others may hold the 'breaks' in a more prominent view. Part III contains assessments and conclusions arising from both Parts I and II and discusses directions and issues in Orthodox theology at the beginning of the twenty-first century.

An important underlying theme running through Orthodox thinking from the Russian Slavophiles of the mid-nineteenth onwards is the restoration or emergence of properly Orthodox thought, gradually freeing itself from the accumulation of the dust of ages and non-Orthodox influences. This agenda became increasingly urgent as Orthodox lands in parts of the Ottoman Empire became free from foreign domination, only to be faced with the new challenges of modernity in all its forms. If at first Orthodoxy appeared ill-equipped to deal with these challenges, it soon demonstrated that it could rise to the occasion, and respond, if not completely or satisfactorily, to the modern world into which it was increasingly thrust. Certain foundations preserved during the long centuries after the fall of Constantinople to the Turks made this possible. Most significant of these was the continuity of the Orthodox liturgical and spiritual traditions, marked dramatically by the publication of the *Philokalia*, a collection of major ascetic

[2]'Breaks and Links' (*Razryvy i sviazi*) is the title of the concluding chapter of Florovsky's *The Ways of Russian Theology* (1937). Translation in Gallaher and Ladouceur, eds., *The Patristic Witness of Georges Florovsky*, 159–83.

texts, first published in Greek in 1782 and subsequently in Slavonic (1793) and in Russian (1877).[3] The *Philokalia* can be considered an Orthodox counterpoint to Denis Diderot's famous *Encyclopédie* published between 1751 and 1772,[4] or alternatively as an Orthodox rejoinder to Emmanuel Kant's *Critique of Pure Reason* published in 1781,[5] the year before the *Philokalia*. Standing against both of these major manifestations of the Enlightenment adulation of reason as the supreme human quality and virtue, the *Philokalia* affirms the primacy of faith and the need for asceticism as an essential element to achieve union with God, or *theosis*, as the true fulfilment of human existence. Despite this powerful affirmation of the Orthodox tradition, more than a half-century would pass after the publication of the *Philokalia* before Orthodox theological reflection began to develop in an original form among a small group of cultivated Russian believers, the Slavophiles.

It has proven impossible to cover all aspects of modern Orthodox theology in the scope of one book. Thus in geographic terms, the book focuses mainly on theology in Greece, Romania, Russia and Orthodox theologians in Western Europe and North America. Very little is said of theology in other countries of Orthodox tradition, such as Bulgaria, Georgia and Serbia, or of theology in the Oriental or non-Chalcedonian Orthodox churches. The selection of issues included in Part II of the book is also necessarily limited. We have nonetheless sought to include the most important theological questions in Orthodoxy over the past century and half, especially those on which there have been and in many cases continue to be divergent and conflicting views. While wishing to present accurately conflicting theologies, in most cases we advance our own conclusions on the issues at stake. Many other questions could have been covered, such as the theology of icons, of the environment, and questions of bioethics, but by and large there has been more cohesion of Orthodox thought, and hence less overt conflict, in these areas than those included in this book.

We have sought to highlight and cite key passages of writings by leading theologians to present the various movements and themes of modern Orthodox thought. These constitute the primary sources for our study. There are, of course, many excellent studies by both Orthodox and non-Orthodox scholars relevant to the period under consideration, but we minimize our references to these, without in any way questioning their value, especially for the study of individual theologians and particular issues. Important studies are noted in the Selected Bibliography for each chapter.

---

[3]The most complete English translation is by G. E. H. Palmer, Philip Sherrard and Kallistos Ware: *The Philokalia: The Complete Text Compiled by St Nikodimos of the Holy Mountain and St Makarios of Corinth*, 4 volumes (London: Faber and Faber, 1979–95) (fifth and final volume forthcoming).

[4]Denis Diderot and Jean le Rond d'Alembert (until 1759), eds., *Encyclopédie, ou dictionnaire raisonné des sciences, des arts et des métiers* (Encyclopaedia, or a Systematic Dictionary of the Sciences, Arts, and Crafts) (Paris: 1751–72). The *Encyclopédie*, the first to include contributions from many authors, aimed to incorporate all world knowledge into one publication, weaning learning away from the control of the Catholic Church. The *Encyclopédie* became a symbol of the secular learning and thought of the Enlightenment.

[5]Emmanuel Kant's *Kritik der reinen Vernunft* (Critique of Pure Reason) (1781) is one of the most influential works of modern philosophy.

At the same time, we draw frequently on general studies of Orthodox thinking by leading Orthodox personalities of the very movements in which they actively participated. These studies include notably Georges Florovsky's *The Ways of Russian Theology* (1937), Nicolas Berdyaev's *The Russian Idea* (1946), the histories of Russian philosophy by Vasily (Basil) Zenkovsky (1950) and by Nicolas Lossky (1952), Nicolas Zernov's *The Russian Religious Renaissance* (1963), *Le Christ dans la pensée russe* (Christ in Russian Thought) (1970) by Paul Evdokimov and *Orthodoxy and the West* (1992) by Christos Yannaras.[6] These are more than academic studies; they are personal statements by important and astute thinkers and observers in the development of modern Orthodox theology and are thereby invaluable signposts and testimonials by key participants in the very subject of this book.

Earlier versions of portions of several chapters were published as follows: 'The Name-of-God Conflict in Orthodox Theology', *St Vladimir's Theological Quarterly* 56, no. 4 (2012), 415–436; 'Treasures New and Old: Landmarks of Orthodox Neopatristic Theology', *St Vladimir's Theological Quarterly* 56, no. 2 (2012), 191–228; 'Two Orthodox Visions of Ecumenism: Sergei Bulgakov and Georges Florovsky', *Ecumenism* no. 192–193 (2015), 35–39; Review of Lawrence Farley, *Feminism and Tradition: Quiet Reflections on Ordination and Communion* (Yonkers NY: St Vladimir's Seminary Press, 2012), *St Vladimir's Theological Quarterly* 60, no. 3 (2016), 415–421; 'Religious Diversity in Modern Orthodox Thought," in Special Issue of *Religions*: "Inward Being and Outward Identity: The Orthodox Churches in the 21st Century," John Jillions, ed., *Religions*, 8 (5), no. 77 (2017); 'On Ecumenoclasm: Anti-Ecumenism in Orthodox Theology', *St Vladimir's Theological Quarterly* 61, no. 3 (2017), 323–355; 'Social and Political Thought in the Russian Religious Renaissance', *Review of Ecumenical Studies* (Sibiu) 10, no. 2 (2018), 141–155; 'Christ, The Fathers and Feminism: Dialogue with Fr Lawrence Farley', *St Vladimir's Theological Quarterly* 62, no. 3 (2018), 287–295.

Acknowledgements

This book grew out of graduate courses on modern Orthodox theology at the Orthodox School of Theology at Trinity College (Toronto School of Theology, University of Toronto), and the Montreal Institute of Orthodox Theology (in affiliation with Université Laval and previously, Université de Sherbrooke, Quebec). Many persons associated with these institutions and others in several countries have contributed directly or indirectly to this book, and I am pleased to acknowledge them here.

[6]Translations: Georges Florovsky, *The Ways of Russian Theology*, in *The Collected Works of Georges Florovsky*, Vols. 5–6 (Belmont, MA: Nordland, 1979); Nicolas Berdyaev, *The Russian Idea* (New York: Macmillan, 1947; Hudson, NY: Lindisfarne Press, 1992; V. V. (Basil) Zenkovsky, *A History of Russian Philosophy* (New York: Colombia University Press, 1953); Nicolas Lossky, *A History of Russian Philosophy* (London: Allen and Unwin, 1952); Nicolas Zernov, *The Russian Religious Renaissance of the Twentieth Century* (New York: Harper & Row, 1963); Paul Evdokimov, *Le Christ dans la pensée russe* (Christ in Russian Thought) (Paris: Le Cerf, 1970; 2011) (no English translation); Christos Yannaras, *Orthodoxy and the West: Hellenic Self-Identity in the Modern Age* (1992) (Brookline, MA: Holy Cross Orthodox Press, 2006).

I am deeply indebted to my friend and colleague Professor Brandon Gallaher (University of Exeter) for our many discussions over the years on a wide range of issues considered in this book. Our collaboration in the preparation of an edition of the major writings of Georges Florovsky[7] proved invaluable not only concerning the contributions of Georges Florovsky to Orthodox thought, but to a better appreciation of the contours of the entire range of Orthodox philosophy and theology in modern times.

I am particularly grateful to Maria Simakova (Trinity College, University of Toronto), who readily applied her profound knowledge of Orthodoxy, especially Russian theology, and her finely tuned academic skills to reviewing many chapters. Her inspired reading of the manuscript greatly assisted in articulating balanced presentations and more nuanced assessments on numerous issues.

Dr Athanasios Giocas (Montreal Institute of Orthodox Theology) also brought a keen mind and broad intellectual culture to bear on a number of chapters, contributing to a sharpening of the analysis and the precision of conclusions.

A number of leading scholars of Orthodox theology provided valuable comments on individual chapters, bringing their specialized knowledge to bear on what must remain a general study. These include notably late Fr Matthew Baker (PhD, Fordham University), Fr Radu Bordeianu (Duquesne University), Fr Andrew Louth (Professor Emeritus, Durham University), Lucian Leustean (Aston University), Sotiris Mitralexis (City University, Istanbul), Aristotle Papanikolaou (Fordham University), Teva Regule (Massachusetts Institute of Technology), Norman Russell (St Stephen's House, Oxford) and Lucian Turcescu (Concordia University).

Academic exchanges and discussions over the years with other scholars permitted me to draw on an even wider range of backgrounds and specializations in tracing this portrait of modern Orthodox theology. These include Metropolitan Kallistos Ware (University of Oxford), Fr Andreas Andreopoulos (University of Winchester), Antoine Arjakovsky (Collège des Bernardins), Nikolaos Asproulis (Volos Academy for Theological Studies), Fr Demetrios Bathrellos (University of Cambridge and Hellenic Open University), Fr John Behr (St Vladimir's Orthodox Theological Seminary), Ionut Biliuta (Babeş-Bolyai University), Peter Bouteneff (St Vladimir's Orthodox Theological Seminary), Will Cohen (University of Scranton), Paul Gavrilyuk (University of St Thomas), Edith Humphrey (Pittsburgh Theological Seminary), Fr John Jillions (Orthodox Church in America), Pantelis Kalaitzidis (Volos Academy for Theological Studies), Nikolaos Loudovikos (University Ecclesiastical Academy of Thessaloniki), Paul Meyendorff (St Vladimir's Orthodox Theological Seminary), Alexei Nesteruk (University of Portsmouth), Michael Plekon (City University of New York), Marcus Plested (Marquette University), Michel Stavrou (Institut de théologie orthodoxe Saint-Serge), Elizabeth Theokritoff, Vera Shevzov (Smith College), Gregory Tucker (University of Regensburg), Anca Vasiliu (Centre national de la recherche scientifique) and David Wagschal (Toronto School of Theology).

I have greatly benefited from the friendship and wisdom of my colleagues at the Orthodox School of Theology at Trinity College (University of Toronto): Dean Christopher Brittan and

[7]Gallaher and Ladouceur, eds., *The Patristic Witness of Georges Florovsky*.

former Dean David Neelands; Professor Richard Schneider and Fr Geoffrey Ready; and at the Montreal Institute of Orthodox Theology: Dr John Hadjinicolaou and Dr Athanasios Giocas.

The Faculty of Divinity of Trinity College (University of Toronto) extended financial support for the research and writing of this book. I also acknowledge the assistance of the libraries of the University of Toronto (especially the John P. Robarts Research Library, the John W. Graham Library of Trinity College and the John M. Kelly Library of St Michael's College).

I wish to thank Milutin and Peter Drobac, and Bojana, Luc and Emilja Lafond for their kind and generous hospitality during my numerous visits to Toronto.

I also thank my dear friend Monique Vallée for her support during the long period of incubation and completion of this book.

Finally, I am grateful for the encouragement of Anna Turton, the eminently supportive and patient Theology Editor at Bloomsbury/T&T Clark, and Sweda R of Deanta Global Publishing Services for the fine copy-editing, typesetting and indexing of this book.

Paul Ladouceur
Rawdon, Quebec, Canada.
Forefeast of the Samaritan Woman, 2018.

1

Prolegomena to Modern Orthodox Theology

Chapter Outline

Overview of Orthodox theology to the fall of Constantinople[1]

The central issue of Christian theology is the reply to Jesus' question to the apostles: 'Who do you say I am?' (Mt. 16.15). The answer to Jesus' question determines the central Christian dogmas, those of Christ and the Trinity. From its very beginnings, Christianity encountered the highly developed culture of Hellenism, the dominant intellectual and cultural feature of the Roman Empire, derived basically from ancient Greek culture and thought, especially philosophy. This encounter is present in the New Testament, for example, in Pilate's response to Jesus in the form of a philosophical question: 'What is truth?' (Jn 18.38). Jesus does not answer Pilate, but he had answered the question experientially in his exchange with Thomas at the Last Supper: 'I am the Way and the Truth and the Life' (Jn 14.6). Truth in Christianity is not a coherent series of abstract axioms, but a Person. We also see the tension in the Christian encounter with Greek thought in St Paul's famous contrast between the 'wisdom of this world' and the 'wisdom of God' manifested in the 'foolishness' of the Cross, Christ crucified as 'the power of God and the wisdom of God' (1 Cor 1.18-25). The flip side of the coin is Paul's preaching to the Athenians in the Acts – clearly Paul is addressing an educated audience and his message is formulated accordingly, in more abstract and philosophical terms than his preaching to other audiences (Acts 17.22-33).

[1]For general references to the history of Eastern Christian theology to the fourteenth century, see the Selected Bibliography for this chapter.

The encounter of the two messages concerning human existence, that of the Gospel, founded on divine revelation culminating in Jesus Christ, and that of Hellenistic philosophy, based on human reasoning, lies at the origin of Christian theology. The central concern of the early Fathers of the Church was first and foremost and indeed always to expound and to defend Christ's teaching as conveyed by the apostles (*kerygma*) and the experience of the church. Since some Christians put forward teachings inconsistent with those of the apostles and the experience of the church, it became necessary to elaborate more precisely the full significance of Jesus' teachings, using a language intelligible to the educated classes of antiquity. The earliest theological writings were those of apologists such as St Justin Martyr and St Irenaeus of Lyons (mid- to late second century). Their writings were aimed at defending the faith both against non-Christian, pagan thinkers and against early forms of deviations from the mainstream of Christian thought, especially Manichaeism and the Gnosticism, dualistic philosophies which emphasized the struggle between good and evil, darkness and light, conceived broadly as the spiritual and the material realms.

The intellectual centre of the Roman Empire in these centuries was Alexandria, not Rome. The leading early Christian thinkers of Alexandria were Clement and Origen (late second to mid-third centuries). The other main centre of Christian thought was in Latin North Africa. The earliest Christian Latin writers were all from North Africa: St Cyprian of Carthage, Tertullian and St Augustine of Hippo. The fourth century was perhaps the greatest century of Christian theology, dominated by the necessity to express correctly Christ's relationship with God and consequently that of the Holy Spirit. The fourth century is sometimes, not entirely accurately, called the 'Trinitarian century', because theological debates focused on the Trinity. The denial of Christ's divinity by the Alexandrian priest Arius and his followers triggered the development of theological language, borrowing and adapting terms familiar in Greek philosophy, to express what Christians believed concerning God and Christ. The basic Christian dogma of the Trinity was proclaimed at the First Ecumenical Council of Nicea in 325 and subsequently expanded at the Second Ecumenical Council of Constantinople in 381. The Nicene-Constantinoplean Creed was thus finalized by the end of the fourth century, with the central idea that Christ and the Holy Spirit are consubstantial (*homoousios*) with the Father: three Persons in one God. The theological giants of this period were three Cappadocians, St Basil the Great, St Gregory Nazianzus and St Gregory of Nyssa, together with St Athanasius of Alexandria and St John Chrysostom.

The Trinitarian dogma was a partial answer to Jesus' question 'Who do you say I am?' While most Christians accepted that Christ was God, this left open the question of how Christ could be divine and human at the same time. The fifth century is sometimes referred to as the 'Christological century', because theology focused on Christ's divinity and humanity. The basic elements of Christology were put in place at the Third Ecumenical Council in Ephesus in 431 and further refined at the Fourth Ecumenical Council in Chalcedon in 451. Chalcedonian Christology hinges on the distinction between nature and person: Christ has two natures (*physeis* or *ousia*), divine and human, in one Person (*hypostasis*), the Logos, the Son of God, the second Person of the Holy Trinity. The leading theological figure of this period was St Cyril of Alexandria.

But linguistic, cultural, social and personal factors resulted in a major split in the Christian community in the fifth century, between those who accepted Chalcedonian Christology, overwhelmingly Greek- and Latin-speaking Christians, and those who refused it, mainly non-Greeks, Semitic Christians, Copts, Syrians and Armenians. The Fifth Ecumenical Council in 553 and the Sixth Ecumenical Council in 680 dealt with challenges to the Chalcedonian dogma, as emperors and patriarchs sought to elaborate Christological definitions which would bring together the Byzantine Empire, deeply divided between Chalcedonians and non-Chalcedonians. These Councils basically re-affirmed the Chalcedonian dogma, while rejecting attempts to modify it by saying that Christ has only one will (monothelitism) or one energy (monoenergism). The principal theologians of these centuries were St John of Damascus and St Maximus the Confessor.

The Seventh Ecumenical Council in 787 dealt with the veneration of icons, in the face of the iconoclastic movement, which sought to deny the appropriateness of representations of Christ, thus challenging, in the eyes of the defenders of icons, the reality of the Incarnation, the human nature of Christ. This issue dragged on after the Seventh Ecumenical Council and was only definitively resolved in 842, with the final restoration of icons.

The last great period of Byzantine theology was during the fourteenth century, dominated by St Gregory Palamas. The fourteenth-century quarrel over hesychasm revolved around the possibility of knowing and experiencing God. This quarrel pitted the monks of Mount Athos, led by Palamas, against rationalist or scholastic theologians, some educated in Western Europe, who argued that it was impossible for humans to know or experience God because God is unknowable in his essence, and that therefore experience of God could only be indirect, or mediated by created substances or grace. The principal dogmatic outcome of the quarrel was a clarification of the ancient distinction between God's essence or nature and his energies. The divine essence is indeed beyond comprehension by all creatures, while God acts and makes himself known in creation by his divine energies. The divine energies are also God, not a created intermediary between God and creation, including humans. Local councils in Constantinople between 1341 and 1351 confirmed the essence-energies distinction and that created beings participate in God through God's energies, while the divine essence remains unknowable. This is the basis of the Orthodox understanding of the doctrine of *theosis* (deification or divinization).

By the time of Gregory Palamas, the Byzantine Empire was already considerably weakened, as a result of Latin domination during the half-century after the sack of Constantinople in 1204 by the Fourth Crusade and the installation of a Latin imperial regime, and of the steady inroads into Byzantine territory by Islamic Arabs and Turks. Syria and Palestine passed to Arab rule between 634 and 641, Egypt between 639 and 641 and North Africa between 670 and 708. The Turks steadily expanded their territory from Persia through Asia Minor at the expense of the Byzantines over a period of centuries, reaching the Sea of Marmara on the doorsteps of Constantinople in 1308 and Trace in 1321. Greece and most of the rest of Balkans fell to the Turks in subsequent decades. By the early fifteenth century, little remained of the Byzantine Empire other than Constantinople itself and few pockets of territory here and there in Greece and the Mediterranean islands. The Byzantine Empire was on its knees. Even the last-minute attempt to rally assistance from the Latin West following a negotiated union of the Orthodox and Catholic churches at the Council of Ferrara-Florence in 1439 failed, as the Orthodox repudiated the terms of union with the Catholic Church, and no help from the West was forthcoming. Constantinople fell to the Turks on 29 May 1453. The Turks subsequently continued to expand their rule to include the Orthodox lands of present-day Bulgaria, Serbia, Macedonia and Romania.

Although the Russian Slavophiles of the mid-nineteenth century mark the true beginning of modern Orthodox theology, their thinking must be seen in the light of Orthodox theology in the preceding centuries. The fall of Constantinople in 1453 ushered in an entirely new era in Orthodoxy and it is at this point that we begin our study of modern Orthodox theology.

Part I

Modern Orthodox Thought in Historical Perspective

2

Theological Encounters with the West: Orthodox Theology from the Fifteenth Century to the Nineteenth Century

Chapter Outline

The Council of Ferrara-Florence and the fall of Constantinople

The fourteenth century marked the last great period of Orthodox theology until modern times. After the fall of Constantinople in 1453, much of the Orthodox world, with the exception of Russia, then still emerging from a century and a half of Mongol domination, was under Muslim rule and the Orthodox Church and faithful were hard pressed to survive under rulers who tolerated the presence of non-Muslims in their lands, but with severe restrictions, pressure to convert to Islam and not infrequent persecution. In these circumstances, theology was relegated to a secondary role in Orthodox communities and energies were devoted to ensuring the survival of the faith in a generally hostile environment.

Much of Orthodox theology from the fourteenth century onwards was stimulated by Western initiatives or influences. Even St Gregory Palamas (1296–1359) elaborated his theology of the divine energies in reaction to challenges from Renaissance humanism, influential in Constantinople at the time, and represented especially by the Calabrian monk Barlaam. Barlaam challenged the validity of the experience of divine light asserted by the hesychasts of Mount Athos by expounding a doctrine to the effect that it is not possible for humans to have a direct experience of God, since God is utterly transcendent in his nature to creation, including humanity. This led Palamas to draw on and to develop the ancient patristic distinction between the divine essence, which remains unknowable by creatures, and the divine energies, by which God makes himself known in creation and in which humans are called to participate. Palamas exposed his theology primarily in a series of writings called the *Triads in Defence of the Holy Hesychasts.*[1] He also played the lead role in the preparation of the 'Declaration of the Holy Mountain in Defence of Those who Devoutly Practise a Life of Stillness', also called the *Hagioretic Tome*, a statement supporting Palamas's theology issued in 1341 by the superiors and principal monks of the monasteries of Mount Athos.[2] The Palamite theology of the divine energies was approved in several councils of the Church of Constantinople between 1341 and 1351, which condemned Palamas's opponents as heretics.[3] Palamas also wrote a short *Confession of the Orthodox Faith*, an expanded version of the Nicene Creed which emphasizes relations among the Persons of the Holy Trinity, especially the procession of the Holy Spirit from the Father, and the major doctrinal pronouncements of the seven ecumenical councils, while rejecting the teachings of Barlaam.[4]

The other major Orthodox writer of the period was St Nicholas Cabasilas (c. 1319/1323–92), a lay disciple of Gregory Palamas. Cabasilas was an important figure in late fourteenth-century Byzantine politics, but he is known primarily for his religious writings. His *Commentary on the Divine Liturgy* can be considered as initiating liturgical theology, and his work *The Life in Christ*, a spiritual treatise based on the principal sacraments as the means of sanctification, is a classic

---

[1]Gregory Palamas's main works have been edited and translated by John Meyendorff: Jean Meyendorff, *Grégoire Palamas, Défense des saints hésychastes* (2 vols.) (Louvain: Spicilegium sacrum lovaniense, 1959). Partial English translation: Gregory Palamas, *The Triads* (Mahwah, NJ: Paulist Press, 1983). For studies of Palamas, see especially Jean Meyendorff, *Introduction à l'étude de Grégoire Palamas* (Paris: Seuil, 1959). The English translation is incomplete: John Meyendorff, *A Study of Gregory Palamas* (London: Faith Press, 1964; Crestwood, NY: St Vladimir's Seminary Press, 1974). See also Meyendorff's *St Gregory Palamas and Orthodox Spirituality* (1965) (Crestwood, NY: St Vladimir's Seminary Press, 1974; 1998).

[2]In G. E. H. Palmer, Philip Sherrard and Kallistos Ware, eds. and trans., *The Philokalia: The Complete Text Compiled by St Nikodimos of the Holy Mountain and St Makarios of Corinth*, vol. IV (London: Faber and Faber, 1995), 418–25.

[3]See *Synodical Tome of 1341* and *Synodical Tome of 1351*, in Jaroslav Pelikan and Valerie Hotchkiss, eds., *Creeds and Confessions of Faith in the Christian Tradition* (4 vols), vol. I (New Haven, CT: Yale University Press, 2003), 320–74.

[4]Gregory Palamas, *Confession of the Orthodox Faith*, in Pelikan and Hotchkiss, *Creeds and Confessions*, I:375–8.

of Orthodox spirituality.[5] Among his other writings are a number of sermons and several philosophical, legal and political texts.

Fifteenth-century Orthodox theology was marked by a major event, the Council of Ferrara-Florence (1438–9),[6] held as a last-minute attempt by the Byzantine Emperor John VIII Palaiologos (reigned 1425–48) to rally the support of the West against the inexorable advance of the Turks. By then the Turks already controlled much of what had been the Byzantine Empire, including all of Asia Minor; for all practical purposes, by the late 1430s, only the city of Constantinople itself remained in Greek hands. The motivation for the council was thus largely political, not theological or ecclesiastical: the Byzantines knew that the re-establishment of union between the Eastern and the Western churches was essential if there was to be any hope of Western support against the Turks.

The Council was held initially in the Italian city of Ferrara, then displaced to Florence, and was attended by the emperor, the patriarch of Constantinople and representatives of the patriarchs of Alexandria, Antioch and Jerusalem, and a large number of bishops and other clergy. There were four issues on the table: the Filioque, the Western doctrine of purgatory, the use of azymes for the Eucharist and papal claims to supreme authority in the church. After prolonged discussions, an agreement was reached in July 1439 and signed by all the Orthodox bishops present at the Council except one – Mark Eugenicus (1392–1445), archbishop of Ephesus. Mark was canonized in 1734 and is considered a champion of Orthodoxy for his resistance to the terms of the union agreement. The union was based on a twofold principle: agreement on doctrinal questions and respect for the rites and traditions of each church. The Orthodox accepted papal claims to universal authority, the Filioque and Roman teaching on purgatory. Even though the actual agreement on these points was somewhat vague, it appeared to the mass of the strongly anti-unionist lower clergy and Orthodox faithful that the emperor and the hierarchs had betrayed the Orthodox cause for political expediency. Concerning the Eucharist, it was agreed that the Orthodox could continue to use leavened bread and the Latins unleavened bread. In modern times, of the questions considered at Ferrara-Florence, the Filioque and the status and authority of the pope remain significant outstanding issues between the Orthodox and the Roman Catholic churches.

The union of Florence was unpopular both in Constantinople and in Russia, the principal Orthodox powers. The Byzantine emperor did not dare to proclaim the union publicly until 1452, thirteen years after the agreement at Florence; by then, many of the bishops who signed the union had retracted their signatures and the Metropolitan of Moscow was deposed on his return to Russia. The union remained a dead letter in the East.

Although the Council of Florence was primarily a political and ecclesial event, it produced some notable theology in the form of the expositions of the Orthodox positions, primarily those of St Mark of Ephesus on the Latin doctrines of the Filioque and purgatory. St Mark was highly regarded by the emperor and in the church both for his holiness and for his learning. He wrote a

---

[5]Nicholas Cabasilas, *A Commentary on the Divine Liturgy* (London: SPCK, 1960; Crestwood, NY: St Vladimir's Seminary Press, 1960); *The Life in Christ* (Crestwood, NY: St Vladimir's Seminary Press, 1974).

[6]The Greeks participated in the 'union council' from April 1438 to July 1439, but the council continued its deliberations on matters pertaining to the Catholic Church until 1445.

large number of theological works on a wide range of subjects, but is most known for his involvement in the Council of Florence, where he was the principal Greek spokesman. Mark of Ephesus occupies an ambiguous place in the history of Christianity: for the Orthodox, he is a saint, a defender of Orthodoxy at a time when the emperor, the patriarch and the other bishops were prepared to compromise on essential Orthodox doctrines for political expediency; but for most Western and especially Catholic historians, he is a narrow-minded and uncompromising demagogue who symbolized 'Byzantium's fanatical hatred of the Latins'.[7] A more balanced view is that Mark was initially open-minded about the desirability of an agreement with the Roman Church, but became increasingly disenchanted with the proposed terms of union, by which the Orthodox accepted the Latin doctrines, with only vague promises of Western assistance against the Turks.[8]

Mark's major line of critique on the Filioque was not against the doctrine as such but rather that the insertion of the doctrine into the Nicene-Constantinoplean Creed was non-canonical, since any change to the Creed had been expressly forbidden by the Third Ecumenical Council (Ephesus, 431). To support his argument Mark used an array of historical evidence from later ecumenical councils and pointed out that the important dogmatic proclamations of the Third Council (concerning Mary as the Theotokos) and the Fourth Council (concerning the two natures of Christ) did not result in amendments to the Creed.[9] In addition to the canonical argument against the inclusion of the Filioque in the Creed, Mark also addressed the theological and philosophical soundness of the Filioque, employing familiar Greek arguments from Scripture, the councils and the Fathers – which the Latins countered with their own set of arguments from the same sources.[10] Mark's main argument was that the Filioque introduces two causes and two principles, a diarchy, in the Trinity, and confuses and even destroys the traditional concept of personal attributes of the Father, the Son and the Holy Spirit.

Mark's more enduring theological contribution, preserved in three documents from the Council of Florence, is his teaching on the soul after death, aimed directly at refuting the Latin doctrine of purgatory. The point of dispute was not whether there was a process of purification of the soul after death, for both sides agreed on the existence of a 'middle state', a state between heaven for the just and hell for those guilty of mortal sin without repentance. The issue was rather whether there was punishment or purification by fire for those in the 'middle state'. Mark argued that the 'fire' in Scripture applies to the eternal fire of hell and that no Greek or Latin Father teaches a punitive fire in the 'middle state'. He also displayed the typically Greek aversion to the legalistic notion of a

---

[7]As characterized by Alexander Schmemann, 'St. Mark of Ephesus and the Theological Conflicts in Byzantium', *St Vladimir's Seminary Quarterly*, 1, 1 (1957), 11. For a discussion of Catholic critiques of Mark of Ephesus, see Constantine Tsirpanlis, *Mark Eugenicus and the Council of Florence: A Historical Re-evaluation of His Personality* (New York: Center for Byzantine Studies, 1979), 95–103. For a less defensive short account of the Council of Florence, see Deno J. Geanakoplos, 'The Council of Florence (1438-39) and the Problem of Union between the Byzantine and Latin Churches', in his *Byzantine East and Latin West: Two Worlds of Christendom in Middle Ages and Renaissance* (Oxford: Basil Blackwell, 1966), 84–111.

[8]Constantine Tsirpanlis argues this forcibly. He writes, for example, that Mark 'was motivated by profound and genuine love for an honourable, true and durable union with Rome, a union based upon mutual recognition and the Tradition of the undivided Church, and not on political opportunism or expediency'. Tsirpanlis, *Mark Eugenicus*, 21. See also ibid., 58–9 and 104.

[9]See the summary of Mark's arguments in Tsirpanlis, *Mark Eugenicus*, 85–94.

[10]A summary of Mark's arguments against the Filioque is contained in his *Confession of Faith* presented during the Council of Florence. Text in Pelikan and Hotchkiss, *Creeds and Confessions*, I:380–4.

necessary satisfaction of offended divine justice through punishment by 'fire'. The Greeks accepted only 'immaterial or allegorical purification, i.e. captivity, darkness, ignorance, remorse, shame'.[11] The final decree of the Council of Florence is vague regarding purgatory, referring to 'purgatorial punishments', not fire.[12]

After Florence, Mark spent the remaining five years of his life leading an anti-unionist movement. In the end, no significant military help from the West materialized and Constantinople fell to the Turks on 29 May 1453.

In the last days of the Byzantine Empire and the first years of Turkish rule, Georgios Kourtesios (c.1400–c.1473), an erudite lay scholar (hence his epithet 'Scholarios'), came into prominence. He attended the Council of Ferrara-Florence, at first defending the union of Florence. However, in June 1445, at the request of Mark of Ephesus, then dying, he agreed to lead the opposition to the union, as Mark had done. With the fall of Constantinople in 1453 and the execution of the ruling patriarch, the Turkish sultan Mehmed II appointed Scholarios as patriarch. Ruling as Gennadius II, he was deposed and restored twice. In response to the sultan's question 'What do you Christians believe?', Gennadius composed a short confession of faith in which he deals in particular with Muslim accusations that Christians are polytheists and idolaters.[13] Although Gennadius energetically explains and defends the doctrines of the Trinity and the Incarnation, some of his statements are loosely worded and ambiguous, for example: 'The life of the Christ in his flesh was the life of a supremely holy man, and the power of his wisdom and his deeds was the power of God.'[14] By itself this statement could be interpreted as denying the divinity of Christ and hence as Arian or even Ebionite. Elsewhere in his confession, however, Gennadius fully affirms the two natures, divine and human, in the one Person of Christ.

With the end of the Byzantine Empire, for nearly two centuries there was no real centre or locus of Orthodox theology and the theological documents that were produced were primarily the work of individual hierarchs, often in response to initiatives from the West. In the absence of a propitious climate for the study and furtherance of theology, Orthodox thought was characterized by a basic conservatism or traditionalism. Kallistos Ware writes,

> Greek thought underwent an ossification and a hardening which one cannot but regret; yet conservatism had its advantages. In a dark and difficult period the Greeks did in fact maintain the Orthodox tradition substantially unimpaired. The Orthodox under Islam took as their guide Paul's words to Timothy: 'Guard the deposit: keep safe what has been entrusted to you.' (1 Tim. 6.20)[15]

But even this was insufficient to isolate Orthodoxy from Western influences, especially after the Reformation. Greek learning was next to impossible under Islam rule and those aspiring to higher education had to study in the non-Orthodox world – in Italy, Germany, France and England.

---

[11]Tsirpanlis, *Mark Eugenicus*, 84. On St Mark's theology of the afterlife and the debate concerning purgatory, see the excellent essay by Demetrios Bathrellos: 'Love, Purification, and Forgiveness versus Justice, Punishment, and Satisfaction: The Debates on Purgatory and the Forgiveness of Sins at the Council of Ferrara-Florence', *Journal of Theological Studies*, NS 65, 1 (2014), 78–121.

[12]See Tsirpanlis, *Mark Eugenicus*, 84.

[13]Text in Pelikan and Hotchkiss, *Creeds and Confessions*, I:387–91.

[14]Pelikan and Hotchkiss, *Creeds and Confessions*, I:388.

[15]Timothy Ware (Bishop Kallistos of Diokleia), *The Orthodox Church* (London: Penguin Books, 1997), 92 (2015 edition, 88–9).

Most Orthodox theologians in the centuries after the fall of Constantinople were trained in the Roman Catholic or Protestant centres of education. This provided avenues for Catholic and Protestant thought to enter the Orthodox world, including Russia, even though Russia remained politically independent of Islam once it had rid itself of the Mongols. Kallistos Ware writes of Orthodox who studied in the West:

> Greek students in the West read the Fathers, but they only became acquainted with such of the Fathers as were held in esteem by their non-Orthodox professors. … It was difficult for them not to look at theology through Western spectacles; whether consciously or not, they used terminology and forms of argument foreign to their own church.[16]

One of the principal victims of the severance of Orthodox theology from its patristic roots was, somewhat ironically, St Gregory Palamas, the last of the great Byzantine Fathers, whose teachings on the divine energies were quietly forgotten by most Orthodox theologians until the twentieth century. It was to characterize the Catholic and Protestant influences in Orthodox theology that Georges Florovsky employed the famous neologism *pseudomorphosis* – 'a false imitation of the form': Orthodox theology falsely imitated the 'form' (and often the content) of Western theology, thereby betraying its own theological heritage.[17] Nonetheless, this Western influence never penetrated deeply into the liturgical or the spiritual life of the Orthodox Church, with some exceptions. The tradition of the great theological and ascetic Fathers of the Church was still there, but was increasingly neglected and their writings accumulated layers of dust as the centuries passed. Nonetheless, the invasive Western influences in traditionally Orthodox lands did not prevent the great Philokalic revival of Orthodox spirituality beginning in the late eighteenth century with the Kollyvades movement on Mount Athos and the publication of the *Philokalia* in 1782. Although the Byzantine liturgy survived these long centuries more or less intact, Orthodox thinking on the sacraments adopted some important aspects of Roman Catholic sacramental theology, which did not affect the actual rites themselves.

The Orthodox-Lutheran dialogue (1573–81)

The most important theological statements during the period between the Council of Florence and the nineteenth century were the Orthodox-Lutheran exchanges of correspondence in the late sixteenth century, the 'confessions of faith' or 'symbolic books' of the seventeenth century and the exchange of correspondence with the English Non-Jurors in the early eighteenth century.

---

[16]Ware, *The Orthodox Church* (1997), 92–3; (2015), 89.

[17]Georges Florovsky's first public use of the term 'pseudomorphosis' was in his 1936 paper 'Western Influences in Russian Theology', in Brandon Gallaher and Paul Ladouceur, eds., *The Patristic Witness of Georges Florovsky: Essential Theological Writings* (London: T&T Clark, 2019), 137, 141, 143, 149. His first use of the term concerned the replacement of patristics by scholasticism. In *The Ways of Russian Theology* (1937), he refers to pseudomorphosis with respect to the establishment of the Uniate Church under Rome in Western Russia in the late sixteenth century and the Westernized legacy of Peter Moghila (a 'Latin pseudomorphosis'). Georges Florovsky, *The Ways of Russian Theology* (2 vols.), in *The Collected Works of Georges Florovsky*, vols. 5 and 6 (Belmont, MA: Nordland, 1979), I:37; 85.

In the late sixteenth century, Lutheran scholars attempted to interest the patriarch of Constantinople in the Reformation, no doubt hoping to rally Orthodox support in a united front against Rome and to initiate a 'reformation' within Orthodoxy. In 1573 a delegation of Lutheran scholars from Tübingen in Germany visited Constantinople and gave Patriarch Jeremiah II a copy of the Augsburg Confession – the basic Lutheran confession of faith – translated into Greek. This visit initiated an exchange of correspondence over the next eight years.[18] In his three letters to the Tübingen theologians (dated 1576, 1579 and 1581), Jeremiah adhered strictly to traditional Orthodox positions and showed no inclination to Protestantism.

The Patriarch's answers are important as the first authoritative Orthodox critique of the principal doctrines of the Reformation. His first letter is an article-by-article commentary on the Augsburg Confession. From the onset, Jeremiah affirms the adherence of the Orthodox Church to tradition as the foundation of her teaching:

> In responding, then, we shall say nothing originating of ourselves, but (what is pertinent) from the holy seven Ecumenical Synods with which, as you write, you acquiesce and you accept. We shall further speak in accordance with the opinion of the divine teachers and exegetes of the divinely inspired Scripture, whom the catholic church of Christ has received in common accord, for their words and miracles illuminated the universe like another sun.[19]

Against the Reformation doctrine of *sola scriptura*, Jeremiah posits the authority of the church, as reflected in the ancient Fathers, in interpreting Scripture:

> All these things which we have spoken, beloved, are founded, as you very well know, upon the inspired Scriptures, according to the interpretation and the sound teaching and explanation of our wise and holy theologians [the Fathers of the Church]. For we may not rely upon our own interpretation and understand and interpret any of the words of the inspired Scripture except in accord with the theologizing Fathers who have been approved by the Holy Synods, inspired by the Holy Spirit for a pious purpose.[20]

In his second letter (1579), Jeremiah reinforces the Orthodox position by citing the Sixth Ecumenical Council: 'For it is a stipulation of the holy and Sixth Ecumenical Synod directing that the Holy Scriptures be understood as the tried and proved teachers of the church have interpreted them and not as those who, by their own sophistry, wish to interpret such matters superfluously.'[21]

The Reformation doctrines of *sola fide* and *sola gratia* ('faith alone' and 'grace alone') inaugurate a debate on the relative roles of faith, divine grace and 'good works' in salvation. Jeremiah emphasizes the Orthodox teaching that both faith and works are necessary for salvation, that human agency ('works') plays a role in salvation, not divine grace alone: 'We say that faith precedes,

[18]Translations of the correspondence in George Mastrantonis, *Augsburg and Constantinople: The Correspondence between the Tübingen Theologians and Patriarch Jeremiah II of Constantinople on the Augsburg Confession* (Brookline, MA: Holy Cross Press, 1982). Pelikan and Hotchkiss include Jeremiah's first letter of 1576, in the Mastrantonis translation – see *Creeds and Confessions*, I:394–474.

[19]Mastrantonis, *Augsburg and Constantinople*, 31.

[20]Ibid., 102.

[21]Ibid., 151–2.

and then the works follow and are necessary according to the commandment of God. The one who fulfils them, as he must, receives reward and honour in everlasting life. Indeed, good works are not separate from, but necessary for, true faith.'[22]

Jeremiah returns to this theme in his comments on article 20 of the Augsburg Confession, which deals with faith and good works but dismisses most Christian pious practices:

> The twentieth [article] says that you do not forbid good works. Yet you characterise feasts, ceremonies, fixed fasts, brotherhoods, monastic life and other similar works as useless. This is not good, nor does it agree with the Holy Fathers. For if you love all good works, as you say you do, you should love these also because they are good works.[23]

Although there appeared to be agreement on a wide range of issues, the subsequent exchanges made it clear that the gulf between the two parties was wide indeed and that neither was prepared to yield to the other's arguments. At the end of his third letter to the Tübingen theologians in June 1581, Jeremiah brought the correspondence to a close, feeling that matters had reached a deadlock, especially over the seemingly irreconcilable attitudes towards tradition, the authority of the ecumenical councils and the Fathers of the Church:

> You honour and exalt them [the 'luminaries and theologians of the church'] in words, but you reject them in deeds. For you try to prove our weapons which are their holy and divine discourses as unsuitable. And it is with these documents that we would have to write and contradict you. ... Therefore, going about your own ways, write no longer concerning dogmas; but if you do, write only for friendship's sake.[24]

The correspondence between the Lutheran theologians and Patriarch Jeremiah was the first formal theological encounter between the Reformation and Orthodoxy, a significant ecumenical endeavour by any standards.[25] The exchanges were carried out at a high theological level, each side seriously considering the arguments of the other and drawing on its best theology. Despite many points of agreement between the two parties – for instance, both stood in opposition to the hegemonic claims of Rome – it became clear that there were major points of disagreement between Orthodoxy and the Reformation. These issues became an 'agenda' for further relations between Orthodoxy and the Reformation over the ensuing centuries: the relative roles of Scripture and tradition in Christianity; the Filioque; divine grace, human free will and predestination; the place of faith and works in salvation; the nature of the Eucharist; the number and form of sacraments; the nature of the church; prayers for the deceased; monasticism; and the veneration of saints, icons and relics. On most of these issues, Orthodoxy is closer to Catholicism than to the Reformation, the exceptions being the Filioque and the nature of the church, specifically the role of the pope. But in

---

[22]Ibid., 42.
[23]Ibid., 83.
[24]Ibid., 306.
[25]For an assessment of the Augsburg-Constantinople correspondence in an ecumenical perspective, see Georges Florovsky, 'An Early Ecumenical Correspondence (Patriarch Jeremiah II and the Lutheran Divines)' (1950), in *Christianity and Culture*, in *The Collected Works of Georges Florovsky*, vol. 2 (Belmont, MA: Nordland, 1974); and 'The Orthodox Churches and the Ecumenical Movement Prior to 1910' (1954), also in *Christianity and Culture*.

the sixteenth century, serious dialogue between the Orthodox and the Catholic churches was still some four centuries in the future.

Orthodoxy and the Counter-Reformation

Orthodox contact with the Catholic Counter-Reformation took place largely in context of the struggle between the two churches in Polish-controlled Western Ukraine for the loyalty of the hierarchs, clergy and faithful. The outcome of this struggle was the Council of Brest-Litovsk in 1596 and the establishment of the Ukrainian Catholic Church, based on the acceptance of some of the Orthodox bishops of the terms of the Council of Florence – the origin of the Greek Catholic or 'Uniate' Church. The Orthodox who accepted the authority of Rome were allowed to retain the Byzantine liturgy and Orthodox rites and practices, such as married priests. No significant theological documents were produced by this process, which was almost entirely dominated by secular and ecclesial politics.

Persecution invigorated the Orthodox Church in the Ukraine. Although many Orthodox nobles joined the Uniates, many of the lower clergy, the Orthodox Brotherhoods and the faithful stood firm against the incursions and proselytism of the Catholic Church. Despite their oppressed status, the Ukrainian Orthodox organized their own schools and published books defending Orthodoxy. Kallistos Ware writes that 'by 1650 the level of learning in the Ukraine was higher than anywhere else in the Orthodox world; scholars from Kiev, travelling to Moscow at this time, did much to raise intellectual standards in Great Russia.'[26] Under the inspired direction of Peter Mogila, Metropolitan of Kiev and Galicia in the mid-seventeenth century, Kiev became the intellectual centre of the Orthodox world.

The Orthodox confessions of the seventeenth century

Orthodox theology in the seventeenth century was noteworthy especially for the Orthodox confessions, or statements of faith, inspired initially by the Protestant tradition of such confessions. In the Orthodox tradition, the essential 'confession' or 'symbol of faith' is the Nicene-Constantinopolitan Creed. Several of the seventeenth-century confessions go well beyond the Nicene Creed to cover many subjects in far more detail than the Creed – especially the Confession of Peter Mogila, which is more properly called a 'catechism'. These confessions, together with other declarations of faith, are sometimes referred to as the 'Symbolic Books' of the Orthodox Church.

---

[26] Ware, *The Orthodox Church* (1997), 95; (2015), 92.

This term is of Protestant origin and has no status in Orthodoxy. The lists of the Symbolic Books vary, but the following are usually included:

1. The Confession of Faith of Patriarch Gennadius II (1455–6).
2. The replies of Ecumenical Patriarch Jeremiah II to the Tübingen theologians on the Augsburg Confession (1576–81).
3. The Confession of Faith of Metrophanes Critopoulos, Patriarch of Alexandria (1625).
4. The Orthodox Confession of the Catholic and Apostolic Eastern Church of Peter Mogila (1638/1642).
5. The Confession of Dositheus II Notaras and the Synod of Jerusalem (1672).[27]

The *Confession of Faith* of Mark of Ephesus (1439) is also considered an important Orthodox affirmation of faith, as well as earlier documents such as the *Encyclical Letter* of Photius the Great to the Bishops of the East (866), the *Synodical Tomes* of the Councils of Constantinople of 1341 and 1351 and the *Confession of the Orthodox Faith* of Gregory Palamas.[28] Later major doctrinal statements include the replies of the Oriental Patriarchs to the English Non-Jurors (1718 and 1723), the *Encyclical of the Eastern Patriarchs* of 1848 and the reply of the Synod of Constantinople to Pope Leo XIII in 1895.[29]

The confession usually *excluded* from the lists of Symbolic Books of the Orthodox Church is *The Eastern Confession of the Christian Faith* of Cyril Lucaris (1633), because of its decidedly non-Orthodox character. The less well-known Confession of Metrophanes Critopoulos (1625) is also often not listed despite its orthodoxy.

The Confession of Metrophanes Critopoulos (1625)

The earliest and least known of the seventeenth-century confessions of faith is that of Metrophanes Critopoulos (1589–1639). Metrophanes was a monk of Mount Athos sent by Cyril Lucaris to study theology in the West. He spent thirteen years (1617–30) in England, Germany, Switzerland and Venice before returning to Egypt in 1631, where he became a bishop and served as Patriarch of Alexandria from 1636 to 1639. His Confession,[30] written while he was still in Western Europe, can be seen as an early attempt by a young Orthodox theologian to reopen theological dialogue with the West, with a certain degree of 'ecumenical goodwill and doctrinal flexibility'.[31]

From the outset of his Confession, Metrophanes tackles the issue of the Filioque, affirming that 'the Holy Spirit proceeds from the Father alone', while at the same time introducing the ambiguous

[27] See Ware, *The Orthodox Church* (1997), 203; (2015), 197.
[28] See Pelikan and Hotchkiss, *Creeds and Confessions*, I:245–384.
[29] See Kallistos Ware, *The Orthodox Church* (1997), 203; (2015), 197.
[30] Text in Pelikan and Hotchkiss, *Creeds and Confessions*, I:477–548.
[31] Pelikan and Hotchkiss, *Creeds and Confessions*, I:475.

formula that the Holy Spirit 'is the spirit of both Father and Son'.[32] His exposition of the Orthodox position on the Filioque is well grounded in the Fathers and he explains the ambiguous statement about the Holy Spirit by saying that

> the Holy Spirit is said to be of the Father and of the Son, but he is of the Father both because he has his hypostasis from him and also as being consubstantial with him; but he is of the Son because he will be said to be consubstantial with him, and very rightly so; and moreover because he is inseparable from him, and his constant companion; but nowhere in the inspired Scriptures is it found that he also has his hypostasis from the Son.[33]

On some contentious questions, Metrophanes is also ambiguous, while on others he presents a clearly Orthodox point of view. On the thorny question of predestination, he points to the distinction between 'foreknowledge' and 'predestination', arguing that if God's foreknowledge of the worthiness of the elect means that they are predestined, 'then it necessarily follows that the unworthiness of the damned comes also from God', to which he objects: 'But that is quite wrong! Because that would mean that God is neither good nor just, if he is the Creator of all alike, but yet foreordains good things for some but the opposite for others.'[34] Yet later he refers to 'those whom God by his foreknowledge had predestined and chosen, [those] he collected together through the preaching of the gospel, and made his own through giving them a share in his grace'[35] – which is very close to ecclesiologies which see the church as a gathering of the elect. In effect, Metrophanes is uncertain about his ecclesiology: he does not state outright that the Orthodox Church is the true Church of Christ, but is content to say 'the whole matter is so uncertain and confused, with each group thinking that they alone are orthodox and considering everyone else to be of no account'.[36] On issues such as the real presence of the Body and Blood of Christ in the Eucharist, the veneration of icons and relics, the invocation of saints in prayer, monasticism and prayers for the deceased, Metrophanes affirms and explains the Orthodox position against Protestant theology.[37] Similarly, although with some ambiguity, on the value of 'works' in salvation, Metrophanes advances the necessity of good works while refusing to place the discussion in the dichotomy of 'faith' versus 'works': 'Therefore good works are essential for the chosen. First, so that it may be clear that their faith is not dead, but living and fruitful. And that through the fruit that they bear they may be good examples to others and that God may be glorified in them.'[38]

Unlike his patron Cyril Lucaris, whose Confession is manifestly Protestant on a number of doctrines, Metrophanes maintains a fundamentally Orthodox perspective. The Greek theologian Ioannis Karmiris (1903–92) considers his Confession 'the most original, independent, and the

---

[32]Ibid., I:479.
[33]Ibid., I:486.
[34]Ibid., I:504.
[35]Ibid., I:507.
[36]Ibid., I:512.
[37]See Pelikan and Hotchkiss, *Creeds and Confessions*, I:516–42.
[38]Pelikan and Hotchkiss, *Creeds and Confessions*, I:510–11.

most free from heterodox influence, of the four confessions of faith produced in the seventeenth century by Orthodox writers'[39] – which is not to say that it is entirely Orthodox. Metrophanes's Confession was never endorsed by a church council and failed to achieve the pre-eminence of the later confessions. Metrophanes saw the errors in the Confession of his former patron and in 1638 he signed the anathemas pronounced against Cyril Lucaris for Calvinism.

The Confession of Cyril Lucaris (1629)

Cyril Lucaris (1572–1638), Patriarch of Alexandria (as Cyril III) from 1601 to 1620 and Patriarch of Constantinople (as Cyril I) from 1620 until he was murdered by the Turks in 1638, developed a strong animosity towards the Church of Rome following theological studies in Wittenberg and Geneva, where he was exposed to Calvinism, and after his involvement in the Western Ukraine during the struggle between the Orthodox and the Catholic churches for the control of the Orthodox under Polish rule. When he became patriarch he devoted his full energies to combating Catholic influence in the Ottoman Empire. He obtained assistance from the embassies of the Protestant countries at Constantinople, while his Jesuit opponents were supported by the diplomatic representatives of the Roman Catholic powers. Cyril Lucaris sought to reform the Orthodox Church and to this end he sent many young Greek theologians to study in Switzerland, the Netherlands and England. The Confession ascribed to Cyril was first published in Latin at Geneva in 1629 and in English, French and German translations, and subsequently in Greek under the title *Eastern Confession of the Christian Faith*.[40]

The major non-Orthodox doctrines of this distinctively Calvinist Confession are the following:

1. An ambiguous formulation of the Filioque: 'the Holy Spirit proceeding from the Father through the Son' (Article 1).[41]
2. The authority of Scripture is above that of the church (*sola scriptura*): 'We believe the Holy Scriptures to be taught of God, whose author is the Holy Spirit and no other. … And so the witness of the Holy Scripture is of higher authority than that of the church' (Article 2).[42]
3. Predestination of those who will be saved and those damned: 'We believe the most good God to have, before the foundation of the world, predestined those whom he has chosen without any regard for their works and having no motivating cause for this election except his good pleasure and his divine mercy. In like manner before the world was made, he has rejected those whom he would reject; and of this rejection, looking to the absolute power and

[39]Ioannis Karmiris, *Heterodoxoi epidraseis epi tas homologias tou IZ' Aionos* (Jerusalem, 1949), 73, cited in Colin Davey, *Pioneer for Unity: Metrophanes Kritopoulos (1589-1639) and Relations between the Orthodox, Roman Catholic and Reformed Churches* (London: British Council of Churches, 1987), 187; and in Jaroslav Pelikan, *Credo: Historical and Theological Guide to Creeds and Confessions of Faith in the Christian Tradition* (New Haven, CT: Yale University Press, 2003), 421.

[40]Text in Pelikan and Hotchkiss, *Creeds and Confessions*, I:551–8.

[41]Pelikan and Hotchkiss, *Creeds and Confessions*, I:551.

[42]Ibid., I:551.

authority of God, his will is the cause; but looking toward the laws and principles of good order which God's providence uses in governing the world, his righteousness is the cause, for God is merciful and righteous' (Article 3).[43]

4 Salvation is by faith alone (*sola fide*): 'We believe that a man is justified by faith and not by works. … Truth itself teaches us that works are not to be neglected, for they are necessary means for a witness to faith and confirmation of our calling. But human frailty witnesses it to be false that works are sufficient for our salvation, that they can enable one to appear boldly at the tribunal of Christ, and that of their own merit they can confer salvation' (Article 13).[44]
5 The doctrine of 'utter depravity' (or 'total depravity'): 'We believe that free will is dead in the unregenerate, because they can in no way do what is good and whatever they do is sin; but in those who are regenerate by the All-holy Spirit, free will is revived and operates but not without the assistance of grace. So, therefore, for a regenerated man to do what is good, it is necessary that he be guided and preceded by grace' (Article 14).[45]
6 There are but two sacraments 'which the Lord instituted in the Gospel' (Article 15), baptism and the Eucharist. Baptism effects the forgiveness of the ancestral sin (Article 16). The Confession affirms 'the true and real presence of our Lord Jesus Christ' in the Eucharist, but denies 'the arbitrarily invented doctrine of transubstantiation', and gives a spiritual interpretation of the experience of communion: 'The body of our Lord Jesus Christ is not that which is seen with the eyes and received in the sacrament but that which faith spiritually apprehends, presents and bestows to us. From whence it is true that we eat and partake and have communion if we believe' (Article 17).[46]

The Protestant doctrines contained in this Confession stimulated Orthodox reflection on the nature of the Orthodox faith vis-à-vis the Western churches and confessions during the rest of the seventeenth century. But almost from the beginning, doubts arose concerning the authorship of the Confession and whether it really reflected Cyril's thinking. The evidence is inconclusive. Supporters of Cyril point to the Orthodoxy of his other writings, to his denials of authorship of the Confession and to his steadfast opposition to Roman influence, especially in Eastern Europe. They also argue that Cyril was caught in the crossfire between Catholic and Protestant European countries, recognizing that he did indeed turn to the embassies of the Protestant powers for support against the intrigues of the Jesuits and the Catholic ambassadors at Constantinople against him. Those who think that the Confession truly reflects Cyril's views cite evidence of Calvinism in certain letters and the fact that Cyril never issued a public denunciation of the Confession.[47]

[43]Ibid., I:551–2.

[44]Ibid., I:553.

[45]Ibid., I:554.

[46]Ibid., I:554–5.

[47]For a summary of the main arguments on both sides see especially George P. Michaelides, 'The Greek Orthodox Position on the Confession of Cyril Lucaris', *Church History*, 12, 2 (1943), 118–29. A resolutely pro-Cyril and anti-Catholic view is expressed by Archbishop Chrysostomos of Etna (Old Calendrist) in 'The Myth of the "Calvinist Patriarch"' http://orthodoxinfo.com/inquirers/ca4_loukaris.aspx (28 May 2014). An article on the website of the Ecumenical Patriarchate is relatively neutral: Athanasios Paliouras, 'Cyril I Lucaris'. www.ec-patr.org/list/index.php?lang=en&id=202 (28 May 2014).

Cyril died a martyr's death in the church, strangled by Janissaries on 27 June 1638 on the orders of Sultan Murad IV.

The Confession of Peter Mogila (1638–42)

The Calvinism of Cyril's Confession was sharply and speedily repudiated by his fellow Orthodox; his Confession was condemned by no less than six local councils between 1638 and 1691. Two other important Orthodox hierarchs, Peter Mogila of Kiev and Dositheus of Jerusalem, produced confessions of their own. As we saw above, Peter Mogila (1595/6–1646/7), Metropolitan of Kiev and Galicia from 1632/3 until his death in 1646/7, played a major role in the revival of Orthodoxy in the Western Ukraine after the 1596 Union of Brest-Litovsk by strengthening the position of those Orthodox who remained independent of Rome. But Peter was himself a 'Latiniser' who favoured and introduced Latin education, modelled on Jesuit institutions in Poland; Latin and Polish became languages of religious education in the Ukraine.

Mogila's *Orthodox Confession of the Catholic and Apostolic Eastern Church*,[48] written initially in 1638 and presented to a church council in Kiev in 1640, was based directly on Roman Catholic manuals.[49] The Confession is indeed a highly structured catechism in the typical Western format of questions and answers, divided into three parts based on the three 'theological virtues', faith, hope and charity.

The first and longest part on faith is a commentary on the twelve articles of the Nicene Creed, the seven gifts of the Holy Spirit, the nine fruits of the Holy Spirit, the nine precepts of the church and the seven sacraments. The gifts and fruits of the Holy Spirit and the precepts of the church are characteristically Roman, not Orthodox enumerations. An example of Western theology is Mogila's account of original sin and baptism:

> Q. I.24. As all mankind, during the state of innocence, was in Adam; so in him all men, falling from what he fell, remained in a state of sin. Wherefore mankind has become, not only subject to sin, but also, on account of sin, to punishment. ... This is called ancestral sin, first, because before this, man was free from all sin; although the devil was then corrupt and fallen, by whose temptation this ancestral sin sprang up in man; and Adam becoming guilty, we all likewise, who descend from him, become also guilty. Secondly, this is called original sin, because no mortal is conceived without this depravity of nature.[50]

> Q. I.102. Baptism is a washing away and rooting out of the ancestral sin, by being thrice immersed in water, the priest pronouncing these words: 'In the name of the Father, Amen; and of the Son, Amen; and of the Holy Ghost, Amen.'[51]

---

[48]See English translation of Part I of the Greek text (revised by Meletios Syrigos and ratified by the Council of Jassy in 1642) in Pelikan and Hotchkiss, *Creeds and Confessions*, I:561–612.
[49]See Florovsky, *The Ways of Russian Theology*, I:76, for likely sources.
[50]Pelikan and Hotchkiss, *Creeds and Confessions*, I:573.
[51]Ibid., I:602.

Mogila returns to the relation of baptism and original sin in Part III, where he says notably:

> Q. III.20. Original Sin is the transgression of that Law of God which was given to Adam, the father of all men. … This original sin spreads over all human nature, inasmuch as we were all then contained in Adam. Wherefore by one Adam sin passed into us all. And we are conceived and born with this blemish. … This hereditary sin cannot be rooted out or abolished by any repentance whatever, but only by the grace of God, through the work of redemption, wrought by our Lord Jesus Christ, in taking upon him our flesh and pouring out his precious blood. And this is done in the mystery of holy baptism, and whoever is not a partaker thereof remains unabsolved from his sin, and continues in his guilt, and is liable to the eternal punishment of the divine wrath.[52]

This treatment of original sin and baptism relies on the Augustinian doctrine that the 'guilt' of original sin is inherited by all the descendants of Adam and is abolished by baptism. A more authentically Orthodox theology insists that guilt for sin is personal and cannot be transmitted; Adam's descendants inherit the consequences of original sin, notably death and suffering and a weakened will reflected in an inclination towards sin, but not the actual guilt.

Another example of Latin theology is the use of the Greek equivalent (*metousiōsis*) of the scholastic term 'transubstantiation' (*transsubstantiatio*) to describe the transformation of the Holy Gifts into the Body and Blood of Christ during the Divine Liturgy:[53]

> Q. I.107. At these words [the epiclesis] there is wrought a change [*metousiōsis*] in the elements, and the bread becomes the very body of Christ, and the wine his very blood, the species only remaining, which are perceived by the sight.[54]

The doctrine of transubstantiation relies on the Aristotelian distinction between substance (the reality of a thing) and accident (its outward appearances or *species*), subsequently taken up in scholastic theology. The final version of the Confession ascribes transubstantiation to the epiclesis, not to the consecration or words of institution as in the initial version of the Confession. This is but a slight change from the pre-eminence accorded to the consecration in Catholic theology to the Orthodox retention of the epiclesis. More traditional Orthodox sacramental theology does not use the notion of transubstantiation, nor does it pronounce on the relative importance of the consecration or the epiclesis. Metrophanes Critopoulos more accurately reflects Orthodox reluctance to be precise on this question when he says that

> the manner in which they are changed is unknown to us and cannot be explained. The clarification of such things is reserved for the elect when they enter the kingdom of heaven. For the time being their simple faith and lack of curiosity will win them greater grace from God. But those who want to discover a reason for everything lose their reason and find ignorance.[55]

Mogila does nonetheless adhere to traditional Orthodox theology by rejecting typically Western doctrines such as predestination (Q.I.26), purgatorial fire (Q. I.66) and the Filioque (Q. I.71).

---

[52]Adapted from the 1772 translation by Philip Lodvel as edited by J. J. Overbeck in 1898: Peter Moghila, *The Orthodox Confession of the Catholic and Apostolic Eastern Church* (London: Thomas Baker, 1898), 132.
[53]See Pelikan, *Credo*, 424–5.
[54]Pelikan and Hotchkiss, *Creeds and Confessions*, I:604.
[55]Ibid., I:520–1.

The second part of Mogila's Catechism treats of hope and contains an exposition of the Lord's Prayer and the nine Beatitudes (Mt. 5.3-11). It discusses the means of salvation, grace, prayer and works of mercy. Part Three treats of love of God and man, and deals with the three cardinal virtues of prayer, fasting and almsgiving; the four general virtues which flow out of them (prudence, justice, fortitude and temperance); the distinction between mortal and 'non-mortal' sins; the seven general mortal sins (pride, avarice, fornication, envy, gluttony, desire of revenge and sloth); the sins against the Holy Spirit (presumption or temerity, despair, persistent opposition to the truth and renouncing of the Christian faith), and concludes with an exposition of the Decalogue. This entire structure is basically Roman Catholic and there are many Catholic elements, such as the distinction between mortal and 'non mortal' (or 'venial') sins (Q. III.17–43).

The list of categories of sins under seven (sometimes eight) broad headings is of Eastern origin, specifically in Evagrius of Ponticus in the late fourth century.[56] But whereas in Orthodox spirituality the various types of sins are called 'passions' and are considered illnesses of the soul which can be cured, in Western spirituality they become the 'seven deadly (or mortal) sins', with decidedly more legalistic and moralist overtones than the passions of the Eastern ascetic Fathers.

Mogila's Confession was a reaction to both the Calvinist Confession of Cyril Lucaris and the continued efforts of Catholic and Reformed missionaries to convert the Orthodox in the Ukraine. The Confession was approved by a council in Kiev in 1640, which nonetheless introduced amendments, and it was subsequently approved by a council in Jassy, Moldavia, in 1642, after it had been revised by a Greek, Meletios Syrigos. The principal substantive changes concerned the passages about the consecration in the Eucharist (which Mogila initially attributed solely to the words of institution, as in Catholic theology) and about the existence of purgatory (contained in the first version of the Confession, and ignoring completely St Mark of Ephesus's rejection of the Roman doctrine at the Council of Florence).[57]

Subsequently two versions of the Confession existed, one published in 1645 by Peter Mogila in Polish and Slavonic, close to his original text, and the amended version in Greek. The Greek version was approved by the patriarchs of Constantinople, Jerusalem, Alexandria and Antioch in 1643 and published in 1695. In 1696 a Slavonic translation of the Greek version was published in Moscow with the approval of Patriarch Adrian and Peter the Great.[58] Yet, as Kallistos Ware writes: 'Even in its revised form the Confession of Mogila is still the most Latin document ever to be adopted by an official council of the Orthodox Church.'[59] Despite the formal approval of the Confession by senior Orthodox authorities, it enjoyed only 'a very relative authority'[60] because of its manifest Latinizing tendencies. Mogila also published a large and a small catechism, and a *Trebnik* or *Euchologion*,

[56]Evagrius of Pontus, *Practicos*. Translated by Robert Sinkewicz as 'The Monk: A Treatise on the Practical Life', in *Evagrius of Pontus: The Greek Ascetic Corpus* (Oxford: Oxford University Press, 2003). A fuller treatment of the passions is found in *The Institutes* by Evagrius's disciple John Cassian. See John Cassian, *The Institutes*, Ancient Christian Writers 58 (New York: Newman Press, 2000).

[57]See Florovsky, *The Ways of Russian Theology*, I:75.

[58]On the publication history of Moghila's Confession, see Florovsky, *The Ways of Russian Theology*, I:76.

[59]Ware, *The Orthodox Church* (1997), 97; (2015), 93.

[60]George A. Maloney, *A History of Orthodox Theology since 1453* (Belmont, MA: Nordland, 1976), 35.

which served to introduce Latinisms into Russian liturgical practice. Georges Florovsky severely chastises Mogila's Confession for its 'crypto-Romanism':

> It is true that in Mogila's Confession key Roman doctrines, including the primacy of the pope, are repudiated. Nevertheless, much of the substance and the whole of the style remain Roman, and not even Syrigos' editing at Iasi could alter that fact. After all, as was customary for Greeks in the seventeenth century, Syrigos had gone to a Latin school. ... It was not so much the doctrine, but the manner of presentation that was, so to speak, erroneous, particularly the choice of language and the tendency to employ any and all Roman weapons against the Protestants even when not consonant in full or in part with Orthodox presuppositions. And it is here that the chief danger of Mogila's Latin 'pseudomorphosis' or 'crypto-Romanism' surfaces. The impression is created that Orthodoxy is no more than a purified or refined version of Roman Catholicism. ... Mogila's 'crypto-Romanism', in spite of its general faithfulness to Orthodox forms, was for a long time to bar the way to any spontaneous and genuine theological development in the East.[61]

The Confession of Dositheus of Jerusalem (1672)

Dositheus (Notaras) (1641–1707), Patriarch of Jerusalem from 1669 to 1707, was known for his firm stand against Catholic and Protestant influences on Orthodoxy, especially the role of the Catholic Church, through the Franciscan Order, in Palestine and the Holy Land. Although he convened the Council of Jerusalem to refute the Calvinist Confession of Cyril Lucaris, Dositheus himself, like Peter Mogila, drew heavily on Latin sources in writing his Confession. His Confession[62] was ratified in 1672 by the Council of Jerusalem. Dositheus's Confession takes the form of a rebuttal of the Protestant influences in the Confession of Cyril Lucaris, especially concerning the relationship of Scripture and tradition; free will, grace and predestination; justification through faith and/or works; ecclesiology; the number and nature of the sacraments; and the veneration of icons.[63] In affirming the equality of authority of Scripture and tradition, the Confession of Dositheus introduces the notion of the infallibility of the church, though without engaging the Catholic doctrine – not yet formally proclaimed – of the infallibility of the pope:

> 2. ... The witness of the catholic church is, we believe, not inferior in authority to that of the Divine Scripture. For one and the same Holy Spirit being the author of both, it is quite the same to be taught by the Scripture and by the catholic church. Moreover, when anyone speaks from himself, he is liable to err, to deceive and be deceived. But for the catholic church, as never having spoken or speaking from herself but from the Spirit of God – who being her teacher, she is unfailingly rich forever – it is impossible to err in any way, or to deceive at all or be deceived; but like the Divine Scripture, she is infallible, and has perpetual authority.[64]

---

[61] Florovsky, *The Ways of Russian Theology*, I:76–7.
[62] Text in Pelikan and Hotchkiss, *Creeds and Confessions*, I:615–35.
[63] See Ware, *The Orthodox Church* (1997), 97; (2015), 93.
[64] Pelikan and Hotchkiss, *Creeds and Confessions*, I:616.

Against the Calvinist doctrine of predestination, the Confession of Dositheus affirms more clearly than that of Peter Mogila the distinction between foreknowledge and predestination and the role of good works in salvation, insisting notably on God's respect for human free will, recurring themes in Orthodox dialogue with Western theology:

> 13. We believe that a man is not simply justified through faith alone, but through faith that works through love, that is to say, through faith and works. But the notion that faith, fulfilling the function of a hand, lays hold on the righteousness which is in Christ and applies it to us for salvation, we know to be far from all true piety. For faith thus understood would be possible in all, and so none could miss salvation, which is obviously false. But on the contrary, we rather believe that it is not the correlative of faith, but the faith that is in us, which, through works, justifies us with Christ. But we regard works not as witnesses certifying our calling, but as being fruits in themselves, through which faith becomes efficacious.[65]

The Confession does nonetheless employ the typically Western distinctions of 'illuminating grace', 'prevenient grace' and 'particular grace'. Such distinctions are unknown in Eastern theology and appear founded on the Western notion of created grace rather than on the Eastern concept of uncreated grace.

Against the Calvinist notion of the 'utter depravity' of fallen humanity, the Confession affirms, without explicitly appealing to the patristic distinction between the 'divine image' and the 'divine likeness,' a permanent human dignity which leaves open the possibility of doing good and the patristic notion of divine-human cooperation (synergy) in the work of salvation:

> 14. We believe that man in falling by his transgression became comparable and similar to the beasts; that is, he was utterly undone and fell from his perfection and impassibility, yet did not lose the nature and power that he had received from the supremely good God. … He still has the same nature in which he was created, and the same power of his nature, that is free will, living and operating, so that by nature he is able to choose and do what is good, and to avoid and hate what is evil. … A man, therefore, before he is regenerated, is able by nature to incline to what is good, and to choose and work mortal good. … But for the regenerated to do spiritual good – for the works of the believer, being contributory to salvation and wrought by supernatural grace, are properly called 'spiritual' – the guidance and provenience of grace is necessary, as has been said in treating of predestination; so that he is not able of himself to do any work worthy of a Christian life, although he has it in his own power to will, or not to will, to co-operate with grace.[66]

In a number of other affirmations Dositheus reflects Western rather than Orthodox theology, for example, in stating unequivocally that there can be neither more nor less than seven sacraments (article 15); in stating that baptism effects the 'remission of the ancestral sin' or 'original sin' (article 16); in his employment, like Peter Mogila, of the Latin term 'transubstantiation' with respect to the

[65]Ibid., I:623.
[66]Ibid., I:624.

Eucharist (article 17); and in defending prayers for the dead, he comes very close to the Roman doctrine of purgatory, without actually using the word purgatory itself (article 18).[67] Concerning transubstantiation, Dositheus is in fact even more explicitly scholastic than Mogila:

> We believe that after the consecration of the bread and of the wine, there no longer remains the substance of the bread and of the wine, but the very body and blood of the Lord, under the species and form of bread and wine, that is to say, under the accidents of the bread and the wine.[68]

On the whole, however, the Confession of Dositheus is less Latin than that of Mogila, and is the most 'orthodox' of all the seventeenth-century confessions, despite its Latinizing tendencies. John Meyendorff considers it to be 'the most important Orthodox dogmatic text of this period'[69] and Kallistos Ware writes that, despite Dositheus's use of Latin arguments, 'the faith which he defended with these Latin weapons was not Roman, but Orthodox.'[70] The Orthodoxy of Dositheus can be seen in doctrines such as his affirmations that the Holy Spirit proceeds from the Father alone (article 1); that the 'ancestral sin' is transmitted to Adam's posterity as 'an inclination toward sinning', but not as actual sin (or guilt), 'for such approaches that lack assent and not put into practice are not sin' (article 6);[71] the validity of the intercession of the Mother of God, the saints and the angels (article 8); the role and dignity of the episcopate (article 10); the divine institution of the sacraments (article 15) and the real presence of Christ in the Eucharist (article 17).

The Russian theological academies (1635–1798)

In 1635 Peter Mogila founded the Collegium of Kiev, which became the Kiev Theological Academy by the end of the seventeenth century. The Kiev Academy was modelled after Jesuit schools in Catholic Poland and instruction was given in Latin, typically using Latin theological manuals grounded in Augustinian theology and Thomistic scholasticism. It became the leading Orthodox educational institution, introducing Western European educational standards into Russia, but also opening the door for additional Western (especially Latin/Catholic) influence in Orthodoxy. Georges Florovsky sees the Academy of Kiev as a prime source of the 'pseudomorphosis' of Russian

---

67 The paragraph dealing with the intermediate state after death is absent from the Pelikan and Hotchkiss rendition of Dositheus's Confession, which is translated from the edition of Ioannes Karmirēs, *Ta dogmatika kai symbolika mnēmeia tēs orthodoxou katholikēs ekklēsias* (The Dogmatic and Symbolic Monuments of the Orthodox Catholic Church) (Graz: Akademische Druck- und Verlagsanstalt, 1968). A translation of the paragraph in question occurs in *The Acts and Decrees of the Synod of Jerusalem*, trans. J. N. W. B. Robertson (London: Thomas Baker, 1899). A slightly modified version is online at www.crivoice.org/creeddositheus.html (14 May 2014).

68 Pelikan and Hotchkiss, *Creeds and Confessions*, I:629.

69 John Meyendorff, *The Orthodox Church: Its Past and Its Role in the World Today* (1981) (Crestwood, NY: St Vladimir's Seminary Press, 4th ed., 1996), 86. See also 'The Significance of the Reformation in the History of Christendom', in *Orthodoxy and Catholicity* (New York: Sheed & Ward, 1966), 136.

70 Ware, *The Orthodox Church* (1997), 97; (2015), 94.

71 Pelikan and Hotchkiss, *Creeds and Confessions*, I:618.

theology, not a 'free encounter' with the West, but rather 'captivity, or more precisely, surrender'.[72] The result was catastrophic for Orthodox theology:

> A scholastic tradition was developed and a school begun, yet no spiritually creative movement resulted. Instead there emerged an imitative and provincial scholasticism, in its literal sense a *theologica scholastica* or 'school theology' ... in the process theology was torn from its living roots. A malignant schism set in between life and thought ... the aura of doom hovered over the entire movement, for it comprised a 'pseudomorphism' of Russia's religious consciousness, a 'pseudomorphosis' of Orthodox thought.[73]

Three other theological academies were founded in Russia modelled on the Kiev Academy. The Moscow Theological Academy and Seminary, located within the Trinity-St. Sergius Lavra in Sergiev Posad north of Moscow, had its origin as the Greek Latin School organized in Moscow in 1687. The St Petersburg Spiritual (or Theological) Academy was founded in 1797 and was the leading theological academy in Russia in the nineteenth century and until its closure by the Bolsheviks in 1918. The Kazan Theological Academy was founded in 1797 and in the nineteenth century, it had a strong missionary orientation.

During the first half of the nineteenth century, Russian gradually replaced Latin as the language of instruction. By the end of the nineteenth century, the Russian theological academies had attained a high academic level. Among their main achievements were translations of the Fathers of the Church into Russian and a large number of learned studies of the patristic period and the Fathers of the Church. The establishment of forerunner of the Kiev Theological Academy in 1635 may be considered the starting point for 'academic theology' or 'school theology', sometimes also called the 'moral school' or the 'historical school'.[74] This type of theology dominated the theological educational systems of countries of Orthodox tradition, especially Russia, Greece and Romania, until well into the twentieth century.

Correspondence with the English Non-Jurors (1716–25)

In the late seventeenth century there was some contact between Orthodoxy and the Church of England, but little came of this. From 1716 to 1725 there was correspondence between the Orthodox and the Non-Jurors, a group of Anglicans, including a number of bishops and a large number of clergy, who separated from the main body of the Church of England in 1688, rather than swear allegiance to the usurper of the throne William of Orange and his wife Mary as King and Queen

[72]Florovsky, *The Ways of Russian Theology*, I:85.

[73]Ibid. See also his 'Western Influences in Russian Theology', in Gallaher and Ladouceur, eds., *The Patristic Witness of Georges Florovsky*, 129–151.

[74]Paul Evdokimov calls it the 'moral school' and Georges Florovsky the 'historical school'. See Paul Evdokimov, *Le Christ dans la pensée russe* (Christ in Russian Thought) (Paris: Le Cerf, 1970), 121–43; and Florovsky, *The Ways of Russian Theology*, II:105–228.

of England, Scotland and Ireland. The Non-Jurors approached both the four Eastern Patriarchs and the Church of Russia in the hope of establishing communion with the Orthodox, with the patriarch of Jerusalem as their chief interlocutor. The replies of the Orthodox (1718 and 1723) were rather severe and patronizing and it appeared that the Orthodox were seeking not reunion or intercommunion, but 'complete submission to the patriarch of Jerusalem'.[75] In the end the Non-Jurors could not accept the Orthodox teaching on several key questions, notably the authority of the ancient ecumenical councils; the real presence of Christ in the Eucharist ('transubstantiation'); the veneration and invocation of the Mother of God and the saints; and icons – aspects of Orthodoxy which continued to trouble Protestants long afterwards.

The Encyclical of the Oriental Patriarchs of 1848

We conclude this discussion of Orthodox confessions of faith with the *Encyclical of the Eastern Patriarchs*,[76] a letter sent in May 1848, by the Oriental patriarchs of the Orthodox Church in reply to Pope Pius IX's *Epistle to the Easterns* (*Ad Orientales*, 6 January 1848). This was an apostolic letter sent in January 1848 to the bishops and clergy of the Orthodox churches not in communion with the Pope, urging them to rejoin Rome. Rather than being a private letter to Pius IX, the reply, signed by the patriarchs of Constantinople, Alexandria, Antioch and Jerusalem and their respective synods, was addressed to 'All the Bishops Everywhere'. The Encyclical restates the Orthodox position on the major outstanding theological questions between the Orthodox and the Catholic churches, notably the Filioque, called a 'heresy' added by the Catholic Church to the Nicene-Constantinopolitan Creed (paragraphs 5 and 6), and papal supremacy – indeed, most of the Encyclical is devoted to the status and role of the pope in the church.

Against the doctrine of papal infallibility, the patriarchs – perhaps inspired by their Russian contemporary, Metropolitan Philaret of Moscow – held that the preservation of faith resides in the total body of the church, that is to say, in the people itself:

> 17. … Neither patriarchs nor councils could then have introduced novelties amongst us, because the protector of religion is the very body of the church, even the people themselves, who desire their religious worship to be ever unchanged and of the same kind as that of their fathers.[77]

This statement does not advance directly the idea of the infallibility of the church as a basic principle of ecclesiology, but it does incorporate a notion of the church as the 'people of God', a notion which nineteenth-century Russian theologians such as Philaret of Moscow and the Slavophiles developed.

[75]H. W. Langford, 'The Non-Jurors and the Eastern Orthodox', a paper read to the Fellowship of St Alban and St Sergius Conference at Durham 26 June 1965. http://anglicanhistory.org/nonjurors/langford1.html (14 May 2014).
[76]Text in Pelikan and Hotchkiss, *Creeds and Confessions*, III:266–88.
[77]Pelikan and Hotchkiss, *Creeds and Confessions*, III:282.

The Encyclical also censures the papacy for Catholic missionary activities among Orthodox Christians (proselytism) and terminates with a vibrant appeal to the Orthodox clergy and faithful to cultivate 'the devotion of [their] whole soul and heart to the blameless, holy faith of our fathers, and love and affection to the Orthodox Church'.[78]

Although not a 'confession of the Orthodox faith' as such, the Encyclical is the major formal nineteenth-century statement of the Orthodox position on several key matters concerning the relationship of the Orthodox Church and the Catholic Church.

Conclusion

Contemporary Orthodoxy has an ambivalent attitude towards the 'Symbolic Books'.[79] On the one hand, they are major Orthodox responses to stimuli from external sources and some have ecclesial status. They thus have a certain historical value, yet none can be considered definitive doctrinal statements. Jaroslav Pelikan characterizes them as 'equal and opposite reactions' to challenges from the Christian West, both Catholic and Protestant, and from Islam.[80] Most originated during the long centuries when many Orthodox churches were under Turkish and Arabic rule, and when Orthodox theology was weak or even practically non-existent – even in Russia theology remained underdeveloped until the nineteenth century. The seventeenth-century confessions, with the possible exception of Peter Mogila's, which is in the form of a catechism, were not intended to serve a pedagogical role within the Orthodox Church and had no practical impact on Orthodox life and spirituality. Despite the theological inadequacies of the confessions, they are nonetheless important witnesses to the continuity of the faith during this period of trial and they constitute the most significant theological documents emerging from the long centuries when Eastern Christianity was unable to engage in creative and independent theological reflection, the five centuries after Gregory Palamas in the fourteenth century until the mid-nineteenth century.[81]

Most Orthodox consider as adequate expressions of the Orthodox faith the Nicene-Constantinoplean Creed, together with certain major dogmatic pronouncements of later ecumenical councils, especially those pertaining to Christology and, as some Orthodox theologians contend, the proclamations of the councils of Constantinople of 1341 and 1351 on Palamite theology – the distinction, without separation, between the divine essence and the divine energies.[82] Non-Orthodox have tended to attach far more importance to the Symbolic Books than Orthodox – most Orthodox have never heard of them. Sergius Bulgakov, writing in the mid-

---

[78]Ibid., III:286.

[79]See Pelikan, *Credo*, 399ff.

[80]Pelikan, *Credo*, 419–26.

[81]For a general survey of other aspects of Greek theology after the fall of Constantinople, see Maloney, *A History of Orthodox Theology Since 1453*, 89–210. Theology in Russia will be considered in the next chapter.

[82]See the discussion on this point under the heading 'Theologoumenon or Dogma?' by Kallistos Ware, 'God Hidden and Revealed: The Apophatic Way and the Essence-Energies Distinction', *Eastern Churches Review*, 7 (1975), 136. Ware refers to the distinction between essence and energies as 'an indispensable part of the faith', and he cites Ioannis Karmiris who maintains the same position.

1930s primarily for a Western audience, is categorical in pointing out that the Symbolic Books identified in Orthodoxy especially by Protestant theologians have no particular status as confessions of faith among the Orthodox themselves, but are rather personal documents:

> In recent times there has appeared the idea of 'symbolic books' or 'confessions' of Orthodoxy which, like the symbolic books in Protestantism, are supposed to expound the dogmatic constitution or basic law of the church. Certain documents called by that name (the answer of the Eastern Patriarchs to Pius IX, the profession of Orthodox faith of Mogila, etc.) may have more or less authority. Nevertheless, they are not symbols of faith: symbolic books, in the strict sense of the word, have no place in Orthodoxy. If they existed, they would replace and abolish the living tradition they are supposed to express. The symbolic books of Protestantism are constitutional charts which serve as foundation for new ecclesiastical societies who do not accept tradition for themselves. Strictly speaking, these books make a beginning of church tradition for Protestant societies. It is evident that in this sense symbolic books are not characteristic of Orthodoxy. What answer to that name are simply the responses of the hierarchy to questions asked by Protestants, or definitions of Orthodoxy, given by itself, as evidence in relation to another confession. Thus pragmatically, and in a certain historic context, these writings also can certainly be submitted to revision.[83]

Other modern Orthodox theologians accord these statements of faith somewhat more status than Bulgakov. In assessing the early ecumenical contacts between Orthodox and Western churches, the seventeenth-century confessions of faith and councils, Kallistos Ware arrives at a balanced judgement:

> Looking back on the work of Mogila and Dositheus, on the councils of Jassy and Jerusalem, and on the correspondence with the Non-Jurors, one is struck by the limitations of Greek theology in this period: one does not find the Orthodox tradition in its *fullness*. Nevertheless the councils of the seventeenth century made a permanent and constructive contribution to Orthodoxy. The Reformation controversies raised problems which neither the Ecumenical Councils nor the church of the later Byzantine Empire was called to face: in the seventeenth century the Orthodox were forced to think more carefully about the sacraments, and about the nature and authority of the church. It was important for Orthodoxy to express its mind on these topics, and to define its position in relation to the new teachings which had arisen in the West; this was the task which the seventeenth-century councils achieved.[84]

If Cyril Lucaris's Confession leaned explicitly towards Calvinism, those of Peter Mogila and Dositheus sought to employ both Orthodox and Catholic arguments to redress the balance, but unfortunately on some issues they espouse Roman positions or use Latin terminology to the detriment of authentic Orthodox theology. Nonetheless, the Confession of Dositheus in particular lays out basic Orthodox teaching on such crucial questions as the assertion of the importance of the tradition of the church, human free will, divine-human synergy and the infallibility of the church. While Georges Florovsky is correct in citing Mogila's Confession as an example of the

---

[83]Sergius Bulgakov, *The Orthodox Church* (1935) (Crestwood, NY: St Vladimir's Seminary Press, 1988), n. 1, 35.
[84]Ware, *The Orthodox Church* (1997), 99; (2015), 95–6.

'pseudomorphosis' of Orthodox theology,[85] it has to be seen in relation to the Protestant excesses of Lucaris's Confession on the one hand, and the later, more balanced, if still Latin-leaning, Confession of Dositheus on the other.

The seventeenth-century Orthodox confessions of faith constitute the major Orthodox theological statements of the time and indeed up to the middle of the nineteenth century. The 'agenda' of the confessions was largely determined by the need to define the Orthodox faith in relation to the Western confessions of faith, and especially to take a stand on the conflict between Protestantism and Catholicism. Since the agenda of the Confessions was determined by external stimulation from the West, it is perhaps not surprising that we look in vain for such characteristically Orthodox theological notions as apophatism and negative theology, the distinction between the divine essence and the divine energies and theosis as the goal of human existence. These are central notions in the patristic tradition of the Greek Fathers from the Apologists to Gregory Palamas but are decidedly muted or inexistent in Western theology and did not feature in the exchanges between Christian East and Christian West. It was not until the revival of patristic theology well into the twentieth century that they returned to centre stage in Orthodox thought.

Although Orthodox theology was weak and inadequate, for good historical reasons, for several centuries after the fall of Constantinople, the faith was still vibrant in the countries of Orthodox tradition, as shown by several indicators. The achievements of religious art in Russia, mainly icons, from the fourteenth to the sixteenth centuries are prodigious. Monasticism expanded considerably in Russia and the icon workshops of Moscow, Novgorod, Pskov, Tver and Vladimir reached their zenith during this period. There was a spiritual decline in the seventeenth and eighteenth centuries, which nonetheless witnessed several remarkable saints, such as Nil Sorski (c. 1433–1508), Juliana Lazarevskaia (1530–1604), Tikhon of Zadonsk (1724–83) and Dimitri of Rostov (1651–1709). In the remnants of the Byzantine Empire, the strength of the faith was evident in the continuity of the church among the Christian population, and in the witness of 'new martyrs', often simple laymen falsely accused of having become Muslim and then reverted to Christianity – an offence punishable by death under Islamic law. The *New Martyrologion* of 1799, prepared by St Nicodemus of the Holy Mountain,[86] describes the lives and martyrdom of eighty-seven neo-martyrs and the lives of at least thirty others are known between 1800 and 1867, prior to the systematic massacres of large numbers of Christians that marked the late nineteenth century and the early twentieth century. The persistence of the faith under adverse circumstances laid the groundwork for the spiritual and theological renaissance which took place beginning in the late eighteenth century, initiated by the return to the traditional sources of Orthodox spirituality, symbolized notably by the publication of the collection of writings of the ascetic Fathers known as the *Philokalia* in 1792, which inaugurated a broad, patristically based spiritual and theological revival in Orthodoxy.[87]

---

[85]Florovsky, *The Ways of Russian Theology*, I:77.

[86]See L. J. Papadopoulos and G. Lizardos, eds., *New Martyrs of the Turkish Yoke* (Seattle, WA: St. Nectarios Press, 1985); and Leonidas Papadopoulos, *Slain For Their Faith – Orthodox Christian Martyrs Under Moslem Oppression* (Ellensburg, WA: Leo Papadopoulos, 2013).

[87]See Ch. 5, 95–6.

3

Theology in Imperial Russia

Chapter Outline

The conflict between the 'Possessors' and the 'Non-Possessors'

A series of interrelated events in the history of the Russian Orthodox Church (ROC) set the stage for emergence of modern theology in the nineteenth century.[1] The first was a conflict over the nature of monasticism. Russian monasticism experienced a period of great flowering in the fourteenth and fifteenth centuries, inspired to a considerable extent by the renewal of the hesychastic tradition on Mount Athos, supported by the theology of the divine energies defended by St Gregory Palamas (1296–1359), ratified by several councils of the Church of Constantinople between 1341 and 1351. The most important figure of the spiritual renewal and monastic reform in Russia was St Sergius of Radonezh (1314–92) and under his inspiration and that of his spiritual successors, monasticism became firmly implanted as an essential feature of Russian Christianity. But by the late fifteenth century, Russian monasticism was

[1]For general references to the history of the Church of Russia, see the Selected Bibliography for this chapter.

marked by two different conceptions of monastic life and the role of monasteries, sustained by two different groups of monks. One party, known as the 'Non-Possessors', advocated an ascetic and mystical vision of monasticism, inherited from the Desert Fathers and the hesychastic tradition of Mount Athos. In this vision, monasticism entails a detachment from the world in order to devote oneself entirely to spiritual undertakings, to pray for the world and to set an example of ideal Christian life. The monastic vow of poverty signifies both personal and institutional poverty; hence monasteries should live essentially from their own income and should not possess great domains, even if these were offered as gifts. This vision of monasticism was represented by St Nil (or Nilus) Sorski (1433–1508). Nilus spent several years on Mount Athos and after his return to Russia he disseminated hesychastic spirituality among Russian monks, promoting monastic poverty and the creation of small monastic foundations with only a few monks, more conducive to prayer and spiritual growth than large monasteries.

The 'Possessors' emphasized the social responsibility of monasteries towards the sick, the poor, travellers and visitors, teaching, healing and assisting those in need. Hence, they argued, monasteries were justified in accepting substantial donations from the wealthy and in owning large estates to produce the revenue required to finance extensive charitable undertakings. At the time about one-third of the land in Russia belonged to monasteries, as a result of donations by pious Russian landowners. In this vision of monasticism, the vow of poverty applies to individuals, not to monasteries. The principal representative of this vision of monasticism was St Joseph of Volokolamsk (1439–1515). Joseph was also one of the leading opponents of a heresy whose adherents were known as Judaizers. The Judaizer heresy, initiated by Jews in dialogue with Christians in Novgorod about 1470, advocated the superiority of the Old Testament over the New and denied the Trinity and hence Christ's divinity and resurrection. The heresy gained considerable support among the clergy and high society in Moscow.

The advocates of both views of monasticism claimed their spiritual heritage from St Sergius of Radonezh. To some extent both were right – but in St Sergius the two aspects of monasticism existed harmoniously in one person who was able to combine an intense spiritual life with active service on behalf of the needy. The Possessors and the Non-Possessors existed in parallel until the conflict on the issue of monastic properties came into the open at a council of the ROC in 1503. Then and subsequently a majority of church leaders supported the Possessors. In the years that followed, the disciples of Nil Sorski, also called the trans-Volga hermits, were persecuted and the tradition of St Nilus was driven underground.

Several other characteristics of the Possessors were important for the future of the Russian Church and theology in Russia. Firstly, following the lead of Joseph of Volokolamsk, they held a severe attitude towards religious dissenters, believing that heretics, especially the Judaizers, should be treated harshly, even tortured and executed, in contrast with an attitude of tolerance towards dissenters aimed at their re-education and forgiveness advocated by Nilus and his followers. Secondly, the Possessors emphasized a strict adherence to ecclesiastical rules in such areas as monastic practice (dress, fasting, silence, attendance at services, etc.) and the celebration of liturgical services – maintaining to the letter all the external 'pomp', the beauty and dignity of

Orthodox liturgical services. Thirdly, Joseph and other Possessors believed in the close association of the church and the state in governing the people, an echo of the 'symphony' theory of government inherited from the Byzantine Empire, although Joseph also supported disobedience to unjust rulers. Finally, many Josephites believed that Russia, and more specifically Muscovy, had become the 'Third Rome' of Christendom: the ancient Church of Rome was the First Rome; Constantinople was the Second Rome, and now Moscow the Third Rome, since the First Rome had fallen into heresy and schism as a result of the Filioque, and Constantinople had accepted the union with Rome at the Council of Florence and had come under Turkish rule. This meant that Muscovy, the Third Rome, was now the legitimate leader of Orthodoxy. The self-proclamation of the autocephaly (ecclesiastical independence) of the Russian Church from Constantinople in 1448, after Constantinople's support for the Union of Ferrera-Florence, and the election of the first patriarch of Moscow in 1589 reinforced the Third Rome theory.

The ascendancy of the Josephite view of monasticism and the church resulted in the increasing isolation and provincialism of the Russian Church, its growing dependence on and subservience to the state, and the domination of ritualism and formalism over intellectual and spiritual creativity in the upper echelons of the church.

The schism of the 'Old Believers' (*Raskolniki*)

The triumph of the Possessors over their spiritual rivals set the stage for a major and catastrophic event in the history of the Russian Church in the middle of the seventeenth century. Patriarch Nikon of Moscow (1605–81), who ruled from 1652 until his resignation in 1658, was a firm admirer of the Greek Church. He set out to reform Russian liturgical practice where it differed from contemporary Greek practice, in particular the service books and certain rituals, in appearance minor, but in reality symbolic of Russian adherence to its own traditions as distinct from those of the Greek Church, viewed as compromised because of the union of Florence and the Turkish conquest. These rituals included the way of making the Sign of the Cross (two fingers crossed – the old Russian way; or three fingers crossed – the Greek way); the recitation of 'Alleluia' during services (twice instead of three times); and the manner of making processions in the church (clockwise, the Russian way, or counterclockwise, the Greek way).

Nikon encountered strong resistance from portions of the clergy who saw no reason to emulate Greek practice as found in the contemporary Greek liturgical manuals. The reforms were implemented in 1654–5 and the dissenters were persecuted – the leader, Avvakum (1620–82), was exiled for ten years in Siberia and imprisoned for twenty-two years before being burnt at the stake with three of his close companions. A pan-Orthodox Council held in Moscow in 1666–7, attended by the patriarchs of Alexandria and Antioch, excommunicated the dissenters, driving them out of the ROC. In addition to Avvakum, other leaders of the dissenters were imprisoned and executed, and many dissenters protested by self-immolation. The conflict produced a profound division in Russian society and a lasting schism (the *raskol*) in the Russian Church. Important segments of the church broke away, becoming known as the 'Old Believers' (more accurately the 'Old Ritualists'), the *Raskolniki*.

Nikon also attempted to exercise a decisive influence in secular affairs, but he went too far, notably by asserting the superiority of the church over the state, and after a quarrel with tsar Alexei (ruled 1645–76), he was forced to resign in 1658 and to retire to a monastery. He was formally deposed by the Moscow Council of 1666–7, although his liturgical reforms remained in place. The persecution of the Old Believers, who split into many factions, continued, even though they may have accounted for up to one-third of Russia's population at the time.

The reforms of Peter the Great

The conflict resulting from Patriarch Nikon's ill-fated reforms and his ill-advised involvement in secular affairs set the stage for the reforms of Peter the Great (1672–1725), who reigned for forty-three years, from 1682 to 1696 with his half-brother Ivan, then as sole ruler until his death. Peter was determined to modernize Russia in all respects along Western lines and he acted vigorously to replace many Russian traditions with European ones, including a centralized absolute monarchy with unrestrained authority over both state and church. To facilitate Russia's contacts with the West, he built a new capital, Saint Petersburg, on the shores of the Baltic Sea, with direct sea access to Western Europe.

Peter's ecclesiastical policy was inspired above all by his determination to insure that the Russian Church could no more attempt to place itself above the state, as Nikon had sought to do. Peter subordinated the church to the state. After the death of Patriarch Adrian in 1700, Peter refused to allow the appointment of a successor and in 1721 he issued a decree known as the *Spiritual Regulation*. This abolished the patriarchate and set up in its place a commission, the Spiritual College or Holy Synod, composed of twelve members, three of whom were bishops, and the rest drawn from the heads of monasteries or from the married clergy. The constitution of the Synod had no precedence in Orthodoxy and was not based on Orthodox canon law, but was copied from Protestant ecclesiastical synods in Germany. Its members were not chosen by the church but appointed by the emperor, who could dismiss them. A government official, the Chief Procurator, was the link between the government and the Holy Synod. Although not formally a member of the Synod, the Chief Procurator was a sort of 'executive secretary' who was responsible for the agenda of the Synod and conveyed its decisions to the emperor for his approval. In practice the Procurator wielded considerable power over church affairs and was in effect a 'minister of religious affairs'. Peter's reforms ended the uneasy balance of authority that had previously existed between patriarch and tsar, suppressing ecclesiastical criticism of the ruler and state policy and transforming the church into a department of the imperial administration, a 'ministry of religion'.

As the Westernization of Russia continued after Peter's death in 1725, the wealth of Russian monasteries attracted the attention of emperors (and empresses) eager to fill their coffers to carry out their ambitious dreams of grandeur along Western European lines. Monasticism was increasingly placed under severe restrictions. New monasteries were not to be founded without special permission; monks were forbidden to live as hermits; and no woman under the age of fifty was allowed to take vows as a nun. Peter and his successors drastically circumscribed the wealth and influence of the monasteries. Anna (1693–1740; reigned 1730–40), Peter's niece, initiated a reign of terror against the church aimed at eliminating any opposition to state supremacy. Elizabeth, Peter's daughter (1709–62; reigned 1741–62), confiscated most of the monastic estates, and Catherine the Great, more German and Lutheran than Russian and Orthodox (1729–96; reigned 1762–96), suppressed more than half the remaining monasteries and imposed a strict limitation to the number of monks. Bishops, monks and priests who raised their voice against state policy were subject to imprisonment, torture and execution. The lower clergy, often ill suited for their pastoral responsibilities, became a poverty-struck and socially inferior self-perpetuating clerical caste.

Thus the triumph of the monastic vision of the Possessors in the early sixteenth century ultimately resulted in a major disaster for the Russian Orthodox Church and contributed to the subordination of the church to the state. The system of ecclesial government which Peter the Great established remained in force with few modifications for two centuries, until it was abolished during the Russian Revolution of 1917.

Russian theology from the time of Peter the Great until the mid-nineteenth century was a sort of hundred years' war between Protestant and Catholic influences. In this period of pseudo-theology, Orthodox theology, with its biblical and patristic base, remained very much in the background, awaiting its time to emerge. Under Peter the Great, the Protestant tendency gained the upper hand, typified especially by Theophane Prokopovitch (1681–1738), the cruel and ambitious archbishop of Novgorod, author, with Peter, of the *Spiritual Regulation* which subjected the church to the state in the manner of German Lutheran principalities and paved the way for the introduction of other Protestant notions into Russian theology. Prokopovitch's Protestantism, a reaction to the Roman influence of Peter Mogila and the Theological Academy of Kiev, spread deeply in the church through the Seminary of Saint Petersburg, which Prokopovitch founded in 1725, and the Moscow Theological Academy and Seminary. But by the early nineteenth century the Protestantizers were forced to yield to a new generation of Catholicizers, typified by Nicholas Protasov (1798–1855), who served as Procurator of the Holy Synod, and to a lesser degree, by Metropolitan Philaret (Drozdov) (1782–1867). There was an aggressive repudiation of Protestant tendencies in theology and a marked return to the theology of Peter Mogila and the Academy of Kiev, with Roman influences on specific questions, a period that Georges Florovsky characterizes as the 'return to scholasticism'[2] but which nonetheless laid the groundwork for the full blossoming of Russian academic theology in the second half of the nineteenth century.

[2]Georges Florovsky, *The Ways of Russian Theology* (2 vols.) in *The Collected Works of Georges Florovsky*, Vols. 5 and 6 (Belmont, MA: Nordland, 1979). I:201–12. See a summary of this dark period in the history of the Russian Orthodox Church in Dimitri Pospielovsky, *The Orthodox Church in the History of Russia* (Crestwood, NY: St Vladimir's Seminary Press, 1998), 105–17.

The spiritual revival of the nineteenth century

Despite the weaknesses and failings of the 'Synodal' period of the ROC, the subordination of the church to the state and the Westernization of the ecclesiastical education system, Russia experienced a great spiritual revival during the nineteenth century. This revival was sparked by a renewal of hesychastic spirituality on Mount Athos and in Romania and the publication of the Slavonic and the Russian translations of the *Philokalia*. The *Philokalia*, first published in Greek in 1782, in Slavonic in 1793 and in Russian in 1877, is a collection of spiritual and ascetic writings from the fourth to the fourteenth centuries, focusing on hesychastic spirituality and the practice of the Jesus Prayer. The Russian spiritual revival was marked by such great spiritual figures as St Seraphim of Sarov (1759–1833) and the holy elders (*startsi*) of the monastery of Optino, as well as saintly bishops. Seraphim of Sarov, the most beloved of modern Russian saints, spent his long monastic life first in the monastery of Sarov, then as a hermit in the forest and finally as a recluse in the monastery. It was only in the final years of his life that he received visitors and welcomed all those who came to see him for his prayers, his blessing and his spiritual counsel. His canonization in 1903, with the Tsar Nicholas II and the royal family in attendance, was the last great public manifestation of 'Holy Russia'.

St Seraphim did not have successors of his stature and after his death another monastic community, the monastery of Optino, or rather its dependency, the skite of St John the Baptist, became the heart of hesychastic spirituality in Russia, thanks to a succession of illustrious *startsi*, from the 1820s until the Bolsheviks closed the monastery in 1923. As with St Seraphim, crowds of visitors came to meet and to receive counsel from the saintly igumens of Optino, one or two of whom inspired the figure of the starets Zosima in Dostoyevsky's novel *The Brothers Karamazov*.

St Ignatius Brianchaninov (1807–67) and St Theophan the Recluse (1815–94) were closely associated with the 'Philokalic revival' of Russian spirituality in the nineteenth century. Although both were bishops, they were not primarily involved with the administration of the church, but were rather spiritual leaders. Briantchaninov was ordained bishop in 1857, but after an illness, he was allowed to retire to a monastery four years later. Similarly, Theophan (Govorov) was ordained bishop in 1863, but in 1866, inspired by Briantchaninov, he resigned his see and spent the remainder of his a life as a recluse in a small monastery. Both became influential spiritual figures as a result of their writings, extensive correspondence and spiritual counsels. Theophan the Recluse prepared the Russian edition of the *Philokalia* and was closely associated with the revision and publication of the *Tales of a Russian Pilgrim*, an anonymous popular work of fiction centred on the Jesus Prayer, first published in 1881.

In the absence of a patriarch, the metropolitan of Moscow was usually the most prestigious hierarch of the ROC, followed by the metropolitan of Saint Petersburg. The most eminent metropolitan of Moscow during the nineteenth century was Philaret (Drozdov) (metropolitan from 1822 to 1867). Philaret was an able administrator, a man of prayer and an excellent preacher. Philaret's saintly if forceful personality and his long tenure assured his influence in the church for over half a century. Philaret was succeeded by the more modest but also saintly Innocent (Veniaminov) (1797–1879). He was a missionary priest in Alaska, then a Russian possession, and, after the death of his wife, he served as Bishop of Alaska from 1840 to 1867 and Metropolitan of Moscow from 1867 to 1879.

One of the last major saintly figures of imperial Russia was Father John of Kronstadt (John Sergiyev, 1829–1908). Canonized by the Patriarchate of Moscow in 1990, John of Kronstadt was a pious and saintly priest of a poor parish in an industrial part of Saint Petersburg, and was noted especially for his devoted celebration of liturgy, his compassion and caring for the poor and his advocacy of frequent communion, as well as for his miracles.

The period from the 1830s until the end of the nineteenth century also witnessed a great flowering of the Russian literature and music. The remarkable achievements of Russian poetry, short stories and novels during this period are referred to as the 'Golden Age' (or 'Golden Era') of Russian letters. Religious themes feature prominently in literary productions, especially the novels of Nicholas Gogol (1809–52), Feodor Dostoevsky (1821–81) and Leon Tolstoy (1828–1910), to such an extent that they are considered major philosophical and theological figures in their own right. Dostoevsky and Tolstoy are important personalities of the Russian religious renaissance of the late nineteenth and early twentieth centuries, which will be considered in detail in Chapter 4.

The *Catechism* of St Philaret of Moscow

Metropolitan Philaret was unquestionably the most important hierarch of the Russian Orthodox Church in the nineteenth century. In the first part of his ecclesiastical service, Philaret was concerned mainly with theological education. After his graduation from the Moscow Theological Academy and Seminary in 1803, he taught Latin and Greek there until 1809, when he was assigned to the St Petersburg Academy. He was deeply involved in the reform of the Russian theological academies at the time, and in 1812 became the rector of the St Petersburg Academy.

Language issues were very prominent in the Russian Church in those years – whether instruction in the theological academies and seminaries should continue to be in Latin or should be in Russian; and whether the Bible should be translated into Russian, or should continue to exist only in Slavonic. Philaret engaged a lengthy battle in favour of the use of Russian in religious education and a Russian Bible. Latin was abandoned progressively but it was only in the 1840s that it was dropped completely as a language of theological instruction. The publication of the Bible in Russian took even longer. Although the Gospels were published in Russian in 1816 and the entire New Testament and the Psalter in 1822, the first complete Russian Bible, the 'Synodal Bible', was finally published only in 1876, after long delays because of conflicts over the propriety of publishing the Bible in Russian.[3]

Philaret was ordained bishop in 1817, and in 1821 he was appointed archbishop of Moscow then Metropolitan of Moscow in 1826, serving for 51 years. Most of his published works consist of sermons. His major theological work is his *Catechism*, which first appeared in a short version in 1823 and the *Longer Catechism* in 1830, with several later revisions and re-editions. An English

---

[3]See Florovsky, *The Ways of Russian Theology*, I:188–201. The entire Russian Bible was actually printed in 1825, but it was seized and destroyed before it could be distributed.

translation was published as early as 1845,[4] and it was also published in German, Greek, Romanian, Serbian and Bulgarian. Although Philaret's *Catechism* was long influential in countries of Orthodox tradition, it was never formally approved by a pan-Orthodox authority, unlike the sixteenth-century Confessions of Peter Mogila and Dositheus.

Philaret's *Catechism* contains 611 questions and answers and, like Peter Mogila's Confession, is divided into three parts based on the three 'theological virtues', faith, hope and charity:

Introduction: Deals with revelation, tradition and Scripture.
Part I. Faith: A commentary on the Nicene Creed and on the sacraments, which are discussed after the tenth article of the Creed (baptism);
Part II. Hope: A short section on prayer, followed by a commentary on the Lord's Prayer, the Doxology and the Beatitudes;
Part III. Love: A commentary on the Decalogue.
Conclusion: A short section on 'The Application of the Doctrine of Faith and Piety'.

Although Philaret is much less Latin in his theology than Mogila nearly two centuries earlier, still the general tone of his catechism is often more Western than Orthodox. He nonetheless omits entirely treating the seven gifts of the Holy Spirit, the nine fruits of the Holy Spirit and the nine precepts of the church – typically Roman Catholic subjects taken up by Mogila. Like Mogila and Dositheus, he rejects the Filioque (Q. 541–2), the Protestant notion of predestination (Q. 123) and the Catholic doctrine of purgatorial fire (Q. 372). Philaret does not mention 'original sin' at all, but instead of the Augustinian notion of the inheritance of Adam's guilt by his descendants, he appeals to the more typically patristic teaching that the consequences of Adam's sin in the form of 'the curse and death' are transmitted to his descendants:

> Because all have come of Adam since his infection by sin, and all sin themselves. As from an infected source there naturally flows an infected stream, so from a father infected with sin, and consequently mortal, there naturally proceeds a posterity infected like him with sin, and like him mortal. (Q. 168)

As a corollary, baptism has nothing do with original sin, but its function is death 'to the carnal life of sin' and rebirth 'of the Holy Spirit to a life spiritual and holy' (Q. 288). Again, unlike Mogila, Philaret makes no mention of the Western distinction between mortal and 'non-mortal' (venial) sins. In the later editions of the *Catechism*, Philaret, while retaining the word 'transubstantiation' for the Eucharist, follows the Encyclical of the Eastern Patriarchs of 1848, ascribing to the term a definition unrelated to the Aristotelian categories of substance and accident:

> The bread and wine are changed, or transubstantiated, into the very Body of Christ, and into the very Blood of Christ. … In the exposition of the faith by the Eastern Patriarchs, it is said that the word transubstantiation is not to be taken to define the manner in which the bread and wine are changed into the Body and Blood of the Lord; for this none can understand but God; but only thus much is

[4] *The Longer Catechism of the Orthodox, Catholic, Eastern Church* (also known as the 'Catechism of St. Philaret, Metropolitan of Moscow') in Philip Schaff, *The Creeds of Christendom with a History and Critical Notes*, 3 Vols. (New York: Harper, 1876). This reproduces the translation by R. W. Blackmore in *The Doctrine of the Russian Church* (Aberdeen, 1845). Online at the Christian Classics Ethereal Library. www.ccel.org/s/schaff/creeds2 (30 May 2014).

signified, that the bread truly, really, and substantially becomes the very true Body of the Lord, and the wine the very Blood of the Lord. (Q. 339–340)

Georges Florovsky has a very high opinion of Philaret, despite a certain harshness in Philaret's character. Philaret is one of the very few Russian theological figures who receive even a passing grade from Florovsky in his *Ways of Russian Theology*:

> His *Sermons and Addresses* remains his principal theological legacy. Philaret never constructed a theological system. His sermons are only fragments, but they contain an inner wholeness and unity. It is not a unity of system, it is a unity of conception. These fragments reveal a living theological experience tormented and tempered in an ordeal of prayer and vigil. Philaret of Moscow was the first person in the history of modern Russian theology for whom theology once more became the aim of life, the essential step toward spiritual progress and construction. He was not merely a theologian, he lived theology. … His sermons dwelled most frequently on the Word of God. He did not consult Holy Scriptures for proofs: he proceeded from the sacred texts. In [Alexander] Bukharev's apt phrase, for Philaret bibical texts 'were the thoughts of the Living and All-wise God emanating from his unknowableness for our understanding'. His thoughts lived in the Biblical element. He pondered aloud while sifting the nuances of a Biblical image or story. Philaret, notes Bukharev, never allowed his theology to become a 'legal investigation governed by a dogmatic code of laws', as was usually the case before Philaret's time and as too often recurred during the epoch of the 'return to the time of scholasticism'.[5]

Academic theology in the nineteenth century

One positive effect of the strong Western influence in the Russian theological academies was a significant improvement in the standard of Russian theological scholarship during the nineteenth century, such that by the end of the century, theological scholarship was at a very high level, especially in such fields as patristics, biblical studies and church history. Both Alexander Schmemann and Kallistos Ware praise the achievements of pre-revolutionary academic theology:

> A new interest in church history and Church Fathers (a virtually complete translation of their writings was achieved in theological academies), in liturgy and in spirituality, led progressively to a dogmatic revival. By the end of the nineteenth century, Russian academic theology stood on its own feet, both in terms of quality (Harnack learned Russian in order to read a monograph on Theodoret of Cyr) and inner independence.[6]
>
> By 1900 Russian academic theology was at its height, and there were a number of theologians, historians, and liturgists, thoroughly trained in western academic disciplines.[7]

---

[5]Florovsky, *The Ways of Russian Theology*, I:212. Surprisingly, Florovsky quotes approvingly Alexander Bukharev (1829–71), whom Florovsky severely castigates later in *The Ways of Russian Philosophy* (II:119–22).

[6]Alexander Schmemann, 'Russian Theology: 1920-1972: An Introductory Survey', *St Vladimir's Theological Quarterly*, 16, 4 (1972), 174–5.

[7]Timothy (Kallistos) Ware, *The Orthodox Church* (London: Penguin, 1993), 124.

Russian academic theology had learned from its Western models and had learned its lessons well. What it lacked was a truly creative appropriation of the spirit of patristic theology and, indeed, theological creativity in general; the heavy, formal structures of church administration and the empire stifled rather than encouraged creativity. Nicolas Berdyaev caustically remarks: 'In Russian Orthodoxy, there existed no theology at all for a long while, for there existed only an imitation of Western scholasticism.'[8] But Berdyaev's hasty dismissal of academic theology must be weighed against the real achievements of the academic theologians, not the least attempts to engage with the same questions that the Slavophiles grappled with, especially the nature of Orthodoxy and its relationship to the Christian West. Much of this discussion took place in the last quarter of the nineteenth century and the first years of the twentieth century, as academic theologians somewhat belatedly sought to assimilate, favourably or critically, the Slavophile analysis of the relationship between Eastern and Western Christianity.[9]

One of the most characteristic features of academic theology, in Russia and elsewhere, was manuals or textbooks of dogmatic theology – unfortunately too much modelled or even copied from Western manuals, either Catholic or Protestant. 'In terms of theological systems, the mid-nineteenth century remained entirely scholastic in its approach and style,' writes Olga Nesmiyanova.[10] The most important theological manuals in the nineteenth century were those of Macarius Bulgakov (1816–82), who served as Metropolitan of Moscow from 1879 to 1882. His *Orthodox Dogmatic Theology*, originally published in six volumes in 1847–53, is largely a collection of biblical and patristic citations arranged according to the typical structure of Western manuals of dogmatic theology. Together with his one-volume *Introduction to Orthodox Theology* (1855), and a summary of dogmatic theology, Macarius's works remained popular textbooks until the end of the imperial regime. He also wrote a twelve-volume *History of the Russian Church*, which became a standard work.

Macarius was far from an original thinker and, like many of his predecessors in Russia, he drew freely from Western sources and methodology in his writings. His theology nonetheless represents a stage in the movement to eliminate the Protestant influence in Russian theology in the wake of Peter the Great, represented in particular by Theophan Prokopovich (1681–1736). Nineteenth-century Russian dogmatic theology sought to redress the undue or even exclusive importance attached to Scripture as source of theology by highlighting the role of natural revelation and more importantly, of tradition and of the church itself, as the guardian and interpreter of Scripture while at the same asserting the superiority of revelation over reason.[11]

Despite positive aspects of the *Dogmatica* of Macarius Bulgakov and other contemporary Russian theologians, commentators have not been kind to Macarius. Already in the mid-nineteenth

---

[8]Nicolas Berdyaev, *The Russian Idea* (New York: Macmillan, 1948), 156.

[9]For an overview of this discussion in the Russian academic community prior to the revolution, see Vera Shevzov, 'The Burdens of Tradition: Orthodox Constructions of the West in Russia (late 19th – early 20th cc.)', in George Demacopoulos and Aristotle Papanikolaou, eds., *Orthodox Constructions of the West* (New York: Fordham University Press, 2013).

[10]Olga Nesmiyanova, 'Russian Theology', in David Fergusson, ed., *The Blackwell Companion to Nineteenth-Century Theology* (Chichester, UK: John Wiley-Blackwell, 2010), 221.

[11]See Nesmiyanova, 'Russian Theology', 218–20.

century, Alexei Khomiakov refers to Macarius's *Dogmatic* as 'delightfully stupid'.[12] Georges Florovsky's critique of Macarius's manual and the spirit – or rather lack of spirit – that lies behind it is devastating:

> The *Orthodox Dogmatic Theology* also of Macarius Bulgakov, later Metropolitan of Moscow and an outstanding historian of the Russian Church, remains despite all its merits a dead book, a monument to dead erudition, unrefreshed by the spirit of true church life – and thus again, a Western book.[13]
>
> There was something bureaucratic in his writing style and exposition. His dogmatic theology lacked precisely a 'sense of the church'. He dealt with texts, not with evidence or truths. Hence he had such a lifeless and uninspired style which carried no conviction. … Macarius had no personal views. He was more objective than others, for he had no opinions of his own. His was an objectivity from indifference. Many were irritated by the inner indifference and soullessness in Macarius's books from the day they appeared. … Macarius's book was outdated the day it first saw the light, and it remained unneeded and without a role to play in Russian theological consciousness.[14]

Paul Evdokimov writes similarly of Macarius's *Dogmatic Theology*: '[It is] a work strangely devoid of dogmatic sense, written with an objectivity which borders on indifference. … Impressive, but without a soul and absolutely no internal dialectic of dogmatic consciousness.'[15]

The manuals of dogmatics and other theological textbooks patterned on Macarius had a long life even after the end of the empire. Many were reprinted when Stalin permitted the reopening of theological schools in 1943 and persisted even after the fall of the Communist regime. Metropolitan Hilarion Alfeyev noted in 2000:

> Works by pre-revolution authors continued to be used as textbooks since contemporary theological literature proved practically inaccessible to Russian theological schools. This situation continues in theological seminaries and academies to this day. During the 1990s vast numbers of religious books published prior to the revolution have been reprinted, but the original theological studies by contemporary authors can be counted on the fingers of one hand.[16]

Academic theology began to shake off the influence of Western theology during the nineteenth century, although this liberation was gradual and was far from complete even by 1917. Philaret played a major role in initiating this movement and for this is praised by Florovsky:

> *Russian theology's true overcoming not only of specific Western influences, but of Westernism in general, first begins with Philaret.* This happened in a way – the one and only way – that can lead to lasting successes: namely, through creatively harking back to the holy *patristic foundations and sources*, and through the *return to patristics*, which served as a true source of delight for Philaret, setting the standard for his own work.[17]

---

[12]Cited in Berdyaev, *The Russian Idea*, 162.

[13]Georges Florovsky, 'Western Influences in Russian Theology' (1937), in Brandon Gallaher and Paul Ladouceur, eds., *The Patristic Witness of Georges Florovsky: Essential Theological Writings* (London: T&T Clark, 2019), 145.

[14]Florovsky, *The Ways of Russian Theology*, I:257–9.

[15]Paul Evdokimov, *Le Christ dans la pensée russe* (Paris: Le Cerf, 1970), 60–1.

[16]Hilarion Alfeyev, 'Orthodox Theology on the Threshold of the 21st Century: Will There Be a Renaissance of Russian Theological Scholarship?' *The Ecumenical Review*, 52, 2 (2000), 312.

[17]Florovsky, 'Western Influences in Russian Theology', 144.

Paul Evdokimov seeks to find a cause for the weakness of original thought reflected in the manuals in the Russian character: 'In this domain we must recognise a certain failure: Russians are not gifted for the construction of great systems, because they feel themselves too constricted.'[18] But he seems to overlook here the philosophical-theological system created by Vladimir Soloviev, Pavel Florensky and Sergius Bulgakov around the notion of Divine Wisdom. And the theological scene was no better in Greece and Romania, where manuals of dogmatic theology *à la* Macarius Bulgakov also held sway until late in the twentieth century.

The generation of senior ecclesiastics who were confronted with the steady rise of discontent with the imperial regime and with the official church as the nineteenth century rolled into the twentieth was schooled in precisely these manuals of theology, which did not recognize the possibility of free theological inquiry and different theological viewpoints among sincere Christians. The atmosphere in the upper echelons of the church was as autocratic and conformist as that of the imperial state itself. It is not surprising that the hierarchs and professors of the theological academies were ill-equipped to engage with Christian thinkers nurtured in the more open and creative intellectual and cultural atmosphere outside the formal structures of the Russian Orthodox Church. The first stirrings of creative theology in fact take place far from the theological academies which stood at the apex of Russian theological education.

The Slavophiles

A new form of Russian theology began to emerge in the 1840s and with it the inauguration of modern Orthodox theology. The theology of the Slavophiles also marked an important turn in Russian philosophy, a turn which Basil Zenkovsky characterizes as 'the return to the ecclesiastical world-view', a radical shift from the rationalist moralistic humanism and aesthetic humanism, which, taking their cues from Enlightenment philosophy, dominated Russian thought in the early decades of the nineteenth century.[19] In the early nineteenth century, after the Napoleonic Wars, even after a century of Westernization, much of Russia was still backward by Western European standards. Peter the Great and his successors introduced certain Western ideas and practices but within strict limits: Russia remained an aristocratic and autocratic state; there was no parliament; industrialization lagged behind Western Europe; and Russian society was highly stratified as a semi-feudal society, with the mass of peasants still tied as serfs to the land and the landowners. Indeed the condition of the peasants had only worsened in the eighteenth century.

It is in this context that throughout most of the nineteenth century and up to the Bolshevik revolution of October/November 1917, Russian thought was dominated by one major question: What is the future of Russia? As the nineteenth century advanced, with increasing industrialization and gradual improvements in education and living standards, it was clear that the quasi-feudal

[18]Evdokimov, *Le Christ dans la pensée russe*, 60.

[19]See V. V. Zenkovsky, *A History of Russian Philosophy* (Paris, 1948) (London: Routledge & Kegan Paul; New York: Columbia University Press, 1953), 171 ff.

Russian society was increasingly anachronistic and that tremendous pressures were building up for major changes to accommodate social and economic modernization. But the imperial system was well entrenched, powerful, bureaucratized and wealthy, and was able to keep the lid on the situation for a century after the Napoleonic Wars.

The question of Russia's future prompted a long reflection in Russian intellectual circles, with an extremely wide range of solutions advanced, most involving the abolition of the monarchy and the establishment of a more representative system of government. The nineteenth century was marked by major political events reflecting the growing frustration felt in Russian society by the immobility of the aristocracy, including a first attempted revolution in December 1825 (the 'Decembrist Revolt'), the assassination of Tsar Alexander II in 1881 by a nihilist revolutionary and the failed revolution of 1905 – the last warning signal that the old order could no longer endure. Significant reforms during this long period were undertaken mainly in the 1860s, with the abolition of serfdom in 1861 (although on terms unfavourable to the peasants), the creation of a modern judicial system, the establishment of a system of local government and the reform of the army. These important steps were not, however, accompanied by political reforms or changes in the governance of the church.

The centralized, bureaucratic and autocratic government first put in place by Peter the Great at the end of the seventeenth century continued little changed until 1917, with curtailment of criticism, repression, exile and imprisonment of political opponents instead of political and social reform. The Russian Church and Russian theology could not avoid being affected profoundly by the atmosphere of immobility at higher political and social levels, especially the 'official' church, integrated into the Russian state apparatus since Peter the Great. This was the social, political and religious context which witnessed the rise of the first truly modern Orthodox theology.

A major new religious and theological development occurred in the mid-nineteenth century: the emergence of lay Orthodox thinkers, outside the formal structures of the Russian Orthodox Church and the theological academies. They represented a Christian current in the seething river of philosophical and religious enquiry that marked Russian intellectual and cultural circles in the century preceding the Revolution. In their thinking, there was no distinction between philosophy and theology, nor for that matter between literature and art and theology or religion.[20] Some were primarily theologians and religious writers (such as Alexei Khomiakov (1804–60), Ivan Kireevsky (1806–65), Basil Rosanov (1856–1919), Dimitri Merezhkovsky (1865–1940), Pavel Florensky (1882–1937)); others philosophers (Nicholas Fedorov (1828–1903), Vladimir Soloviev (1853–1900), Nicolas Lossky (1870–1965), Peter Struve (1870–1944), Nicolas Berdyaev (1874–1948) and Simeon Frank (1877–1944)); novelists (Nicholas Gogol (1809–52), Leon Tolstoy (1828–1910) and Feodor Dostoyevsky (1821–81)); poets (Alexander Blok (1880–1921), Andrei Bely (1880–1934) and Vyacheslav Ivanov (1886–1949)); or artists (Alexander Ivanov (1806–58) and Mikhail Nesterov

---

[20]Paul Evdokimov writes: 'In Russia, there is no clear distinction between theology and religious philosophy and one must add that the most lively theological thought was often found outside the official schools. A whole group of religious thinkers, Khomiakov, Soloviev, Fedorov, Gogol, Dostoyevsky, Rosanov, Merejkovsky, Frank, [Nicholas] Lossky, Chestov, Berdiaev and many others did not belong to the milieu of the theological academies, yet they made substantial theological contributions.' Evdokimov, *Le Christ dans la pensée russe*, 65.

(1862–1942)). Early in his career, Sergius Bulgakov (1871–1944) was primarily an economist and philosopher and after 1920 his works were more properly theological. All contributed to the religious expression of the time, but with the exception of Florensky, ordained in 1911, and Bulgakov, in 1918, none were members of the clergy and only Florensky taught at a theological academy (Moscow).

The earliest group of original Russian religious thinkers are known as the Slavophiles, the most prominent of whom were a group of six young landowners, Constantin Aksakov, Alexei Khomiakov, Ivan and Peter Kireevsky, Alexander Koshelev and Yuri Samarin. The Slavophiles and their intellectual opponents, known as the 'Westernizers', represented two strands of thought on the role and future of Russia which emerged in the late 1830s. The debate between the two camps was stimulated by the publication in 1836 of the first 'Philosophical Letter', written in French in 1829, by Peter Chaadaev (1794–1856). Chaadaev postulates that, in contrast with a vastly overdrawn and idealized portrait of Europe united and fortified by Christianity, Russia has no history of its own, not 'a single cherished memory, a single venerable monument', that it belongs to neither East nor West, that it has not been touched by education, and that, having no culture of its own, it never contributed to universal culture:

> We do not belong to any of the great families of the human race; we are neither of the West nor of the East, and we have not the traditions of either. Placed, as it were, outside of time, we have not been touched by the universal education of the human race. ... From the outset of our existence as a society, we have produced nothing for the common benefit of mankind; not one useful thought has sprung from the arid soil of our fatherland; not one great truth has emerged from our midst; we have not taken the trouble to invent anything ourselves and, of the inventions of others, we have borrowed only empty conceits and useless luxuries.[21]

Hidden away in this broad indictment of Russian history is a reference to what subsequently became the principal theme of Slavophile thought: the church. For Chaadaev, the 'supreme principle of *unity*', which comes closest to 'the true spirit of religion', is 'wholly contained in the idea of the fusion of all the moral forces in the world into a single thought, a single emotion, and in the progressive establishment of a social system, or *church*, which is to make truth reign among men'.

In response to Chaadaev's *cahier de doléances* against Russia, the remedy to Russia's ills, argued the Westernizers, lay in the continued importation of Western technology, ideas and values begun under Peter the Great – Russia should continue to Westernize its technology, economy and culture to become a truly modern state and to take its rightful place in the concert of nations dominated by the Western powers. The Westernizers looked to Western philosophy, especially German idealism and romanticism, for intellectual and cultural inspiration.

Against Chaadaev's dim view of Russia's past, the Slavophiles invoked the uniqueness of old Russian culture, which led them directly to the Orthodox tradition, representing the continuity and fullness of the original Church of Christ. The Slavophiles were not inherently anti-Western;

---

[21]Peter Chaadaev, 'Letters on the Philosophy of History' (1836), in Marc Raeff, ed., *Russian Intellectual History: An Anthology* (New York: Harcourt, Brace & World, 1966), 161; 167.

indeed, Khomiakov referred to the West as having been 'the land of holy miracles',[22] now in a period of spiritual and culture decline. In the eyes of the Slavophiles, the weaknesses of Western Christianity and culture were the result of deviations from true Christianity: the authoritarianism and centralization of the Catholic Church on the one hand and the individualism of Protestantism on the other. The result was the exaltation of reason over faith, of individual over communal values, and destructive egoism, competitiveness and aggressiveness in personal, social and national relations – all of which was embodied in the social and religious policies and reforms of Peter the Great, reinforced by the Enlightenment. The Slavophiles advocated a return to authentic Russian social, cultural and religious values, as exemplified in traditional Russian communal life and in Orthodoxy. It is in this context that Georges Florovsky sees Slavophilism as 'a religious philosophy of culture'.[23]

On a more philosophical level, the Westernizers emphasized a personalist approach to history, society and religion, 'the primacy of the principle of personhood in history and social life, as well as the autonomy, value and liberty of the individual'[24] – central ideas of the Enlightenment, reflected in the American and French Revolutions and Declarations of Rights. Personhood was the key to participation in world culture. The Slavophile response to what they perceived as unbridled and selfish individualism was the affirmation of communal values based on Christian love; in this, they argued, lay true and unique Russian culture. Against the exaltation of reason and rationalism of the Westernizers, the Slavophiles posited the validity of intuitive, non-rational knowledge, experience and testimony, and they centred their thinking on the Orthodoxy tradition as the key to the Russian soul and future. The boundaries between the two strands of thought were not well defined and even the appellation 'Slavophile' is a misnomer, since this group of thinkers attached primacy to Orthodoxy rather than to Slavic culture in a more ethnic sense.[25]

Alexei Khomiakov (1804–60) may rightfully be considered the first modern Orthodox theologian.[26] Nicolas Berdyaev praises Khomiakov as 'the first Russian free theologian ... the first *Orthodox* theologian to be an independent thinker ... the founder of Russian theology'[27] – 'free' and 'independent', always crucial values for Berdyaev, because Khomiakov, as a layman outside the structure of the ecclesial education, was not formally bound by church discipline, nor was his outlook fixed by the strictures of Western modes of thought, especially scholasticism. Khomiakov was a landowner and retired cavalry officer. His major theological interest was the Orthodox

---

[22]From Khomiakov's poem 'Rêverie' (1834), a famous phrase quoted rather sarcastically by Feodor Dostoyevsky in his *Winter Notes on Summer Impressions* (1863), an account of his first journey to Europe the previous year.

[23]Georges Florovsky, *The Ways of Russian Theology*, II:21.

[24]Sergey Horujy, 'Slavophiles, Westernisers and the Birth of Russian Philosophical Humanism', in G. M. Hamburg and Randall Poole, eds., *A History of Russian Philosophy 1830-1930: Faith, Reason and the Defense of Human Dignity* (Cambridge: Cambridge University Press, 2010), 39.

[25]See Zenkovsky, *A History of Russian Philosophy*, 206–7; 236–7.

[26]Kallistos Ware writes that Khomiakov was 'perhaps the first original theologian in the history of the Russian Church' (*The Orthodox Church*, 123). George Maloney goes so far as to say that Khomiakov 'can be called the most influential Russian lay theologian of the modern age' (*A History of Orthodox Theology*, 57). Maloney has little regard for later Russian lay theologians such as Nicolas Berdyaev and Vladimir Lossky.

[27]Nicolas Berdyaev, *Aleksei Stepanovitch Khomiakov* (1912), cited in Boris Jakim and Robert Bird, eds., *On Spiritual Unity: A Slavophile Reader* (Hudson, NY: Lindisfarne Books, 1998), 326, 327, 328.

Church, both as distinct from Western Christianity and as a vessel for Russian culture. The Slavophile concern to define a truly Russian culture involved breaking with the Catholic and the Protestant influences which largely dominated Russian society and the church. For Khomiakov and his fellow thinkers this meant a return to the true sources of Orthodoxy, in particular the Greek Fathers of the Church, largely ignored in Western Christianity, which focused its attention mostly on Augustine and the other Latin Fathers, Thomas Aquinas and the scholastics. The outlook of the Slavophiles also meant, in keeping with patristic theology, a return to the experience of the church 'as the source and measure of all theology ... a return to the school of the church which adores and prays'.[28]

Khomiakov maintained an active correspondence with Western religious figures, especially with leading Anglicans, such as William Palmer (1811–79), an Anglican clergyman who examined the practicability of intercommunion between the Anglican and Orthodox churches but later converted to Catholicism. Khomiakov's writings, printed posthumously by his friends and disciples, exerted profound influence on later Russian thinkers such as Fyodor Dostoyevsky, Konstantin Pobedonostsev and Vladimir Soloviev.

Khomiakov's most important theological writing is a short treatise, written in Greek in about 1850 but not published in Russian until 1863, under the title 'The Church is One'. The startling title is, as Florovsky writes, 'the theme and the thesis, the premise and the conclusion'.[29] In contrast with the elaborate systems of proof of academic theology, Khomiakov jettisons attempts to 'prove' his theses; rather, in the manner of the 'Centuries' of ancient Fathers, he proceeds largely by affirmation, he 'testifies and describes'.[30] His essay was originally included in a letter to an Anglican correspondent. Khomiakov's ecclesiology had a strong impact on the thinkers of the Russian religious renaissance at the end of the nineteenth century and the beginning of the twentieth century, and on Russian thinkers in exile (see Chapter 11).

The opening sentences of this work are a classic foundational statement of modern Orthodox ecclesiology:

> The church is one. Her unity follows of necessity from the unity of God; for the church is not a multitude of persons in their separate individuality, but a unity of the grace of God, living in a multitude of rational creatures, submitting themselves willingly to grace. Grace, indeed, is also given to those who resist it, and to those who do not make use of it (who hide their talent in the earth), but these are not in the church. In fact, the unity of the church is not imaginary or allegorical, but a true and substantial unity, such as is the unity of many members in a living body.[31]

Khomiakov's vision of the church is basically mystical; the church is the Body of Christ before being a visible institution on earth: 'The church, the Body of Christ, is manifesting forth and fulfilling herself in time, without changing her essential unity or inward life of grace. And therefore, when we speak of the church visible and invisible, we so speak only in relation to man.' This vision

---

[28]Evdokimov, *Le Christ dans la pensée russe*, 66.
[29]Florovsky, *The Ways of Russian Theology*, I:43.
[30]Ibid.
[31]Alexei Khomiakov, 'The Church is One', 193–4.

of the church allows Khomiakov and his theological successors, especially among the religious philosophers, to assert the subsistence of the unity of the church amidst visible division: 'The church is one, notwithstanding her division as it appears to a man who is still alive on earth. It is only in relation to man that it is possible to recognise a division of the church into visible and invisible; her unity is, in reality, true and absolute.'[32]

For Khomiakov the church is founded on love and freedom, the basis of central Slavophile idea of the church as *sobornost'*, a difficult term which connotes approximately the community of the faithful and is translated typically as 'catholicity' or 'conciliarity' (also as 'togetherness', 'symphony' or 'integrality'). In Slavophile thought, *sobornost'* above all connotes 'communion in love', a human faculty superior to reason:

> Of the universal laws of the willing reason or the reasoning will, writes Khomiakov, the first, supreme, most perfect law is, for the undistorted soul, the law of love. Consequently, accord with this law can pre-eminently strengthen and expand our mental vision, and top this law we must subjugate and with it we must harmonize the stubborn discord of our intellectual powers. … Communion in love is not only useful but wholly necessary for the attainment of the truth, and the attainment of the truth is based on this communion and is impossible without it. … This feature sharply distinguishes Orthodox teaching from all other teachings: from Latinism, which depends on external authority; and from Protestantism, which emancipates the individual into the desert of rational abstraction.[33]

In contrast with the weaknesses they saw in the Western churches, the Slavophiles thought to have discovered the model of the church in the Russian peasant communal organization known as the *obshchina* or *mir*, which served as village government and agricultural cooperative, and which, it was claimed, was an ancient, pre-bourgeois and unique institution which distinguished Russia from other countries. Like the West, Russia had deviated from true Christianity, mainly as a result of the reforms of Peter the Great and the Europeanizing of the Petrine and post-Petrine era. It was in this context that the Slavophiles elaborated the key notion of the church as *sobornost'*. Critical to the Slavophile conception of the church is a rejection of the notion of the church as merely an institution in favour of an organic conception of the church, inherently close to Paul's figuration of the church as the Body of Christ, with Christ as the Head of the Church and the faithful as the members of the Body (Col. 1.18; 2.19).

Yuri Samarin (1819–76), Khomiakov's disciple, biographer and editor, in Florovsky's words 'faithfully reproduced what was most basic in Khomiakov's understanding of the church's self-perception' in his well-known statement: 'The church is not a doctrine, not a system, and not an institution. The church is a living organism, an organism of truth and love, or more precisely: *truth and love as an organism*.'[34] In a similar vein, Berdyaev characterizes *sobornost'* as 'the organic union of freedom and love, community', while Nicolas Lossky summarizes the Slavophile conception of

---

[32]Ibid., 195; 193.

[33]Cited in Nicolas Berdyaev, *Aleksei Stepanovitch Khomiakov*, in Jakim and Bird, eds., *On Spiritual Unity*, 338–9.

[34]Yuri Samarin, 'On the Theological Writings of Alexei Khomiakov', in Jakim and Bird, eds., *On Spiritual Unity*, 171. Samarin's essay is the introduction to the first Russian edition of Khomiakov's theological writings (Prague, 1867), which Samarin edited. See Florovsky, *The Ways of Russian Theology*, II:53.

sobornost' as 'the combination of freedom and unity of many persons on the basis of their common love for the same absolute values'.[35] Berdyaev also emphasizes that for Khomiakov *sobornost'*, as 'communion in love', was 'not a philosophical idea, taken from Western thought, but a religious fact, taken from the living experience of the Eastern Church'.[36]

Another major notion put forward by Khomiakov, in keeping with the central Slavophile idea of the church as the community of the faithful, is the infallibility of the church, a counterpoint to the Roman doctrine of papal infallibility and to the Protestant rejection of the authority of the church in matters of dogma and interpretation of Scripture: 'The church knows nothing of partial truth and partial error, but only the whole truth without admixture of error. … The church herself does not err, for she is the truth, she is incapable of cunning or cowardice, for she is holy.'[37]

As a corollary of this doctrine, Khomiakov draws a distinction between the infallibility of the church and the possibility of erroneous teachings of individuals in the church, again in opposition to the claim of papal infallibility:

> The church, by her very unchangeableness, does not acknowledge that to be error, which she has at any previous time acknowledged as truth; and having proclaimed by a General Council and common consent, that it is possible for any private individual, or any bishop or patriarch, to err in his teaching, she cannot acknowledge that such or such private individual, or bishop, or patriarch, or successor of theirs, is incapable of falling into error in teaching; or that they are preserved from going astray by any special grace. … The grace of faith is not to be separated from holiness of life, nor can any single community or any single pastor be acknowledged to be the custodian of the whole faith of the church, any more than any single community or any single pastor can be looked upon as the representative of the whole of her sanctity.[38]

Another corollary of the infallibility of the church is that pronouncements of church councils are insufficient in themselves to define the Orthodox faith: they must be received by the people, the church as a whole, as a demonstration of their truly divine-human ('theandric') nature. In his essay 'On the Western Confessions of Faith', Khomiakov refers approvingly to the *Encyclical of the Eastern Patriarchs* of 1848:

> The Eastern patriarchs, having assembled in council with their bishops, solemnly pronounced in their reply to the Encyclical Letter of Pius IX that 'infallibility resides solely in the *ecumenicity* of the church bound together by mutual love, and that the unchangeableness of dogma as well as the purity of rite are entrusted to the care not of one hierarchy but of all the people of the church, who are the Body of Christ.'[39]

Khomiakov goes on to reject the notion of a 'teaching church' within the church, a 'bifurcation' which he sees as 'the common feature of both western confessions' (Catholicism and the Reform):

[35]Berdyaev, *The Russian Idea*, 161; Nicolas Lossky, *History of Russian Philosophy* (London: George Allen & Unwin, 1952), 14.
[36]Berdyaev, *Aleksei Stepanovitch Khomiakov*, in Jakim and Bird, eds., *On Spiritual Unity*, 339.
[37]Alexei Khomiakov, 'The Church is One', 196.
[38]Ibid., 196–7.
[39]Alexei Khomiakov, 'On the Western Confessions of Faith' (1864), in Alexander Schmemann, *Ultimate Questions: An Anthology of Modern Russian Religious Thought* (Crestwood, NY: St Vladimir's Seminary Press, 1977), 55.

'The whole church teaches – the church in all her fullness. The Church does not acknowledge a teaching church in any other sense.'[40] Referring to councils whose doctrines were rejected by the church, he writes,

> Why were these councils rejected, when outwardly they did not differ from the ecumenical councils? Solely because their decisions were not acknowledged as the voice of the church *by the whole people of the church*, by that people and within that world where, in questions of faith, there is no difference between a scholar and an untutored person, between cleric and layman, between man and woman, king and subject, slaveowner and slave, and where, if in God's judgment it is needed, a youth receives the gift of knowledge, a word of infinite wisdom is given to a child, and the heresy of a learned bishop is confuted by an illiterate cowherd, so that all might be joined in that free unity of living faith which is the manifestation of the Spirit of God.[41]

For Slavophiles, socialism and capitalism were equally repugnant offspring of Western decadence; the West failed to solve human spiritual problems because it stressed rationality and competition at the expense of cooperation. Neither Catholicism nor Protestantism was capable of maintaining the necessary harmony between freedom and unity. As one scholar expresses the Slavophile view: 'As Catholicism emphasises external unity at the expense of freedom, Protestantism sacrifices unity to a personal freedom so unrestrained that it ends as anarchy.'[42] In Khomiakov's idealized vision of Orthodoxy, the Orthodox Church combined both unity and freedom.

Although open to dialogue with Western Christians, Khomiakov was realistic about the obstacles involved. In his correspondence with William Palmer, Khomiakov stresses the significance of genuine unity as the basis of the church:

> The church cannot be a harmony of discords; it cannot be a numerical sum of Orthodox, Latins, and Protestants. It is nothing if it is not perfect inward harmony of creed and outward harmony of expression (not withstanding local differences in the rite). The question is, not whether Latins and Protestants have erred so fatally as to deprive individuals of salvation. … The question is whether they have the truth, and whether they have retained the ecclesiastical tradition unimpaired. If they have not, where is the possibility of unity?

While recognizing the affinity of Anglicans to the Orthodox, he points out that Anglicanism is far from unified itself:

> Many bishops and divines of your communion are and have been quite orthodox. But what of it? Their opinion is only *an individual opinion*, it is not *the Faith of the Community*. Ussher is almost a complete Calvinist; but yet he, no less than those bishops who give expression to Orthodox convictions, belongs to the Anglican Church.[43]

---

[40]Alexei Khomiakov, 'On the Western Confessions of Faith', 58.
[41]Ibid., 62.
[42]Joseph Wieczynski, 'Khomyakov's Critique of Western Christianity', *Church History*, 38, 3 (1969), n. 12, 295.
[43]Alexei Khomiakov, 'Third Letter to William Palmer', in W. J. Birkbeck, ed., *Russia and the English Church during the Last Fifty Years* (London: Eastern Church Association, 1895), 69–70.

Khomiakov is critical of both the Roman Catholic Church and Protestantism, both of which he accuses of being imbued with 'the spirit of utilitarian rationalism' and of dividing the church into 'the teaching church and the church of pupils'. He flails the Catholic Church especially for her assertion of the universal authority and infallibility of the pope and Protestantism for undermining tradition: 'Protestantism means the expression of doubt in essential dogma. In other words, the denial of dogma as a living tradition; in short, a denial of the church.'[44]

Despite the limited nature of Khomiakov's theology, even his ecclesiology, his thinking had a powerful impact on the emergence of modern Orthodox theology and he ranks high in the eyes of later Orthodox theologians. Georges Florovsky, for one, is rather favourable towards Khomiakov and he cites approvingly Berdyaev's characterization of Khomiakov as a 'Knight of the Orthodox Church'.[45] Florovsky writes,

> In his day Khomiakov's voice resounded as a reminder of the reality of the church – a reminder that the experience of the church is the primary source and measure of every genuine effort to construct theology. A sign was thereby given for a return – a return from the school to the church, which explains why the summons confused even the best of the contemporary 'school theologians'. Contemporary Western European theology provided them with a more familiar context than that afforded by the restless and unexpected expanses of patristic theology and asceticism.[46]

Major weaknesses in Khomiakov's thought are the limited importance or even outright neglect of the liturgical, sacramental, mystic and hierarchical dimensions of the church and the absence of such major themes as evil, the death and resurrection of Christ and eschatology.[47] Paul Florensky recognizes the 'good fruits' of Khomiakov's thought in 'all that is fresh in theology'. At the same time he is concerned over the potentially negative impact on Orthodoxy of Khomiakov's critique of the canonical order of the church, the Catholic doctrine of the sacraments and the Protestant doctrine of the divine inspiration of Scripture, a line of thought which leads Florensky to accuse Khomiakov of 'Protestantism'. He sees in Khomiakov's doctrine of the church a 'flavour' of Protestant *immanentism*, in the sense of 'humanity's intention to create all reality out of itself, outside of and apart from God'. For Florensky, Khomiakov's insistence that the legitimacy of church doctrines derive from their definition in unity ('communion in love') represents a departure into immanentism, in contrast with the essence of Orthodoxy as *ontologism*, 'the 'reception of reality from God' as given, not as created by humanity' – truth as an ontological reality apart from human agreement or disagreement.[48] Georges Florovsky dismisses Florensky's central critique of Khomiakov's ecclesiology as more 'invective than critical' and concludes that

[44]Alexei Khomiakov, 'On the Western Confessions of Faith', 40.

[45]Florovsky, *The Ways of Russian Theology*, II:39. The reference is from Nicolas Berdyaev's study of Khomiakov published in 1912. The original comparison of Khomiakov to a 'knight' is from Alexander Herzen (1812–70), one of Khomiakov's Westernizing opponents.

[46]Florovsky, *The Ways of Russian Theology*, II:53.

[47]See Evdokimov, *Le Christ dans la pensée russe*, 72. In 'The Church is One', Khomiakov does in fact write at length about the sacraments.

[48]Pavel Florensky, 'Around Khomiakov' (1916), in Jakim and Bird, eds., *On Spiritual Unity*, 321–5.

> No matter how socially ambiguous the Slavophiles could be in presenting their philosophical views, Khomiakov's doctrine of the church remains completely true to fundamental and ancient patristic tradition. He merely models his polemic on the ancient church's custom of juxtaposing the church and heresy above all as love and discord, or community and isolation – as did St Irenaeus, Tertullian, Origen, and, most pronouncedly of all, St Augustine, who shifted the stress in a particularly expressive way precisely to love.[49]

In a vein similar to Florensky, Nicolas Berdyaev, in his 1912 book on Khomiakov, concludes that despite Khomiakov's 'great theological achievements', his 'religious consciousness was limited, confined, incomplete', because Khomiakov accorded little or no attention to the prophetic and creative aspects of the church, a divine-human process at work in the church, religious cosmology, eschatology and apocalypse, including 'cosmic transfiguration', and he displays 'insufficient sensitivity to the mystical side of Christianity'.[50] Like Florensky, Berdyaev recognizes that Slavophile theology represented 'a jet of fresh air' which brought religious themes into Russian philosophy and literature.[51]

Ivan Kireevsky (1806–65) was a Russian literary critic and philosopher who, together with Alexei Khomiakov, is credited as a co-founder of the Slavophile movement. Kireevsky was well versed in Western philosophy from his travels in the West and he supported Khomiakov against the Westernizers. In his later life Ivan Kireevsky was closely associated with the Monastery of Optino and the Optino startsi. Kireevsky produced few writings of his own, but was involved in the production of Russian translations of the Fathers undertaken by the monks of Optino. Like Khomiakov, Kireevsky was interested in the theology of the church and he coined a definition of *sobornost'* – a word which Khomiakov never used – which made it the equivalent of the 'communion of saints': 'The sum total of all Christians of all ages, past and present, comprise one indivisible, eternal living assembly of the faithful, held together just as much by the unity of consciousness as through the communion of prayer.'[52]

From a fascination with European cultural development in the early 1830s, Kireevsky moved to a critique of Western Europe for its estrangement from its Christian roots, in contrast with Russia, which, he contended, maintained the purity of its Christian culture. In his one major philosophical work, 'On the Necessity and Possibility of New Principles in Philosophy' (1856), he reviews and finds inadequate the most popular philosophical systems of the day, notably those of Hegel and Schelling. Like Khomiakov, the fundamental problem that Kireevsky identified in Western thought was an excessive reliance on reason, the exaltation of reason 'as the highest instrument of cognition' and hence its tendency to 'limit truth to that aspect of cognition that is accessible only to this

[49]Florovsky, *The Ways of Russian Theology*, II:46.
[50]Berdyaev, *Aleksei Stepanovitch Khomiakov*, in Jakim and Bird, eds., *On Spiritual Unity*, 333–5. Berdyaev also criticizes Khomiakov for ignoring the later Solovievian themes of Sophia, the world-soul and the eternal feminine, themes which Berdyaev himself subsequently discarded. Ibid., 335.
[51]Berdyaev, *Aleksei Stepanovitch Khomiakov*, in Jakim and Bird, eds., *On Spiritual Unity*, 332.
[52]Quoted in Ninian Smart, John Clayton, Patrick Sherry and Steven T. Katz, eds. *Nineteenth-Century Religious Thought in the West* (Cambridge: Cambridge University Press, 1988), 183.

strictly rational manner of thinking'.[53] Kireevsky turns to the Fathers of the Church for his model of Christian philosophy: 'Schelling sought the expression of theological dogmas in the writings of the Holy Fathers without appreciating their speculative concepts of reason and laws of higher cognition." Russia, on the other hand, has retained "lofty examples of religious thought in the ancient Holy Fathers and in the great spiritual writings of all times.'[54] Kireevsky spells out the way forward towards 'an independent philosophy that will correspond to the basic principles of ancient Russian civilisation and be capable of subordinating the divided civilisation of the West to the integral consciousness of believing reason'.[55]

Khomiakov discovered among Kireevsky's papers after his death and published under the title 'Fragments' a partially developed text and reflections that would likely have constituted the positive side of Kireevsky's proposal for the future of Russian thought. In the 'Fragments' Kireevsky contrasts the 'borrowed civilisation', the 'foreign civilisation', based on 'a logical culture, a sensual-empirical culture' that the Russian upper classes imported from the West, with the 'primordial culture of Russia … preserved in its arrested development in the mores, customs and inner mindset of the so-called common people', the 'pure faith' of the Russian people.[56] The remedy for Russia's plight, Kireevsky argues, lies in the re-appropriation of the 'profound, loving, and pure philosophy of the Holy Fathers, which represents the embryo of this superior philosophical principal'. This 'new science of thinking … would destroy the unhealthy contradiction between mind and faith, between inner convictions and external life.' In the final analysis, the experience of faith is superior to the conclusions of reason:

> Believing philosophy will accept the guidance of the Holy Fathers as the first grounds for its self-comprehension, all the more as this guidance cannot be surmised by abstract thinking. For the truths expressed by the Holy Fathers were achieved by them from immediate, inner experience and are communicated to us not as a logical conclusion, which is also possible for our own reason, but rather as the testimony of eyewitnesses concerning a country they have been to.[57]

Kireevsky is not advocating a simple return to the thinking of the Fathers, but rather the development of the 'embryo of this future philosophy' in terms of 'modern civilisation': 'To think that we have a philosophy ready, contained in the Holy Fathers, would be extremely erroneous. Our philosophy must yet be created … not by a single individual; it should grow in common view through the sympathetic cooperation of a unanimity in thought.'[58]

Kireevsky's prophetic call for a 'return to the Fathers' was partly reflected at the time in the theology of Metropolitan Philaret and, later in the century, by several of the religious philosophers, but it was not until after the Russian Revolution that Georges Florovsky and Vladimir Lossky and other Russian exiles internalized and realized the full import of Kireevsky's visionary call. Florovsky

[53]Ivan Kireevsky, 'On the Necessity and Possibility of New Principles in Philosophy', in Jakim and Bird, eds., *On Spiritual Unity*, 266–7.
[54]Kireevsky, 'New Principles in Philosophy', 273.
[55]Ibid.
[56]Kireevsky, 'Fragments', in Jakim and Bird, eds., *On Spiritual Unity*, 276–7.
[57]Ibid., 282–3.
[58]Ibid., 281.

has a high opinion of Kireevsky for his 'ascetic effort', 'conversion and renunciation', and 'the overcoming of romanticism', but he stops short of seeing in Kireevsky a precursor to his own neopatristic project and himself as Kireevsky's successor.[59]

Alexander Bukharev

Alexander Bukharev (Archimandrite Theodore) (1829–71) occupies a unique position mid-way between the Slavophiles and the religious revival of the late nineteenth century, and also a middle position between official 'academic theology' and the 'free theology' of the religious philosophers. Bukharev was educated at the Moscow Theological Academy, where he became a priest and a monk and began his teaching career. He became aware of the gulf that had already developed between the church and academic theology on the one hand, and the Russian upper classes and intellectual society on the other hand. Bukharev thought that the church should seek to bridge this gulf and he moved in this direction initially within the bounds of the church itself. But his readiness to dialogue with the secular world was too much for his ecclesiastical superiors, not the least, Metropolitan Philaret, and he fell into disfavour.

After his first falling-out with Philaret, Bukharev was 'exiled' from Moscow to the Theological Academy of Kazan. He was restored to favour after a few years, but because he continued to advocate the engagement of the Russian Church with secular culture, he became a target for conservative lay journalists. He lost the public relations battle, which resulted in the censorship of his writings, notably a commentary on the Book of Revelation, and his relegation to a monastery. He then took the dramatic step of asking to be released from his monastic vows and reduced to lay status. This was granted in July 1863 and a few weeks later, Bukharev married. He was subsequently shunned by both the church and the state for employment and publication and he and his wife Anna lived in great poverty. Their only child, a daughter, died in infancy, much to the chagrin of the Bukharevs.

Aware of the potential dangers involved in the developing split in the Russian society, Bukharev's principal message was the need for the church to engage in a dialogue 'with the world', to bring Christ's message to those who had become or were becoming estranged from Christ and the church. This concern is evident in the very title of his main book, *On Orthodoxy in Relation to the Modern World* (1860), a collection of fifteen essays and a short conclusion dealing with a wide range of topics.[60] The largest group of essays (five) takes a biblical theme as starting point, three church history, three a liturgical subject, two deal with the Old Believers, and one with art and another with civic affairs. Bukharev uses the subject of each essay to articulate his main thesis, that

---

[59]Florovsky, *The Ways of Russian Theology*, II:26–7.

[60]Alexander Bukharev, *O Pravoslavii v otnochenu k sovremennosti* [On Orthodoxy in Relation to the Modern World] (Saint Petersburg, 1860; 2nd ed., 1906). Very little of Bukharev's writings is available in translation. Valliere presents a summary and commentary on the sixteen essays of *On Orthodoxy in Relation to the Modern World* in *Modern Russian Theology* (35–72), and Elisabeth Behr-Sigel comments on it in *Alexandre Boukarev – Un théologien de l'Église orthodoxe russe en dialogue avec le monde moderne* (Paris: Beauchesne, 1977), 64–72.

Orthodoxy must engage with the modern world. Each essay becomes a platform from which Bukharev can hammer home his central theme:

> We should defend all aspects of humanity as the property of Christ. ... The repression, constraint and especially the repudiation of anything truly human, is an infringement of Christ's grace. ... Orthodoxy should shine like a sun in all civil life, in the whole circuit of our sciences, arts and official relations.[61]

Bukharev represents an attempt, however timid and inept, to develop an Orthodox theology of culture, to see the light of Christ and sense 'the "hidden warmth" of Christ's Church, at just those points where there was no external evidence of Christ's presence', an attempt to re-establish 'the "appurtenance to Christ" of these seemingly non-Christian phenomena'.[62] Bukharev wrote that he himself 'was blinded by the *abundance of Christ's light which there revealed itself to believing thought*'.[63]

Paul Valliere summarizes Bukharev's theological outlook and mission:

> Orthodoxy is a heavenly treasure, but the Orthodox people obscure the fact by apathy, lack of faith and failure to share the treasure with their neighbours, including the West. Theodore summons his fellow Orthodox 'not to bury but to use' the gift entrusted to them. He exhorts them to remember the truth of Christ is not their private possession but 'a treasure for the whole world, and consequently that we who possess this treasure are debtors before the whole world'. He reminds his fellow Russians that they bear particular responsibility for the Orthodox cause because Russia, alone among the eastern Christian countries, is strong and independent.[64]

Bukharev's appeals were an attempt to surpass the polarization reflected in the Slavophile-Westernizer debate a generation earlier by invoking the moral responsibility of the church and the Orthodox faithful to witness to Christ in society as it is, not as this or that group thought it should be.

But Bukharev's pathetic voice was ignored by both sides – the Russian Church and the intelligentsia – as each went its own way, unconcerned with the premises and preoccupations of the other. Bukharev died a lonely death in 1871 at the age of forty-two. At the end of the nineteenth century and the beginning of the twentieth century, thanks to the efforts of his wife, a few friends and an admirer in the person of Pavel Florensky, to keep his memory alive, his writings were revived and republished, a witness to the failure of the Russian Orthodox Church, increasingly isolated as an ally of the hated autocratic regime, to come to grips with the modernity and to open lines of communication with religious thinking outside its own domain.

Bukharev's legacy remains controversial. Georges Florovsky is merciless about Bukharev, seeing in him 'a utopian dreaminess', 'the stubbornness of a visionary', completely lacking 'any sense of historical perspective', with 'no spiritual sense of proportion', an absence of 'creative force' with no 'ascetical courage'; his renunciation of the priesthood was 'a convulsion of dreamy perplexity, a genuine mystical suicide', 'a convulsive and impotent protest of a utopian fantasy against the tragic

---

[61] Bukharev, *O Pravoslavii*, 20; 316. Cited in Zenkovsky, *A History of Russian Philosophy*, I:317.
[62] Zenkovsky, *A History of Russian Philosophy*, I:317.
[63] Bukharev, *O Pravoslavii*, cited in Zenkovsky, *A History of Russian Philosophy*, I:318.
[64] Valliere, *Modern Russian Theology*, 39. The citation is from *O Pravoslavii*, 90–2.

complexity of life'; his book *On Orthodoxy and the Modern World* 'contains much more that is artificial than is genuinely perceived', a 'lacklustre' effort, with 'very few luminous pages'. Bukharev, concludes Florovsky, was an utter failure: 'He could not bear his own cross and hence his collapse. His is an agitated image, but certainly not a prophetic or heroic one.'[65]

And yet Florovsky's spiteful tirade against Bukharev does not prevent him from summarizing reasonably well the core of Bukharev's thinking and his crusade:

> Basic to Bukharev's worldview is the very illuminating experience of an unfolding salvation. The Lamb of God has accepted and removed the sin of the world; the barrier of sinfulness has been smashed and destroyed. Bukharev's wholly unrestrained optimism and joy at reconciliation stem from this belief. In Christian experience sinfulness loses its sting, the heart overflows with the feeling of God's redeeming mercy. One must become a crusader, suffer with the Lamb, co-experience and, as it were, take upon oneself all the sinfulness and faults of others. Only through such common suffering, only through the power of such a compassionate love is it possible to enter into the power of the blessing of the Father and the love of the Lamb. Hence an acute sense of Christian responsibility for life arises. By the power of the immutable incarnation, in the image of the God-man, each and every human deed or act has been assigned a higher purpose.[66]

Florovsky sees Bukharev from the same perspective as Bukharev's pugnacious critic and detractor the publicist Victor Askochenski (1813–79), and Bukharev's ecclesiastic superiors who insured that Bukharev could not succeed in getting his message across (even if it was the light of Christ) in civilian life.

Subsequent views of Bukharev paint a very different picture. Basil Zenkovsky is positive towards him, as are Paul Evdokimov, Nadejda Gorodetski,[67] Elisabeth Behr-Sigel and Paul Valliere.[68] Zenkovsky writes: 'Bukharev offered a positive exhibition of the Orthodox view of the contemporary world. … His overcoming of secularism from within is an important contribution and one for which he will always be remembered.'[69] Zenkovsky considers that subsequent Russian religious thought, Bulgakov and Basil Rozanov, are in direct continuity with Bukharev's theology of culture. Evdokimov sees in Bukharev 'a precursor of 'Orthodox culture and of cultural theology', with the astonishing ability 'to perceive everywhere the Light of the Logos'. Bukharev fell afoul of official theology because he accused it of failing, in its unwillingness to dialogue with modernity, to grasp the full implications of the Incarnation: 'For him, any attempt to separate the spiritual, and therefore the church, from the flesh of the world, from humanity, from culture, borders on the monophysite heresy,' a reflection of 'fear of the divine and the Light of the Logos'.[70]

In the conclusion of her study of Bukharev, Elisabeth Behr-Sigel puts the finger on the nature of his prophetic vision:

---

[65]Florovsky, *The Ways of Russian Theology*, II: 119–22.
[66]Florovsky, *The Ways of Russian Theology*, II: 121.
[67]Nadejda Gorodetski, *The Humiliated Christ in Modern Russian Thought* (London: SPCK, 1938), 115–26.
[68]Valliere, *Modern Russian Theology*, 99–106.
[69]Zenkovsky, *A History of Russian Philosophy*, I:319.
[70]Evdokimov, *Le Christ dans la pensée russe*, 85–9.

> A contemporary of a Russia barely emerging, for the great majority of her people, from a rural and patriarchal civilization, Bukharev perceived the signs announcing the birth of a new world. He felt and profoundly grasped the great aspirations of modern man, the powerful dynamism which on one hand leads him to the conquest of the material world thanks to the instruments of western rationality, science and technology, and on the other hand to the construction of a more just world and a culture in which human creativity can freely express itself. At the same time, he is aware of the catastrophes whose seeds lay within this promethean undertaking: dehumanization of man torn away from his cosmic and spiritual roots and the profanation of a world delivered to the appetites of human vultures. Penetrating and analyzing with perspicacity the problem of modern Russia, Bukharev grasped its universal implications. In a world still apparently stable, in an official church inclined to triumphalism, he perceived – like his contemporary Dostoyevsky – the subterranean groaning which pointed to the great dislocations of the twentieth century.[71]

Florovsky was unable to see anything positive in Alexander Bukharev because Bukharev's thinking does not fit into Florovsky's vision of what Orthodox theology should be. Florovsky was scandalized by Archimandrite Theodore's renunciation of his ordination and his monastic vows, which prevented Florovsky from seeing the positive and prophetic nature of Bukharev's life and work. Florovsky is hard to put to find Western influences in Bukharev, so he dismisses him on other grounds. Behind Florovsky's bitter criticism lies no doubt a disappointment that Bukharev, unlike Ivan Kireevsky, had not turned to the ancient Fathers of the Church for inspiration, which would have made him, like Kireevsky, a prophet of neopatristic theology.

Conclusion

In contrast with preceding centuries, the nineteenth century witnessed a noticeable shift in the locus of theological and philosophical thought from a concentration in the Russian Orthodox Church and its institutions to a much broader circle of educated lay persons largely outside the church's control. The expression of ideas and lively intellectual debate spread widely in different social circles throughout the nineteenth century, a consequence of the extension of education, rising wealth, contact with the West and the decline of the legitimacy of the church-state apparatus. The Westernization of Peter the Great undermined the traditional aristocracy centred on the old Muscovy kingdom and the subordination of the church to the state weakened the ability of the church to inspire (and, ironically, to stifle) theological innovation outside its institutional limits.

Westernization opened Russia to the introduction not only of Western technology and culture; it also permitted the penetration of Western philosophical and theological thought into the Russian fabric. This obliged Russian intellectuals committed to Orthodoxy to reflect on the nature of the Orthodox tradition in relation to the West, producing the first truly original modern Orthodox philosophical-theological movement, Slavophilism. The ill-defined dynamic of debate between the

---

[71]Behr-Sigel, *Alexandre Boukharev*, 92–3.

Slavophiles and the Westernizers in the mid-nineteenth century provided the impetus for the more robust and broader-based Russian religious renaissance of the late nineteenth and early twentieth centuries.

Alexander Bukharev remains a solitary prophetic figure of the mid-nineteenth century. His central message of the urgent necessity for the church to bring the message of Christ to the broad educated elite alienated from the church became critically urgent towards the end of the nineteenth century as the decaying imperial regime, increasingly unable to control the ferment in Russian society, moved inexorably towards its own apocalypse. Just as there was a revival of interest in Bukharev among the religious philosophers at the beginning of the twentieth century, so there has been a reaction against George Florovsky's entirely negative judgement of him. Positive assessments of Bukharev focus precisely on his perspicacity in seeing the tragic rift between the church and the educated and cultured classes in Russian society and his courage in attempting to bridge the gap. He was a failure in the eyes of the Russian Church and society, but apparent failure is the fate of most prophets and it is only in retrospect that their wisdom becomes evident. In his emphasis on the all-encompassing implications of the Incarnation – 'and Word became flesh' (Jn 1:14) – and his appeal for engagement with contemporary society, Bukharev properly anticipates major themes of the Russian religious renaissance.

The theological vision of the leading Slavophiles contains more than a little religious and socio-political romanticism and idealism, bordering on utopianism, reflected especially in their vision of the church as an organic unity and social harmony of the people inspired by Christian love. Nonetheless, such Slavophile notions as *sobornost'*, the infallibility of the church residing in the whole people of the church and the rejection of formal distinction between a 'teaching church' and a 'learning church' have found their way into the mainstream of modern Orthodox ecclesiology. The Slavophile vision of the church is reflected especially in the ecclesiology of later theologians who emphasize the church as the Mystical Body of Christ, as distinct from those who focus more on the historical and institutional aspects of the church.[72]

Later in the nineteenth century, Slavophilism became distorted from its original intent and transformed into support for pan-Slavic political ideas, notably the unification of all Slavic peoples under the leadership of the Russian tsar and the independence of the Balkan Slavs from Ottoman rule. This political momentum culminated in the Russo-Turkish War of 1877–8, by which Bulgaria was freed from the Ottoman Empire and Serbia and Montenegro formally proclaimed their independence. In another vein, politically inspired Slavophilism degenerated into aggressive

---

[72]The more mystical approach to the Church is exemplified by Sergius Bulgakov, *The Bride of the Lamb* (1945) (Grand Rapids, MI: Eerdmanns, 2001); Georges Florovsky, essays on 'Ecclesiology and Ecumenism' in Gallaher and Ladouceur, *The Patristic Witness of Georges Florovsky*, 247–307; Dumitru Staniloae, *The Church: Communion in the Holy Spirit* (1978) (Vol. 4 of *The Experience of God: Orthodox Dogmatic Theology*) (Brookline, MA: Holy Cross Orthodox Press, 2012); and Boris Bobrinskoy, *The Mystery of the Church* (2003) (Yonkers, NY: St Vladimir's Seminary Press, 2012). For more historical-institutional views of the Church, see Hilarion Alfeyev, *Orthodox Christianity. Vol. I: The History and Canonical Structure of the Orthodox Church* (Yonkers, NY: St Vladimir's Seminary Press, 2011), and *Vol. II: Doctrine and Teaching of the Orthodox Church* (Yonkers, NY: St Vladimir's Seminary Press, 2011), Part Five: 'The Church' (387–488); and Jean-Claude Larchet, *L'Église, Corps du Christ Vol. I. Nature et structure. Vol. II. Les relations entre les Églises* (Paris: Le Cerf, 2012). The Alfeyev, Bobrinskoy and Larchet books are reviewed in our article 'Three Contemporary Orthodox Visions of the Church', *St Vladimir's Theological Quarterly*, 58, 2 (2014), 217–34.

Russian nationalism, especially in the context of the abortive January Uprising in Poland-Lithuania against the Russian Empire (1863–4). Nineteenth-century political Slavophilism and the even narrower Russian nationalism derived from it, including its modern revival after the fall of the Communist regime in Russia, retained only what Berdyaev calls the 'pagan-nationalistic elements' which emerge from a constricted interpretation of Slavophile thought.[73] It is the religious philosophers of the end of the nineteenth century who are the true philosophical and theological successors of the Slavophiles and in this sense the Slavophiles can be considered the initiators and precursors to the broader and more vibrant religious thinking of the late nineteenth century.

Slavophile reflection on the nature of the church, especially the notion of *sobornost'*, has had a powerful impact on the development of modern ecclesiology and even with its weaknesses it formed the starting point for the development of twentieth-century Eucharistic ecclesiology by Nicholas Afanasiev, John Zizioulas and others, as we will explore in later chapters. Similarly, the notion of the infallibility of the people of God has gone a long way in modern Orthodox ecclesiology.

---

[73]Berdyaev, *Aleksei Stepanovitch Khomiakov*, in Jakim and Bird, eds., *On Spiritual Unity*, 348.

4

The Russian Religious Renaissance

Chapter Outline

Russian theology in the late nineteenth century

By the late nineteenth century, Russian theology existed in three broad religious and theological traditions, with complex and often conflicting relationships among them. As we saw in the previous chapter, *formal church or academic theology* was the theology taught in the seminaries and theological academies and featured in official church publications. Academic theology suffered from both external and internal constraints. Externally, it was constrained by the close relationship of the Russian Orthodox Church (ROC) with the imperial regime and was subject to censorship, while internally it suffered from Western methodological, philosophical and theological influences, especially scholasticism in dogmatic theology. Academic theology nonetheless achieved a partial emancipation from its 'Western captivity' during the nineteenth century, especially following the reforms of the theological schools in the early nineteenth century. And despite the constraints, the achievements of Russian academic theology were considerable in some domains, such as biblical studies and translations and studies of the Fathers of the Church.

Official church theology was marked by the repression of original thought and suspicion or outright rejection of the possibility of real dialogue with issues and thinking outside the Russian

Church, as Alexander Bukharev discovered in the mid-nineteenth century. The weaknesses of academic theology, and the often external and ritualistic faith that accompanied it, became all too evident after the revolutions of 1917. As one seminary rector during the revolution reflected afterwards:

> Spiritual life and the fire of religious zeal had by then started dwindling and weakening. Faith had become mere duty and tradition, prayer a cold and routine ritual. Inside us and those who surrounded us there was no fire. … Neither then, nor now, am I in the least surprised that we inspired no one to follow us; how could we, who were not burning ourselves, set other souls ablaze? … We were cold inside. Should we be surprised, how the faithful even held out with us in church any longer? But they were simple souls. … We could no longer inspire intelligent people or higher circles, nor even maintain them in the churches, in the faith.[1]

It is not surprising that in late imperial Russia the seminaries, practically the only avenues of education open to the sons of lower clergy, were breeding schools for atheism and revolutionary politics.

Most of the leaders of the *Russian religious renaissance* at the end of the nineteenth century and the early twentieth century were lay philosophers and theologians, as well as artistic and literary figures, operating outside the formal framework of the church and hence freer to express themselves than academic theologians. Nonetheless in the early twentieth century this group included one priest, Fr Pavel Florensky, and Sergius Bulgakov, who became the most prominent figure of this group, was ordained in 1918. As we suggested in the previous chapter, the Russian religious philosopher-theologians were the true spiritual and theological successors of the early Slavophiles.

The leaders of the religious renaissance were part of a broad grouping within the educated echelons of Russian society known as the intelligentsia. Although there is little agreement on what constituted the Russian intelligentsia, it certainly was not educated people in general, but rather a broad intellectual, social and political movement characterized by several key features.[2] These included notably a deep concern for Russia's social problems, especially the situation of the poor and the oppressed, a critical and even hostile attitude towards the government and the aristocracy which maintained fundamentally oppressive and unjust political and social structures, and a certain self-consciousness of its own existence. For many *intelligenty*, this configuration of ideas coalesced around one central goal: the abolition of the monarchy and with it the entire aristocratic and autocratic socio-political structure of Russian society, and its replacement with a modern social, economic and political system inspired by Western models. Another characteristic of much of the intelligentsia was opposition to the church, at least to the church's role in society because of its close association with the detested imperial regime. Finally, looking back at the Slavophile-Westernizer

---

[1]Metropolitan Benjamin (Fedchenkov) (1880–1961), 'On the Threshold of Two Eras' (Moscow, 1994), 135, quoted in Hilarion Alfeyev, 'Orthodox Theology on the Threshold of the 21st Century: Will There Be a Renaissance of Russian Theological Scholarship?' *The Ecumenical Review*, 52, 3 (2000), 310.

[2]There are numerous studies of the intelligentsia. For attempts to define the intelligentsia, see notably Nicolas Zernov, *The Russian Religious Renaissance of the Twentieth Century* (New York: Harper & Row, 1963), 1–34; Christopher Read, *Religion, Revolution and the Russian Intelligentsia, 1900-1912: The Vekhi Debate and Its Intellectual Background* (London: Macmillan, 1979), 1–6; and Martin Malia, 'What Is the Intelligentsia?' and Richard Pipes, 'The Historical Evolution of the Russian Intelligentsia', in Richard Pipes, ed., *The Russian Intelligentsia* (New York: Columbia University Press, 1961).

debate of the mid-nineteenth century, the intelligentsia represented in a way the triumph of Western ideas in Russia, while those who claimed the Slavophile heritage were conservative nationalists who condemned all shades of thought among the *intelligenty.*

Nicolas Zernov refers to the intelligentsia as an 'Order'[3] – but this appellation suggests that the intelligentsia had some sort of formal structure, which was far from being the case. In fact, the intelligentsia was divided into numerous intellectual, philosophical, cultural and political groups. Some groups favoured the violent destruction of Russia's existing social and political structures to achieve their goals, while others advocated the establishment of legal and political systems which would limit the powers of the state, along the lines of Western liberalism and democracy. Philosophical positivism, materialism and atheism underpinned the thinking of much of the intelligentsia. The failure of the imperial regime to move decisively towards genuine political and social reform, especially after the aborted revolution of 1905, served to radicalize even further wide segments of the intelligentsia, of whom the most radical were the Marxists under the leadership of Lenin and Trotsky. The principal means of expression of the intelligentsia were various print media, books, scholarly and more popular journals, pamphlets, as well as open lectures and discussion groups of all sorts.

By the end of the nineteenth century, the mid-nineteenth-century rivalry between Slavophiles and Westernizers had been superseded by more fundamental conflict between positivists-materialists and idealists – with both parties grounding their thinking on different strands of Western thought. Positivism maintains that information derived from sensory experience and from logical analysis is the exclusive source of valid knowledge, and thus denies the validity of realities which cannot be verified empirically, rejecting any transcendent reality. Positivism is the basis of modern science, and positivists, following the French sociologist Auguste Comte (1798–1857), consider that human society, like the non-human world, operates according to general laws. Materialism holds that only physical reality exists and that all phenomena, including mental constructs and consciousness, are the result of material interactions. The leading nineteenth-century materialists were the Germans Ludwig Feuerbach (1804–72), Karl Marx (1818–83) and Friedrich Engels (1820–95), whose revolutionary and atheistic historical and social theories had a powerful influence on important segments of Russian intelligentsia.

In contrast, idealism considers that reality, or at least reality as we can know it, is fundamentally mental, an immaterial construction of the mind, and it thus affirms the existence of non-empirical reality. Russian religious philosophy was strongly influenced by German idealism, beginning with Immanuel Kant (1724–1804), and including Johann Gottlieb Fichte (1762–1814), Georg Wilhelm Friedrich Hegel (1770–1831), Friedrich Wilhelm Joseph Schelling (1775–1854) and Arthur Schopenhauer (1788–1860). Idealism attracted some prominent members of the intelligentsia and for several major figures of the religious renaissance constituted a philosophical mid-point, a way-station, between atheistic positivism-materialism and Christianity. While the emerging Christian intelligentsia shared with the rest of the intelligentsia a vivid social conscience, reflected especially in the goal of seeking the end of the imperial regime, it was set apart from the others by its adherence

[3]Zernov, *The Russian Religious Renaissance*, 17ff.

to Christianity broadly defined, often with only nominal adherence to Orthodoxy. By the late nineteenth century many in the Russian upper classes, both the aristocracy and educated persons from lower social groups, had turned away from the church and from Christianity in general and there was little contact between the ROC and even the Christian intelligentsia, a tragic situation that Alexander Bukharev had anticipated a generation earlier. The ROC looked askance at the rather personalized image of Christianity held by many Christian intellectuals and at their nominal or even non-existent adherence to the Orthodox Church. The major exception to alienation of educated people from the church was the imperial family and those close to it, who maintained their strong commitment to Orthodoxy and the church.

The religious intelligentsia was thus intermediary between the church and the non-Christian intelligentsia, a group hard put to establish its credibility both to the 'right' and to the 'left'. To the 'right', the ROC refused to see the religious intelligentsia as loyal 'sons and daughters of the church', certainly prior to the fall of the monarchy and the Council of ROC in 1917–18, at which some lay theologians, such as Sergius Bulgakov, played a major role. To the 'left', vis-à-vis the non-Christian intelligentsia, the religious intelligentsia sought to inject a Christian perspective and voice into the debates on Russia's future, to be a witness of the faith among the intelligentsia. This was in a sense a belated response to Bukharev's call for the church to become engaged with modernity – but it took place largely outside church structures. But for the non-Christian intelligentsia, Christianity simply had nothing to offer to the debate about Russia's future.

A related aspect of the religious intelligentsia was that it was never able to reach widely into Russian society. It remained a brilliant but mostly elite movement, largely restricted to the intellectual and literary circles of Saint Petersburg and, to a lesser extent, Moscow and Kiev. Years later, Nicolas Berdyaev (1874–1948), one of the leaders of this group, confessed frankly in an article:

> The weakness of the Russian spiritual renaissance was in its absence of a broad social base. It emerged among the cultural elite. The struggle for spirit, for spiritual life and spiritual creativity led to a rift with the broad social movement and mass of the people and at the same time it was not in union with the traditional-conservative popular religiosity. The isolation of the creators of spiritual culture at the beginning of the century increased all the more. The need for surmounting the isolation pushed some to the right, they hoped to merge themselves with those of the Old Russia, from which the intelligentsia were cut off. But no one was properly successful at this.[4]

St Maria of Paris (Mother Maria Skobtsova, 1891–1945), a young participant in cultural and intellectual circles in Petersburg just before the First World War, wrote similarly of this period in her memoirs:

> We lived in the middle of a vast country as if on an uninhabited island. Russia was illiterate, whereas in our milieu was concentrated all the culture of the world: the Greeks were quoted by heart, we welcomed the French symbolists, we thought of Scandinavian literature as our own, we were

[4]Nicolas Berdyaev, 'The Russian Spiritual Renaissance of the Beginning of the XXth Century and the Journal *Put'* (For the Tenth Anniversary of *Put'*)' *Put'*, 49 (1935). Online at: www.chebucto.ns.ca/Philosophy/Sui-Generis/Berdyaev/essays/rsr.htm (2 February 2017).

familiar with the philosophy, theology, poetry and history of the whole wide world, in this sense we were citizens of the universe, the keepers of humanity's cultural museum. This was Rome in the time of its decline. ... We played out the last act of the tragedy concerned with the rift between the intelligentsia and the people. Beyond us stretched out the Russian Empire's snowy desert, a country in fetters: it was as ignorant of our delights as of our anguish, while its own delights and anguish had no effect on us. ... Everybody stood for revolution; the most responsible utterances were made on the subject. Yet they left me more disenchanted with ourselves than ever before. For no one, positively no one was prepared to die for it. Moreover, if they were to learn that people do die for it, they would have evaluated this too somehow, they would have approved or disapproved, they would have understood it at its highest level and discussed it at the top of their voices – until the breakfast-time fried eggs were served.[5]

The third theological tradition was the continuity of *Orthodox ascetic and spiritual theology*, the 'Holy Russia' of the mystical theology of St Seraphim of Sarov (1754–1833), the revival of hesychastic spirituality after the publication the Slavonic and Russian editions of the *Philokalia*, the *startsi* (elders) of Optino Monastery (between the 1830s and 1923), the saintly bishops Ignatius Brianchaninov (1807–67) and Theophan the Recluse (1815–94), the popular book *The Way of the Pilgrim* (1884) and Archimandrite Hilarion, author of the book *On the Mountains of the Caucasus*, which ignited the Name-of-God controversy (onomatodoxy) just prior to the First World War.[6] Georges Florovsky reminds the readers of *The Ways of Russian Theology* of this tragic split that developed within the church itself, between the hierarchy and official theology and the great body of the faithful:

The history of Russian theology exhibits disarray in its creative development. Most painful has been the strange gulf between theology and piety, between theological scholarship and devotional prayer, between the vagaries of theological schools and the life of the church. This was the rupture and schism between the 'intelligentsia' and 'the people' within the church itself. ... Theological scholarship came to Russia from the West. For much too long it remained a foreign entity, even insisting on speaking in its own alien tongue[7] – neither the language of common life, nor the language of prayer. It remained a kind of heterodox insertion into the organic fabric of the church. It developed in an artificial and all-too isolated environment, becoming and remaining an academic enterprise. As it turned into a subject of instruction, it ceased being a quest for truth or a confession of faith. Theological thought lost the habit of listening to the heartbeat of church life and gradually lost access to this heart. It attracted little attention or sympathy in wider circles of church society or among the people.[8]

[5]Mother Maria Skobtsova, 'Recollections of Blok: For the 15th Anniversary of His Death', cited in Sergei Hackel, *Pearl of Great Price: The Life of Mother Maria Skobtsova, 1891-1945* (Crestwood, NY: St Vladimir's Seminary Press, 1981), 80–1.

[6]See Ch. 15 and Paul Ladouceur, 'The Name-of-God Conflict in Orthodox Theology', *St Vladimir's Theological Quarterly*, 56, 4 (2012).

[7]A reference to the use of Latin as the principal language of instruction in Russian theological education.

[8]Georges Florovsky, 'Breaks and Links' (conclusion of *The Ways of Russian Theology*), in Brandon Gallaher and Paul Ladouceur, eds., *The Patristic Witness of Georges Florovsky: Essential Theological Writings* (London: T&T Clark, 2019), 162–3.

A Christian intelligentsia

The major figures of the Russian religious renaissance, sometimes referred to as 'the God-seekers' (*Bogoiskateli*),[9] included many philosophers, lawyers, historians and publicists, and also literary figures, novelists, poets, artists and literary critics. The religious renaissance overlapped with the Silver Age of Russian letters in the decades prior to the revolution of 1917, a time of great literary flowering and intellectual ferment, with a wide variety of often ill-defined and competing religious and artistic trends. Two events in particular marked the coming of age of the religious renaissance. Beginning in January 1877, Vladimir Soloviev delivered twelve lectures on the theme of 'Godmanhood' (*bogochelovechestvo*).[10] Soloviev's audacious and powerful ideas in these lectures and in other writings set the tone for a great deal of Russian Christian thought until the end of the Second World War. Among those who followed Soloviev's lectures were the already-prominent novelists Fyodor Dostoyevsky and Leo Tolstoy. Dostoyevsky's last and greatest novel, *The Brothers Karamazov*, was published in instalments between January 1879 and November 1880. The novel showed the influence of both Soloviev's thought and the nineteenth century spiritual revival in Russia stimulated by the *Philokalia* and hesychasm.

After Soloviev's death in 1900, the most influential philosophers of the religious renaissance were Nicolas Berdyaev, Nicolas Lossky, Simeon Frank, Peter Struve and Basil Zenkovsky. Few of the Russian religious renaissance personalities were theologians in the modern sense, although several moved gradually into the theological domain, such as Sergius Bulgakov, initially an economist and philosopher. Pavel Florensky was a true polymath, at once a philosopher, mathematician, linguist, scientist and theologian. Elizabeth Kuzmina-Karavaeva (née Pilenko), the future Mother Maria Skobtsova, was a poet, artist, social activist, politician and theologian.

There were two broad groups among the Christian philosopher-theologians in terms of relations with the ROC. The first group, numerous prior to the First World War, were on the fringes of the church or clearly estranged from the church. The most well-known personalities of this group included Soloviev and Tolstoy, together with those loosely associated under the banner of the 'new religious consciousness'. The second group consisted of those in formal relation with the church, which included initially only one priest, Fr Pavel Florensky, ordained in 1911. As a result of the 'return to the church' movement, this group expanded slowly prior to the Revolution and more dramatically among the Christian intelligentsia in exile in the 1920s.

In the last decades of the nineteenth century, the novelists *Leo Tolstoy* (1828–1910) and *Fyodor Dostoyevsky* (1821–81) expressed in their writings a fundamentally Christian view of Russia. The focus of both novelists was the search for meaning in life, which they saw in Christianity. Both, but especially Tolstoy, had personalized views of Christianity, and both had contacts with the Optino

---

[9]Nicolas Berdyaev uses this expression to refer to Russian philosophers and literary figures from Peter Chaadaev (1794–1856) and the Slavophiles to Soloviev and the other personalities of the Russian religious renaissance. See Nicolas Berdyaev, 'Russkie Bogoiskateli' (Russian God-Seekers) (1907), in his book, *Dukhovnyi krisis intelligentsia* (1910). Translation in Nicolas Berdyaev, *The Spiritual Crisis of the Intelligentsia*): *Articles on Societal and Religious Psychology (1907–1909)* (Portsmouth, NH: Vilnius Press, 2014), 27–37.

[10]Vladimir Soloviev, *Lectures on Godmanhood* (1881) (London: Dennis Dobson, 1948; Hudson, NY: Lindisfarne Press, 1995).

Monastery. There are important differences, however, between the two novelists. Tolstoy had a rather rationalist view of Christianity: He denied the divinity of Christ yet at the same time believed in Christ's teachings as though Christ were indeed divine.[11] Tolstoy was a moralist who accepted neither the church nor the state. Nor did he accept secularized society and he remained aloof from the institutional church. Some saw him as a nihilist or even a 'Christian anarchist', exemplified especially in his 1894 philosophical work *The Kingdom of God Is Within You*, which became a key text for non-violent resistance movements worldwide. In later life, his teachings concentrated exclusively on the moral lessons of the Gospels, especially the Sermon on the Mount. His non-violence inspired Gandhi, who had a correspondence with the Russian novelist in the early twentieth century, and also Martin Luther King.

Conversely, in his later years Dostoyevsky's faith was solidly Orthodox and he was closer to the church than Tolstoy. His major novels are impregnated with Christian themes and values, even in seemingly non-religious characters. Dostoyevsky, accompanied by Vladimir Soloviev, used his visit to Optino as an inspiration for the setting and some of the characters in *The Brothers Karamazov* (1880) – although the monks of Optino denied that the monk Zosima in the novel was based on the starets Ambrosii of Optino, whom Dostoyevsky had met.

Vladimir Soloviev (1853–1900) was a brilliant Russian philosopher, poet and mystic whose bold thinking had a powerful, even determining influence on much of the philosophy, theology and art of the religious renaissance. In his teens, Soloviev, son of the famous historian Sergius Soloviev, renounced Orthodoxy for nihilism, but he soon returned to Christianity and to the ROC. As a philosopher, he was a critic of Western philosophy, especially positivism. The major themes of his philosophy revolved around a search for a principle of 'total unity', unifying all existence. Basil Zenkovsky calls Soloviev's philosophical system 'a modernised pantheism', a label which others have also applied to Soloviev's thought.[12] 'Total unity' found its most dramatic expression in the ideas of divine Sophia, whose presence Soloviev claimed to have experienced in several visions, including one in the British Museum, while doing research on Sophia, and another in the Egyptian desert; Godmanhood , the implications for humanity and the cosmos of the Incarnation; and *sobornost'*, which Soloviev adapted from the Slavophiles in his search for a unifying principle for humanity. His ideas about the divine Sophia are generally considered to be outside the limits of Christian dogma. He was accused of seeing divine Sophia as a kind of fourth, feminine divine hypostasis, but he defended himself against this accusation.[13] Soloviev himself never considered that he was deviating from the Orthodox faith and it is unfortunate that later interest for Soloviev focused largely on his mystical experiences and his unconventional ideas of Sophia, the world-soul and the eternal feminine, distracting attention from equally if not more significant aspects of his thought, notably the articulation of Christian moral and legal philosophies. Leading figures of the

[11]See Paul Evdokimov, *Le Christ dans la pensée russe* (Christ in Russian Thought) (Paris: Le Cerf, 1970), 92.

[12]V. V. Zenkovsky, *A History of Russian Philosophy* (2 vols.) (in Russian) (Paris, 1948–50) (English translation: London: Routledge & Kegan Paul; New York: Columbia University Press, 1953; 2003), vol. 2, 530. We will discuss total-unity and sophiology in more detail in Ch. 9.

[13]See Judith Deutsch Kornblatt, *Divine Sophia: The Wisdom Writings of Vladimir Solovyov* (Ithaca, NY: Cornell University Press, 2009), 11.

religious renaissance benefited from Soloviev's Christian ethics in such crucial domains as legal, social and political theory, major preoccupations in the fatal years prior to the revolutions of 1917. Soloviev's forceful but often incomplete, obscure and ambiguous if not self-contradictory thinking had a powerful influence on contemporary and later religious thinkers, such as Berdyaev, Bulgakov, Florensky, Nicolas Lossky and Simeon Frank, the novelists Dostoevsky and Tolstoy, new religious consciousness figures such as Vasily Rozanov, Dimitri Merezhkovsky and Zinaida Gippius, and the poets Andrei Bely and Alexander Blok. While not all accepted his more daring ideas, all recognized him as an original Christian thinker and seeker after the truth.

Pavel Florensky (1882–37) had specialized knowledge in many different fields, including mathematics, physics, art, linguistics, philosophy and theology, and he published works in most of these fields. He knew most European languages as well as Latin, Greek and Hebrew and several Central Asian languages. His upbringing was a-religious and his interests were mainly in science. As an adolescent he underwent a spiritual crisis brought about by a perceived inability of science alone to account for truth which lay beyond the reaches of scientific determinism. Florensky overcame this crisis by the study of mathematics and philosophy at the University of Moscow, which led him to Orthodoxy. He went on to study at the Moscow Theological Academy in Sergiyev Posad, graduating in 1908, and immediately began teaching philosophy at the Academy. During this period he had a considerable influence on his close friend Sergius Bulgakov. The notion of Sophia, both divine and created, inherited from Soloviev, features in his theology – yet his main theological study, *The Pillar and Ground of the Truth* (1914), passed the religious censors.[14] Unlike virtually all the prominent Orthodox philosophers and theologians of the time who either left Russia voluntarily after the Bolshevik revolution or were expelled by Lenin in 1922, Florensky explicitly elected to remain in the Soviet Union. After the revolution, he worked for the state body responsible for the electrification of Russia. Florensky was arrested for the first time in 1928, but was quickly freed after the intercession of friends. In 1933 he was arrested again and sentenced to ten years in the labour camps. In 1934 he was moved to the island of Solovki in the White Sea, a former monastery converted to a labour camp, where many members of the clergy were interned and executed. Florensky was executed in 1937.

In the early years of the twentieth century, disenchantment with the failure of positivism and other fundamentally non-Christian or anti-Christian philosophies to account properly for the fullness of human existence, especially the human thirst for the absolute, the transcendental and the eternal, led several former atheists and Marxists to look to Christianity and to the Orthodox Church. Among these figured four leading Marxists: Nicolas Berdyaev, Sergius Bulgakov, Simeon Frank and Peter Struve. Nicolas Zernov says of these 'Four Notable Converts':

> The long and hard struggle of the Russian intelligentsia against the autocracy, which involved the rejection of the church, was brought to a sudden end by the collapse of the St Petersburg Empire in 1917. On the eve of this momentous event four leading Marxists became converts to Christianity and abandoned their former materialistic outlook. … Independently they all passed through the same stages of inner evolution and eventually found their spiritual home in the Orthodox Church. There

[14]Pavel Florensky, *The Pillar and Ground of the Truth: An Essay in Orthodox Theodicy in Twelve Letters* (1914) (Princeton, NJ: Princeton University Press, 1997).

is a striking similarity in the destiny of these four men whose spiritual pilgrimage was symbolic of the order they represented. They were born in the seventies of the nineteenth century and all died at the same age. They began their careers as Marxists and revolutionaries, but ultimately became convinced Christians, and all suffered exile for the sake of their religious convictions.[15]

Nicolas Berdyaev (1874–1948) was born in Kiev and in his early teens began to read major German philosophers, notably Hegel, Schopenhauer and Kant. He entered Kiev University in 1894, became a Marxist and in 1897 was arrested in a student demonstration and expelled from the university. His involvement in illegal activities led to three years of internal exile in Central Russia. In 1904 Berdyaev moved to Saint Petersburg, where he participated actively in intellectual and spiritual debates, departing from radical Marxism to focus his attention on philosophy and spirituality. In the years before the revolution, Berdyaev published several books and was involved in a number of literary undertakings. He became an Orthodox Christian, but was often critical of the institutional church.

Although Berdyaev did not accept the Bolshevik regime because of its authoritarianism and the domination of the state over the freedom of the individual, he was permitted to continue to lecture, to write and to organize the Free Academy of Spiritual Culture in Moscow. In September 1922, he was among a group of prominent writers, scholars and intellectuals sent into exile in Western Europe. At first Berdyaev and many other émigrés went to Berlin, but economic and political conditions in Weimar Germany caused him and his wife to move to Paris in 1923.

In the years that he spent in France, Berdyaev wrote fifteen books, including his most important works. His major philosophical and theological themes were the human person, creativity and freedom. He has been characterized as 'rebellious prophet', 'Christian existentialist' and 'apostle of freedom'.[16] Berdyaev's works were rapidly translated into the major European languages and up to about the 1960s, he was the most well-known Orthodox thinker in non-Orthodox circles. Berdyaev was a tireless organizer of intellectual circles and discussion groups; he founded or chaired such groups in Saint Petersburg prior to the Revolution, in Moscow until he was expelled from the Soviet Union, in Berlin and in Paris. Berdyaev was particularly active in promoting exchanges of ideas between exiled Russian thinkers and the French intellectual community. He also founded and edited the journal *Put'* (The Way), the leading Orthodox intellectual journal in Paris from 1925 to 1940, and was a close friend and associate of Mother Maria Skobtsova.

Sergius Bulgakov (1871–1944) was born into a clerical family stretching back six generations. He studied at Orel seminary, lost his faith and became a Marxist, or, as he expressed it later, 'I fell victim to a gloomy revolutionary nihilism.'[17] In 1894 he graduated in law from the University of Moscow, where he also studied political economy. He was one of the leading Marxist philosophers and economists, but a study of the economics of rural Russia had convinced him that Marxism was incorrect in its major premises. By the turn of the century he was an idealist, contributing an

[15]Zernov, *The Russian Religious Renaissance*, 131.

[16]See Donald A. Lowrie, *Rebellious Prophet: A Life of Nicolai Berdyaev* (London: Victor Gollanz, 1960); Donald A. Lowrie, ed., *Christian Existentialism: A Berdyaev Anthology* (London: Allen & Unwin, 1965); and Michel A. Vallon, *An Apostle of Freedom: Life and Teachings of Nicolas Berdyaev* (New York: Philosophical Library, 1960).

[17]Sergius Bulgakov, 'Autobiographical Notes' (1946), in James Pain and Nicolas Zernov, eds., *A Bulgakov Anthology* (London: SPCK, 1976), 4.

important essay to the collection *Problems of Idealism* (1902) and later to *Vekhi* (1909). His return to Orthodoxy took place gradually over a period of several years and was complete in 1908.

Bulgakov rapidly became a major figure in the Russian religious renaissance in the early years of the twentieth century. His thinking was initially strongly influenced by Vladimir Soloviev and subsequently by his friend Pavel Florensky. He was an important lay participant in the 1917–18 Council of the ROC and was ordained to the priesthood the day after Pentecost 1918, shortly before the end of the Council. During the Russian Civil War he taught philosophy at the University of Simferopol in the Crimea. He was a prolific writer, but it was only from 1917 onwards that his books became properly theological. Bulgakov expounded his mature theology in exile, notably in what has become known as the minor or little trilogy: *The Burning Bush* (on the Mother of God) (1927); *The Friend of the Bridegroom* (on St John the Baptist) (1927); and *Jacob's Ladder* (on angels) (1929); and the major or great trilogy: *The Lamb of God* (1933) (on divine-humanity, Sophia and Christ), *The Comforter* (1936) (on the Holy Spirit) and *The Bride of the Lamb* (1945) (on creation, the church and eschatology).[18]

In December 1922 the Bolshevik government expelled Bulgakov and his family, together with other prominent opposition intellectuals. In 1923 he became professor of church law and theology at the school of law of the Russian Research Institute in Prague and in 1925 he moved to Paris, where he was one of the founders of the Saint Sergius Institute of Orthodox Theology. He served as professor of dogmatic theology and dean until his death from throat cancer in July 1944. Bulgakov was a powerful thinker and a man of deep conviction, unafraid to defend ideas which broke with current thinking in the church. His teachings on Sophia (sophiology) and on ecumenism resulted in major theological controversies in the mid-1930s. (These will be explored in greater detail in Chapters 9 and 11.)

Peter Struve (1870–1944) trained as a lawyer and acquired a specialized knowledge of economics. He was very active in politics, first as a legal Marxist and a leader in the Social Democratic Party, but by 1900 he broke with Marxism and moved to idealism and liberalism, becoming a leading figure in the Constitutional Democratic Party (Kadets), and then to Orthodoxy. The conversion to Christianity of this former leading Marxist public figure was more scandalous to his erstwhile intellectual colleagues than those of the other 'notable converts'. He served as a member of the Second Duma (1907), edited a liberal literary-political monthly *Russkaya mysl* [*Russian Thought*] and contributed to both *Problems of Idealism* and *Vekhi*. He was active in the 'White' contra-revolution movement and in exile he was associated with the conservative wing of the liberal movement.

Simeon Frank (1877–1950), son of a Jewish doctor, was initially attracted to Marxism, but after being forced to study in Germany because of his radical student activities in Russia, he published a critique of Marxism's labour theory of value. He moved to idealism and political liberalism, and became Orthodox in 1912. Frank was close to Struve throughout much of his adult life. In 1921 Frank was associated with Berdyaev in the Free Academy of Spiritual Culture in Moscow and he was exiled in 1922. In exile, Frank wrote many philosophical and religious works. His philosophy

[18]All are published by Eerdmans in English translation between 2003 and 2010.

was centred on the 'metaphysics of total-unity', a major theme for several Christian philosophers influenced by Vladimir Soloviev.

In addition to the four leading Marxists who returned to Christianity, several other prominent members of the Russian intelligentsia also reconciled with the Orthodox Church after a period of estrangement. *Nicolas Lossky* (1870–1965) was expelled from school for his atheist convictions and subsequently converted to Christianity, very likely around 1914. He became professor of philosophy at the University of Saint Petersburg and was expelled from Russia, together with his family, including his son Vladimir Lossky (1903–58), on Lenin's orders in 1922. He initially taught in Prague, then in Bratislava and from 1946, at St Vladimir's Orthodox Seminary in New York. His most well-known work is his *History of Russian Philosophy* (1952).[19] Paul Evdokimov attributes the conversion of Nicolas Lossky to Pavel Florensky's book *The Pillar and Ground of the Truth* – a conversion which undoubtedly opened the door to that of his son Vladimir, who was eleven at the time of the publication of Florensky's book in 1914.[20] *Alexander Izgoev* (pen name of Aron Lande) (1872–1935), another former Marxist, was a publicist, journalist and politician who contributed to the *Vekhi* (1909) and *De Profundis* (1918) symposia. *Basil Zenkovsky* (1881–1962) was a philosopher who went through a period of atheism as an adolescent and young adult, but returned to the church prior to completing his university studies in Kiev. He taught philosophy at the Saint Sergius Institute in Paris and was president of the Russian Student Christian Movement (ACER) for nearly forty years. He wrote a monumental if somewhat neglected *History of Russian Philosophy* (1948).[21]

Elizabeth Kuzmina-Karavaeva (née Pilenko, *Mother Maria Skobtsova*, St Maria of Paris, 1891–1945) may have been a Marxist for a brief period during her adolescence, but she certainly was directly associated with the Socialist Revolutionary Party for several years, at least until 1918. She was a poet and artist but distanced herself from the rarefied atmosphere of the Petersburg literary salons just prior to the First World War. She was baptized as an infant, but her family was non-practising and her formal return to the church dates from the death of her four-year-old daughter Anastasia in Paris in 1926. After several years of social involvement with the Russian Student Christian Movement in France, in 1932 she became a nun and launched a number of social initiatives, all the while continuing to write articles on a wide range of theological and spiritual subjects, especially on the 'social gospel'. She was arrested in 1943 for helping Jews in German-occupied Paris during the Second World War and died in March 1945 in the Ravensbrück Concentration Camp in Germany. She was canonized by the Ecumenical Patriarchate in 2004, together with Fr Dimitri Klepinin, the chaplain of her chapel in Paris, her son George (Yuri) and the editor Ilya Fondaminski, all of whom died in German concentration camps.[22]

---

[19]Nicolas Lossky, *History of Russian Philosophy* (London: George Allen & Unwin, 1952).

[20]See Evdokimov, *Le Christ dans la pensée russe*, 175.

[21]Zenkovsky, *A History of Russian Philosophy*, 1953. Zenkovsky's *History* is more highly considered than Nicolas Lossky's shorter but more well-known work. For a review of assessments of the Zenkovsky book and comparisons with Lossky's, see Kare Johan Mjor, *Reformulating Russia: The Cultural and Intellectual Historiography of Russian First-Wave Émigré Writers* (Leiden & Boston: Brill, 2011), 253–6.

[22]Selections of Mother Maria's principal writings are available in Maria Skobtsova, *Mother Maria Skobtsova: Essential Writings* (Maryknoll, NY: Orbis Books, 2003); and in Paul Ladouceur, ed., *Sainte Marie de Paris (Mère Marie Skobtsova 1891-1945), Le Jour du Saint-Esprit* (Paris: Le Cerf, 2011).

The new religious consciousness

The principal personalities grouped under the epithet of the 'new religious consciousness' were Vasily Rozanov (1856–1919), Dimitri Merezhkovsky (1865–1941) and his wife Zinaida Gippius (or Hippius) (1869–1945), all brilliant writers, and several leading literary figures, such as the poets Vyacheslav Ivanov (1866–1949), Andrei Bely (1880–1934) and Alexander Blok (1880–1921), major figures of the Russian Silver Age. They and their entourage and followers held a wide range of shifting religious views. Some associated with the new religious consciousness were neo-pagans, hostile to Christianity; most were attracted to Christ and Christianity, but interpreted Christianity from a very personal perspective. They exemplified the failure of the Russian Orthodox Church to communicate the Christian message in terms meaningful to intellectual and cultural milieus. They saw Christ as a moral and spiritual leader; some acknowledged his divinity, but they could not accept the established Russian Church, which they viewed as compromised because of its close association with the detested imperial regime and by the rigidity of its doctrines, rituals, morality and hierarchical structures. The new religious consciousness was also marked by neo-romantic aestheticism and sensibility, not only as style but as world view. This was accompanied by an emphasis on 'natural religion', on the importance of emotions, feelings and psychological sensitivity, and a certain 'a-dogmatism', which itself became a new dogmatism. Disenchantment with the historical 'visible church' and conscious opposition to doctrine and ecclesial forms led to an emphasis on the importance of the 'invisible church', the church in the heart of the believer. In her diary, Zinaida Gippius expresses the disappointment of many Christian intellectuals with the ROC, not without a certain sadness:

> I speak now, *knowingly*, from my experience, and believing in the authenticity and the truth of the yet invisible [inner] church. But not believing that it is the last, the final church, which has already encompassed everything within itself. For it is not without reason that the visible church, consisting of such people, has its present appearance. After pushing aside all those who belonged to it only externally, the church has received *only* Father John [of Kronstadt] and those close to him. Is the whole of human understanding, are all the answers to our pain and torments, is the whole significance of Christ *already* manifest in the holiness of Father John? Alas, alas! How can we cut off our *understanding* of love, our thirst for the holiness of prayers *with knowledge* – about life, about thought, about every man, about everything in his entire contemporary essence? 'I shall pray with my heart – I shall pray with my mind …,' said the apostle. But Father John and the whole church do not teach us how to pray with our minds *also*.[23]

For Merezhkovsky, Gippius and others in their circle, the answer to this unsatisfactory state of affairs could only be the establishment of a 'new church': 'A *church* is needed as an image of the evangelical, Christian religion of the Flesh and Blood,' mused Gippius in 1899. 'The *Existing* Church can satisfy neither us nor the people close to us in the *Zeitgeist* [the spirit of the age] because of

[23]Zinaida Gippius, 'About the Cause', in Temira Pachmuss, ed., *Between Paris and St. Petersburg: Selected Diaries of Zinaida Hippius* (Urbana, IL: University of Illinois Press, 1975), 133. The reference to 'the Apostle' may be a very approximate rendition of 1 Cor. 14:19: 'Yet in the church I had rather speak five words with my understanding [mind]…', together with Jesus' teaching on the First Commandment (Mt. 22:37).

the way it is constructed.'[24] The Merezhkovskys referred to the idea of a new church as 'the Cause', which became bound up in the personal relations of the couple and their close friend Dmitri Filosofov (1872–1940), with whom they lived for many years in a ménage à trois, one of several scandalous causes célèbres at the time. Reflecting on those close to her, including Merezhkovsky, Filosofov and Rozanov, Gippius wrote that 'all sought God, were pitiful, and could not find him.'[25]

Following the lead of the Merezhkovskys, many of those associated with the new religious consciousness looked forward to a 'third revelation' or testament, associated with the Holy Spirit, which would go beyond the Old and the New Testaments and lead to a widespread spiritual renaissance. In this theory, the first phase of human history represented the realm of God the Father, reflected in the Old Testament as the revelation of divine power and authority as truth; the second phase was that of Jesus Christ, God the Son, the realm of the New Testament and the revelation of truth as love; and the third phase or Third Testament, embodied in a church of the Third Testament, the realm of the Holy Spirit, which would reveal love as freedom and resolve the duality or antitheses of the human condition: earth and heaven, flesh and spirit, sex and asceticism, individuality and sociality, hatred and love.[26]

Vasily Rozanov and others of his circle interpreted Soloviev's notion of divine-humanity as a duality of Holy Spirit and Holy Flesh, which they felt could only be resolved in a Third Testament, since historical Christianity – the church – was so strongly oriented to the Spirit that it disregarded and even annihilated the flesh and humanity's connection with the earth. In a similar vein Rozanov criticized historical Christianity for being a 'religion of Golgotha' – strongly focused on Christ's passion and death – as distinct from the true Christianity of Bethlehem, symbol of the Incarnation. For Rozanov, the revelation of the Word made Flesh is a source of joy not sorrow: 'Among all the philosophic and religious doctrines there is no world-view more luminous and full of the joy of life than that of Christianity.'[27] Yet Rozanov's focus on the flesh and on sex as the highest expression of human solidarity with the earth was neither hedonistic nor Freudian; nor was sex separated from marriage and family – procreation and family are major, perhaps central themes in Rozanov's thinking. For Rozanov, as for the Merezhkovskys and their circles, the failure of the church to incorporate adequately humanity's own 'incarnation' – that is, its connection with the earth, nature and the cosmos – into ecclesial anthropology was sufficient grounds to look to a new revelation which would restore genuine Christianity.

As Basil Zenkovsky points out in his generally sympathetic account of Rozanov's thinking, Rozanov's 'metaphysics of sex' was an aspect of a truly cosmic vision, in which the sacred mystery of sex, as the generation of life and of personhood, is 'the sphere in man which mysteriously connects him with all of nature' (Zenkovsky), and even 'transcends the boundaries of nature; it is

[24]Gippius, 'About the Cause', 101.
[25]Ibid., 104.
[26]For a summary of the religious beliefs of the Merezhkovskys and those of their circle, see the introduction to Temira Pachmuss, ed., *Between Paris and St. Petersburg*, especially 17–19, and her monograph *Zinaida Hippius: An Intellectual Profile* (Carbondale, IL: Southern Illinois University Press, 1971), 103–65.
[27]Vasily Rozanov, *Okolo tserkovnykh sten* [By the Walls of the Church] (Saint Petersburg, 1906), I:15, cited in Zenkovsky, *A History of Russian Philosophy*, 1:457.

extra-natural and supernatural' (Rozanov).[28] Zenkovsky defends Rozanov against the accusation of 'mystical pantheism' levied against his philosophy.

Other commentators fail to consider the personalities of the new religious consciousness as serious thinkers and summarily dismiss them. Georges Florovsky characterizes Rozanov as 'religiously blind',[29] with 'no sense of responsibility for his thoughts',[30] a thinker who remained outside Christianity. According to him, Rozanov failed to perceive 'the true mystery of Bethlehem [as] the fiery mystery of the divine incarnation', seeing it only as a 'pastoral scene or picture of family devotion. The [true Christian] joy is not so much that of human birth, but rather of the glory of God's condescension.'[31] Florovsky, unlike Zenkovsky, sees no value in Rozanov's 'vision of flesh and sex', and labels it as 'diseased and unhealthy'.[32] Nicolas Zernov, while more restrained than Florovsky in his discussion of Rozanov, nonetheless describes Rozanov's religious attitude as 'fundamentally pagan', worshipping 'an unknown God who was beyond good and evil'.[33]

Other orientations, including unconventional sexual behaviour ranging from homosexual unions to common-law couples and unconsummated marriages,[34] within the new religious consciousness were also provocative and controversial, even with their erstwhile friends and associates among the philosopher-theologians. Some of the symbolist poets, especially Alexander Blok, Georgy Chulkov (1879–1939) and Vyacheslav Ivanov, promoted 'mystical anarchism'. Others associated with the new religious consciousness were drawn to marginally Christian occult and esoteric beliefs, such as those of Helena Blavatsky (1831–1891) (theosophy) and Rudolf Steiner (1861–1925) (anthroposophy), then popular in Russia. Most focused on love and especially sexual love as the highest human state, promoting marriage and family and objecting to asceticism and monasticism. The Merezhkovsky-Gippius group developed its own quasi-Christian prayers and rituals used at its weekly prayer sessions in Russia and during frequent stays abroad, considering that this was consistent with the group's inner union with the existing church and its outward separation from it.

Direct relations between those associated with the new religious consciousness and the more intellectually inclined Christian leaders were limited. Among the latter, Nicolas Berdyaev was for some years closest to the leading new religious consciousness figures. In the first phase of his intellectual and religious journey from Marxism, and even after his adhesion to the church in 1908, Berdyaev was associated with Rozanov, Merezhkovsky, Gippius and other personalities of the new religious consciousness. He later describes the atmosphere surrounding this group as if it were under a 'magic spell', following a 'strange mythology', caught up in 'hysterical naturalism', with

---

[28]Zenkovsky, *A History of Russian Philosophy*, 1:460.

[29]Georges Florovsky, *The Ways of Russian Theology* (2 vols.), *The Collected Works of Georges Florovsky*, vols. 5 and 6 (Belmont, MA: Nordland, 1979), II:240.

[30]Florovsky, *The Ways of Russian Theology*, II:241.

[31]Ibid., II:241–2.

[32]Ibid., II:242.

[33]Zernov, *The Russian Religious Renaissance*, 181; 182.

[34]See the fine study by Olga Matich, *Erotic Utopia: The Decadent Imagination in Russia's Fin de Siècle* (Madison, WI: University of Wisconsin Press, 2005).

views often far removed from historical Christianity.[35] Berdyaev quickly became aware of 'something unwholesome in the prevailing atmosphere' and he found little satisfaction in the 'emotional and intellectual confusion which reigned among the "neo-Christians".'[36] As a result, writes Berdyaev, his reaction against the atmosphere created by the Merezhkovskys 'speeded me on my way to the Orthodox Church'.[37] Berdyaev remained nonetheless impressed and attracted by the Merezhkovskys' 'intense awareness of ideas and by a complete absence in them of the commonplace'.[38]

Theological contacts and frictions

The profound divisions among Russia's religious and theological groups rendered communication among them difficult and most contacts were marked by conflict. The relations between two highly visible leaders of the Christian intelligentsia and the ROC illustrate only too well the church's inability to accommodate Christian thinking outside the confines of official church structures and theology. Vladimir Soloviev, the most profound and influential philosopher of the Russian religious renaissance, ran afoul of the ROC. In 1891 he was denied communion by his confessor, then a not uncommon penitence in Orthodoxy. In 1896 Soloviev took communion during a liturgy celebrated by a Greek Catholic ('Uniate') Russian priest. Some interpreted this gesture as a 'conversion' to Catholicism, but there is ample evidence against a simple conversion as normally understood. His act should be seen rather in the context of his ecumenical conviction, shared by many Russian intellectuals, that the unity of the church in Christ was never broken, despite the visible splits among the different Christian confessions. As Lev Gillet remarks, 'He wanted to recognize, acknowledge, declare and solemnly profess a union which, he believed, already existed.'[39] Nicolas Zernov comments on this incident: 'His communion at the Roman altar was a prophetic act demonstrating his belief that no barriers built by men could break the unity within the Church of Christ.'[40] Soloviev saw himself as a universal Christian, at once Orthodox and Catholic.[41] The church never condemned any of Soloviev's teachings and he died in 1900 within the Orthodox Church.

---

[35]Nicolas Berdyaev, *Dream and Reality: An Essay in Autobiography* (1949) (original English title: *Self-Knowledge: An Essay in Philosophical Autobiography*) (London: Bles, 1950), 145; 146; 147.

[36]Berdyaev, *Dream and Reality*, 143; Zernov, *The Russian Religious Renaissance*, 156.

[37]Berdyaev, *Dream and Reality*, 146.

[38]Ibid., 147.

[39]'Un Moine de l'Église d'Orient' [Lev Gillet], 'La signification de Soloviev' (The signficance of Soloviev) in *L'Église et les églises, 1054-1954; Neuf siècles de douloureuse séparation entre l'Orient et l'Occident* (The Church and the Churches, 1054-1954: Nine Centuries of Painful separation between the East and the West), Vol. 2 (Chevetogne, BE: Éditions de Chevetogne, 1955), 372.

[40]Nicolas Zernov, *Three Russian Prophets: Khomiakov, Dostoevsky, Soloviev* (London: SCM Press, 1944), 132.

[41]For a balanced review of the positions on Soloviev's 'conversion', see François Patrimonio, 'La profession de foi catholique de Soloviev', (The Catholic profession of faith of Soloviev) in *Colloque Vladimir Soloviev* (Paris: Institut catholique de Paris, 1978–1979). Other commentators also situate Soloviev's 'communion' gesture in the context of his ecumenical outlook. See Gillet, 'La signification de Soloviev', 369–79; Zernov, *Three Russian Prophets*, 131–2; and Paul Marshall Allen, 'Regarding Soloviev's "Conversion"', in *Vladimir Soloviev: Russian Mystic* (Blauvelt, NY: Steinerbooks, 1978), 411–16.

In February 1901 the Synod of the ROC excommunicated Leo Tolstoy for his unconventional philosophical and theological views. Many regarded this drastic step as a profound mistake, a symbol of the gulf separating the church and the contemporary culture, of the church's inability to cope adequately with Russia's changing intellectual landscape.

The fate of the Saint Petersburg Religious-Philosophical Assemblies, held between November 1901 and April 1903, also illustrates the nature of the profound gap that separated the church from its potential ally in Russian society, the Christian intelligentsia. Zinaida Gippius had the idea of a forum where members of the ROC could meet and discuss openly with leaders of the religious renaissance, and it was Merezhkovsky and his friends who sought and obtained official authorization for the meetings from Constantine Pobedonostsev (1827–1907), the all-powerful Procurator of the Holy Synod and a bulwark of conservatism, authority and autocracy, and from Anthony (Vadkovsky) (1846–1912), the liberal Metropolitan of Saint Petersburg. The idea of a dialogue between the church and leaders of the Christian intelligentsia also had the support of other reformed-minded hierarchs, such as Bishop (later Metropolitan and Patriarch) Sergius (Stragorodsky) (1867–1944) and lay officials of Holy Synod, notably Valentin Ternavtsev (1866–1940) and Vasily Skvortsov (1859–1932).

The series of public meetings between the church representatives and members of the Christian intelligentsia constituted a major attempt to bridge the gap between two parties, both nominally Christian, yet suspicious and even hostile towards each other: 'For both, the other side was an unknown world. They met as two strangers eager to become acquainted with each other's outlook and concerns.'[42] The fundamental question which underlay the Assemblies was 'How could Christianity again become influential in life?'[43] Ternavtsev, who had close connections among the intelligentsia, pleaded in the initial paper 'The Intelligentsia and the Church', in language reminiscent of Alexander Bukharev:

> The time has come for all of Christianity to demonstrate not just in doctrinal word but in deed that the church embodies more than a beyond-the-grave ideal. The time has come to reveal the truth about the world concealed in Christianity. … The time has come to witness to the religious vocation of the secular powers and our common salvation in Christ.[44]

But the expectations of the two groups were widely divergent. The intelligentsia figures eagerly resorted to prophetic and apocalyptic language as they looked for an opening and reforms on the part of church leaders which would serve to bridge the gap between the church and world and lead to the awaited 'third revelation'. On the other side, many of the church representatives saw the Assemblies as a mission among the intelligentsia and they sought above all the adhesion of the intelligentsia to the church. Many intelligentsia participants considered most church representatives as rigid, narrow minded, puritanical and uncultured, while the church spokesmen thought that their interlocutors were irresponsible, ignorant of church doctrine and history and self-opinionated.

---

[42]Zernov, *The Russian Religious Renaissance*, 90.
[43]Florovsky, *The Ways of Russian Theology*, II:253.
[44]Cited in Florovsky, *The Ways of Russian Theology*, II:253.

Bishop Sergius (Stragorodsky), then rector of the St Petersburg Theological Academy and future de facto head of the ROC from 1925 to 1944, chaired the sessions, twenty-two in all, and over 200 people attended regularly. With the exception of the final two sessions, revised and censored proceedings of the Assemblies were published in *Novyi Put'* (*The New Way*), a popular intelligentsia review founded by Dimitri Merezhkovsky and Zinaida Gippius. The most important subjects discussed at the Assemblies were dogma and the possibility of a new revelation (dear to the hearts of many of those associated with a new religious consciousness); freedom of conscience; the religious views of the novelists Nicholas Gogol, Leo Tolstoy and Fyodor Dostoyevsky; celibacy, sex, procreation and marriage (five sessions, favourite themes of Rozanov and Merezhkovsky); asceticism; and priesthood.

Apart from a fundamental division between the two groups, the church representatives and the lay religious thinkers, there was a wide range of opinion within each group – even the church representatives were far from being a unified block. In response to the hoped-for new revelations and the anti-dogmatic views of Merezhkovsky and the mystical poet Nicholas Minsky (1855–1937), Peter Leporsky, professor of the St Petersburg Theological Academy, presented a rigid view of dogma as fixed and not subject to fuller development or understanding, while his colleague Alexander Brilliantov advanced the view that revelation is subject to variations in interpretation, and Fr I. Slobodskoy declared 'that it was possible to penetrate still more deeply into Christian truth without substantially altering its content'.[45] In the Assemblies, leading figures of the new religious consciousness played the main role on the part of the Christian intelligentsia, while the main philosopher-theologians were less involved.

There were major problems of communication between the two groups: 'The language used by professional theologians and the intelligentsia was at times quite unintelligible to the opposite party,' writes Zernov.[46] At the first meeting, on 29 November 1901, Valentin Ternavtsev delivered the initial paper, an analysis of the key characteristics of the two parties, the intelligentsia and the church. His assessment of the church is severe:

> Our church has not forsaken the Russian people in the hour of their misfortune and tribulation, but it has become indifferent to social improvements. It is unable to give people Christian hope, joy or real help. It treats material calamities as God-sent trials which must be accepted on bended knees. The absence of any social programme sanctioned by religious convictions is the cause of the helplessness of the church. It is unable to master its practical tasks because it has become too other-worldly. … As Christians, however, we must believe in the possibility of Russia's revival, which can only be achieved with the help of religion; but from whence can this inspiration come? The church in its present state is unable to assist the country, and it shrinks from its social responsibility, and yet [adds Ternavtsev in a truly prophetic warning] church leaders will be obliged very soon to meet not only their local enemies, but also world-wide anti-Christian powers face to face.[47]

---

[45]Zernov, *The Russian Religious Renaissance*, 94.

[46]Ibid., 95.

[47]Zinaida *Gippius, Dimitri Merezhkovsky (in Russian) (Paris, 1951)*, 100-1, cited in Zernov, *The Russian Religious Renaissance*, 92–3.

His comments on the intelligentsia are perhaps overly positive. He points to the high social ideals of the intelligentsia while neglecting to elaborate on the dark side of the thinking of the non-religious majority of the intelligentsia, as Gippius herself points out:

> It is a mixed body; some of its members will never accept Christ. Opposition to him will lead them far away to places which they do not foresee at present and which they will not like when they find themselves there, but I do not want to speak about them at present. There are also others who are ready to be reconciled with Christianity. The intelligentsia as a whole has many merits. It is endowed with intellectual and moral energy, and it has its own enlightened teachers and martyrs. It has achieved so much that it cannot be dismissed as a body altogether foreign or hostile to Christian truth. The noblest intentions of its members are inspired by humanism at its best. These men and women believe that mankind will eventually discover its oneness. The problems of the organization of labour, of capitalist exploitation and of private property preoccupy their minds. They are attracted by world-wide schemes; they are neither a mere crowd nor a political party; they are a body which is captivated by the vision of a new society built upon a sound spiritual foundation.[48]

Like Alexander Bukharev a generation earlier, Ternavtsev calls on the church to engage with what he called 'the truth on earth': 'The times is coming for all Christianity to show not only in words, in teachings, but also in deed, that the church holds more than an ideal of afterlife. The time has come to reveal the Truth about the world hidden in Christianity.'[49]

Despite a certain amount of good will on both sides, in Merezhkovsky's words, 'The union of the church and the world did not take place.'[50] The meetings were stopped in April 1903 at the request of Constantine Pobedonostev, who became disturbed at the overly outspoken character of the meetings, especially the criticism of the church, and criticism of the meetings in conservative newspapers. In his assessment of the Assemblies, Dimitri Merezhkovsky remarks sarcastically that the church establishment was preventing the *intelligenty* interested in Christianity from entering the church:

> Christianity is surprising and festive for us in the highest degree. We – the wayfarers on the high road, the publicans, sinners, adulterers, robbers, tramps, anarchists and nihilists – are precisely the unsummoned, uninvited guests at the feast. We are still in the darkness of our night, but we have already heard the second call of the bridegroom. Timidly, ashamed of our ugly, unspiritual and unchurchly appearance, we approach the wedding chamber and are blinded by the radiance of the festivities. Yet dead academics – those old servants of the master – will not let us in. Although we have come to rejoice at the feast, they do not wish to believe it under any circumstances. ... The theologians have become too accustomed to Christianity. For them it is as drab as workdays.[51]

---

[48]Gippius, *Dimitri Merezhkovsky*, 99–100, cited by Zernov, *The Russian Religious Renaissance*, 91–2.

[49]Cited in Matich, *Erotic Utopia*, 217. In her discussion of the Religious-Philosophical Assemblies, Matich focuses on the discussions on sex, celibacy and marriage (*Erotic Utopia*, 222–33).

[50]Quoted by Florovsky, *The Ways of Russian Theology*, II:252.

[51]Cited by Florovsky, *The Ways of Russian Theology*, II:257, and by Zernov, *The Russian Religious Renaissance*, 95. Merezhkovsky's remarks echo the parable of the wedding feast (Mt. 22.1-14) and Jesus' words about the Pharisees and Scribes preventing others from entering the Kingdom (Mt. 23.13).

The church leaders and the lay professors of the academies were ill-equipped to dialogue with religious thought outside the strict confines of official theology, while the intelligentsia representatives, impatient to apply Christianity to Russia's very real problems, were inadequately aware of Christian doctrine, history and anthropology to engage in meaningful dialogue – as the church representatives at the Assemblies correctly pointed out. The church representatives were themselves far from a uniform bloc. Gippius noted in her dairy the diversity of attitudes among the church representatives:

> We came to know many new people and were constantly finding out more and more about those *who* comprised the Orthodox Church, which, as it seemed to us then, needed further evolution, the acceptance of new values, and changes. For its stagnation could not satisfy the spirit within us. … These are the people who made up the teaching church: those believing blindly, as the ancients did, as children, with an infantile yet genuine holiness, for example, Father John of Kronstadt. He thought that we ourselves, our needs, our life, and *our* belief were incomprehensible, unnecessary, and even accursed. [The church also consisted] of the indifferent and obtuse ecclesiastical officials; of disinterested though very pleasant half-liberals: Antony [Vadkovsky, Metropolitan of St Petersburg]; of the kind and peaceful semi-Buddhists: Father Sergei [Bishop Stragorodsky]; of the wild and evil ascetics of thought; of the formal positivists, shallow, vain, and base: Father Sollertinsky; of the strict positivist-moralists with ambition: Father Grigory Petrov. One did come across such brilliant and interesting scholars of wisdom and fortitude as Bishop Antonin [of Narva], and of course there were absolute heretics who did not believe in the authenticity of the historical life of Christ. … The professors of the Theological Academy were almost all positivists – sometimes even careerists. But there were also professors endowed with young, student souls;[52] however, they understood little, for they were profoundly uncultured as a result of their upbringing. [53]

Although the Religious-Philosophical Assemblies produced no specific results, they nonetheless marked a willingness on the part of some members of the two Christian groups to enter into dialogue. The Assemblies signalled an opening on the part of representatives of the new religious consciousness to see if the ROC could satisfy their religious aspirations. The failure of the Assemblies served to highlight the profound divisions between the official church and academic theology, and the religious renaissance. The monthly review *Novy Put'* [The New Way], which the Merezhkovskys launched during the Assemblies, continued as an outlet for new religious consciousness literature and thought and for the discussion of social and political issues, led by the former Marxists Bulgakov and Berdyaev. In January 1905, *Voprosy zhizni* [Questions of Life] replaced *Novy Put'*, with a focus on social and political questions rather than art and literature. Similarly, the Religious-Philosophical Society, launched by Berdyaev with government authorization, was a sort of successor to the Assemblies. But both the periodicals and the society suffered from the absence of church representatives, the essential basis of the Assemblies, restricting the dialogue to the Christian intelligentsia itself. As Berdyaev wrote years later: 'In Russian Christian thought

[52]Gippius is referring here to Anton Kartashev and Vasili Uspensky, with whom Merezhkovsky and Gippius remained in contact after the termination of the Religious-Philosophical Assemblies.

[53]Gippius, 'About the Cause', 132–3. A slightly different version appears in Gippius's *Dimitri Merezhkovsky*, cited by Zernov, *The Russian Religious Renaissance*, 95–6.

of the nineteenth century ..., something new about man was revealed. But official Orthodoxy, official ecclesiasticism, was unwilling to listen to it.'[54] The inconclusive experience of the Religious-Philosophical Assemblies constituted a backdrop for both the consummation of the separation of church and society in the Bolshevik revolution, and for the partial reconciliation of the church and Christian intellectuals at the Council of the ROC held in 1917–18.

On another level, individual members of the Christian intelligentsia had personal contacts with members of the Russian Orthodox Church, more frequently charismatic spiritual figures rather than members of the church hierarchy. In some cases these contacts proved decisive in the return of intellectuals to the church. Nicolas Berdyaev had a difficult relationship with the Russian Orthodox Church and in 1913 he was even accused of blasphemy for a fiery article criticizing the Holy Synod over the Name-of-God controversy. Found guilty, he could have been exiled for life to Siberia, but the World War and the Bolshevik revolution prevented the matter coming to trial. He visited Optino Monastery, but his contacts with elders there were unsatisfactory. Finally it was his acquaintance with Fr Alexis Metchev (1859–1923), a parish priest in Moscow (canonized in 2000) that marked his return to the church. Berdyaev writes in his autobiography:

> [Fr Alexis] belonged to the married clergy and was regarded by many as a 'white' *starets*. There was indeed something about him reminiscent of Dostoyevsky's starets Zosima. He seemed to belong to a wholly different spiritual world from that of the majority of the Russian clergy. ... Through him I came to feel a new bond with the historical Orthodox Church, which had in fact never been completely broken, despite all my non-conformity and protestations against it. In this respect, there was something in common between my own religious position and that of Soloviev, although his objectives were different.[55]

Berdyaev's sister-in-law, who edited his posthumously published writings, adds the following comment on this passage:

> Berdyaev frequently made his confessions and received Holy Communion in Fr Alexis's church. The latter had a large following and deeply impressed the huge crowds who came to his services in search of consolation and help. There were among them Red Army soldiers and even Communists. Fr Alexis could pick out those in the crowd who were in particular need at the moment and called them out to see him personally. He had the gift of second sight. Berdyaev went to say goodbye to Fr Alexis a few days before his expulsion from Russia. He was deeply distressed by this ejection from his native land. Berdyaev could on several occasions have escaped from the Communists but he always refused to do so, wishing to share the destiny of the people. He returned shaken after his visit. He told his sister-in-law: 'Fr Alexis was dressed in white and it seemed to me that his entire being was illuminated by rays of light. I told him how painful to me was the separation from Russia. "You must go," answered the priest, "the West must hear your words".'[56]

Another important contact took place between Sergius Bulgakov, then a lay philosopher, and the academic theologian Anton Kartashev (1875–1960). Kartashev, professor of church history

---

[54]Nicolas Berdyaev, *The Russian Idea* (New York: Macmillan, 1948), 96.

[55]Berdyaev, *Dream and Reality*, 204. For the accusation of blasphemy, see 202–3, and for his visit to Optino, 188–90.

[56]Quoted in Zernov, *The Russian Religious Renaissance*, 60.

at the St Petersburg Theological Academy (1900–5) and at the University College for Women (1906–18), was for a few months the last Procurator of the Holy Synod of the Russian Orthodox Church and Minister of Religion in the ill-fated Provisional Government of 1917, until the October Revolution. He was also on friendly terms with the Merezhkovskys and was at times a part of their inner circle, until he committed himself entirely to the Orthodox Church. After he went into exile in 1919, he was one of the founders of the Saint Sergius Institute in Paris, where he taught until his death. Kartashev wrote years later about his first meeting with Bulgakov:

> Bulgakov came to see me in the spring of 1905 at my flat which was attached to the Theological Academy. Our discussion centred upon church reform and the need for promoting Christian participation in political and social activities. I expected from him an emphasis on socialism for he was reputed to be a staunch Marxist. I was surprised to hear him say: 'Yes, social problems, but not Marxism, for Karl Marx is organically anti-Christian. As a Jew he is full of eschatology. But his eschatology is an earthly one and it is opposed to the teaching of the Gospels.' These words penetrated into the darkness of my ignorance of Marxism as if by the rays of a searchlight. ... After that discussion I realised that Bulgakov was no longer a lay humanist, but a theologian with the Biblical outlook.[57]

Sergius Bulgakov, still hesitant about his place in the church after his adherence to idealism around 1900, had a determining encounter with an elder at a critical juncture in his spiritual journey back to the church. In his *Autobiographical Notes*, he describes this encounter as a mystical experience which marked his reintegration into the church:

> One sunny autumn day in 1908 I made my way to a solitary hermitage lost in the forest, where I was surrounded by the familiar sights of northern nature. I was still in the clutches of doubt and hesitation. I had come there as a companion of a friend; secretly I hoped that I might meet God. But my determination deserted me, and while I was at Vespers I remained cold and unfeeling. When the prayers for those preparing for confession began, I almost ran out of the church. I walked in deep distress towards the guest house, seeing nothing around me, and suddenly found myself in front of the elder's cell. I had been led there. I intended to go in another direction but absent-mindedly made a wrong turn in the confusion of my distress.
>
> A miracle had happened to me. I realized it then without any doubt. The Father, seeing his prodigal son, ran to meet me. I heard from the elder that all human sin was like a drop of water in comparison with the ocean of divine love. I left him, pardoned and reconciled, trembling and in tears, feeling myself returned as on wings within the precincts of the church. ... The bells were calling to prayer. I listened to them as if I heard them for the first time in my life, for they invited me also to join the fellowship of believers. I looked on the world with new eyes. The next morning at the Eucharist I knew that I was a participant in the Covenant, that our Lord hung on the cross and shed his blood for me and because of me; that the most blessed meal was being prepared by the priest for me, and that the gospel narrative about the feast in the house of Simon the leper and about the woman who loved much was addressed personally to me. It was on that day when I partook of the blessed Body and Blood of my Lord.

[57] Anton Kartashev, 'My Early Encounters with Fr Sergius', *Pravoslavnaya Mysl* (Orthodox Thought), III (Paris, 1951), 51. Quoted in Zernov, *The Russian Religious Renaissance*, 97–8.

Another sad clash among the three major religious traditions in Russia took place in the years immediately prior to the First World War, as the Russian religious scene was marked by a major conflict over the theology of the Name of God, an offshoot of the use of the Jesus Prayer in monastic and lay settings. This conflict initially pitted a large group of Russian monks on Mount Athos against other Athonite Russian Monks, the predominantly Greek Athonite monasteries, the Ecumenical Patriarchate and the ROC, backed by the state. The dissenting monks were rounded up by Russian military and sent back to Russia in warships. Several leading members of the Russian religious renaissance, including Bulgakov, Berdyaev, Florensky, Vladimir Ern (1882–1917) and Alexei Losev (1893–1988), rallied to the defence of the beleaguered advocates of 'Name-Praising' (*onomatodoxy* from the Greek or *imyaslavie* in Russian), against the power of the church. This three-sided conflict was yet another illustration of the chasm that separated the official church not only from the Christian intelligentsia, but also from its own mystical and charismatic tradition. This conflict will be examined in greater detail in Chapter 15.

Three symposia and a church council

An important and early collective manifestation of the abandonment of positivist philosophies by a significant if very much minority portion of the intelligentsia was the publication in 1902 of the volume *Problems of Idealism*.[58] Peter Struve conceived of the volume as a sort of idealist manifesto dedicated to the general themes of freedom of conscience, the unconditional significance of personhood, political liberalism and the imperative of ethical norms in social and political life, thus constituting an explicit rejection of the materialist, positivist and revolutionary maximalist tendencies that dominated among the intelligentsia. The book appeared under the editorship of Peter Novgorodtsev (1866–1924), a professor of law and leading personality in the Constitutional Democratic (Kadet) Party. There were twelve contributors, including Berdyaev, Bulgakov, Frank and Struve. In his Foreword, Novgorodtsev refers to the idealist principles as responding to 'the categorical imperative of morality, which gives primary importance to the principle of the absolute significance of personhood'.[59] For the former Marxists, philosophical idealism constituted a short-lived stage on their intellectual and spiritual journey from positivism to Christianity. Increasingly they regarded the majority of the intelligentsia, in Berdyaev's words, as mired in 'persistent conservatism ... rigid materialistic and positivistic orthodoxy and agnosticism ... inertia and blindness'.[60] Berdyaev considers that his contribution to *Problems of Idealism* marked 'a first attempt to formulate the idea of personalism which came to be my *idée maîtresse*'.[61] It is illustrative of the increasingly divergent tendencies in the Christian intelligentsia that the leading philosopher-

[58]Randall Poole, trans. and ed., *Problems of Idealism: Essays in Russian Social Philosophy* (New Haven, CT: Yale University Press, 2003).
[59]Poole, trans. and ed., *Problems of Idealism*, 83.
[60]Berdyaev, *Dream and Reality*, 136–7.
[61]Ibid., 133.

theologians published *Problems of Idealism* during the Petersburg Religious-Philosophical Assemblies, in which they played at best a discrete role.

As a follow-up to *Problems of Idealism*, in 1903 Sergius Bulgakov published his own book, *From Marxism to Idealism*, which further elaborated the idealist theses and his own philosophical transition to idealism.

Another major milestone in the intellectual and spiritual journey from idealism to Christianity by leading intellectuals was the publication in 1909 of the book *Vekhi* [Signposts]. The Revolution of 1905 occurred between the publication of *Problems of Idealism* and *Vekhi*. The traumatic experience of the failed revolution served on the one hand to reinforce the beliefs of the majority of the *intelligenty* that only violent revolution, with the participation of the popular masses, could bring down the monarchy, and on the other hand, to confirm the idealists that their commitment to personhood, freedom and the spiritual dimension of humanity was correct and imperative, and for many, could only be achieved in Christianity. The idealists saw the failed revolution as a disavowal of positivism and atheism, which had resulted in a mounting spiral of violence and repression, by the state against dissenters, and by revolutionaries against state agents, especially local officials.

Vekhi contains contributions by seven leading representatives of the Russian religious renaissance, including the four former Marxist philosophers (Berdyaev, Bulgakov, Frank and Struve) and three others, Mikhail Gershenzon (scholar, essayist and editor; 1869–1925), Bogdan Kistiakovsky (professor of legal philosophy at the University of Kiev; 1868–1920) and Alexander Izgoev (brilliant political, social and cultural commentator, active in the Constitutional Democratic Party; 1872–1935).[62] Not included among the *Vekhi* authors were representatives of the literary, cultural and esoteric religious renaissance such as Rozanov, Merezkovsky and Gippius, nor of course any church figure.

The book was immensely popular, a cause célébre among the intelligentsia: Within a year it went through five printings (23,000 copies), elicited some 200 published rejoinders and was hotly debated at numerous public meetings. It was strongly criticized by the revolutionaries, who saw the book in the service of the upper classes; by even the moderate intelligentsia, who could see no value in a Christian approach to Russia's problems or to life in general; and by the conservatives, who saw the book either as part of a broad conspiracy against Holy Russia perpetrated by the *intelligenty*, students and Jews, or alternatively as another example of the importation of Western thought – while considering it as a useful attack on revolutionary extremism.[63]

In the words of Simeon Frank, *Vekhi* 'asserted the necessity of a religious foundation for any consistent philosophy of life, and at the same time sharply criticized the revolutionary and

---

[62]There are two English translations of *Vekhi*: Boris Shragin and Albert Todd, eds., *Landmarks: A Collection of Essays on the Russian Intelligentsia, 1909* (New York: Karz Howard, 1977); and Marshall S. Shatz and Judith E. Zimmerman, eds., *Vekhi: Landmarks: A Collection of Articles about the Russian Intelligentsia* (Armonk, NY: M. E. Sharpe, 1994). For a summary of the *Vekhi* essays, see Zernov, *The Russian Religious Renaissance*, 111–30; and Read, *Religion, Revolution and the Russian Intelligentsia*, 106–20.

[63]See summaries of the debate over *Vekhi* in Read, *Religion, Revolution and the Russian Intelligentsia*, 106–20; and Leonard Schapiro, 'The *Vekhi* Group and the Mystique of Revolution', in Ellen Dahrendorff, ed., *Russian Studies* (London: Collins Harvill, 1986), 68–92.

maximalist tendencies of the radical-minded Russian intelligentsia'.[64] Leonard Schapiro positions *Vekhi*'s authors 'midway between the Slavophiles and the Westerners':

> They accepted the Slavophile veneration of Russian national tradition, while rejecting their romantic idealisation of innate Russian virtues as a substitute for the more usual civic virtues. They accepted the Westerners' desire to learn from the countries of the West, while rejecting their atheism, their socialism and their utilitarianism.[65]

The main ideas which the *Vekhi* authors retained from the West were civic culture and responsibility, public education, the rule of law and public order. Even though they differed on many issues, *Vekhi* authors shared a personalist viewpoint against the collectivist vision of the majority of the intelligentsia, and idealism against the majority's positivism and materialism. Several authors, notably Berdyaev, stressed the need for personal responsibility and a spiritual revolution. The book prophetically warned the intelligentsia of the dangers of rigid Marxist and revolutionary philosophies which had scant regard for freedom in their quest for power. The almost universally negative reaction to *Vekhi* showed that its authors had struck a vital nerve. Particularly galling was the accusation that the intelligentsia displayed 'conservatism' in continuing to adhere blindly to its belief that any means, especially violence and revolution, are justified to bring about changes in social structure and political institutions, when the failed revolution of 1905 demonstrated both philosophically and historically that this belief was detrimental to true human progress and transformation.

A sign of a certain reformist tendency in the ROC after the failed 1905 revolution and perhaps a residue of the Religious-Philosophical Assemblies were proposals to hold a major church council aimed at reforming aspects of the church no longer in keeping with Russia's requirements and aspirations. Concrete preparations were undertaken between 1906 and 1916, including pre-conciliar commissions and the soliciting of views of hierarchs and other members of the church. But these efforts bore little fruit and no council was convoked prior to the outbreak of the First World War: 'The conciliar process appeared to have sunk into a certain bureaucracy'.[66] After the collapse of the monarchy in the February Revolution of 1917 and a reform of the Holy Synod, the Synod convoked the council *in extremis*, amidst increasing revolutionary activity. The fall of the monarchy effectively broke the formal subordination of the church to the state. Anton Kartashev, who became Procurator of the Holy Synod under the Kerensky government in July 1917, moved quickly to abolish the now redundant post and he became Minister of Confessions. The All-Russian Church Council met in Moscow from 15 August 1917 to 7 September 1918.[67] The Council was animated by a spirit of *sobornost'*, with laymen forming a majority of voting delegates (299 out of

[64]Simeon Frank, *A Biography of P.B. Struve* (New York: Chekhov Publishing House, 1956), 82, translation in Zernov, *The Russian Religious Renaissance*, 111.

[65]Schapiro, 'The *Vekhi* Group and the Mystique of Revolution', 79.

[66]Hyacinthe Destivelle, *The Moscow Council (1917-1918): The Creation of the Conciliar Institutions of the Russian Orthodox Church* (Notre Dame, IN: University of Notre Dame Press, 2015), 44.

[67]Destivelle's study of the Council contains a translation of the Constitutions and Decrees of the Council. Destivelle, *The Moscow Council*, 191–351.

564 voting members, most of whom were themselves elected by various church bodies) – but with the bishops retaining a right of veto over decisions passed by the general assembly.

The Council's agenda covered a full range of issues dealing with virtually all aspects of the status, governance, institutions and activities of the church. Theological questions other than those arising from ecclesiology did not feature prominently, with the exception of the Name-of-God controversy. Sergius Bulgakov was named to head a sub-commission on this issue, but the Council wound up before the sub-commission could complete its work. The Council's main decisions concerned the establishment of a system of church administration in the spirit of *sobornost'*, with joint clergy-lay governance of the church at all levels. Because of the triumph of the Bolsheviks in the October revolution, only one major Council decision was implemented: the restoration of the patriarchate, almost two centuries after Peter the Great had formally abolished it. The election of the saintly Tikhon (Belyavin) (1865–1925), then Metropolitan of Moscow, as Patriarch of the ROC, the first in over two centuries, symbolized the formal emancipation of the church from state control. But almost immediately the church fell under the wrath of the Communists, who were determined to eradicate not only the church as an institution but also religious belief itself in the new Soviet state.

With the triumph of the Bolsheviks in the October Revolution of 1917, most of the leading representatives of religious renaissance went into exile, many voluntarily, or they were expelled by the Communists. One of the last manifestations of the Christian intelligentsia in Russia was a collection of essays under the title *Out of the Depths* (*Iz glibiny*, *De profundis*, from Ps. 21/22, and the title of Simeon Frank's essay in the volume), by eleven prominent non-Marxist intellectuals, including five of those who had contributed to *Vekhi* in 1909, dealing with the causes and nature of the Revolution.[68] This symposium was a bitter reproach over the consequence of ignoring the message of *Vekhi*: The intelligentsia's continued pursuit of radicalism and revolutionary maximalism was now bearing fruit in the triumph of Bolshevism, marked by the suppression of all forms of dissidence from Marxist ideology and Communist rule. Many of *Vekhi*'s Christian themes reappear here, such as the importance of ethical standards and repentance, and the incompatibility of materialism with Christianity. The book was a pungent testimony to the defeat of liberal and religious social and political thought and ideals at the hands of Bolshevik atheistic materialism. Although a pessimistic tone overshadows most of the essays, several express the hope that out of the ashes a new Russian phoenix would arise. It was a sign of the times that the book was never distributed in Russia. Printed in the autumn of 1918, *Out of the Depths*, as a religiously inspired anti-Bolshevik book, could not be freely circulated and only a few copies survived.

[68]William Woehrlin, ed. and trans., *Out Of the Depths (De Profundis): A Collection of Articles on the Russian Revolution* (Irvine, CA: Charles Schlacks, 1986). See accounts in Schapiro, 'The *Vekhi* Group and the Mystique of Revolution', 81–4; and Zernov, *The Russian Religious Renaissance*, 207–9.

Revolution and exile

Despite the increasing restrictions on free expression after the Bolshevik triumph, non-Marxist intellectuals attempted to retain some measure of open intellectual culture and discourse by establishing societies devoted to cultural, philosophical and even spiritual themes. The Bolshevik leaders tolerated their existence for a few years. In September 1919 Berdyaev and others formed the Free Academy of Spiritual Culture in Moscow, devoted to 'maintaining and developing spiritual culture in Russia'.[69] The Free Academy sponsored extremely popular lectures on a wide range of philosophical issues, with religious idealism as the dominant leitmotiv. But the Bolsheviks soon closed down the Free Academy and deported Berdyaev.

The Communists could not tolerate the existence of independent thinking in the new Soviet Union and moved to eliminate or silence all sources of possible dissent or opposition, especially from the non-Marxist intelligentsia who had not gone into voluntary exile. In August 1922, Lenin ordered the arrest and expulsion from the Soviet Union of a large number of Russian intellectuals who did not support the Bolsheviks. The best estimate of the number actually banished from the Soviet Union is about eighty, together with their immediate families, while many others were sent into internal exile.[70] Among those deported were several leading members of the religious renaissance, notably Nicolas Berdyaev, Sergius Bulgakov, Simeon Frank, Lev Karsavin and Nicolas Lossky. In September and December 1922, many non-Marxist intellectual and cultural leaders and their families were put on ships in the Baltic Sea and sent to Germany – this incident became known as the 'philosophers' steamboat'. The one leading philosopher-theologian who was not expelled and chose to stay in Russia was Pavel Florensky.

Many of the Russian expatriates in Eastern and Western Europe saw the large exile community as the repository of the true Russia, which had been usurped by the Bolsheviks. The expatriates felt that 'Russia Abroad',[71] as it was known in the interwar period, had a responsibility to preserve and to further authentic Russian culture and values, centred in three areas in particular: Orthodoxy, culture and the Russian language. The exiles formed associations of all sorts, organized Russian schools and publications and attempted to minimize assimilation into host societies. The written word – newspapers, journals of all sorts, books – was the principal means of communication and coherence among the widely dispersed expatriate communities. Initially, the expatriates believed that the communist regime would soon collapse and that they could return to assume their rightful place in Russian society and politics. But as the years went by and the Soviets consolidated their grip over the country, it became increasingly evident that what was first seen as a temporary exile was becoming permanent. The Second World War put an end to many expatriate initiatives and publications and any remaining dreams of return to a Russia freed of communism.

---

[69]Cited in Stuart Finkel, *On the Ideological Front: The Russian Intelligentsia and the Making of the Soviet Public Sphere* (New Haven, CT: Yale University Press, 2007), 105.

[70]Finkel, *On the Ideological Front*, 9.

[71]The title of a book by Marc Raeff, *Russia Abroad: A Cultural History of the Russian Emigration, 1919-1939* (New York: Oxford University Press, 1990). See also Mjor, *Reformulating Russia*, 27–51.

After the war, the 'first wave' of emigrants fleeing the Bolshevik triumph was joined by refugees escaping from the conflict and from oppression under communist rule and the centre of Russian emigrant life shifted from Europe to the United States. Physical return to Soviet Russia was impossible for most and only a 'metaphysical return' – by means of publications and, after the Second World War, radio broadcasts – could be envisaged. But the Soviets prevented any significant dissimulation of immigrant thinking in the Soviet Union until after the fall of communism.

Many of the émigrés initially arrived in Constantinople, Sofia and Belgrade, but few stayed long in Constantinople, while Sofia and Belgrade remained important émigré centres in the interwar years, especially for more conservative political and ecclesiastical groups. Berlin quickly became the principal centre of the exiled Russian intelligentsia. Berdyaev was instrumental in forming the Russian Religious Philosophical Academy in Berlin as a successor to the Free Spiritual Academy in Moscow. With increasing economic problems in Germany, many of those who went initially to Berlin moved on, especially to Prague or to Paris. The Czech government, under the leadership of the sympathetic Tomas Masaryk, founder and President of Czechoslovakia from 1918 to 1935, encouraged the Russian refugees, especially in education. Russian intellectuals founded a short-lived but influential Russian Law Faculty and other educational bodies. But most of the former Christian intelligentsia soon departed for Paris, especially after the founding of the Saint Sergius Theological Institute in 1925.

The initial faculty of Saint Sergius included the best minds of Russian theology in exile. Fr Sergius Bulgakov was invited to head the school and he became professor of dogmatic theology. Other representatives of the pre-revolutionary Christian intelligentsia and academic theologians who taught at Saint Sergius are the historians Georges Fedotov (1886–1951) and Anton Kartashev, and the philosophers Boris Vysheslavtsev (1877–1954) and Basil Zenkovsky. Among the younger staff members prior to the Second World War were Nicholas Afanasiev (canon law; 1893–1966), Cassian Bezobrazov (biblical studies; 1892–1965), Georges Florovsky (patristics; 1893–1979), Cyprian Kern (liturgy and patristics; 1899–1960) and Leon Zander (philosophy; 1893–1964).

Once in exile, many religious intellectuals of the pre-revolutionary era returned to the Orthodox Church, joining those who had returned to the church prior to the First World War. But some stood apart from the church, notably those associated with the new religious consciousness movement. Vasily Rozanov, who died in January 1919, was reconciled with the church in his dying days at the Monastery of Trinity Saint Sergius near Moscow, where he and his wife were assisted by Pavel Florensky. Alexander Blok died a sad and lonely death in Russia in 1921. Vyacheslav Ivanov went to Italy in 1924 and joined the Russian Greek Catholic Church. He died in Rome in 1949. Dimitri Merezhkovsky and Zinaida Gippius, fiercely anti-Bolshevik, fled to Paris in 1920, where they fostered Russian literary and anti-Bolshevik causes and hosted a literary and philosophical society under the name 'The Green Lamp' from 1927 to 1939. They remained faithful to their own vision of Christianity and never accepted the Orthodox Church, even in the extreme circumstances of the church in exile, no longer under the shackles of the imperial regime. Merezhkovsky died in 1941 and Gippius in 1945.

Berdyaev began his exile in Berlin in late 1922 but quickly moved to Paris, where he remained until his death in 1948. During his Parisian years, he wrote most of the books for which he became well known.[72] Berdyaev also played a key role in promoting the intellectual pursuits of his companions in exile as editor and publisher of works by the leading Russian religious, literary, philosophical and theological exiles in the 1920s and 1930s. He notably directed the important publishing house YMCA-Press (named for its principal financial backer, the American branch of the YMCA), and he edited the journal *Put'*, the most influential periodical of the exiled Russian intelligentsia between 1925 and the last of its sixty-one issues in March 1940.[73]

Berdyaev's major philosophical-theological themes are the primal significance of the human person and its correlates, freedom and creativity; Russian thought; and analysis of the Russian Revolution, Marxism and modernity. He also wrote an important intellectual autobiography (*Dream and Reality: An Essay in Autobiography*, 1949). Berdyaev's broad spiritual and intellectual culture and his Christian-inspired but not always explicitly Christian thinking on human existence and the modern world touched sensitive chords in European circles from the late 1930s until about the 1960s. During this period he was by far the most well-known modern Orthodox religious-philosophical thinker, but his popularity faded considerably in the last decades of the twentieth century. Even among Orthodox he became more often considered an idiosyncratic figure, only remotely connected with mainstream Orthodoxy. Undoubtedly Berdyaev's failure to see in the Church Fathers the true source of Christian philosophy, together with a perception that he was an existentialist philosopher,[74] contributed to the decline of his star in the wake of the revival of patristic theology in both Orthodox and non-Orthodox circles in the second half of the twentieth century.

Most of the Russian thinkers in exile attempted to recreate as best as they could the intellectual environment which they had known in Russia. A sign of this was that virtually all of the older generation of the intelligentsia wrote their works in Russian, and their writings were initially published by Russian publishing houses, especially YMCA-Press in Paris (despite its name, it published exclusively in Russian until after the Second World War), and in Russian journals in Western Europe, especially Paris and Berlin. Many of the exiles viewed their prime audience as the Russian exile community itself, as a stepping stone to a hoped-for return to Russia or at least an audience in Russia itself. In addition, while many of this generation were familiar with major Western European languages and could speak English, French and/or German, they were perhaps not sufficiently at ease in foreign languages to write major substantive philosophical and theological works. A related indicator of the problem of acculturation of the older generation of theologians was the use of Russian as the language of instruction at the Saint Sergius Institute – it was only in the 1970s that French became the language of instruction. The change from Russian to French as the language of instruction had the effect of broadening the vocation of Saint Sergius from a

[72]These include *The Meaning of History* (1923); *The End of Our Time* (*The New Middle Ages*) (1924); *Freedom and the Spirit* (1928); *The Destiny of Man* (1931); *Christianity and Class War* (1931); *The Fate of Man in the Modern World* (1934); *The Origin of Russian Communism* (1937); *Slavery and Freedom* (1939); *The Russian Idea* (1946); *Spirit and Reality* (1946); *The Realm of Spirit and the Realm of Caesar* (1949); *The Divine and the Human* (1949). All these books were published in English translation, many in the 1930s, the remainder in the late 1940s and early 1950s.

[73]See the detailed study by Antoine Arjakovsky, *The Way: Religious Thinkers of the Russian Emigration in Paris and Their Journal* (Notre Dame, IN: University of Notre Dame Press, 2013).

[74]See Andrew Louth, *Modern Orthodox Thinkers: From the Philokalia to the Present* (London: SPCK, 2015), 64–5.

Russian-only student body to a pan-Orthodox one, with the admission of students from other cultural backgrounds, especially Greek, Romanian, Arabic and, of course, French.

Initially, few of the works of the Russian theologians published in Paris were translated – the major exception being Berdyaev's writings, which appeared in Western languages shortly after their publication in Russian. It was easier for some of the younger theologians, such as Georges Florovsky, Leon Zander and Nicolas Zernov, and of course for 'second generation' theologians such as Paul Evdokimov, Vladimir Lossky and Alexander Schmemann, to adapt themselves to the culture of their countries of exile and to acquire a better grasp, both spoken and written, of Western languages than the older generation. Many of the members of the younger generation – the children of those exiled – were educated partly or entirely in the West and they wrote mainly in Western European languages.

The agenda of the exiled Russian thinkers necessarily shifted as a result of the Bolshevik revolution and the triumph of communism. From a concern over the future of Russia, an intellectual agenda which the Christian thinkers in exile shared with the pre-revolutionary intelligentsia as a whole, attention turned to several other major themes. They sought to understand the causes and nature of the Russian Revolution, including the evident failure of the church to ascertain the momentous changes festering beneath the surface in Russian society, to exercise spiritual and intellectual leadership, and to react constructively to modernism. Although the exiled intellectuals continued to analyse the political situation of Russia, especially the nature of Marxism and the reasons for the triumph of communism, this was now more an academic exercise than anything else; the Christian thinkers were no longer actors in the drama as they were prior to the Revolution, but only spectators and commentators. A related theme was the study, publication and denunciation of communist persecution of the church and indeed of all forms of dissent and opposition to the totalitarian regime.

Another theme which emerged among the exiled intellectuals was social justice – the 'social gospel'. Mother Maria Skobtsova was the most active in this area, through her activities as itinerant secretary of the ACER (Russian Student Christian Movement) prior to her becoming a nun in 1932, and subsequently, in several hostels for the poor that she founded in Paris. She also inspired her entourage, including Nicolas Berdyaev, Ilya Fondaminski and the literary critic Constantine Mochulsky (1892–1948), who were closely associated with her in the organization that she founded, *Action orthodoxe*. Mother Maria wrote many articles and even several plays ('mysteries') on the theme of the social gospel – the 'second gospel commandment'.[75] This group founded the periodical *Novyi grad – The New City* – to expound a Christian view of modern society.

During the 1920s and 1930s, the Russian intellectuals in Western Europe had increasing contacts with sympathetic Western Christians – Anglicans, Catholics and Protestants. The nature of the church and the significance of ecumenism emerged as major areas of reflection and engagement. A number of the leading Russian theologians were very active in the ecumenical movement

[75]Mother Maria Skobtsova, 'The Second Gospel Commandment', in *Mother Maria Skobtsova: Essential Writings*. See translations of her 'mystery plays' and important social articles in Ladouceur, ed., *Sainte Marie de Paris, 247–394.*

beginning in the late 1920s, especially Sergius Bulgakov, Georges Florovsky, Sergius Chetverikov, Leon Zander and Nicolas Zernov, with whom was associated Fr Lev Gillet (1893–1980), a French Catholic priest who became Orthodox in 1928. This theme will be examined in more detail in Chapter 12.

The Sophia controversy and the decline of religious philosophy

By the late 1920s, Fr Sergius Bulgakov was the leading representative of the Russian religious renaissance. He was widely respected both in the Russian exile community and among non-Christian theologians and churchmen. In the mid-1930s, Bulgakov became embroiled in two important theological controversies, one over his teachings on Divine Wisdom or sophiology, and the other concerning his proposal for intercommunion with Anglicans.[76] Bulgakov developed the idea of Sophia into an integrated but complex theology, reflected in his major theological works.[77] Bulgakov's sophiology raised numerous questions and protests, which culminated in the great sophiological controversy of 1935–36.[78] More than any other idea of Russian religious philosophy, sophiology provoked a profound division among exiled Russian theologians. Nicolas Berdyaev, for one, did not adhere to sophiology: 'I do not myself share the views of the sophiological school.'[79] But Berdyaev praises sophiology for 'an indication of creative thought in Russian Orthodoxy', and he defends Bulgakov's 'line of thought in Orthodoxy' and his 'statement of new problems'.[80] For Georges Florovsky, sophiology marked the dividing line between the inheritors of Soloviev's philosophy and theology and the nascent alternative approach to theology, which he later referred to as the 'neopatristic synthesis'. Indeed, opposition to sophiology can be seen as the substratum

---

[76]The 'intercommunion' controversy will be considered in Ch. 12, 289–298.

[77]The theological and philosophical aspects of sophiology will be considered in more detail in Ch. 9, 199–205.

[78]The secondary literature on the Sophia dispute is considerable even in the absence of a full-length monograph. See Arjakovsky, *The Way: Religious Thinkers of the Russian Emigration,* passim, but especially 384–402; Antoine Arjakovsky, *Essai sur le père Serge Boulgakov* (Essay on Fr Sergius Bulgakov) (Paris: Parole et Silence, 2006); Élisabeth Behr-Sigel, 'La sophiologie du père Serge Boulgakov' (The sophiology of Fr Sergius Bulgakov) (1939), *Le Messager orthodoxe*, 57, 1972; Evdokimov, *Le Christ dans la pensée russe*; Vladimir Lossky, *The Mystical Theology of the Eastern Church* (Crestwood, NY: St Vladimir's Seminary Press, 1976), Ch. 3, 'God in Trinity'; Aidan Nichols, *Light from the East: Authors and Themes in Orthodox Theology* (London: Sheed & Ward, 1995), Ch. 4, 'Sergei Bulgakov and Sophiology'; Paul Valliere, *Modern Russian Theology: Bukharev, Soloviev, Bulgakov: Orthodox Theology in a New Key* (Grand Rapids, MI: Eerdmans, 2000), 287–9; Zernov, *The Russian Religious Renaissance*, Ch. 11, 'The Divine Wisdom'. See also the special issue of *St Vladimir's Theological Quarterly* devoted to Sergius Bulgakov (49, 1–2, 2005), especially the articles by Brandon Gallaher and Irina Kukota, Bryn Geffert and Alexis Klimoff.

[79]Nicolas Berdyaev, *The Russian Idea* (New York: Macmillan, 1948), 241. Berdyaev had written more emphatically earlier: 'I myself did not stand in the Platonic-sophiological line of Russian religious philosophy. I am not a Platonist and not a sophiologist, unlike V. Soloviev, unlike P. Florensky, unlike Fr Bulgakov.' Nicolas Berdyaev, ' The Russian Spiritual Renaissance of the Beginning of the XXth Century and the Journal *Put*" (For the Tenth Anniversary of *Put*') (in Russian) *Put*', 49 (1935). Translation: www.chebucto.ns.ca/Philosophy/Sui-Generis/Berdyaev/essays/rsr.htm (13 March 2017).

[80]Berdyaev, *The Russian Idea*, 241.

underlying major aspect of Florovsky's theology, amply illustrated by his 1928 essay 'Creation and Createdness'.[81]

In the mid-1930s, Bulgakov's teachings on Sophia were condemned by two different and mutually hostile factions of the ROC – Metropolitan Sergius (Stragorodsky) (1867–1944), the self-appointed 'guardian of the patriarchal throne' of the Patriarchate of Moscow and the 'Karlovtsy Synod' of Russian bishops abroad, which became the ROC Outside of Russia (ROCOR). Hierarchs of the Karlovtsy Synod criticized Bulgakov's theology as early as 1924, but the 1930s' phase of the dispute was set in motion by a report on Bulgakov's sophiology prepared, at the request of Metropolitan Eleutherius (Bogoyavlensky) of the Moscow Patriarchate, by the young theologian Vladimir Lossky (1903–58), firmly attached to the Moscow Patriarchate, and Alexis Stavrovsky (1905–72), who had attended the Saint Sergius Institute, but did not complete his studies. It is unlikely that Metropolitan Sergius ever actually read Bulgakov's works himself, but instead he relied on summaries provided by the hostile commentators.

In general terms, the Lossky-Stavrovsky report concluded that Bulgakov's teaching on Sophia, as expounded notably in Bulgakov's book *The Lamb of God* (1933), was pantheist, removing distinctions between God and creation. In response, Metropolitan Sergius issued a decree (*ukaz*) on 24 August 1935, which describes Bulgakov's teaching as 'an eccentric and arbitrary (*svoeobraznym i proisvolnym*) Sophianic interpretation, frequently perverting the dogmas of the Orthodox faith', and finds that some of its possible conclusions may be 'even dangerous for spiritual life' and that the teaching is 'foreign' to the Orthodox Church. But the *ukaz* stops short of describing Bulgakov's doctrines as heretical.[82] The ROCOR Bishops' Council had no such qualms and in October 1935, after a lengthy study of the issue by Archbishop Seraphim (Sobolev) (1881–1950), it flatly condemned Bulgakov's teachings on Sophia as heretical.[83]

Bulgakov replied to both sets of critics and, in 1936, Vladimir Lossky expanded his critique of Bulgakov's teachings in a small book (his first and indeed one of only three books published in his lifetime) called *Spor o sofii* (The Dispute over Sophia).[84] The book sets out Lossky's theological objections to Bulgakov's sophiology, but also goes on to attack other aspects of Bulgakov's theology: his Trinitarian theology, his Christology, his use of gender analogies in theology, his concept of tradition and pan-human ecclesiology, the idea of Godmanhood, the use of historical analogies and the importance of dogma in the church, or, as Paul Valliere puts it, 'the distinction … between

[81]For this argument see Paul Gavrilyuk, *Georges Florovsky and the Russian Religious Renaissance* (Oxford and New York: Oxford University Press, 2013), especially Ch. 8, 'The Sophiological Subtext of Neopatristic Theology', 132–58; and Brandon Gallaher and Paul Ladouceur, 'Introduction: Georges Florovsky and the Mind of the Fathers', in *The Patristic Witness of Georges Florovsky: Essential Theological Writings* (London: T&T Clark, 2019), 1–29. On sophiology itself, see Ch. 9 of this book, 199–205.

[82]Cited in Paul Anderson, 'Memorandum on Ukaz Concerning the Rev. Sergius Bulgakoff' (Paris: 30 October 1935), in 'Memoranda Regarding the Sophiological Controversy', Archives of the Fellowship of St Alban and St Sergius. www.sobornost.org/Archives_Bulgakov-Sophia.pdf (7 November 2016).

[83]'A Decision of the Bishops' Council of the Russian Orthodox Church Abroad of 17/30 October 1935 Concerning the New Teaching of Archpriest Sergei Bulgakov on Sophia, the Wisdom of God'. Cited in Ludmila Perepiolkina, *Ecumenism: A Path to Perdition* (Saint Petersburg: Self-published with Archimandrite Alexei (Makrinov), 1999). http://ecumenizm.tripod.com/ECUMENIZM/id17.html (7 November 2016).

[84]Vladimir Lossky, *Spor o Sofii: 'Dokladnaia' Zapiska prot. S. Bulgakova i smysl ukaza Moskovskoi Patriarkhii* (Paris, 1936). The book was reprinted in Russia (Moskva: Izdatel'stvo Sviato-Vladimirskogo Bratstva, 1996), but no translation in English has been published, although there is an unpublished translation by William Kevin Fisher.

the church and a debating society'.[85] It is not exactly a 'manifesto' for a new approach to theology, yet it challenges many aspects of Bulgakov's theology.

The canonical status of both condemnations is questionable. ROCOR, then headquartered in Serbia, broke with the Church of Russia in 1922 and was technically in schism. It represented the more traditional, conservative side of Russian Orthodoxy. Metropolitan Sergius had no authority either from Patriarch Tikhon or from a council of the ROC, or the Holy Synod, to act as de facto head of the Moscow Patriarchate. It was not possible for the Russian Church to elect a successor after the death of Patriarch Tikhon in 1925 and the three *locum tenens* that Tikhon appointed to act in his place should he be arrested or die were themselves imprisoned or dead. Sergius simply stepped in to fill the breach created in the absence of any decision-making organ in the Russian Church. In condemning Bulgakov's teachings, he acted in his own name.

Ecclesiastical politics played a major and even determining role in the condemnation of Bulgakov's teaching on Sophia. Bulgakov and the Saint Sergius Institute belonged to the third Russian jurisdiction, headed by Metropolitan Evlogy (Georgievsky) (1868–1946), who was appointed by Patriarch Tikhon in 1922 to head the Russian Church in Western Europe. Evlogy faced an impossible situation. He tried to be faithful to the suffering church in Russia by remaining within the Moscow Patriarchate, but the compromises of Metropolitan Sergius with the Bolsheviks, especially after 1927, made this increasingly difficult – the Moscow Patriarchate could not even recognize its own martyrs to the Communist yoke. At the other extreme, ROCOR denounced the 'Red Church' as captured by the Communists. Metropolitan Evlogy was caught in the crossfire and his position in the Moscow Patriarchate became increasingly untenable. In 1930, Metropolitan Sergius attempted to remove Evlogy for having participated in ecumenical prayer services for the suffering church in Russia and early in 1931 Evlogy placed himself and his jurisdiction under the Ecumenical Patriarchate of Constantinople.[86] Thus the condemnations of Bulgakov's theology in the mid-1930s were a convenient way for the other two Russian jurisdictions to embarrass and humiliate Evlogy by attacking his protégé, Fr Sergius Bulgakov.

Evlogy defended Bulgakov, but felt obliged to appoint a commission to examine Bulgakov's controversial teachings. The commission basically found that Bulgakov's teachings were not heretical, but required clarification on a number of points.[87] One of those appointed to the commission, which was composed mostly of professors of the Saint Sergius Institute, was Georges Florovsky, much against his will. Although Florovsky was highly critical of Bulgakov's sophiology, he was unwilling to join in a public campaign against Bulgakov and limited his involvement in the commission as best he could.[88]

---

[85] Valliere, *Modern Russian Theology*, 396.

[86] See Paul Ladouceur, 'On Ecumenoclasm: Anti-Ecumenical Theology in Orthodoxy', *St Vladimir's Theological Quarterly*, 61, 3 (2017), 345–6.

[87] Translation of the Reports and discussion in Bryn Geffert, 'The Charges of Heresy against Sergius Bulgakov: The Majority and Minority Reports of Evlogii's Commission and the Final Report of the Bishops' Conference', *St Vladimir's Theological Quarterly*, 49, 1–2 (2005).

[88] See Alexis Klimoff, 'Georges Florovsky and the Sophiological Controversy', *St Vladimir's Theological Quarterly*, 49, 1–2 (2005); and Paul Ladouceur, '"Aimons-nous les uns les autres": Serge Boulgakov et Georges Florovsky' ('"Let us love one another': Sergius Bulgakov and George Florovsky), *Contacts*, 64, 237 (2012).

In the end, Bulgakov retained his chair of dogmatic theology at Saint Sergius, with the undertaking not to teach the Sophia doctrine in his classes – although it is not clear to what extent he actually refrained from teaching sophiology. There was no publication ban and Bulgakov continued to write about sophiology. His small book on the subject appeared in English in 1937,[89] and several of his major theological writings, which continued to espouse sophiology, were published subsequent to the 1935–36 quarrel.

In 1939, Bulgakov contracted a cancer of the throat and had an operation which left him almost unable to speak, although he continued to teach, to write and to celebrate the Divine Liturgy. Bulgakov died in 1944, but several of his major books were published after his death: *The Bride of the Lamb* (on creation, the church and eschatology), *The Philosophy of the Name* (which deals with the onomatodoxy question), a book on revelation, as well as his *Autobiographical Notes*.[90]

Bulgakov's successors were not of the same calibre as the master himself and apart from a few notable publications after the war by those close to him, the approach to theology that he incarnated quickly declined in importance. Bulgakov's main direct successors were Leon Zander, who was active especially in the ecumenical field, Nicolas Zernov (1898–1980), who taught at Oxford University and was closely associated with the Fellowship of St Alban and Saint Sergius, and Constantine Andronikof (1916–97), professor of liturgical theology at Saint Sergius and dean from 1991 to 1993, and translator of most of Bulgakov's major writings into French. Paul Evdokimov (1901–70) and Olivier Clément (1921–2009), while not direct successors of Bulgakov, nor followers of sophiology, were open to certain interests and ideas of the older generation of the religious renaissance, especially Bulgakov, as well as to the emerging neopatristic approach to theology. Evdokimov studied under Bulgakov at Saint Sergius Institute in the mid-1920s – he was in the first graduating class – while Olivier Clément studied under Evdokimov, as well as with Vladimir Lossky, in the 1950s.[91]

Conclusion

The Russian religious renaissance of the late nineteenth century and the beginning of the twentieth century represents an apex of Orthodox thought in the centuries after the fall of the Byzantine Empire. The leaders of the renaissance inherited the spirit of theological reflection from the mid-nineteenth-century Slavophiles, but considerably broadened the scope of issues under consideration to a full range of dogmatic and moral questions, in response both to their own inquisitive spirit

[89]Sergius Bulgakov, *The Wisdom of God: A Brief Summary of Sophiology* (London: Williams & Norgate, 1937).

[90]Translations of extracts of *Avtobiograficheskie zametki* (Autobiographical Notes) (1946) appeared in James Pain and Nicolas Zernov, eds., *A Bulgakov Anthology* (London: SPCK, 1976), and the full text in French: *Ma vie dans l'Orthodoxie Notes autobiographiques* (Geneva: Syrtes, 2015). Bulgakov's *Apokalipsis Ioanna: opyt dogmaticheskogo istolkovaniia* (The Apocalypse of John: A Dogmatic Interpretation) was published in 1948 and his *Filosofiia imeni* (The Philosophy of the Name) in 1953. French translation: *La Philosophie du Verbe et du Nom* (Lausanne: L'Âge d'homme, 1991).

[91]For biographies and studies of Lossky and Evdokimov, see Olivier Clément, *Orient-Occident: Deux Passeurs: Vladimir Lossky et Paul Evdokimov* (East-West: Two Mediators: Vladimir Lossky and Paul Evdokimov) (Geneva: Labor et Fides, 1985).

and to the needs of the times. They were Christian voices in the far-reaching and increasingly urgent debates on the future of Russia, debates dominated by non-Christian and anti-Christian philosophies. The official church and its institutions, including the theological academies, beholden to the imperial regime, proved incapable of responding to the existence of religious thought outside its own confines. Despite a certain goodwill shown in the St Petersburg Religious-Philosophical Assemblies of 1901–3, and proposals for a church Council after 1905, the Russian Orthodox Church was unable to find common ground with other Christian groups in Russia. There was fault on both sides of the *dialogue manqué*. To a scholastic and ecclesial rigidity of discourse on the part of many church officials at the Assemblies corresponded a doctrinal rigidity on the part of religious intelligentsia. Some questions and challenges of the intelligentsia simply could not be answered in the affirmative by the church leaders because an affirmative answer would be fundamentally non-Christian or non-Orthodox – there were some genuinely neo-pagan strands in the religious thinking of the intelligentsia. The clash between church representatives and members of the religious intelligentsia during the Religious-Philosophical Assemblies and resultant impasse were not simply a failure of the church to speak the language of intelligentsia or to answer its questions, but arose from a profound irreconcilability of their respective world views, beliefs and doctrines.

Even on the eve of the First World War, the conflict over the Name-of-God demonstrated the estrangement of the church leadership from important Christian groups who were potential allies in a social and political environment increasingly hostile to the imperial regime and everything associated with it, including the church.

There were two broad groupings within the Russian religious renaissance, which we have named the philosopher-theologians and the new religious consciousness. Philosopher-theologians such as Berdyaev, Bulgakov and other former idealists represented an intellectual Christian approach to the problems of Russian thought and society, while the leaders of the new religious consciousness represented essentially a cultural and literary manifestation of the religious renaissance, in the spirit of neo-romanticism and poetic symbolism. Although the personalities of the highly fragmented new religious consciousness could be dismissed as pseudo-Christian aesthetes and confused spiritual dilettantes, they did not, like the positivists, materialists and other atheists who made up the majority of the intelligentsia, dismiss Christ and Christianity outright, even if they objected to many aspects of historical Christianity and distanced themselves from the ROC. Most of this group adhered to basic idealist values such as the uniqueness and inviolability of the person and the necessity of ethical norms, accepted Christ in some fashion and were sincere seekers after truth. The subsequent history of Russian theology focuses mostly on the philosophical-theological personalities of the religious renaissance, while accounts of the Silver Age of Russian letters concentrate mainly on its literary and artistic expressions, closely associated with the leading figures of the new religious consciousness.

The leaders of the Russian religious renaissance reflected an engagement with contemporary problems from a Christian perspective; they offered an applied theology. The publication of *Vekhi* in 1909 in particular and the reaction to it showed, on the one hand, that there existed powerful Christian thinkers within the intelligentsia, and on the other hand, that they were a minority voice among the intelligentsia as a whole, which was viscerally hostile to Christianity. In the end, neither the philosopher-theologians nor the new religious consciousness had a significant impact on the revolutionary movement – or on the ROC. *Vekhi* turned out to be a prophetic warning, for exactly what the authors foresaw happened – the most radical and violent faction of the intelligentsia, the Bolsheviks, triumphed in 1917 and immediately turned against the more moderate intelligentsia, even their erstwhile socialist allies, eliminating them as potential ideological and political rivals.

The Moscow Council of 1917–18 of the Russian Orthodox Church embodied exactly the type of open attitude and reform spirit that the Christian intelligentsia had hoped for fifteen years earlier in the Religious-Philosophical Assemblies. It marked a partial reconciliation between the church, freed from its formal subordination to the now-vanished imperial regime, and leading representatives of the Russian religious renaissance. This reconciliation deepened in the exile situation in which many of the philosopher-theologians soon found themselves. Despite the inability of the ROC to implement the decisions of the Council of 1917–18, the Council remains a symbol – and a challenge – of a vision of the church in keeping with the best theological reflection on the church from the Slavophiles to the philosopher-theologians of the Russian religious renaissance.

The presence of the exiled elite of the Christian intelligentsia in Paris, especially at the Saint Sergius Institute, is the origin of the so-called 'Paris School' – a misleading term, since it could suggest a unified theological approach. In fact the Orthodox thinkers present in Paris in the interwar period and the immediate post-war period represented a wide range of religious, philosophical and theological personalities, from Nicolas Berdyaev and Sergius Bulgakov to Georges Florovsky and Vladimir Lossky, who hardly embody a unified 'school' of thought. The term is best understood as a geographic designation – in the same sense as the 'School of Athens' refers to all Athenian philosophers, who certainly did not have a unified system of thought.

One of the most striking aspects of modern Orthodox theology is the rapid decline of the type of philosophical-theological thought represented by the leaders of the religious renaissance, even among theologians of Russian origin in exile. Several factors account for this development. First, cut off from its roots in Russia, this mode of thought and its native social, cultural and political context were simply too foreign in the setting of intellectual, literary and personal exile in which the leaders of the religious renaissance found themselves after 1920. The brilliant but exotic flower of Russian religious thought could not bloom for long when it was transplanted unto a far-away soil. Religious philosophy developed in the intellectual ferment of the late imperial regime and it presented Christian perspectives on the future of Russia. This context was no longer relevant in exile. In exile, the Christian intellectuals were a poor social, cultural and religious minority in countries dominated by Western culture and Western Christianity. Few of the older generation of Russian thinkers really adapted themselves to the exile situation in which they found themselves – Berdyaev, by far and away the most cosmopolitan of the group, was an exception.

Secondly, as we noted above, it proved difficult to communicate the major interests and themes of Russian religious thought beyond the Russian context itself. With the exception of the books of Nicolas Berdyaev and some works of Sergius Bulgakov, during the 1930s and in the immediate post-war years, virtually all writings of the Russian exiles were published only in Russian, which limited access to non-Russian audiences. There has been no equivalent of Russian religious thought in other major countries of Orthodox tradition, such as Greece and Romania and even Serbia and

Bulgaria. With the growing internationalization of Orthodox theology in the second half of the twentieth century, Russian religious thought appeared to many as a somewhat provincial and dated attempt to develop a modern Orthodox theology.

In addition, in the exile setting certain internal weaknesses and inadequacies in the religious philosophical-theological approach to Orthodoxy became more evident, especially its deficient grounding in patristic theology, the Byzantine liturgical tradition, church history and Orthodox spirituality. The great theological controversies of the mid-1930s over sophiology and intercommunion, with Sergius Bulgakov at the epicentre of each, certainly contributed to the decline of religious philosophy from its apogee prior to the Russian Revolution. For many of the younger generation of Russian theologians, especially Georges Florovsky and Vladimir Lossky, the major ideas of religious renaissance – notably all-unity and sophiology, even as grafted, somewhat artificially, to the Orthodox tradition by as great a genius as Bulgakov – were perceived as too dependent on Western philosophy, too speculative in nature and too distant from Orthodox tradition contained in patristic thought, especially the theology of the Greek and Byzantine Fathers.

The successors of the leaders of the Russian religious renaissance, especially those of Sergius Bulgakov, were unable to sustain the intellectual momentum and creativity of the older generation, nor to communicate to a younger generation educated largely in the West the enthusiasm of the religious renaissance for ideas such as all-unity and sophiology. For the younger theologians, the gap between the approach and ideas of the philosopher-theologians and patristic theology was simply too great to satisfy the criterion of faithfulness to Orthodox tradition and they set out to re-establish theology in more direct continuity with the patristic thinking. By the end of the Second World War, this alternate project for the renewal of Orthodox thought, centred on a return to patristic sources, was already well advanced, thanks to the work of Georges Florovsky, Vladimir Lossky, Dumitru Staniloae and others who promoted a revival of Palamite theology in Orthodoxy. Chapter 5 will focus on the origins and nature of what subsequently became known as neopatristic theology or the neopatristic synthesis.

In the second part of this book, we will examine in more detail some of the main ideas of the Russian religious renaissance, especially those which found their way into the neopatristic mode of theology, or which were subjects of conflict among Orthodox theologians: the relationship between God and creation (Chapter 9); divine-humanity and the theology of the person (Chapter 10); ecclesiology and ecumenism (Chapters 11 and 12); the 'churching' or 'Christification' of life (Chapter 13); social and political theology (Chapter 14); and the Name-of-God quarrel (Chapter 15).

5

The Origins and Nature of Neopatristic Theology

Chapter Outline

The origins of neopatristic theology

Neopatristic theology originated both in continuity with earlier developments in Orthodox thought and in reaction to certain modes of early twentieth-century theology which the founding fathers considered incompatible with the mainstream of Orthodox tradition going back to the ancient Fathers. Ramifications of the patristic revival in Orthodox thought and practice are found in several strands of Orthodox theology, even though it was Georges Florovsky and Vladimir Lossky and others who consciously practised and advocated a 'return to the Fathers' – to patristic theology – as the fundamental basis of Orthodox theology. Nevertheless, with nuances of emphasis and interests, many of those typically associated with the academic, ascetic-mystical and the religious philosophy theological strands of the nineteenth and early twentieth centuries were also patristic in their own ways.

The roots of the broad neopatristic movement in modern Orthodoxy can be traced to the late eighteenth century. The publication of the *Philokalia* in 1782 by St Macarius of Corinth (1731–1805) and St Nicodemus of the Holy Mountain (1749–1809) was a major undertaking on the part of important spiritual and theological figures to restore patristic thought to its true place in Orthodoxy.[1] The *Philokalia* is a cornerstone of the modern patristic edifice. The interest of its editors was primarily in ascetic writings, but they and their successors in Moldavia and Russia also promoted more properly theological patristic writings. Nicodemus, for example, prepared an edition of the works of Gregory Palamas, which unfortunately was seized and destroyed by the Austrian police in Venice before it could be printed. In nineteenth-century Russia, the Slavophile Ivan Kireevsky, and academic scholars and monastic figures such as Macarius of Optino, promoted the translation and publication of the Greek Fathers in Russian, as well as scholarly studies of patristic theology. In a similar vein, the leading figures of the Russian religious renaissance, notably Pavel Florensky and Sergius Bulgakov, considered that they were working within the spirit of the Fathers. In retrospect, there has indeed been a broad, identifiable neopatristic movement in Orthodox thought since the late eighteenth century, on which twentieth-century neopatristic theology built and carried forward.

The main types of theology against which neopatristic theology posed itself as an alternative approach were academic or school theology and the type of theology which characterized the Russian religious renaissance, considered too liberal and modernist by its critics. Academic theology dominated the theological educational systems of the major countries of Orthodox tradition, especially pre-revolutionary Russia, Greece and Romania. Academic theology was a prime example of what Georges Florovsky called the 'pseudomorphosis' and even the 'Latin captivity' of Orthodox theology, the principal theme of his *The Ways of Russian Theology* (1937).[2] This theology is characterized by an attempt to systematize theological discourse into a unified framework, often inspired in structure, language and in some cases even doctrines, by Western theology and theological treatises, both Roman Catholic and Protestant, and is often reflected in 'manuals' of dogmatic theology. This is not a traditional Orthodox approach to theology. There is only one significant historical example of an integrated theological treatise among the writings of the early Fathers, *The Exact Exposition of the Faith* (*De fide orthodoxa*) of St John of Damascus (c. 676–749). Manuals of dogmatic theology are typical of scholastic theology – a rational approach to theology, rather than the more characteristically Orthodox mystical and liturgical approach, which seeks to deepen the experience of the faith while respecting the mystery of the faith. The emancipation of Orthodox theology from an essentially scholastic approach began in the

[1]English translation: [St Nicodemus of the Holy Mountain and St Makarios of Corinth, eds.], G. E. H. Palmer, Philip Sherrard and Kallistos Ware, trans., *The Philokalia: The Complete Text*, Vols. I-IV (London: Faber and Faber, 1983–95). A fifth volume will contain the remaining texts from the original *Philokalia*.

[2]Georges Florovsky devotes Chapter VII of *The Ways of Russian Theology* to 'The Historical School', which includes academic theology, religious journalism and 'moralists' such as Leo Tolstoy, Maksim Tareev, Constantine Pobedonostsev, Anthony Khrapovitsky and Viktor Nesmelov. See *The Ways of Russian Theology*, vol. II (Vaduz, LI: Büchervertriebsanstalt, 1987), 105–228. Paul Evdokimov refers to the latter group of religious authors, together with others such as the poet Vyacheslav Ivanov and the literary critic Dimitri Merezhkovsky, as 'the moral school' in *Le Christ dans la pensée russe* (Christ in Russian Thought) (Paris: Les Éditions du Cerf, 1970), 121–46. Florovsky refers to the 'Latin capivity' of the Russian theological academies in 'Western Influences in Rssian Theology' in Brandon Gallaher and Paul Ladouceur, eds., *The Patristic Witness of Georges Florovsky: Essential Theological Writings* (London: T&T Clark, 2019), 143. John Zizioulas subsequently employed the expression 'Babylonian captivity' in a similar sense. See John Zizioulas, *Being As Communion: Studies in Personhood and the Church* (Crestwood, NY: St Vladimir's Seminary Press, 1985), 20. The expression gained popularity in modern times from Martin Luther's treatise *Prelude on the Babylonian Captivity of the Church* (1520). The expression 'Western captivity' is also widely attributed to Florovsky. Although it conveys his notion of pseudomorphosis, Florovsky does not seem to have used it.

nineteenth century, but the progress was slow and is far from complete even in the early twenty-first century.

As we saw in Chapter 3, the *Orthodox Dogmatic Theology* (5 vols., 1849–53) of Metropolitan Makarius (Bulgakov) of Moscow (1816–82) and other similar works long dominated theological instruction in Russia. Examples of the same tradition in Greece are the *Dogmatics of the Eastern Orthodox Church* (1907) of Christos Androutsos (1869–1935), which held sway for many decades in Greek theological education, and the *Dogmatics of the Orthodox Catholic Church* (3 vols., 1959–61) of Panagiotis Trembelas (1886–1977). Another modern example of a treatise of dogmatic theology is the one-volume manual *Orthodox Dogmatic Theology* (1963) by Fr Michael Pomazansky (1888–1988), which enjoys considerable popularity in some Orthodox circles.

The origins of the neopatristic strand of Orthodox theology can be traced to three theologians, working more or less separately from each other – even though for a time in the early 1930s, all three were present in Paris: Fr Georges Florovsky (1893–1979), Vladimir Lossky (1903–58) and Fr Dumitru Staniloae (1903–93). Although Florovsky was not the sole initiator of neopatristic theology, he was by far its most ardent, articulate – and outspoken – representative. In his theological vision, Orthodox theology sorely needed to return to the school of the Fathers as its sole authentic foundation, to re-appropriate patristic theology, rather than lose its soul in the byways of other theological horizons. By the late 1940s he characterized this theological turn in the catchy slogan 'neopatristic synthesis'. Other leading early neopatristic theologians such as Vladimir Lossky did not write explicitly about their approach to theology and it is to Florovsky that we must turn for the clearest exposition of what constitutes neopatristic theology.

Georges Florovsky was born in 1893 in Odessa, Russia (now in the Ukraine), as the fourth child of an Orthodox priest. Inspired by the erudite environment in which he grew up, he learned English, German, French, Latin, Greek and Hebrew to varying degrees while still a schoolboy. At eighteen, he started to study philosophy and history at the University of Odessa. After his graduation, he taught for three years at high schools in Odessa and in 1919 at the University of Odessa. But in 1920 the Florovsky family was forced to leave Russia. Georges Florovsky made his way to Sofia and then to Prague, where he taught at the Russian Law Faculty and became acquitted with Fr Sergius Bulgakov and other exiled leaders of the religious renaissance. In Sofia he wrote a master's thesis on Alexander Herzen (1812–70), considered the father of Russian socialism, but he never concluded the writing of a monograph on Herzen.[3]

In 1925 Bulgakov moved to Paris to teach dogmatics at the newly founded Saint Sergius Institute of Orthodox Theology, and at Bulgakov's suggestion, in 1926 Florovsky was invited to teach patristics at the Institute. It is in the study of the ancient Fathers that Florovsky found his vocation. Although Florovsky did not have an academic degree in theology, he plunged himself into the study of the Fathers of the Church, finding in the Fathers the foundation and enduring basis for Orthodox theology. In 1932 he was ordained to the priesthood. Florovsky spent the war years in Serbia, then returned to Paris to teach at Saint Sergius for a few years. During this period Florovsky

[3]Paul L. Gavrilyuk, *Georges Florovsky and the Russian Religious Renaissance* (Oxford: Oxford University Press, 2013), 80–1.

and Vladimir Lossky had considerable contact with each other; it was Florovsky who introduced Lossky into the Fellowship of St Alban and St Sergius. Previously, they had little contact, in part because of jurisdictional issues (Florovsky was a member of the Russian jurisdiction under Metropolitan Evlogy, whereas Lossky remained with the Moscow Patriarchate), and also because of Lossky's role in the sophiology affair. Although Florovsky contested Bulgakov's sophiology, he disapproved of the way that Bulgakov was treated during the controversy, disagreed with the two condemnations and considered that his differences with Bulgakov were theological but not dogmatic in a narrow sense.[4]

In 1949 Florovsky accepted a teaching position at St Vladimir's Orthodox Theological Seminary in New York and in 1950 he became its Dean. In a few years he considerably raised the academic level of St Vladimir's, in part by recruiting such figures as Alexander Schmemann, and by converting the seminary into a graduate institution. But Florovsky was not easy to get along with and he had conflicts with other staff members, students and the hierarchs who oversaw St Vladimir's. In 1955 he was asked to step down as dean and leave the seminary. His ecumenical friends found him a position at the Harvard School of Theology and subsequently at Princeton University. From the mid-1930s until about 1970 Florovsky was very active in the ecumenical movement and he was the most well-known Orthodox representative in ecumenical circles for some thirty years.

The revival of the apophatic tradition, Palamite theology and theosis

The initial development of a neopatristic mode of theology took place in parallel with a more specific movement in Orthodoxy to recover three closely interrelated theological notions: the apophatic tradition or 'negative theology', the theology of the divine energies as distinct from the divine essence and deification or theosis as the ultimate human destiny, notions which stand as hallmarks of Orthodox theology in relation to traditional Western theology.

By affirming that God is above human conceptions and language yet makes himself known in creation, apophatism seeks to retain both God's self-revelation and the divine mystery. Orthodox theology emphasizes that only the Persons of the Holy Trinity know the divine essence, which remains unknowable to any created being, angels or humans. For some Orthodox theologians, notably Vladimir Lossky, apophatism is closely related to antinomies in Christian theology, which create a constant tension between two apparently contradictory or at least antagonistic principles: God is One and Trinity; God is transcendent and immanent; God is knowable and unknowable; the Logos is God and Man; Christ is the eternal Son of God and the Son of the Virgin Mary. This mode of thought and of conceiving truth, which features strongly in Florovsky and Lossky, less so in other neopatristic theologians such as Staniloae, is disconcerting to the rational, Cartesian mind, especially when it is combined with its close pendant, intuitive knowledge.

[4]Unpublished interview with Andrew Blane recorded between 1969 and 1971 (as summarized by Fr Matthew Baker (1977–2015) in a private communication).

Apophatism or antinomic thought is deeply rooted in the early Fathers and has a long history in Orthodox theology, certainly up to Gregory Palamas in the fourteenth century. But scholastic and Enlightenment influences in Orthodoxy, as we have seen, dulled these and other aspects of the Orthodox tradition, which did not fit easily into a more rational approach to theology and which are muted or absent in Western Christian theology. The return of theosis as a prominent feature in Orthodox discourse can be traced to the publication of the *Philokalia*, which marked the beginning of the modern patristic revival in Orthodoxy in the late eighteenth century. The Preface to the *Philokalia*, anonymous but attributed to St Nicodemus of the Holy Mountain, is a masterly overview of hesychastic spirituality, with theosis as the major theme – theosis is mentioned over twenty times in this short text.[5]

Apophatism features in both the Russian religious renaissance and neopatristic theology, with somewhat different emphases and expression. Antinomic thought and intuitive knowledge are two typical characteristics of Russian religious thought. These characteristics make Russian thought more open to new ideas and sources of inspiration, including personal experience, than strictly rational, deductive and abstract thinking. Although many of the Russian religious thinkers sought a principle which could encompass and reconcile the antinomies, some were comfortable with the idea that truth could contain apparent contradictions and that aspects of truth escaped human knowledge and formulation. 'To explain logically the mystery of this contradictory situation', writes Simon Frank concerning antinomies in integral knowledge, 'to explain it in such a way that it stops being a mystery, is impossible'.[6]

Antinomies are an important element in the thinking of Pavel Florensky and Sergius Bulgakov. In the Sixth Letter of *The Pillar and Ground of the Truth* under the title 'Contradiction', Florensky seeks to reconcile the apparent dilemma of the Hegelian dialectic: 'The thesis and the antithesis together form the expression of truth. In other words, truth is an antinomy, and it cannot fail to be such.'[7] Russian thinkers, in Florensky's words, accept that 'both the one and the other are true, but each in its own way. Reconciliation and unity are higher than rationality.'[8] For Florensky, the resolution of philosophical and theological antinomies can only be spiritual and eschatological, for in the Holy Trinity there is but one truth:

> In Heavenly Jerusalem, there are no contradictions. … Then, there will be no contradictions, and no rationality tormented by contradictions. … the Truth of the Triradiant Light shown by Christ and reflected in the righteous, the Light in which the contradiction of the present age is overcome by love and glory. … In heaven, there is only the one Truth.[9]

The first part of Bulgakov's *Unfading Light* (1917), entitled 'The Divine Nothing', is a study of antinomy in theology and philosophy, from the Greek philosophers to the Fathers of the

[5]St Nicodemus the Hagiorite, 'Proem', *The Philokalia: Writings of Holy Mystic Fathers* (1782) (Belmont, MA: Institute for Byzantine and Modern Greek Studies, 2008), 27–40.
[6]Simon Frank, *The Light Shineth in Darkness: An Essay in Christian Ethics and Social Philosophy* (1949) (Athens, OH: Ohio University Press, 1989), 9.
[7]Pavel Florensky, *The Pillar and Ground of the Truth* (1914) (Princeton, NJ: Princeton University Press, 1997), 109.
[8]Florensky, *The Pillar and Ground of the Truth*, 118.
[9]Ibid., 117.

Church to Western theology and philosophy. Bulgakov sets the tone for this exploration in the opening sentences:

> The fundamental content of *religious* experience, as contact with the transcendent, outside-the-limits, divine world contains in an obvious manner a contraction for rational thinking. The object of religion, God, is something that on the one hand is completely *transcendent*, of a different nature, and external to the world and the human being, but on the other hand *is revealed* to religious consciousness, touches it, enters inside it, and becomes its immanent content. Both moments of religious consciousness are given simultaneously, like poles, in their mutual repulsion and attraction.[10]

Bulgakov sees this fundamental antinomy of religious consciousness reflected in the two basic types of theology, negative and positive.[11] Neopatristic theologians, in appropriating their predecessors' reception of antinomic thought, sought to dispel the ambiguities brought about by an excessive reliance on philosophical notions of antinomies and on a certain romantic wistfulness in Russian religious thought by providing a firmer grounding for the divine mystery in patristic apophatism.

Closely related to apophatism is the notion of intuitive knowledge. Intuitive knowledge arises as a spontaneous certainty, a sudden and unexpected understanding or enlightenment, rather than as a result of other modes of learning, such as observation, experiment or rational deduction. Intuitive knowledge is thus close to the knowledge of faith and personal experience, especially interior, spiritual and mystical experience. This 'intuitivism', in whole or in part, is found throughout Russian religious philosophy, from Khomiakov to Soloviev, Berdyaev to Florensky and Bulgakov, where it frequently takes the form of knowledge arising from direct experience. Berdyaev says of his philosophical approach: 'My philosophical thought does not have a scientific format, it is not logical-rational, but is living intuition; it rests upon a spiritual experience and it is passionately directed towards liberty. I do not think discursively; I do not as much go towards truth as I begin with truth.'[12]

Florensky affirms in the opening lines 'To the Reader' that the general theme of his *The Pillar and Ground of the Truth* is that 'Living religious experience [i]s the sole legitimate way to gain knowledge of the dogmas. ... Only by relying on immediate experience can one survey the spiritual treasures of the church and come to see their value.'[13] The appeal to experience can easily be considered spiritual romanticism, but it has to be seen primarily as a reaction against the rational, scholastically inspired theology of the academies, and it attracted the experientially oriented leaders of the religious renaissance in Russia. One of the main criticisms of Florensky's book is precisely that it relies too much on personal experience – in the eyes of critics, this makes it 'subjective' and hence of limited validity, – as distinct from church dogmas and patristic teachings, founded on revelation and supported by Christian philosophy. Florovsky writes: 'Florensky's book is deliberately and eminently subjective ... he presents his personal preferences as a confession of

---

[10]Sergius Bulgakov, *Unfading Light: Contemplations and Speculations* (1917) (Grand Rapids, MI: Eerdmans, 2012), 103.
[11]Bulgakov, *Unfading Light*, 110.
[12]Nicolas Berdyaev, *Essai de métaphysique eschatologique: Acte créateur et objectivation* (Essay on Eschatological Metaphysics: The Creative Act and Objectification) (Paris: Aubier, 1946), 5.
[13]Florensky, *The Pillar and Ground of the Truth*, 5.

catholic experience.'[14] But Florovsky's critique of Florensky's approach to theology as overly personal is vastly overdrawn, and is certainly no basis per se for minimizing or diminishing the importance of Florensky's theology. Reflection on personal experience in the light of revelation is a door to ascertaining fundamental reality, as for example in Florensky's portrayal of the relationship among the four major concepts, derived from Platonism, that fascinated other Russian religious thinkers – truth, love, good and beauty:

> In love and only in love is real knowledge of the Truth conceivable. On the other hand, knowledge of the Truth is revealed by love: he who is with Love is unable not to love. … 'Truth, Good and Beauty.' This metaphysical triad is not three different principles, but one principle. It is one and the same spiritual life, but seen from different points of view. Spiritual life as emanating from 'I', as having its centre in 'I', is the Truth. Perceived as the immediate action of another, it is Good. Objectively contemplated by a third, as radiating outward, it is Beauty.[15]

Thus, the resolution of the inherent tension and duality between the knowing subject and the object known is found in love, which alone can unite subject and object in harmony. Berdyaev writes along the same lines:

> Love is recognized as the principle of apprehension; it guarantees the apprehension of truth; love is a source and guarantee of religious truth. Corporate experience of love, *sobornost'*, is the criterion of apprehension. Here we have a principle which is opposed to authority; it is also a method of apprehension which is opposed to the Cartesian *cogito ergo sum*. It is not *I* think, but *we* think, that is to say, the corporate experience of love thinks, and it is not thought which proves my existence but will and love. … Love is the principal source of the knowledge of Christian truth, and the church is a unity of love and freedom.[16]

By affirming that humans are more than simply rational creatures, religious philosophy surpasses and replaces the rationalist Cartesian axiom '*Cogito ergo sum* – I think, therefore I am' with an adage along the lines of 'I love, therefore I am.'[17] This resolves, but does not dissolve the subject-object duality and fully respects and affirms the theology of the person, a major aspect of modern Orthodox thought (see Chapter 10).

The distinction between the divine essence, unknowable by creatures, and the divine energies, by which God makes himself known in creation and in which humans can participate, originated with the Cappadocian Fathers and was brought to full development by St Gregory Palamas in the fourteenth century. Although the Palamite theology of the divine energies was formally approved by councils of the Church of Constantinople between 1341 and 1351, it virtually disappeared from the Orthodox theological scene after the fall of Constantinople in 1453, partly as a result of Western influences on Orthodox theology. For several centuries, Orthodox academic theology, expressed

[14]Florovsky, *The Ways of Russian Theology*, II:276–7.
[15]Florensky, *The Pillar and Ground of the Truth*, 56.
[16]Nicolas Berdyaev, *The Russian Idea* (New York: Macmillan, 1948), 161; 164.
[17]Adopted as the title of a study on Archimandrite Sophrony (Sakharov): Nicholas Sakharov, *I Love, Therefore I Am: The Theological Legacy of Archimandrite Sophrony* (Crestwood, NY: St Vladimir's Seminary Press, 2002).

essentially in Western, especially scholastic, theological categories and language, largely followed the Western lead in ignoring apophatic theology, the essence-energies distinction and theosis.

The leading Russian philosopher-theologians were aware of the Palamite theology of the divine energies, and indeed drew on it in their defence of the Russian monks during the 'Athonite controversy' concerning the veneration of the names of God (*onomatodoxy* or *imiaslavie*) immediately prior to the First World War (see Chapter 15). In his work *Unfading Light*, Sergius Bulgakov presents an accurate summary of the Palamite teaching on the divine energies, in the context of a general survey of the apophatic tradition in Eastern and Western theology.[18] But this awareness of Palamism among leading Russian theologians did not extend beyond Russia at the time.

More important as a stimulating factor for the re-emergence of Palamite theology in the 1920s and 1930s was severe criticism of Palamism by several Roman Catholic theologians, notably Adrian Fortescue (1874–1923), Martin Jugie (1878–1954) and Sébastien Guichardan.[19] Jugie, writing on Palamas' 'strange theology' in the early 1930s, repeats the ancient criticism that the notions of the divine energies and a real distinction between the divine essence and the divine Persons are attacks on divine simplicity; by undermining divine simplicity Palamas 'gravely adulterates the notion of God', leading to 'monstrous errors'.[20] For Jugie the fundamental error of Palamas's 'system' is 'to recognize in God a composition of nature and persons, of substance and accidents, of essence and physical properties flowing from the essence, of primary element and secondary element'.[21] Jugie also attacks what he perceives as other 'erroneous and close to heretical' Palamite theses of uncreated deifying grace, the uncreated gifts of the Holy Spirit, the power and light by which one sees the uncreated glory of God and the inhabitation of the divine Persons in the soul of the just.[22] A final critique undermines the very premise of hesychastic theology: 'For Palamas, in effect, the divine Persons, any more than the divine essence, are not in direct relation with creatures. What is given to the just is not the Person of the Holy Spirit, but his operation.'[23] Returning to his anti-Byzantine polemics in 1941, Jugie solemnly declared that in any case 'Palamism as a dogma in the Greco-Russian Church is indeed dead' and he doubted that 'the current sympathetic consideration of a few Russian émigrés' would be sufficient to revive it.[24] For several Orthodox theologians, misrepresentations and biased critiques of Palamas confirmed the

[18]Bulgakov, *Unfading Light*, 131–4.

[19]Adrian Fortescue, 'Hesychasm', in *The Catholic Encyclopedia*, Vol. 7 (New York: Robert Appleton, 1910). www.newadvent.org/cathen/07301a.htm (19 May 2017); Martin Jugie, 'Palamas Grégoire' (Gregory Palamas) and 'Palamite (Controverse)' (The Palamite Controversy) in *Dictionnaire de théologie catholique*, Vol. 11.2 (Paris: Letouzey et Ané, 1932), cols. 1735–76 & 1777–1818; Martin Jugie, 'De Theologia Palamitica' (On Palamite Theology) *Theologia Dogmatica Christianorum Orientalium*, Vol. II (Paris: Letouzey et Ané, 1933), 47–183; Sébastien Guichardan, *Le Problème de la simplicité divine en Orient et en Occident aux XIVe et XVe s.: Grégoire Palamas, Duns Scott, Georges Scholarios* (The Problem of Divine Simplicity in the East and West in the 14th and 15th Centuries: Gregory Palamas, Duns Scotus and George Scholarios) (Lyons: Legendre, 1933).

[20]Jugie, 'Palamas Grégoire', in *Dictionnaire de théologie catholique*, 11.2:1763.

[21]Ibid., 11.2:1764.

[22]Ibid., 11.2:1764–5.

[23]Ibid., 11.2:1764.

[24]Martin Jugie, *Le Schisme byzantin: Aperçu historique et doctrinal* (The Byzantine Schism: Historical and Doctrinal Overview) (Paris: Lethielleux, 1941), 383.

urgent necessity of accurately presenting Palamite theology and of reviving Palamism as a living feature in Orthodox thought.

Jugie's 1941 diagnosis of the status of Palamite theology in Orthodoxy was not far off the mark, but he vastly underestimated the strength of the Palamite revival already underway in the 1930s. An early work on Palamas was the master's thesis completed in Saint Petersburg in 1905 of a Greek theologian, Gregorios Papamichael (1875–1956), but even the published thesis had no impact, even on Greek theology, still in the firm grip of neo-scholasticism.[25] Some of the leading early twentieth-century Russian theologians, notably Pavel Florensky and Sergius Bulgakov, appealed to the Palamite theology of divine essence and divine energies in their defence of *imyaslavie* during the 'Name-of-God' quarrel (onomatodoxy) on Mount Athos and in Russia prior to the First World War.[26] But they did not adopt Palamism as a central element of their theologies, since it appeared to be incompatible with their vision of Divine Wisdom, Sophia, as the key to the relations between God and the creation (see Chapter 9). Nonetheless, Bulgakov, for one, considered that his sophiology was a form of Palamism.

Among the future neopatristic theologians, Georges Florovsky first highlighted the importance of apophatism, the energy-essence distinction and theosis, initially in private letters to Bulgakov as early as 1925, and more substantially in his essay 'Creation and Createdness', first published in 1928.[27] The essay is an exploration of patristic thought on the meaning of creation and the nature of the relationship between Creator and creation. This fine piece can be seen as part of Florovsky's 'shadow-boxing' with the theology of the Russian religious renaissance, especially that of Bulgakov, over sophiology, although neither Bulgakov nor Divine Sophia is mentioned in the article. Florovsky points to the inseparable links which bind together the essence-energies distinction, apophatism (which relates in particular to the unknowable divine essence) and theosis (by which creatures can participate in the divine energies, thereby becoming themselves divinized). Although not directly relying on Palamas, this article makes extensive use of Palamite theology in its central argument that the fundamental distinction between divine nature and human nature is that between uncreated and created.

---

[25]Gregorios Papamichael, *Cho agios Grigorios ho Palamás archiepískopos Thessaloníkis* (St Gregory Palamas, Archbishop of Thessaloniki) (Saint Petersburg & Alexandria, 1911). See Panagiotes Christou, 'Neohellenic Theology at the Crossroads', *Greek Orthodox Theological Review*, 28, 1 (1983), 53.

[26]On the theology of Name of God, see Hilarion Alfeyev, *Svyashchennaya taina tserkvi. Vvedenie v istoriyu i problematiku imyaslavskikh sporov*, 2 Vols. (Saint Petersburg, 2002). French translation: *Le Nom grand et glorieux* (The Great and Glorious Name) (Paris: Éditions du Cerf, 2007); and *Le Mystère sacré de l'Église. Introduction à l'histoire et à la problématique des débats athonites sur la vénération du nom de Dieu* (The Sacred Mystery of the Church: Introduction to the History and the Problematic of the Athonite Debates concerning the Veneration of the Name of God) (Fribourg, CH: Academic Press, 2007). For an overview of the theological aspects of onomatodoxy, see Paul Ladouceur, 'The Name-of-God Conflict in Orthodox Theology', *St Vladimir's Theological Quarterly*, 56, 4 (2012); and Ch. 14.

[27]Georges Florovsky, 'Tvar i tvarnost', *Pravoslavnaya mysl*, 1 (Paris, 1928). Translation: 'Creation and Createdness', in Gallaher and Ladouceur, eds., *The Patristic Witness of Georges Florovsky*, 33–63. A shorter version also appeared in French in 1928: 'L'idée de la création dans la philosophie chrétienne' (The idea of creation in Christian philosophy) *Logos*, 1 (Romania, 1928); and in English as 'The Idea of Creation in Christian Philosophy', *Eastern Churches Quarterly*, 8, 3 (1949). We return to 'Creation and Createdness' more extensively in Ch. 9.

But Florovsky was not the only Orthodox theologian who realized the importance of Palamite theology, as several other Orthodox theologians also sought to recover Palamite theology.[28] In the 1930s, two other Orthodox theologians, working independently, published major works on Palamite theology. The first modern Orthodox study is that of Archimandrite Basil Krivoshein (1900–85), then a Russian monk on Mount Athos. Krivoshein's methodical presentation was first published in 1936 in Russian in Prague and a translation appeared in the English Catholic periodical *Eastern Churches Quarterly* in 1938 and a German translation in 1939.[29] The English translation of this text was the first major Orthodox writing on Palamas in a Western language. It relies exclusively on Palamas's writings then available in printed form – not all of Palamas's works had been printed; some were still only in manuscript.

Also published in 1938 was a major work on Palamas by Fr Dumitru Staniloae, a Romanian theologian. Staniloae studied the theology and writings of Palamas in Berlin, Paris and Constantinople in 1929 and 1930 and copied manuscripts of some of Palamas's unpublished works. Staniloae's book, *The Life and Teachings of Gregory Palamas* (in Romanian), included translations of extracts of the Palamas's *Triads* and two other tracts.[30]

Vladimir Lossky became interested in apophatism and Palamas early in his theological studies. His first published articles, in 1929 and 1931, dealt with apophatism and analogies in Pseudo-Dionysius.[31] Lossky drew heavily on the Palamite theology of the divine energies in his groundbreaking *The Mystical Theology of the Eastern Church*, first delivered as lectures in Paris in 1942 and published in 1944.[32] Another Orthodox theologian interested in Palamas was Archimandrite Cyprian Kern, professor of liturgical theology and patristics at the Saint Sergius Institute. In 1942 a translation of his article on 'Spiritual Predecessors of St Gregory Palamas' appeared in the United Kingdom and he also published an article on Palamas in French in 1947 and a study of the anthropology of St Gregory Palamas in 1950 (in Russian).[33]

Together with Florovsky's article 'Creation and Createdness', Basil Krivoshein's article, Dumitru Staniloae's book and Vladimir Lossky's *Mystical Theology* marked the beginning of the revival of

---

[28]Although Florovsky was a pioneer of the neo-Palamite revival, in his later work he does not attach as much importance to Palamas or to apophatism as do other modern Orthodox theologians such as Lossky and Staniloae. Athanasius, Augustine and Chrysostom are more important for Florovsky's Christocentric theology than Palamas.

[29]Basil Krivoshein, 'The Ascetic and Theological Teaching of Gregory Palamas' (in Russian), *Seminarium Kondakovianum, Recueil d'études d'archéologie et histoire de l'art, études byzantines*, VIII (Prague, 1936); in English in *Eastern Churches Quarterly*, 3 (1938), 26–33; 71-–84; 138–56; 193–214 (reprinted as a monograph in 1954 (London: Geo. E. J. Coldwell) and in 1968); in German in *Das östliche Christentum*, 8 (1939); in French in Basile Krivochéine, *Dieu, l'homme et l'Église. Lecture des Pères* (Paris: Les Éditions du Cerf, 2010).

[30]Dumitru Staniloae, *Viața și învățătura Sfântului Grigorie Palama cu trei tratate traduse* (Life and Works of St Gregory Palamas, with Three Tracts in Translation) (Sibiu, Romania, 1938); reprinted in Bucharest in 1993 and 2006. It has not yet (2018) been published in a Western European language.

[31]Vladimir Lossky, 'Otritsatel'noe bogoslovie v uchenii Dionisiya Areopagita' (Negative theology in the doctrine of Dionysius the Aeropagite), *Seminarium Kondakovianum*, 3 (1929); and 'La notion des "Analogies" chez Denys le pseudo-Aréopagite' (The notion of analogies in Denis the Aeropagite), *Archives d'histoire doctrinale et littéraire du Moyen Age*, 5 (1931).

[32]Vladimir Lossky, *Essai sur la theologie mystique de l'Eglise d'Orient* (Paris: Aubier, 1944), English translation: *The Mystical Theology of the Eastern Church* (London: J. Clarke, 1957; Crestwood, NY: St Vladimir's Seminary Press, 1976).

[33]Cyprian Kern, 'Spiritual Predecessors of St. Gregory Palamas', *Theological Thought* (1942); 'Les éléments de la théologie de Grégoire Palamas' (Elements of the theology of Gregory Palamas) *Irénikon*, 20 (1947); *Antropologiya svyatogo Grigoriya Palamy* (The Anthropology of St Gregory Palamas) (Paris: YMCA-Press, 1950; Moscow: Palomnik, 1996).

Palamite theology in Orthodoxy (although the influence of the Staniloae work remained limited since it was not translated into Western European languages). The restoration of Palamite theology in Orthodoxy, often referred to as 'neo-Palamism', continued after the Second World War, reaching a high point with the publication in 1959 of studies on Palamite theology by Fr John Meyendorff (1926–92), which we will consider in more detail in Chapter 9.

The triumph of neopatristic theology

In addition to stirrings of a revival of Palamite theology in the late 1920s and the 1930s, several other major events and publications in the 1930s marked the public beginning of the new patristic approach to Orthodox theology. Two major theological disputes erupted almost simultaneously and in parallel, both involving the theology of Fr Sergius Bulgakov: the quarrel over sophiology, and another concerning his proposal for 'limited intercommunion' among Anglicans and Orthodox in the context of meetings of the Fellowship of St Alban and St Sergius. We will consider the sophiology dispute in more detail in Chapter 9 and the controversy over limited intercommunion in Chapter 12.

The dispute over sophiology in the mid-1930s is the most serious controversy in twentieth-century Orthodox theology. It generated a number of substantial publications, both those attacking Sergius Bulgakov's teachings on Sophia and his replies to his critics. The ashes are still smouldering over the Sophia controversy and a detached and thorough account has yet to be published.

Georges Florovsky played a discrete role in the heat of the Sophia controversy. Although he was strongly critical of sophiology and of other aspects of Bulgakov's theology, in his writings he took an indirect approach, seeking to undermine the principal arguments used by the sophiologists, without attacking sophiology head-on. While he criticized Bulgakov and sophiology privately, he was unwilling to participate in public attacks on Bulgakov proffered by the Patriarchate of Moscow and the Russian Orthodox Church outside of Russia (ROCOR), and by some members of Metropolitan Evlogy's own jurisdiction, especially Fr Sergius Chetverikov (1867–1947).

Late in 1936, Florovsky delivered two papers at the First Congress of Orthodox Theology, held in Athens from 29 November to 4 December 1936. Both Bulgakov and Florovsky, together with Anton Kartashev and Basil Zenkovsky, attended this meeting on behalf of the Saint Sergius Institute, but history remembers Florovsky's papers.[34] His longer paper, 'Western Influences in Russian Theology' (delivered in German, the principal language of the meeting), is a summary of the main themes and conclusions of Florovsky's *The Ways of Russian Theology*, which had not yet

[34]The proceedings of the Congress are published in Hamilcar S. Alivisatos, ed., *Procès-verbaux du premier Congrès de théologie orthodoxe à Athènes, 29 novembre-6 décembre 1936* (Proceedings of the Congress of Orthodox Theologians) (Athens: Pyrsos, 1939). For a fascinating report of the Congress by a Roman Catholic observer, see E. Stéphanou, 'Le premier Congrès de théologie orthodoxe (Athènes, 29 novembre-3 décembre 1936)' (The first Congress of Orthodox Theologians), *Échos d'Orient*, no. 36, 186 (1937).

been published.[35] It is an overview or catalogue of the various negative influences of Western theology on Russian thought up to the early twentieth century. It was in this paper that Florovsky introduced his catchphrase *pseudomorphosis* to characterize most of Russian theology up to his day. In mineralogy, a *pseudomorph* is a mineral or mineral compound that appears in an untypical form, resulting from a substitution process in which the original appearance and dimensions remain constant, but the mineral or material is replaced by another – a typical example is petrified wood. Florovsky took the term from the German historian and philosopher Oswald Spengler (1880–1936), especially his book *The Decline of the West* (*Der Untergang des Abendlandes*) (1918–23), in which Spengler puts forth a cyclical theory of the rise and decline of civilizations. In Spengler's historiography, pseudomorphosis refers to 'those cases in which an older alien Culture lies so massively over the land that a young Culture, born in this land, cannot get its breath and fails not only to achieve pure and specific expression-forms, but even to develop fully its own self-consciousness.'[36] The 'young Culture' takes on the 'form' of the 'older alien Culture', thereby preventing it from achieving its full potential. For Florovsky, the concept of pseudomorphosis aptly characterized Russian theology, beholden to various forms of Western thought, from scholasticism to the Reformation, the Counter-Reformation, pietism, Protestant mysticism, esoteric sects, Free-Masonry, romanticism and last but far from least, various forms of German philosophy, especially idealism. Already in the early 1920s, Florovsky considered that Russian theology, in seeking to imitate or to adopt key ideas and modes of thought from one or another or several Western theologies or philosophies, had strayed from the real basis of Orthodox thought, the theology of the Fathers. This line of thought formed the basis of his 'Western Influences in Russian Theology' and *The Ways of Russian Theology*: 'The Orthodox were compelled to think in categories foreign to their essence and to articulate themselves using non-customary terms and concepts.'[37]

Florovsky's second paper, only a few pages long, 'Patristics and Modern Theology', delivered in English, can be considered the first explicit 'manifesto' of neopatristic theology as Florovsky conceived it.[38] If 'Western Influences in Russian Theology' represented the critical, negative side of Florovsky's thought, 'Patristics and Modern Theology' constitutes the positive side: how Orthodox theology can recover its true foundations in the almost-forgotten writings of the Fathers.

In the following year, 1937, two publications further demarcated the dividing line between the two principal strands of theology represented in the Parisian Russian community. Florovsky's *The Ways of Russian Theology* is a masterly but highly opinionated history of Russian thought up to the beginning of the First World War. Florovsky's thesis is that Russian religious thought was largely dominated by non-Orthodox influences, both methodological and doctrinal, from the time of Peter Mogila onwards and he finds Western influence just about everywhere. Only a few Russian religious thinkers, such as Alexei Khomiakov and Metropolitan Philaret of Moscow, get passing

[35]Georges Florovsky, 'Westliche Einflüsse in des Russischen Theologie' (Western influences in Russian theology), *Kyrios*, 2, 1 (1937). English translation in Gallaher and Ladouceur, eds., *The Patristic Witness of Georges Florovsky*, 129–51.

[36]Oswald Spengler, *The Decline of the West* , vol. II (1922) (London: George Allen & Unwin, 1928), 189.

[37]Florovsky, 'Western Influences in Russian Theology', 141.

[38]Florovsky, 'Patristics and Modern Theology' (1937), in Gallaher and Ladouceur, eds., *The Patristic Witness of Georges Florovsky*, 153–7.

marks from Florovsky. Major figures of theological renewal and renaissance, notably Alexander Bukharev and Pavel Florensky, are strongly condemned. Sergius Bulgakov gets off rather lightly – Florovsky only considers Bulgakov's more philosophical writings prior to the revolution, not his major theological works published in exile. The conclusion of *The Ways of Russian Theology*, 'Breaks and Links', is an important milestone in the development of Florovsky's programme for a new direction in Orthodox theology. The book was poorly received in the Russian intellectual community in Paris, which mostly preferred to ignore it. Florovsky, thick skinned as he was, never fully recovered from the negative reception of his chef d'oeuvre. Nicolas Berdyaev, for one, wrote a scathing and highly emotional review in the intellectual periodical *Put'*, which he edited.[39]

Also in 1937, the Saint Sergius Institute published a collection of eleven essays under the title *Living Tradition: Orthodoxy in the Modern World*.[40] Valliere describes the book as 'a summary of the theology of the Russian school', asserting the divine-human nature of tradition.[41] The book contains essays by the teaching staff of the Saint Sergius Institute, Florovsky excluded: Nicholas Afanasiev, Sergius Bulgakov, Anton Kartashev, Cyprian Kern, Georges Fedotov, Leon Zander and Basil Zenkovsky.[42] The title of the book showed that the leading members of the religious renaissance considered that their theology was based in tradition, including the teachings of the Fathers – perhaps an implicit response to the emerging neopatristic theology, which could not pretend to have a monopoly on tradition.[43]

The two books, *The Ways of Russian Theology* and *Living Tradition*, did not quite neutralize each other. Florovsky's *The Ways of Russian Theology*, despite its essentially polemical and negative approach, had far more influence on young aspiring theologians than *Living Theology*, which Valliere describes as representing 'the losing side of a bitter in-house debate'.[44]

While the Second World War slowed the promotion of the neopatristic approach to theology, it permitted a deepening of reflection on what such a theology really entails. The publication in 1944 of Vladimir Lossky's *The Mystical Theology of the Eastern Church*, apart from being a major publication in its own right, showed what neopatristic theology could look like in a major study. Written and initially published in French, Lossky's book grew out of a series of lectures delivered in Paris and was aimed essentially at a Western audience. It is a masterly and articulate presentation of the major themes of patristic theology, including the revival of the major neglected or 'lost' aspects of Orthodox theology: apophatic theology, the Palamite essence-energies distinction, theosis or

---

[39]Nicolas Berdyaev, 'Orthdoksiya i chelovechnost' (Orthodoxia and humanness), *Put'*, 53 (1937). Review of Georges Florovsky, *The Ways of Russian Theology* (Paris: YMCA-Press, 1937).

[40]*Zhivoe predanie: pravoslavie v sovremennosti* (Living Tradition: Orthodoxy in the Modern World) (Paris: YMCA-Press, 1937).

[41]Paul Valliere, *Modern Russian Theology: Bukharev, Soloviev, Bulgakov: Orthodox Theology in a New Key* (Grand Rapids, MI: Eerdmans, 2000), 384.

[42]The essays by Afanasiev, Bulgakov, Kern and Zander are translated in Michael Plekon, ed., *Tradition Alive: On the Church and the Christian Life in Our Time* (Lanham, MD: Rowman and Littlefield, 2003). Paul Valliere presents a summary of the main articles of *Zhivoe predanie* in *Modern Russian Theology*, 383–95.

[43]Paul Valliere characterizes the purpose of the book somewhat more narrowly, in negative terms: to oppose a theological proposition – 'that patristic theology should be the primary guide of Orthodox theology and Orthodox life which, as the authors believed, sanctioned the attack on Bulgakov and threatened to diminish the freedom and scope of Orthodox theologizing.' Valliere, *Modern Russian Theology*, 383.

[44]Valliere, *Modern Russian Theology*, 384.

deification as the aim of Christian life, and the intricate relationships among philosophy, theology and mysticism in Orthodoxy. Lossky's theology is not without its critics. Major critiques are that he exaggerates the tensions between East and West even in the patristic period, that he overemphasizes the apophatic approach, that he underemphasizes Christology, and that unduly separates the 'economy of the Son' and the 'economy of the Holy Spirit' in the world.[45]

Despite criticisms of aspects of Lossky's theology by both Orthodox and non-Orthodox theologians, by any accounts Lossky's book is a great classic and is likely the single most important and influential book of Orthodox theology of modern times. Rowan Williams describes the book as 'vastly influential'; Christos Yannaras writes that the Greek translation of *The Mystical Theology of the Eastern Church* in 1964 became 'a best-seller' and that it is 'one of the most influential Orthodox books of the twentieth century'; and Andrew Louth refers to it as 'virtually a handbook of the neopatristic synthesis'.[46] With the publication of Lossky's *Mystical Theology*, neopatristic theology reached a certain maturity and rapidly became the leading approach in Orthodox theology.

Sergius Bulgakov died in 1944. Although several major works, notably *The Bride of the Lamb* (on the church and eschatology), *The Philosophy of the Name* and his study on the Apocalypse, as well as his *Autobiographical Notes*, were published posthumously after the Second World War, his successors were not of his calibre and the type of speculative theology that he incarnated rapidly lost ground to neopatristic theology as the dominant mode of Orthodox theology. Leadership in Orthodox theology shifted from Paris to New York, as three major practitioners of the new approach left the Saint Sergius Institute to teach at the fledgling St Vladimir's Orthodox Theological Seminary in New York: Georges Florovsky in 1948; Alexander Schmemann in 1951 and John Meyendorff in 1959. Florovsky, as dean of St Vladimir's Seminary between 1948 and 1955, and subsequently as professor of theology at Harvard School of Divinity and at Princeton University, became the chief spokesman for neopatristic theology as a popular teacher, lecturer and writer – he wrote dozens of articles, but never published a full-length book after *The Ways of Russian Theology*.[47]

---

[45]For criticisms of Lossky's *Mystical Theology*, see John Zizioulas, 'The Church as Communion: A Presentation on the World Conference Theme', in Thomas F. Best and Günther Gassmann, eds., *On the Way to Fuller Koinonia: Official Report of the Fifth World Conference on Faith and Order* (Geneva: World Council of Churches Publications, 1994), 103–11; Georges Florovsky's review of the English translation of *The Mystical Theology* in *The Journal of Religion*, 38, 3 (2008), 207–8; Serge Verkhovskoy's review of *The Mystical Theology* in the *St Vladimir's Theological Quarterly*, 2, 2 (1958), 52–4; and Petros Vassiliadis, 'Greek Theology in the Making, Trends and Facts in the 80s – Vision for the 90s', *St Vladimir's Theological Quarterly*, 35, 1 (1991), 49–50.

[46]Rowan Williams, 'Eastern Orthodox Theology', in David Ford and Rachel Muers, eds., *The Modern Theologians: An Introduction to Christian Theology since 1918*, 3rd ed. (Oxford: Blackwell, 2005), 578; Christos Yannaras, *Orthodoxy and the West: Hellenic Self-Identity in the Modern Age* (Brookline, MA: Holy Cross Orthodox Press, 2006), 292; Andrew Louth, 'The Patristic Revival and Its Protagonists', in Mary B. Cunningham and Elizabeth Theokritoff, eds., *The Cambridge Companion to Orthodox Christian Theology* (Cambridge: Cambridge University Pres, 2008), 194.

[47]For a bibliography of Georges Florovsky, see Andrew Blane, ed., *Georges Florovsky: Russian Intellectual and Orthodox Churchman* (Crestwood, NY: St Vladimir's Seminary Press, 1993), 347–401. *The Collected Works of Georges Florovsky* (1972–89) in fourteen volumes contains a wide selection of his writings, but is nonetheless incomplete and the texts are 'often not reliable' (Blane, *Georges Florovsky*, 401; and Gallaher and Ladouceur, eds., 'Editorial Introduction', *The Patristic Witness of Georges Florovsky*, xvii). For secondary literature on Florovsky to 2013, see Matthew Baker, 'Bibliography of Literature on the Life and Work of Father Georges V. Florovsky', *Theologikon* (Veliko Turnovo) 2, 1 (2013), 253–331; earlier version: 'Bibliography of Literature on the Life and Work of Father Georges V. Florovsky', *Transactions of the Association of Russian-American Scholars in the USA*, 37 (2011–12), 473–547.

The neopatristic synthesis

Georges Florovsky first used the term 'neopatristic synthesis' in an article published in Swedish in 1947, and in a public address in English in 1948, at the formal beginning of the academic year of St Valdimir's Seminary in New York, published in 1949.[48] Although Florovsky often referred to his theology as a 'neopatristic synthesis', he never really completely clarified what he meant by this rather catchy name. The neopatristic synthesis is Florovsky's antidote to the *pseudomorphosis* or 'captivity' of Orthodox theology that he exposes so thoroughly in *The Ways of Russian Theology*. Theology based on the ancient Fathers was the only correct way for Orthodox theology, hence an alternative both to dry academic theology and to the speculative theology of the Russian religious renaissance. For Florovsky, both were 'tainted' by Western influences, but not the same ones: scholasticism for the first and German philosophy for the second.

It is peculiar that Florovsky should use the term 'synthesis' to describe the theological approach that he advocated. The term 'synthesis' (from the ancient Greek σύνθεσις σύν 'syn' 'with' and θέσις 'thesis' 'placing') refers generally to a process which combines together two or more pre-existing elements resulting in the formation of something new. In philosophy, the triad *thesis, antithesis, synthesis* refers to a dynamic thought process in which the *thesis* is an intellectual proposition, the *antithesis* the negation of the thesis, a reaction to the proposition, and finally the *synthesis* resolves the conflict between the thesis and antithesis by reconciling their common truths and forming a new proposition. The philosophical triad thesis-antithesis-synthesis is often but incorrectly associated with Hegel and with the dialectical materialism of Marxism-Leninism, but Florovsky no doubt had in mind the common semantic meaning when he adopted the term 'synthesis' to describe his theological method.

For Florovsky, as for the history of Christian thought in general, the *patristic synthesis* involved on the one hand biblical revelation and on the other, Greek philosophy. But neither in his references to the 'patristic synthesis' nor even to 'neopatristic synthesis' was Florovsky using the word 'synthesis' in its strict philosophical, especially Hegelian sense, but rather as an approximate synonym for 'system' – a unified and consistent theological project. Thus revelation and philosophy are not dialectical opposites, but rather two poles of a continuum, ways of knowing God. The patristic synthesis is thus Judeo-Christian revelation explored, expressed and made comprehensible, to the extent possible, in Christianized Hellenic terms. This synthesis resulted in Christian theology. Thus Florovsky describes patristic theology as 'the traditional synthesis', 'the Christian synthesis' and 'the Hellenic synthesis'.[49] The Fathers adopted no particular philosophical tradition, but they 'attempted a new philosophical synthesis on the basis of the revelation' and they 'linked the divine message they had to deliver with the aspirations of the Hellenic mind'. Philosophy is then

---

[48]Georges Florovsky, '*In Ligno Crucis*: Kyrkofädernas Lära om Försoningen, Tolkad från den Grekisk-ortodoxa Teologiens Synpunkt', *Svensk Teologisk Kvartalskrift*, 23 (1947). English translation: '*In Ligno Crucis*: The Church Fathers' Doctrine of Redemption', in Gallaher and Ladouceur, eds., *The Patristic Witness of Georges Florovsky*, 71–9; and 'The Legacy and the Task of Orthodox Theology' (1949), in Gallaher and Ladouceur, eds., *The Patristic Witness of Georges Florovsky*, 185–91.

[49]Georges Florovsky, 'Patristics and Modern Theology', and 'Breaks and Links', Conclusion to *The Ways of Russian Theology*, in Gallaher and Ladouceur, eds., *The Patristic Witness of Georges Florovsky*, 153–7; 159–83.

understood as 'simply the vocation of the human mind to apprehend the ultimate Truth, now revealed and consummated in the incarnate Word'.[50]

In his provocative but prophetic conclusion, 'Breaks and Links', to *The Ways of Russian Theology*, Florovsky sets out five major characteristics of the 'new theology' that he is advocating:

1. *The recovery of the 'patristic style' in Orthodox theology*, not the letter of patristic teachings but the spirit of the Fathers: 'The road "to the Fathers" in any case leads only forward, never back. The point is to be true to the patristic *spirit*, rather than to the *letter* alone.' Florovsky was well aware of potential danger of merely restating the words of the Fathers, a 'theology of repetition', and he frequently came back to the theme of the need to acquire the 'style' or the 'spirit' or the 'mind' of the Fathers, rather than merely repeating what they said.
2. *The need for 'catholic consciousness' in Orthodox theology*: Personal consciousness acquires 'the ability and the power to perceive and express the consciousness and life of the whole. This kind of "catholic transfiguration" can occur only in the conciliarity [*sobornost'*] of the church.' Here Florovsky picks up the creedal notion of the catholicity of the church, drawing on the Slavophile-religious philosophy term *sobornost'*, contrasting this with 'individualism' and 'one's private niche'. Florovsky is in effect asserting that theology must be conducted in the church, for the church and as a reflection of the testimony and tradition of the church.
3. *Theology must take place in the context of history*: 'Theological consciousness must become *historical* consciousness and can attain catholicity only to the extent of its historicity. … A keen sense of history is a mandatory qualification for any theologian. … To theologise in the church is to theologise in the historical mode, because the life of the church (*tserkovnost'*) is, in fact, Holy Tradition.' The 'history' of which Florovsky speaks includes both the history of salvation but also, and perhaps more importantly in this context, the history of the church, including of course the role and thinking of the Fathers in shaping the doctrine and life of the church.
4. *Orthodox theology must be fundamentally Hellenistic*: 'Russian theological thought must yet be rigorously schooled in Christian Hellenism. Hellenism can be said to have become a perpetual dimension of the church, having been incorporated into the very fabric of church life as an eternal category of Christian existence.' Florovsky's insistence on theological Hellenism allows him to critique theologies employing other schools of Christian thought and modern philosophies, particularly idealism, which could distort or even falsify authentic Christian theology.
5. *Orthodox theology has an ecumenical responsibility*: 'Orthodoxy is summoned to witness. … And Orthodox theology is called upon to show that the 'ecumenical question' can only be resolved in the fulfilment of the church, within the totality of a catholic tradition,

---

[50]Florovsky, 'Preface to *In Lingo Crucis*' (1939), in Gallaher and Ladouceur, eds., *The Patristic Witness of Georges Florovsky*, 68.

> uncontaminated and inviolable, yet ever renewed and ever growing.' This implies going beyond mere rejection of undesirable Western influences and replacing them with the true patristic foundations of theology; this 'purified' Orthodox theology must return to the West in order to 'bear witness' to Orthodox theology as the authentic Christian theology. This formed the basis of Florovsky's ecumenical vision. Although he was committed to Christian unity, he was realistic about the obstacles, primarily dogmatic, that stood in the way of unity and hence he emphasized 'Orthodox testimony': 'An Orthodox theologian must bring his testimony to this world as well, a testimony drawn from the reservoirs of the church's inner memory.'[51]

Florovsky's address at the formal opening of the 1948–9 academic year of St Vladimir's Seminary and Academy in November 1948 brings further precision to his concept of neopatristic synthesis. Following up on the fifth theme from 'Breaks and Links', Florovsky places Orthodox theology squarely in an ecumenical context, stressing that Christian East and Christian West 'have the same ancestry and the same historical roots, and have succeeded to the same parental society, Hellenic and Roman'. They are in fact 'sister civilisations', 'Siamese twins', 'fragments of a disrupted world and they belong together despite the Schism'. He goes on to sketch out the role of Orthodox theology in the context of a broad ecumenical patristic revival and reiterates in particular the need to avoid both 'servile repetition of the patristic letter' and 'biblical fundamentalism'.[52]

Behind Florovsky's rhetoric lies a profound conviction of the relevance of patristic theology to the problems of the modern world. This represents a refinement of the conviction that Orthodoxy could and must fruitfully dialogue with the modern world as articulated by Alexander Bukharev and the contributors to *Problems of Idealism* (1902), *Vekhi* (1909), *De Profundis* (1918) and *Living Tradition* (1937).[53] Florovsky was sympathetic to the efforts of Catholic theologians of the 'modernist' movement to make the church more relevant to the modern world, and to the objectives of the religious philosophers. In his 1948 address Florovsky was considerably kinder to the theologians and philosophers of the Russian religious renaissance than many of his often severe judgements in *The Ways of Russian Theology*, even going so far as to refer to their 'noble endeavour and a daring and courageous one', and calling on his listeners 'to walk in their steps', even while not endorsing 'their findings and speculations'.[54] This part of his address remains a largely isolated attempt by Florovsky to bridge the gap between his neopatristic theology and the religious renaissance. In any case, within a decade religious philosophy had become largely irrelevant to contemporary Orthodox theology.

In a paper delivered in 1959 at the Faith and Order Orthodox Consultation in Kifissia, Greece, Florovsky spoke at some length about the neopatristic synthesis – again, without clearly defining

---

[51]All citations from Georges Florovsky, 'Breaks and Links', in Gallaher and Ladouceur, eds., *The Patristic Witness of Georges Florovsky*, 159–83.

[52]All citations from Florovsky, 'The Legacy and the Task of Orthodox Theology', in Gallaher and Ladouceur, eds., *The Patristic Witness of Georges Florovsky*, 185–91.

[53]See Ch. 4, 80–83; and 107 in this chapter.

[54]Florovsky, 'The Legacy and Task of Orthodox Theology,' 190.

how he conceived it.[55] He does, nonetheless, make some key points which assist in understanding his conception of the neopatristic synthesis. In the first place, the conciliar phrase 'following the Holy Fathers' is legitimate because the church, in addition to being '*Apostolic*' is also '*patristic*': 'And only by being "*patristic*" is the church continuously "*Apostolic*".' He goes on:

> The Fathers testify to the Apostolicity of the tradition. There are two basic stages in the proclamation of the Christian faith. *Our simple faith had to acquire composition*. There was an inner urge, an inner logic, an internal necessity, in this transition – from *kerygma* to *dogma*. Indeed, the *dogmata* of the Fathers are essentially the same 'simple' *kerygma*, which had been once delivered and deposited by the apostles, once, for ever.
>
> 'The mind of the Fathers' is an intrinsic term of reference in Orthodox theology, no less than the word of the Holy Writ, and indeed never separated from it. The Fathers themselves were always servants of the Word, and their theology was intrinsically exegetical.[56]

Thus the core of Florovsky's theological methodology consists in 'acquiring the mind of the Fathers' – *ad mentem Patrum*:

> It is utterly misleading to single out certain propositions, dogmatic or doctrinal, and to abstract them from the total perspective in which only they are meaningful and valid. It is a dangerous habit just to handle 'quotations', from the Fathers and even from the Scripture, outside of the total structure of faith, in which only they are truly alive. 'To follow the Fathers' does not mean simply to quote their sentences. It means *to acquire their mind*, their *phronema*.

But he does not indicate further what 'acquiring the mind of the Fathers' actually means – beyond the notion that the teachings of the Fathers are essentially the *kerygma* of the apostles 'properly articulated and developed into a consistent body of correlated testimonies'.

He gives two other basic indications in this text. The first is a reply to the question 'Who are the Fathers?' Referring to St Jerome's remark that the Spirit breathes in all ages, Florovsky mentions some later Fathers, but he does not venture past Gregory Palamas, although he does state that '"the age of the Fathers" still continues alive in the "Worshipping Church"'. Another component of the 'mind of the Fathers' is a strong emphasis on Christ: 'The synthesis must begin with the central vision of the Christian faith: Christ Jesus, as God and Redeemer, Humiliated and Glorified, the Victim and the Victor on the Cross.' Much of Florovsky's theology is strongly Christological. Among Florovsky's specific critiques of Pavel Florensky is that his *The Pillar and Ground of the Truth* (1913) does not contain a chapter on Christ and Florovsky claimed that he influenced Bulgakov to write a book on Christ.[57]

---

[55]All quotations here and following from Florovsky, 'The Ethos of the Orthodox Church' (1960), in Gallaher and Ladouceur, eds., *The Patristic Witness of Georges Florovsky*, 289–302.

[56]In appearing to place 'the mind of the Fathers' on the same footing as Scripture, Florovsky is treading on thin ice; some further clarification is certainly required here.

[57]Florovsky, *The Ways of Russian Theology*, II:278–9. Bulgakov's book on Christ is of course *The Lamb of God* (1933), which turned out to be the wolf in the sheepfold in the Sophia controversy.

Acquiring the patristic mind

Clearly Florovsky was well aware of potential danger of merely restating the words of the Fathers, a 'theology of repetition', as he often disparagingly described it, and hence his emphasis on 'acquiring the mind of the Fathers'. Some modern Orthodox theology is in fact a 'theology of repetition', an informed and often useful collation and analysis of writings of the Fathers on this or that subject, but this does not characterize the more creative end of the neopatristic theology, as we will see in later chapters. Florovsky certainly had in mind more than the mere repetition of the original deposit of the faith contained in revelation as expressed in classical patristic times; the neopatristic synthesis was much more than a restatement of patristic teaching in modern language. If neopatristic theology were only this, then good translations of the writings of the Fathers would surely do the trick, or at best a contemporary restating of patristic theology. The neopatristic synthesis also means more than dealing with the same issues that the Fathers faced, but with better tools, such as better biblical texts and critical editions of the works of the Fathers themselves. In 1936 Florovsky had said:

> This call to '*go back*' to the Fathers can be easily misunderstood. It does not mean a return *to the letter* of old patristic documents. To follow in the steps of the Fathers does not mean *jurare in verba magistri* [to swear by the words of the masters]. What is really meant and required is not a blind or servile imitation and repetition, but rather a further *development* of this patristic teaching, both homogenous and congenial. We have to kindle again the creative fire of the Fathers, to restore in ourselves *the patristic spirit*.[58]

In his 'theological will' some forty years later, he says of the neopatristic synthesis:

> In the first two years of my professorship in Paris I read systematically the works of the major Fathers, partly in original, partly in translations. I studied primary sources before I turned to the learned literature. It is probably for that reason that I appear to be so much 'old-fashioned'. I did not start with the 'higher criticism', and for that reason was never confused or corrupted by it. But, for the same reason, I was immunized forever against the routine, against that 'theology of repetition' which is addicted simply to archaic forms and phrases, but so often misses completely the quickening spirit. Fathers have taught me Christian Freedom. They were more than simply legislators, they were true prophets, in the true sense of this word – they beheld the mystery of God. (They were first of all men of insight and faith.) They were men of God, seers. It is by that way that I was led quite early to the idea of what I am calling now 'the neopatristic synthesis'. It should be more than just a collection of patristic sayings or statements. It must be a *synthesis*, a creative reassessment of those insights which were granted to the Holy Men of old. It must be *patristic*, faithful to the spirit and vision of the Fathers, *ad mentem Patrum*. Yet, it must be also *neo*-patristic, since it is to be addressed to the new age, with its own problems and queries.[59]

---

[58]Florovsky, 'Patristics and Modern Theology', 155.

[59]Georges Florovsky, '"Theological Will"', in Gallaher and Ladouceur, eds., *The Patristic Witness of Georges Florovsky*, 242. The original is from Andrew Blane, 'A Sketch of the Life of Georges Florovsky', in Blane, ed., *Georges Florovsky*, 153–4.

Florovsky clearly saw the necessity for Orthodox theology to address the 'problems and queries of the new age', the modern world, modernity and modernism. On this, the religious philosophers would agree wholeheartedly: This was essentially their project from the beginning, from the time that Alexander Bukharev, by his life and writings, first challenged the Church of Russia to come to grips with modern society, to the religious renaissance itself, which advanced Christian perspectives on the future of Russia.

The conclusion of this exploration is that Florovsky's 'neopatristic synthesis' does not refer to a 'synthesis' in a dialectical sense, but rather it is a broad theological methodology, the application of patristic theology – the 'patristic mind', as Florovsky liked to refer to it, – to modern problems.

Since Florovsky never spelled out what actually constitutes the 'patristic mind', some interpret it as an equivalent of *consensus patrum,* to which Florovsky also often referred.[60] While some of Florovsky's statements about 'the mind of the Fathers' may lend themselves to this reading, he himself noted differences between the Fathers on certain issues, between Alexandria and Antioch on a range of issues, between Cyprian and Augustine on the church, between Augustine and the Cappadocians on the Trinity.[61] The internal coherence of Florovsky's thinking suggests that he meant 'learning to theologise like the Fathers', not merely 'to quote the Fathers', to engage in a 'theology of repetition' that he frequently warned against; Florovsky's notion of the patristic mind is more than a *consensus patrum*, however this nebulous concept may be defined.

Neopatristic theology in an ecumenical context

Parallel with the emerging patristic turn in Orthodox theology was a similar movement in Catholic theological circles, a delayed fallout from the modernist controversy which shook the Roman Catholic Church in the late nineteenth and early twentieth centuries. Catholic modernism was a belated response to Enlightenment rationalism in both philosophy and science, with battle lines drawn particularly around a rational approach to Scripture, along the lines of nineteenth-century biblical criticism. Other departures from conventional Catholic theology would open the door, it was argued, to relativism and change in such areas as essential dogma, ecclesiology and morals. Rome came up with the term 'modernism' to cover a host of intellectual challenges arising in Catholic circles, especially in France, England and Italy, and associated it with opposition to European philosophical, theological and political liberalism, evolution and a host of other related

[60]This is, for example, John Behr's interpretation of what Florovsky meant by 'the mind of the Fathers': 'The point is not to quote the Fathers, but to acquire their mind. Their particular differences are not ignored, but neither are they in view: it is the consensus of the Fathers, their *phronema*, that is important. Any differences between them are also likewise elided: differences are recognized, but the particular voice of each Father is not important, for what alone is "authoritative and binding" is their consensus, expressing "the mind of the Catholic and Universal Church".' John Behr, 'Passing Beyond the Neo-Patristic Synthesis', paper delivered at the conference on 'Patristic or "Post-Patristic" Theology: Can Orthodox Theology Be Contextual?' Volos, Greece, 3–6 July 2010.

[61]See for example Florovsky's review of Lossky's *The Mystical Theology of the Eastern Church, in Journal of Religion*, 38, 3 (1958), 207.

evils creeping into Catholic thought. Rome condemned modernist thinking as early as 1864 and more explicitly as 'the synthesis of all heresies' by Pope Pius X in 1907, subsequently requiring Catholic theologians to take an anti-modernist oath.

The anti-modernist campaign accelerated the revival of medieval scholasticism already underway in Catholic circles. This neo-scholasticism (or neo-Thomism), which in its extreme form insisted on a rigid adherence to the thought and methods of Thomas Aquinas, resembled the dry academic theology predominant in Russia and other countries of Orthodox tradition until well into the twentieth century. More progressive Catholic theologians, especially in France, unable to turn to modern thought for inspiration, and aware of the constraints of scholastic theology, sought safe refuge in historical theology, and more specifically in the Greek Fathers, long neglected in Catholic thought. It was in this context that they encountered the interest among Russian theologians in the Fathers. While the modernist tendencies within the Catholic Church could have some parallels with aspects of Russian religious thought prior to the First World War, the 'return to the sources', biblical and patristic, in Catholic circles was closer to the return to patristic thought in Orthodox circles in the 1920s and 1930s. The movement within the Catholic Church became known as *ressourcement* (literally here 'resourcing'; in the context, seeking theological inspiration in the ancient Fathers, not only in the medieval scholastics). After the Second World War its critics and detractors pejoratively called the movement *nouvelle théologie*, implying a departure from accepted Catholic theology, defined in the neo-scholastic mode. To conservative Catholics, *ressourcement* looked like a latter-day revival of modernism in a different garb and Pope Pius XII condemned the *nouvelle théologie* in his 1950 encyclical *Humani generis*. Subsequently, several of the key *ressourcement* leaders, including the Dominican Yves Congar (1904–95) and the Jesuit Henri de Lubac (1896–1991), both future cardinals, were forbidden to teach and their works were withdrawn from seminary libraries. But the censorship and banishment of the *ressourcement* leaders did not last long: by the early 1960s the wind was blowing in a different direction in the Catholic Church and the leaders of the *nouvelle théologie* were not only rehabilitated, but also became leading lights of the Second Vatican Council (1962–65), which opened the windows (if not the doors) of the Catholic Church to the outside world.[62]

Nicolas Berdyaev, indefatigable initiator of philosophical-theological discussion groups, launched a Religious-Philosophical Academy in Berlin in 1922, a reconstitution of similar undertakings in Saint Petersburg and then in Moscow. The Academy, also known as the 'Berdyaev Colloquium', transferred with him to Paris in 1924. This loose gathering soon became a lively ecumenical forum for Orthodox, Catholics and Protestant philosophers and theologians. The main Orthodox participants were Berdyaev; Bulgakov; Florovsky; Boris Vysheslavtsev (1877–1954), professor of philosophy at the Saint Sergius Institute; Myrrha Lot-Borodine (1882–1957), medievalist and scholar of Orthodox mysticism and spirituality; and Basil Zenkovsky (1881–1962), professor of philosophy at the Saint Sergius Institute. While Berdyaev and Bulgakov were leaders of the Orthodox contingent, others, such as Lot-Borodine, made important contributions to the

[62]Studies on *ressourcement*/*nouvelle théologie* are contained in Gabriel Flynn and Paul D. Murray, eds., *Ressourcement: A Movement for Renewal in Twentieth-Century Catholic Theology* (Oxford: Oxford University Press, 2012).

colloquium. Myrrha Lot-Borodine, who came to France initially for studies in 1906, completed her doctorate in medieval literature and married the distinguished French medieval historian Ferdinand Lot (1866–1952). She became interested in patristic theology and delivered major papers, subsequently published, in the Berdyaev colloquia on the patristic doctrine of deification, the *Mystagogia* of Maximus the Confessor and on Nicolas Cabasilas.[63]

The Catholic participants initially included both representatives of the neo-Thomist stream and some who emerged in the *ressourcement* movement: Jacques Maritain (1882–1973), a leading neo-Thomist philosopher; Gabriel Marcel (1889–1973); Charles du Bos (1882–1939); Lucien Laberthonnière (1860–1932); occasionally Jules Lebreton (1873–1956); Étienne Gilson (1884–1978), with Maritain, a major neo-Thomist; and Édouard Le Roy (1870–1954). Leaders of French Protestantism were Marc Boegner (1881–1970), long-time president of the Protestant Federation of France; Wilfred Monod (1867–1943), professor at the Faculty of Protestant Theology in Paris; and Pierre Maury (1890–1956), translator of Barth. Discussions in the group constituted 'at once an encounter and a confrontation', as Florovsky recalled years later, and 'confrontation was often rather sharp and heated, but always in the spirit of mutual respect and confidence'.[64] After a few years the Vatican objected to theological discussions involving Catholics and Protestants, but the group continued privately in Berdyaev's home with only Orthodox and Catholics.

Berdyaev's colloquium was Georges Florovsky's first involvement in an ecumenical group. Florovsky, a junior participant in these discussions, nonetheless presented as papers 'the first specimens of his "neopatristic synthesis"': 'Creation and Createdness' (published in Russian in 1928); 'Of the Death on the Cross' (1930); the first version of 'Revelation, Philosophy and Theology' (1931); and 'Mysticism and Liturgy' (unpublished).[65] In the late 1920s and 1930s, Florovsky was in dialogue with Anglicans through the Fellowship of St Alban and Saint Sergius, founded in 1928 to promote understanding and progress towards unity between Orthodox and Anglicans, and with Protestants in the context especially of the great international gatherings of the 1930s which preceded the establishment of the World Council of Churches (WCC) in 1948. Again, Florovsky was at first a junior Orthodox participant, overshadowed by senior figures such as Metropolitan Evlogy and Sergius Bulgakov, in both the Fellowship and the Faith and Order conferences, but he soon came into his own because of the attractiveness of his theological programme founded on Scripture and the Fathers, the force of his personality and his command of English and German.

Florovsky also had contacts with major Protestant theologians, partly on a personal basis and partly through his ecumenical activities. In June 1931 Florovsky participated in Karl Barth's

---

[63]Myrrha Lot-Borodine, *Un Maître de la spiritualité byzantine au XIVe siècle: Nicolas Cabasilas* (A Byzantine Spiritual Master of the 14th Century: Nicholas Cabasilas) (Paris: L'Orante, 1958) (articles published between 1935 and 1953); *La Déification de l'homme selon la doctrine des pères grecs* (The Deification of Man according to the Doctrine of the Greek Fathers) (Paris: Les Éditions du Cerf, 1970) (articles published in 1932–3). Her translation of Maximus' *Mystagogia* was published in *Irénikon*, 13, 14 and 15 in 1936–8). See Andrew Louth, *Modern Orthodox Thinkers: From the Philokalia to the Present* (London: SPCK, 2015), 94–6.

[64]Georges Florovsky, 'The Ecumenical Dialogue' (1964), in Gallaher and Ladouceur, eds., *The Patristic Witness of Georges Florovsky*, 303.

[65]George H. Williams, 'Georges Florovsky: His American Career (1948-1965)', *Greek Orthodox Theological Review*, 11, 1 (1965), 32.

seminar at the University of Bonn, where he presented his seminal paper on 'Revelation, Philosophy and Theology'.[66] Barth was a leader in the post-First World War movement in Protestant theology variously called crisis theology, dialectical theology and even neo-orthodoxy. A Protestant *ressourcement* in the wake of the carnage of the Great War, the core of this movement involved a rejection of certain aspects of liberal Protestantism of the nineteenth century, which was heavily influenced by Enlightenment rationalism, and a return to the biblical and Reformation basis of Protestantism, as distinct from a return to patristic sources characteristic of the contemporaneous movements in Orthodox and Catholic theological milieus. Florovsky and Barth had major theological differences and their first encounter ended in 'manifest mutual disagreement'.[67] Their disagreements revolved around the relationship of revelation, philosophy and theology, the present significance of eschatology and its relation to history, the nature of the church, the role of human agency in salvation and the use of analogy and apophatism in theology.[68] Barth was unimpressed by Florovsky's commitment to patristic theology as the legitimate foundation of Christian theology. Yet despite their theological differences, Florovsky and Barth collaborated in the ecumenical movement; both are among the founders of the WCC and played important roles notably at the Amsterdam conference of 1948 and the Evanston conference of 1954.

Some leaders of the neopatristic movement pursued other ecumenical paths. Beginning in the 1930s, Vladimir Lossky had frequent contacts with Catholic *ressourcement* theologians and philosophers in Paris. During the Second World War, he participated in colloquia organized by the well-known Catholic writer Marcel Moré (1887–1969). These meetings brought together a wide range of theologians and philosophers and it was here that Lossky delivered a series of lectures in 1944 on Orthodox mystical theology, published the same year under the title *Essai sur la théologie mystique de l'Église d'Orient*, his now classic *Mystical Theology of the Eastern Church*.

From these colloquia developed a periodical, *Dieu vivant: Perspectives religieuses et philosophiques*, founded in 1945 by Louis Massignon (Islamist; 1883–1962), Marcel Moré and the future Cardinal Jean Daniélou (1905–74). The Catholic intellectuals and theologians behind *Dieu vivant* represented a new voice in Catholic theology. *Dieu vivant* was a public expression of the patristic turn in Catholic theology and its orientation was decidedly eschatological, often on the fringes of, or even opposed to, official Catholic theology. From the start *Dieu vivant* was ecumenically oriented. The editorial committee, which reviewed manuscripts, consisted of a Catholic (Gabriel Marcel), a Protestant (the philosopher Pierre Burgelin, 1905–85), an Orthodox (Vladimir Lossky) and a non-believer (the philosopher Jean Hyppolite, 1907–68).[69] Lossky contributed an article on St Gregory

[66]First published as 'Offenbarung, Philosophie, und Theologie', in *Zwischen den Zeiten*, 9, 6 (Munich, 1931); translation in Gallaher and Ladouceur, eds., *The Patristic Witness of Georges Florovsky*, 115–27.

[67]Matthew Baker, '"*Offenbarung, Philosophie, und Theologie*": Karl Barth and Georges Florovsky in Dialogue', *Scottish Journal of Theology*, 68, 3 (2015), 300.

[68]Baker presents overviews of both theological differences and convergences between Florovsky and Barth. Convergences include opposition to a rejection of patristic Christology in neo-Protestant circles and to natural theology. Baker suggests that a close examination of both theologians reveals more congruity in their positions on some points of dispute than first meets the eye. See Baker, '"*Offenbarung, Philosophie, und Theologie*"', 325–6.

[69]For an overview of *Dieu vivant*, see Étienne Fouilloux, 'Une vision eschatologique du christianisme: *Dieu vivant* (1945-1955) (An eschatological vision of Christianity: *Dieu vivant* [1945–1955])', *Revue d'histoire de l'Église de France*, 57, 158 (1971).

Palamas to the first issue of *Dieu vivant* and published another major article in the journal in 1948.[70] During its short existence (1945–55), *Dieu vivant* was an influential if controversial periodical on the French intellectual scene. Other major Orthodox figures who published articles in the journal were Elisabeth Behr-Sigel (1907–2005), Paul Evdokimov (1900–70) and Myrra Lot-Borodine (1882–1957).

Vladimir Lossky also participated in the *Centre catholique des intellectuels français* (CCIF), founded clandestinely in 1941 by Catholic philosophers and historians as a meeting-place for French Catholic intellectuals to reflect on the place of Catholic Christianity in modern society and to take part in the great intellectual debates of the time. This group was especially active after the war and played an important role in the preparation of the Second Vatican Council. Open to the active participation of non-Catholics and non-believers, several Orthodox thinkers (Lossky, Paul Evdokimov and the iconographer Gregory Krug (1908–69)) were invited to take part in the discussions.[71] By participating in the CCIF, Lossky sought 'to identify in Western mystical movements those which are related to Eastern spirituality'[72] and 'to witness to the universality of Orthodoxy'.[73]

In 1939, Vladimir Lossky met Jean Wahl (1888–1974), a renowned French philosopher of Jewish origin, forced into exile during the Second World War. After the war, Lossky participated in the *Collège philosophique*, which Wahl founded in 1946 as a centre for non-conformist intellectuals, an alternative forum to the more conservative Sorbonne. Lossky was a regular participant in the *Collège philosophique*, contributing five major papers to its discussions.[74] In a similar vein, in 1945–46 Lossky gave a series of lectures on the vision of God in patristic and Byzantine theology at the *École pratique des hautes études*, a leading French secular institution for research and higher education affiliated with the Sorbonne.[75]

Although the Reformation doctrine of *sola scriptura* long put a damper on Protestant interest in the Fathers and patristic theology, it is noteworthy that the early landmarks of a 'patristic revival' in English-speaking Christianity were due to the efforts of Anglican, Episcopalian, German Reformed and Presbyterian theologians, who published two milestone collections of translations

---

[70]Lossky's articles in *Dieu vivant* were 'La théologie de la lumière chez saint Grégoire Palamas' (The theology of light in the thought of St Gregory Palamas), *Dieu vivant*, 1, 1945; and 'Du troisième attribut de l'Église' (Concerning the third mark of the church), *Dieu vivant*, 10, 1948 (translations in the posthumous collection *In the Image and Likeness of God* (Crestwood, NY: St Vladimir's Seminary Press, 1974)).

[71]Lossky participated in discussions of 'Transcendence and Negative Theology', 'Dogma and Mystery' and 'The Myth'.

[72]Claire Toupin-Guyot, *Les Intellectuels catholiques dans la société français* (Catholic Intellectuals in French Society) (Rennes: Presses universitaires de Rennes, 2015), § 44. http://books.openedition.org/pur/8731?lang=en (1 June 2017).

[73]Claire Toupin-Guyot, 'Modernité et Christianisme. Le Centre Catholique des intellectuels français (1941–1976). Itinéraire collectif d'un engagement' (Modernity and Christianity: The Centre Catholique des intellectuels français (1941–1976. Collective journey of a commitment)) (Doctoral thesis, Université Lumière-Lyon II, 2000), 56. http://theses.univ-lyon2.fr/documents/lyon2/2000/toupin_c#p=0&a=top (9 June 2017).

[74]Lossky's papers at the Collège philosophique were: 'Ténèbres et lumière dans la connaissance de Dieu'; (Darkness and light in the knowledge of God) 'L'apophase et la théologie trinitaire' (Apophasis and Trinitarian theology); 'La notion théologique de la personne' (The theological notion of the human person); 'La théologie de l'image' (The theology of the image); and 'La rose et l'abîme (la notion de l'être créé chez Maître Eckhart)' (The rose and the abyss (the notion of created being in Meister Eckhart)). All except the last are contained in *In the Image and Likeness of God*.

[75]These lectures were published in French in 1962 and in English as *The Vision of God* (London: The Faith Press, 1963; Crestwood, NY: St Vladimir's Seminary Press, 1983).

of major patristic texts between 1867 and 1900, the well-known *Ante-Nicene Fathers* (ANF) (10 volumes) and *Nicene and Post-Nicene Fathers* (NPNF) (28 volumes).[76]

An important manifestation of the patristic revival has been the publication of critical editions of patristic writings, of which the most extensive collection is the *Sources chrétiennes*, published by the Catholic Éditions du Cerf. *Sources chrétiennes* was launched in 1943 under the direction of the Jesuits Jean Daniélou and Henri de Lubac. Each volume contains the original text, with French translation on the facing page, a theological and technical introduction and detailed footnotes. The volumes cover both Greek and Latin Fathers and other ancient writings, such as the works of Philo of Alexandria. The collection is vast, with some 600 volumes published (2018). No works of Gregory Palamas have been published in *Sources chrétiennes* – perhaps because Palamite theology is still sensitive in some Catholic circles, but more practically, a critical edition of Palamas has been published in Greece, and English and French translations of several of his most important works were published by John Meyendorff and in the translations of the *Philokalia*.[77] The existence of *Sources chrétiennes* is vital for patristic studies, but Orthodox collaboration in the collecion itself has been minimal.[78] Other important collections of original patristic texts include the *Corpus Christianorum* published by Brepols (based in Belgium), with over 500 works (as of 2015) and the *Patrologia Orientalis*, launched in 1905 and now also published by Brepols, specializing in Oriental Christian texts (240 volumes as of 2015). There also are significant collections of translations of patristic writings in major European languages.[79]

A continuing manifestation of a broad ecumenical patristic revival are the International Conferences on Patristic Studies, which are held at Oxford every four years since 1951, with the regular publication of conference papers under the title *Studia patristica*. These conferences are credited for playing 'a central role in the spectacular flourishing of patristics for the rest of the [twentieth] century'.[80] The conferences bring together Catholic, Orthodox and Protestant scholars from around the world, with Orthodox scholars much in the minority.

In contrast with the *neo*-orthodox movement in Protestant theology in the post-Second World War period, the *paleo*-orthodox movement in the late twentieth-century Protestant circles, especially in the United States, is explicitly patristic, seeking the essentials of Christian theology in the theology of the church, the pronouncements of the Ecumenical Councils and the teachings of

---

[76]Alexander Roberts and James Donaldson, eds., *Ante-Nicene Christian Library* (Edinburgh: T&T Clark, 1867–73); reissued by A. Cleveland Coxe, ed., as *The Ante-Nicene Fathers* (Buffalo, NY and New York: Christian Literature Company, 1885–96), with volume 9 issued in Edinburgh by T&T Clark in 1897. Philip Schaff and Henry Wace, eds., *A Select Library of the Nicene and Post-Nicene Fathers of the Christian Church* (Edinburgh: T&T Clark; New York: Christian Literature Company, 1886–1900).

[77]The maturation of the Palamite revival in modern Orthodox thought will be considered in Ch. 8, 'The Restoration of Patristic Thought'.

[78]Orthodox theologians involved in the *Sources chrétiennes*, mostly in the writing of introductions and notes, include Hilarion Alfeyev (on Symeon the Pious, spiritual father of Symeon the New Theologian), Placide Deseille (on Guerric d'Igny, a medieval Cistercian author), Basil Krivoshein (on Symeon the New Theologian), Jean-Claude Larchet (on Maximus the Confessor) and Michel Stavrou (co-editor of a symposium on the Fathers of the Church and Europe).

[79]The major series of patristic works in English translation are *Oxford Early Christian Texts* (Oxford University Press); *The Fathers of the Church* (Catholic University of America Press); *Ancient Christian Writers: The Works of the Fathers in Translation* and *Classics of Western Spirituality* (Paulist Press); *Popular Patristics Series* (St Vladimir's Seminary Press).

[80]Charles Kannengiesser, *Handbook of Patristic Exegesis: The Bible in Ancient Christianity* (Leiden, NE: Brill, 2004), I:62.

the Fathers prior to the separation of Eastern and Western Christianity and the Reformation. This revival of patristic theology in several Protestant denominations owes a great deal to the discovery in evangelical circles that the ancient Fathers and councils were biblically based and that in fact a large portion of patristic writings are biblical commentaries. It is a re-insertion of a certain notion of 'tradition' into modern descendants of a movement founded on the *sola scriptura* doctrine. One of the outcomes of this movement is the series *Ancient Christian Commentary on Scripture* (twenty-nine volumes, 1998–2010), which brings together patristic commentaries on individual books of the Bible. Methodist paleo-orthodox theologian Thomas Oden (1931–2016), who had connections with Orthodox theologians, writes that he wants 'to begin to prepare the postmodern Christian community for its third millennium by returning again to the careful study and respectful following of the central tradition of classical Christianity',[81] and that he takes as his 'subject of advocacy not modern theological opinion about Christianity but the common faith of the ancient ecumenical church gathered repeatedly in general council in its first millennium, a *consensus fidelium* that understood itself to be grounded in the heart of early Christian scriptures'.[82] Such programmatic statements certainly echo Georges Florovsky's calls from the mid-1930s onwards for a return to patristic theology in Orthodoxy.

While the historical origins and denominational settings of Orthodox neopatristic theology, Catholic *nouvelle théologie* and Protestant neo-orthodox and paleo-orthodox movements are different and largely unrelated, these movements have some points in common, such as reaction against the continuing influence of Enlightenment rationalism, whether in the form of liberal Protestantism, German idealist philosophies or neo-scholasticism, and a desire to seek theological inspiration in the thinking of the Fathers of the first millennium, the period of the 'Undivided Church'.[83]

Conclusion

By the late 1920s a move towards a more patristically based theology began to emerge in Orthodox theological circles, mainly among a younger generation of theologians, primarily Russian, who had not been on the front line of the intellectual jousting that characterized the last decades of imperial Russia. The stimulus came from three directions: dissatisfaction with the dryness and weariness of spirit of official academic theology; growing unease and even outright opposition to what was perceived as excesses of the speculative theology of the Russian religious renaissance, with sophiology as the flashpoint; and the rediscovery of patristic apophatism, the Palamite theology of the divine energies and theosis. Palamite theology had been lost in the academic theology that

[81]Thomas C. Oden, *Agenda for Theology* (San Francisco, CA: Harper & Row, 1979), 31. See also Thomas C. Oden, *After Modernity … What? Agenda for Theology* (Grand Rapids, MI: Zondervan, 1990), 34.
[82]Oden, *Agenda for Theology*, 17; See also Oden, *After Modernity … What?*, 13–17, 37–8.
[83]From the title of Volume XIV of the series *Nicene and Post-Nicene Fathers*, edited by Philip Schaff and Henry Wace: *The Seven Ecumenical Councils of the Undivided Church*, first published in 1899.

dominated Orthodox theological education for several centuries and was under attack by Catholic theologians who argued that Palamism, if not actually heretical, bordered on heresy. The two strands, a broad return to patristic theology and the revival of Palamism, occurred in parallel with close interrelationships.

Of the main founding fathers of neopatristic theology, Georges Florovsky, Vladimir Lossky and Dumitru Staniloae, it was Florovsky who articulated the return to the Fathers as an explicit theological method and programme. Beginning in the mid-1930s, Georges Florovsky advanced a theological programme centred on a recovery of patristic theology. In broad terms, Florovsky saw a return to the theology of the Fathers as an antidote to both the sterility of academic theology detached from the life of the church and strongly influenced by Western scholasticism, and from the excessive speculations of religious philosophy, too indebted, in his view, to Western philosophies, especially German idealism, and venturing too far from the church's doctrines, the 'faith of the Fathers'.

Despite Florovsky's own repudiation and direct critique of what he considered to be the excessively personal, emotional and intuitive undertones of religious philosophy, his own personal experience in studying the Fathers in Paris in the 1920s and 1930s resulted in another form of intuition – the profound conviction that the Fathers and the Fathers alone, although almost exclusively the Greek Fathers (including Augustine!) – are the key to true Christian theology. And it was precisely this intuition which subsequently was seen as the Achilles's heel of the neopatristic synthesis, a weak point in Florovsky's theological project.

Although Florovsky spoke and wrote about his theological vision on a number of occasions, he never fully explained what he meant by the expressions 'neopatristic synthesis' and 'acquiring the mind of the Fathers' that he used to characterize his approach to theology. Nonetheless, based on the clues that Florovsky gave over the years as we have discussed above, the following elements appear to enter into Florovsky's notion of what constitutes the 'patristic mind': Scripture as the foundation of all theology; Christ as the centre of theological reflection; a historical awareness, both of the history of salvation as revealed in Scripture, and the history of the church; a 'catholic consciousness', theology in the context of the church; fidelity to the Hellenistic-Byzantine theological tradition; a focus on contemporary issues and problems; and the integration of theology with the prayer and sacramental life of the church – as Florovsky emphasized, the Fathers were 'Holy Men of Old', not only 'theologians' in the modern sense.[84]

To these notions of the 'patristic mind', Florovsky adds the ecumenical responsibility of Orthodox theology, as he sets out his programme in *The Ways of Russian Theology*: 'An Orthodox theologian must bring his testimony to this world as well, a testimony drawn from the reservoirs of the church's inner memory.'[85] In this light Orthodox involvement with theologians and churchmen of other denominations, Anglican, Catholic and Protestant, in the broad ecumenical patristic revival of the twentieth century has been very much in keeping with Georges Florovsky's insistence on the ecumenical vocation of Orthodox theology.

[84]See Georges Florovsky, '"Theological Will"', 242.
[85]Florovsky, 'Breaks and Links', 175.

Andrew Louth presents a somewhat different assessment of Florovsky's 'method of the neopatristic synthesis', based on Florovsky's introduction to the 1972 re-edition of his patristic manuals of the 1930s. Florovsky states that patristic literature must be studied both as ancient Christian literature and as the history of doctrine, 'a kind of Christian philosophy', with emphasis on 'the theological character of patrology'.[86] This indeed characterizes Florovsky's approach to patristics, but does not adequately cover Florovsky's constant emphasis on 'the acquisition of the patristic mind' as the fundamental trait of his conception of neopatristic theology. Later in Louth's text, he emphasizes 'the centrality of Christ' in Florovsky's theology in general and in his pursuit of the neopatristic synthesis in particular – one of the aspects of Florovsky's notion of 'the mind of the Fathers' that we highlighted above.[87]

Although Florovsky's vision of the patristic basis of theology set the tone for the development of much of Orthodox theology in the second half of the twentieth century, this does not mean that all theologians identified with neopatristic theology were somehow 'disciples' of Georges Florovsky. Indeed there are as many varieties of Orthodox theology during this period as there are theologians. Some theologians remained closer to Florovsky's vision than others, some were more comfortable than others with ideas arising from the Russian religious renaissance than others, and some tackled ideas and issues that had not featured in patristic times but are clearly relevant to an engagement of Orthodox thought with the modern world. Following the lead of the founders of neopatristic theology, especially Florovsky and Lossky, theologians in other major centres of Orthodox thought also adopted a patristic approach to theology. Most Orthodox theologians of the second half of the twentieth century loosely grouped under the neopatristic umbrella benefited from the insights of their predecessors among the Slavophiles and the leading philosopher-theologians of the Russian religious renaissance.

[86]Florovsky, 'Introduction', *Vostochnye ottsy IV-go veka* (The Eastern Fathers of the 4th Century) (reprint: Gregg International, 1972; original: Paris, 1931), quoted in Louth, *Modern Orthodox Thinkers*, 84.
[87]Louth, *Modern Orthodox Thinkers*, 92.

6

Theology Old and New in Greece

Chapter Outline

Academic theology in Greece

Prior to the 1960s, theology in Greece was dominated by the same type of academic theology that prevailed in Russia before the 1917 revolution, using the same formalistic approaches to theology based on Western theological models, especially scholasticism.[1] Aristotelian philosophy, medieval scholasticism and the humanistic spirit of the Renaissance in Western Europe began to make inroads in Byzantine society and learning even prior to the fall of Constantinople in 1453. Despite the triumph of the Palamite theology of the divine energies in the hesychast controversy of the mid-fourteenth century, Renaissance and Enlightenment thought penetrated deeply into Greek intellectual circles during the long Turkish occupation. Greek higher education was forbidden in the Ottoman Empire and Greeks wishing to do advanced studies were obliged to

[1]For an overview of Greek theology after Palamas, see Christos Yannaras, *Orthodoxy and the West: Hellenic Self-Identity in the Modern Age* (1992) (Brookline, MS: Holy Cross Orthodox Press, 2006). Yannaras's book is in many ways the Greek equivalent of Georges Florovsky's *The Ways of Russian Theology* (1937), with a similar intellectual programme: to expose and denounce Western influences in Greek thought and piety. Yannaras is just as opinionated as Florovsky, and indeed Yannaras is perhaps even more strident than Florovsky in his denunciation of Western thought. For a more academic but less illuminating study, see George Maloney, 'The History of Orthodox Theology among Greek-Speaking Churches', in Part II of his *History of Orthodox Theology since 1453* (Belmont, MA: Nordland, 1976), 89–210.

study in the West, which further increased Western influence on Greek theology. Theophilos Korydalleus (1570–1645), a noted Aristotelian scholar who studied in Italy, set Greek education in an Aristotelian-scholastic pattern that dominated for over two centuries. Korydalleus was sympathetic towards the Calvinism of Cyril Lucaris (1572–1638) and after the death of Lucaris, in 1639 Korydalleus delivered an impassioned defence of Lucaris. As in Russia with Peter Mogila (1596–1646) about the same time, under Korydalleus, theology in Greece was largely cut off from its biblical and patristic roots and was dominated by scholastic rationalism, with a disregard for the experiential and apophatic nature of patristic theology.

Eustratios Argenti (1687–c.1758) was a lay theologian of the early eighteenth century, known primarily for his polemical works against Catholicism, especially his *Manual Concerning Baptism* (c. 1755), published during a controversy provoked by Orthodox questioning, sustained by Argenti's work, of the validity of Latin baptism by aspersion. Vikentios Damodos (1700–52) wrote the first Greek manual of dogmatic theology in 1730, based on the *Dogmatica theologica* of the French Jesuit Denys Petau (1583–1652). This set the tone for other similar works in the eighteenth and nineteenth centuries. One effect of the Damodos manual and later ones was to reinforce the isolation of theology as essentially an intellectual undertaking, cut off from the experience and practice of the church. The basic structure, topics, methodology and even in some cases, dogmas, were based on or even copied from Western manuals of dogmatic theology, along the same lines as those produced in Russia in the nineteenth century.

Eugenius Bulgaris (Voulgaris) (1716–1806) was the most illustrious Greek theologian of the eighteenth century. After studies in theology, philosophy and European languages in Padua, in 1753 he was asked by the Patriarch of Constantinople, Cyril V, to establish an academy on Mount Athos, with the objective of raising the educational level of the monks. The Athonite Academy or *Athoniada* was situated at Vatopedi Monastery and attracted many students, but Bulgaris was forced to resign in 1759. Bulgaris, who translated Locke and Voltaire, was open to the ideas of the Enlightenment and he sought to promote an intellectual renaissance in Greek thought based on the Orthodox tradition, but bolstered by the Greek classics and also the new ideas of the Enlightenment. After his departure from Athos, he taught briefly at the Patriarchal Academy in Constantinople, then went to Leipzig and to Saint Petersburg, where Catherine the Great recruited him to take charge of her library. He spent the remainder of his life in Russia. Bulgaris was also one of the initiators of a linguistic reform which aimed to produce a 'purified' Greek by introducing elements of classical Greek into the contemporary vernacular language or demotic Greek. This eventually resulted in the formation of *katharevousa* Greek, which became the official language of the independent Greek state and of Greek scholarship.

Greek independence in 1833 reinforced the cleavage between school theology and the church and faithful. The Faculty of Theology of the University of Athens was founded in 1837 and that of Thessalonica a century later, in 1941, but the inspiration was the same. From the beginning, schools of theology were copied from Protestant German models, isolated from the life of the church and the faith of the people; theology was an academic subject like any other. But for much of the nineteenth century the staff of the Athens Faculty of Theology consisted of only one or two professors, with a handful of students, so its actual impact on the church in Greece was limited. Only after 1900 did the teaching staff and student body in theology expand. For the first century of the Faculty, all of the theology professors, almost all laymen, did higher studies in Germany, except for two who studied in Russia.

St Nectarius of Aegina (Anastasius Kephalas, 1846–1920) studied at the Athens Faculty of Theology from 1882 to 1885, with the support of Patriarch Sophronius IV of Alexandria. Despite the scholastic inspiration of the theology taught at the Faculty, Nectarius made good use of his theological training throughout his life, especially in his sermons and numerous books and pamphlets. Nectarius was fully grounded in the life of the church, and from 1894 to 1908 he headed the Rizarios Ecclesiastical School in Athens, established in 1844 for training priests. His writings are nonetheless often marked by a certain formalism and dryness characteristic of scholastic philosophy and theology.[2]

The dominant figure in Greek theology for most of the twentieth century was Christos Androutsos (1869–1935), who taught at the University of Athens from 1912 until 1935. Androutsos authored books on a wide range of philosophical and theological subjects ranging from ancient Greek philosophy to modern thinkers such as Fredrich Nietzsche, Sigmund Freud and Henri Bergson. But it was his *Dogmatics of the Eastern Orthodox Church* (1907) which set the tone for Greek theology for a good part of the twentieth century. Androutsos sets out to provide a strong philosophical basis for theology, using Orthodox dogmas 'as sources and norms for speculation while using human reason to strengthen the defined dogmas'.[3] Despite his good intentions, Androutsos, like his predecessors in Greece and elsewhere, was nonetheless inspired by a rational rather than a mystical and liturgical approach to theology, and he follows the typical scholastic structure of treatises of dogmatic theology, examining successively God, creation, providence, the world, humanity, original sin, salvation, the Incarnation, Christ, grace, the sacraments and eschatology. Like his predecessors in the eighteenth and nineteenth centuries, Androutsos found his inspiration mainly in Western treatises rather than the Orthodox tradition. Nonetheless, his *Dogmatics* had a powerful impact on theological education in Greece for well over half a century, and was, as Christos Yannaras (b. 1935) reluctantly admits, 'considered in Greece as the authentic formulation of Orthodox dogmatic teaching'.[4] Yannaras sees Androutsos's *Dogmatics* as prime example of the 'Western captivity' of Greek theology: 'His *Dogmatics* is typical: the culmination of the unconscious process of the Westernization of Greek scholars that had begun in the fourteenth century … On every page scholasticism masquerades as "Orthodox" dogmatics.'[5] Non-Orthodox aspects of Androutsos's theology include the experiential inaccessibility of dogma, which is subject only to rational clarification; emphasis on the divine essence rather than the divine Persons;

[2]Very little of St Nectarius's abundant writings has been translated. Selected passages are contained in Constantine Cavarnos, *St. Nectarius of Aegina* (Belmont MA: Institute for Byzantine and Modern Greek Studies, 1988), 154–87, and in St Nectaire d'Égine, *Lettres pastorales aux moniales d'Égine* (Pastoral Letters to the Nuns of Aegina) (Bagnolet, FR: Lis et parle, 2011).

[3]Maloney, *A History of Orthodox Theology since 1453*, 197.

[4]Christos Yannaras, 'Theology in Present-Day Greece', *St Vladimir's Theological Quarterly*, 17, 4 (1972), 199.

[5]Yannaras, 'Theology in Present-Day Greece', 200; *Orthodoxy and the West*, 203–4. In these and other comments on Greek academic theology, Yannaras does not utilize Florovsky's term 'pseudomorphosis', but the rhetorical intent is the same.

absence of the distinction between the divine essence and divine energies and acceptance of the juridical notion of salvation, based on Anselm of Canterbury. Androutsos's approach to faith is simultaneously emotional and rational, in which revelation plays only a supporting role. He writes on the one hand that faith is 'the sentiment by which man experiences and acknowledges the presence of God in the natural and moral world', yet at the same time.

> The comprehension of dogmas is given to the intellect. The more devoutly we study them, the more deeply we understand them in all their aspects. … It is by the study and knowledge of dogmas that Christian knowledge and wisdom progress in each of the faithful and in the church as a whole.[6]

The other major representative of Greek academic theology in the twentieth century was Panayiotis Trembelas (1886–1977). His literary output was enormous, covering most aspects of theology, including dogmatics, biblical commentaries and studies, apologetics, liturgy, homiletics, catechetics and canon law, as well as philosophy. Trembelas taught at the University of Athens from 1939 to 1957. He was one of the founders of the Zoe Brotherhood of Theologians in 1907 and was closely associated with Zoe from 1911 until 1960, when he joined the break-away Sotir (Saviour) Brotherhood. Among Trembelas's publications, his three-volume *Dogmatics* stands out as the last great monument of Greek academic theology. Published in 1959–61, it appeared in French shortly afterwards.[7] The major change from Androutsos's *Dogmatics* is that Trembelas introduces an anthology of patristic references to buttress the essentially unchanged rationalistic, scholastic structure and exposition of Orthodox dogmas as found in Androutsos's work a half-century earlier.

Ioannis Karmiris (1904–92), one of last of the major Greek academic theologians, taught symbolics, dogmatics and Christian ethics at the University of Athens. He wrote *A Synopsis of the Dogmatic Theology of the Orthodox Catholic Church* (1957) and prepared a very useful edition of Orthodox statements or symbols of faith and confessions.[8]

While certainly monumental, Trembelas's *Dogmatica* is neither inspired nor inspiring. For Kallistos Ware, the treatise represents 'a faithful picture of the kind of theology taught over the past half century in Greek universities', it is 'outstanding of its type', 'exhaustive and highly methodical', but it requires 'several emphatic reservations' because of the 'the style of theology that it represents'.[9] Ware criticizes the book on these points in particular: the *Dogmatica* is a 'very *self-confident* book … magisterial in tone, monolithic and even "triumphalist"'; it is focused almost entirely on Greek theologians and hence is 'a somewhat *provincial* book'; it is fundamentally a Western approach to theology 'the *method* is definitely occidental ... the order and arrangement of subjects, the treatment of each topic, much of the terminology and categories invoked, bear unmistakably the stamp of the West'; it is out of date, even with respect to Western theologians: 'The West on

---

[6]Christos Androutsos, *Dogmatikí tis Orthodóxou Anatolikís Ekklisías* (Dogmatics of the Eastern Orthodox Church) (1907), cited in Yannaras, 'Theology in Present-Day Greece', 200.

[7]Panagiotis N. Trembelas, *Dogmatique de l'Église orthodoxe* (Dogmatica of the Orthodox Church) (Bruges, BE: Chevetogne/Desclée de Brouwer, 1966–8). 3 vols., 1744 p.

[8]Ioannis Karmiris, *Ta Dogmatiká kai Symvoliká Mnimeía tis Orthodóxou Katholikís Ekklisías* (Dogmatic and Symbolic Monuments of the Orthodox Catholic Church), 2 Vols. (Athens, 1952–3; Graz, 1968).

[9]All citations from Kallistos Ware, 'Review of Panagiotis N. Trembelas, *Dogmatique de l'Église orthodoxe*', *Eastern Churches Review* 3, 4 (1971), 477–80. See also the severe critique of Trembelas's *Dogmatica* by Yannaras, *Orthodoxy and the West*, 208–12.

which he has drawn is that of the past rather than the present' – there is no mention of twentieth-century Catholic or non-Greek Orthodox theologians; the book is descriptive rather than analytical, containing 'long and fascinating *catena* of patristic quotations ... We are told what the Fathers *said*; but at times we are still left asking "What exactly did they *mean*?"'; and finally, the book is '*academic* and *scholastic* rather than liturgical and mystical', 'a theology of the lecture hall and examination schools rather than a theology of mystery, adoration and divine glory'. Ware cites in particular the inadequate treatment of the apophatic approach to theology, the essence-energies distinction in God, the connection between the church and the Eucharist and the absence of Eucharistic ecclesiology and the dogmatic implications of the hesychast controversy. There are only three references to Gregory Palamas, while Isaac the Syrian and Symeon the New Theologian not mentioned, nor are such prominent modern Orthodox theologians as Vladimir Lossky or Georges Florovsky, who were already well known at the time of publication of the Greek edition of the *Dogmatica*. Trembelas ignores both the Russian religious renaissance and emerging neopatristic theology, which had already taken flight in Western Europe and North America by the late 1950s.

On the positive side, Trembelas's *Dogmatica* contains a useful compendium of patristic sources relevant for a full range of theological issues. And his theology is more faithful to the Orthodox tradition than the seventeenth-century confessions of faith. While these confessions reject such obvious Western doctrines as the *Filioque* and papal supremacy over the entire church, they tended to follow Western doctrines in more subtle areas such as the divine energies, theosis, original sin and transubstantiation.

In his discussion of the knowledge of God, Trembelas constantly stresses that the full knowledge of God is unattainable since the divine essence is beyond conception and expression, and yet God makes himself known through revelation. Trembelas seeks to steer between the ancient teachings of the knowability of the divine essence, and modern mysticism and pantheism which make the same claim, and an exaggeration of the unknowability of God, by invoking the biblical and patristic notions of imperfect and incomplete knowledge of God by human intelligence. Although Trembelas mentions briefly the doctrine of the divine energies, it is clear that he is more at ease with classic philosophical notions such as divine simplicity, divine attributes and the names of God. He emphasizes that the attributes and names of God are not to be understood as defining or limiting the divine essence, which is beyond all understanding (I:171–84).[10] Although he states that, distinct from the divine essence, the energies are 'operations *ad extra*' and in time, nowhere does he state clearly that the energies are themselves divine. He refers to Athanasius, Basil, Cyril of Alexandria, Mark of Ephesus, the Tomos of the Council of 1351 and even Bulgaris and Karmiris on the divine energies, but he studiously avoids any mention of Gregory Palamas (I:209–15). Trembelas refers briefly to theosis in his treatment of eschatology, as the 'completion of the divinisation already commenced here below', and as the ultimate objective of the Incarnation, as proclaimed by the Fathers, citing Athanasius, Gregory of Nazianzus and Gregory of Nyssa – but he does refer to the *Philokalia* (III:522–3).

[10]References are to Trembelas, *Dogmatique de l'Église orthodoxe*, (Volume:page [s]).

Trembelas considers original sin in the descendants of Adam to be 'the inheritance of a sinful state', not as fault or guilt (I:622). The effects of original sin are a degrading of the divine image in humans, marked by darkening of rationality and a weakening of the will in resisting evil (I:612–17). Trembelas is faithful to Orthodox thinking on original sin when he rejects the doctrines of the complete destruction of the divine image and the inheritance of the guilt of original sin by the descendants of Adam and its transmission by sexual intercourse and the conception of children. Hence Trembelas sees the purpose of baptism as regeneration by the Holy Spirit, granting of a new life in Christ and membership in the church, not the forgiveness of inherited original sin (III:79–80).

Although Trembelas explicitly rejects Anselm of Canterbury's juridical soteriology (Christ's sacrifice was necessary to satisfy divine justice outraged by sin), in the end his own doctrine of salvation is implicitly based on a notion of Christ's 'merits' and comes close to Anselm: 'We can speak of the superabundant satisfaction of the Lord's sacrifice, in the sense that it not only sufficed to eradicate God's anger towards us and to reconcile us with his justice, but that it became the source of superabundant gifts and graces' (II:202–4).

In his discussion of the term 'transubstantiation' concerning the Eucharist, Trembelas recognizes that the term came into Orthodox usage in the confessions of faith, yet Peter Mogila and Dositheus use the term as equivalent to the more patristic 'change' and 'conversion', without necessarily describing the mode by which the bread and the wine are converted to the Body and Blood of the Lord. Trembelas somewhat ambiguously accepts the scholastic distinction between 'substance' and 'accidents', without committing himself to the term 'transubstantiation' (III:209–210).

In comparison with the seventeenth-century Orthodox confessions of faith, there is in Trembelas's *Dogmatica* a partial recuperation of the Orthodox tradition in key doctrines, even if he presents these in an essentially scholastic framework and largely in the form of patristic references. In comparison with Vladimir Lossky, for example, and indeed neopatristic theology in general, Trembelas lacks above all a clear grasp of the interrelation of apophatism in theology, the divine energies and theosis. Although he mentions these doctrines, especially in their historic context, they remain disconnected and marginal to his own theology. In Trembelas's *Dogmatica*, Greek patristic theology is still largely enmeshed in a scholastic framework and mentality.

For the critics, the scholasticism of academic theology and the pietism of the Greek religious fraternities are the Scylla and Charybdis of Western theological influence in Orthodoxy. Christos Yannaras considers Trembelas's *Dogmatica* as a manifestation of both:

> Trembelas's stature is sadly diminished by his entrapment in a Western theological outlook. ... His vast output is steeped in pietistic moralism, accompanied by rationalistic apologetic ... For Trembelas, Orthodoxy was simply moral purity of life and the emotional convictions which sustained it, and every page he wrote proves it.[11]

Trembelas's last work, *Mysticism-Apophatism, Cataphatic Theology*, published in 1974, was a rearguard action devoted to refuting the stirrings of the 'new theology', in particular two of its major

[11]Yannaras, *Orthodoxy and the West*, 207–8.

pillars, apophatism and mystical experience. These aspects of the new theology in Greece stood in opposition to the intellectualism and moralism of academic theology and the theology of the Zoe Brotherhood and thus 'threatened the missionary ideal to which he [Trembelas] had dedicated his life and the theological ideas which his writings supported'.[12] In any case, academic theology was rapidly outflanked by the emergence of neopatristic theology in Greece during the 1960s.

The sad state of Greek theology up to the 1950s was evident even to otherwise sympathetic external observers. Peter Hammond (1921–99), an Anglican priest who spent nearly two years studying the Church of Greece, describes the 'theology of the schools' as 'earth bound and wholly academic: a theology of manuals which bears little relation to holy living'.[13] A. M. (Donald) Allchin (1930–2010), long-time active participant in the Fellowship of St Alban and St Sergius and other ecumenical endeavours, writes about Androutsos's *Dogmatic Theology* that 'the whole subject seems dead, cut off from the life and worship of the church on the one hand, and from the life and the struggle of the world on the other. One has the impression of a perfect academic system existing in a world of its own and for its own sake.'[14] Allchin refers to a profound distrust between the faculties of theology and the monasteries and a suspicion of theology even in movements such as Zoe.

Greek religious movements

The religious history of modern Greece has been strongly marked by religious movements, especially the Zoe ('Life') Brotherhood of Theologians.[15] Zoe and its predecessors in the nineteenth century were created in response to the difficult conditions of the Church of Greece after the liberation of Greece from the Ottoman Empire. Under the Turks, the church was tolerated but just barely: Only worship was permitted, religious education and the teaching of Greek language and culture were discouraged, heavy taxes were imposed on Christians and conversion to Islam was encouraged. Church life was reduced to a minimum and consisted primarily of the sacraments. In many villages, the priesthood became hereditary and little distinguished the priest from other poor and uneducated villagers.

Religious movements in Greece thus arose in the context of the profound needs of the Greek people for effective teaching of the faith and the fulfilment of spiritual needs. The weakness of the Orthodox Church of Greece until well into the twentieth century prevented it from implementing

---

[12]Ibid., 212.

[13]Peter Hammond, *The Waters of Marah: The Present State of the Greek Church* (London: Rockliff, 1956), 148.

[14]A. M. Allchin, 'Some New Tendencies in Greek Theology', *Sobornost*, 4, 8 (1963), 456.

[15]Useful references on the Greek religious movements are: Astérios Argyriou, *Spirituels Néo-Grecs, XVe–XXe siècles* (Neo-Greek Spiritual Figures, 15th–20th Centuries) (Namur, BE: Soleil Levant 1967); Demetrios J. Constantelos, 'The Zoe Movement in Greece', *St Vladimir's Theological Quarterly* 3 (1959); Basil Jioultsis, 'Religious Brotherhoods: A Sociological View', *Social Compass*, 22, (1975); Vasilios Makrides, 'The Brotherhoods of Theologians in Contemporary Greece', *Greek Orthodox Theological Review*, 33 (1988); Emmanuel Psilopoulos, 'Le mouvement Zoï dans l'Église orthodoxe de Grèce' (The Zoe movement in the Greek Orthodox Church), *Revue des sciences religieuses*, 40 (1966); Christos Yannaras, *Orthodoxy and the West: Hellenic Self-Identity in the Modern Age* (Brookline, MS: Holy Cross Orthodox Press, 2006), especially chapter XVII: 'The Extra-Ecclesial Organizations'.

a true home missionary program. The twentieth-century religious movements originated in the Greek tradition of itinerant preachers, of whom the most illustrious were St Cosmas of Aetolia (c. 1714–79), the lay preachers Cosmas Flamiatos (1786–1852) and Papoulakos (Christophoros Panagiotopoulos) (1785–1861), the monk Ignatios Lampropoulos (1814–69) and especially Apostolos Makrakis (1831–1905). Makrakis, a controversial figure, was a philosopher, writer and talented preacher who wrote a detailed commentary on the New Testament and established his own school, called Logos. These preachers were strongly motivated charismatic figures deeply committed to the conversion of the faithful and the reform of the church, but they were essentially solitary and did not establish lasting movements which survived them. It was nonetheless Makrakis who laid the groundwork for the establishment of Zoe, the first and most important of the religious brotherhoods.

Zoe was founded by Archimandrite Eusebius Matthopoulos (1845–1929), a disciple of Makrakis. From 1884 to 1900 Matthopoulos undertook itinerant missionary work in Greece based on Scripture and the liturgical life, creating small groups for mutual assistance and spiritual support. He became convinced of the need for a more formal structure than an itinerant preacher could provide. In 1907 he brought together theologians and theology students in the Zoe Brotherhood of Theologians. The objectives of Zoe were both the spiritual growth of its members and the renewal of spiritual life in Greece, based on an active presence throughout the country. Matthopoulos directed Zoe until 1927 and the movement was a reflection of his ideas and personality. His book *The Destiny of Man*, first published in 1913, became the essential reference manual, spiritual guide and programme of Zoe over the years. After the Bible, it was the most popular religious book in Greece for many decades, with sixteen editions to 1987. Matthopoulos and his followers employed Western missionary and evangelization methods, emphasizing personal piety and morality above all, centred on the 'imitation of Christ', notion more typical of Western than Orthodox spirituality, which speaks rather of union with Christ and deification (theosis). 'The destiny of man', writes Matthopoulos, 'consists in the imitation of Christ and in the enjoyment in God of eternal glory and beatitude for the glorification of the supreme and good God'.[16] As Basil Jioultsis summarizes Zoe's theological and spiritual perspectives: 'Morality took precedence over dogma, so that individual morality and piety came to be overemphasized and apparently dependent upon known Western conceptions of piety (moral introspection, natural theology, religion of the emotions, religious civilization).'[17]

Zoe, imitated by later movements, adopted some aspects of traditional monasticism and for this reason the religious fraternities are sometimes called 'monastic brotherhoods'. The members of Zoe, both clergy and laity, after a novitiate lasting six years or more, took a solemn promise to follow the three traditional monastic practices (poverty, chastity and obedience), but did not take formal vows. Lay members could leave the brotherhood and return to civil life. Members of Zoe lived in community in the main house of the fraternity in Athens, but brothers residing

---

[16]Eusebius Matthopoulos, *The Destiny of Man* (1913), extract in Argyriou, *Spirituels Néo-Grecs*, 149.
[17]Jioultsis, 'Religious Brotherhoods', 71.

elsewhere in the country lived alone. The number of members of Zoe peaked around 1959, with about 150 members.

Zoe founded its call for spiritual renewal in three areas: Bible study, preaching and participation in the sacraments. Zoe organized Sunday schools, Bible study groups and summer camps for students and maintained an extensive publication programme. Until the end of the Second World War, preaching was Zoe's main activity, but with the emergence of a large middle class in Greece and a higher level of education, Zoe gave more importance to the written word. Zoe and its affiliates published numerous editions of the Bible, Bible commentaries, books of spirituality and magazines and publications for children, youth and adults. These included twenty-one illustrated novels for children, with a total of over a million copies. The books of Matthopoulos and his equally charismatic successor, Archimandrite Seraphim Papacostas (1892–1954), who headed Zoe from 1927 to 1954, enjoyed enormous success.[18] To address the needs of different sectors of the population, Zoe created about twenty parallel agencies, which pursued the same objectives as Zoe, with activities adapted to the interests of different audiences. These agencies included sisterhoods with catechetical and social vocations, and Christian associations of professionals, intellectuals, educators, students, parents, youth and workers, each with its own activities and publications. Zoe also founded schools for training catechists, a School of General Christian Studies to provide a Christian perspective for students in higher education, a theological centre and two publishing houses.

Members of Zoe were required to follow strict moral and behavioural rules and personal austerity. Spiritual practices included regular confession, participation in the liturgical community, frequent communion and study of Scripture. Zoe attached great importance to clothing and appearance, and personal expenses were set at bare minimum; cigarettes, movies and worldly books and associates were prohibited.

Zoe sparked a broad religious renewal at a time when the Greek Church was weak; parish clergy and even bishops were often poorly educated and ill prepared for teaching the faith. The church, subject to the Greek state, had little authority, politicians interfered in the life of the church, especially in episcopal nominations, and simony was widespread. The people had little respect for the clergy and the hierarchy, while Zoe proposed a strict morality, reflected in the lives of its members. Zoe adopted the effective methods and often the teaching materials of Western missionaries, all the while retaining an Orthodox appearance, especially the liturgy. The rapid urbanization of Greece, especially after the Second World War, also initially favoured Zoe, which concentrated its efforts in urban areas.

Zoe's relations with the Church of Greece were ambiguous, often characterized by tension as Zoe appeared to offer itself as an alternative to the church, a sort of parallel church. Zoe maintained its own places and style of worship, which set it apart from the Church of Greece. At the same time many church leaders recognized that Zoe was far more effective at evangelization than the official

---

[18]Seraphim Papacostas's most popular book is *Repentance* (Athens: Zoe Brotherhood of Theologians, 1987; 3rd ed., translated from the 12th Greek edition). Other well-known titles are *The Parables of Christ*; *The Miracles of Christ*; *The Sermon on the Mount*; *Baptism, A Handbook of the Divine Liturgy*; *The Problem of Parenthood and Birth Control*; *Morality and Health*; *Between the Two Wars*; *Postwar Problems*; and *For the Hours of Pain* (all in Greek).

church. Twice, in 1914 and 1923, Zoe was formally accused of heresy, but both times Zoe successfully defended itself before the Holy Synod of the Church of Greece. Although the church never condemned Zoe or other fraternities, relations between the church and Zoe were strained in many dioceses, in part because representatives of Zoe were responsible to their superiors in Athens rather than to local bishops.

In the late 1950s internal dissention erupted between more conservative Zoe leaders seeking to maintain the brotherhood's traditional approach and activities, and more progressive members who saw a need for Zoe to adapt itself to changing conditions in Greek society and Greek theology. In 1960 about a third of the members of Zoe, the 'old guard', formed a new fraternity called Sotir (Saviour). Archimandrite Elias Mastroyannopoulos (b. 1919), elected head of Zoe in 1957, attempted to reform Zoe in the early 1960s, but he was deposed in 1965. Several other brotherhoods were formed after the Second World War, but none acquired the scope of Zoe or even of Sotir.

Assessments of observers of the Greek religious movements are far from unanimous. Some praise the movements, others are severely critical, some are more nuanced, acknowledging the services that Zoe rendered to Greek Orthodoxy, while pointing to its mistakes and weaknesses. John Meyendorff, after a visit to Greece in 1959, wrote a generally positive assessment of Zoe, especially its liturgical renewal, calling Zoe 'the most lively and active part of the entire modern Greek Church'. Of the liturgical renewal Meyendorff wrote: 'This liturgical renewal, of which many of us dream, is there entirely accomplished, without fanfare and unhealthy emotions, in accord with the tradition of the Church.'[19] Yannaras would certainly take sharp exception to this favourable assessment. Elisabeth Behr-Sigel is more nuanced than Meyendorff about Zoe as is Metropolitan Kallistos Ware.[20]

Until the crisis of 1958–60, criticisms of Zoe were rather limited, but during the crisis, several younger members left the brotherhood and became formidable critics. Criticism covers a wide range of aspects, most fundamentally that the religious movements were based on Western models, rather than being grounded in Orthodox tradition. Because they operated largely independently of the Church of Greece, they are sometimes called 'para-ecclesial' or even 'extra-ecclesial' organizations.[21] The brotherhoods are also accused of political and social conservatism, a charge which included a close association between the brotherhoods and the detested 'colonels' regime' which ruled Greece from 1967 to 1974. Several members of the junta had close personal ties with Zoe and Sotir. On 11 May 1967, shortly after the military coup on 21 April 1967, Archbishop Chrysostomos (Hadjistavrou) (1880–1968) was pressured to resign as head of the Church of Greece. He was succeeded by the candidate of the military junta, the conservative Hieronymos (Kotsonis) (1906–88), under whose leadership, from 1967 to 1973, more progressive hierarchs were replaced by members of Zoe or Sotir.

[19]John Meyendorff, 'Zoï', *Le Messager orthodoxe*, 5 (1959), 27.
[20]Elisabeth Behr-Sigel, 'Rencontre avec la Grèce chrétienne' (Encounter with Christian Greece), *Contacts* 16, 45 (1964), 58–62; Kallistos Ware, *The Orthodox Church* (Harmondsworth UK: Penguin Books, 2nd ed., 1993), 142.
[21]Christos Yannaras refers to the religious fraternities as 'Extra-Ecclesial Organisations', in *Orthodoxy and the West*, 217–250.

The most articulate and vocal critic of the religious movements has been Christos Yannaras.[22] In his youth and as a young adult, Yannaras was deeply involved with Zoe, but he broke with the movement in 1964, prior to departing for studies initially Germany, then in France, since Paris remained a leading centre of neopatristic theology, even if many leading figures had moved to the United States. Yannaras and other critics see the theology and spirituality of the religious movements as heavily inspired by Western pietism, incompatible with Orthodoxy. Yannaras considers pietism 'the great heresy of our age', which transposes salvation from participation in the Body of Christ, the church, to the fulfilment of personal religious duties (including participation in the sacraments, which thus become acts of personal piety), a scrupulous morality and the imitation of the 'virtues' of Christ. The church becomes an assembly of those who are individually justified, to complement and support personal piety, not the place and the means of salvation.

Positive assessments of the religious movements are usually based on their performance and impact on Greek religious life, at least up to the 1960s:

> The impact of Zoe upon the Greek people was impressive. Through stressing the necessity to change one's life, frequent confession and holy communion, and spreading the Christian message to the modern world, Zoe initiated an important revival of religious life at a time when the official church was by far ineffective for this purpose. … It is evident that the religious revival of the people with regard to Orthodox spirituality originated in this century from private initiative and not from the official church.[23]

The theology of Greek religious movements reflects many aspects of Western, especially Protestant, theology in support of morality and individual piety: the primacy of the Bible over the teaching of the church and patristic tradition; a juridical doctrine of salvation; deification (theosis), to the extent that it is retained, is seen as a 'character development' rather than participation in divine life; a legalistic view of the transmission of original sin; the denial of the distinction between divine essence and divine energies; the rejection of the neptic tradition and hesychastic spirituality; an anti-monastic attitude (even if the movements borrowed some traditional monastic elements); autonomy of the laity in the church and overemphasis of the universal priesthood of the laity and the replacement of icons by religious works of the Renaissance and traditional Orthodox Church music by Western hymns and music in religious activities outside the liturgy itself. One scholar even refers to Zoe as an 'Orthodox Reformation'.[24]

Are the fraternities part of the Church of Greece? Yannaras places them outside the church on the grounds of their autonomous and secular legal status, while other commentators consider

[22]In addition to Yannaras's book *Orthodoxy and the West*, see also his 'Pietism as an Ecclesiological Heresy', Ch. 8 of his *Freedom of Morality* (Crestwood, NY: St Vladimir's Seminary Press, 1984), 119–36; and 'Additional Note'. http://orthodoxinfo.com/inquirers/pietism.aspx (2 November 2015).Yannaras writes extensively about his involvement with Zoe in his autobiographical work *Katafugio ideōn* (Refuge of Ideas) (Athens: Domos, 1987). See a résumé in Evaggelia Grigoropoulou, 'The Early Development of the Thought of Christos Yannaras', Ph.D. thesis, University of Durham, 2008, 14–30.

[23]Makrides, 'The Brotherhoods of Theologians in Contemporary Greece', 169–70; 173. Yannaras and others would dispute Makrides's remark that Zoe promoted 'Orthodox spirituality'.

[24]Christoph Maczewski, *Dei Zoi-Bewegung Griechenlands* (The Zoe Movement of Greece) (Göttingen, DE: Vandenhoeck u. Ruprecht, 1970), cited by Christos Yannaras, *Orthodoxy and the West*, 244.

them within the church, since they were not condemned by the church, and their members, including priests and bishops, were indeed members of the church. Despite the personal adherence of its members to the Church of Greece, formally the fraternities were not structures of the Church of Greece.

Are the brotherhoods truly 'monastic'? As suggested above, some characteristics lean in this direction, but at the same time, the brotherhoods exhibit features which differentiate them from traditional monasticism: Except in Athens, members of fraternities live "in the world" rather than in a monastery; the importance attached to active missionary work as distinct from communal and personal prayer; a centralized and hierarchical structure parallel to the church; an independent and critical attitude towards the church and a rejection of traditional monastic spirituality. It is mainly for these reasons that traditional monks have not considered members of the movements as monastic brothers. In effect, the religious brotherhoods resemble more Roman Catholic religious communities with social and educational vocations than Orthodox monastic communities.[25] In 1975, the Holy Community of Mount Athos (which brings together the igumen of the Athonite monasteries) issued a statement condemning both academic theology and pietism, in response to Trembelas's book *Mysticism-Apophatism-Cataphatic Theology*:

> A scholastic and spiritually jejune theology is useless for the salvation of man. And a dogmatically spineless pietism which thinks that deification is an improvement in character should by its very nature be rejected. Such a theology is at its last breath; and such a way of life is powerless to withstand the general crisis of our era. The two together, theology and pietism, form one of the causes and the consequences of the spiritual decadence of our times.[26]

The 'Theology of the '60s'

In the first half of the twentieth century, theology in Greece was caught between academic theology patterned after scholasticism, represented by Androutsos and Trembelas and others, and the moralistic and pietist-inspired theology of the Zoe Brotherhood and its imitators. Greek theology too went through a long period of 'pseudomorphosis', to use Florovsky's term. Although Florovsky was writing specifically about the Russian experience, the 'Western captivity' of much of Orthodox theology lasted well into the twentieth century, later in Greece and Romania than in the theology of the Russian theologians in exile. Yannaras, for one, considers that much of Greek theology as late as 1992 continued to suffer from the formalism typical of the manuals of dogmatic theology, the absence of dialogue and criticism and confusion or an absence of criteria and principles. The result was a blind clinging to the formulas of the past represented by Androutsos and Trembelas, and a rejection of any innovation in the name of safeguarding traditional Orthodoxy:

---

[25]Fr Theoklitos of the Athonite monastery of Dionysiou refers to the members of the religious fraternities as 'lay preachers'. Cited by Irénée Doens in 'Chronique religieuse: Monastères orthodoxes en Grèce' (Religious chronicle: Orthodox monasteries in Greece), *Irénikon*, 34 (1961), 377.

[26]From *Athonitikoi Dialogoi* (1975), 20–7; cited in Yannaras, 'Additional Note'.

> Any new formulation, any new development of dogma beyond the presently accepted norms in Greece is judged to be suspect and dangerous, even before it has been seriously considered. There are Greek academic theologians for whom the whole theological movement of the Orthodox Russians of the diaspora is suspect, at times even unacceptable, simply because it involves something new for Greece. A few years ago, Professor Constantine Mouratidis, a theologian of the faculty of theology of Athens, wrote that apophatism, since in itself it signifies a negation, is inadmissible for Orthodox theology![27]

Yannaras cuts to the core in his criticism of academic theology: 'We might say that academic theology in Greece is not fundamentally Greek since it is cut off from both the continuity of tradition and the intellectual life of the country.'[28] He invokes Florovsky, familiar with Greek theology from his visits to Greece, who observed that Greek theologians were not touched by the fundamentally Greek dimension of Orthodox theology in the Hellenism of dogmas, worship and icons.

Hamilcar Alivisatos (1887–69), professor of canon law and practical theology in Athens from 1919 to 1956, wrote in 1949: 'Today, patristic theology is recognised as the right point of departure for Greek theology.'[29] Alivisatos was aware of the interest among Russian theologians in the Fathers. He was one of the principal organizers of the First Congress of Orthodox Theologians held in Athens in 1936 and he edited its proceedings. He met both Sergius Bulgakov and Georges Florovsky and was familiar with Florovsky's two interventions at the Congress with their critique of Western influence in Russian theology and a clear call for a return to patristically based theology. But there was no immediate follow-up to Alivisatos's a mild suggestion for a patristic turn in Greek theology.

Nevertheless, within a decade light was beginning to shine on the rather gloomy scene of Greek theology. The Russian theologians in exile provided the initial stimulus for a renewal of Greek theology initiated in the late 1950s and the 1960s – Florovsky's call for a neopatristic synthesis did not fall on deaf ears in Greece. In 1971 Christos Yannaras could write:

> One can sense the beginning of a renewal. … Withal, there are indications of new tendencies and trends that give us great reason to hope – first of all, in the academic realm. True, they are generally under the influence of the theological circles of the Russian diaspora in Europe and America. The return to the apophatic and mystical theology of the Eastern tradition, the so-called neo-palamite theology, the theology of icons and of the Orthodox liturgy and finally the dialogue between this theology with the spirit and problematics of the contemporary Western world are at last beginning to have a serious impact in Greece. The school of the Russian diaspora has made possible an orderly advance beyond the scholastic and rationalistic spirit of Greek academicism, without the risk of theological acrobatics.[30]

A younger generation of Greek theologians, many of whom completed their higher education abroad, was reaching maturity in the late 1950s and early 1960s. They were exposed to the thinking of Russian theologians and familiar with the ideas of the neopatristic synthesis, as well as with trends

[27]Yannaras, 'Theology in Present-Day Greece', 204.

[28]Ibid., 206.

[29]Cited by Norman Russell, 'Modern Greek Theologians and the Greek Fathers', *Philosophy & Theology* 18, no. 1 (2006), 79.

[30]Yannaras, 'Theology in Present-Day Greece', 207.

in Catholic theology, especially the *théologie nouvelle* movement, which also involved a return to patristic inspiration for theology, and in philosophy, especially existentialism. The publication of the theses and early writings of the younger theologians punctuated the early 1960s, challenging the well-entrenched academic theology of Androutsos, Trembelas and Karmiris. The chief architects of the neopatristic renaissance of Greek theology were Savas Agouridis, George Mantzarides, Panayiotis Nellas, Nikos Nissiotis, John Romanides, Christos Yannaras and John Zizioulas.

A key event which symbolically marked the beginning of the new trend in Greek theology was the publication in 1957 of the doctoral thesis of Fr John Romanides (1927–2001), *The Ancestral Sin*, despite strong objections by Panagiotis Trembelas and Panagiotis Bratsiotis (1889–1982) of the Athens Faculty of Theology. Romanides and Trembelas engaged in heated written exchanges over Romanides's thesis, primarily over the status and creditability of the theologians of the Russian diaspora which Romanides invokes in support of his patristic approach to original sin.[31]

Romanides was born in Greece, but his parents emigrated to the United States shortly after his birth. After studies at the Hellenic College in Brookline, Massachusetts, and the divinity schools of Yale and Harvard, he returned to Greece for doctoral studies. From 1956 to 1965 he taught dogmatic theology at Holy Cross Theological School and was close to Georges Florovsky during this period. In 1968 he was appointed professor of dogmatic theology at the University of Thessalonica, a position he held until his retirement in 1982, after which he taught at the Balamand Theological School in Lebanon.

Romanides's theology is predicated on a historiography which sees an irreconcilable rift between the Christian East, considered the true successor to the Christianized Roman Empire, and a Western Christianity usurped by the converted barbarian tribes, especially the Franks and the Goths, who sought to dominate the Orthodox East, in part through the papacy, and to supplant their erroneous theology for that of the Greek Fathers. Despite this structural anti-Western stance, Romanides was active in ecumenism, serving on the Central Committee of the World Council of Churches (WCC) and in the theological dialogues with the Lutherans and the Oriental Orthodox. Romanides's influence has been considerable, but aspects of his theology, especially as derived from his theory of the *romiosyne* ('romanity') of Orthodoxy, posited in opposition to the *francosyne* of Western Christianity, remains controversial.[32] Also controversial is Romanides's attribution of the source of the West's deviation from (Greek) patristic Christianity to Augustine. For Romanides, the West's key theological errors can be traced back to Augustine: the doctrines of original sin and the procession of the Holy Spirit from the Father and the Son. These doctrines in turn led to the rejection of the essence-energies distinction in God and hence also theosis, and the substitution in

---

[31]The correspondence was published much later: Georgios Metallinos, ed., *Encheirídion: Allilografía p. I. S. Romanídou kai kath. P. N. Trempéla (Katagrafí enós theologikoú dialógou)* (Enchiridion: Handbook of the Correspondence between Fr. I. S. Romanides and Professor P. N. Trembelas: Chronicle of a Theological Dialogue) (Athens: Harmos, 2009).

[32]Romanides has ardent supporters and equally ardent critics. Among the critics, see Pantelis Kalaitzidis, 'The Image of the West in Contemporary Greek Theology', in George E. Demacopoulos and Aristotle Papanikolaou, eds., *Orthodox Constructions of the West: Orthodox Christianity and Contemporary Thought* (New York: Fordham University Press, 2013), 144–50. This essay is based on his thesis: Pantelis Kalaitzidis, 'Hellenicity and Anti-Westernism in the Greek "Theology of the '60s"' (Doctoral Thesis, Aristotle University of Thessalonica, School of Theology) (Thessalonica, 2008).

their stead of philosophical notions of the divine essence to develop theological discourse about God, the Trinity, relations between God and creation, grace, predestination and salvation.[33]

Romanides's thesis on original sin marked a sharp break with the juridical concept of sin and salvation, originating in Augustine and developed by Anselm of Canterbury, and his thesis signalled a revival of the soteriology of the Greek Fathers. Romanides argues for a return to the concept in the early church of the 'ancestral sin' of Adam, as distinct from the Augustinian notion of 'original sin', and the transmission of Adam's guilt to all his descendants.[34] The Eastern Christian notion of 'ancestral sin' points to the transmission of the effects of the first sin to the human race in the introduction of death, a weakened will and an inclination towards evil – but not the actual guilt, which remains personal. As we have seen previously with respect to the sixteenth-century confessions of faith, the Western notion of the transmission of Adam's guilt to his descendants frequently crept into Orthodox theology. Romanides's book *The Ancestral Sin* is a wide-ranging treatment of major themes in patristic theology such as creation, the divine energies and anthropology and is marked by 'a fairly strident anti-Westernism',[35] including attacks on Western notions such as the Filioque, Anselm's juridical soteriology and the medieval idea of *analogia entis*, by which aspects of creation (*entis*) are held to reflect (*analogia*) divine characteristics.

In this context, the restoration of the apophatic tradition and Palamite theology to their just places in Orthodox theology was a major aspect of theological renaissance in Greece. A sign of change in the academic environment, at least at the Faculty of Theology in Thessalonica, was a symposium held in Thessalonica in 1959 to mark the sixth centenary of the death of St Gregory Palamas, to which were invited many international scholars, including Georges Florovsky, who was awarded an honorary doctorate of theology. Florovsky's main address, delivered in Greek, was on 'St. Gregory Palamas and the Tradition of the Fathers'.[36] The move to restore Palamism in Greek theology was bolstered by the publication of a critical edition of *The Writings of St. Gregory Palamas* (1960–96), and a translation of Palamas into modern Greek, under the direction of Panayiotis Chrestou (1917–96) of the University of Thessalonica.[37] The publication of the first volume of the writings of Palamas was followed in 1963 by a study of the theology of Gregory Palamas on theosis, the doctoral dissertation, under Chrestou's direction, of George Mantzaridis (b. 1935), who became one of the leading theologians of the new generation. Mantzaridis subsequently published several other studies on Palamas, collected under the title *Palamika* in 1973, as well as an important study

[33]See George Demacopoulos and Aristotle Papanikolaou, 'Augustine and the Orthodox: The "West" in the East', in George Demacopoulos and Aristotle Papanikolaou, eds., *Orthodox Readings of Augustine* (Crestwood, NY: St Vladimir's Seminary Press, 2008), 28–30; and Andrew Louth, *Modern Orthodox Thinkers: From the Philokalia to the Present* (London: SPCK, 2015), 228–9. Romanides develops his argumentation concerning *romiosyne* notably in *Romiosýni-Romanía-Roúmeli* (Thessalonica: Pournaras, 1975) and in *Franks, Romans, Feudalism, and Doctrine: An Interplay Between Theology and Society* (Brookline, MA: Holy Cross Orthodox Press, 1981).

[34]John Romanides, *The Ancestral Sin* (1957) (Ridgewood, NJ: Zephyr, 2002), 157–62.

[35]Louth, *Modern Orthodox Thinkers*, 227.

[36]Georges Florovsky, 'St Gregory Palamas and the Tradition of the Fathers' (1960), in Brandon Gallaher and Paul Ladouceur, eds., *The Patristic Witness of Georges Florovsky: Essential Theological Writings* (London: T&T Clark, 2019), 221–32.

[37]See also Panayiotis Chrestou, *Partakers of God (Patriarch Athenagoras Memorial Lectures*, 1982) (Brookline, MA: Holy Cross Orthodox Press, 1984).

on theosis.[38] These publications were contemporaneous with the publication of Fr John Meyendorff's studies of Palamas, which first appeared in French in 1959.[39]

In 1964 Vladimir Lossky's *The Mystical Theology of the Eastern Church* appeared in Greek translation. This quickly became a theological bestseller and set the tone for the development of neopatristic theology in Greece, as it had done earlier in Russian exile circles and in the English-speaking world. Christos Yannaras and others were strongly influenced by Lossky's book, especially in the development of Greek thinking on apophatism and the theology of the human person.

And in 1965 Nikos Nissiotis (1925–86) published two books, *Prolegomena to Theological Epistemology* and *The Philosophy of Religion and Philosophical Theology*. Nissiotis studied theology and philosophy in Athens, Zurich, Basel and Leuven, completing a ground breaking doctorate in 1956 in Athens on existentialism and Christianity, focusing on Kierkegaard, Jaspers, Heidegger and Sartre.[40] Nissiotis was deeply involved in ecumenism, as an Orthodox observer at the Second Vatican Council and from 1966 to 1974 as director of the Ecumenical Institute at Bossey, Switzerland, the educational arm of the WCC. His main thesis in *Prolegomena to Theological Epistemology* is that knowledge of God through philosophy, psychology and natural theology is ultimately inadequate, and that God can be known only in faith and love, in Christ through the Holy Spirit and in the church, This mystical and experiential approach to knowledge of God constituted a direct challenge to the scholastic rationalism of Greek academic theology. Nissiotis died tragically in an automobile accident in August 1986.

Also in 1965 was the publication of the doctoral dissertation of John Zizioulas (b. 1931), *The Unity of the Church in the Holy Eucharist and the Bishop during the First Three Centuries*, which marked a refinement in Eucharistic ecclesiology first elaborated by Nicholas Afanasiev.[41] Between 1960 and 1964 Zizioulas studied under Georges Florovsky at Harvard University. After teaching at the University of Athens, Zizioulas taught in Edinburgh and Glasgow and at King's College, London. In 1986, he was elected titular metropolitan of Pergamon and was appointed Professor of Dogmatics in the Faculty of Theology in Thessalonica. Zizioulas has been a major Orthodox figure in ecumenical circles, especially in the WCC, where he worked in the Secretariat, and in the Orthodox-Catholic theological dialogue, which he co-chaired with a senior representative of the Catholic Church, retiring in 2016. We will consider Zizioulas's major theological contributions, to the theology of the person in Chapter 10, and to ecclesiology, in Chapter 11.

In 1969 Panayiotis Nellas (1936–86), who taught in an Athenian secondary school, published his first study on Nicholas Cabasilas, followed by a more detailed monograph in 1974. These works served to make better known the liturgically based theology and spirituality of Cabasilas, a contemporary of Gregory Palamas. The main thrust of Nellas's theology is that the destiny of

---

[38]George Mantzaridis, *The Deification of Man: St Gregory Palamas and the Orthodox Tradition* (Crestwood, NY: St Vladimir's Seminary Press, 1984).

[39]Full references in Ch. 9, n. 85, 209 in this book.

[40]Nikos Nissiotis, *Existentialism and Christian Faith: Existential Thought in Philosophy and Christian Faith as the Inevitable and Fundamental Problem for Thought according to Søren Kierkegaard and the Contemporary Existentialist Philosophers Karl Jaspers, Martin Heidegger and Jean-Paul Sartre* (in Greek) (Athens: Ekdoseis Minima, 1956).

[41]John Zizioulas, *Eucharist, Bishop, Church: The Unity of the Church in the Divine Eucharist and the Bishop During the First Three Centuries* (1965) (Brookline, MA: Holy Cross Press, 2001).

human beings, must be seen, not from the moral outlook of Zoe, but from the perspective of patristic anthropology, as a reaching forth to eternity in God – that is, as theosis, and hence the title of his major work, *Deification in Christ*, published in 1979.[42]

Savas Agouridis (1921–2009) was a pioneer in Greek biblical studies over many decades as professor of the New Testament. After postgraduate studies in the United States in the late 1940s, he taught at the University of Thessalonica (1955–68) and the University of Athens (1968–85). Agourides was associated with the theology of the 60s, but unlike several others, his theological outlook was not coloured by anti-Westernism, and he was himself critical of the systemic anti-Westernism of other contemporary Greek theologians.[43]

Beyond the academy

Parallel with the ferment in Greek academic circles in the 1960s were several developments outside academia also moving towards a return to patristic theological foundations. A key figure in non-academic circles was Demetrios Koutroubis (1921–83), who had become a Roman Catholic, entered the Jesuit Order and had studied in Western Europe, especially at the important Jesuit centre in Lyons, France. After teaching at a Catholic university in Lebanon, he returned to the Orthodox Church and to Greece in 1954 and played a major though discreet role in promoting patristic-based theology. Koutroubis wrote very little himself and his influence was largely personal, through his discussions with younger theologians and a wide range of Greek and foreign religious figures in what he called the 'theological seminar', conducted in his own house.[44] He was instrumental in making the thinking of the contemporary Russian theologians known in Greece, thanks in part to his friendship with Archimandrite Elias Mastroyannopoulos, the leader of the Zoe movement from 1959 until 1965. Mastroyannopoulos had a cautiously open theological outlook and he encouraged Koutroubis's patristic initiatives. These included the publication in 1960 of two articles on Gregory Palamas in the Zoe periodicals *Aktines* and *Anaplasis*, based on John Meyendorff's work on Palamas, and one on Nicholas Cabasilas, inspired by Myrrha Lot-Borodine's study on Cabasilas.[45]

In 1962, Zoe published an innovative book under the title *Theology – Truth and Life*, edited by Koutroubis. The book was innovative in Greek theology because it contained translations of writings of leading Russian neopatristic theology theologians (Florovsky, Lossky, Schmemann and

[42]Panayiotis Nellas, *Deification in Christ: Orthodox Perspectives on the Nature of the Human Person* (Yonkers, NY: St Vladimir's Seminary Press, 1987).

[43]See Pantelis Kalaitzidis, 'New Trends in Greek Orthodox Theology: Challenges in the Movement towards a Genuine Renewal and Christian Unity', *Scottish Journal of Theology*, 67, 2 (2014), 133.

[44]See 'In Memoriam Demetrios Koutroubis', with four obituaries, by Kallistos Ware, Christos Yannaras, Elias Mastroyannopoulos and A. M. Allchin, in *Sobornost*, 6, 1 (1984), 67–77; and Andrew Louth, 'Dimitris Koutroubis', *Modern Orthodox Thinkers: From the Philokalia to the Present* (London: SPCK, 2015), 251–4.

[45]See Myrrha Lot-Borodine, *Nicolas Cabasilas: Un maître de la spiritualité byzantine au XIVe siècle* (Nicholas Cabasilas: A Byzantine Spiritual Master of the 14th Century) (Paris: Éditions de l'Orante, 1958).

Meyendorff), and the Serb Justin Popovitch, as well as three essays by young Greek theologians, two from Zoe (Mastroyannopoulos and Demetrios Trakatellis (b. 1928)[46]) and Nikos Nissiotis, already prominent as assistant director of the Ecumenical Institute at Bossey, Switzerland.[47] This marked the first time that writings of leading representatives of neopatristic theology were available to a wide public in Greece and it was a forward-looking attempt on the part of the Zoe leadership to build bridges to the emerging neopatristic renaissance at home and abroad. In his introductory essay, 'Some Characteristics of Orthodox Theology', Mastroyannopoulos expands on the sense of the title of the book, stressing the intimate connection between true theology and the life of the church and the faithful, a theology developed 'in the fervent atmosphere of prayer and communion with God' and 'in participation in the liturgical prayer of the church', as contrasted with a theology 'shut up in its study', a 'theology of professors' – a slap at academic theology.[48] Nissiotis's essay, 'Theology as Science and Glorification', continues on the same line, arguing that theology is not properly speaking a science, but begins in God and finishes in God. The theologian works as a living member of the church, offering 'the voice of thanksgiving of all the members of the church'.[49] Trakatellis's essay 'Our Theology Yesterday and Tomorrow' characterizes the 'theology of yesterday' as drawing on themes and attitudes from Western theology and divorced from the church and from life – Florovsky's inspiration is manifest (even if a Florovsky text did not feature in the anthology). The theology of the future must be a theology of the living God and of the incarnate God, a theology of the whole world, a reflection of the universal quality of God's love, a theology of the 'Yes', 'endless, confident, clear and inspired by love'.[50] The language of the essays by the Greek theologians in this volume is a far cry from the *Dogmatica* of Androutsos and Trembelas and marked an important patristic overture on the part of the Zoe leadership.

In 1963 Zoe published two other anthologies prepared by Koutroubis, one on the liturgy and Eucharistic theology, with studies by Mastroyannopoulos, Alexander Schmemann and Olivier Clément, and the other, entitled *Monasticism and the Modern World*, on early Christian ascetic spirituality. Under Mastroyannopoulos, Zoe also demonstrated an ecumenical opening. In October 1962, Mastroyannopoulos participated in a conference of the Conference of European Churches held in Nyborg, Denmark, where he delivered an inspired address on the subject 'The Task of the Churches Today'.[51] The opening to the theologians of the Russian diaspora was accompanied by a greater awareness of the *ressourcement* or *nouvelle théologie* movement in Catholic theology, with an early awareness of the writings of figures such as Yves Congar, Jean Daniélou and Hans Urs von Balthasar.

From 1960 to 1964 Koutroubis and Mastroyannopoulos organized an annual theological seminar called *Ephesos* for Zoe theologians, postgraduates, professors from the theological faculties and some bishops. These seminars exposed the participants to developments in Orthodox theology

---

[46]Demetrios Trakatellis was ordained to the priesthood in 1964, to the episcopate in 1967 and he became archbishop of the Greek Orthodox Archdiocese of America in 1999.

[47]See a review of the book by Allchin, 'Some New Tendencies in Greek Theology', 458–64.

[48]Citations in Allchin, 'Some New Tendencies in Greek Theology', 459.

[49]Ibid., 460–1.

[50]Ibid., 462–3.

[51]Elias Mastroyannopoulos, 'The Task of the Churches Today: Some Forgotten Obligations', *Sobornost*, 4, 8 (1963), 415–19.

in Western Europe and North America.[52] After 1964, the theological conferences continued for another six years, but outside the framework of Zoe.

Zoe had extensive connections with the worshipping church and the lives of the faithful that neither the academic theologians nor the handful of emerging neopatristic theologians possessed. The book *Theology – Truth and Life* was a sort of Greek neopatristic manifesto which could have played the same role as Florovsky's addresses at the conference of Orthodox theologians in 1936 and his *The Ways of Russian Theology*. But the initiatives undertaken by Koutroubis and Mastroyannopoulos were short-circuited when Mastroyannopoulos was overthrown in 1965. Zoe returned to a narrow conservativism, and the Mastroyannopoulos years represented an aborted opportunity both to reform Zoe's own theology and spirituality and to make theology more relevant to Greek religious life.

The formation of the Theological Syndesmos, in which the biblical scholar Petros Vassiliadis (b. 1945) of the University of Thessaloniki played a leading role, was 'a response to the increasing alienation of modern Greek society from the values and the authentic sprit of Orthodoxy'. The declaration of this group, centred mostly in Thessalonica, is highly critical of the old 'academic theology', describing it as marked by 'intellectualism, elitism, folklorism, aristocratism'; it is a theology 'which falls short of concrete action'; but nonetheless, it 'keeps a slow pace in its effort to land in reality'. It is even more critical of the more conservative tendency in Greek theology, which displays 'an uncritical, stagnant, negative and offensive reaction against all free expressions'; it remains 'incurably fanatic and racist'. Needless to say, the declaration was not well received everywhere, and Vassiliadis complains that the 'theological climate' is still 'heavily occupied by the clouds of the old school of formalistic thought' – that is, by academic theology.[53]

Developments in Greek culture, especially literature, also supported the move away from both scholasticism in theology and pietism in religious life. The dean of modern Greek Orthodox literary figures was the novelist, short-story writer and poet Alexandros Papadiamandis (1851–1911). His characters, especially the priests, are drawn mostly from the simple lives in Greek villages and islands and are manifestations of practical virtue and wisdom. It is the living Orthodox tradition of the people, far from faculties of theology and learned treatises. Papadiamandis is often referred to as 'Greece's Dostoyevsky' for his sensitivity to the spiritual element in the human condition and to the Orthodox tradition.[54] Other novelists, poets, essayists, playwrights and artists also reflected what Christos Yannaras calls 'the theology of transfiguration, the theology of the liturgical spirituality of a people that continues to incarnate the reality of the Body of Christ'.[55]

---

[52] Yannis Spiteris writes that Florovsky, Lossky, Schmemann, Meyendorff and Justin Popovitch of Serbia participated in the 1962 symposium. Certainly Elisabeth Behr-Sigel was present, but Spiteris's list of foreign participants is erroneous. Lossky died in 1958, and there is no independent indication that the others he names attended. Spiteris appears to have confused the list of foreign participants with the authors of the texts translated in book *Theology – Truth and Life* (1962), which he asserts was the Acts of the symposium. Yannis Spiteris, *La teologia ortodossa neo-greca* (Neo-Greek Orthodox Theology) (Bologna: Edizione Dehoniane, 1992), 213. The same list of prominent attendees appears in Norman Russell, 'Modern Greek Theologians', 80.

[53] Petros Vassiliadis, 'Greek Theology in the Making, Trends and Facts in the 80s – Vision for the 90s', *St Vladimir's Theological Quarterly*, 35, 1 (1991), 36–42.

[54] See Anestis Keselopoulos, *Greece's Dostoevsky: The Theological Vision of Alexandros Papadiamandis* (Protecting Veil Press, 2011).

[55] Yannaras, 'Theology in Present-Day Greece', 212.

The testimony concerning the living reality of Orthodoxy in everyday that Greek literary figures brought to light in their writings stood in contrast if not contradiction with the formalism of school theology and the pietistic moralism of the religious brotherhoods.

The role of cultural figures in the invigoration and transformation of Greek religious thought is reminiscent of the Russian religious renaissance, where the novelists, poets and essayists of the 'new religious consciousness' embodied a Christian approach, often quite unconventional, to society, politics, economics and culture. Unlike many of the major figures of the Russian religious renaissance, however, the personalities of the religious renaissance in Greek culture remained much closer to mainstream Orthodox theological and spiritual traditions.

From 1964 to 1967, a group of former Zoe members close to Koutroubis and led by Christos Yannaras, published the journal *Synoro* (*Frontier*), with thematic issues exploring the relevance of Orthodoxy to contemporary issues in art, society, politics, drawing on both Russian theologians and Greek thinkers and artists. *Synaro* closed in silent protest to the seizure of power by the military junta. After the fall of the junta, Panayiotis Nellas, keenly intent to make Greek theology relevant to contemporary Greek society, promoted a new Greek theological journal in the early 1980s. The theological quarterly *Synaxi*, which Nellas launched in 1982, was a successor to *Synoro*. The very title of the journal was a mission statement: to bring together and to promote dialogue among the scattered theological and spiritual voices in Greek society. *Synaxi* quickly became a major focal point for the new theology in Greece, with articles on a wide range of theological and other issues, not only by academics, but also by artists, lay intellectuals, monks and non-Greeks.[56] After Nellas's untimely death at the age of fifty in 1986, Sotiris Gounelas (b. 1949) assumed responsibility for *Synaxi*, followed by Athanasios Papathanassiou (b. 1959) in 1997. Both successfully maintained a dynamic team of contributors, sustaining *Synaxi*'s importance as the leading Greek theological publication, generating 'new approaches in modern Greek theological thinking', in part by making better known the thought of the Russian diaspora and by engaging a wider circle of intellectuals, including from Mount Athos, in the shaping of Greek theological reflection.[57]

During this period Christos Yannaras emerged as one of the principal leaders of the new theology in Greece. Yannaras's intellectual scope is far-reaching and his literary corpus is enormous, with over seventy books and numerous essays and newspaper and magazine articles stretching over more than half a century. While his prime focus is on the philosophical aspects of Orthodoxy, as for the Russian religious philosophers of the early twentieth century, philosophy and theology blend into a sophisticated Orthodox intellectual discourse. After his break with Zoe in 1964, Yannaras subsequently studied philosophy in Germany and in France. As a philosopher, he is close to the existentialist school, and has been influenced by Martin Heidegger. Like several of leading figures of the Russian religious renaissance, Yannaras bridges the gap between philosophy and theology. In 1970, he was awarded a doctorate from the Sorbonne for a thesis in philosophy entitled 'Metaphysics of the Body: A Study on John Climacus', but the University of Athens rejected the

[56]A selection of major articles in *Synaxi* published between 1982 and 2002 appeared in English translation: John Hadjinicolaou, ed., *Synaxis: An Anthology of the Most Significant Orthodox Theology in Greece Appearing in the Journal Synaxi from 1982 to 2002*, 3 vols. (Montreal: Alexander Press, 2006).
[57]See Vassiliadis, 'Greek Theology in the Making', 36.

thesis because of its emphasis on Christian love as erotic.[58] Also in 1970, Yannaras was awarded a doctorate in theology from the University of Thessalonica for a thesis on 'The Ontological Content of the Theological Concept of the Person', subsequently published as *Person and Eros*.[59] After being refused a post in theology at the University of Athens, Yannaras taught in Crete, and was finally appointed in 1981 to a chair in philosophy at the Panteion University of Social and Political Philosophy in Athens. His nomination was controversial since the institution was dominated by non-Christian scholars, who objected to the appointment of a committed Christian thinker seen more as a theologian than a philosopher.

Yannaras's book *Person and Eros* develops the key notions that underlie much of Yannaras's thought: that the proper mode of human existence is personal, in relation with other persons, both divine and human; humans cannot grasp the divine essence but we can know and experience God through a personal relationship; love is the ultimate fulfilment of human existence. Yannaras asserts the primacy of the person over essence or being, which is taken to express the core of Greek-Byzantine philosophy and theology, as distinct from the primacy accorded to essence over person, said to characterize Western philosophy and theology. For Yannaras, the intellectual understanding of the God, human existence and world in Western thought gave rise to a culture founded on rationality and manifested in scholasticism, the Enlightenment, individualism and modernism, and in positivist and materialist philosophies. This is the source of atheistic, or at best, non-theistic secularism which has dominated Western thought since the Enlightenment and which is the principal foundation of Western-inspired global culture.

Yannaras considers his critique of the foundations of modern Western culture as self-critique from within a globalized Western way of life which includes Greece, a society 'radically and unhappily Westernised'. 'My critical stance towards the West is self-criticism', he writes in the preface to the English edition of his *Orthodoxy and the West*, 'it refers to my wholly Western mode of life. I am a Western person searching for answers to the problems tormenting Western peoples today.'[60] It is in this perspective that Yannaras is equally critical of aspects of modern Greece, especially the articulation of the Greek state and the Church of Greece in terms of Greek nationalism, summarized in the expression 'Nationalism spells the demise of Hellenism'[61]:

> Nationalism in general, the Greek state's recent version of it in particular and the like, which have divided this land so deeply and tormented it so much, are typical products of the narrowness of the myopic parochialism of the state: they have nothing to do neither with the civilizational identity of Hellenism nor with the universality of Orthodoxy.[62]

---

58 Norman Russell, 'Christos Yannaras', in S. J. Kristiansen and Svein Rise, eds., *Key Theological Thinkers: From Modern to Postmodern* (Farnham UK: Ashgate, 2013), 726.

59 Christos Yannaras, *Person and Eros* (Brookline, MA: Holy Cross Orthodox Press, 2008).

60 Yannaras, *Orthodoxy and the West*, viii–ix.

61 See for example Christos Yannaras, 'Póte téleiose istoriká o Ellinismós' (When Hellenism ended) (2009). www.kathimerini.gr/715529 (21 March 2018).

62 Christos Yannaras, *Kefálaia Politikís Theologías* (Principles of Political Theology) (Athens: Grigoris, 1983), 201. See also Christos Yannaras, *Alítheia kai Enótita tis Ekklisías* (The Truth and the Unity of the Church) (Athens: Grigoris, 1977), 78–80. I am grateful to Sotiris Mitralexis for these references.

Consistent with his critique of a narrow view of Hellenism, Yannaras warns against the injection of particularistic notions into the church:

> The most important danger for the universal unity of the local Orthodox churches during the last centuries has been *nationalism* or *phyletism*. This is the substitution of the truth concerning the nature of the church – and this nature is the 'new' mode of Trinitarian existence 'in Christ', – with the objective unity of a race or nation; a relativization of the divine-human common nature of the church for the sake of 'individual' otherness (national or racial).[63]

Yannaras's perspective is thus a universal or 'catholic' Hellenism, which brings together the apophatic tradition of the Greek Fathers, the Palamite theology of the divine energies and the theology of the person developed in the thinkers of the Russian religious renaissance, especially, for Yannaras, in Vladimir Lossky. In this respect Yannaras's Hellenism approximates that of Georges Florovsky, who cannot be suspected of covert Greek nationalism, even if his prime theological referent is almost constantly the Greek-Byzantine Fathers.

Yannaras's critique of Western culture in a Hellenistic-Orthodox perspective is subtle and complex, but his excesses of language and rigid categorization can easily lead to a superficial dismissal of his thinking on a wide range of issues as a simple blend of 'Greek nationalism, anti-Westernism, anti-modernism and Orthodoxy'.[64] Although Yannaras's alternatives or cures for the problems of modernity are less well articulated than his diagnosis of its illnesses, his stature as modern Orthodox thinker can only increase as more of his writings are translated.

Stelios Ramfos (b. 1939) is a well-known and controversial personality in Greece. His intellectual and personal journey took him from Marxism to Orthodoxy in the early 1970s, and after 1996, to a critic of Greek ineptitude in adapting to the modern world and a growing estrangement from Orthodoxy. He studied law in Athens and philosophy in Bonn and Paris, where he taught philosophy from 1969 to 1974. He returned to Greece after the fall of the colonels' regime and became a popular lecturer and author. His book *Yearning for the One* explores the notions of the individual and the person in Greek and Western thought.[65] Here Ramfos raises questions about the validity of the standard narrative of the contrast between the person and personhood as valued in Orthodox theology and the individual or individualism which is taken to characterize Western thought. We will return to Ramfos's approach to personalism in Chapter 10.

A broad 'reaching out' of Orthodox theologians in the 1980s to the wider Greek intellectual community became known as the 'neo-Orthodox movement'.[66] The origin of neo-Orthodoxy lay in

---

[63]Yannaras, *Alítheia kai Enótita tis Ekklisías*, 79; *Vérité et unité de l'Église* (Grez-Doiceau, BE: Axios, 1989), 45.
[64]Victor Roudometof, 'Orthodoxy as Public Religion in Post-1989 Greece', in Victor Roudometof, Alexander Agadjanian and Jerry Pankhurst, eds., *Eastern Orthodoxy in a Global Age: Tradition Faces the Twenty-First Century* (London: AltaMira Press, 2005), 92.
[65]Stelios Ramfos, *Yearning for the One: Chapters in the Inner Life of the Greeks* (2000) (Brookline, MA: Holy Cross Orthodox Press, 2011).
[66]On the neo-Orthodox movement, see notably four articles on 'Le mouvement "néo-orthodoxe" en Grèce' (The 'neo-Orthodox' movement in Greece) in *Contacts*, 36, 124 (1984): Claudio Mésoniat, 'Un aperçu du mouvement' (An overview of the movement); Claudio Mésoniat, 'Un entretien avec Dionissis Savopoulos)' (An interview with Dionysis Savvopoulos); Jacques Touraille, 'Marxisme et Orthodoxie' (Marxism and Orthodoxy); and Panayote Dimitras, 'L'anti-occidentalisme grec' (Greek anti-Westernism). Also Vasilios Makrides, 'Byzantium in Contemporary Greece: The Neo-Orthodox Current of Ideas', in David Ricks and Paul Magdalino, *Byzantium and the Modern Greek Identity* (Aldershot UK: Ashgate, 1998).

a religious quest of certain intellectuals and literary and cultural figures on the political left, seeking to identify the basis for authentic Greek culture. This quest spawned a lively dialogue between Christian and Marxist intellectuals, but the term 'neo-Orthodoxy' soon came to refer to a wide range of personalities and ideas, to the point that some despair of being able to define it meaningfully or to consider it as a 'movement' at all.[67] The most prominent Orthodox personalities identified as 'neo-Orthodox' include, in addition to Christos Yannaras and Stelios Ramfos, Fr Georgios Metallinos (b. 1940) and Theodoros I. Ziakas (b. 1945), together with Marxist interlocutors such as Kostas Zouraris (b. 1940) and Kostis Moskoff (1939–98).

Like the Russian Slavophiles of the mid-nineteenth century, those identified with the neo-Orthodox movement recognized the critical importance of Christianity and Byzantine culture in the formation of the Greek identity, and they turned to Greek Orthodoxy as the key to the definition of Greekness in the face of Western culture and values. Pantelis Kalaitzidis characterizes the principal features of the neo-Orthodox movement as 'a return to tradition of the Fathers, a return to the people, Greek uniqueness, and a radical critique and rejection of the West, the Enlightenment, modernity etc.'[68] The movement had some surprising facets, including Orthodox-Marxist/Communist dialogue, considerable interest in traditional monasticism and hesychastic spirituality among Greek intellectuals and students and positive assessments of Orthodoxy by several popular cultural figures, such as the composer-singers Mikis Theodorakis (b. 1925) and Dionysis Savvopoulos (b. 1944). Neo-Orthodoxy was also associated with the marginal Greek Christian Democracy Party (ChD) and its student and youth arm, the Greek Christian Democratic Youth Organisation (Exon). But as the neo-Orthodox trend turned more towards Greco-Orthodox nationalism, the secular intellectuals withdrew from the dialogue. Little united the disparate personalities lumped under the neo-Orthodox label other than recognition of the importance of the Orthodox-Byzantine tradition in the formation of modern Greece and a critique of the West articulated from different perspectives. After the fall of communism in Eastern Europe, the basis of the Christian-Marxist dialogue disintegrated and the Orthodox associated with this trend followed other paths, even if the neo-Orthodox label persisted in popular parlance.

At the same time that neopatristic theology was appearing in Greek academic and para-academic circles, monasticism in Greece and especially on Mount Athos was undergoing a period of renewal. After decades of steady decline in the numbers of Athonite monks, in the early 1970s a marked renewal was visible on Mount Athos. This monastic renewal involved not only an increase in the number of monks on the Holy Mountain, but also a spiritual renaissance focused on the revival of hesychastic spirituality centred on the practice of the Jesus Prayer. Again, this revival, which continued from the mid-1960s at least until the beginning of the twenty-first century, involved a return to the patristic, ascetic and liturgical foundations of the Orthodox spiritual tradition, a far cry from the abstract spirituality flowing from scholastic theology and the moralistic spirituality of

[67]See Sotiris Mitralexis, '"A Luscious Anarchism in All of This": Revisiting the '80s and '90s Greek "Neo-Orthodox" Current of Ideas', *Journal of Modern Greek Studies* (forthcoming 2019).

[68]Pantelis Kalaitzidis, *Orthodoxy and Political Theology* (Geneva: WCC Publications, 2012), 33.

the religious brotherhoods.[69] Although the monastic renewal is broadly welcomed, the often vociferous opposition of the Athonite monasteries to ecumenism is less appreciated and has resulted in anti-monastic sentiments in more progressive theological circles.[70]

The language question

The language question has been a thorny issue in Greek theology for several reasons. The basic problem is that modern spoken and literary Greek (*dimotiki* or demotic Greek) is quite different from both the classical Greek of the pre-Christian period and the Hellenistic Greek of the early Christian period, *koiné*. In addition to modern Greek, there was another linguistic idiom, called *katharevousa* or 'pure language', used in legislation and other government documents, and in most university writings, until the late twentieth century. This 'pure language' was created by Greek intellectuals in the early nineteenth century with a view to 'ennobling' spoken Greek by giving it elements of classical Greek. *Dimotiki* became the official language of Greece only in 1976 and by the end of the twentieth century full *katharevousa* had become obsolete. *Katharevousa* nonetheless influenced the development of modern Greek, which now contains certain elements of *katharevousa*.

Language has been a theological issue on two fronts, the language of theology and the translation of the Bible into modern Greek. From the outset, Greek theology used exclusively the *katharevousa* idiom, thereby adding to the isolation of Greek academic theology from both Greek society as a whole, including non-academic intellectual circles, and the church. Christos Yannaras wrote in 1971:

> The problem of language in Greece is not limited to linguistic forms and to the preference given to one idiom over the other. It is a barrier that divides Greek intellectuals as profoundly and starkly as the division between the Slavophiles and 'Westerners' in nineteenth century Russia. 'Pure language' has always been the hallmark of Greek intellectuals influenced by the West, of the representatives of Western humanism and Enlightenment, of the romanticists of classicism who rejected or despised the Byzantine period of Greek civilization and the admirable popular culture of the Turkish domination. There are many exceptions of course. But this has been the rule.[71]

The move away from the use of *katharevousa* in theological publications began in the 1960s, and *Synaxi*, the most dynamic theological publication in Greece, never used it. The first Greek translation in 1964 of Vladimir Lossky's hugely influential *The Mystical Theology of the Eastern Church* was in *katharevousa*, but the 1970 translation of Alexander Schmemann's *For the Life of the World*

---

[69]On the monastic renewal on Mount Athos see Graham Speake, *Mount Athos: Renewal in Paradise* (New Haven, CN: Yale University Press, 2002); Georgios I. Mantzaridis, 'Athonite Monasticism at the Dawn of the Second Millennium'. http://www.elpenor.org/athos/en/e21813.asp (5 November 2015); Kallistos Ware, 'Wolves and Monks: Life on the Holy Mountain Today', *Sobornost'*, 5, 2 (1983); Kallistos Ware, 'Athos after Ten Years: The Good News and the Bad', *Sobornost'*, 15, 1 (1993).

[70]See the chapter 'Orthodoxy or Death!' in the polemical work by Ludmilla Perepiolkina, *Ecumenism: A Path to Perdition* (1999). http://ecumenizm.tripod.com/. On Athonite opposition to the dialogue between the Orthodox churches and the Oriental Orthodox churches, Paul Ladouceur, 'Orthodox Critiques of the Agreed Statements between the Orthodox and the Oriental Orthodox Churches', *St Vladimir's Theological Quarterly*, 60, 3 (2016), 335–6; 342; 345; 353–4; 365.

[71]Yannaras, 'Theology in Present-Day Greece', 206.

was apparently the first theological book in Greek published in vernacular *demotiki* Greek,[72] marking the beginning of the demise of *katharevousa* in Greek theology.

Arguments over the translation of Bible into modern Greek include linguistic, historical, theological, hermeneutical and even constitutional questions. Translations of the New Testament into modern Greek appeared as early as 1638, with another in 1703, but these translations, printed in Geneva and London, did not have much impact. The first attempt to translate the Bible into modern Greek was made shortly after Greek independence. The initiative came from a group of theologians sympathetic to Protestantism, under Theokletos Pharmakides and Neophytos Vamvas, called the Koraists, after Adamantios Koraes (1748–1833). This translation was made on the basis of the Protestant text of the Bible, which excludes the deuterocanonical books contained in the Orthodox canon of the Old Testament.[73] The translation, published by the Bible Society, a Protestant organization, was in literary *katharevousa* Greek. The Ecumenical Patriarchate banned this translation because it did not use the Orthodox canon of the Bible and because the original *koiné* text was not included in parallel columns with the translation. The church saw this translation as part of a proselytizing movement by Protestants among the Orthodox. The Patriarchate proceeded to commission its own translation, which was produced by a member of hierarchy, Hilarion of Tirnovo in Bulgaria, using a more popular linguistic form than that of the Bible Society. In 1901, another translation of the Gospels into modern Greek, prepared by Alexandros Pallis (1851–1935), provoked a similar controversy, even though the Ecumenical Patriarchate eventually authorized this translation in 1911.

The question of a new translation of the Bible into modern Greek came up again in the 1980s, following a translation seminar in 1977, initiated by the biblical departments of the faculties of theology of both Athens and Thessalonica and the Bible Society in Greece, which by then had majority Orthodox participation.[74] A pilot edition of the new translation appeared in 1985, but ran into stormy waters, with the result that the translation was initially condemned by the Church of Greece. After an extensive theological debate, the final edition of the new translation was published in 1989, with only minor changes from the pilot text, and with the blessing of the Church of Greece, the Ecumenical Patriarchate and the other Greek-language Patriarchates.

Towards post-patristic theology?

Great diversity characterized theology in Greece in the last decades of the twentieth century and the beginning of the twentieth century. This theological multi-polarity includes at least

[72]Sotiris Mitralexis, 'The Reception of the Theology of the Russian Diaspora by the Greek Theology of the '60s: A Case Study'. Paper for the conference '1917-2017: A Critical Reflection on the Theological Legacy of the Russian Diaspora' (University of Winchester, 11–13 January 2018), 5.

[73]See Panayiotis Crestou, 'Neohellenic Theology at the Crossroads', *Greek Orthodox Theological Review*, 28 (1983), 49.

[74]See Petros Vassiliadis, 'Greek Theology in the Making, Trends and Facts in the 80s – Vision for the 90s', *St Vladimir's Theological Quarterly*, 35, 1 (1991), 43.

six important modes of theology: vestiges of academic theology, especially in the theological educational system; the neopatristic approach to theology carried forward from the theology of the '60s, embodied notably by John Zizioulas; the theological moralism of the still-active but less prominent religious brotherhoods; theological conservatism or neo-traditionalism among certain academics, hierarchs, and monastic figures; the 'neo-Orthodoxy' of Christos Yannaras and others; and revisionist critiques of neopatristic theology emerging from engagement with modernity and associated with the unfortunate expression 'post-patristic theology'. While some aspects of this theological fertility became familiar outside Greece, primarily through the translations of the works major personalities such as Christos Yannaras, John Zizioulas, Hierotheos (Vlachos) of Nafpaktos (b. 1945) and younger figures such as Pantelis Kalaitzidis and Nikolaos Loudovikos, the works of many Greek theologians remain untranslated and little studied outside Greece. Even for such a prominent figure as Christos Yannaras, many of his numerous books, not to speak of his voluminous other writings, are published only in Greek. In this section, we focus mainly on those aspects of the Greek theological scene of the late twentieth century and early twenty-first centuries which have achieved a certain measure of international visibility, with an emphasis on younger theologians, at the risk of skewing the fullness of modern Greek theology considered from an internal perspective.

Prominent representatives of the younger generation of Greek theologians in the early twenty-first century include Fr Demetrios Bathrellos (b. 1968), who teaches at the Hellenic Open University (Athens) and at the Institute for Orthodox Christian Studies (Cambridge): Pantelis Kalaitzidis (b. 1961), director of the Volos Academy for Theological Studies: Fr Nikolaos Loudovikos (b. 1959), who teaches at the University Ecclesiastical Academy of Thessaloniki and at the Cambridge Institute for Orthodox Christian Studies; and Athanasios N. Papathanasiou (b. 1959), editor of the journal *Synaxi* since 1997.

Demetrios Bathrellos is primarily a scholar of Byzantine theology, a specialist on Maximus the Confessor. His thesis on Maximus's Christology is published in English,[75] and his books in Greek cover dogmatic theology, Christianity in the public square and the sinlessness of Christ. He has also written an important extended essay on the teaching of St Mark of Ephesus on the afterlife and Orthodox participation in the Council of Ferrara in 1438.[76]

Nikolaos Loudovikos has published works on Maximus the Confessor and ecclesiology, and has waded into the middle of contemporary Orthodox thought on personalism and ecclesiology.[77] Initially a student of John Zizioulas, Loudovikos took his distance from Zizioulas and is now a

[75]Demetrios Bathrellos, *The Byzantine Christ: Person, Nature, and Will in the Christology of St Maximus the Confessor* (Oxford: Oxford University Press, 2004).

[76]Demetrios Bathrellos, 'Love, Purification, and Forgiveness versus Justice, Punishment, and Satisfaction: The Debates on Purgatory and the Forgiveness of Sins at the Council of Ferrara-Florence', *Journal of Theological Studies*, NS 65, 1 (2014). See Paul Ladouceur, Review article 'Orthodox Theologies of the Afterlife', *St Vladimir's Theological Quarterly*, 62, 1 (2018).

[77]Loudovikos's most important publications in English translation are *A Eucharistic Ontology: Maximus the Confessor's Eschatological Ontology of Being as Dialogical Reciprocity* (Brookline, MA: Holy Cross Orthodox Press, 2010); and *Church in the Making: An Apophatic Ecclesiology of Consubstantiality* (Yonkers, NY: St Vladimir's Seminary Press, 2016). For a summary of his critique of John Zizioulas, see 'Person Instead of Grace: and Dictated Otherness: John Zizioulas's Final Theological Position', *Heythrop Journal*, 48 (2009); and his critique of Christos Yannaras: 'Hell and Heaven, Nature and Person. Chr. Yannaras, D. Stăniloae and Maximus the Confessor', *International Journal of Orthodox Theology*, 5, 1 (2014).

formidable critic of his former teacher's personalism and ecclesiology, and of the personalism of Christos Yannaras. For Loudovikos, Yannaras, Zizioulas and others have strayed from the healthy patristic balance between person and nature. Modern Orthodox thought in this area, while developing a robust theology of the human person, has, in the eyes of Loudovikos and others such as Jean-Claude Larchet, gone too far in denigrating the notion of human nature, which becomes associated with necessity constraining the person, and ultimately with the primordial fall and even hell. We will consider the Loudovikos's approach to personalism and ecclesiology in more detail in Chapters 10 and 11.

Pantelis Kalaitzidis identifies four major settings and institutions open to new trends in Greek theology: the journal *Synaxi*, at its foundation in 1982 originally an outlet for neopatristic theology, which subsequently opened to broader tendencies; *Theologia*, the scholarly journal of the Church of Greece; the independent biblical foundation Artos Zoes and the Volos Academy for Theological Studies.[78] In a similar vein, the Danish scholar Trine Stauning Willert identifies as 'spaces of progressive theological thought', *Synaxi* and the Volos Academy, and also KAIROS, the Greek Theological Association for the Improvement of Religious Education, founded in 2010 with a view to reform religious education in Greek schools along progressive lines.[79]

Athanasios N. Papathanasiou is a well-known figure in Greek theology and public circles as editor of *Synaxi*, instructor at the Hellenic Open University and frequent participant in conferences and Greek social media. Papathansiou focuses on the engagement of Orthodoxy with modernity, especially Orthodox mission, social justice and political theology. He stresses scriptural, patristic and canonical texts which highlight the indissolubility of Christian faith and practice and social with economic justice, developing a liberation perspective along the lines of liberation theology in the Catholic Church. Papathanasiou espouses an Orthodox theology of liberation which calls on Orthodox to seek justice, solidarity and freedom in contemporary society. 'Theology is the elevation of the Christian faith', he writes, 'to encounter and confront the injustice of this age, while maintaining the metaphysical fullness of the faith'.[80] At the same time he is aware of the tension in Orthodoxy between emphasis on personal salvation and social concern and action, and the ambiguous attitude in the early church and the Byzantine Empire towards social justice, including slavery.[81]

Papathanasiou's social engagement is reflected notably in his extended essay 'Social Justice and Orthodox Theology' (2001)[82] and in a collection of short pieces under the title *The Clash with Nothingness* (2015), previously published in newspapers and magazines, even on his

---

[78]Kalaitzidis, 'New Trends in Greek Orthodox Theology', 157–60.

[79]Trine Stauning Willert, *New Voices in Greek Orthodox Thought: Untying the Bond between Nation and Religion* (Farnham, Surrey: Ashgate, 2014), 55. The book focuses on the thinking of Pantelis Kalaitzidis and the Volos Academy (chapters 1 to 3) and the teaching of religion in Greek schools (chapters 4 to 7).

[80]Athanasios N. Papathanasiou, *I Ríxi me to Midén: Sfinákia Politikís Theologías* (Rupture with Nothingness: Snippets of Political Theology) (Athens: Armos Publications, 2015), back cover. See reviews by Nikolaos Asproulis, *Synaxis*, 135 (2015) (in Greek); *Orthodoxes Forum*, 30:1 (2016) (in German); and by Maro Triantafyllou. https://marotriantafyllou.wordpress.com/2015/10/13 (19 February 2018).

[81]See Athanasios N. Papathanasiou, 'Liberation Perspectives in Patristic Thought: An Orthodox Approach', *Scientific Review of Post-Graduate Program Studies in Orthodox Theology*, 2 (Patras: Hellenic Open University, 2011).

[82]Athanasios N. Papathanasiou, *Koinonikí Dikaiosýni kai Orthódoxi Theología* (Social Justice and Orthodox Theology: A Proclamation) (Athens: Akritas, 2001).

Facebook page, and covering a wide range of current social, cultural and political issues. Major themes include solidarity with the victims of history, acceptance of the foreigner – refugees and migrants, – separation of church and state, and rejection of neo-liberalism, fundamentalism and the nationalism of the far right. Faith and theology lead to political engagement: 'Theology here is a profoundly *political* voice: it is a proposition on the meaning of our common life. Faith is not a private and privatized affair, but comes forth to confront the unfairness and inhumanity of this world.'[83]

In these and in other publications, Papathanasiou advances an engaged faith which seeks to understand contemporary society from a Christian perspective and to participate actively in national and international social and political issues. He writes: 'Is Christian participation in a global movement to eradicate abusive and usurious [national] debts anything other than a requirement of the very mystery of faith?'[84] While the church must not exercise state power, a Christian must be in the public domain, a citizen active in the concerns of his society. The public square is 'a forum of dialogue and confrontation', where religion must expose 'what threatens human life and dignity or, on the contrary, what constitutes hope.'[85] Papathanasiou's reflections on refugees and migrants are a noteworthy example of his social commitment: 'The stranger I accept, the stranger I become,' he writes.[86]

Pantelis Kalaitzidis has a high international visibility outside Greece, thanks to the activities of the Volos Academy, of which he is the director, and to his numerous publications in Western Europe and North America. Following studies in theology in Thessalonica and philosophy in Paris, Kalaitzidis completed his doctoral thesis in 2008 at the University of Thessalonica. He is a determined critic of many aspects of neopatristic theology, especially a perceived anti-Westernism and its frequent fellow travellers: the exaltation of an idealized vision of the Byzantine Empire; religious nationalism; anti-ecumenism; the difficulty of neopatristic theology to engage meaningfully and constructively with modernity and contemporary social, political and ethical issues; concentration on patristic theology to the neglect of other fields such as biblical studies; a strong focus on the hierarchical aspect of the church and the neglect of the royal priesthood of the faithful and the role of the laity, especially women, in the church.[87] Some features of neopatristic theology under fire, especially the trio of anti-Westernism, 'Byzantinism' and anti-ecumenism, are perhaps stronger in the Greek context than elsewhere in Orthodoxy, but an anti-Western undertone is indeed a characteristic of Orthodox neopatristic theology (see Chapter 17).

---

[83]Papathanasiou, *The Clash with Nothingness*, back cover.

[84]Ibid., 30.

[85]Ibid., 72.

[86]Athanasios N. Papathanasiou, 'O xénos pou déchomai, o xénos pou gínomai' (The stranger I accept, the stranger I become), *Planodion*, 48 (June 2010). http://e-theologia.blogspot.ca/2010/10/blog-post_26.html (25 February 2018). See also the collection of texts in his *O Theós mou o allodapós: Keímena gia mian alítheia pou eínai 'tou drómou'* (My God, the Stranger: Texts for Truth 'On The Road') (Athens: Akritas, 2002).

[87]See Pantelis Kalaitzidis, 'New Trends in Greek Orthodox Theology: Challenges in the Movement towards a Genuine Renewal and Christian Unity', *Scottish Journal of Theology*, 67, 2 (2014), 136–56. In addition to the points mentioned above, Kalaitzidis sees other weaknesses in neopatristic theology: devaluation of eschatology; overemphasis on monasticism, ascetic practices and the role of elders (*geronda* or *startsi*) in the church; and the neglect of mission. See also his 'Orthodoxy and Hellenism in Contemporary Greece', *St Vladimir's Theological Quarterly*, 54, 3–4 (2010).

The Volos Academy rapidly emerged in the new millennium as a dynamic feature in Greek theology and a major force in global Orthodox thought. The Volos Academy, founded in 2000, operates under the aegis of the Greek Metropolis of Demetrias, with the strong support of Metropolitan Ignatios (Georgakopoulos) (b. 1956), who has headed the metropolis of Demetrias since 1998. Volos is not a teaching institution, but is rather a research centre and publishing house, with considerable international visibility and support.[88] Its formal areas of interest are conventional enough: liturgical chant and musicology; the manuscript tradition of the New Testament; canon law; interreligious studies and Byzantine and post-Byzantine monuments and relics. A large part of the Academy's activities is centred on the organization of studies, conferences and colloquia, frequently in collaboration with academic institutions in Eastern Europe, Western Europe and the United States. The Volos Academy, operating outside the formal university structure but within the Church of Greece, has more freedom than a university faculty, and it has successfully mobilized financial support for its many conferences, publications and other activities. Despite its high external visibility, Volos appears to have limited influence within Greece itself, in comparison with other theological actors, such as leading figures of the older generation, notably Christos Yannaras, the journals *Synaxi* and *Theologia*, younger theologians such as Nikolaos Loudovikos and Athanasios Papathansiou and neo-traditionist figures such as Hierotheos Vlachos.

The tone of the Volos Academy was set by Kalaitzidis's doctoral thesis, entitled 'Hellenicity and Anti-Westernism in the Greek "Theology of the '60s"'.[89] The thesis is an indictment of hellenocentrism, the identification of Orthodoxy with the Greek nation and Greek culture, the nostalgic idealization of the Byzantine Empire and of Greek anti-Westernism. Kalaitzidis's main targets are John Romanides, Archimandrite Vassilios Gontikakis (b. 1936; former Abbot of the Athonite monasteries of Iviron and Stavronikita), Nikos Matsoukas (1931–2006; professor of dogmatics at the University of Thessalonica) and Georges Florovsky, especially Florovsky's notion of Christian Hellenism, an influential theme in the theology of the '60s, but most especially Christos Yannaras. Kalaitzidis reads Yannaras's critique of Western thought and culture as systematic, structural and persistent, but he seems to overlook Yannaras's proclaimed perspective as a critic within Westernism itself, his universal rather than ethnic or national vision of Hellenism and his engagement with issues of modernity in a number of books and other publications.[90]

Kalaitzidis's study is an inverse image of Florovsky's *The Ways of Russian Theology* (1937) and of Yannaras's *Orthodoxy and the West* (1992). Just as Florovsky set out to identify and denounce Western influence in Russian thought, and Yannaras to point the finger at Western influences in Greek Orthodoxy, so Kalaitzidis sets out to identify and denounce anti-Westernism in modern Greek thought. Florovsky himself gets off rather lightly in Kalaitzidis's analysis. Despite Florovsky's

[88]See the Volos annual programme, for example *Orthodoxy and 'Open Society'. Academic Year 2014-15: Program and Parallel Events* (Volos, GR: Volos Academy for Theological Studies – Research Center, c. 2014).
[89]Pantelis Kalaitzidis, 'Hellenicity and Anti-Westernism in the Greek "Theology of the '60s"' (in Greek) (Doctoral Thesis, Aristotle University of Thessalonica, 2008).
[90]Examples of Yannaras's treatment of issues of modernity include his books *Orthós Lógos Kaí Koinonikí Praktikí* (Rationality and Social Practice) (Athens: Domos, 1984) and *Tó Pragmatikó Kaí Tó Fantasiódes Stín Politikí Oikonomía* (The Real and the Imaginary in Political Economy) (Athens: Domos, 2006). These and many more of Yannaras's books are in Greek only.

thesis of Hellenism as '*a standing category of Christian existence*,'[91] Florovsky, like Yannaras for that matter, saw Hellenism in theological and universal terms, not as an ethnic or cultural category, and certainly neither can be accused of promoting religious nationalism. Nonetheless, for Kalaitzidis a simplified reading of Florovsky by some Greek theologians served to promote an unhealthy, ethnically based Christian Hellenism. In other writings, Kalaitzidis considers that neopatristic theology as a whole has been profoundly infected by the canker of anti-Westernism. In this, he has a sympathetic audience among other Orthodox theologians in several countries.

The positive side of the Kalaitzidis-Volos theological agenda focuses on the universalism of Orthodoxy, and engagement with modernism from an Orthodox perspective, instead of simplistic and vociferous (and largely futile) denunciations of modernity, ecumenism and religious pluralism, typical of neo-traditionalist circles in Greece and elsewhere. The engagement with aspects of modernity is clear in themes addressed by the Volos Academy: Orthodox Christianity and modernity; theology and culture; religion in the public square; women and laity in the church; ecumenism and multiculturalism or religious pluralism.

In 2001–2, the Volos Academy hosted a lecture series on the theme 'Orthodox Christianity and Modernity'.[92] In a lengthy introduction to the collected papers, Pantelis Kalaitzidis issues a clarion call for Orthodox engagement with modernity, especially central notions such as the emergence of the autonomous subject, the affirmation of rationality, human rights, the religiously neutral secular state and the separation of church and state (typically accompanied by the relegation of religion to the private sphere). This stance contrasts sharply with the rejection of modernity by many Orthodox theologians, for whom the fundamental achievements of modernity 'have remained essentially alien to Orthodoxy'.[93] Kalaitzidis sees in modern Orthodox theology of the person one of the principal foundations for a fruitful Orthodox encounter with modernity. He supports his argument by drawing a parallel between the encounter of Christianity with Hellenic culture in the early centuries of the church, which resulted in the adoption (and adaptation) of many notions of Greek philosophy into Christian theology, and the awaited encounter of Orthodoxy with modernism resulting from the Enlightenment in particular. Together with other Christian authors, Kalaitzidis argues that modernity has a Christian basis, which some refer to as 'non-religious Christianity'. He is nonetheless confident that Orthodoxy can engage in 'a creative encounter and a serious theological dialogue with whatever challenges modernity poses', without losing its soul. The book is a revisionist manifesto which sets forth the philosophical, theological and historical foundations for the engagement of Orthodoxy with modernity, especially in the public square.

The activities of the Volos Academy and the thinking of Pantelis Kalaitzidis are disturbing in the Greek context, in some ways reminiscent of the initial reaction to same theology of the '60s that

---

[91]Georges Florovsky, 'Patristics and Modern Theology' (1939), in Gallaher and Ladouceur, eds., *The Patristic Witness of Georges Florovsky*, 157.

[92]The lecture series: Pantelis Kalaitzidis and Nikos Ntontos, eds., *Orthodoxía kai neoterikótita* (Orthodox Christianity and Modernity) (Athens: Indiktos Publications, 2007). The Introduction is published separately: Pantelis Kalaitzidis, *Orthodoxía kai neoterikótita: Prolegomena* (Orthodoxy and Modernity: An Introduction) (Athens: Indiktos Publications, 2007).

[93]Kalaitzidis, *Orthodoxy and Modernity: An Introduction*, passim. I am grateful to Pantelis Kalaitzidis for access to a draft English translation by Elizabeth Theokritoff.

Kalaitzidis criticizes. A broadly based revisionist movement in Orthodox theology, with the Volos Academy in the front ranks, was manifest at a conference held at Volos in 2010 on the theme 'Neo-Patristic Synthesis or Post-Patristic Theology: Can Orthodox Theology Be Contextual?' (see Chapter 17).

There is an anti-Volos reaction in neo-traditionalist quarters of the Church of Greece and Greek universities. Taking a cue from Volos's own modus operandi, Metropolitan Seraphim (Mentzelopoulos) of Piraeus (b. 1956) organized a symposium on 4 February 2012 with the polemical title 'Patristic Theology and Post-Patristic Heresy'.[94] The well-attended event was a generalized attack on a good part of modern Orthodox theology, except for John Romanides, Panayiotis Trembelas, and, to some extent, Georges Florovsky and a few others. The symposium was stimulated largely by the 2010 Volos conference, with opposition to the very idea of 'post-patristic theology' as the *leitmotif* and Romanides as the knight in shining armour who saves Orthodoxy from heretical theological revisionism.

Despite its limited internal impact, the progressive strand of modern Greek theology, represented by the Volos Academy and Pantelis Kalaitzidis, is the darling of studies of the Greek religious scene.[95] Studies nonetheless note the intellectualism of the Academy and its restricted audience of a relatively closed circle of initiates, in comparison with the wider appeal of the more traditionally oriented 'neo-Orthodox' strand in Greek theology, powerfully represented by Christos Yannaras, and, we could add, the neo-traditionalist strand, which also enjoys support in the Church of Greece, the universities and the monasteries.

Conclusion

In an article published in 1972, Christos Yannaras presents a scathing assessment of academic theology in Greece:

> Morality was separated from dogma. Dogmas remained a body of theoretical principles without any immediate relationship to the spiritual life of the faithful. Morality was based on rationalistic concepts and in particular on the juridical conception of the relationship between God and man, which has always been the hallmark of Western piety. ... Academic theology was totally indifferent to the people and to their spirituality. It could not see how it might find its roots and its truth in them. Dedicated to science and to its methods, it remained totally apart from the life and spirituality of the

[94]An English translation of the conference proceedings, with most of the papers, was published on the website of the Pantocrator Monastery of Melissochori: www.impantokratoros.gr/99150D71.en.aspx (8 October 2015). See also Ch. 17 concerning this conference.

[95]In addition to Willert's *New Voices in Greek Orthodox Thought* mentioned above, see also Catharina Raudvere, Krzysztof Stala and Trine Stauning Willert, eds., *Rethinking the Space for Religion: New Actors in Central and Southeast Europe on Religion, Authenticity And Belonging* (Lund, SE: Nordic Academic Press, 2012); Victor Roudometof and Vasilios N. Makrides, eds., *Orthodox Christianity in 21st century Greece: The Role of Religion in Culture, Ethnicity and Politics* (Farnham: Ashgate, 2010); Trine Stauning Willert and Lina Molokotos-Liederman, eds., *Innovation in the Greek Orthodox Tradition? The Question of Change in Greek Orthodox Thought and Practice* (Farnham: Ashgate, 2012). On the intellectualism and low public profile of progressive theologians, see Willert, *New Voices in Greek Orthodox Thought*, 60–1; 74; 77; 79–80.

> church. And this attitude prevailed during the entire duration of the free Greek state, up to the present time [1972].[96]

Although some of his remarks are overdrawn, in his denunciation of Western influence in Greek academic theology Yannaras parallels Florovsky's similar denunciation of Western influence in Russian theology. In a similar vein, Panayiotis Chrestou characterized this type of Greek theology as having 'its heart rooted in Orthodoxy, its mind fed by Protestantism and its argumentation derived from scholasticism'.[97]

On another theological front, the religious fraternities, Zoe and its imitators, were a striking feature of the Greek religious scene until late in the twentieth century. Formally Zoe was never a heretical or schismatic organization, but in many ways it operated as a kind of parallel church. Its accomplishments were prodigious in terms of the promotion of personal and family piety, publications, Bible study groups and Christian organizations of all sorts. But its spirit and many of its methods were not Orthodox and it served as a vehicle to further Western influence on Greek Orthodoxy, not the scholastic and rationalist Western influence which affected Greek theology, but rather Anglican and Protestant pietism. Although Zoe was a powerful force in Greek religious life for many decades, its impact on theology in Greece was minimal, even if Panagiotis Trembelas, the leading Greek academic theologian of the second half of the twentieth century, remained closely associated with the movement throughout most of his long career.

Zoe's influence reached a peak in the 1940s and the 1950s, but declined sharply after the 1960 split in the movement, a messy and much-publicized affair. Several other major developments accelerated the decline of religious brotherhoods in the 1960s: the presence and activities of major spiritual figures, both on Mount Athos and elsewhere in the country, firmly attached to the church, who undermined the notion of a separation between the church as an institution and the praying church and personal piety[98]; a strong monastic revival on Mount Athos; greater maturity of the Greek Orthodox Church, marked for example by a rising level of education of priests and its own missionary activities; the major turn in Greek theology to a more patristic-based theology; and rising materialism and indifference which affected all forms of religious participation among broad sectors of the population. The upshot of these developments was that after the fall of the colonels' regime in 1974, the religious fraternities were no longer major forces in Greek society and Greek Orthodoxy, but their legacy continues and they remain the subject of much debate.

Recognition of the new patristic-based theology was not universal in Greece. The theological faculty of Athens in particular continued for a long time to be a bastion of traditional academic theology, more so than the faculty of theology at Thessalonica. In a 1983 lecture at the Orthodox Theological Society in America, Panayiotis Chrestou, speaking on 'Neohellenic Theology of the Crossroads', purports to find 'the way for true renewal in neohellenic theology' among the academic

---

[96]Christos Yannaras, 'Theology in Present-Day Greece', *St Vladimir's Theological Quarterly*, 14, 4 (1972), 197. See also the chapter on 'The Theological Schools', in *Orthodoxy and the West*, 193–216.

[97]Panayiotis Chrestou, 'Neohellenic Theology at the Crossroads', *Greek Orthodox Theological Review*, 28, 1 (1983), 51.

[98]The most important modern spiritual figures of Greece and Mount Athos feature in Herman Middleton, *Precious Vessels: The Lives and Counsels of Contemporary Elders of Greece* (Thessalonica and Ashville, NC: Protecting Veil Press, 2003).

theologians of Athens and Thessalonica – but he makes no mention of the leaders of the new theology already identified by Christos Yannaras twenty years earlier. Chrestou evokes the 'patristic turn' in a few sentences at the end of his lecture, summarized in one short statement: 'The tendency of turning to patristic sources is stronger today.'[99] Clearly academic theology enjoyed a long life in Greece.

The neo-Orthodox label applied to Greek theology covers a broad scope of personalities, the most prominent of whom is Christos Yannaras, who, like Georges Florovsky, sees a universal feature in Hellenism which defines the true nature of Orthodoxy. John Romanides and Christos Yannaras, despite fundamental differences between them, provide the link between neo-Orthodoxy and the broader neopatristic theological movement characterized as 'the theology of the '60s'. An unfortunate collateral effect of the neo-Orthodox movement was that neopatristic theology as a whole became, in the eyes of critics, tainted with the same conservative, nationalist and anti-modernist brush as they perceived, however, incorrectly, in neo-Orthodoxy. Religious studies scholars in particular seem to confound neopatristic theology with the neo-Orthodoxy of the 1980s and 1990s, collapsing the former into the latter.[100]

The theology of the '60s, a shorthand for the revival of patristic theology in Greece, is deeply indebted to the Russian theologians in exile, especially Vladimir Lossky and Georges Florovsky, and also Alexander Schmemann and John Meyendorff. The principal channels from the Russians to the Greeks were John Romanides, the circle around Demetrios Koutroubis, and Christos Yannaras. Yannaras considers that it was in fact 'the presence of the theology of the Russian diaspora, together with further turns to the Fathers such as the *nouvelle théologie*, that sparked the Greek renaissance and made it possible.'[101] There were, of course, other influences, including individuals such as John Romanides and John Zizioulas, the revival of Greek monasticism, especially on Mount Athos, and the work of the faculty of theology of Thessaloniki under Panayiotis Chrestou. The inception of neopatristic theology in Greece was a sort of theological revolution, for Yannaras and others 'a truly new and different way to conceive and speak of theology, Christianity, tradition, the patristic legacy, and the church.'[102]

The new millennium saw the emergence of critiques of established types of theology, both from the theological 'left' and the theological 'right', making a sharp polarization among Greek theologians. Sotiris Mitralexis characterizes the poles as marked by 'a *fervent anti-Westernism*' – *sola traditio*, – and a '*rampant anti-Easternism*' – *sola modernitas*[103] – anti-Easternism in the sense of opposition to anything that highlights Eastern Christian or Orthodox particularism in the face of Christian universalism. There is clearly a wide diversity of views between the two poles. The more conservative or neo-traditionalist pole, with leading figures such as Metropolitans Hierotheos

---

[99]Christou, 'Neohellenic Theology at the Crossroads', 54.

[100]Willert dismisses Greek neopatristic theology in a few sentences under the heading 'Neo-Orthodox Revival and Anti-Westernism'. See Willert, *New Voices in Greek Orthodox Thought*, 49–50.

[101]As interpreted by Sotiris Mitralexis, 'The Reception of the Theology of the Russian Diaspora by the Greek Theology of the '60s', 4.

[102]Ibid., 6.

[103]Sotiris Mitralexis, 'Modern Greek Theology', in Andrew Louth and Andreas Andreopoulos, eds., *Oxford Handbook of Orthodox Theology* (Oxford: Oxford University Press, forthcoming).

Vlachos and Seraphim Mentzelopoulos, typically targets as opponents Metropolitan John Zizioulas, and indeed a good part of neopatristic theology, both Greek and international. The more progressive or modernist pole, typified by figures such as Pantelis Kalaitzidis, in addition to criticizing neo-traditionalist theology, also attacks neopatristic theology for its perceived underlying anti-Westernism and its difficulty in coming to grips with modernity. In some ways Christos Yannaras towers above these polarities as a unique prophetic voice inadequately understood and insufficiently studied both inside and outside Greece.

Neopatristic theology has come under fire from younger theologians, who feel that the practice of this approach to theology in Greece has become tainted with an unhealthy introspective spirit characterized by anti-Westernism, an undue exaltation of the Byzantine Empire and an a priori rejection of modernity. These critiques coalesce around the polemical slogan 'post-patristic theology'. The term 'post-patristic' was no doubt a hastily launched trial balloon which soon burst, making its advocates easy targets for accusations of betraying Orthodox tradition. This serves to distract attention from the main trusts of the progressive theologians, especially the necessity of engaging the modern world beyond mere denunciation. Despite the controversial idea of 'post-patristic' theology, the ferment in Greek theology, reinforced by similar developments in Orthodox theology elsewhere, may nonetheless open new possibilities for Orthodoxy theology to overcome some of the weaknesses inherent in neopatristic theology. The current theological revisionism could also provide a framework for the now conventional neopatristic approach to recognize the origins of some of its key concepts in earlier theology, especially in the enduring aspects of Russian religious philosophy. We will return to these themes in the concluding chapters of this book.

7

Theology in Romania

Chapter Outline

Overview of theology in Romania

The region which now forms the modern state of Romania has a long history of Christian culture, extending back to the legendary preaching of the apostle Andrew along the shores of the Black Sea. From the fifteenth to the seventeenth centuries, and again in the nineteenth and twentieth centuries, the Romanian lands witnessed a flowering of hesychastic spirituality, nourished by frequent contacts with the monasteries of Mount Athos – Romania is even described as having a 'hesychastic culture'.[1] The Romanian principalities of Walachia and Moldavia were generous patrons of the monasteries of Mount Athos and of Christian communities in the Christian Middle East, especially the Patriarchate of Jerusalem. Monasticism in Romania remained a constant source of spiritual uplifting of the Romanian faithful over the centuries. St Paisius Velichkovsky (1722–94), who transferred his monastic community from Mount Athos to Moldavia in 1784, undertook the translation of ancient spiritual and ascetic writings into Slavonic and Romanian, which resulted in the first publication of a Slavonic *Philokalia*, the

[1]From the title of the classic study by Metropolitan Serafim Joanta, *Treasures of Romanian Christianity: Hesychastic Tradition and Culture* (Toronto, ON: Cross Meridian, 2013). This is a revised translation of the French original: Romul Joanta, *Roumanie: Tradition and Culture hésychastes* (Bégrolles, FR: Abbaye de Bellefontaine, 1987).

Dobrotoliubie, in 1793. This provided a major impetus for a widespread spiritual renewal in Russia from the early nineteenth century onwards.

The Romanian principalities were exposed to both Roman Catholic and Protestant influences, in particular as a result of the rule of Austria-Hungary from 1688 to 1919 over the mixed Romanian-Hungarian region of Transylvania, and from the influence of Western missionaries in Romania and of Romanians who studied in the West. Austrian pressure led to the formation of a Byzantine rite Romanian Greek Catholic Church in union with Rome in 1700 in Transylvania, and Catholic ascendency in Transylvania was accompanied by the development of schools and theological education along Western lines. The formation of modern Romania by the union of Walachia and Moldavia in 1859 was followed by a secularization which saw the nationalization of many monastic properties. A robust monasticism nonetheless endured as a major aspect of Romanian Orthodoxy. There was an important spiritual revival in Romania in the twentieth century, which not even the forty years of communist rule was able to extinguish.[2]

As in Russia, formal theology developed slowly in Romania.[3] The first major theological event which took place in Romania in modern times was the Council of Jassy (Iaşi) in 1642, convened by Metropolitan Varlaam of Jassy (1590–1657; canonized in 2007) to consider the Confession of Faith of Peter Mogila, written to counteract the Calvinistic leanings of the Confession of Cyril Lucaris. As we saw in Chapter 2, the Council of Jassy approved Mogila's Confession of Faith, as modified by the Greek hieromonk Melitos Syrigos, although even this modified version still contained elements of Latin theology. Metropolitan Varlaam wrote two major works directed against Calvinist theology, a catechism and a defence of the seven sacraments. Other religious works published during this period were translations into Romanian of the Bible, liturgical books, the lives of the saints and some patristic writings.

A number of seminaries modelled on Russian seminaries were established in Romanian dioceses in the early nineteenth century, two of which, those of Bucharest (founded in 1836) and of Sibiu (1849), developed into higher-level theological academies, as in Russia. Teaching materials for the seminaries consisted of translations of Greek and Russian texts. Metropolitan Grigorie (Dascalul) of Wallachia (1765–1834; canonized in 2005), who translated a number of patristic works into Romanian, wrote the first Romanian *Dogmatica* in 1806. The second half of the nineteenth century also saw the publication of translations of complete works from Greek and Russian and adaptations and compendia of theological texts from patristic and other sources.

As in Russia and Greece, theology in Romania in the nineteenth and twentieth centuries was dominated by scholastically inspired academic theology. Romanian translations of the dogmatic treatises of Russian and Greek theologians of the nineteenth and early twentieth centuries,

---

[2]See notably Joanta, *Treasures of Romanian Christianity*, 247–75; and Un Moine de l'Église orthodoxe de Roumanie (André Scrima), 'L'avènement philocalique dans l'Orthodoxie roumaine' (The advent of the Philokalia in Romanian Orthodoxy), *Istina*, 3 & 4 (1958).

[3]For a more detailed presentation of traditional theology in Romania, see George Maloney, 'The Rumanian Orthodox Church', in his *History of Orthodox Theology since 1453* (Belmont, MA: Nordland, 1976), 271–98. Maloney focuses primarily on academic theology, according scant attention to neopatristic theology. He mentions Dumitru Staniloae only briefly, mainly with respect to Staniloae's *Filocalia* (294).

notably those of Makarius Bulgakov and Christos Androutsos (the latter translated by Dumitru Staniloae in 1930), were prominent among Romanian theological publications. Bishop Melchizedek Stefanescu (1823–92) published several theology textbooks between 1846 and 1862. His *Teologia dogmatică a Bisericii Ortodoxe catolice de Răsărit* (Dogmatic Theology of the Orthodox Catholic Church of the East) appeared in 1855, and four other *Dogmatica* were published between 1862 and 1916. Stefanescu also translated the *Catechism* of Philaret of Moscow (1857).

Many of the professors of the theological academies were well trained, both in Romania and abroad. Of the teaching staff of twenty-one at the Bucharest Faculty of Theology in 1961, sixteen had studied abroad prior to 1940, many in Paris and Strasbourg, others in Germany, Rome, Warsaw or Oxford.[4] In the 1950s future Patriarch Iustin (Moisescu) (1910–86; patriarch 1977–86) initiated and supervised the production of series of manuals for use in the Romanian theological schools, covering all major traditional disciplines: Old Testament, New Testament, patristics, church history, history of the Romanian Church, dogmatic theology, ethics, homiletics, catechetics, liturgical theology, pastoral theology, canon law, symbolics, as well as an introductory volume of fundamental theology and volumes on the history of religions, the history of education and general education.[5]

The most important of these manuals was the popular manual of dogmatic theology, first published in 1958, the *Teologica Dogmatica si Simbolica* (Dogmatic and Symbolic Theology), written by Professors Nicolae Chitescu, Isidor Todoran, I. Petreuta and Dumitru Staniloae.[6] This work follows very closely the *Dogmatica* of Christos Androutsos.[7] The 'Symbolics' portion of the book deals mainly with comparisons of Orthodox theology with Roman Catholic and Protestant theology. Another version of this work, under the title *Teologica Dogmatica, Manual pentru seminariile teologice* (Dogmatic Theology, A Manual for Theological Seminaries), by Isidor Todoran and Ioan Zagrean, was published in 1991, after the fall of the communist regime.

Ioan Coman (1902–87) was a well-known Romanian patrologist. He studied theology, the history of religions and Byzantine studies in Bucharest and he also studied at the Protestant Theology Faculties in Strasbourg, Montpellier and Paris and at the Faculty of Catholic Theology in Strasbourg. He taught patristics and Byzantine history in Bucharest from 1944 until 1970 and was the author of the influential *Patrologie* textbook, used for teaching patristics in Romanian academies and seminaries.

[4]Alf Johansen, *Theological Study in the Romanian Orthodox Church under Communist Rule* (London: Faith Press, 1961), 4–5. Johansen, a Lutheran theologian from Denmark, visited Romania four times between 1956 and 1961, studied at the Bucharest Faculty of Theology and had several meetings with Patriarch Justinian. Some consider that he was duped and used by the communist regime for propaganda purposes.

[5]See brief summaries and comments on the volumes in Johansen, *Theological Study in the Romanian Orthodox Church*, 10–47. Johansen had access to both the volumes that had been printed, as well as those still in typescript in 1961.

[6]Nicolae Chițescu, Isidor Todoran, I. Petreuță, *Teologia Dogmatică și Simbolică*, Vol. I–II (Cluj-Napoca, RO: Editura Renașterea, 2004). Dumitru Staniloae was one of the co-authors of the book, but he had been arrested by the time of its publication and was not named as one of the authors.

[7]See Johansen, *Theological Study in the Romanian Orthodox Church*, 21; Maloney, *A History of Orthodox Theology*, 292.

The theology of Fr Dumitru Staniloae (1903–93) stands in sharp contrast to the formal academic theology of Romanian theological education. Dumitru Staniloae was the leading representative of the 'new theology' in Romania for a good part of the twentieth century and one of the major figures of neopatristic theology. As we saw in Chapter 5, his monograph on St Gregory Palamas published in 1938 was the first modern book-length study of Palamas, and included translations of several of Palamas's works. Staniloae's literary output is enormous and includes many books and numerous articles intended for learned and for general audiences on a wide range of theological subjects. We will consider Staniloae's theology in more detail later in this chapter.

The little-known theologian Anca Manolache (1923–2013) was a lonely voice in the Romanian Orthodox Church in the latter years of the communist regime and after the fall of communism in 1989. Originally educated in law and philology, she studied theology during the communist years, but was imprisoned for 'omitting to denounce her friends' from 1959 to 1964 (the same years that Dumitru Staniloae was imprisoned). She subsequently worked for the Biblical and Missionary Institute in Bucharest, acting as editor for Staniloae's Romanian translations of the *Philokalia* and for Stanilaoe's *Orthodox Dogmatic Theology* (*The Experience of God* in English translation). Her main theological interest was the role of women in Christianity and especially in Romania and she published a number of articles pointing to the systematic discrimination against women and their subservient and secondary roles in Romanian society and the church.[8] But her mildly progressive views on the social and ecclesiastical roles of men and women were too much for the conservative Romanian Orthodox Church and she remained largely ignored and under-appreciated.[9]

The Romanian Orthodox Church was influenced by extreme tendencies in Romanian society and politics in the interwar period, during the Second World War and after the war. Nationalist and conservative thinking dominated Romanian politics in the years prior to the Second World War. One right-wing group, the Legion of the Archangel Michael, more commonly known as the Iron Guard or the Legionnaire Movement, founded in 1927 by the charismatic Corneliu Codreanu (1899–1938), combined nationalism and religion in an explosive cocktail.[10] The movement's wide appeal, especially among university students, was based on a fascist agenda which mingled ultra-nationalism, Romanian ethnicity, antisemitism, anti-communism, anti-capitalism and Orthodox Christianity. Many members of the church, including clergy and some hierarchs, were attracted to the Iron Guard because of its religious and mystical dimension, especially as united with Romanian nationalism, as an alternative to secularism and communism. The fusion of these disparate elements is referred to as 'sacralised politics', 'clerical fascism'[11] or more broadly 'religious fascism', which in

---

[8]A number of Anca Manolache's articles are collected her book *Problematica feminină în Biserica lui Hristos: Un capitol de antropologie creștină* (Feminine Problematics in the Church of Christ: A Chapter of Christian Anthropology) (Timisoara: Mitropoliei Banatului, 1994).

[9]See Lucian Turcescu, 'A Woman's Lonely Voice in the Romanian Orthodox Church: Introducing Anca Manolache', *Orthodoxy in Dialogue* (24 May 2018). https://orthodoxyindialogue.com/2018/05/24/ (29 August 2018).

[10]See Ionut Biliuta, 'The Archangel's Consecrated Servants. An Inquiry in The Relationship Between the Romanian Orthodox Church and the Iron Guard (1930-1941)'. PhD dissertation (Central European University, Budapest, 2013).

[11]See Roger Griffin, 'The "Holy Storm": "Clerical Fascism" through the Lens of Modernism'; and Valentin Sandulescu, 'Sacralised Politics in Action: The February 1937 Burial of the Romanian Legionary Leaders Ion Moța and Vasile Marin', in *Totalitarian Movements and Political Religions*, 8, 2 (2007). Ionut Biliuta refers to the Iron Guard as 'religious fascism' ('The Archangel's Consecrated Servants', iii).

the case of the Iron Guard includes a 'legionary theology'. This theology involves notably the extension of the Christian notion of salvation to the ethnic nation.[12]

In January 1941, members of the Iron Guard led an anti-Jewish pogrom in Bucharest and revolted against the fascist government of General Ion Antonescu (1882–1946). The revolt resulted in the formal dissolution of the movement, but former Iron Guard members continued to play an important role in Romania until the communist takeover after the Second World War. Iron Guard members participated in the brutal government-sponsored pogrom in the Transylvanian city of Iasi in June 1941, during which between 13,200 and 15,000 Jews were massacred. Former Iron Guard leaders, members and sympathizers became important targets for repression after the installation of the communist regime in 1948.

After the Soviet invasion of Romania at the end of the Second World War and the consolidation of power by the communists, the leadership of the Romanian Orthodox Church came under strong communist influence. Shifting allegiances to the other end of the political spectrum, important church figures associated publically with socialism and communism after 1948, either from personal conviction or from a shrewd assessment of the best stance for the survival of the church under the communist regime – and for their personal survival.

The social apostolate and the servant church

During the communist period the Romanian Orthodox Church promoted a doctrine known as the social apostolate, with a refinement called the servant church. Both sought to effect an artificial and uneasy rapprochement between the church and the communist authorities, as the leaders of the Romanian Orthodox Church sought to ingratiate themselves with Romania's communist government in order to preserve some measure of freedom for religious activities in the face of official atheism and anti-religious persecution. The social apostolate is particularly associated with Patriarch Justinian (Marina) (1901–77; patriarch 1948–77), often called the 'Red Patriarch',[13] and is expounded in twelve volumes of his collected sermons, speeches and writings on the social role of the church, intended mainly for the edification of the clergy.[14] Theology, declares Justinian, must be mobilized 'to serve life and the current problems that the church and the contemporary world face, and theological study and research must constitute real and useful contributions from the church towards solutions as much to its own problems as to those of contemporary humanity'.[15]

---

[12]See Ionut Biliuta, 'The Foundation of the Iron Guard's Theology (1934-1937)', Ch. V of 'The Archangel's Consecrated Servants', 183–234.

[13]Justinian's two immediate successors, like Justinian, also became patriarch with the support of the Communist Party: Iustin (Moisescu) (1910–86; Patriarch from 1977 to 1986) and Theoctist (Arăpașu) (1915–2007; Patriarch from 1986 to 2007).

[14]Patriarch Justinian (Marina), *Apostolat social, pilde și indemnuri pentru cler* (Social Apostolate, Examples and Advice for the Clergy) (1948–76).

[15]Cited in Olivier Gillet, *Religion et nationalisme: L'Idéologie de l'Église orthodoxe roumaine sous le régime communiste* (Religion and Nationalism: The Ideology of the Romanian Orthodox Church during the Communist Regime) (Bruxelles: Éditions de l'Université de Bruxelles, 1997), 20–1.

The social apostolate was based on three principal thrusts: support for the new social and political orientations of the Romanian state; the mobilization of theology in the struggle for peace and progress; and engagement in ecumenism to foster unity in progress towards social justice, peace and disarmament, and against discrimination and colonialism. The church must become a servant church, actively engaged in building the new people's republic, 'with clergy dedicated to the service of society, as good citizens devoted to the state and the people'.[16] The social apostolate justified ecclesial support of ideas such as collective ownership of the means of production, the foundation of the 'ideal city' on earth (equated with the Kingdom of God), the identification of the people with the state, the only guarantor of individual happiness; and the training of clergy to further communist theories and activities.[17]

In practice the elaboration of the social apostolate was closely tied to support for Romanian nationalism. Church apologists argued from the New Testament and the Fathers to demonstrate that Christians owed allegiance and obedience both to God and to the state, and that patriotism was firmly grounded in the Gospel and the Fathers. Just as 'the Orthodox Church has understood that it must collaborate closely with the state,' so the citizen must submit to civil authorities: 'According to the teaching of our church, the state and the authority of the state are God's will and the Christian has the sacred duty to submit [to this authority] since the state represents the principle of order in the world.'[18] One apologist, E. Vasilescu, an Orthodox priest, appeals to patristic support for patriotism by citing Origen, Tertullian, Gregory of Nazianzus, John Chrysostom, Augustine Ambrose of Milan, Isidore of Pelusium and Maximus the Confessor. 'For to the holy Fathers,' writes Vasilescu, 'the authority of the state was conceived for human well-being and hence when Christians submit themselves to this authority, they fulfill the will of God.'[19]

Leading Romanian Church officials defended the social apostolate doctrine as a continuation of the venerable Byzantine symphony theory of co-equal church and state authority, the prevalent political theology of the Byzantine Empire and of the old Muscovy Kingdom before the reforms of Peter the Great.[20] The social apostolate was in fact a radical departure from the 'symphony' doctrine in that the church was clearly subordinate to the state, not its equal, and of course the People's Republic of Roamnia, ideologically atheist and opposed to all forms of religion and religious belief, was far removed from the at least nominally Christian Byzantine Empire. In the vision of Justinian, his successors and the ecclesiastical apologists, the Gospel, as viewed through the prism of the social apostolate, required the church to become an active collaborator with the communist regime, since it promoted the well-being of the population, despite its atheistic ideology and its persecution of members of the church.

---

[16]Gillet, *Religion et nationalisme*, 21.

[17]Cristian Sonea, 'Patriarhul Justinian Marina şi Apostolatul social în contextul societăţii socialiste. Repere pentru o mărturie creştină în lumea contemporană' (The Patriarch Justinian Marina and the Social Apostolate in the context of the socialist society), *Studia Universitatis BabesBolyai: Theologia Orthodoxa*, 1 (2009), 147–52.

[18]S. Vlad, cited in Gillet, *Religion et nationalisme*, 54; and N. V. Dura, 59.

[19]E. Vasilescu, cited in Gillet, *Religion et nationalisme*, 58.

[20]For the views of a prominent Romanian apologist and long-time official of the World Council of Churches, see Ion Bria, 'Évolution et originalité de l'Église locale de Roumanie' (Evolution and originality of the local Church of Romania) in *Autre visage de l'orthodoxie, Église de Roumanie* (Another Face of Orthodoxy: The Church of Romania) (Geneva, 1981).

The notion of the servant church was further expounded by the future Metropolitan of Transylvania, Antonie (Plamadeala) (1926–2005) in his doctoral thesis at Heythrop College (University of London), under the title 'The Servant Church in Western Thought: An Orthodox Assessment'.[21] Plamadeala, seen as 'firmly among the collaborationist clergymen of the communist period',[22] developed the notion of the servant church as an extension of the social apostolate. Plamadeala refers to differences in nature, purpose and structure of the church and the state, but at the same time he sees no strict separation between the Orthodox Church and the Romanian people, nor between the church and the Romanian state:

> After 1944, the Romanian Orthodox Church … adapted itself to the new social, political, economic and spiritual realities … It manifested its loyalty to the state and carried on its activity in its own field, avoiding any interference with the secular field of the state. … The Romanian Orthodox Church has a well-defined and important position in the life of the Romanian people within our socialist state in line with the good relations which had existed for centuries between the church and the Romanian people, between the church and the Romanian state, no matter what form the latter took.[23]

Plamadeala defends the notion of the servant church by appealing to Scripture (for example, the early Christian community described in Acts (2.44-47; 4.34-37)), and the Fathers of the Church. The church must imitate Christ who became incarnate 'not to be served but to serve and to give his life as a ransom for many' (Mk 10.45):

> Service itself is essential to the existence-in-communion of the church, and flows from its relationship with humanity which was included in the work of Christ. Service should therefore be regarded not only as a simple historical or pastoral necessity but also as a co-responsibility before humanity, for which, by its very foundation, mission and destiny, the church was called.[24]

Plamadeala sees in the social preaching and ministries of John Chrysostom and other Fathers precursors of Marxism, and he even finds in Chrysostom's sermons Marx's theory of surplus value. But he fails to mention that Chrysostom and other socially minded Fathers maintained their independence from the Byzantine state, even criticizing publically the failings of the imperial family and suffering the consequences, as did Chrysostom.[25]

Yet by emphasizing the primacy of the church's social responsibility, Plamadeala's challenging thesis neglects other aspects of the church's mission, notably its main purpose, to bring the Gospel, the 'good news' of salvation in Christ, to humanity, as well as the liturgical and sacramental

---

[21]A Romanian version of Plamadeala's thesis was published under the title 'Biserica slujitoare în Sfânta Scriptură, Sfânta Tradiţie şi în teologia contemporană' (The Servant Church in Holy Scripture: Holy Tradition and Contemporary Theology) in *Studii Teologice*, 14, 5–8 (1972), 325–641. This also contains a summary of the conclusions from the otherwise unpublished English version of the thesis (642–51).

[22]Cristian Romocea, *Church and State: Religious Nationalism and State Identification in Post-Communist Romania* (London: Continuum, 2011), 165, n. 101.

[23]Antonie Plamadeala, 'Church and State in Romania', *Church and State: Opening a New Ecumenical Discussion* (Faith and Order Paper 85) (Geneva: WCC, 1978), 95; 102.

[24]Antonie Plamadeala, 'Some Conclusions', *Studii Teologice*, 14, 5–8 (1972), 649.

[25]See Roman Braga, 'Between God and Satan', in *On the Way of the Faith* (Rives Junction, MI: Dormition of the Mother of God Orthodox Monastery, 1997), 184–7.

functions of the church. Plamadeala does not resolve the ambiguity inherent in the notion of 'servant church': 'servant' to whom, Christ, humanity – or the government of the day? In Palmadeala's theory of the servant church, we are a long way from the theology of the church as the continuation of Christ's ministry as Priest, King and Prophet, and from the church as the One, Holy, Catholic and Apostolic Body of Christ.

The commitment of the Romanian Orthodox Church to support the social ideals of the communist government and its foreign policy, notably the Soviet-inspired 'struggle for peace', was a reflection of both political expediency and the apparently genuine social convictions of some senior church leaders, especially Patriarch Justinian. His social views corresponded in major areas with communist policies, including the collectivization of agriculture. Most hierarchs and many priests, willingly or not, were collaborators of the regime and became agents of the secret police. They supported socialist objectives through preaching, pastoral letters, articles in theological journals and books, but Marxist ideology is little reflected in the theological manuals produced in the 1950s and 1960s.[26] Hierarchs who did not 'toe the line' were quickly removed or otherwise rendered innocuous to the regime and overtly dissident priests were imprisoned and defrocked.

In its essence, the doctrine of the social apostolate declares that the church owes its allegiance to the government of the day and should support government promotion of the social well-being of the population. The theory aimed at adapting the church to reality of the new communist Romania and more particularly at preserving a major, if subservient role for the Romanian Orthodox Church at the centre of Romanian public life. In terms of *realpolitik*, the social apostolate 'meant a mutually beneficial relationship: on the one hand, the church enjoyed the preservation of its religious dominance and its influence in society, while on the other hand, the state benefited from continuing to control the church and using its spiritual authority as a political tool.'[27] The accommodation between the Romanian Orthodox Church and the communist government of Romania was indeed mutually beneficial: the church received financial support from the state budget, including salaries for priests and professors of theology and subsidies for rebuilding churches (simultaneous with the forcible closure and destruction of churches), while the regime was assured of the church's loyalty and its commitment to subdue potentially dissident voices in its ranks. But the political stance of the Romanian Orthodox Church became increasingly untenable in the later years of the harsh rule of the communist dictator Nicolae Ceausescu (1918–89; in power 1965–89), with the growing social and economic privations of the great mass of the population. Nonetheless, the church continued to support the Ceausescu regime until the last days and was caught off guard when a popular revolt finally toppled Ceausescu on 25 December 1989.

Despite the incongruities in the political and social theology of the Romanian Orthodox Church, uncritical external commentators, such as Demetrios J. Constantelos, see in Justinian's social apostolate and Plamadeala's servant church a continuation of the social concerns of the early church, especially St John Chrysostom:

[26]Johansen, *Theological Study in the Romanian Orthodox Church*, 55.

[27]Lucian Leustan, *Orthodoxy and the Cold War: Religion and Political Power in Romania* (Basingstoke, UK: Palgrave Macmillan, 2009), 74.

> One of the encouraging developments in the Orthodox Church in Romania is the contribution of its theologians toward a better understanding of the church as servant. The work of Bishop Antonie Plamadeala has contributed to the rediscovery of the church's moral and social theology and to more philanthropic activities of the Romanian Orthodox Church.[28]

Paul Tarazi of St Vladimir's Orthodox Theological Seminary in New York writes: 'Under Patriarch Justinian's impetus, this Chrysostomian spirit pervaded the life of the church in Romania also on the intellectual level – witness the monumental and timely doctoral dissertation of Antonie Plamadeala.'[29] Tarazi's remarks may not reflect a close reading of Justinian's writings or Plamadeala's thesis, nor do they take adequately into account their collaboration with the oppressive policies of the communist regime, but rather are based on a broad appreciation of their support for the social improvement of the hard-pressed Romanian people. More typical is the assessment that the communist regime successfully marshalled a largely amenable hierarchy to support the regime. 'All the intellectuals of the church are mobilised and asked to write in defence of the atheistic regime,' creating a 'Marxist theology',[30] writes one commentator, Fr Roman Braga (1922–2015), himself a victim of communist persecution. Other commentators of the Romanian Church during the communist period also stress the extent of the subjugation of the church, especially the hierarchy, to the regime:

> During the communist period the church was used as an instrument to control the population through which the regime extended its propaganda and identified its possible dissidents. … The regime allowed the church to continue its activity mainly because the hierarchy was politically controlled. By having their own people in the hierarchy and fostering internal clerical clashes for ecclesiastical power, the communists sought domination of the entire church. The church was actively engaged in the propagandistic message of the battle for peace and the Holy Synod adopted regulations and elected hierarchs imposed by the regime as representing the will of the church.[31]

Despite widespread collaboration of church officials with the communist regime, important segments of the Romanian Church retained their independence from the regime, as symbolized by Fr George Calciu-Dumitreasa (1925–2006) on the part of the parish clergy, and by Elder Cleopa Ilie (1912–98), abbot of the Sihastria Monastery in Moldavia, from the monastic community. During Great Lent 1978, Fr George Calciu delivered seven sermons, intended for Romanian seminarians, in which he was overtly critical of Marxism and the communist regime. He was persecuted by both the church and the regime, defrocked, imprisoned, tortured and exiled in 1985.[32] Elder Cleopa

---

[28]Demetrios J. Constantelos, 'Origins of Christian Orthodox Diakonia: Christian Orthodox Philanthropy in Church History' (unpublished paper, 2004). http://www.rondtb.msk.ru/info/en/Constantelos_en.htm (27 May 2015).

[29]Paul Nadim Tarazi, 'St. John Chrysostom Exegesis for Preaching and Teaching', *Journal of the Orthodox Center for the Advancement of Biblical Studies*, 4, 1 (2011) (paper presented at the International Theological Conference on St. John Chrysostom, University of Bucharest, Romania, 12–14 November 2006), 11.

[30]Braga, 'Between God and Satan'.

[31]Leustan, *Orthodoxy and the Cold War*, 189. Much of the same text is in Lucian Leustean, ed., *Eastern Christianity and the Cold War, 1945-91* (Abingdon, UK: Rutledge, 2011), 54.

[32]Fr George Calciu is the author of several books in Romanian, published mostly after his death in 2006. In English see *Christ Is Calling You. A Course in Catacomb Pastorship* (Platina, CA: St Herman of Alaska Brotherhood, 1997) (this contains the 1978

escaped harassment and arrest by fleeing three times, for a total of almost eight years, into the forests of Moldavia, but he managed to exercise his charismatic function of starets between his periods of exile and after his definitive return to cenobitic life in 1964.[33]

The Burning Bush Group

With the Second World War still raging, a number of Romanian intellectuals sought to further their interest in the spiritual tradition of the Eastern Church, especially hesychasm. During the first week of August 1943, Sandu Tudor (born Alexandru Teodorescu; 1896–1962), a renowned poet, author and publisher who became a monk under the name of Fr Daniel, and Fr Benedict Ghius (1904–90), abbot of the All Saints Monastery in Bucharest[34], organized a week-long retreat in Cernauti, Bukovina, newly attached to Romania (now Chernivtsi in the Ukraine). The retreat included church services, prayer, lectures and discussions, centred on Romania's hesychastic heritage. In the autumn of the same year, a hieromonk former Optina hermitage in Russia, Fr Ivan (Ioan/John Kulighin) (1885–c.1950), who came to be known as 'Father John the Foreigner', was freed from a Soviet concentration camp by Romanian troops retreating from the Soviet Union and brought to Bucharest. Fr John supported Sandu Tudor's efforts to nurture broader interactions and exchanges among spiritually inclined Romanian intellectuals. The Burning Bush Group evolved from the August 1943 retreat and Fr John's arrival in Romania. The group was initially an informal gathering of individuals with no structures, meeting at the Antim Monastery. John the Foreigner became the spiritual mentor of the Burning Bush Group. His spirituality was based on traditional hesychasm and he drew heavily on the *Philokalia* and the *Pilgrim's Tale* for his inspiration. After the Soviet Army occupied Romania, Fr John was arrested and in early 1947 deported to Siberia, where he died in the 1950s. Fr John's testimony to his spiritual children is a brief farewell letter in the form of mystical treatise concerning spiritual direction.[35]

The other members of the Burning Bush Group were mostly intellectuals, university professors, doctors, monks and students. Some of the Group's older members had associations with the Iron Guard. Important figures were the doctor and poet Vasile Voiculescu (1884–1963), university professor and journalist Alexandru Mironescu (1903–73), poet and culture critic Paul Sterian (1904–84), composer Paul Constantinescu (1909–63), architect Constantin Joja (1908–91), historian and Byzantinist Alexandru Elian (1910–98) and philosopher Anton Dumitriu (1905–92).

'Seven Words to Young People'); and *Father George Calciu: Interviews, Talks, and Homilies* (Platina, CA: St Herman of Alaska Brotherhood, 2010).

[33]Several biographies and books of the teachings of Elder Cleopa have appeared in Romanian. In English see *The Truth of Our Faith: Discourses from Holy Scripture on the Tenets of Christian Orthodoxy* (Thessalonica, GR: Uncut Mountain Press, 2001); and Ioanichie Balan, *Shepherd of Souls. The Life and Teachings of Elder Cleopa* (Platina, CA: St Herman of Alaska Brotherhood, 2000).

[34]The All Saints Monastery in Bucharest is usually referred to as the Antim or Anthim Monastery in honour of its founder St Anthim (Iverieli) (Anthim the Iberian or Georgian, 1650–1716; Metropolitan of Bucharest 1708–15).

[35]A translation of Father John's farewell letter is included as an Annex to Athanasios Giocas and Paul Ladouceur, 'The Burning Bush Group and Father André Scrima in Romanian Spirituality', *Greek Orthodox Theological Review*, 52, 1–4, 2007 (published in 2010), 55–7.

Among the students were Valeriu Anania (future Metropolitan Bartolomeu) (1921–2011), Roman Braga (future priest and missionary in Brazil) (1922–2015), André Scrima (future priest and theologian) (1925–2000), Leonida Plamadeala (future Metropolitan Antonie) (1926–2005) and George Vasii (future poet and architect) (1935–2011). Dumitru Staniloae, already a noted theologian, attended some meetings of the Group but was not considered to be a formal member. The monks at Antim were well educated and had an openness which stood in contrast to populist and closed piety typical of Romanian Orthodoxy. Fr Benedict, the abbot, was a progressive monk who had completed doctoral studies in Strasbourg. The Group had access to the monastery's library and to the personal libraries of its members and to English, French and German translations of the works of the Russian religious thinkers of twentieth century and they drew inspiration from the first four volumes of Staniloae's Romanian *Filocalia*, published between 1946 and 1948.[36]

For André Scrima, the Burning Bush Group represented the intimate identity of a family sharing the same spirit.[37] The Group emphasized respect for the person and freedom of thought and its free and open discussions covered a wide range of subjects in theology, philosophy, history and literature. Like the Christian intelligentsia in pre-revolutionary Russia, the Group sought to establish links between Orthodox theology and spirituality and the modern world. They saw Orthodoxy as spiritual culture open to new ideas and to the universal, a liberating rather than a constraining force.

In June 1958, all the members of the Burning Bush Group except André Scrima, who was out of the country, were arrested. Some think that the *Securitate* moved against the Burning Bush Group following favourable comments on the Group in publications outside Romania, particularly articles by the French Orthodox theologian Olivier Clément and by André Scrima.[38] The communist government considered that the Group, despite its non-political nature, was a 'secret society' hostile to the order of the socialist state. Scrima was spared the ordeal of imprisonment and trial that the other members of the Burning Bush Group suffered. The members of the Group were sent to prison, where some of them died, including Fr Daniel (Sandu Tudor) in 1962, and many suffered a broken health from their harsh treatments in prison.

Dumitru Staniloae

By the strength of his personality, his faith, his personal witness, his learning and the quality and volume of his written works, Fr Dumitru Staniloae (1903–93) was both a leading Romanian

---

[36]André Scrima, *Timpul rugului aprins: Maestrul spiritual în tradiția răsăriteană* (The Time of the Burning Bush: The Spiritual Master in the Eastern Tradition) (Bucharest: Humanitas, 1996). Citations from an unpublished French translation by Anca Vasiliu, 'Le Temps du Buisson Ardent', 62.

[37]Scrima, 'Le Temps du Buisson Ardent', 45.

[38]Olivier Clément, 'L'Eglise orthodoxe roumaine et le Buisson Ardent', (The Romanian Orthodox Church and the Burning Bush), *Réforme*, 644 (Paris, 20 July 1957); and Scrima (under the pseudonym 'Un moine de l'Église orthodoxe de Roumanie'), 'L'avènement philocalique dans l'Orthodoxie roumaine' (1958). See Radu Dragan, 'Une figure du christianisme orientale du XXe siècle: Jean l'Étranger' (A 20th century personality of Eastern Christianity: John the Foreigner), in *Politica Hermentica*, 20 (L'Âge d'Homme: Lausanne, 2006), 136–8.

theologian and a spiritual figure, 'the principal author of the Philokalic renewal in Romania after the [Second World] War',[39] and one of the founders and leaders of the neopatristic approach to theology. His theology marks a sharp break with the formal academic theology that dominated almost all Romanian theology in the twentieth century.

Dumitru Staniloae studied at the Universities of Cernauti and Bucharest and completed his doctorate at the University of Athens with a thesis on the relations between Patriarch Dositheus of Jerusalem (1641–1707) and the Romanian principalities. Beginning in 1929 Staniloae taught at the Theological Academy of Sibiu, becoming its rector in 1936. During this period he was a frequent contributor to the magazine *Telegraful român* (Romanian Telegraph), a social, cultural and ecclesiastical magazine based in Sibiu, and he served as its director.

Staniloae was also closely associated with the journal *Gândirea* (Thought), a leading Romanian literary and political journal in the 1920s and 1930s, often involved in cultural and political conflicts during this turbulent period of Romanian history. From 1928 to 1944 *Gândirea* was directed by the controversial theologian and literary and artistic critic Nichifor Crainic (1889–1972). Crainic moved the journal from an original modernist stance at its foundation in 1921 to a traditionalist and nationalist position, even advocating pro-fascist and anti-Semitic policies in the late 1930s and during the Second World War.[40] It was closed down in 1944 with the fall of the fascist regime and Romania's turn-about in the war, as Romania switched from its alliance with the Axis powers to a pro-Allied policy.

In 1946, under communist pressure, Staniloae was obliged to resign as rector of the Sibiu Theological Academy and was transferred to the Faculty of Theology at the University of Bucharest, where he remained until his retirement in 1973. Staniloae was close to several members of the Burning Bush Group and after the communists arrested its leading members in June 1958, Staniloae himself was arrested in November 1958 for his association with the Group and possibly for his pre-war sympathies with right-wing and nationalist groups, especially the Iron Guard. He was imprisoned for five years, until January 1964. While he subsequently spoke little of his years of imprisonment, he made an important remark to his friend Olivier Clément (1923–2009): 'It was the only time in my life that I was able to "sustain" the Jesus Prayer in an uninterrupted invocation.'[41] After Staniloae's release from prison, the communist government, seeking to create an image of religious freedom in Romania, allowed the publication of his theological works, and, after 1968, permitted him to travel abroad to attend international meetings.

Already by the time of his imprisonment Staniloae had acquired an international reputation, which undoubtedly spared him from the severe mistreatment of other Christian prisoners of conscience at the hands of the dreaded *Securitate*, and eventually secured his release. Until the publication of his works in English translation, Staniloae was known especially in France, in part through traditional ties between Romanian and French intellectual and cultural circles, and

[39]Joanta, *Romania: Its Hesychast Tradition and Culture*, 248.

[40]For a study of Nichifor Crainic and *Gândirea* see Christine Hall, *Pancosmic Church – Specific Românesc Ecclesiological Themes in Nichifor Crainic's Writings between 1922 and 1944* (Uppsala: Uppsala Iniversitet, 2008).

[41]Cited by Olivier Clément, 'In Memoriam Dumitru Staniloae (1903-1993)', *Contacts*, 45, 161 (1993), 293.

because of Staniloae's friendship with Olivier Clément. Clément was the first Orthodox theologian to recognize Staniloae's stature as a major Orthodox theologian.

Staniloae's major publications begin with his 1938 study of St Gregory Palamas. In 1943 he published *Iisus Hristos sau restaurarea omului* (Jesus Christ or the Restoration of Man), which treats of the ontology of salvation through Christ's Incarnation; Christ is the ultimate meaning of human existence and the only way to achieve true humanity. After the war Staniloae undertook the publication of a Romanian *Philokalia*. Despite the essential role played by St Paisius Velichkovsky and his Romanian and Slavic monks in the Moldavian monasteries at the end of the eighteenth century and the beginning of the nineteenth century, no Romanian *Philokalia* was published at the time. Staniloae managed to publish the first four volumes of his *Filocalia* in Sibiu between 1946 and 1948, and it was only several years after his release from prison in 1963 that the communists allowed the publication of six additional volumes between 1976 and 1981, with two further volumes appearing in 1990 and 1991.[42]

Staniloae's *Filocalia* is more than a translation of the original Greek *Philokalia*; it is rather an original Romanian anthology of spiritual and ascetic writings. Staniloae adds to the *Philokalia* notably texts exploring the theological, doctrinal and mystical foundations of hesychasm, particularly from two of his preferred authors, Maximus the Confessor and Gregory Palamas, and other texts, from writings of Barsanuphius and John, Dorotheus of Gaza, John Climacus, Isaac the Syrian and Isaiah the Hermit. He also provides a survey of hesychasm in Romania. Staniloae added substantive explanatory footnotes and commentaries throughout the text to facilitate the understanding of the now often obscure language and references of many ascetic writings and to illustrate the relevance of ancient Christian theological and ascetic writings to the modern world. Staniloae's *Filocalia* is an important feature of the broad revival of hesychastic spirituality in Romania which began in the monasteries and among intellectuals during the interwar period and continued into the communist period, with such manifestations as the revival of monastic life, the Burning Bush Group and a number of luminous spiritual figures such as Fr Ilie Cleopa.[43]

Staniloae's major theological works are a trilogy covering dogmatic theology, ascetical and mystical theology and liturgical theology. His most important writing is his *Teologia dogmatică ortodoxă* (Orthodox Dogmatic Theology), published in three volumes in 1978.[44] This work, which stands in sharp contrast with the *Dogmatica* of Romanian academic theology, establishes Staniloae as one of the leaders of Orthodox neopatristic theology. Staniloae's book *Spiritualitatea ortodoxă Ascetica și Mistica* (Orthodox Ascetic and Mystical Spirituality) (1992) is based on a course on

[42]For a summary of the contents of Staniloae's *Filocalia*, see Maciej Bielawski, 'Dumitru Staniloae and His Philokalia', in Lucian Turcescu, ed., *Dumitru Stăniloae: Tradition and Modernity in Theology* (Iasi; Oxford; Palm Beach, FL; Portland OR: Center for Romanian Studies, 2002), 34–50.

[43]See Scrima, 'L'avènement philocalique dans l'orthodoxie roumaine', 319.

[44]This has been translated in six volumes under the general title *The Experience of God*. Dumitru Staniloae, *Orthodox Dogmatic Theology: The Experience of God*, Vol. 1: *Revelation and Knowledge of the Triune God*; Vol. 2: *The World: Creation and Deification*; Vol. 3, *The Person of Jesus Christ as God and Savior*; Vol. 4: *The Church: Communion in the Holy Spirit*; Vol. 5: *The Sanctifying Mysteries*; Vol. 6: *The Fulfillment of Creation* (Brookline, MA: Holy Cross Orthodox Press, 2005–13).

mystical theology that he taught at the Bucharest Faculty of Theology in the 1950s.[45] It is a synthesis of the Orthodox ascetic tradition, centred on theosis or deification, seen as the union of the Christian with God in Christ, and is structured around the three 'stages' or 'steps' of the spiritual life traditional in both Eastern and Western Christianity, purification, illumination and perfection. The third work in Staniloae's trilogy, *Spiritualitate și Comuniune* în *Liturghia Ortodoxă* (Spirituality and Communion in the Orthodox Liturgy), published in 1986, has not been translated. Staniloae's other books include a course on the theme 'God Is Love', first published in 1971, and a book on the Jesus Prayer published in French.[46]

Staniloae sees Christianity as a divine-human culture, uniting East and West, 'an original synthesis between the open, joyous and luminous Latin spirit, and the mystical spirituality, the profundity, of Orthodoxy',[47] an equilibrium between the rational and mysteric.[48] Staniloae's major concerns throughout his writings are to create a harmonious and holistic theology uniting the heights of ancient Christian speculative thought and formal church dogmas with constant attention to the contemporary situation and experience of the faithful seeking to work out their salvation in a vastly changed world from that of the early centuries of Christianity.

Staniloae unites God, humanity and the rest of creation in a unified cosmic vision in Jesus Christ. His cosmic Christianity attaches considerable importance to the revelation and contemplation of God in nature, drawing on Maximus's *logoi* of created things and the Palamite theology of the divine energies: the world, humans, living creatures, inanimate creation, all are infused with God's presence.[49] In this cosmological theology and spirituality, the world is a gift of God's love, and the locus of dialogue between God and humanity and among human beings. Staniloae refers to the contemplation of God in creation, a key aspect of the illuminative stage of the spiritual life, as 'a symbolic knowledge of the world', 'the spiritual understanding of nature', and consideration of the objects of creation as 'rays of divine glory, love and all powerfulness'.[50]

Staniloae places considerable emphasis on the theology of the person, both divine and human, and the corollaries of personhood, freedom and love, the basis of the divine image in humans: 'Our

---

[45]Dumitru Staniloae, *Orthodox Spirituality: A Practical Guide for the Faithful and a Definitive Manual for the Scholar* (South Canaan, PA: St Tikhon's Seminary Press, 2003).

[46]Dumitru Staniloae, 'Dunezeu este iubire (Ioan 4:8)' (God is Love), *Ortodoxia*, 23, 3 (1971); *Dieu est Amour* (God Is Love) (Geneva: Labor et Fides, 1980); *Prière de Jésus et expérience de l'Esprit Saint* (The Jesus Prayer and the Experience of the Holy Spirit) (Paris: Desclée de Brouwer, 1991).

[47]Ion Bria, 'Homage to Fr Dumitru Staniloae on His Sixtieth Birthday', *Ortodoxia*, 30, 4 (1978), 639. Cited in Joanta, *Treasures of Romanian Christianity*, 249.

[48]The secondary literature on Staniloae's theology is ample and growing. For short overviews see Ion Bria, 'The Creative Vision of D. Staniloae: An Introduction to His Theological Thought', *The Ecumenical Review*, 33, 3 (1981); Olivier Clément, 'In Memoriam Dumitru Staniloae (1903-1993)', *Contacts*, 45, 161 (1993); Andrew Louth, 'The *Orthodox Dogmatic Theology* of Dumitru Staniloae', *Modern Theology*, 13, 2 (1997) (included in Turcescu, ed., *Dumitru Stăniloae: Tradition and Modernity*); Radu Preda, 'Dix chapitres sur le père Dumitru Staniloae. Bref portrait du théologien orthodoxe roumain d'aujourd'hui' (Ten chapters on Fr Dumitru Staniloae: A brief portrait of the Romanian Orthodox theologian today) *Contacts*, 45, 161 (1993); and Kallistos Ware, Forward to Staniloae's *Orthodox Dogmatic Theology: The Experience of God* (Vol. 1).

[49]See notably 'The Being of God and His Uncreated Operations', Ch. 7 of Staniloae's *The Experience of God*, Vol. 1, 125–39.

[50]See 'The Contemplation of God in Creation', in *Orthodox Spirituality*, 203–23; also 'Natural Revelation', Chapter 1 of *The Experience of God*, Vol. 1, 1–14; and 'Creation: The Visible World', and 'The World as Gift and Word', Chs 1 and 2 of *The Experience of God*, Vol. 2, 1–66.

love finds its explanation in the fact that we are created in the image of the Holy Trinity, the origin of our love.'[51] Since the Trinity is the 'divine image in the human person,'[52] 'the plenitude of personhood in communion,'[53] love is the language of God and the language about God and humanity, the universal theme of Staniloae's mature years:

> The mystery, the divine image of our person and of the person of others, discloses itself and becomes actual in communion. It is in communion with our fellow human beings, however, that the mystery of the interpersonal divine presence is most clearly revealed.[54]

Theosis or deification is thus the true achievement of full human personhood and existence; human persons only become fully human in surpassing limited human nature by uniting with God in and through Christ and the Holy Spirit:

> The goal of Orthodox spirituality is none other than living in a state of deification or participation in the divine life. ... Deification is realised through the believer's participation in the divine powers [energies], by flooding him with boundless divine things [charisms]. ... The believer is raised higher than the level of his own powers, not of his own accord, but by the work of the Holy Spirit.[55]

In his discussion of theosis, Staniloae carefully distinguishes theosis as the full realization of human personhood in communion with a personal God from oriental and esoteric spiritualities which envisage the finality of human existence in the dissolution of personal identity in an impersonal divinity:

> More infinity and more joy are to be found in communion with the personal God than in any act of being submerged in an ocean of infinity, for this communion is rest in the love of the infinite Person.[56]
>
> I do not lose myself in this infinity, because it is the infinity of a personal God whose love is my delight; I depend on his love.[57]
>
> Orthodox spirituality has as its goal the deification of man and his union with God, without being merged with him.[58]

Staniloae sees theology and spirituality, contemplation and action as a continuous whole, an Orthodox culture which unites mysticism and asceticism with theology and action in the world. 'A theology which feeds on the prayer and spiritual life of the church,' writes Staniloae, 'is a theology which expresses and deepens the church's thinking, her spiritual life and her work of sanctification and serving.'[59] Prayer is the fundamental human action, especially prayer for others: 'The saint is

---

[51] Staniloae, *The Experience of God*, 1:245.
[52] Ibid., 2:99.
[53] Kallistos Ware, Forward to Staniloae's *Orthodox Dogmatic Theology: The Experience of God*, xx.
[54] Staniloae, *The Experience of God*, 2:99.
[55] Staniloae, *Orthodox Spirituality*, 22.
[56] Staniloae, *The Experience of God*, 2:99.
[57] Dumitru Staniloae, *Prayer and Holiness: The Icon of Man Renewed in God* (Oxford: SLG Press, 1982), 10.
[58] Staniloae, *Orthodox Spirituality*, 46.
[59] Staniloae, *The Experience of God*, 1:87.

the person who includes all humanity in his prayer.'[60] Prayer is more important than theology: 'The thought about God interrupts the direct relation with God.'[61]

Tradition is at the service of both the church and the individual Christian:

> [Tradition is] the totality of the various ways by which Christ passes over into the reality of human lives under the form of the church and all his works of sanctification and preaching. … Tradition has the role of putting and keeping the successive generations of Christians in contact with Christ because of the fact that tradition, by its very nature, is both the invocation of the Holy Spirit (*epiklesis* in a broad sense) and the reception of the Holy Spirit.[62]

Staniloae's ecclesiology is also cosmic. The church is a 'laboratory of resurrection', uniting 'both the eternal and the temporal … the uncreated and the created … spiritual things of all categories and matter'; 'the union of all that exists, or, in other words, she is destined to encompass all that exists: God and creation. She is the fulfilment of God's eternal plan: the unity of all.'[63] The church is the eschatological fulfilment of creation; she has a theandric constitution: 'The church is Christ extended with his deified body in humanity … Her content consists of Christ united with the Father and the Spirit according to his divine nature, and united with us according to his human nature.'[64] This metaphysical and eschatological vision of the church as the union of all creation has some parallels in the search of the Russian religious philosophers for the principle of all-unity, mostly closely in the ecclesiology of Sergius Bulgakov (see Chapters 4 and 9).

Staniloae has a mixed attitude towards Western theology, on the one hand critical of many aspects of Western thought, while at the same time accepting certain Western categories as organizing principles for his own theology. His *Dogmatica* generally follows a conventional scholastic structure typical of most textbooks of dogmatic theology, moving from sources and nature of revelation, to God and the Trinity (Vol. 1 in the English translation), to creation of the world, humanity, angels, the fall and deification (Vol. 2), the Incarnation, Christology and salvation (Vol. 3), the church, the Holy Spirit and again salvation (Vol. 4), the sacraments (Vol. 5), and terminating with eschatology (Vol. 6). It is admittedly difficult to avoid the general structure of scholastic *Summae* if one wishes to bring all of Christian thought into the compass of a single vision – even Vladimir Lossky employs this structure in his classic work *The Mystical Theology of the Eastern Church*. Staniloae uses the now widely employed threefold ministry of Christ as Prophet, Priest and King in his discussion of Christology, a categorization which originates with Eusebius but was greatly developed by Reform theologians, especially Calvin. Staniloae also retains the Western number of seven sacraments, although at times the Orthodox tradition has also identified other liturgical rites as sacraments (such as consecration of churches, monastic vows and anointing of rulers). Despite Staniloae's use of structural principles typical of Western theology, he infuses these structures with the wisdom of patristic theology and with his own profound insights.

---

[60]Quoted in Olivier Clément, 'In Memoriam Dumitru Staniloae', 301.
[61]Dumitru Staniloae, *Prière de Jésus et Saint-Esprit*, 41.
[62]Staniloae, *The Experience of God*, 1:48.
[63]Ibid., 4:13.
[64]Ibid., 4:14.

Ethno-theology

Ethnic nationalism was a powerful social and political force in Romania in the interwar period, especially in the years immediately prior to the Second World War and during the period of Romania's alliance with Nazi Germany. The Romanian Orthodox Church adopted this nationalist and anti-Semitic discourse, supporting government measures against Romania's then substantial Jewish population.[65] Leading nationalist and anti-Semitic Orthodox intellectuals of the pre-war period include Nichifor Crainic, the philosopher Nae Ionescu (1890–1940), and his student Gheorghe Racoveanu (1900–1967), Fr Nicolae Neaga (1902–2003) and Fr Liviu Stan (1910–73).[66] They openly voiced a religious ethno-nationalist ideology in association with the notorious Iron Guard, which staged brutal pogroms against Romania's Jewish population and played an important role in Romanian politics until its attempted revolt in January 1941, suppressed by the Romanian and German armies.

A difficult aspect of Dumitru Staniloae's life and theology is his association with Romanian ethno-religious nationalism. This ethno-theology is reflected in a number of his writings in the 1930s and the early 1940s, and he returned to this theme sporadically during and after the communist period. In several articles published in *Telegraful român* and in *Gândirea*, Staniloae, following Nichifor Crainic's 'ethnocratic' political theology, advances a theological justification for nationalism, arguing that ethnic nations are an aspect of God's plan for humanity; nations are 'divine thoughts' and thus intrinsically good. This theological grounding of nationalism is reinforced when nationality and religion are historically linked, as in the Romanian people.[67] An example of this religious nationalism was the reaction in Romania, especially in religious circles, to the deaths of two Iron Guard leaders, Ion Mota (1902–37) and Vasile Marin (1904–37), killed on 13 January 1937 fighting for the Nationalists (pro-Franco) in the Spanish Civil War. The dead Iron Guard militants were treated as national heroes; Dumitru Staniloae hailed them as 'martyrs for Christ'.[68]

In Staniloae's writings of the 1930s and up to 1940, as for Nichifor Crainic and many other Romanian nationalists, Orthodoxy and Romanianhood are one. There is 'an intrinsic and deep unity between Romanian ethnicity and the Orthodox Church', an 'Orthodox Romanianness'.[69]

---

[65]See Ionut Biliuta, 'Sowing the Seeds of Hate. The Antisemitism of the Romanian Orthodox Church in the Interwar Period', *Shoah: Intervention, Methods, Documentation*, 3, 1 (Vienna, 2016).

[66]See Ionut Biliuta, 'The Afterlife of the 1930s Orthodoxism-Nationalism beyond Nichifor Crainic and Nae Ionescu', *Anuarul Institutului de Cercetări Socio-Umane* (2009); and his 'Sowing the Seeds of Hate'.

[67]See Dumitru Staniloae's articles: 'Orthodoxie şi naţiune' (Orthodoxy and nation), *Gândirea*, 14, 2 (1935); and 'Românism şi Ortodoxie' (Romanianness and Orthodoxy), *Gândirea*, 14, 8 (1936); and Ionita Biliuta, 'Between Orthodoxy and the Nation: Traditionalist Definitions of Romanianness in Interwar Romania' (MA Thesis, Central European University, Budapest, 2013).

[68]Dumitru Staniloae, 'Martiri pentru Hristos' (Martyrs for Christ), *Telegraful român*, 85, 4 (1937), 2. Cited in Biliuta, 'The Archangel's Consecrated Servants', 254. See also Sandulescu, 'Sacralised Politics in Action'.

[69]Romocea, *Church and State*, 201. See also Roland Clark, 'Nationalism, Ethnotheology, and Mysticism in Interwar Romania', *The Carl Beck Papers in Russian & East European Studies*, No. 2002 (Pittsburgh, OH: Center for Russian and East European Studies, 2009); Mihail Neamtu, 'Between the Gospel and the Nation: Dumitru Stăniloae's Ethno-Theology', *Studia Archaeus* (Bucarest) 10, 3 (2006); Maciej Bielawski, *The Philocalical Vision of the World in the Theology of Dumitru Staniloae* (Bydgoszcz, HU: Homini, 1997), 33ff.; 200–3; and Lavinia Stan and Lucian Turcescu, *Religion and Politics in Post-Communist Romania* (Oxford: Oxford University Press, 2007), 45.

The emphasis on the correspondence of Romanian ethno-cultural identity and Orthodoxy leaves no room for non-ethnic Romanians (such as Jews, Hungarians and Romani) and non-Orthodox (such as Roman Catholics and Jews) in Romania.

Staniloae's arguments are summarized in a few passages:

> God created Adam and Eve in the beginning. In them were virtually present all nations. These are revelations in time of the images which have existed eternally in God. Every nation has an eternal divine archetype that it has to bring about more fully. There is one instance when nations may not be from God and we would have to fight against them: when human diversification into nations would be a consequence of sin and a deviation from the way in which God wanted to develop humanity. In that case, the duty of every Christian would be to get humanity out of that sinful state and to fuse all nations into one. [70]
>
> The Romanian nation (*neam*) is a biological-spiritual synthesis of a number of elements. The most important of them are the Dacian element, the Latin element, and the Christian Orthodox element. … The parts are stamped with a new, unifying, and individualizing stamp which is Romanianhood (*românitatea*). Therefore, we can say that the highest law for our nation (*neam*) is Romanianhood. … Which is the Romanian way of communion with the transcendental spiritual order? History and the current life of our people tell us that it is Orthodoxy. Orthodoxy is the eye through which Romanians gaze at heavens and then, enlightened by the heavenly light, they turn their eye toward the world while continuing to attune their behaviour to it. We also know that this is the only eye that is correct and healthy. … Orthodoxy is an essential and vital function of Romanianism. The permanent national ideal of our nation can only be conceived in relation with Orthodoxy.[71]

Staniloae does not elaborate on what is included in his notion of nations resulting from 'a consequence of sin and a deviation from the way in which God wanted to develop humanity'. From the story of the Tower of Babel in Genesis (Gen. 11.4-9), it can be argued that all ethic nations are 'a consequence of sin', founded on divisions of humanity into groups based on linguistic, cultural and historical characteristics which are not essential aspects of human nature. On the contrary, ethnic nations can easily become causes of friction and conflict, opposing the unity in Christ sought by Jesus in his priestly prayer (Jn 17.22-23) and by Paul in his epistles (Gal. 1.27-29; Col. 3.11). And of course modern pluralistic states are not based on ethnic nationality; these appear to fall outside Staniloae's framework.

In several articles in the late 1940s and again in the 1970s, Staniloae approved the forced dissolution of the Romanian Greek Catholic Church and its absorption into the Romanian Orthodox Church, on the grounds that the Greek Catholic Church was only 'a mere expression of

---

[70]Dumitru Staniloae, 'Brief Theological Interpretations of the Nation' (in Romanian), *Telegraful Român*, 82, 15 (1934), 2. Trans. Lucian Turcescu in Witte and Alexander, *The Teachings of Modern Orthodox Christianity*, 340–1. Also cited in Romocea, *Church and State*, 212.

[71]Dumitru Staniloae, 'The Moral Aspect of Nationalism' (in Romanian), *Telegraful Român*, 88, 47 (1940), 1–2. Trans. Lucian Turcescu in John Witte and Frank Alexander, eds., *The Teachings of Modern Orthodox Christianity on Law, Politics, and Human Nature* (New York: Columbia University Press, 2007), 340. Also cited in Romocea, *Church and State*, 202. Staniloae's principal writings in the 1930s on religious nationalism were republished in the volumes *Ortodoxie si românism* (Orthodoxy and Romanianism) (Sibiu, 1939), and *Natiune si creşitinism* (Nation and Christianity) (Bucharest: Elion Press, 2003).

the Roman Catholic proselytising action within the traditional boundaries of Orthodoxy', which had the effect of separating previously Orthodox Romanians in Transylvania from their Orthodox brothers and sisters in other Romanian principalities.[72] Staniloae returned to the theme of religious nationalism after the fall of the communist regime in his book *Reflecții despre spiritualitatea poporului român* (Reflections on the Spirituality of the Romanian People (Craiova, 1992)).

André Scrima

André Scrima (1925–2000) provided a link among the various strands of theology, mysticism and spirituality, largely inspired by hesychasm, which characterized the quest of many Romanian intellectuals in the post-Second World War period. Scrima studied philosophy, mathematics, physics and theology at university, completing a thesis on apophatic theology. He took part in the activities of the Burning Bush Group and was strongly influenced by Fr John the Foreigner. Tonsured a monk in 1956 at Slatina Monastery, he taught at the seminary at Neamts. Acting as interpreter for Patriarch Justinian, he had the occasion to meet the Sarvepalli Radhakrishnan (1888–1975), an Indian philosopher and former Oxford professor then serving as vice-president of India. Through him, Scrima was able to study Hindu spirituality in India. He spent two years at the Banaras Hindu University in Varanasi, preceded by a pilgrimage to Western and Eastern Christian monastic settings in France, Mount Athos and Lebanon. In India, he learned Sanskrit and wrote a thesis on a school of Hindu philosophy concerned with the self-realization by which one understands the ultimate nature of reality. He also wrote a seminal article in French on the hesychastic renewal in Romania.[73]

While Scrima was in India, the Securitate dismantled the Burning Bush Group. Unable to return to Romania, Scrima went to Lebanon where he was ordained to the priesthood and became the spiritual father of the monastery of St George at Deir-el-Harf. He also taught at the Holy Spirit University in Kaslik, a private Catholic institution. Under the leadership of Fr Georges Khodr (b. 1923; future Metropolitan of Byblos, Botris and Mount Lebanon), a spiritual renewal within the Patriarchate of Antioch was taking place at that time, with the involvement of Fr Lev Gillet (1893–1980; 'A Monk of the Eastern Church'), and Scrima became an important figure in this spiritual renewal. In 1961, Scrima became an Archimandrite of the Ecumenical Throne and he served as Patriarch Athenagoras's personal representative in the theological discussions with the Roman Catholic Church, contributing to the lifting of the anathemas of 1054 at the historic meeting in Jerusalem of Patriarch Athenagoras and Pope Paul VI in January 1964, and serving as official observer of the Ecumenical Patriarchate at the Vatican II Council. From 1961 until his return to

[72]Neamtu, 'Between the Gospel and the Nation', 24–6.

[73]Scrima, 'L'avènement philocalique', 295–328, 443–74. See also his 'The Hesychastic Tradition: An Orthodox-Christian Way of Contemplation', in Yusuf Ibish and Ileana Marculescu, eds., *Contemplation and Action in World Religions: Selected Papers from the Rothko Chapel Colloquium Traditional Modes of Contemplation and Action* (Houston, TX: Rothko Chapel, 1978), 136–50.

Romania in 1992, he divided his time between Lebanon, Italy, France and the United States, returning to Romania after the fall of communist regime.

Scrima's penetrating and analytical writings seek to convey non-obvious meanings as subtly as possible, bringing novel insights into important and recurring themes of Orthodox theology and spirituality. His major themes include the relationships between hesychasm and monasticism, the role of monasticism in the world as a characteristic witness of Orthodoxy, the importance of spiritual guidance in the Christian life (a theme greatly inspired by his experience with John the Foreigner), and he advocated a biblically and liturgically based spirituality (in the footsteps of Fr Lev Gillet, whom Scrima met on numerous occasions in Lebanon).[74] Scrima saw the necessity of an open dialogue between Orthodoxy and modernity and non-Christian religions, and he considered hesychasm as a major key in dialogue between Hindus and Christians, placing Orthodoxy in a unique position as a Christian bridge to Hindu spirituality.[75]

Conclusion

As in other countries of Orthodox tradition, Romanian theology in the nineteenth century and much of the twentieth century was largely characterized by a neo-scholastic framework inspired by Western models, imported directly from the West or indirectly from Russian and Greek sources. The typical manifestation of this academic theology was the textbook of dogmatic theology and other related theological manuals covering most theological disciplines. This intellectual and abstract approach to theology stood in sharp contrast with traditional Romanian spirituality, centred around hesychasm and the monastic life, which blossomed particularly in the fourteenth and fifteenth centuries, in the early nineteenth century, in the wake of the publication of the *Philokalia* in 1782, and, perhaps more surprisingly, during much of the twentieth century, even during the long decades of the communist regime. The vibrant, patristically based theology of Dumitru Staniloae stands in sharp contrast with 'school theology'. But during the period between the two world wars and sporadically since, aspects of Romanian Orthodoxy came under the spell of Romanian nationalism, which sees Orthodoxy as an essential aspect of true Romanian ethnic and state identity.

The Burning Bush Group, despite its limited membership and influence in wider society during its existence, remains a luminous episode in the otherwise bleak period of the communist regime. The Burning Bush Group and the major religious personalities that preceded it during the interwar period are perhaps the closest equivalent to the Russian religious renaissance outside of Russia itself. Orthodox personalities such as Nichifor Crainic were deeply involved in Romanian cultural, social and political life in the interwar period, like their Russian counterparts prior to the revolution. But these Romanian Christian intellectuals were caught up in ethnic nationalism in a way that the

[74]For a more detailed presentation of André Scrima's theology, see Athanasios Giocas and Paul Ladouceur, 'The Burning Bush Group and Father André Scrima in Romanian Spirituality', *Greek Orthodox Theological Review*, 52, 1–4, 2007 (published 2010).
[75]Scrima, 'L'avènement philocalique', 450.

Christian intelligentsia in Russia never was. And as in Russia, attempts by a Christian intelligentsia to dialogue with the modern world came to abrupt end with the arrival of communism.

Unlike the major figures of the Russian religious renaissance, the members of the Burning Bush Group were not directly involved in public and political discourse – impossible in any case after 1948 – , yet they too represented an attempt to bridge the gap between Orthodoxy and society and culture. The members of the Burning Bush Group included philosophically and theologically inclined intellectuals, and representatives of the arts and culture, brought together far more harmoniously than in Russia in the years preceding the revolution.

During the communist period, the social apostolate and the doctrine of the servant church were attempts to reconcile desirable aspects of Marxist social objectives with Christianity. But instead of appealing exclusively to Scripture and patristic thought as the basis of a Christian social theology, the social apostolate adopted elements of Marxist ideology and rhetoric, including the notion of class struggle and uncritical denunciations of capitalism and the West, resulting in 'a unique and unprecedented ideological symbiosis' between Marxism and Christianity.[76] The social apostolate was sufficiently Christian to attract Christian intellectuals and sufficiently Marxist to be pleasing to the communist regime, but it represented a major compromise of Christian principles in the name of political expediency.

While the study of the social theology of the early Fathers is certainly commendable, it is an error to attribute proto-Marxism to them, or to overlook that they were not blind servants of the imperial political system, but were critical of the rulers when they overstepped the limits of Christian charity and morality – Chrysostom being a prime example. A major problem with Justinian's social apostolate and Plamadeala's servant church is that the Romanian Church leaders saw no inconsistency in subordinating the church to an atheistic anti-religious regime, in return for a certain relative peace for the church. Some studies also suggest that Romanian Orthodoxy failed to develop a coherent opposition to communism because of nationalist and ethnic preoccupations.[77]

The doctrines of the social apostolate and the servant church, and indeed the relationship of the senior hierarchy of the Romanian Orthodox Church with the communist regime, particularly the notorious secret police, the Securitate, remained controversial issues in the decades after the fall of communism in 1989. Many commentators of the Romanian religious scene are critical of the overtly pro-regime behaviour of the senior leadership of the Romanian Orthodox Church. But some see in the behaviour and discourse of senior church officials, including even their collaboration with the Securitate, an astute tactic intended to secure a certain degree of toleration by the communists which allowed the church to survive, and even to flourish in some respects, despite official atheist propaganda, closures of monasteries and parishes, restrictions on monastics, the imprisonment of priests, monks and faithful, and the destruction of churches.[78] It is an open question whether it was justifiable to go so far as to advance theologies acceptable to the communist

---

[76]Romocea, *Church and State*, 3.

[77]See Romocea, *Church and State*, 3.

[78]See Roman Braga, 'On Compromise in the Hierarchy During the Communist Yoke'. www.orthodoxytoday.org/articles6/BragaChurch.php (3 November 2014).

authorities, such as the doctrines of the social apostolate and the servant church, to preserve the existence of the church as an institution during the communist regime. After Stalin's restoration of the church in Russia during the Second World War, church officials were expected to mouth support for Soviet foreign and domestic policy, but the Russian Orthodox Church did not adapt its theology to suit communist ideology. Lavinia Stan and Lucian Turcescu write:

> The Communist Party controlled the Orthodox Church by appointing obedient patriarchs. The three 'red' patriarchs – Justinian Marina (1948-1977), Iustin Moisescu (1977-1986), and Teoctist Arăpaşu [1986–2007] – only rarely had the courage to place the interests of their church ahead of the interests of the party-state, and they never openly defied the authorities or informed foreign governments of the plight of their religious group. Instead of opposing religious persecution, they turned a blind eye to it and constantly denied any form of discrimination, thus condoning the communist regime's actions against their church.[79]

Under various guises, religious ethno-nationalism has been a feature of the Romanian religious and national scene since the interwar period, adapting itself to the political regime of the day, whether conservative, fascist, communist or democratic. Religious ethno-nationalism is a troublesome aspect of Staniloae's theology in particular, but it is secondary in relation to the depth and range of his theology and his overall contribution to the development of Orthodox theology and spirituality in general. It is possible that Staniloae intended his advocacy of religious ethno-nationalism mainly for internal consumption; it does not feature in his monumental *Orthodox Dogmatic Theology*, nor in his *Orthodox Spirituality*. Staniloae's apology for ethno-theology remains incomplete and inadequate and requires further study.

The influence of Dumitru Staniloae extends well beyond Romania, to Orthodox theology as a whole and indeed in non-Orthodox theological circles familiar with his work. Yet despite the great prestige attached to Staniloae's theology, his *Dogmatica* has not systematically replaced the more traditional textbooks of the academic theology used in Romania's seminaries and faculties of theology and he appears to be little read in Romania itself.

[79]Lavinia Stan and Lucian Turcescu, *Religion and Politics in Post-Communist Romania* (Oxford: Oxford University Press, 2007), 23.

8

Tradition and the Restoration of Patristic Thought

Chapter Outline

Tradition and the nature of theology

While Orthodox theologians of all persuasions accept the importance of tradition, there is a wide range of views on the meaning and role of tradition and its significance for modern Orthodox theology. The most fundamental difference between the theologians of the Russian religious renaissance and later neopatristic theologians may perhaps lie in their attitudes towards the Fathers. For the theologians of the religious renaissance, the thinking of the Fathers, certainly on non-dogmatic issues, is a helpful, even indispensable guide to theological reflection, but not an absolute norm – they were prepared to look elsewhere than the classical Fathers for sources of inspiration to bring Christ's message to the modern world. For the neopatristic theologians, the thinking of the ancient Fathers is largely considered an absolute norm for all subsequent theology, and an appeal to any other philosophical or theological is suspect if not rejected outright. The issue is thus what status is accorded to the patristic tradition? Is it indicative or normative?

Orthodoxy places a very high value on tradition and since neopatristic theology involves a revival of the thinking of the Fathers within the context of the tradition of the church, the more precise question is: What is the authority of the Fathers? Once we are beyond the realm of what is clearly dogmatic as enunciated in the Nicene-Constantinopolitan Creed and dogmatic pronouncements of ecumenical councils, are the teachings of the Fathers to be regarded as normative, authoritative beyond question, or are they indicative, guidelines in orientating contemporary theological reflection?

In his critique of George Florovsky's *The Ways of Russian Theology*, Nicolas Berdyaev accuses Florovsky of having yielded to 'the temptation of historicism', which he sees as the 'absolutization' of history, specifically the history of Greek-Byzantine theology, as the norm for all Christian thought and indeed of Christianity itself.[1] In a later work Florovsky quotes with approval Marc Bloch's statement that 'Christianity is a religion of historians' and he goes on to say that 'Christianity is basically a vigorous appeal to history.'[2] The question is not so much 'history' as a concept as history as the source of tradition. The history that Florovsky evokes is first and foremost the history of salvation as revealed in the Bible, and Florovsky most likely understood Bloch's statement in the sense that 'Christianity is a religion of tradition'. Berdyaev and others perceive a danger in absolutizing tradition such that it becomes the sole acceptable theological criterion, and, in the absence of a notion of tradition as dynamic, as 'living tradition', there is a risk of transforming 'tradition' into 'traditionalism'. Traditionalism freezes religious thought and practices in exactly the same patterns as those already existing: The Spirit can no longer 'blow where he pleases' (cf. Jn 3.1) but only where he has blown in the past.

The initial fault line on tradition, especially the place of the Fathers in Orthodox theology, was articulated by Sergius Bulgakov and Georges Florovsky. For Bulgakov, no mean patristic scholar himself, the writings of the Fathers must be seen first and foremost historically:

> The writings of the Holy Fathers in their dogmatic proclamations must also be understood within their historical context. One must not apply to them a meaning that is not inherent in the nature of the problems they were actually concerned with. One cannot seek in the writings of one period answers to the questions inherent in another. In any case the writings do not possess a universality applicable to all periods in history. The writings of the Fathers are historically conditioned and therefore limited in their meaning. This does not prevent them from having an eternal value insofar as they are woven into the dogmatic conscience of the church, but it is important to establish that the writings of the Fathers are not the Word of God and cannot be compared to it or made equal to it. In principle, nobody is making such an equation nowadays, as was done before, but in fact it does happen, and this approach is harmful when put to ill use. We say this not to diminish the authority of the Fathers of the Church but so that this authority may be taken for what it is.[3]

In contrast to Bulgakov's cautious and relativizing approach towards patristic teachings, Florovsky saw immutable values in the 'ancient patristic tradition'. Florovsky objects to the approach to theology of Vladimir Soloviev and 'his intellectual descendants and those continuing his work, and from them into the *present religio-philosophical tradition*'[4] (read Bulgakov in particular) to cast theology in the language and concepts of contemporary philosophy, especially German idealism.

---

[1]Nicolas Berdyaev, 'Orthdoksiya i chelvechnost' (Orthodoxia and Humanness) *Put'*, No. 53 (Paris, 1937), 53–65. Review of Georges Florovsky, *The Ways of Russian Theology* (Paris: YMCA-Press, 1937). Trans. Stephen Janos. www.berdyaev.com/Berdyaev/berd_lib/1937_424.html (13 May 2015).

[2]Georges Florovsky, 'The Predicament of the Christian Historian' (1959), in Brandon Gallaher and Paul Ladouceur, eds., *The Patristic Witness of Georges Florovsky: Essential Theological Writings* (London: T&T Clark, 2019), 193.

[3]Sergius Bulgakov, 'Dogma and Dogmatic Theology' (1937), in Michael Plekon, ed., *Tradition Alive: On the Church and the Christian Life in Our Time* (Lanham, MA: Rowan & Littlefield, 2003), 71.

[4]Georges Florovsky, 'Western Influences in Russian Theology' (1937), in Gallaher and Ladouceur, eds., *The Patristic Witness of Georges Florovsky* (emphasis in original), 147.

Instead, Florovsky posits the Greek-Byzantine patristic tradition as the only true philosophy and the only true theology; philosophy is dependent on theology and not vice versa. In Florovsky's conception, the task of theology consists:

> not so much translating the tradition of faith into contemporary language – into the code of the most current philosophy, so to speak – as *learning to find the immutable basic principles of the Christian love of wisdom in the old ancient patristic tradition*; not revising dogmatic theology in line with modern-day philosophy, but rather the reverse: *building up philosophy on the basis of the experience of faith itself, so that the experience of faith becomes the source and standard of philosophical contemplation.*[5]

The temptation to absolutize tradition is particularly acute when it comes to the Fathers of the Church. It is only too easy to use quotations from the Fathers as proof texts on the same level of authority as Scripture. In some of Florovsky's statements advocating the neopatristic synthesis, he seems in fact to equate the Fathers and Scripture. In a paper delivered in 1959 to the Faith and Order Orthodox Consultation in Kifissia, Greece, Florovsky stated:

> The Fathers testify to the Apostolicity of the tradition. There are two basic stages in the proclamation of the Christian faith. *Our simple faith had to acquire composition.* There was an inner urge, an inner logic, an internal necessity, in this transition – from *kerygma* to *dogma*. Indeed, the *dogmata* of the Fathers are essentially the same 'simple' *kerygma*, which had been once delivered and deposited by the apostles, once, for ever. ... 'The mind of the Fathers' is an intrinsic term of reference in Orthodox theology, no less than the word of the Holy Writ and indeed never separated from it. The Fathers themselves were always servants of the Word, and their theology was intrinsically exegetical.[6]

For Bulgakov, the teachings of the Fathers reflect underlying verities, an eternal theology, which could be set into different philosophical systems, using language different from that of the Fathers. For Florovsky, it is not possible to articulate the truths of Christianity other than in the same concepts, the same philosophy, indeed the same vocabulary, as those of the Greek Fathers in particular. Florovsky devoted a great of energy expounding and defending his vision of the vital significance of patristic tradition in Orthodoxy and more specifically Greek-Byzantine theology as the essential norm for not only for Orthodox theology, but for Christian theology as a whole.

In his argument on the significance of the patristic tradition, Bulgakov introduces an important distinction among dogma, doctrine and *theologoumena* (although in practise he tends to fuse the latter two): 'The number of dogmas is limited and, in the case of many if not the majority of questions, we are presented only with theological doctrines. Popular opinions in any case are not dogmas but *theologoumena*.'[7] In this sense, doctrines include teachings of the Fathers which are not formal dogmas and it is here that ancient Fathers may have differing and even conflicting

---

[5]Idem, 147–8.

[6]Georges Florovsky, 'The Ethos of the Orthodox Church' (1959) in Gallaher and Ladouceur, eds., *The Patristic Witness of Georges Florovsky*, 293.

[7]Bulgakov, 'Dogma and Dogmatic Theology', 67.

views. Consistent with his overall approach to the Fathers, Florovsky rejects the validity of Bulgakov's distinction between dogma and doctrine, which he calls a 'a forced distinction'.[8] Florovsky's main concern was to prevent the expression of Christian doctrine in any system of thought other than the Hellenism of the Greek Fathers and he does not resolve the issue of having to consider all patristic teachings as equally valid and significant.

The tension between the two primal approaches to patristic tradition has continued unabated and has become more acute in recent years with renewed questioning of the soundness and pertinence of the neopatristic approach to Orthodox theology on the one hand, and the rise of Orthodox fundamentalism on the other, with the attendant risk of falling into a rigid traditionalism. Already in 1937 Bulgakov characterized the tendency to 'canonize' the *writings* of the Fathers as a 'patrological heresy'.[9] The church canonizes the *persons* of Fathers for their holiness, but it does not canonize their *writings*. In a similar vein, later Orthodox theologians refer to the tendency towards patristic traditionalism as a 'patristic fundamentalism' (Petros Vassiliadis), 'patristicism' (Alan Brown), a 'fundamentalism of tradition' or a 'fundamentalism of the Fathers' (Pantelis Kalaitzidis).[10]

In a 1990 lecture at St Vladimir's Theological Seminary, Petros Vassiliadis (b. 1945), while recognizing the impact of Florovsky's call for Orthodox theology to go 'back to the Fathers' on theology in Greece, nonetheless points to this tendency towards traditionalism:

> This revival, despite Florovsky's own remarks not to return to the dead letter of the Fathers, has seldom become nationwide a liberating force leading to a holistic understanding of all aspects of theology and everyday church life. Very often, 'return to the Fathers' was understood in a fundamentalist way, similar to the biblical fundamentalism of the Protestant world. Some have regretted this kind of patristic fundamentalism that has replaced a biblical fundamentalism that flourished during the climax of the activities of the religious organizations in Greece.[11]

Indeed the dividing line between contemporary critics and defenders of neopatristic theology is much the same as it was when the neopatristic approach first appeared on the scene in the 1930s: What role and authority should Orthodox theology accord to the teachings of the Fathers on non-dogmatic questions?[12]

Neopatristic theologians attempt to build in some safeguards against traditionalism, notably in the distinction between 'Tradition' and 'traditions' and in the concept of 'living tradition'.[13] There

---

[8]Georges Florovsky, 'Patristics and Modern Theology' (1936), in Gallaher and Ladouceur, eds., *The Patristic Witness of Georges Florovsky*, 153.

[9]Bulgakov, 'Dogma and Dogmatic Theology', 71.

[10]Petros Vassiliadis, 'Greek Theology in the Making, Trends and Facts in the 80s – Vision for the 90s', *St Vladimir's Theological Quarterly*, 35, 1 (1991), 34; Alan Brown, 'On the Criticism of *Being as Communion* in Anglophone Orthodox Theology', in Douglas Knight, ed., *The Theology of John Zizioulas: Personhood and the Church* (Aldershot UK: Ashgate, 2007), 64, 76; Pantelis Kalaitzidis, 'From the "Return to the Fathers" to the Need for a Modern Orthodox Theology', *St Vladimir's Theological Quarterly*, 54, 1 (2010), 8.

[11]Vassiliadis, 'Greek Theology in the Making', 34.

[12]Kalaitzidis, 'From the "Return to the Fathers" to the Need for a Modern Orthodox Theology'. See also John Meyendorff's collected essays in *Living Tradition: Orthodox Witness in the Contemporary World* (Crestwood, NY: St Vladimir's Seminary Press, 1978) – the title is taken deliberately from the 1937 volume.

[13]See the discussion in Paul Valliere, *Modern Russian Theology: Bukharev, Soloviev, Bulgakov: Orthodox Theology in a New Key* (Grand Rapids, MI: Eerdmans, 2000), 382–3.

are two principal aspects of the attempt to distinguish 'Traditions' from 'traditions'. The first is the affirmation, long-standing in both the Orthodox and the Catholic churches, of the importance of tradition in Christianity, in contrast to the *sola scriptura* doctrine of the Reformation. In the Orthodox perspective, scripture and tradition do not stand as alternatives, but rather as essential and complementary aspects of the church; indeed, scripture itself is a part of tradition, since it was created within the church. But this externally directed aspect of tradition must be completed by an internally directed distinction between what is immutable in tradition and what is transient and subject to change. In a 1952 essay Vladimir Lossky advanced a mystical notion of tradition as 'the life of the Holy Spirit in the church, communicating to each member of the Body of Christ the faculty of hearing, of receiving, of knowing the Truth in the Light which belongs to it'.[14] This approach conceives tradition as 'the unique mode of receiving Revelation, a faculty owed to the Holy Spirit', 'a faculty of judging in the Light of the Holy Spirit',[15] rather than revelation itself. If Lossky does not really clarify what he understands by 'Tradition', John Meyendorff does so by expanding on Lossky:

> No clear notion of the true meaning of Tradition can be reached without constantly keeping in mind the well-known condemnation of 'human tradition' by the Lord himself [cf. Mt. 15.3-9]. The one Holy Tradition, which constitutes the self-identity of the church through the ages and is the organic and visible expression of the life of the Spirit in the church, is not to be confused with the inevitable, often creative and positive, sometimes sinful, and always relative accumulation of human traditions in the historical church.[16]

Peter Bouteneff spells this out even more clearly:

> It is important, then, to distinguish among the teachings that are found within the life of the church. Not everything that is taught by someone in the church is dogmatically binding. Not everything that we read in one or another the Church Fathers' writings is a dogma. Nor is every rule described in Scripture dogmatic. … Teachings are dogmatic when they are shown to have been clearly defined – usually by an ecumenical council – and have been universally accepted by all the churches that recognize themselves as Orthodox.[17]

Without a distinction between Tradition and traditions, there is indeed a danger of dogmatizing or 'canonizing' almost everything in the church, including all the writings of the Fathers, as Bulgakov pointed out, and all decisions of the ecumenical councils, whether truly dogmatic, disciplinary or organizational (such as the liturgical calendar).

---

[14]Lossky's essay 'Tradition and Traditions' first appeared as the introductory chapter to Leonid Ouspensky and Vladimir Lossky, *The Meaning of Icons* (1952). Reprinted in Vladimir Lossky, *In the Image and Likeness of God* (Yonkers, NY: St Vladimir's Seminary Press, 1985), 141–68; here at 152.

[15]Lossky, 'Tradition and Traditions', 155.

[16]John Meyendorff, 'The Meaning of Tradition', *Living Tradition: Orthodox Witness in the Contemporary World* (Crestwood, NY: St Vladimir's Seminary Press, 1978), 21. This is based on his earlier article 'Tradition and Traditions', *St Vladimir's Theological Quarterly*, 6, 3 (1962).

[17]Peter Bouteneff, *Sweeter than Honey: Orthodox Thinking on Dogma and Truth* (Yonkers, NY: St Vladimir's Seminary Press, 2006), 199.

As a middle course between considering patristic teachings and concepts as absolute, universal and immutable, and a rejection of much of patristic theology as outdated and irrelevant, some Orthodox theologians propose a 'contextual approach' to patristic theology, along the lines of Bulgakov's historical perspective. Hilarion Alfeyev outlines what this means:

> Phenomena can only receive adequate judgement from within the context of their origin and development. Thus the theology of each Church Father should be studied, as far as possible, from within the historical, theological, cultural and linguistic world in which he lived. ... One should not apply criteria applicable in one context to a patristic author who belongs to a totally different milieu.[18]

The contextual approach to patristic theology appears to be closer to Bulgakov's thinking than to Florovsky's: 'The writings of the Fathers are historically conditioned and therefore limited in their meaning,' wrote Bulgakov in 1937.[19] But not everything that the Fathers wrote should be seen only contextually or historically: on major dogmatic questions, especially concerning the Trinity and Christ, the teachings of the Fathers found their way into formal Christian dogmas. It is in this sense that the somewhat fluid notion of *consensus patrum* has some value. But beyond a relatively small number of formal dogmas (such as the Trinity and the two natures of Christ), *consensus patrum* is problematic. The difficulty is to draw the line between what is absolute because it relates to dogma and what is more properly contextual, useful guidance for contemporary theology but far from definitive. The other danger in a strictly contextual approach to the Fathers is that of relegating patristic writings to academic or literary museums, interesting, beautiful perhaps, but hardly relevant to everyday life.

Ironically, later in life, Florovsky seems to have moved closer to Bulgakov's position on the contemporary authority of the Fathers. In a letter written in December 1963 to his friend the Anglican Arthur Dobbie Bateman,[20] Florovsky, after stating that he dislikes the phrase *consensus patrum* writes: 'The "authority" of the Fathers is not a *dictatus papae*. They are guides and witnesses, no more. Their *vision* is "of authority", not necessarily their words.'[21] Florovsky's main concern was the struggle against a mere 'theology of repetition', but the statement that the Fathers are 'guides and witnesses, no more', is closer to Bulgakov's thinking, as expressed in his 1937 paper on 'Dogma and Dogmatic Theology', than to Florovsky's own earlier more unqualified exaltation of patristic thought.

The 'development of doctrine' is an issue related to the role of tradition in contemporary theology. Orthodox are uncomfortable with the notion of doctrinal development, because of a

---

[18]Hilarion Alfeyev, 'The Patristic Heritage and Modernity', *Orthodox Witness Today* (Geneva: World Council of Churches, 2006), 156. Alfeyev goes on to castigate Florovsky's *Ways of Russian Theology* as 'neither adequate nor fair' for its judgement of Russian patristics from a Byzantine perspective. The Volos Academy for Theological Studies in Greece has been promoting a contextual approach to Orthodox theology, notably by sponsoring, with other institutions, seminars on 'Can Orthodox Theology Be Contextual?' in 2010 and in 2013.

[19]Bulgakov, 'Dogma and Dogmatic Theology', 71.

[20]Arthur F. Dobbie Bateman (1897–1974) was an early leader of the Fellowship of St Alban and St Sergius and one of the first English critics and translators of modern Russian philosophy, theology and spirituality.

[21]Georges Florovsky, 'On the Authority of the Fathers', letter to A. F. Dobbie Bateman, 12 December 1963, in Gallaher and Ladouceur, eds., *The Patristic Witness of Georges Florovsky*, 238.

deeply ingrained conviction that Christ gave the full deposit of the faith once and for all in his life and in his teachings, as received by the apostles, recorded in the New Testament and transmitted in the church. At the same time Orthodox vehemently oppose the idea that the utilization of concepts originating in Greek philosophy to describe the faith constituted a profound distortion of the faith of the apostles, a critique of early Christian theology most forcibly articulated by the German historian of dogma Adolf von Harnack (1851–1930). But Orthodox have difficulty in articulating why early Christian theology, especially the Trinitarian theology and the Christology of the fourth and fifth centuries, and even the Palamite theology of the divine energies, does not constitute 'development of doctrine' as understood in Catholic and Protestant theologies, yet are valid and even necessary expressions of the Christian faith.

Andrew Louth addresses this issue in a paper entitled 'Is Development of Doctrine a Valid Category for Orthodox Theology?' His answer is a clear 'No': 'The idea of development itself is not an acceptable category on Orthodox theology.'[22] But this 'No' does in fact require qualification to avoid wandering accidently into the von Harnack camp. Louth quotes with approval the Romanian theologian Mihail Neamtu: 'The profound dogmatic elaborations of the fourth century … did not bring the apostolic faith somewhere further, on to a deeper level of understanding.' Yet Louth states on the following page: 'The central theological task, as the Fathers see it, is to interpret the writings of the *theologoi*, that is, the Scriptures, in the light of the mystery of Christ. … There is no development beyond seeking, again and again, to deepen our understanding of the Scriptures in the light of the mystery of Christ.'[23] The distinction is subtle: Orthodox reject the notion of doctrinal development in the sense of the discovery of new doctrines, but accept that there is deepening or development in our understanding and articulation of the deposit of the faith as revealed by Jesus Christ. This safeguards the dogmatic expression of the faith in the Nicene Creed and other received dogmatic statements (against the critiques of von Harnack et al.), and still permits Orthodox theology to deal with new issues, not present in apostolic or even patristic times, using notions borrowed notably from Greek philosophy or not fully developed in earlier times, such as the theology of the human person and social and political theology (against the accusation of traditionalism).

In this same paper Louth also advances the position that

> We do not hope to surpass the Fathers in our grasp of the mystery of Christ; rather, we look to them to help us to a deeper understanding. We do not stand over against the Fathers; we come to them to learn from them. This entails that if development [of doctrine] means that there is an historical advance in Christian doctrine, making our understanding of the faith deeper or more profound than that of the Fathers, at least in principle, then such a notion of development cannot be accepted as a category of Orthodox theology. We shall not advance beyond the faith of the Fathers, nor shall we advance beyond the faith of the apostles.[24]

---

[22]Andrew Louth, 'Is Development of Doctrine a Valid Category for Orthodox Theology?' in Valerie Hotchkiss and Patrick Henry, eds., *Orthodoxy and Western Culture, A Collection of Essays Honoring Jaroslav Pelikan on His Eightieth Birthday* (Crestwood, NY: St Vladimir's Seminary Press, 2006), 61. See also similar statements on pages 55 and 57.
[23]Louth, 'Is Development of Doctrine a Valid Category for Orthodox Theology?' 60–1.
[24]Ibid., 55.

One question here is who are the Fathers? The apostles? The Fathers up to the fourth century? Or fifth? Or the fourteenth? Or the more open-ended view of Kallistos Ware:

> It is dangerous to look on 'the Fathers' as a closed cycle of writings belonging wholly to the past, for might not our own age produce a new Basil or Athanasius? To say that there can be no more Fathers is to suggest that the Holy Spirit has deserted the church.[25]

Hilarion Alfeyev quotes these last sentences of Kallistos Ware with approval and adds:

> The confession of a 'patristic faith' not only implies the study of patristic writings and the attempt to bring the legacy of the Fathers to life, but also the belief that our era is no less patristic than any other. The 'golden age' inaugurated by Christ, the apostles and the early Fathers endures in works of the Church Fathers of our days, to last for as long as the Church of Christ will stand on this earth and for as long as the Holy Spirit will inspire it.[26]

Georges Florovsky was also open, if cautious, on the question of latter-day Fathers of the Church: 'The church is still fully authoritative as she has been in the ages past, since the Spirit of Truth quickens her now no less effectively as in the ancient times'; '*There should be no restriction at all*' in the time frame of the normative authority of the church.[27] But in naming 'Fathers', he does not venture later than Mark of Ephesus (fifteenth century).

A subsidiary aspect of the debate over tradition is found in the 'slogans' meant to characterize one or another approach to the Fathers: 'Back to the Fathers' or 'Beyond the Fathers'. 'Back to the Fathers', said to characterize neopatristic theology, sees the Fathers as normative expressions of Christianity, whereas 'Beyond the Fathers', associated with the Russian religious renaissance, considers the Fathers as a starting point for the further development of Christian thought in relation to contemporary problems and needs (and not, as some maintain, an outright rejection of the Fathers). Paul Valliere sets out to discredit neopatristic theology as a 'Back to the Fathers' movement bent on immobility, but he overstates his case by downplaying or ignoring altogether the dynamic element in Georges Florovsky's project and especially Florovsky's constant warning about the dangers of 'a theology of repetition'.[28]

But any debate over such slogans is dangerous and a needless distraction from the underlying issues. Like other slogans, they oversimplify and misrepresent the complex foundations of the major approaches to the Fathers in modern Orthodox theology. A synthesis between the slogans is suggested by the expression 'Forward with the Fathers', used by Augustine Casiday as a chapter title

---

[25]Kallistos Ware, *The Orthodox Church* (London: Penguin Books, 1993), 204.

[26]Hilarion Alfeyev, 'The Neopatristic Heritage and Modernity', in *Orthodox Witness Today*, 148. Alfeyev's theological openness in the quotation is to some extent somewhat blurred by his own *dogmatica*, *Orthodox Christianity, Vol. II, Doctrine and Teaching of the Orthodox Church* (Yonkers, NY: St Vladimir's Seminary Press, 2012). This is virtually a summary of patristic theology. See our review of this book in *St Vladimir's Theological Quarterly*, 58, 4 (2014).

[27]Georges Florovsky, 'Saint Gregory Palamas and the Tradition of the Fathers', in Gallaher and Ladouceur, eds., *The Patristic Witness of Georges Florovsky*, 226.

[28]See Paul Valliere, 'The Limits of Tradition', conclusion to his book *Modern Russian Theology: Bukharev, Soloviev, Bulgakov: Russian Theology in a New Key* (Edinburgh: T&T Clark, 2000), especially 376–83. See also the critique of Valliere's position in Augustine Casiday, *Remember the Days of Old: Orthodox Thinking on the Patristic Heritage* (Yonkers, NY: St Vladimir's Seminary Press, 2014), 42–61.

of his book on the patristic heritage.[29] 'Forward with the Fathers' is certainly closer to Florovsky's thinking than merely 'Back to the Fathers', and at least has the advantage of maintaining a dynamic approach to patristic theology, opening the door to the possibility of new insights, faithful to the patristic way of doing theology, as we suggested in Chapter 5, rather than merely repeating what the Fathers wrote.

The restoration of patristic thought and patristic studies

As we argued earlier, the major achievement of neopatristic theology has been the restoration of patristic thought at the very heart of Orthodox theology, with the revival of apophatism, the Palamite distinction between the divine essence and the divine energies and theosis as the keystone doctrines. The revival of these three central doctrines went hand-in-hand with a broader renaissance of patristic theology. Georges Florovsky initially conceived the neopatristic project in the mid-1930s as a response to the 'pseudomorphosis' of Orthodox theology in the preceding centuries, a theology extensively influenced by Western ideas, both scholasticism and Western philosophies. For Florovsky, the answer to this sad state of affairs was a return to the sources, the recovery of patristic thought as the basis for Orthodox theology, the acquisition of 'the mind of the Fathers', a 'neopatristic synthesis', to address the problems of the day. Admittedly, his project had weaknesses from the outset, not the least of which is that Florovsky never really clearly explained what he meant by 'the mind of the Fathers' and he himself rarely ventured into uncharted theological waters, generally staying within themes already explored by the Fathers.

Although Georges Florovsky, Vladimir Lossky and their successors consciously undertook to 're-habilitate' patristic theology within Orthodox thought, a broad patristic movement began long before. The publication of the *Philokalia* in 1782 by St Macarius of Corinth (1731–1805) and and St Nicodemus of the Holy Mountain (1749–1809) is a cornerstone of the modern patristic edifice. The interest of the editors of the *Philokalia* was primarily in ascetic writings, but they and their successors in Moldavia and Russia also promoted more 'theological' writings – Nicodemus prepared an edition of Gregory Palamas, which unfortunately was seized and destroyed by the Austrian police in Venice before it could be printed. In nineteenth-century Russia, the Slavophile Ivan Kirievsky (1806–56), academic scholars and monastic figures such as Macarius of Optino (1788–1860) promoted the translation of the Greek Fathers into Russian, as well as scholarly studies of patristic theology. In a similar vein, the leading figures of the Russian religious renaissance, notably Pavel Florensky and Sergius Bulgakov,

[29]Casiday, *Remember the Days of Old*, 141. Florovsky does not appear to have used the expression 'Forward with the Fathers' attributed to him, although he did write something similar in 'Breaks and Links', the conclusion to *The Ways of Russian Theology* (1937): 'The road "to the Fathers" in any case leads only forward, never back. The point is to be true to the patristic *spirit*, rather than to the *letter* alone, to light one's inspiration at the patristic flame rather than engaging in a collection and classification of ancient texts'. Gallaher and Ladouceur, eds., *The Patristic Witness of Georges Florovsky*, 166.

considered that they were working within the spirit of the Fathers. In short, the twentieth-century neopatristic movement built on and carried forward a patristic revival initiated over a century and a half earlier.

A corollary of neopatristic theology has been the flowering of patristic studies by Orthodox theologians, even though Orthodox remain a minority among patristic scholars. Indeed, as Fr Cyril Hovorun (b. 1974) points out, for many Orthodox, patristics has a psychological and social meaning as a 'socio-religious phenomenon', in addition to a theological one: 'For the Orthodox, patristics is more than just patristics. It is an essential part of their confessional identity.'[30] Somewhat cynically, he adds that 'The Orthodox like to identify themselves and their tradition with the Fathers, but they do not often care about what the Fathers really thought and what they did write …; they will never say that they do not care about what the Fathers wrote; they just do not read them.'[31] More than a theological point of reference, the ancient Greek Fathers become a sort of trademark supposedly differentiating Orthodoxy from Western Christianity

The modern Orthodox neopatristic revival beginning in Paris in the 1930s developed in parallel with a similar movement, the *nouvelle théologie*, among Roman Catholic theologians and indeed the two existed in a mutually beneficial symbiotic relationship. At that time, the Catholic hierarchy frowned on theological speculation as part of its crackdown on modernism in the Church. At the same time, Catholics were forbidden to engage in the ecumenical endeavours spearheaded by Protestant denominations. Patristics was thus a safe refuge for Catholic theologians. Orthodox theologians in Paris who fostered a patristic revival within Orthodoxy, such as Vladimir Lossky and Myrrha Lot-Borodine, found themselves 'in good company' with their Catholic counterparts, both neo-Thomists such as Étienne Gilson (1884–1978) and Maurice de Gandillac (1906–2006) and *nouvelle théologie* scholars such as the Jesuits Jean Daniélou (1905–74), Henri du Lubac (1896–1991) and Claude Mondésert (1906–90), the Dominican Yves Congar (1904–95) and the Oratorian Louis Bouyer (1913–2004).

The French patristic community launched a gigantic patristic project during the Second World War: the establishment of critical editions and the publication of translations with ample scholarly notes and references for the major writings of both Greek and Latin Fathers, with the aim of eventually replacing the standard patristic reference, the monumental collection (386 volumes) of Greek and Latin Fathers published by the French priest Jacques-Paul Migne (1800–75) between 1844 and 1865. Since the Second World War, many Anglican and Protestant scholars have also devoted themselves to patristic studies, including the establishment of critical texts and translations of major patristic writings, and the publication of scholarly studies of the Fathers, including the clarification of the authorship of certain works, such as those of Evagrius of Pontus, Denys the Areopagite and Macarius of Egypt. Non-Orthodox scholars have also discovered and published hitherto unknown works, such as catechetical homilies of John Chrysostom and Theodore of Mopsuestia, and additional writings of Isaac the Syrian. Understanding of such major figures as

[30]Cyril Hovorun, 'Patristics after Neo-Patristics', in Justin A. Mihoc and Leonard Aldea, eds., *A Celebration of Living Theology: A Festschrift in Honour of Andrew Louth* (London: T&T Clark, 2014), 206.
[31]Hovorun, 'Patristics after Neo-Patristics', 206.

Evagrius, Macarius, Symeon the New Theologian, Maximus the Confessor, John of Damascus and Gregory Palamas has been greatly advanced by the work of non-Orthodox scholars.[32]

While Orthodox attention to Gregory Palamas represents, as we have seen, a special case, Orthodox scholars have also focused their attention on other major Fathers, such as Symeon the New Theologian (studies by Basil Krivoshein and Hilarion Alfeyev) and Maximus the Confessor (studies by Hilarion Alfeyev, Andrew Louth and Jean-Claude Larchet). Orthodox scholars have also produced major synthetic studies of patristic thought, such as those of John Behr relating to the development of Christian dogmas contained in the Nicene Creed.

Conclusion

For most Orthodox theologians at the beginning of the twenty-first century, religious philosophy, prevalent in much of Russian theology up to the Second World War, and the 'academic-moral' school have largely been relegated to historical theology or are considered to subsist only on the fringes of mainstream Orthodox thought. The current 'Bulgakovian revival' is found mainly in non-Orthodox academic circles, and one is hard put to identify more than a few true 'Bulgakovian' Orthodox theologians.[33] Yet academic theology is still alive and well in more conservative Orthodox circles – one can point to the continued availability and popularity, even on the internet, of Fr Michael Pomazansky's *Orthodox Dogmatic Theology, A Concise Exposition*,[34] a characteristic monument of this type of theology, and to a revival of the pre-revolutionary theology textbooks in the Russian seminaries and academies and in other Orthodox countries after the fall of communism. But by and large, the patristic mode of theology has had widespread acceptance in Orthodox circles since the 1950s. Whether patristic thought on any particular issue is considered normative or indicative, it is inconceivable that credible Orthodox theology today can be done without an acute awareness of the thinking of the Fathers. The starting points of Orthodox theology are the twin pillars of Scripture and the Fathers – even if who actually are the 'Fathers' remains an open question.

It is fair to say that we now have a much better appreciation of the Fathers than since the end of classical patristic age. This is fine and commendable: the problem is that a great deal of Orthodox

[32]For an overview of the patristic revival in an ecumenical context, see Andrew Louth, 'The Patristic Revival and Its Protagonists', in Mary B. Cunningham and Elizabeth Theokritoff, eds., *The Cambridge Companion to Orthodox Christian Theology*, especially pages 192–3 and 197–9.

[33]Antoine Arjakovsky is one of the few who employs and advocates Bulgakov's theology, including sophiology. See his *Essai sur le père Serge Boulgakov, philosophe et théologien chrétien* (Essay on Father Sergius Bulgakov, Christian Philosopher and Theologian) (Paris: Parole et silence, 2006); and *The Way: Religious Thinkers of the Russian Emigration in Paris and their Journal* (Notre Dame, IN: University of Notre Dame Press, 2013). The recent publication of English translations of Bulgakov's 'major trilogy' (*The Lamb of God* (1933), *The Comforter* (1936) and *The Bride of the Lamb* (1945), English translations in 2008, 2004 and 2002 respectively) promotes interest in Bulgakov, but has not necessarily resulted in an active revival of his theology.

[34]In the Annex to his *Orthodox Dogmatic Theology*, entitled 'New Currents in Russian Philosophico-Theological Thought', Pomazansky critiques Russian religious philosophy, not neopatristic theology, which he does not mention. See Michael Pomazansky, *Orthodox Dogmatic Theology: A Concise Exposition (1963)* (Platina, CA: St Herman of Alaska Brotherhood Press, 1984), 357–372.

'theological energy', which must be considered a scarce and shrinking resource, is devoted to patristic studies, which largely remain in a closed circuit, disconnected from contemporary theological issues and problems. Certainly it is easier to study the thinking of one Father or one issue across several Fathers, than to tackle complex modern issues which were not a concern in patristic times. Florovsky himself produced many scholarly patristic studies, but patristic studies as such were not what he intended when he spoke about the need to 'acquire the mind of the Fathers', a 'patristic mind-set'. Even though Florovsky himself rarely ventured into uncharted theological waters, major exceptions being ecclesiology and ecumenical theology, his basic platform for the neopatristic synthesis clearly called for tackling contemporary issues using a patristic base.

The emphasis on patristic studies has distracted attention and resources from the study of contemporary issues which were not a concern or simply did not exist in classical patristic times. Even leading Orthodox figures typically associated with the modern revival of patristic theology expressed doubts concerning the actual practice of theology among patristically inclined Orthodox. Alexander Schmemann, in a revealing reflection stimulated by a remark of John Meyendorff, expresses the limits of the neopatristic revival, not so much as it was originally conceived by Georges Florovsky, but rather as it was seen and practised by others:

> Once, Father John M[eyendorff] told me in a moment of candour that he cannot understand why people are obsessed with the Fathers. So many people propagate this fashion, which prevents them from understanding anything in the real world, and at the same time are convinced that they serve the church and Orthodoxy. I'm afraid that people are attracted not by the thoughts of the Fathers, not by the content of their writings, but by their style. It is quite close to the Orthodox understanding of liturgical services: love them without understanding; and inasmuch as they are not understood, come to no conclusion. We sit in our shell, charmed by a melody, and do not notice that the church is suffering, and for a long time already has left the battlefield.[35]

We will consider assessments of neopatristic theology more thoroughly in Chapter 18.

[35]Alexander Schmemann, *The Journals of Father Alexander Schmemann, 1973-1983* (Crestwood, NY: St Vladimir's Seminary Press, 2000), 269 (entry for Thursday, 2 October 1980).

Part II

Themes and Conflicts in Modern Orthodox Theology

9

God and Creation

Chapter Outline

The problem of how God, as infinite, eternal, uncreated, immaterial and transcendent, relates to the finite, contingent and material and immaterial created world has long challenged human thought. Orthodox philosophers and theologians from the late nineteenth century onwards approached this question from several perspectives and proposed different solutions. We will consider here six modern Orthodox approaches to God-creation relationships: all-unity and cosmism; sophiology; divine energies; panentheism; the *logoi* of things and the contemplation of God in creation. These approaches are not mutually exclusive, but since they start from different presuppositions and employ different concepts and vocabulary, it is often difficult to see the relationships among them and to reconcile them. All of these approaches must be considered in the light of the Incarnation of Christ and his mission in the world, inseparable from the activity of the Holy Spirit. There is, nonetheless, a tendency to isolate Christ and the Incarnation from God-creation relationships in general, which turns the question of how God relates to the created world into more of a philosophical issue than a properly theological one. To some extent as well, the perspectives that we are considering are historically conditioned, arising at particular times and within broad approaches to theology, and they are often associated with specific personalities in the modern Orthodox thought. Nevertheless, all seek to shed light on how God relates to creation.

All-unity and cosmism

Among the philosopher-theologians of the Russian religious renaissance, the notions of all-unity (*vseedinstvo*), divine-humanity or Godmanhood (*bogochelovechestvo*) and Divine Wisdom or Sophia (sophiology) are intimately intertwined in the search for an understanding of how God relates to creation. In this chapter we will, somewhat artificially we recognize, consider all-unity and sophiology as distinct yet interrelated approaches to this issue, leaving a more detailed consideration of divine-humanity to Chapter 10.

The idea of a principle of unification of all that exists has its roots in ancient philosophies. It features prominently, for example, in Plato ('the One') and in Plotinus ('the First'). In early Christian thought, God as Creator is the de facto principle of unity in creation, but for many thinkers of the Russian religious renaissance, the challenge was to identify a basis of all-unity which would encompass both the Creator and the created, the spiritual and the material, in a single all-inclusive vision of total knowledge and existence. Although the idea of the totality of all beings forming an absolute unity occurs as early as Peter Chaadaev (1794–1856), it was Vladimir Soloviev (1853–1900) who made all-unity, together with divine-humanity, the centrepieces of his thinking. To express the idea of the unity of all beings, Soloviev coined the term *vseedinstvo*, all-unity (also translated as total-unity, pan-unity, uni-totality and all-encompassing unity). It is in this light that Nicolas Lossky (father of Vladimir Lossky) (1870–1965) describes the characteristic feature of Russian philosophical thought as 'the search for an exhaustive knowledge of reality as a whole and the concreteness of metaphysical conceptions … the whole being understood not as a chaotic multiplicity but as a systematic pan-unity'.[1] This all-unity is discovered first in contemplation and in prayer: 'In dialoguing with God', summarizes the Catholic theologian Tomáš Špidlík, 'we discover the profound sense of the universe and its unity: the Russians call this *vseedinstvo*, "all-unity", for them a key expression in gnoseology.'[2] From Soloviev onwards, all-unity was a powerful, even hypnotic notion in Russian thought, 'bewitching and subjugating men's minds', writes Basil Zenkovsky (1881-1962).[3] Other figures of the Russian religious renaissance who pursued the quest for all-unity, or the closely related concept of integral knowledge, at some stage in their intellectual development include Nicolas Berdyaev (1874–1948), Sergius Bulgakov (1871–1944), Simeon Frank (1877–1950), Lev Karsavin (1882–1952), Alexei Losev (1893–1988), Nicolas Lossky (1870–1965), Sergius Troubetskoy (1862–1905) and Eugene Troubetskoy (1863–1920), as well as the leading poets of the Silver Age of Russian letters prior to the First World War, such as Alexander Blok (1880–1921) and Vyacheslav Ivanov (1866–1949).

Vladimir Soloviev set out to unify the three forms of knowledge, the empirical, the metaphysical and the mystical, which must be integrated with the aesthetic, with beauty.[4] Beauty in this sense is

---

[1]Nicolas Lossky, *History of Russian Philosophy* (London: George Allen & Unwin, 1952), 95.

[2]Tomáš Špidlík, *L'Idée russe: Une autre vision de l'homme* (The Russian Idea: Another Vision of the World) (Troyes, FR: Fates, 1994), 86.

[3]V. V. Zenkovsky, *A History of Russian Philosophy*, 2 vols. (London: Routledge & Kegan Paul, 1953), II:874.

[4]See Soloviev's essay 'Beauty in Nature', in Vladimir Wozniuk, ed., *The Heart of Reality: Essays on Beauty, Love and Ethics by V.S. Soloviev* (Notre Dame, IN: University of Notre Dame Press, 2003).

not merely an aesthetic quality isolated from ethics and truth, but is rather beauty as a manifestation of goodness and truth. Soloviev first referred to the principle of unity in creation as the 'world-soul' (*anima mundi*), a term inherited from Stoic and Neo-Platonist philosophy and more directly from the German idealist Friedrich Schelling (1775–1854). Through this notion of the world-soul, Soloviev sought to reconcile divine unity and the multiplicity of creation: 'The soul of the world is both *one* and *all*; it occupies a mediating position between the plurality of living entities and the unconditional unity of the Deity. … The soul of the world is a *dual* entity: it includes both the divine principle and created being.'[5] For Soloviev, divine fullness or actuality *includes* multiplicity, the unity of a multiplicity of ideas and potencies, 'the primordial unity of the divine Logos', writes Soloviev in his *Lectures on Godmanhood* (1881).[6] The cosmic 'fall' is thus a fall from divine unity-in-multiplicity to creaturely disunity-in-multiplicity: 'Having fallen away from the divine unity, the natural world appears as a chaos of discordant elements.'[7]

Soloviev conceived the principle of all-unity manifested in the world-soul as a mirror of the divine world, which unites the Platonic triad beauty, truth and goodness:

> *The absolute actualises goodness in beauty, through truth.* Since they are only different aspects or positings of a single subject, these three ideas, or universal unities, form, in their interpenetration, a new concrete unity. This unity constitutes the complete actualisation of the divine content, the integral totality of the absolute essence, the realisation of God as the *all-One*, in whom 'dwells all the fullness of the Godhead bodily' [Col. 2.9][8]

For Soloviev, love is the overarching principle of unity of the goodness-truth-beauty triad which brings together the different orders of existence:

> Goodness is the unity of the all or of all individuals; it is love as what is willed, or desired; it is the beloved. Consequently, here we have love in a special and preeminent sense as the idea of ideas; its unity is *essential*. Truth is also love; that is, it is the unity of the all, but as objectively represented; its unity is ideal. Finally, beauty is also love (that is, the unity of all individuals). But it is love as manifested or made available to the senses; its unity is real.[9]

Soloviev saw the world as all-unity in the state of becoming, whereas the Absolute is the All-Unity, as Lossky explains:

> The world contains the divine element, all-oneness, as a potentiality, an idea; but it also contains the non-divine, natural, material element, the dispersed, the multiplex of the particular which is not all-oneness. However, every particular being tends to become all-oneness and gradually moves toward that goal, uniting oneself with God. The process of establishing all-oneness in the world is the development of the world.[10]

---

[5]Vladimir Soloviev, cited in Zenkovsky, *A History of Russian Philosophy*, II:505–6.
[6]Vladimir Soloviev, *Lectures on Godmanhood* (also *Lectures on Divine Humanity*) (1881) (Hudson, NY: Lindisfarne Press, 1995), 131.
[7]Soloviev, *Lectures on Godmanhood*, 135.
[8]Ibid., 103–4.
[9]Ibid., 103.
[10]Lossky, *History of Russian Philosophy*, 104.

Prince Myshkin, the main character of Feodor Dostoyevsky's novel *The Idiot* (1868), expresses the core idea of the unity of the good, truth and beauty in the often quoted but often misunderstood phrase: 'Beauty will save the world.'[11] Soloviev concurs with Dostoyevsky:

> In his convictions [Dostoyevsky] never separated truth from good and beauty; in his artistic creativity he never placed beauty apart from the good and the true. And he was right, because these three live only in their unity. The good, taken separately from truth and beauty, is only an indistinct feeling, a powerless upwelling; truth taken abstractly is an empty word; and beauty without truth and the good is an idol. For Dostoevsky, these were three inseparable forms of one absolute Idea.[12]

For the religious philosophers, only God is supreme Goodness-Truth-Beauty and Christ is supreme Goodness-Truth-Beauty incarnate and can thus unite God and the entire cosmos as a single reality. The search for beauty becomes the search for the divine presence in the world and in this light we can understand the interest in nature and in art of the major figures of the Russian religious renaissance. It is all too easy to assimilate this concern for beauty to a form of exalted and misguided romanticism or aestheticism. This is what George Florovsky (1893–1979) does when he describes Pavel Florensky (1882–1937) as seeking 'aesthetic solitude'.[13] In the vision of the Russian religious thinkers, God creates the world in beauty as a manifestation of his love towards creation. Thus the created beauty of the world is not merely 'aesthetic'; it is a visible manifestation and seal of divine love and of God's intimate connection with the world, which has a correlate in the aesthetic ideal of beauty as the goal of the human creative process.[14]

One corollary of the notion of the all-unity is a vision of creation, the cosmos, which emphasizes that humanity is a part of the cosmos, rather than sees the cosmos as something 'out there' and humanity as irreconcilably different from the rest of creation. This cosmic outlook sees the world first and foremost as a divine creation reflecting divine glory: one has only to open one's eyes to perceive the glory of God. All-unity is thus an unspoken complicity between Creator and created. The sense of wonder experienced in the contemplation of nature becomes a prayer; humanity joins and verbalizes the wordless worship of both inanimate and animate creation for its Creator.

This cosmism, as a sense of unity between humanity and the rest of creation, is reflected in the descriptions of nature in the writings of major personalities of the Russian religious renaissance. In Fyodor Dostoyevsky's *The Brothers Karamazov*, the starets Zosima recounts an event from his youth, when he suddenly calls out to his companions, 'speaking straight from [his] heart':

> Gentlemen, … look around you at the gifts of God, the clear sky, the pure air, the tender grass, the birds; nature is beautiful and sinless, and we, only we, are sinful and foolish, and we don't understand

---

[11]Feodor Dostoyevsky, *The Idiot* (1868), Constance Garnett translation (1913), Part III, chapter V.
[12]Vladimir Soloviev, 'Three Addresses in Memory of Dostoyevsky', in Wozniuk, ed., *The Heart of Reality*, 16.
[13]Georges Florovsky, *The Ways of Russian Theology*, 2 vols., Vols. V–VI of *The Collected Works of Georges Florovsky* (Belmont, MA: Nordland, 1979; Vaduz: Büchervertriebsanstalt, 1987), II:277.
[14]I am grateful to Maria Simakova for these insights.

> that life is heaven, for we have only to understand that and it will at once be fulfilled in all its beauty, we shall embrace each other and weep.[15]

Similarly, after the death of Zosima, Alyosha (Alexei), the youngest of the Karamazov brothers, rushes out into the still night and gazes upwards at the starry night and all around him

> The silence of earth seemed to melt into the silence of the heavens. The mystery of earth was one with the mystery of the stars. … Alyosha stood, gazed, and suddenly threw himself down on the earth. He did not know why he embraced it. He could not have told why he longed so irresistibly to kiss it, to kiss it all. But he kissed it weeping, sobbing, and watering it with his tears, and vowed passionately to love it, to love it for ever and ever.[16]

In his *Autobiographical Notes*, Sergius Bulgakov also describes several experiences which nudged him towards his return to Christianity, after years of intellectual wandering in the byways of Marxism and idealism. The first of these experiences, in the spirit of nineteenth-century romanticism, took place in 1895:

> I was twenty-four years old. For a decade I had lived without faith and, after early stormy doubts, a religious emptiness reigned in my soul. One evening we were driving across the southern steppes of Russia, and the strong-scented spring grass was gilded by the rays of a glorious sunset. Far in the distance I saw the blue outlines of the Caucasus. This was my first sight of the mountains. I looked with ecstatic delight at their rising slopes. I drank in the light and the air of the steppes. I listened to the revelation of nature. My soul was accustomed to the dull pain of seeing nature as a lifeless desert and of treating its surface beauty as a deceptive mask. Yet, contrary to my intellectual convictions, I could not be reconciled to nature without God. Suddenly, in that evening hour, my soul was joyfully stirred. I started to wonder what would happen if the cosmos were not a desert and its beauty not a mask or deception – if nature were not death, but life. If he existed, the merciful and loving Father, if nature was the vesture of his love and glory, and if the pious feelings of my childhood, when I used to live in his presence, when I loved him and trembled because I was weak, were true, then the tears and inspiration of my adolescence, the sweetness of my prayers, my innocence and all those emotions which I had rejected and trodden down would be vindicated, and my present outlook with its emptiness and deadness would appear nothing more than blindness and lies, and what a transformation it would bring to me![17]

But Bulgakov was slow to respond to this invitation to recognize a transcendental reality, the existence of a world beyond the sensory; another thirteen years would pass before his definitive return to the faith and the church.

Pavel Florensky, whose estrangement from the faith was limited to a short time during his adolescence, also intersperses descriptions of experiences of nature in his classic *The Pillar and Ground of the Truth* (1914). Many chapters of the book (in the form of letters to an unnamed friend) begin with an evocation of a natural experience with which he associates a

---

[15]Fyodor Dostoyevsky, *The Brothers Karamazov* (1880), Constance Garnett translation (1912), Part II, chapter VI, 2.

[16]Dostoyevsky, *The Brothers Karamazov*, III, VII, 4.

[17]Sergius Bulgakov, 'My Conversion', from *Autobiographical Notes* (1946), in James Pain and Nicolas Zernov, eds., *A Bulgakov Anthology* (London: SPCK, 1976), 10–11.

theological reflection developed in the rest of the chapter, as in this introduction to Letter Five, on the Comforter:

> Do you remember, my gentle one, our long walks in the forest, the forest of dying August? The silvery trunks of the birches stood like stately palms, and their gold-green tops, as though exuding blood, pressed against the crimson and purple aspens. And above the surface of the earth, the branches of a hazel grove spread like green gauze. There was a holy hush of solemnity beneath the vaults of this temple. My far and yet eternally near Friend, do you remember our intimate conversations? The Holy Spirit and religious antinomies – that, it appears, is what interested us most. And finding ourselves in this solemn grove, we walked at sunset through the cornfield, became drunk with the flaming west, and rejoiced that the question was becoming clear, that we had come independently to the same answer. Then our thoughts flowed out in streams flaming like the vault of heaven, and we grasped each other's thoughts almost before they were spoken.[18]

Orthodox thought after the Russian religious philosophers had difficulty comprehending and accepting the notion of all-unity, tinged with Platonism and romantic cosmism, and sought to bridge the gap between God and creation by other avenues. One weakness of all-unity considered in isolation from Christ, the Incarnation and Divine Wisdom, is that it becomes a philosophical notion which is not specifically Christian and is not dependent on revelation, even though it is not inimical to revelation. For some critics, all-unity is too reminiscent of pantheism for comfort. Basil Zenkovsky describes Soloviev's metaphysics of all-unity as 'a modernised pantheism, in the tradition of Spinoza and Schelling', with the world as Absolute Being, even if 'an Absolute in process of becoming', while recognizing Soloviev's sincere wish 'to place Christian principles at the foundation of all of his theoretical constructions'.[19] Nicolas Lossky also refers to the 'pantheistic flavour'[20] of Soloviev's conception of all-unity as the Absolute and both Zenkovsky and Lossky link what they perceive as implicit pantheism in Soloviev's cosmology to his failure to consider God explicitly as *the* Absolute, the Creator.[21] Yet Soloviev does not emerge as a pantheist in the light of the totality of his writings and of his life. It is true that, unlike Florensky and Bulgakov, Soloviev did not forcefully emphasize the idea of God as Creator – the thrust of Soloviev's intellectual project was to express a unity between God and the world, not to seek out what differentiates them. In Soloviev's later thinking, divine creation becomes bound up with Sophia, Divine Wisdom, both as history and as eschatology, raising further questions for his successors – and for later critics – as in this passage from *Russia and the Universal Church* (1889):

> According to the Book of Genesis, God created the heaven and the earth in this *reshith*,[22] in his essential Wisdom. This signifies that Divine Wisdom not only represents the essential and actual all-unity of God's absolute being or substance, but also contains the power to unify the separated and fragmented cosmic being. Being the finished unity of all in God, Divine Wisdom also becomes the

[18]Pavel Florensky, *The Pillar and Ground of the Truth: An Essay in Orthodox Theodicy in Twelve Letters* (1914) (Princeton, NJ: Princeton University Press, 1997), 80.
[19]Zenkovsky, *A History of Russian Philosophy*, II:530.
[20]Lossky, *History of Russian Philosophy*, 128.
[21]See Zenkovsky, *A History of Russian Philosophy*, II:530; Lossky, *History of Russian Philosophy*, 127–8.
[22]Soloviev equates the Hebrew *reshith* with the Greek *archí* and the Latin *principium*.

unity of God and of extradivine existence. She therefore represents the true cause of creation and the goal of the latter – the principle in which God created the heaven and the earth. … She is *Malkhouth* (*Basileia*, *Regnum*, Kingdom) at the end – the Kingdom of God, the perfect and fully realized unity of the Creator and creation.[23]

Sophia: The Wisdom of God

Divine Wisdom or Sophia is the most well-known idea of the Russian religious renaissance – and the most complex and hotly contested. Sophia is a further step in the exploration of all-unity in the quest for an understanding of God's relations with the world. From Vladimir Soloviev to Pavel Florensky and Sergius Bulgakov, much of Russian religious thought was enraptured by the idea of Divine Sophia, seen as a transformation and even fulfilment of all-unity. Basil Zenkovsky characterizes Sophia as an elaboration of Soloviev's notion of total-unity and as a synthesis of a nature-philosophy: a cosmology founded on 'a conception of the world as a "living whole"'; an anthropology which 'relates man and the mystery of the human spirit to nature and the Absolute'; and a theology of 'the "divine" aspect of the world'.[24] Nicolas Zernov (1898–1980) sees Sophia as the 'potential holiness of matter, the unity and sacredness of the entire creation, and man's call to participate in the divine plan for its ultimate transfiguration'.[25] But Sophia resists straightforward exposition; it is an ethereal, even evanescent concept, assuming different forms depending on the writer or even the particular stage in the evolution of the thinking of certain writers. In Pavel Florensky and Sergius Bulgakov, Sophia is nonetheless a more strongly theistic and Christian endeavour to encompass the divine and the created in a unified vision of existence than Soloviev's more abstract and philosophical notions of all-unity, the world-soul and Sophia itself.

Attempts to express succinctly the essence of sophiology, even by sympathetic commentators, almost invariably stumble over terminology and often appeal to quasi-mystical language, as for example in this passage of Paul Evdokimov (1901–70):

> Sophia, the Wisdom of God, is 'the great root of creatures in their cosmic totality', the divine essence of the world, its truth and its holiness, the object of divine love. … [Its aspects are manifested in] the deified nature of Christ, in the universal humanity integrated into Christ, which is the church, in the chaste integrity of the Theotokos, in the cosmic reality as a whole, bound in love and illuminated by the beauty of the Holy Spirit.[26]

For Soloviev, the starting point of Sophia was not so much intellectual notions as his own mystical experiences, which led him to envisage Sophia as the incarnation of feminine beauty. Sophia is

---

[23]Vladimir Soloviev, *Russia and the Universal Church* extract in Judith Deutsch Kornblatt, *Divine Sophia: The Wisdom Writings of Vladimir Solovyov* (Ithaca and London: Cornell University Press, 2009), 201. See also *Russia and the Universal Church* (London: Geoffrey Bles-Centenary Press, 1948), 159.

[24]Zenkovsky, *A History of Russian Philosophy*, II:840–1.

[25]Nicolas Zernov, *The Russian Religious Renaissance of the Twentieth Century* (New York: Harper & Row, 1963), 285.

[26]Paul Evdokimov, *Le Christ dans la pensée russe* (Christ in Russian Thought) (Paris: Les Éditions du Cerf, 1970), 178.

the hidden soul of the world, of divine origin, the link between God and the world. In his poem *Three Encounters* (1898), Soloviev writes of three mystical experiences with Sophia, first as a child in Moscow, then in the British Museum and finally in Egypt in 1875. He describes a vision of a beautiful woman that he had in Egypt, a woman whom he identifies as Sophia:

> What is, what was, what ever will be -
> Was there embraced in one motionless gaze.
> Below run blue the rivers and the sea,
> And alpine snows and distant forest ways.
> I saw it all, and all I saw was one.
> A single image of all female beauty …
> The immeasurable encompassing its sum.
> You stand alone before me, and within me.
> That desert day I saw you in your fullness …
> Oh, radiant one! You have deceived me not;
> The roses in my soul shall ever flourish.[27]

In his *Lectures on Godmanhood*, Soloviev refers to Sophia as 'the world soul, or ideal humanity (Sophia), which contains within itself and unites with itself all particular living entities, or souls'; Sophia 'occupies a mediating position between the multiplicity of living entities, which constitute the real content of its life, and the absolute unity of Divinity, which is the ideal principle and norm of its life'.[28]

Fr Pavel Florensky, who provides a link between Vladimir Soloviev and Sergius Bulgakov in the development of the doctrine of Divine Wisdom, places his discussion of Sophia in *The Ground and Pillar of Truth* (1914) under the umbrella of all-unity in the saying that introduces it: *Omnia conjungo* (I unite all).[29] Florensky, attempting to anchor Sophia in Trinitarian theology, introduces the problematic idea that Sophia describes Sophia as 'the Great Root', a special, created hypostasis in relation to the three Hypostases of the Trinity:

> Sophia is the Great Root of the whole creation. … Sophia is all-integral creation and not merely *all* creation, Sophia is the Great Root by which creation goes into the intra-Trinitarian life and through which it receives Life Eternal from the One Source of Life. Sophia is the original nature of creation, God's creative love. [30]
>
> Sophia takes part in the life of the Trihypostatic Divinity, enters into the interior of the Trinity, and enters into communion with Divine Love. Since Sophia is a *fourth*, creaturely, and therefore nonconsubstantial Person, she does not 'form' a Divine Unity. … As the *fourth* Person, she, by God's condescension (but in no way by her own nature!) introduces a distinction in relation to herself in the providential activity of the Hypostases of the Trinity.[31]

---

[27]Vladimir Soloviev, 'Three Encounters', in Kornblatt, *Divine Sophia*, 271.
[28]Soloviev, *Lectures on Godmanhood*, 231.
[29]Florensky, *The Pillar and Ground of the Truth*, 231.
[30]Ibid., 237.
[31]Ibid., 252.

But in Florensky's evocative, mystical language, Sophia is also 'the guardian angel of creation, the ideal person of the world', 'the power or force of the being of creation', 'the meaning or truth of creation', 'the spirituality of creation', 'its holiness, purity, and immaculateness, i.e., its beauty', the church, the Body of Christ and the Holy Spirit 'to the extent that he has deified creation'.[32] In this perspective Sophia could be seen as an extended metaphor for creation, both *in via* and deified, or perhaps more precisely, as a symbol or allegory for divine presence in creation. It is in this context that we can place Florensky's emphasis, like Bulgakov after him, on creation as divine kenosis, self-abasement: 'The Holy Trinity *condescends* to this correlation of itself with its own creature and therefore to the determination of itself by its creature, thereby "emptying" itself of absolute attributes. Remaining all-powerful, God treats his creatures as if he were not all-powerful.'[33]

Florensky's hierarchy of creation is then a hierarchy of progressive intensifications of divine presence in creation or of deification, culminating in the Mother of God:

> If Sophia is all of Creation, then the soul and conscience of Creation, Mankind, is Sophia *par excellence*. If Sophia is all of Mankind, then the soul and conscience of Mankind, the Church, is Sophia *par excellence*. If Sophia is the Church, then the soul and conscience of the Church, the Church of the Saints, is Sophia *par excellence*. If Sophia is the Church of the Saints, then the soul and conscience of the Church of Saints, the Intercessor for and Defender of creation before the Word of God, who judges creation and divides it in two, the Mother of God, 'Purifier of the World', is, once again, Sophia *par excellence*. But the true sign of Mary Full of Grace is her Virginity, the beauty of her soul. This is precisely Sophia.[34]

Florensky was no doubt aware of the thorny problems of relating time and eternity, the finite and the infinite and determination and freedom in an understanding of God and creation, but, unlike Bulgakov after him, he did not offer a full-blown theology to resolve the underlying problems.

The advocates of sophiology, especially Bulgakov, draw support from biblical references to Wisdom, particularly the personification of Wisdom in certain passages of the Old Testament, notably in Proverbs, the Wisdom of Solomon, Ecclesiastes, Ecclesiasticus, Job and Psalm 103/104, and also references to the Glory of God (*shekinah*).[35] For Bulgakov, both Wisdom and Glory point to the divine essence (*ousia*): 'In a certain sense … *ousia* stands precisely for Wisdom and Glory.'[36] Bulgakov distinguishes between the two by saying that Wisdom is the 'content' of the Godhead and Glory its 'manifestation', but recognizes that they are inseparable and in practice interchangeable: 'The divinity in God constitutes the divine Sophia (or glory), while at the same time we assume that it is also the *ousia*: *Ousia*=Sophia=Glory.'[37]

---

[32]Ibid., 237; 252–3.

[33]Ibid., 236.

[34]Ibid., 253.

[35]Bulgakov summarizes the most relevant scriptural passages invoked by the sophiologists in his *Sophia, The Wisdom of God: An Outline of Sophiology* (1937) (Hudson, NY: Lindisfarne Press, 1993), 25–30.

[36]Bulgakov, *Sophia, The Wisdom of God*, 33. See also the discussion on Glory and Sophia in Sergius Bulgakov, *The Lamb of God* (1933) (Grand Rapids, MI: Eerdmans, 2008), 107–9; 112; 167–8 and so on.

[37]Bulgakov, *Sophia, The Wisdom of God*, 31; 33.

But it is the personification of Wisdom which retains the most attention. The Book of Wisdom describes Wisdom in glowing terms, as 'a breath of the power of God, and a pure emanation of the glory of the Almighty', 'an image of his goodness', and 'an initiate in the knowledge of God, and an associate in his works'. Wisdom 'pervades and penetrates all things'; 'although she is but one, she can do all things'; 'She reaches mightily from one end of the earth to the other, and she orders all things well'; 'She glorifies her noble birth by living with God, and the Lord of all loves her' (Wis. 7.22–8.4). Going beyond a poetic or metaphoric interpretation of such passages, the sophiologists perceive the revelation of a mysterious but real aspect of divine existence.

The sophiologists also argued their case from the dedication of certain major Orthodox churches, in particular Saint Sophia in Constantinople and Kiev, to Holy Wisdom. And whereas in Byzantine theology Wisdom is identified with Christ, the sophiologists argued that in the Slavic tradition Wisdom is identified with the Mother of God, a notion challenged by Georges Florovsky.[38]

Divine Sophia is reflected in 'creaturely Sophia', the created world, which is an image of its divine prototype. Divine Sophia is also the heavenly church, while the world (or humanity) is the creaturely Sophia 'in the process of becoming', because, although created 'in its fullness and perfection', 'in its present state it is not yet finished'.[39] Divine Sophia and creaturely Sophia come together in the church: 'The Church is Sophia in both of her aspects, Divine and creaturely, in their interrelationship, which is expressed in their union.'[40] In the church, humans, 'creaturely hypostases', are 'fully united in the hypostasis of the God-man'.[41] In a short article in 1936, Bulgakov defines the central problem of sophiology as

> the relationship between God and the world, between God and humanity (which are essentially the same). In other words, it is the problem of the power and the signification of Theanthropy, not only of the God-Man as the Verb incarnate, but precisely of Theanthropy as the unity (*edinstvo*) of God and the created universe, in humanity and by humanity.[42]

For Bulgakov, as indeed for many Russian spiritual figures, divine kenosis or abasement features as an important theological principle. The Incarnation of the Word of God presupposes 'the removal of the [Divine] Glory, not, certainly, in "heaven", in the "immanent" Trinity, but in the world'.[43] For Bulgakov, the Incarnation of Christ 'is, first of all a kenotic act: "The Word was made flesh." For the human essence to be united with the divine essence without being dissolved or annihilated, Divinity had to descend, to diminish itself into the human essence.'[44] In the Incarnation, God renounces or abandons something, not, as some Christian theologians speculate, his divinity,

---

[38]Georges Florovsky, 'Christ, the Wisdom of God, in Byzantine Theology', *Résumés des Rapports et Communications, Sixième Congrès international d'études Byzantines, Supplément* (Summaries of Reports and Communications: Sixth International Congress of Byzantine Studies) (Paris: Comité d'Organisation de Congrès, 1940); another version published as 'The Hagia Sophia Churches', in *Aspects of Church History*, Vol. IV of *The Collected Works of Georges Florovsky* (Belmont, MA: Nordland, 1975).
[39]Bulgakov, *The Lamb of God*, 160.
[40]Sergius Bulgakov, *The Bride of the Lamb* (1946) (Grand Rapids, MI: Eerdmans, 2002), 253.
[41]Bulgakov, *The Bride of the Lamb*, 265.
[42]Sergius Bulgakov, 'Le problème central de la sophiologie' (The central problem of sophiology) (1936), *Le Messager orthodoxe*, 98 (1985), 83.
[43]Bulgakov, *The Bride of the Lamb*, 397. On Christ's kenosis, see Bulgakov, 'The Humiliation of the Lord (the Kenosis)', Ch. 4.II of *The Lamb of God*, 213–47; and Bulgakov, *Sophia, The Wisdom of God*, 88–93.
[44]Bulgakov, *The Lamb of God*, 219.

but rather the Glory of the divinity, not the nature of divinity, but the 'form', 'which the Son of God has as God but which he removes from himself in his humiliation, although he will later once again put on this garment of Glory' (see Jn 17.5).[45] In his kenotic state, Christ retains the 'potential of Glory, which must be actualised anew'[46] (as in the Transfiguration).

Christ's ascension after his resurrection marks the end of this kenosis and the entry of Christ's deified human nature into Divine Glory. Similarly, creation marks a kenosis of Divine Sophia in that creaturely Sophia signifies a diminishing from a state of being to one of becoming, from fullness to potentiality, a kenosis which is proportional to the degree of freedom granted to creatures.[47] There is thus a scale of divine abasement increasing from inanimate creation, bound by the laws of physics, to human freedom.

The sophiologists were aware of the Palamite theology of the divine energies and in fact they appealed to it in their defence of the 'Name-worshipers' during the onomatodoxy quarrel prior to the First World War (see Chapter 15). But they did not consider Palamism a fully adequate explanation of how God relates to creation, even if in the mid-1920s Bulgakov for one virtually equated Sophia with the divine energies of the Cappadocians and Gregory Palamas: 'Essentially, this same distinction [between the essence of God and the activity or energy of the self-revealing Godhead], only in a different light, is expressed in the thought that the Wisdom of God, Sophia, is the revelation of the transcendental substance of God.'[48]

In a seminar in 1928, Bulgakov summarized succinctly his teaching on Sophia:

> Sophia, the Wisdom of God, is the revelation of the life of the Triune God, the manifestation of the nature of the divinity and in this sense the Glory of God. Sophia belongs to the Holy Trinity as a whole as self-revelation of the divinity. Sophia is not hypostatic as such but is hypostatised in each of the divine Hypostases. As divine life *in actu*, Sophia is an energy revealing divine *ousia* or the essence of God and manifests itself in the world as the hidden and revealed depth of divine life, its power and its idea. Sophia, energy, is God, not in the sense of subject but in the sense of complement (not *o Theos* but *Theos* in Greek).[49]

Here again Bulgakov identifies Sophia as 'energy', rather along the lines of the Palamite distinction between divine energies and divine essence. In *The Lamb of God* (1933), Bulgakov again virtually equates Sophia (also called here Divine-Humanity) and the divine energies:

> The Divine-Humanity in God possesses the whole of the absolute *spirituality* that is proper to Divinity. This is the 'energy' of Divinity, which possesses an infinite multitude of radiations of the *ousia* (cf. St Gregory Palamas's doctrine of energies ...).[50]

---

[45]Ibid., 224. See also the summary at 445.
[46]Bulgakov, *The Lamb of God*, 224.
[47]Bulgakov, *The Bride of the Lamb*, 60–1; 142.
[48]Sergius Bulgakov, 'Hypostasis and Hypostaticity: Scholia to *The Unfading Light*' (1925), *St Vladimir's Theological Quarterly*, 49, 1–2 (2005), 24.
[49]Valentin Zander's summary of Bulgakov's tenth seminar (31 December 1928), in Nikita Struve, ed., *Bratstvo Sviatoi Sofii: Materialy i Dokumenty, 1923-1939* (Fraternity of the Holy Wisdom: Materials and Documents) (Paris: YMCA-Press, 2000), 142. French translation in Antoine Arjakovsky, *Essai sur le père Serge Boulgakov (1871-1944): Philosophe et théologien chrétien* (Essay on Fr Sergius Bulgakov: Christian Philosopher and Theologian) (Paris: Parole et Silence, 2006), 43–4.
[50]Bulgakov, *The Lamb of God*, 116.

In *The Bride of the Lamb* (published posthumously in 1946), Bulgakov nonetheless considers that patristic cosmology lacks 'fundamental clarity' and 'does not achieve completeness' because 'patristic sophiology' is 'a kind of sophiological ambiguity'.[51] Sophiology thus becomes an extension or a deepening of the Palamite doctrine of the divine energies, 'which is essentially an unfinished sophiology'.[52] Palamism is a precursor of sophiology: 'By accepting Palamism, the church as definitely entered onto the path of recognizing the sophiological dogma.'[53]

Bulgakov sought to situate Divine Sophia in terms of the classic theological distinction between nature or substance (*ousia/physis*) and person (*hypostasis*). Bulgakov at first adhered to Soloviev's concept of Divine Sophia as a kind of personified heavenly being while noting as early as *The Unfading Light* (1917) that Sophia is different from the three Hypostases of the Holy Trinity, a 'special hypostasis, of a different order, a fourth hypostasis', which, nonetheless is not God, does not participate in inner-divine life, and does not convert the tri-hypostaseity into tetra-hypostaseity.[54] Initially, following Florensky, Bulgakov identified Sophia with the hypostasis side of the *ousia-hypostasis* distinction, but he became increasingly aware of the problems associated with any hint of Sophia as a hypostasis. From 1925 onwards he distanced himself from Soloviev and Florensky's personification of Sophia in no uncertain terms: 'There is no fourth hypostasis, of equal honour and consubstantial with the Most-Holy Trinity, there is not and cannot be; the holy Trinumber is complete in itself and admits no addition.'[55] Wishing to anchor sophiology more firmly in the theological tradition of the church, Bulgakov turned to the substance or essence side of *ousia-hypostasis*, coming up with the puzzling notion of 'hypostaticity' (*ipostasnost'*): 'the capacity to hypostasise oneself [*ipostasirovat'sia*], *to belong* to a hypostasis, to be its disclosure, *to give oneself up* to it'.[56] But even this important qualification is not a fully satisfactory explanation of the relationship between Sophia and the Trinity. In his description of hypostaticity as a 'self-hypostasizing principle', Bulgakov inherits some notions of Sophia from his predecessors: 'This is the power of love ... passive, feminine, self-surrender in the acceptance of love.'[57]

In his final great writing *The Bride of the Lamb* (1946), Bulgakov tries to clarify further his idea of Sophia as divine potentiality of self-revelation, without being a divine hypostasis: 'As divinity, Sophia is nonhypostatic (is not a "fourth hypostasis"). ... She *belongs* to the divine trihypostatic Person as this Person's life and self-revelation. ... The Divine Sophia contains the entire fullness of divine being, but she does not exist in isolation from the divine trihypostatic person.'[58] Sophia is nonetheless a 'living essence' which belongs 'to the personal life of the hypostasis', which

---

[51]Bulgakov, *The Bride of the Lamb*, 18.
[52]Ibid.
[53]Ibid.
[54]Sergius Bulgakov, *Unfading Light: Contemplations and Speculations* (1917) (Grand Rapids, MI: Eerdmans, 2012), 217.
[55]Bulgakov, 'Hypostasis and Hypostaticity', 28. The essay is a 'dogmatic clarification' of Bulgakov's ambiguous and controversial references to Sophia as a 'fourth hypostasis'. See also Bulgakov, *Unfading Light*, 131–4; Bulgakov, *Sophia, The Wisdom of God*, n. 7, 33; the Foreword by Brandon Gallaher and Irina Kukota to Bulgakov's essay in the same issue of *St Vladimir's Theological Quarterly*; and Rowan Williams, ed., *Sergii Bulgakov: Towards a Russian Political Theology* (Edinburgh: T&T Clark, 1999), 125.
[56]Bulgakov, 'Hypostasis and Hypostaticity', 28.
[57]Ibid., 29.
[58]Bulgakov, *The Bride of the Lamb*, 38–9.

'enters into and participates in God's life' (p. 39). The most perfect expression of this participation in divine life is divine love:

> [Sophia] is love, as the ideal-real connection of the *all.* … Logic and aesthetics are also full of love, for a mutual connection of love between Truth and Beauty exists in the Divine Sophia. Love is all-unity, integral wisdom, cosmic altruism. The divine world in itself is an organism of love, a ladder of descending and ascending love.[59]

In the light of the subsequent fate of sophiology and the neo-Palamite revival, Bulgakov was overly optimistic concerning Orthodox acceptance of sophiology as a development of Palamism or as a theology of love. After Bulgakov's death in 1944, the doctrine of Divine Wisdom did not undergo significant further development and it was left to disciples such as Leon Zander (1893–1964), to expound and defend the insights of the great theologian. But the main thrust of Orthodox thinking on God and creation looked increasingly in other directions.

The divine energies and createdness

In Chapter 5 we saw that the revival of Palamite theology of the divine energies[60] went hand-in-hand with a restoration of patristic theology in Orthodox thought, a movement which Georges Florovsky called the neopatristic synthesis. The distinction between the unknowable divine essence and the divine energies by which God manifests himself in creation provided the crucial basis for the elaboration of a theology of relations between God and the world grounded in patristic theology. In retrospect, the revival of Palamism in Orthodoxy was important both as a milestone on the road to overcoming the 'Western captivity' of Orthodox theology, and also as the theological key unlocking the door to a more widely accepted understanding of how God relates to creation than the solutions proposed in the Russian religious renaissance. For the neopatristic theologians, the speculative ideas of all-unity, the world-soul and Sophia of the religious renaissance were too distant from patristic thought, too open to accusations of determinism and pantheism, and too indebted to German philosophy for comfort. They were far more at ease with the patristic emphasis on creation *ex nihilo* and the distinction between the divine essence and the divine energies, seen as fundamental aspects of patristic theology.

It is not that creation *ex nihilo* does not feature in the thinking of the religious renaissance. Sergius Bulgakov for one, unlike Vladimir Soloviev, unambiguously emphasizes divine creation. Thus in *Unfading Light* (1917) Bulgakov writes: '*The world is created out of nothing* – Christian revelation teaches.'[61] In *The Lamb of God* (1933), he opens his discussion of the creation of the world with the statement 'God created the world out of nothing.'[62] The entire Part I of *The Bride of*

---

[59]Ibid., 40.

[60]See an overview of the theology of the divine energies and its modern revival in Ch. 5, 101–5.

[61]Bulgakov, *Unfading Light*, 186.

[62]Bulgakov, *The Lamb of God*, 119.

the Lamb (1946) is devoted to 'The Creator and Creation.'[63] But in Bulgakov creation is bound up in the doctrine of Sophia, with a tendency to blur the boundaries between uncreated and created, and additional problems arising from his perception of freedom and necessity in God and some form of eternal existence of creation in God. For Georges Florovsky and other Orthodox theologians, Bulgakov's thinking on these issues opens the door to incipient pantheism.

Bulgakov's thinking on the relation of freedom and necessity in God is subtle and easily subject to misinterpretation. Bulgakov distinguishes two aspects or moments in divine necessity and freedom. First God-in-himself (the 'immanent Trinity'; God as Absolute) is absolutely free from determination. The plenitude of divine love is realized in intra-divine relations (*perichoresis*/circumincession). God has no need to create, Bulgakov writes in *The Lamb of God*, 'He does not need the world for himself.'[64] In this sense, creation is contingent: 'In relation to the life of the Divinity *itself*, the world did not have to be.'[65] But God freely creates out of love and once having created, though, God is bound – or determined – by his nature as love to love his creation (the 'economic Trinity'; God as Absolute-Relative). In this sense that Bulgakov can also affirm without blushing that

> God *needs* the world, and it could not have remained uncreated. ... God is love, and it is proper for love to love and to expand in love. ... God-Love *needs* the creation of the world in order to *love*, no longer only in his own life, but also outside himself, in creation.[66]

Bulgakov goes on to explain that this is not a 'natural necessity, the necessity of his self-completion', nor is it a necessity 'imposed from outside', but it is rather '*the necessity of love*, which cannot *not* love, and which manifests and realizes in itself *the identity* and *indistinguishability* of freedom and necessity.'[67] Brandon Gallaher summarizes Bulgakov's thinking on divine necessity: 'God freely chooses to be dependent on the world, to be in need to it, and this dependence is an eternal reality that God cannot simply undo.'[68]

Does this ingenious distinction get Bulgakov off the hook for seeing necessity in God? Not entirely in the eyes of Georges Florovsky and other critics. For Florovsky, in line with Greek philosophy and early Christian theology, any notion of necessity in God is untenable in the light of divine freedom: the world is entirely contingent even in the light of divine love.

A related aspect of creation with which both the Russian religious thinkers and the neopatristic theologians grappled is the old problem of whether creation in some form subsists in God from all eternity. Again, we will restrict our consideration here to Sergius Bulgakov and Georges Florovsky, whose approaches to the problem were radically different.

---

[63]Bulgakov, *The Bride of the Lamb*, 3–250.

[64]Bulgakov, *The Lamb of God*, 119.

[65]Ibid.

[66]Ibid., 120.

[67]Ibid.

[68]Brandon Gallaher, *Freedom and Necessity in Modern Trinitarian Theology* (Oxford: Oxford University Press, 2016), 97. For a detailed study of divine freedom and necessity in Bulgakov, see Part I of this book, 'God as Both Absolute and Absolute-Relative in Sergii Bulgakov', 45–114.

Bulgakov's most important premise is that only God truly exists: 'Only the divinity of the existent God is, and there is nothing apart from and outside of divinity,' he writes in *The Bride of the Lamb*.[69] The 'nothingness' of the ancient formula *creatio ex nihilo* is not a 'somethingness' apart from God: '"Out of nothing" means, after all, that there is no matter or force that could contain the possibility of the world and could assure for the world a place *alongside* God, *outside of* or *apart from* God.'[70] Bulgakov concludes from this that 'If God is the Creator, he is the Creator from all eternity.'[71] This in turn implies that Creation somehow exists in God's own being from all eternity, if only as a potentiality, an 'idea' which comes to fruition in the fullness of time:

> God cannot fail to be the Creator, just as the Creator cannot fail to be God. The plan of the world's creation is as co-eternal to God as is his own being in the Divine Sophia. In this sense (but only in this sense), God cannot do without the world, and the world is necessary for God's very being. And to this extent the world must be excluded in God's being in a certain sense.[72]

Aware of the risks that this position entails, Bulgakov explicitly rejects here and elsewhere the pantheistic identification of God and the world, 'according to which God is the world and only the world.'[73]

Florovsky's major essay 'Creation and Createdness' (1928) set the stage for much of subsequent Orthodox thought on creation. Bulgakov (and behind him, Soloviev) is Florovsky's unnamed opponent in 'Creation and Createdness.'[74] Against any possible inclination towards pantheism, throughout the essay Florovsky emphasizes the ontological distance between God as uncreated Creator and the world as created. The first sentences emphatically proclaim: '*The world was created.* In other words, it was made out of nothing and did not exist before.'[75] To counter notions of creation as somehow arising from the divine essence and hence implying some form of necessity, Florovsky draws on the patristic theology of creation as a free act of God's will and thus being contingent and dependent: 'The world exists, but it also *began to exist*, which means that it *might not have existed*, and so its existence is not a matter of any necessity. Created existence is neither self-sufficient nor self-sustaining.'[76] Thus Florovsky rejects both the possibility of chance and arbitrariness in creation and a certain determinism in Bulgakov's doctrine of creation.

Florovsky thus discards the potential existence of creation as an eternal idea in God's 'mind' (here equated with essence), since this 'would introduce the world into the inner life of the Holy

---

[69]Bulgakov, *The Bride of the Lamb*, 43.
[70]Ibid.
[71]Ibid., 45.
[72]Ibid., 45–6.
[73]Bulgakov, *The Bride of the Lamb*, 46. For Bulgakov's rejection of pantheism, see also 4, 6, 34, 35, 212, 220 and 228; in *Unfading Light* (189 and 349); and in *The Lamb of God* (121, 134 and 443).
[74]See the Introduction 'Georges Florovsky and the "Mind of the Fathers"' and the Editors' Notes to 'Creation and Createdness,' in Brandon Gallaher and Paul Ladouceur, eds., *The Patristic Witness of Georges Florovsky: Essential Theological Writings* (London: T&T Clark, 2019), 33; 42; 56; 59.
[75]Georges Florovsky, 'Tvar i tvarnost', *Pravoslavnaya mysl*, 1 (Paris: St. Sergius Institute of Orthodox Theology, 1928). Translation: 'Creation and Createdness', in Gallaher and Ladouceur, eds., *The Patristic Witness of Georges Florovsky*, 34. A shorter version of Florovsky's essay also appeared in French in 1928: 'L'idée de la création dans la philosophie chrétienne', *Logos*, 1 (Romania, 1928); and in English 'The Idea of Creation in Christian Philosophy', *Eastern Churches Quarterly*, 8, 3 (1949).
[76]Florovsky, 'Creation and Createdness', 36.

Trinity as its co-determining principle'.[77] To get around the problem of the origin of the 'idea' of the world, Florovsky postulates two 'types' of eternity, one related to the divine essence (and hence to the eternal existence of the three divine Persons), the other to the divine will (which includes God's eternal 'idea of the world, his plan and intention').[78] Florovsky's concerns are above all to preserve the distinction between divine essence or being and divine will and to attach creation to the divine will, not the divine essence:

> The idea of the world originates *in God's will, not his being*. Instead of 'having' the idea of creation, God 'invents' it, and because he does this freely through the exercise of his will, he in some sense becomes Creator, albeit from eternity. Nevertheless, God could have chosen not to create, and then his 'abstaining' from creation would in no way alter or impoverish his divine nature. It would mean no diminution of it, any more than creating a world enriches divine life.[79]

The philosophical snare that he is trying to avoid is attaching creation to the divine essence, which would compromise divine liberty by introducing necessity (to create) and lead inexorably to pantheism, a major flaw identified in Soloviev's (and by implication, Bulgakov's) metaphysics: 'The world did not have to be and only exists because of God's perfect freedom and unfathomable will. That is the ultimate consequence of the world being created as the "work of God's will"'.[80]

To bridge the gap between God as Creator and the world as creation, Florovsky appeals to the ancient distinctions between 'theology' (God in himself) and 'economy' (God in relation to the world), between the divine essence and the divine will, between essence and energies or actions, the latter being 'real and life-giving manifestations of divine life, and his *ways of relating* to the creation'.[81] Florovsky summarizes the main features of Palamite theology, touching in passing on the question of necessity and freedom in God, 'which must be understood in terms appropriate to divine life', as mirroring the distinction 'between "nature" and "action", or between "substance" and "grace"'[82] – an anticipation of the late twentieth-century debate over nature-determination and person-freedom (see Chapter 10). But the ultimate bridging of the gap between Creator and creation – as indeed for Soloviev and Bulgakov – is of course in the Incarnation of the Word of God, the union of the divine and human natures in Christ, with the possibility of deification for all. Here, somewhat ironically, Florovsky's thinking coincides with that of Soloviev and Bulgakov.

Florovsky's essay is a powerful affirmation of patristic thinking on creation, with the theology of the divine energies, inseparable from the Incarnation, occupying centre stage in his understanding of how God relates to creation. Florovsky considered this essay, together with that on redemption, as 'my best achievements, and probably my only ones'.[83] Clearly Florovsky comes up against the

---

[77]Ibid., 43.
[78]Ibid., 43.
[79]Ibid., 43.
[80]Ibid., 44.
[81]Ibid., 51.
[82]Ibid., 56.
[83]Cited in Andrew Blane, *Georges Florovsky: Russian Intellectual and Orthodox Churchman* (Crestwood, NY: St Vladimir's Seminary Press, 1993), 154. Florovsky never completed his writing on redemption, but most of the text was published in *Creation and Redemption*, Vol. 3 of *The Collected Works of Georges Florovsky* (Belmont, MA: Nordland, 1976). See the discussion of Florovsky's writings on redemption in Matthew Baker, Seraphim Danckaert and Nicholas Marinides, eds., *On the Tree of the*

same issues as his predecessors in the Russian religious renaissance and, like them, introduces a new theological notion, two types of eternity (which could be interpreted as Divine Sophia in new clothing), as an attempt to resolve the problem of how the temporal and created relates to the eternal and uncreated. By anchoring creation in the divine will and calling on the essence-energies distinction, Florovsky sought to be more faithful to patristic theology than the religious philosophers.

As we saw in Chapter 5, Vladimir Lossky's vastly influential book, *The Mystical Theology of the Eastern Church* (1944), a masterly and articulate presentation of patristic theology, included as major themes the long-forgotten but now revived aspects of Orthodox theology: apophatism, the essence-energies distinction and theosis.[84] More than Florovsky's essay 'Creation and Createdness' sixteen years earlier, Lossky's book signalled the return of Palamite theology to the centre stage of modern Orthodox thought.

The revival of Palamism in Orthodox theology reached maturity in the work of John Meyendorff (1926–1992), especially the publication in 1959 of his doctoral thesis *Introduction to the Study of Gregory Palamas*, his translations of Palamas's *Triads* and his more popular work *St Gregory Palamas and Orthodox Spirituality*.[85] For Meyendorff, as indeed for most modern Orthodox theologians, the teaching of Gregory Palamas on the essence-energies distinction in God is critical for a proper understanding of Christian anthropology, of the divine-human relationship, and ultimately of salvation and eschatology. Meyendorff casts the fourteenth-century hesychast controversy between Palamas and his critics as a conflict between two currents of apophatic theology: one which conceives 'the transcendence and unknowability of God as a consequence of the *limitations of the created mind*', and the other which asserts 'divine transcendence as a *property of God*, … which no detachment and no surpassing oneself could make vanish'.[86] Both views of apophatism claim their origin in the Pseudo-Dionysius, but whereas for Meyendorff the first is basically a Thomist interpretation of apophatism, the latter characterizes Palamas and modern neo-Palamism. These contrasting views translate into two rival theological approaches. The first – which Meyendorff calls an 'essentialist' theology – accords absolute priority to the unknowable, unparticipable, indivisible and simple divine essence. The second – which Meyendorff describes as an 'existential' theology – sees the divine energies as the manifestation of divine existence *ad extra*. These energies are inseparable yet not identical with the divine essence, and are not 'accidents' or 'qualities' in a philosophical sense, God being entirely present in the energies – a view that is consistent with a Christian understanding of divine simplicity.[87] Like many of Palamas's

---

Cross: Georges Florovsky and the Patristic Doctrine of Atonement (Jordanville, NY: Holy Trinity Seminary Press, 2016), 129–33; and in Gallaher and Ladouceur, eds., *The Patristic Witness of Georges Florovsky*, 65–6.

[84]Lossky's earliest article on apophatism dates from 1929. See his articles on apophatism and Palamism in *In the Image and Likeness of God* (Crestwood, NY: St Vladimir's Seminary Press, 1974).

[85]Meyendorff's works were initially published in French: Grégoire Palamas. *Défense des saints hésychastes: Introduction, texte critique, traduction et notes* (Louvain: Peeters, 1959); *Introduction a l'étude de Grégoire Palamas, Patristica Sorbonensia*, Vol. 3 (Paris: Éditions du Seuil, 1959); *St Grégoire Palamas et la mystique orthodoxe* (Paris: Éditions du Seuil, 1959). In English: *A Study of Gregory Palamas* (London: Faith Press, 1964); *St Gregory Palamas and Orthodox Spirituality* (Crestwood, NY: St Vladimir's Seminary Press, 1974); *Gregory Palamas: The Triads* (New York: Paulist Press, 1983).

[86]Meyendorff, *A Study of Gregory Palamas*, 203.

[87]The core of Meyendorff's presentation of Palamism is Chapter V, 'An Existential Theology: Essence and Energy', *A Study of Gregory Palamas*, 202–27.

contemporaries, Meyendorff sees St Gregory as 'a representative of traditional Orthodoxy'[88] who restates and clarifies notions already present in the Greek Fathers of the fourth century and safeguards the Christian notion of God as 'a living God, the God of the Bible, whom no philosophical conception can define',[89] and who is the basis of the Christian spiritual life and the real experience of God.

Meyendorff defends Palamas not only against his Byzantine critics (Barlaam, Akindynos and Nicephorus Gregoras), but also against modern Western critics of Palamas, Martin Jugie (1878–1954) and Endre von Iványka (1902–74),[90] as well as against the Russian sophiologists. Against the latter, Meyendorff cites Palamas's understanding of Divine Wisdom as a characteristic of the Father, the Son and the Holy Spirit, 'an essential divine attribute, insomuch as the three hypostases share in the creative act'.[91] Wisdom is neither identified with the divine essence nor is an object of love for God, as the sophiologists claim.[92]

Since Meyendorff, many other Orthodox theologians have written on Palamite theology and the revival of Palamite theology in Orthodoxy has had an impact in non-Orthodox circles. Despite being widely acclaimed, Meyendorff's work also drew rounds of criticism from both Orthodox and non-Orthodox. The major Orthodox critics of Meyendorff have been Elisabeth Behr-Sigel (1907–2005), Basil Krivochein (1900–85) and John Romanides (1927–2001).[93] While broadly welcoming Meyendorff's work and his revival of Palamas, they nonetheless reproach him for various missteps: for an excessive abstraction of the Palamite doctrine from its historical setting, especially its relation to ascetic and mystical doctrines and experiences; for imposing categories of modern philosophy unto the fourteenth-century quarrel – especially seeing Palamas as 'personalist' and 'existentialist' and his adversaries as 'essentialist' and 'nominalist'; for a too-facile characterization of Palamas's anthropology as 'monist' in comparison with Barlaam's 'dualism' and for incorrect translations or misinterpretations of key Palamite texts.

Subsequent studies of the Palamite controversy also tend to downplay the contrasts that form the backbone of much of Meyendorff's analysis: existence-essence; Palamism-Thomism; mysticism-scholasticism and ultimately East-West.[94] John Romanides, who appropriates the basics of Palamism,[95] offers an alternate reading of Meyendorff from his own historical perspective of a fundamental conflict of theologies between Eastern and Western Christianity. Romanides takes

---

[88]Meyendorff, *A Study of Gregory Palamas*, 237.
[89]Ibid., 210.
[90]Ibid., 226.
[91]Ibid., 222.
[92]Ibid., 226.
[93]See John Romanides, 'Notes on the Palamite Controversy and Related Topics', Part I, *Greek Orthodox Theological Review*, 6, 2 (1960–1); Part II, *idem.*, 9, 2 (1963–4); V. Krivoshein, 'Sv. Grigoriy Palama: Lichnost' i ucheniye (po nedavno opublikovannym mat-lam)' (St Gregory Palamas: Personality and teaching (recently published materials), *Messager de l'Exarchat du patriarche russe en Europe occidentale*, 9, 33–4 (1960); Elisabeth Behr-Sigel, 'Réflexions sur la doctrine de Grégoire Palamas' (Reflections on the doctrine of Gregory Palamas) *Contacts*, 12 (1960). Romanides's article is in effect a highly critical extended book review (sixty-six pages) of Meyendorff's publications on Palamas.
[94]See a summary in Andrew Louth, *Modern Orthodox Thinkers: From the* Philokalia *to the Present* (Downers Grove, IL: InterVarsity Press, 2015), 185–8. Louth writes that 'Meyendorff's understanding of nominalism seems muddled' (187).
[95]See John Romanides, *An Outline of Orthodox Patristic Dogmatics* (Rollinsford, NH: Orthodox Research Institute, 2004), 4–11.

Meyendorff to task for presenting Palamas-Barlaam debate as 'a domestic quarrel between certain Byzantine humanists and a large segment of Byzantine monastics and their adherents', rather than 'a clash between Latin and Greek theology, as has been generally believed'.[96] Romanides also attacks Meyendorff for misunderstanding the debate between Palamas and Barlaam concerning the hesychastic practice of 'noetic prayer'; for depicting Palamas's theology as an 'Incarnation mysticism', linking hesychast practices to the Incarnation and baptismal grace; for his claims that Palamas 'applies Christological correctives to the Platonic patristic tradition and its religious experiences and visions of the divine independently of the Incarnate Son of God';[97] for failing to grasp the respective approaches to symbols by Palamas and Dionysius on the one hand and Barlaam and his followers on the other; and more generally for attempting to distance Palamas from the Pseudo-Dionysius, by attributing 'originalities' to Palamas.[98] Contrary to Meyendorff, for Romanides, Palamas remains entirely faithful to Pseudo-Dionysius.[99]

Despite criticism of Meyendorff's interpretation of the fourteenth-century quarrel, Orthodox theologians writing in the wake of Florovsky, Lossky and Meyendorff are almost universally supportive of Palamism as such, although some, such as Christos Yannaras (b. 1935) and John Zizioulas (b.1931), are less enthusiastic than others. Jean-Claude Larchet (b. 1949) criticizes Yannaras for attaching the divine energies to the divine Persons, rather than to the divine essence, as in patristic theology, especially Maximus, and suggests that Zizioulas does the same in attaching divine love to the Person of the Father.[100] More importantly, Zizioulas practically ignores the divine energies in his early writings, while in a later essay, 'On Being Other', he advances a hypostatic rather than an energetic approach to being: 'We should be reluctant to approach being, both created and uncreated, from the angle of energy. Instead, I have been suggesting that, following St Maximus, we must approach it from the angle of *hypostasis* or the "mode of being", that is, the way that it relates to other beings.'[101] This 'reluctance' stems from Zizioulas's constant preference of person over nature, to which, as he recognizes, energies are attached, to the point that he denies any personal or hypostatic quality to the divine energies:

> The divine energies *qua* energies never express God's *personal* presence, since they belong to the level of *nature* and to *all three persons* of the Trinity. If the world and God were to be united through the divine energies *qua* energies, the unity would have been one with *all three persons* simultaneously, and not via the Son – it would not have been a *hypostatic* union.[102]

---

[96]Romanides, 'Notes on the Palamite Controversy', Part I, 186.
[97]Ibid., Part II, 236.
[98]Ibid., Part II, 226–7; 236–49; 257–62; 266. Romanides describes Meyendorff's anti-Platonist quest as 'an obsessed struggle to depict Palamas as an heroic Biblical theologian putting to the sword of Christological Correctives the last remnants of Greek Patristic Platonic Apophaticism and its supposed linear descendants, the Byzantine Platonic-nominalistic humanists'. Ibid., 250.
[99]Romanides, 'Notes on the Palamite Controversy', Part II, 256.
[100]Jean-Claude Larchet, *Personne et Nature: La Trinité – Le Christ – L'homme. Contributions aux dialogues interorthodoxe et interchrétien contemporains* (Trinity-Christ-Man: Contributions to Contemporary Inter-Orthodox and Inter-Christian Dialogues) (Paris: Les Éditions du Cerf, 2011), 305.
[101]John Zizioulas, *Communion and Otherness: Further Studies in Personhood and the Church* (London and New York: T&T Clark, 2006), 94–5.
[102]Zizioulas, *Communion and Otherness*, 29.

Larchet hotly contests Zizioulas here, maintaining that 'the essence and its energies are considered as enhypostatized by the three divine Persons, and having consequently not only a real existence, but the same ontological rank (*degré*) as the Persons themselves.'[103] The divine energies are not impersonal, argues Larchet, 'since, even though they arise from the essence, they belong to the Persons and are manifested by them'.[104]

Even though Zizioulas does not deny the essence-energies distinction, because of his marked preference for person over nature, he considerably discounts its significance, in this standing almost alone among major Orthodox theologians at the beginning of the twenty-first century.

In the 1970s an ecumenical debate on Palamism took place in the pages of scholarly journals in Belgium, France, Germany, the United Kingdom and the United States. The debate was sparked by articles critical of Palamism following the publication of Meyendorff's *Study of Gregory Palamas*, notably by the Austro-Hungarian philologist and Byzantinist Endre von Ivánka, and articles in the French Catholic journal *Istina*.[105] By then, the Palamite revival, advanced by the writings of Vladimir Lossky and John Meyendorff, was well established in Orthodox circles and there was growing interest in Palamism among non-Orthodox.[106] At stake in these debates is the challenge that Palamas poses to conventional Catholic theology which sees no place for the essence-energies distinction, with perhaps a lingering suspicion that this theology may be heretical. Although many Catholic theologians reject Palamite theology, some see no inherent contradiction between Palamas and Aquinas. But the discussion becomes bound up with differing Eastern and Western approaches to theosis, grace and real or nominal distinction between divine essence and divine energies.[107]

Orthodox rejoinders to critiques of Palamas were not long in coming. In 1975 Kallistos Ware presented a paper on Palamism at the Anglican-Orthodox Joint Doctrinal Discussions, subsequently published in the *Eastern Churches Review*.[108] Ware's article is an irenic presentation of Palamism

---

[103]Larchet, *Person et nature*, 310.

[104]Ibid., 310–11.

[105]See Endre von Ivánka, 'Das Dogma der orthodoxen Kirche' (The dogma of the Orthodox Church) in Wilhelm Nyssen et al., *Handbuch der Ostkirchenkunde* (Handbook of Eastern Church Studies), Bd. 1 (Düsseldorf: Patmos Verlag, 1984): I:289–320; and his *Plato Christianus* (Einsiedeln, CH: Johannes Verlag, 1964), 425–30. Articles in *Istina*, 19, 3 (1974): 'Grégoire Palamas' (unsigned editorial); Juan-Miguel Garrigues, 'L'énergie divine et la grâce chez Maxime le Confesseur' (Divine energy and grace in Maximus the Confessor); Jean-Philippe Houdret, 'Palamas et les Cappadociens' (Palamas and the Cappadocians); Marie-Joseph Le Guillou, 'Lumière et charité dans la doctrine palamite de la divinisation' (Light and love in the Palamite doctrine of deification) and Juan Sergio Nadal, 'La critique par Akindynos de l'herméneutique patristique de Palamas' (Akindinos's critique of Palamas's patristic hermaneutic).

[106]For a detailed survey (111 pages!) of Palamite literature during the decade 1962–72, see Daniel Stiernon, 'Bulletin sur le palamisme' (Bulletin on Palamism) in: *Revue des études byzantines*, 30 (1972), 231–341. For earlier periods, see Hans-Georg Beck, *Kirche und theologische Literatur im byzantinischen Reich* (Church and Theological Literature in the Byzantine Empire) (Munich: C. H. Beck'sche Verlagsbuchhandlung, 1959), 713–98; and Mauricius Gordillo, *Theologia Orientalium cum Latinorum comparata: Commentatio historica* (Comparative Oriental and Latin Theology: A Historical Study), I, *Orientalia Christiana Analecta* 158 (Rome: Pontificiae Universitatis Gregorianae-Romae, 1960), 301–21.

[107]For overviews of post-Meyendorff Western and especially Catholic views on Palamism, see Nichols, *Light from the East*, 52–5; Jeffrey Finch, 'Neo-Palamism, Divinizing Grace and the Breach between East and West', in Michael Christensen and Jeffery Wittung, eds., *Partakers of the Divine Nature: The History and Development of Deification in the Christian Traditions* (Grand Rapids, MI: Baker Academic, 2008), 233–49 and Norman Russell, 'The Reception of Palamas in the West Today', *Theologia* (Athens), 83, 3 (2012).

[108]Kallistos Ware, 'God Hidden and Revealed: The Apophatic Way and the Essence-Energies Distinction', *Eastern Churches Review*, 7 (1975).

and its modern revival, without reference to von Ivánka or the *Istina* articles. Specific replies to the *Istina* articles appeared in 1975 in *St Vladimir's Theological Quarterly*, with articles by Georges Barrois and Christos Yannaras.[109] In 1977 the *Eastern Churches Review* featured five articles on Palamism, three by Orthodox authors defending Palamism (George Mantzarides (b. 1935), Gabriel Patacsi (1932–83) and Kallistos Ware), and two articles critical of Palamism, by the Benedictine Dom Illtyd Trethowan (1907–93) and the Anglican Rowan Williams (b. 1950).[110] Ware's article consists mostly of replies to the critiques raised by Trethowan and Williams. Support for Palamas also came from an unexpected source, two articles by the Franciscan patrologist André de Halleux (1929–94).[111]

Subsequently, several other Western scholars – Gerhard Podskalsky (1937–2013), Dorothea Wendebourg (b. 1952) and Dirk Krausmüller (b. 1962) – joined the ranks of those attacking Palamism, mostly repeating or expanding on arguments first advanced by Jugie in the 1930s.[112] Some of the arguments against Palamism are methodological, others substantive. The main lines of the critiques are that Palamas and his latter-day revivalists misconstrue patristic sources to buttress his doctrine of the divine energies; that his teaching involves a false understanding of divine transcendence and incomprehensibility; that it violates the principle of divine simplicity by introducing a differentiation in the divine essence, erecting an epistemological device into an ontological distinction in God (a 'real distinction'); that it sustains doctrines of emanationism and of theosis by participation that are Neo-Platonist rather than Christian; that the essence-energies distinction is unnecessary because all knowledge involves 'union without confusion'; that the Palamite theology of essence and energies is 'a philosophical error, a piece of scholasticism [!] of no vital importance'; that the very notion of theosis as 'participation' in the divine life is problematic; that Ware (among others) confuses the issue by speaking of antinomy in theology; and that Palamism was an Eastern response to Thomism.[113]

Against this barrage of criticism, the supporters of Palamas, including André de Halleux, maintain that Palamas is faithful to his patristic sources and the tradition of the church, which includes the church's ascetic-mystical experience; that antinomies are appropriate in Christian theology, while rational and philosophical notions such as divine simplicity are inadequate; that the opponents of Palamism inappropriately employ scholastic and Thomistic theology to attack

[109]Georges Barrois, 'Palamism Revisited', *St Vladimir's Theological Quarterly*, 19, 4 (1975); and Christos Yannaras, 'The Distinction between Essence and Energies and Its Importance for Theology', *St Vladimir's Theological Quarterly*, 19, 4 (1975).

[110]Articles on 'Palamism Today' in *Eastern Churches Review*, 9 (1977): George Mantzarides, 'Tradition and Renewal in the Theology of Saint Gregory Palamas'; Illtyd Trethowan, 'Irrationality in Theology and the Palamite Distinction'; Rowan Williams, 'The Philosophical Structures of Palamism'; Kallistos Ware, 'The Debate about Palamism'; and Gabriel Patacsi, 'Palamism before Palamas'.

[111]André de Halleux, 'Palamisme et Tradition' (Palamism and tradition), *Irénikon*, 48, 4 (1975); and 'Palamisme et Scolastique. Exclusivisme dogmatique ou pluriformité théologique?' (Palamism and scholasticism: Dogmatic exclusivity or theological pluriformity?), *Revue théologique de Louvain*, 4 (1973).

[112]Gerhard Podskalsky, *Theologie und Philosophie in Byzanz* (Theology and Philosophy in Byzantium) (Munich: Bech, 1977); Dorothea Wendebourg, *Geist oder Energie: Zur Frage der innergöttlichen Verankerung des christlichen Lebens in der byzantinischen Theologie* (Spirit or Energy: On the Inner Divine Grounding of Christian Life in Byzantine Theology) (Munich: Kaiser Verlag, 1980); Dirk Krausmüller, 'The Rise of Hesychasm', in Michael Angold, ed., *The Cambridge History of Eastern Christianity* (Cambridge: Cambridge University Press, 2006). See Russell, 'The Reception of Palamas in the West Today', 15–16.

[113]Summary from Ware, 'The Debate about Palamism', passim.

Palamas; that they reduce complex origins and ideas to a conflict between Aristotelianism and Platonism; that they cast an internal Orthodox debate as an East-West confrontation and that they extract Palamas from his historical context, without which it not possible to understand the fourteenth-century quarrel and its dogmatic dénouement in pronouncements with conciliar authority.

While the scholarly debate of the 1970s over Palamism represents an evolution from the polemical dismissal of Palamism as pantheist and heretical by Catholic writers of the 1920s and 1930s, subsequent engagement between Orthodox and non-Orthodox scholars over Palamas has tended, with some exceptions, to be more irenic. Typical of a later phase of appropriation of Palamas is a colloquium held at Cambridge in 2008, with the participation of leading Anglican, Reformed, Orthodox and Catholic theologians.[114] The six Orthodox scholars represented in the symposium (Constantinos Athanasopoulos, David Bradshaw, Nikolaos Loudovikos, Georgios Martzelos, N. N. Trakakis and Metropolitan Vasilios Karayiannis) defend Palamism, with important nuances among them. Roy Clouser, a philosopher in the Reformed tradition, seeks to build bridges between the essence-energies distinction and Protestant and Reformed thinking on the divine presence in creation, while the Dominican Antoine Lévy brings Palamas and Aquinas into dialogue as two different approaches, sharing common features, to understanding the relationship between God and creation.[115] John Milbank of the Radical Orthodoxy group of Anglicans sees paradigm shifts in conceptions of God-creation relations – in both Eastern and Western Christianity, represented by Palamas and Duns Scotus – from a model which focuses primarily on divine-human/creation participation to one which emphasizes the distinction between an impersonal non-participable aspect of God and the 'sharable' aspect.

The lines of demarcation in modern debates over Palamism, both in the 1920s and 1930s and later in the 1970s, are reminiscent of the general context of the fourteenth-century debates: a structured approach to theology strongly grounded in philosophy encountering a mystical-liturgical approach and being unable to accommodate such a theological vision within its parameters. A similar consideration also characterizes the conflict over the Name-of-God (onomatodoxy) at Mount Athos and in Russia prior to the First World War (see Chapter 15). It is nonetheless an oversimplification of complex theologies to characterize these two approaches solely as 'essentialist' and 'existentialist'. By the early twenty-first century the polemics of denunciation of Palamism as pantheist and heretical had largely given way to concerted attempts to grasp the significance of Palamism in both Eastern and Western theology, with the dividing lines no longer 'East versus West', but rather on an individual basis. In the 2008 Cambridge colloquium, remaining polemics are mostly from the Orthodox side, with some Orthodox theologians (Athanasopoulos, Bradshaw and Loudovikos) positing the inherent superiority of Eastern theology of God-creation relations over Western alternatives.

---

[114]See the proceedings in Constantinos Athanasopoulos and Christoph Schneider, eds., *Divine Essence and Divine Energies: Ecumenical Reflections on the Presence of God in Eastern Orthodoxy* (Cambridge: James Clarke, 2013).

[115]Christoph Schneider summarizes the views and critiques of the authors' positions in the Introduction, 'Beyond Agnosticism and Pantheism', while in the final chapter ('In Defence of the Essence/Energies Distinction: A Reply to Critics'), David Bradshaw replies to the critics of his paper, both those favourable to and those opposed to Palamite theology.

Panentheism

The notion that God is 'in the world' – or alternatively, that the world is 'in God' – is the philosophical and theological position known as *panentheism*, which stands between *pantheism* and *deism*. Pantheism confounds God and creation, denying God's transcendence and retaining only God's immanence, whereas deism admits the existence of divine Being but does not recognize any divine action in the world other than the initial act of creation. The classic eighteenth-century image attributed to deism presents God as a cosmic clockmaker, who, having made the clock, winds it up and withdraws, letting it tick along independently. Most Christian theology, however, is resolutely *theist*. Theism is situated between panentheism and deism: God is the creator of the world and acts in the world, but only metaphorically can we say that God is 'in the world' or that the world is 'in God'.

Panentheism is a neologism composed of the Greek words *pan*, all, *en*, in and *theos*, God. Panentheism understands God and the world to be intimately interrelated, with the world being in God *in some fashion* and, similarly, God being in the world. The fundamental problem of panentheism is the middle term, '*en*/in': How is creation 'in' God? Or God 'in' creation? Panentheism seeks to avoid both separating God from the world, as traditional theism often tends to do, especially in its radical form of deism, and identifying or fusing God with the world as in pantheism. Traditional theistic systems emphasize the difference between God and the world, while panentheism stresses God's active presence in the world. Conversely, whereas pantheism identifies or commingles God and the world, panentheism maintains the identity and significance of both the divine and the non-divine, the distinction between the world as created and God as transcendent, uncreated and the Creator.

Anticipations of panentheist understandings of God and creation occurred in both philosophical and theological writings throughout history, although enthusiastic panentheist readings of ancient authors may be more anachronistic than sound historical theology. A rich diversity of panentheist models of God-world relations has developed in the past century, often in response to scientific theories, especially modern cosmology.[116] Among the earlier generation of Orthodox theologians, Sergius Bulgakov explicitly espoused panentheism, and several modern Orthodox theologians identify themselves as panentheists, including Metropolitan Kallistos Ware (b. 1934), Father Andrew Louth (b. 1944) and the mathematician-theologian Alexei Nesteruk (b. 1957).

To distance himself from Vladimir Soloviev's subtly pantheistic philosophical-theological system, Bulgakov emphasizes God's transcendence to creation and God as Creator while at the same time maintaining the prime panentheist affirmation that God is in creation and creation in God, as in these passages:

---

[116]See the typology in Philip Clayton's concluding essay, 'Panentheism Today: A Constructive Systematic Evaluation', in Philip Clayton and Arthur Peacocke, eds., *In Whom We Live and Move and Have Our Being: Panentheistic Reflections on God's Presence in a Scientific World* (Grand Rapids, MI: Eerdmans, 2004), 251–2. For a more extensive treatment, see John W. Cooper, *Panentheism – The Other God of the Philosophers: From Plato to the Present* (Grand Rapids, MI: Baker Academic, 2006).

> As the object of the providence of God, the world is not only a thing or an object in the hands of God – it possesses its own proper being, given by God at its creation, its own proper nature, its own proper life. And at the same time this created nature does not remain outside God, because ontologically there can be no extra-divine existence. The world abides in God, although it is not God, and the relationship of God to the world in the providence of God is not defined as a unilateral action of God towards a world existing outside of him and alien to him, but rather as an *interaction* of Creator with creation. … Owing to the divinity of its foundation, the world maintains its self-existence in the eyes of God, although it is created *ex nihilo*. As a result of its created nature, it also maintains its own being in the eyes of God. God gave to the world at its creation a genuine *reality*, which he also establishes eternally for the Creator himself. It is by the power of this divine reality and of this unbridgeable difference that the world exists both for itself and for God and the relationship between them can only be on the basis of interaction, however deep, intimate and multifaceted it may be, to the extent of the union of the two natures, divine and human, and the deification of humanity in Christ and the church.[117]
>
> God creates the world, as it were, out of himself, out of the abundance of his own resources. Nothing new is introduced for God by the life of the world of creatures. That world only receives, according to the mode proper to it, the divine principle of life. Its being is only a reflection and a mirror of the world of God. … The world, having been created from 'nothing', in this 'nothing' finds its 'place'. God confers on a principle which originates in himself an existence distinct from his own. This is not pantheism but panentheism.[118]

Bulgakov's cosmology fuses panentheism and sophiology, with which he also assimilates the patristic notion of the divine energies, in a complex and not entirely coherent system that seeks to maintain an antinomic balance between God as utterly transcendent and yet radically immanent.[119] He explicitly defines his theology as panentheist, defending it against the accusation of pantheism brought against Soloviev: 'But is this not a pantheism, an impious deification of the world, leading to a kind of religious materialism? Yes, it *is* a pantheism, but an entirely pious one; or more precisely, as I prefer to call it in order to avoid ambiguity, it is a panentheism.'[120] Bulgakov summarizes his panentheism as 'the truth that all is in God or of God (panentheism)'[121] (1925); or again: 'the world is the not-God existent in God; God is the not-world existent in the world. God posits the world outside of himself, but the world possesses its being in God' (1931).[122]

---

[117]Sergius Bulgakov, *Judas Iscarioth, L'Apôtre félon* (Judas Iscariot, The Perfidious Apostle) (1931) (Geneva: Syrtes, 2015), 102–4. Also cited in Brandon Gallaher, 'Antinomism, Trinity and the Challenge of Solov'ëvan Pantheism in the Theology of Sergij Bulgakov'", *Studies in East European Thought*, 64 (2012), 216–17.

[118]Bulgakov, *Sophia, the Wisdom of God*, 63–4; 72.

[119]For an exploration of the problems in Bulgakov's panentheism see Gallaher, 'Antinomism, Trinity and the Challenge of Solov'ëvan Pantheism', 215–18. Gallaher concludes that Bulgakov falls into the same pantheist difficulties as Soloviev, and that Vladimir Lossky may well be partially right in his critique of Bulgakov's sophiology on this score.

[120]Sergius Bulgakov, *The Comforter* (1936) (Grand Rapids, MI: Eerdmans, 2004), 199–200.

[121]Bulgakov, 'Hypostasis and Hypostaticity: Scholia to the *Unfading Light*', 27.

[122]Sergius Bulgakov, *Icons and the Name of God* (1931) (Grand Rapids, MI: Eerdmans, 2012), 32. The second sentence is cited in Gallaher, 'Antinomism, Trinity and the Challenge of Solov'ëvan Pantheism', 217, but is missing in the English translation.

Kallistos Ware, Andrew Louth and Alexei Nesteruk participated in a symposium on panentheism held in December 2001.[123] Ware's paper focuses on the Palamite doctrine of the divine energies, and Louth's on the *logoi* of Maximus the Confessor. Ware and Louth seek to relate the doctrines of Maximus and Palamas to panentheism. Ware argues that panentheism 'is a label that may legitimately be applied to Palamism', in the sense of 'weak panentheism', since Palamas, in common with the main line of ancient and modern Orthodox theology, 'believes that the divine being is in no way exhausted by the universe, for God remains utterly transcendent in his imparticipable essence'.[124] Nesteruk, proceeding from the ancient Greek and patristic notion of humanity as a microcosm of creation and from *logoi* of things of Maximus, sees the universe 'as inherent in the person of the Logos of God'.[125] But since the universe as a whole is not a personal hypostasis, it cannot relate to God as such, and thus humans, capable of participating 'in the Logos of God', bring non-human creation to its fulfilment in God, acting as 'priests of creation'.[126]

Orthodox critics of panentheism are not lacking, Georges Florovsky being the strongest. He saw Bulgakov's panentheism as little more than Soloviev's pantheist wolf disguised in a theistic sheepskin. But rather than waging a frontal battle against Soloviev and Bulgakov, Florovsky attacked them indirectly, as we saw above in our discussion of his 1928 article 'Creation and Createdness', positing the patristic doctrine of creation as the true Christian theology of relations between God and the world. In this shadow-boxing, Origen and Arius serve as stand-ins for the Russian philosopher-theologians, by implication associating panentheism with ancient heresies.[127]

Ironically, Florovsky's willingness to admit, however reluctantly, that creation has some form of eternal existence in the divine will could be considered a legitimate formulation of panentheism. Florovsky tackles the problem of explaining the relationships between God and creation, time and eternity, in the context of his thesis that the idea of creation existed in God's mind from all eternity, but its realization occurs in time. His solution is not entirely satisfactory, since it seems to run counter to his own categorical assertion that 'Nothing created can ever be part of God',[128] and involves introducing time into eternity:

> God's idea of the world, his plan and intention are without any doubt *eternal*, but in some sense they are *not coeternal or co-exist* with him, as they are 'separated' from his 'essence' by *the exercise of his will*. To put it differently, the eternity of God's idea of the world is of a different type to the eternity of God's being and consciousness.[129]

---

[123]See their essays in Clayton and Peacocke, eds., *In Whom We Live and Move and Have Our Being*: Kallistos Ware, 'God Immanent yet Transcendent: The Divine Energies according to Saint Gregory Palamas'; Andrew Louth, 'The Cosmic Vision of Saint Maximos the Confessor'; and Alexei Nesteruk, 'The Universe as Hypostatic Inherence in the Logos of God: Panentheism in the Eastern Orthodox Perspective'.

[124]Ware, 'God Immanent yet Transcendent', 166.

[125]Nesteruk, 'The Universe as Hypostatic Inherence in the Logos of God', 175.

[126]Ibid., 178–81.

[127]Our analysis here is indebted to Gavrilyuk, *Georges Florovsky and the Russian Religious Renaissance*, especially 106–11 and 145–50.

[128]Florovsky, 'Creation and Createdness', in Gallaher and Ladouceur, eds., *The Patristic Witness of Georges Florovsky*, 45.

[129]Ibid., 43.

Florovsky further muddles his own argument that there are two types of eternity by citations from Gregory of Nazianzus, Augustine, John of Damascus and Maximus the Confessor to the effect that there was some form of divine eternal pre-contemplation of creation before its actual realization.[130] Unlike Bulgakov and later theologians such as Louth, Nesteruk and Ware, Florovsky is unwilling to call a spade a spade – to recognize intimations of panentheism in the ancient Fathers – but in the end his solution appears to be panentheist in all but name.

Florovsky's main target in 'Creation and Createdness' is sophiology, but panentheism suffers collateral damage for being too closely interwoven with sophiology in Bulgakov and for being ultimately reducible, according to Florovsky, to pantheism. Whereas Florovsky sees panentheism as a sub-species of pantheism (hence unacceptable), Bulgakov and other modern Orthodox theologians who espouse panentheism regard it as a sub-species of theism (hence acceptable). Considering the totality of Bulgakov's theology, with the overwhelming evidence that he was a Christian theist, it is not possible to sustain a claim that he was in reality a pantheist, even if his own theological system grounded in sophiology breaks down under close analysis.

Nicolas Lossky was another strong critic of sophiology and panentheism. In his comments on Soloviev's cosmology, Lossky not only speaks of its 'pantheistic flavour', but also implicitly rejects panentheism:

> The problem of connection between God and the world is solved consistently only by the Christian doctrine of God creating the world out of nothing: according to this doctrine God created the world, both in form and in substance, as something entirely new, different from himself, without using for this creation any material either in himself or outside.[131]

Nicolas Lossky, like Florovsky and other critics of sophiology, finds that Bulgakov was unable to prevent his sophiology from slipping into a form of pantheism: 'The non-divine aspect of the world proves to be so characterless that his theory must be regarded as a peculiar variety of pantheism.'[132] Lossky finds that the basic flaw in Bulgakov's system is that he blurs if not eradicates the ontological gulf between God and creation:

> His contention that in the Divine and in the created world all is 'one and identical in content (though not in being)' (*Agnets bozhii*, 148), and all his theories connected therewith contain too great an ontological approximation of the world, and especially of man, to God. … that is logically incompatible with the teaching about God expounded by the negative theology, even if additions be made to it from the positive theology.[133]

Lossky's specific objections to Bulgakov's panentheism, which overlap with his critique of sophiology, are, first, that the idea that God creates from within himself minimizes divine creativity: 'He borrows the whole of the world's content from himself; thus there is no real creativeness, but

---

[130]Ibid., 45–6.
[131]Lossky, *History of Russian Philosophy*, 128.
[132]Ibid., 229.
[133]Ibid., 228.

merely a shifting or externalization of contents already present in God.'[134] Secondly, the line of Bulgakov's argument suggests that humanity is consubstantial with God, an untenable position in Christian theology. Lossky also concludes that panentheism is unable to give a reasonable explanation of the presence of evil in the world, of the freedom of created agents and of their capacity for independent creativity.[135]

In attacking Origen's cosmology, Florovsky implicitly invites the reader to draw a parallel between Bulgakov's sophiology and panentheism and Origen. But another parallel is also valid: even if both Origen and Bulgakov made major theological errors, this did not prevent them from being sincere and pious Christians and outstanding theologians, who were confessors of the faith, Origen suffering physical torture which likely resulted in a premature death and Bulgakov loss of employment and exile.

The *logoi* of things and the contemplation of God in creation

In the development of Christian spirituality, the importance of the contemplation of God in creation was first highlighted by Evagrius of Ponticus, a late fourth-century Desert Father in Egypt. For Evagrius, contemplation includes 'primary natural contemplation', the contemplation of God proper to angels, and 'secondary natural contemplation', the contemplation of God through the ultimate principles or 'reasons' (*logoi*) of visible creation.[136] St Maximus the Confessor (c. 580–662) developed extensively the notion of the *logoi* of created beings, and both Evagrius and Maximus viewed the contemplation of God in creation as a preliminary and even necessary step to the direct contemplation of God. Among modern Orthodox authors, Dumitru Staniloae (1903–93) and Kallistos Ware also stress the importance of the contemplation of God in the natural world.[137] Both rely on Maximus's teaching on the *logoi* in creation and on the Palamite theology of the divine energies. For Staniloae and Ware, Maximus and Palamas formulate a theological understanding of God's immanence, his presence in the world, while safeguarding his absolute transcendence, thus avoiding falling into pantheism. These ancient Fathers were responding to problems of his time, using slightly different concepts and language to articulate the philosophical and theological problem of the relationship of God to creation, but their insights are still valuable for a modern theological understanding of creation.

---

[134]Ibid.

[135]See Lossky, *History of Russian Philosophy*, 229–31.

[136]For Evagrius, the 'gnostic' life (*gnostica*), including natural contemplation, follows the mastery of the passions and the acquisition of a certain degree of impassibility (*apatheia*). See Robert E. Sinkewicz, *Evagrius of Pontus: The Greek Ascetic Corpus* (Oxford: Oxford University Press, 2003), xxxiv.

[137]Dumitru Staniloae, 'The Contemplation of God in Creation', in *Orthodox Spirituality: A Practical Guide for the Faithful and a Definitive Manual for the Scholar* (South Canaan, PA: St Tikhon's Seminary Press, 2002), 203–23; Kallistos Ware, 'Through Creation to the Creator', Third Marco Pallis Memorial Lecture, *Ecotheology*, 2 (London: Friends of the Centre, 1996) www.incommunion.org/2004/12/11/through-creation-to-the-creator (12 March 2011).

In his doctrine of the *logoi*, Maximus connects creation to the divine Logos, the Second Person of the Holy Trinity, through whom God created the universe. Each created thing has a *logos*, God's intention for that thing, which draws it to achieve its divinely ordained purpose. Christ, the Logos of God, is both the source of the *logoi* of things and their ultimate fulfilment, in a cosmic theosis. The universe is thus imbued with divine presence.[138] The *logoi* are not something that a biologist, a geologist or an astronomer will discover but rather the spiritual sense of creation originating in God, God's intention for created things and the goal towards which they strive. In this cosmic vision, all of creation is a theophany, a divine manifestation, and can and should become an occasion for elevating our thoughts and our prayers to God, a spiritual movement that Kallistos Ware characterizes as 'through creation to the Creator'.

Maximus and Palamas approach the same question, how God relates to creation, but from different perspectives. Seven centuries before Palamas, Maximus saw no conflict or incompatibility between his notion of the *logoi* and the essence-energies distinction that he inherited from the Cappadocian Fathers. Kallistos Ware points out that, whereas Maximus's approach is predominantly Christological, in attaching the *logoi* of beings to the divine Logos, Palamas emphasizes the Trinitarian aspect of the divine energies: 'It is an error to say that any one person in the Godhead has an "energy" in which the other two persons do not share.'[139]

Metaphorically, the divine energies may be said to represent the relationship of God to creation from the divine perspective, God as Creator and Sustainer looking towards creation, whereas the *logoi* represent this relationship from the perspective of creation, creation looking towards God as the source, pillar, ground and goal of its existence. Pavel Florensky, without naming either Maximus or Palamas, expresses a similar idea in *The Pillar and Ground of the Truth*:

> The reason of a thing [the *logoi*] is, from the point of view of a creature, love of God and the vision of God that comes from this. This reason is a particular idea of God, *a conditional idea of the Unconditional* [the ground of all *logoi* in the Logos, Christ]. But, from the point of view of divine Being, the reason of a creature is *an unconditional idea of the conditional*, God's idea about a particular thing – the act [energy] by which God … condescends to think about the finite and limited – introduces the meagre semi-being of the creature into the fullness of being of the interior of the Trinity.[140]

Modern readers of Maximus are divided on whether the *logoi* are created or uncreated. In the 2008 Cambridge colloquium mentioned previously, John Milbank (b. 1952) argues that Maximus's *logoi* are created: 'Even though the outgoing *logoi* [i.e. from God] are for Maximus active, shaping forces within the cosmos, they are still created forces. … while for Maximus the *logoi* are the action upon creatures of the Logos, they are always in the material universe.'[141] On the other hand, Vasilios Karayiannis (b. 1948) affirms unambiguously that 'the *logoi* of beings are uncreated as are the

[138]For résumés of Maximus's teaching on the *logoi*, see Louth, 'The Cosmic Vision of Saint Maximos the Confessor'; and Ware, 'Through Creation to the Creator'.
[139]Ware, 'God Immanent yet Transcendent', 161.
[140]Florensky, *The Pillar and Ground of the Truth*, 235.
[141]John Milbank, 'Christianity and Platonism in East and West', in Athanasopoulos and Schneider, eds., *Divine Essence and Divine Energies*, 193.

divine energies which are within the *logoi* of beings.'[142] As summarized by Christoph Schneider, Karayiannis finds in Maximus that 'The *logos* of each being existed already before creation, i.e. it existed timelessly within the eternal will of God.'[143] Karayiannis avoids any suggestion of pantheism and remains within the mainstream of Orthodox thinking by affirming that 'the eternal presence of the *logoi* of beings within God does not mean that creation is also eternal. God as the creator of time, and as the creator of those things within time, is eternal and his *ex nihilo* creation is the result of divine will and not a product of necessity.'[144] Creation is effected by the divine will – *fiat lux* (Gen. 1.3) – as the pre-existing divine ideas of creation are actualized by creation *ex nihilo*. This account of Maximus by Ware, Karayiannis and others places Maximus retroactively in the panentheist camp, although, as we saw above, some Orthodox theologians object to the possibility of creation having any sort of pre-existence in God, even in the divine will. This would, critics argue, cast a doubt on the central doctrine of creation *ex nihilo* because God would be creating from within his own being – a critique articulated by Nicolas Lossky, as mentioned above. Nonetheless, this appears to be the panentheist position and, apparently, that of Maximus, who expands the Cappadocian essence-energies distinction with his theology of the *logoi* in created beings.

The contemplation of God in creation plays an important role in Dumitru Staniloae's theology and his presentation of Orthodox spirituality. Picking up on Evagrius and Maximus, Staniloae situates the contemplation of God in the second stage of the spiritual life, together with the spiritual understanding of Scripture, apophatic knowledge of God and pure prayer.[145] The world as a theophany aflame with the divine presence has a fundamentally spiritual or mystical purpose in the divine economy:

> The existence of the world is seen as having the purpose, among others, of exercising all our spiritual powers in our ascent to God. … The existence of the world itself as a way to God is a proof that the supreme knowledge of God isn't an irrational act, but suprarational; that is, it isn't realised by a premature renunciation of reason. … but by the surpassing of reason. … We are raised to a suprarational, but not anti-rational knowledge of God.[146]
>
> The *logoi* of things don't consist simply of their fleshly utility, but in the revelation of a spiritual sense, of a divine intention.[147]

Staniloae insists strongly on the necessity of 'a long preparation of a pronounced moral character'[148] – the mastery of the passions in classical ascetic terminology – as a pre-condition for discovering the *logoi* in things. Nor does Staniloae allow for the possibility of a spontaneous, unprovoked

[142]Vasilios Karayiannis, 'The Distinction between Essence and Energy according to Maximus the Confessor', in Athanasopoulos and Schneider, eds., *Divine Essence and Divine Energies*, 251. For a fuller treatment, see his *Maxime le Confesseur: Essence et énergies de Dieu* (Maximus the Confessor: The Essence and Energies of God) (Paris: Beauchesne, 1993), especially '*Logoi* des êtres et énergies divines' (The logoi of things and the divine energies), 215–22.

[143]Christoph Schneider, 'Introduction: Beyond Agnosticism and Pantheism', in Athanasopoulos and Schneider, eds., *Divine Essence and Divine Energies*, 24.

[144]Karayiannis, 'The Distinction between Essence and Energy according to Maximus the Confessor', 251.

[145]See Part Two, 'Illumination', of Staniloae's *Orthodox Spirituality*, 195–299.

[146]Staniloae, *Orthodox Spirituality*, 208.

[147]Ibid., 216.

[148]Ibid., 209.

intuitive experience of transcendental reality occasioned by creation, such as those envisioned in Dostoyevsky, Bulgakov and Florensky. Other Orthodox authors, such as Kallistos Ware, insist less than Staniloae on a moral prerequisite for the contemplation of God in creation.

The combination of the theologies of the divine energies and the *logoi* in creation is reflected in two other spheres of modern Orthodox thought, sacramental theology and environmental theology. The contemplation of God in creation is closely related to the notion of the world as sacrament, an idea associated with Alexander Schmemann (1921–83) in particular.[149] Schmemann uses the expression in a pastoral and liturgical context, inviting his readers to reject both a flight from the world and seeing the world 'as something incomprehensible and unmanageable'.[150] Instead, he encourages us to approach the world 'sacramentally through Christ':

> Nature and the world are otherwise beyond our grasp; time also, time that carries all things away in a meaningless flux, causing men to despair unless they see in it the pattern of God's action, reflected in the liturgical year, the necessary road to the New Jerusalem.[151]

In the theology of Alexander Schmemann, John Zizioulas and others, humans are liturgical creatures, priests of the cosmic liturgy who offer creation to God. For Schmemann, 'The world was created as the "matter", the material of one all-embracing eucharist, and man was created as the priest of his cosmic sacrament.'[152] He continues:

> For man can be truly man – that is, the king of creation, the priest and minister of God's creativity and initiative – only when he does not posit himself as the 'owner' of creation and submits himself – in obedience and love – to its nature as the bride of God, in response and acceptance.[153]

The cultic function of a priest is to offer the gifts of the community to God, so that they may be blessed, sanctified and returned to be shared by the community. This act of offering does not add anything to God, but rather is a recognition of God's sovereignty and providence. Humanity as priest of creation offers creation to God, recognizing that it is God's from the outset, as Creator, Sustainer and Finality of all that exists: 'Only the human being', writes John Zizioulas, 'can … unite the world in his hands in order to refer it to God so that it can be united with God and thus saved and fulfilled'.[154] Zizioulas emphasizes that the notion of humanity as priest of creation is superior to the ideas of humans as proprietors of creation, free to exploit the natural world for

---

[149]Schmemann's well-known book *For the Life of the World: Sacraments and Orthodoxy* (1963) (Crestwood, NY: St Vladimir's Seminary Press, 2nd rev. ed. 1973) was published in the UK under the title *The World as Sacrament* (London: Darton, Longman & Todd, 1966), even though this expression does not actually occur in the book.

[150]Alexander Schmemann, 'The World as Sacrament', in *Church, World, Mission: Reflections on Orthodoxy in the West* (Crestwood, NY: St Vladimir's Seminary Press, 1979), 226.

[151]Schmemann, 'The World as Sacrament', 226.

[152]Schmemann, *For the Life of the World*, 15.

[153]Ibid., 85.

[154]John Zizioulas, 'Proprietors or Priests of Creation?' Fifth Symposium on Religion, Science and the Environment (Baltic Sea Seminar, 2 June 2003). www.rsesymposia.org/themedia/File/1151679350Pergamon.pdf (12 November 2016). Reproduced in John Chryssavgis and Bruce V. Foltz, eds., *Toward an Ecology of Transfiguration: Orthodox Christian Perspectives on Environment, Nature, and Creation* (New York: Fordham University Press, 2013), here at 167. See also his 'Man the Priest of Creation: A Response to the Ecological Problem', in Andrew Walker and Costa Carras, eds., *Living Orthodoxy in the Modern World: Orthodox Christianity & Society* (Crestwood, NY: St Vladimir's Seminary Press, 1996).

their own benefit, or as stewards of creation with merely a managerial function. With the Eucharist as the model of the priestly function and offering, Zizioulas stresses that humans are called on to 'improve' nature, as the bread and wine of the Eucharist are the result of nature (wheat and grapes), transformed through human creativity and work: 'The human being is the priest of creation in the sense that the material world he takes in his hands is *transformed* into something better than what it is *naturally*. Nature must be improved through human intervention; it is not to be preserved as it is.'[155] This is not entirely satisfactory, since it opens the door to a brutally interventionist approach towards nature on the grounds of seeking to 'improve' it, as in genetic manipulation of plants, animals and even humans, to overcome apparent defects. In a broader perspective, the idea of humanity as priest of creation does not supplant but rather complements that of humanity as steward of creation, responsible for its good management before God, its true proprietor.

The idea of the world as sacrament is a mystical and liturgical expression of the theology of divine presence in creation as elaborated in the doctrines of the divine energies, panentheism and the contemplation of God in creation. The world as sacrament includes a vision of creation which encompasses several other important features. For instance, creation is not something that occurred once in the past, whether 6,000 years ago (per Genesis and biblical genealogies) or some 14 billion years ago (per modern cosmology), but is a continuous divine act. Nothing can exist without being sustained at every moment by divine will: creation is here and now (cf. Pss. 103/104.27-30; Pss. 138/139.7-12). Creation is simultaneously external to God, yet God creates the world 'not as it were from the outside, but from within'.[156] As in panentheism, the world is somehow in God and God in the world, since nothing can exist apart from God.

The contemplation of God in creation also calls for a heightened awareness of the distinctiveness of each individual being, as Kallistos Ware stresses: 'We are to perceive and to value each thing in and for itself, viewing that thing in sharp relief, appreciating what in the Zen tradition is called the special "Ah!" of each thing, its "is-ness", or *haeccitas*.'[157] The key to the contemplation of God in creation, however, is to see beyond the uniqueness of each thing to the mystical divine presence in all things: 'It is impossible to make sense of the world unless we also look beyond the world; the world only acquires its true meaning when seen as the reflection of a reality that transcends it ... the world [becomes] pellucid, so that it reveals to us the indwelling Creator-Logos.'[158] This is the mystical or spiritual significance of Maximus's doctrine of the *logoi* of things, which remains incomplete if it is considered only as an abstract reflection on God and creation.

The contemplation of God in creation means passing beyond a strictly utilitarian vision of the world to a vision of the world as a manifestation of God's glory, as expressed by Dumitru Staniloae: 'So the world has been set up for us as a road to God. The existence of the world is seen as having the purpose, among others, of exercising all our spiritual powers in our ascent to

[155]Zizioulas, 'Proprietors or Priests of Creation?', in Chryssavgis and Foltz, eds., *Toward an Ecology of Transfiguration*, 170.
[156]Ware, 'Through Creation to the Creator'.
[157]Ibid.
[158]Ibid.

God.'[159] The notion of the world as sacrament – all of creation is sacred, especially all that lives[160] – implies not only a respectful relationship between humans and creation, but also a positive responsibility for creation. This is the theological basis for Orthodox concern for the environment, a prominent feature of Orthodox theology in the late twentieth century and the beginning of the twenty-first century.[161]

Conclusion

Modern Orthodox theology has devoted considerable attention to the issue of how God relates to the world, proposing widely different, overlapping and even conflicting approaches. The related notions of all-unity and sophiology, key themes of the Russian religious renaissance, have not achieved significant and lasting acceptance in Orthodoxy, despite later interest in post-Soviet Russia and in the West. Although all-unity and sophiology and the elaborate theologies associated with them may now be more of historical than current interest, they nonetheless played an important role in the stimulation of other approaches which gained broader support in Orthodox circles. The mainstream of Orthodox thought, while intrigued by a mystical vision of a principle of unity both in the created world and between creation and Creator, was at the same time dismayed by the complexity and artificiality of the philosophical and theological constructs spawned in the elaboration of this unifying principle. It was more reassuring to fall back on notions well grounded in patristic theology and the history of the church – the *logoi* of Evagrius of Ponticus and Maximus the Confessor, the Palamite theology of the divine energies and the contemplation of God in creation – and it is these notions which gained the upper hand in Orthodoxy. These theologies, together with the more troublesome notion of panentheism, have features comparable with all-unity, to the extent that they seek to bridge the gap between Creator and creation.

Patristically inclined theologians perceived all-unity as bound up with Romantic sentimentalism and German idealism and too close to pantheism for comfort. The risk of slipping into a form of pantheism is certainly a danger in all-unity: if a single principle encompasses God and creation, it is all too easy to confound God with creation. But it is difficult to sustain a claim that Soloviev and his later followers were pantheists in a classic sense, for all believed in God's otherness from creation (God as transcendent) and in creation *ex nihilo*. At the same time their cosmologies tend towards a confusion of God (as 'First Absolute', in Soloviev's parlance) and all-unity (or world-soul or 'Second Absolute') as the principle of both unity and multiplicity in creation. It is necessary therefore to counterbalance any notion of all-unity, which emphasizes God's immanence or unity

---

[159]Staniloae, *Orthodox Spirituality*, 208.

[160]From the title of a collection of Kallistos Ware's writings in French: *Tout ce qui vit est saint* (All that Lives Is Holy) (Paris: Le Cerf, 2003).

[161]Orthodox literature on the environment is considerable. For a generous selection of key writings, see Chryssavgis and Foltz, eds., *Toward an Ecology of Transfiguration.* See also Elizabeth Theokritoff, *Living in God's Creation: Orthodox Perspectives on Ecology* (Crestwood, NY: St Vladimir's Seminary Press, 2010).

with the world, with the classical concept of God's transcendence, conventionally expressed in the antinomy that God is at once immanent in the world, yet simultaneously transcendent to it. In Soloviev's later thought, the world-soul evolves into the problematic concept of Sophia, Divine Wisdom, in which form it was inherited by prominent successors such as Pavel Florensky and Sergius Bulgakov. For the critics of all-unity, the pantheistic risk of the metaphysics of all-unity was accentuated in the idea of Sophia, culminating in the conflict over sophiology in the mid-1930s.

Although sophiology loomed large in the first half of the twentieth century, Orthodox theology did not 'receive' sophiology, in the sense of a broad acceptance of its main ideas. In the eyes of critics, sophiology was ultimately irreconcilable with the doctrines of Maximus the Confessor (the *logoi* of things) and especially Gregory Palamas (divine energies). Maximus and Palamas might not have provided all the answers that the sophiologists sought, but the sophiologists were unable to convince sceptics that their doctrine was a consistent development of patristic theology.

In many ways Bulgakov's sophiology represents the culmination of the theology of the Russian religious renaissance. Bulgakov constructed a theological system based on the intuition of Divine Wisdom as the key to the relation between God and the world. He can be faulted for developing a system founded on a doctrine which finds at best only weak support in Scripture, the Fathers and the experience of the church. In setting out to construct a complete theological system, Bulgakov was more in the philosophical tradition than in the tradition of Orthodox theology. Nevertheless, despite the insurmountable weaknesses inherent in sophiology, Bulgakov's principal theological works must be considered among the major writings of modern Orthodox theology.

After the Second World War, sophiology was largely ignored in Orthodox theological circles, except as an aspect of the history of modern Orthodox theology. Bulgakov's vision of sophiology as a development of Palamite theology did not capture the Orthodox imagination. The Palamite revival, already underway in the 1930s, continued to gather momentum after the Second World War and quickly eclipsed sophiology as a more satisfactory approach to a theology of God and creation. Insufficient attention has been paid to understanding the relationship between the Palamite theology of the divine energies and sophiology. The publication of Bulgakov's major theological works in French (in the 1980s) and in English (2002–12) revived a certain interest in sophiology, but more attention is devoted to Bulgakov and sophiology in non-Orthodox academic circles than among Orthodox theologians. By the early twenty-first century, few Orthodox theologians actively subscribed to sophiology.[162] Sophiology is an intriguing and spectacular but flawed and tragic theological insight, now largely relegated to the history of theology. Even if it is fair to say that Orthodox theology has not received sophiology, one can nonetheless affirm that the sophiologists asked the right questions about the relations between God and the world, but gave the wrong answers.[163]

Unfortunately, philosophers and theologians, not unexpectedly, naturally tend to read and understand Sophia through philosophical and theological lenses as a description of a metaphysical

---

[162]The French Orthodox theologian Antoine Arjakovsky is a major advocate of Bulgakov's theology. See Arjakovsky, *Essai sur le père Serge Boulgakov*; and Arjakovsky, *The Way: Religious Thinkers of the Russian Emigration in Paris and their Journal*.

[163]Georges Florovsky used this expression referring to the Eurasians of the 1920s, but it also applies to his attitude towards the sophiologists. See Georges Florovsky, 'Evraziiskii soblazn' (The Eurasian Temptation), *Sovremennye Zapiski*, 34 (1928).

entity or reality of some sort, rather than as a poetic or mystical image of God-in-creation and creation-in-God. In this perspective, Bulgakov set himself on an impossible mission in attempting to solidify the mystical visions of Soloviev and Florensky into a coherent philosophical-theological system compatible with the Orthodox tradition.

Orthodox theologians of the early twentieth century stood on weak ground in defending Palamas, since Palamite theology had largely disappeared from Orthodox thought in the preceding centuries. Absent from nineteenth- and early-to-mid-twentieth-century treatises of dogmatic theology, the divine energies feature prominently in the works of theologians of the neopatristic tradition, such as Georges Florovsky, Vladimir Lossky and John Meyendorff, and in the *Dogmatica* of Hilarion Alfeyev, John Romanides and Dumitru Staniloae.[164] The first order of priority for early practitioners of neopatristic theology was to restore Palamas to his rightful place in Orthodox thought. By the time of the debate on Palamism in the 1970s, this had largely been achieved. As Aidan Nichols wrote in 1995: 'Nowadays most, perhaps all, Orthodox theologians would regard [Palamas's doctrine] as part of the assured dogma of the church, since the particular councils which taught it have themselves been "received" by the generality of the Orthodox.'[165]

Despite the widespread acceptance of Palamism among modern Orthodox theologians, some, such as Justin Popovich and John Zizioulas, do not attach much importance to the doctrine of the divine energies, or ignore it altogether.[166] Nonetheless, the revival and near-universal acceptability of this doctrine in Orthodoxy must rank as one of the most significant achievements of neopatristic theology, perhaps its most important. By the 1970s, Orthodox supporters of Palamism were in a position not only to defend this theology from the solid ramparts of a half-century of Orthodox scholarship, but also to mount an offensive against weak points in corresponding Western theology, while conceding to some of the criticisms, such as aspects of Meyendorff's interpretation of the fourteenth-century debate. The discussion of Palamism is far from concluded but can now be conducted in an open and cooperative ecumenical context, as shown by the Cambridge symposium of 2008 on divine energies.

In his 1928 article 'Creation and Createdness', Georges Florovsky put considerable emphasis on the ontological gulf between Creator and creation, as a counterpoint to the perceived pantheism of all-unity and sophiology. But in itself this emphasis does not resolve the question of how God relates to creation, which is properly the domain of the essence-energies distinction. It is

[164]See Hilarion Alfeyev, 'The Essence and Energies of God', in *Orthodox Christianity, Volume II: Doctrine and Teaching of the Orthodox Church* (Yonkers, NY: St Vladimir's Seminary Press, 2012), 153–8; John Romanides, 'The Distinction between the Essence and the Energies of God', chs. 41 and 65 of his *Patristic Theology: The University Lectures of Fr. John Romanides* (Thessaloniki, GR: Uncut Mountain Press, 2008), 157–60 and 253–9; and Dumitru Staniloae, 'The Being of God and His Uncreated Operations', in *The Experience of God*, Vol. 1 of *The Experience of God: Orthodox Dogmatic Theology*, 6 vols (Brookline, MA: Holy Cross Orthodox Press, 1994), I:125–39.

[165]Nichols, *Light from the East*, 47.

[166]The divine energies do not feature in Justin Popovich's *Dogmatica* entitled *The Orthodox Philosophy of Truth* (3 vols in Serbian, 1932; 1935; 1978); French translation Justin Popovitch, *Philosophie orthodoxe de la vérité: Dogmatique de l'Église orthodoxe* (Orthodox Philosophy of the Truth: *Dogmatica* of the Orthodox Church), 5 vols. (Lausanne: L'Âge d'homme, 1992–7). The relevant volume of this work (vol. 1) was published in 1932, before the Palamite revival had made much headway. It and the second volume (1935) follow closely similar Russian and Greek *Dogmatica*. John Zizioulas does not discuss the divine energies in his *Lectures in Christian Dogmatics* (London: T&T Clark, 2008).

theologically insufficient to point to fundamental differences between Creator and creation; provision must be made for their potential unity, which is rendered possible through the doctrines of divine energies, the *logoi* of things, the Incarnation of the Logos and theosis.

Despite theological weaknesses in the notion of all-unity, the idea of a fundamental, if often vaguely articulated, unity of humanity and the rest of creation – seen in the light of an essential differentiation between God as Creator and the cosmos as created – finds an echo in later Orthodox reflection on the divine energies, as manifested especially in the spiritual and liturgical notions of the contemplation of God in nature, the idea of 'the world as sacrament' and Orthodox concern for the environment.

A well-known patristic adage, inherited from Greek philosophy and found in Basil the Great, Gregory of Nazianzus and Gregory of Nyssa and others, sees humanity as a *microcosm* of creation – humans unite the material or sensible world and the intelligible or spiritual. Humans are thus mediators between different realms that were set in opposition as a result of human sin. Maximus the Confessor insists that humanity's vocation is to reunite the basic divisions in creation and that this role is pre-eminently fulfilled by Christ.[167] Dumitru Staniloae refers to the idea in Maximus that sees humanity as a *macrocosm*, capable of encompassing the entire universe because it is 'called to comprehend the whole world' within itself.[168] Staniloae extends Maximus by referring to the universe as *macroanthropos*, creation called to become humanity writ large by being 'humanized entirely', 'becom[ing] pan-human', 'becom[ing], in its entirety, a humanized cosmos'.[169] Humanity's mission goes well beyond personal salvation to encompass the entire universe, to act with Christ to purify the cosmos of the effects of sin, to vivify it, to humanize it and to 'Christify' the cosmos by offering it to God. In this sense the church encompasses not only human beings, but the entire creation, an idea picked up by Vladimir Lossky and others. Lossky writes: 'The entire universe is called to enter within the church, to become the Church of Christ, that it may be transformed after the consummation of the ages, into the eternal Kingdom of God.'[170]

But this cosmic vision was not universally characteristic of Orthodox theology after the decline of Russian religious philosophy. In the 1937 *Living Tradition* collection of essays, Basil Zenkovsky detects in Orthodox thought a risk of acosmism, a refusal to give non-human creation an ontological status of its own, an exclusively anthropocentric and utilitarian view of non-human creation.[171] Similarly, Nicholas Afanasiev (1888–1977) discerns in the nascent neopatristic movement 'a certain exit of the church from the world: there is only one path – from the world

---

[167]See Maximus the Confessor, 'Ambiguum 41', *On Difficulties in the Church Fathers: The Ambigua*, Vol. 2 (Cambridge, MA: Harvard University Press, 2014), 103–21; and the discussion in Lars Thunberg, *Microcosm and Mediator: The Theological Anthropology of Maximus the Confessor* (1965) (Chicago, IL: Open Court, 1995), 132–43.
[168]Staniloae, *The Experience of God*, I:4.
[169]Ibid.
[170]Lossky, *The Mystical Theology of the Eastern Church*, 113.
[171]Basil Zenkovsky, 'The Problem of the Cosmos in Christianity', in *Zhivoe predanie: Pravoslavie v sovremennosti* (Living Tradition: Orthodoxy in the Modern World) (Paris: YMCA-Press, 1937); summary in Valliere, *Modern Russian Theology*, 393–4.

into the church, but there is no path from the church into the world.'[172] Paul Valliere argues that, in comparison with the earlier theology of the Russian religious renaissance, Orthodox neopatristic theology is weak on cosmology, in particular on 'cosmodicy', Bulgakov's term for 'the right of the world to theological status'.[173]

The concerns of Zenkovsky and Afanasiev in 1937, and Valliere's critique of neopatristic theology as weak in cosmology, while having some merit, have to be considered in light of the strong interest among neopatristic theologians in the theology of the divine energies, Maximus's *logoi*, panentheism, the contemplation of God in creation and the world as sacrament. These theologies represent an engagement with creation which is consistent with the intent of the Russian religious philosophers, but which marshals a different array of arguments, more solidly anchored in patristic thought and the experience of the church. Both religious philosophy and neopatristic theology seek to build bridges between God, humanity and the rest of creation; contemporary thinking reaches beyond a philosophical approach to the articulation of a vision which is at once theological, liturgical and spiritual, with ethical implications in terms of concern for the environment. For instance, the initiatives of the Ecumenical Patriarch Bartholomew concerning the environment are a recognition of the importance of the natural world in its own right and of the responsibility of Christians towards creation.[174]

The different approaches to a theology of God and the world overlap to some extent. Among the early Russian religious thinkers, all-unity flowed easily into sophiology, which ultimately proved to be a theological dead-end. On the other hand, the theology of the divine energies, the *logoi* of things and panentheism appear to be compatible to some Orthodox theologians, who accept all three. These in turn flow into the spirituality of the contemplation of God in creation, concern for the natural world and support for environmental measures. But there are still gaps. The grey areas of the relationship between Palamas's divine energies and Maximus's *logoi* are not fully worked out, and Orthodox theology has yet to deal adequately with the major philosophical and theological objections to panentheism raised by Georges Florovsky and Nicolas Lossky.[175]

Despite the seeming incompatibility of the all-unity and Divine Wisdom of the Russian religious renaissance with the theologies of the divine energies and the *logoi* of things that later gained wide acceptance in Orthodoxy, something of the religious philosophers' mystical-poetic view of the natural world as a reflection of divine Unity-Truth-Beauty-Goodness-Love is found in the idea of the world as sacrament and the contemplation of God in creation, a re-enchantment of the cosmos infused with the divine presence and worthy of human respect and loving-care. Sergius Bulgakov, in a meditation on the theological significance of the legend of the Holy Grail, offers a mystical

---

[172]Nicholas Afanasiev, 'Neizmennoe i vremennoe v tserkovnykh kanonakh' (The unchangeable and the temporary in the church's canons) (1937), in *Zhivoe predanie*, 93. Cited in Valliere, *Modern Russian Theology*, 386.

[173]Valliere, *Modern Russian Theology*, 386.

[174]For an overview of Patriarch Bartholomew's creation theology and environmental activities, see John Chryssavgis's Introduction to John Chryssavgis, ed., *On Earth as in Heaven: Ecological Vision and Initiatives of Ecumenical Patriarch Bartholomew* (New York: Fordham University Press, 2012), 4–15.

[175]Paul Gavrilyuk makes a start, mostly in the form of questions about Florovsky's objections to panentheism, in *Georges Florovsky and the Russian Religious Renaissance*, 149–50.

justification of this vision by reflecting that, after Christ on the cross had been pierced by the soldier's lance,

> The blood and water [from Christ's side] that flowed into the world abide in the world. They sanctify this world as the pledge of its future transfiguration. Through the precious streams of Christ's blood and water that flowed out of his side, all creation was sanctified – heaven and earth, our earthly world, and all the stellar worlds. … The whole world is the chalice of the Holy Grail … The Holy Grail … is not offered for communion but abides in the world as the mysterious holiness of the world, as the power of life, as the fire in which the world will be transfigured into a new heaven and new earth. … All of nature thirsts for the body and blood of Christ and receives them in communion in the blood and water that flowed out of his side when he was on the cross.[176]

The understanding of the relationship of God and creation is only possible in Christ, the Word of God incarnate, the God-man, the union of the Uncreated and the created.

[176]Sergius Bulgakov, 'The Holy Grail' (1932), *The Holy Grail and the Eucharist* (Hudson, NY: Lindisfarne Books, 1997), 33–4.

10

Divine-Humanity, Personhood and Human Rights

Chapter Outline

Two interrelated themes which feature prominently in Orthodox thinking since the late nineteenth century are divine-humanity and the theology of the human person or personhood. Both have their origin in the Russian religious renaissance, especially in the thinking of Vladimir Soloviev (1853–1900), and were inherited by other major figures of the religious renaissance, notably Nicolas Berdyaev (1874–1948) (personhood) and Sergius Bulgakov (1871–1944) (divine-humanity). The theology of the human person was further developed under the umbrella of neopatristic theology, especially by Vladimir Lossky (1903–58), Christos Yannaras (b. 1935) and John Zizioulas (b. 1931), while the more difficult notion of divine-humanity has proven less resilient to the passage of time. Orthodox thinking on human rights, which can be considered an application of the theology of the human person, became a divisive issue in the late twentieth century, and will also be considered in this chapter.

Divine-humanity

Vladimir Soloviev coined the term *bogochelovechestvo* to express the core concept of his philosophical-theological thinking, the subject of his *Lectures on Godmanhood (Divine-Humanity)*

(1878), which heralded the beginning of the Russian religious renaissance.[1] *Bogochelovechestvo* defies accurate definition and translation. It is formed from *Bogochelovek*, 'God-human', a theological and liturgical name for Christ. Standard translations of *bogochelovechestvo* are 'divine-humanity' and 'Godmanhood', but 'God-humanity' or 'God-humanness' are more accurate.[2] Paul Valliere offers a short definition of *bogochelovechestvo* as 'the sum of the conditions, qualities and characteristics united in the person of the God-human', Christ.[3]

Christ is the God-man, but the notion of divine-humanity includes both the downward movement of God towards humanity – and indeed towards creation as whole – exemplified in the Incarnation of the Logos, and also an upward movement of humanity towards God, culminating in theosis or divinization. The Russian religious thinkers sought to grasp all the consequences of the Incarnation of the Son of God, of the incomprehensible union of God and humanity, for the Christian, for all humankind and for the cosmos as a whole. In the mid-nineteenth century, Alexander Bukharev (1822–71) already expressed the central issue: 'Will that spiritual transformation take place among us? and when will it take place? in virtue of which we should begin *to understand all earthly things in terms of Christ*.'[4] Divine-humanity presupposes and confirms faith in God and faith in humanity, in effect restating the patristic idea of the divine image in humanity. Applied to Christ, divine-humanity is consistent with the Christological thinking and doctrines of the early church, in identifying the Person of Christ as the Logos, the Second Person of the Trinity, and in affirming Christ's full divinity and his full humanity. But whereas the central concern of the ancient Fathers of the Church was to reflect on the Incarnation of the Logos and to defend this doctrine against erroneous teachings, for the Russians the Incarnation is taken as a given, and their concern is rather to understand its full cosmic implications, for the divinization of human nature and the sanctification of matter.

Combined with other ideas typical of the Russian religious philosophers, notably all-unity and Sophia, divine-humanity sometimes developed in ways incompatible with patristic theologies of creation and the Incarnation. Soloviev sees Christianity as the fulfilment of all the religious striving of humanity, yet it is more than the sum of all other religions: 'Christianity has its own content, independent of all these elements that have become part of it. This content is uniquely and exclusively Christ. In Christianity as such we find Christ, and only Christ. Although it is often expressed, this truth is not well understood.'[5] In some passages of his *Lectures on Godmanhood*, Soloviev sees Christ in a manner consistent with the main body of patristic Christology: 'The only new teaching [in the Gospel] specifically different from all other religions is Christ's teaching about

---

[1]Vladimir Soloviev, *Lectures on Godmanhood* (1878) (London: Dennis Dobson, 1948; revised trans. Hudson, NY: Lindisfarne Press, 1995).
[2]For a discussion of the difficulty of translating *bogochelovechestvo*, see Paul Valliere, *Modern Russian Theology: Bukharev, Soloviev, Bulgakov: Orthodox Theology in a New Key* (Grand Rapids, MI: Eerdmans, 2000), 11–15. Valliere prefers 'the Humanity of God', which suffers from overstating the human aspect at the expense of the divine.
[3]Valliere, *Modern Russian Theology*, 11.
[4]Cited by Nicolas Berdyaev, *The Russian Idea* (New York: Macmillan, 1948), 185, emphasis added.
[5]Soloviev, *Lectures on Godmanhood*, 105.

himself, his reference to himself as living, incarnate truth: "I am the Way, the Truth and the Life" [Jn 14.6]; "He that believeth in the Son hath everlasting life [Jn 3.36].'"[6]

But Soloviev is pre-eminently a philosopher who sets out to answer the question, 'How, then, is Christ as the life and the Truth to be conceived, or represented to reason?'[7] Soloviev boldly sets out to demonstrate the validity of Trinity 'as much a truth of speculative reason as of Revelation'.[8] Although Soloviev draws on abstract language typical of philosophy to speak of God and Christ, for which he is criticized, he constantly returns to the content of God's being as the living and personal God, and to Christ as the living, personal incarnation of truth, the God-man, without which no revelation of God to man is possible. Thus Christ is the unified expression of divinity in all creation, manifested in a 'particular individual entity':

> The eternal God actualizes himself eternally by actualizing his own content, that is, by actualizing the all. This all, in contrast to the existent God as the absolutely one, is a multiplicity. But this multiplicity is the content of the absolutely one, is conquered by the one, is reduced to unity. … The universal organism, which expresses the absolute content of the divine principle, is preeminently a particular individual entity. This individual entity, the actualized expression of the absolutely existent God, is Christ.[9]

Soloviev refers to the unifying principle in itself as the Logos, whereas the unity produced in creation is Sophia: 'In the divine organism of Christ, the acting, unifying principle, the principle that expresses the unity of that which absolutely is, is obviously the Word, or Logos. The second kind of unity, the produced unity, is called Sophia in Christian theosophy.'[10]

Basil Zenkovsky (1881–1962) identifies Godmanhood (and not all-unity) as the central concept of Soloviev's philosophy, which 'unites Soloviev's cosmology, anthropology and historiosophy'.[11] Zenkovsky sees in Soloviev's metaphysics a determinism which states that God in effect requires creation in order to fulfil himself, in order to be God: 'The dualism of God and the world', writes Zenkovsky of Soloviev's metaphysics, 'is marked by a logically inescapable *necessity*: the "other" (the world) is necessary to God in its "reality"; and evidently this dualism, which is determined by the inner dialectic of God, is primordial.'[12] In this construct, the living Christ of the Gospel runs the risk of being transformed into a cosmic principle reflecting God's fulfilment of himself in creation, resulting in a confusion of Christ and creation, the basis for the accusations of pantheism often levied against Soloviev's system.[13]

---

[6]Ibid.

[7]Ibid., 106.

[8]Cited in Basil Zenkovsky, *A History of Russian Philosophy*, 2 vols (New York: Columbia University Press, 1953), II:497.

[9]Soloviev, *Lectures on Godmanhood*, 106–7.

[10]Ibid., 107–8. Soloviev uses the term 'theosophy' in the general sense of 'wisdom about God', not in the specific sense that it acquired in the religious-philosophical doctrines of the Theosophical Society. Helena Blavatsky's foundational work *The Secret Doctrine* appeared in 1888, ten years after Soloviev's *Lectures*.

[11]Basil Zenkovsky, *A History of Russian Philosophy*, 2 vols (New York: Columbia University Press, 1953), II:483, n. 1.

[12]Zenkovsky, *A History of Russian Philosophy*, II:501.

[13]Basil Zenkovsky and Nicolas Lossky are among those who read pantheism into Soloviev. See the discussion in Ch. 9, 109; 224–5.

Zenkovsky is severe in his assessment of Soloviev's system. Despite Soloviev's sincere Christianity and his intention to 'place Christian principles at the foundation of all of his theoretical constructions',[14] for Zenkovsky he nonetheless distorts, perhaps unintentionally, key Christian doctrines, including that of the Incarnation, turning them into cosmic notions disconnected from their historical context in revelation. In the absence of an ontological distinction between God and the world, signified by the lack of a clear-cut doctrine of creation, Soloviev fuses God, Christ and the world in the metaphysics of total-unity. Zenkovsky says of Soloviev's *bogochelovechestvo*: 'He took the concept of Godmanhood from Christianity, but he transformed it from a concept bound up with the theme of man and history, of sin and salvation, into a general metaphysical concept, thus emptying it almost completely of its Christian content.'[15]

In addition to its importance as the central idea in Soloviev's reflections, divine-humanity figures highly in the thought of Nicolas Berdyaev, Sergius Bulgakov and other philosophical, theological and literary figures of the Russian religious renaissance. Berdyaev offers a succinct summary of the key notions associated with divine-humanity in a fashion consistent with traditional Orthodox thought on the Incarnation, extending the principle of the Incarnation potentially to all humanity:

> In the Person of Jesus Christ there took place the union of divine and human nature and the God-man appeared. The same thing ought to take place in humanity, in human society and in history. The realization of Godmanhood, of divine-human life, presupposes the activity of men. … Christianity is not only belief in God; it is also belief in man, and in the possibility of a revelation of the divine in man. There exists a commensurability between God and man and on that account only is a revelation of God to man possible. … In Jesus Christ the God-man, there is in an individual Person a perfect union of two natures – divine and human. This ought to take place collectively in mankind, in human society. … Godmanhood is a possibility because human nature is consubstantial with the human nature of Christ.[16]

In this light, divine-humanity encompasses in one central dynamic idea the fundamental Orthodox doctrines of the Incarnation, the two natures of Christ and *theosis*, the possibility of human divinization in and through Christ.

Divine-humanity also crowns Bulgakov's theology, contained in his great trilogy, published under the general title of 'Divine-Humanity'.[17] Each of the six volumes of Bulgakov's minor and major trilogies explores divine-human relations in a specific context: in and through Mary, the Mother of God (*The Burning Bush*); the relationship of John the Forerunner and Jesus (*The Friend of the Bridegroom*); the interaction of angels and humans (*Jacob's Ladder*); Christ himself as redeemer (*The Lamb of God*); the sanctifying Spirit (*The Comforter*) and in and through the church and eschatology (*The Bride of the Lamb*). Unlike conventional *Dogmatica* inspired by scholastic

---

[14]Zenkovsky, *A History of Russian Philosophy*, II:530.

[15]Ibid.

[16]Berdyaev, *The Russian Idea*, 91; 172–3.

[17]For an overview of Bulgakov's dogmatics, see Valliere, Chapter 13, 'Dogmatics of the Humanity of God', *Modern Russian Theology*, 291–346.

models, Bulgakov's dogmatics does not begin with a general treatise on the nature and properties of God and he only discusses the Father specifically in an epilogue to *The Comforter*.[18] Throughout his trilogies, Bulgakov appeals to the notion of Sophia to elaborate the positive content of divine relations with creation, especially humanity. As we saw in Chapter 10, in Bulgakov, Sophia is the rite of passage, the hallway, the key by which God and creation enter into relation with each other. This sophiological shadow, which looms over Bulgakov's theology and is edged, in the eyes of some, with overtones of pantheism and determinism,[19] rendered his often brilliant, often obscure, but always challenging dogmatic explorations difficult to accept for some of his contemporaries and for later generations of Orthodox theologians.

In his elaboration of the Christology of divine-humanity, Bulgakov takes Chalcedonian Christology as his starting point. He argues that, whereas Chalcedon's dogmatic declaration of the two natures in the one Person of Christ and its *negative* formulae concerning the union (without confusion, without change, without division, without separation) set the outer boundaries for Christological reflection, it is necessary for Christian theology to elaborate the *positive* content of the Incarnation:

> [The Chalcedonian formula] remained unclarified and unrealized in theological thought. It was more a schema than a doctrine. … The dogma is silent, however, on the positive interrelation of the two natures. … the patristic thought of the epoch … failed to elucidate the *mode* of the union of the natures in relation to one hypostasis. … Patristic theology thus did not find its way to a doctrine of the God-Man and Divine-humanity.[20]

The provision of a positive content to Chalcedon's negative formulations is the task that Bulgakov set for himself in his Christology. Valliere sees in this task 'an appreciation of the humanistic implications of the doctrine',[21] but this perspective focuses too narrowly on the 'humanity' side of divine-humanity and insufficiently on the 'divine' side. Bulgakov sought to maintain equilibrium between the two. Bulgakov's Christology is inclined to see Christ not only as 'a historical individual', but also as a cosmic figure incorporating all humanity, a notion which can be seen as originating in Paul's reference to Christ as the 'Second Man' and the 'Last Adam' (1 Cor. 15.45-48). Christ is 'Man in the sense of Universal Man, and his personality contained all human forms; it was the All-Personality.'[22] While in this formulation, we can hear an echo of Soloviev's all-unity and his vision of Christ's pan-humanity, Bulgakov does not depart from the historical Christ, but rather assigns cosmic implications to the Christ of the Scriptures.

For Bulgakov, the positive content of the Christological dogma of Chalcedon lies primarily in divine kenosis, the voluntary self-emptying of the Son of God in becoming incarnate and assuming human nature. The dominant image of Christ in Russian Thought has been the 'kenotic Christ': the Son

---

[18]Sergius Bulgakov, 'Epilogue: The Father', *The Comforter* (1936) (Grand Rapids, MI: Eerdmans, 2004), 359–94.
[19]See especially the fine analysis in Brandon Gallaher, *Freedom and Necessity in Modern Trinitarian Theology* (Oxford: Oxford University Press, 2016), especially Part I, 'God as both Absolute and Absolute-Relative in Sergii Bulgakov', 45–116.
[20]Sergius Bulgakov, *The Lamb of God* (1933) (Grand Rapids, MI: Eerdmans, 2008), 57; 195; 209; 210.
[21]Valliere, *Modern Russian Theology*, 297.
[22]Bulgakov, *The Lamb of God*, 203.

of God, who, by his Incarnation, takes on the lowly appearance of a servant, laying aside the prerogatives of his divinity and allowing himself to be humiliated, to suffer at the hands of his own creatures, to be crucified and put to death. This aspect of Russian thought takes its cue from St Paul:

> Christ Jesus, who, being in the form of God, thought it not robbery to be equal with God, but made himself of no reputation, and took upon him the form of a servant, and was made in the likeness of men. And being found in the fashion of a man, he humbled himself and became obedient unto death – even the death of the cross (Phil 2:5-8).

The kenotic Christ is the prime Russian image of Christ in popular piety and in literature. Paul Evdokimov writes:

> The religious ideal of a people is formed from its very personal vision of God, from the artistic and iconographic image of Christ. There is a Flemish Christ, a Spanish Christ, a Greek Christ. There is also a Russian Christ, who has an essentially evangelical appearance under the kenotic aspect as the humble Brother of the humiliated, who is always with the poor, the infirm and the suffering.[23]

Russian Christology attaches considerable importance to God's identification with the human condition. For instance, the Christology of Mikhail Tareev (1867–1934), professor of moral theology at the Theological Academy of Moscow prior to the revolution, is centred on the double kenosis of Christ, both the voluntary renunciation of his divine glory and power and the taking on of human abasement and suffering. Similarly, Simeon Frank (1877–1950) writes: 'The idea of God who comes into the world and voluntarily shares the world's suffering – the idea of the suffering God-Man – is *the only possible theodicy*, the only convincing 'justification' of God.'[24]

Bulgakov develops a kenotic Christology under the sophiological umbrella in the core of *The Lamb of God* (1933) under the heading 'The Humiliation of the Lord (the Kenosis)'.[25] For Bulgakov, the Incarnation, from conception to death, is a kenotic act: 'For the human essence to be united with the divine essence without being dissolved or annihilated, Divinity had to descend, to diminish itself to the human essence.'[26] Faithful to the dogma of the two natures in Christ, Bulgakov affirms that, 'In becoming man, God does not stop being God'; rather, 'God renounces something, abandons something, in order to become accessible to man.'[27] To characterize what it is that Christ abandons in the Incarnation, Bulgakov appeals to a distinction between *divine nature* or 'God *according to* himself', and *divine glory*, which he also calls *divine life* and God '*for* himself'.[28]

---

[23]Paul Evdokimov, *Le Christ dans la pensée russe* (Christ in Russian Thought) (Paris: Le Cerf, 1970), 41. The classic study of the kenotic Christ is Nadejda Gorodetsky, *The Humiliated Christ in Russian Thought* (London: SPCK, 1938). See also Michel Evdokimov, *L'Image du Christ dans la tradition et la littérature russes* (The Image of Christ in Russian Tradition and Literature) (Paris: Desclée, 2007); and Elisabeth Behr-Sigel, 'The Kenotic, the Humble Christ', in Michael Plekon and Sarah E. Hinlicky, eds., *Discerning the Signs of the Times: The Vision of Elisabeth Behr-Sigel* (Crestwood, NY: St Vladimir's Seminary Press, 2001).

[24]Simeon Frank, *God with Us: Three Mediations* (1942) (London: Jonathan Cape, 1946), 208.

[25]Bulgakov, *The Lamb of God*, 213–47. Bulgakov drew on German and British kenotic theology in developing his kenotic Christology. See Paul Gavrilyuk, 'The Kenotic Theology of Sergius Bulgakov', *Scottish Journal of Theology*, 58, 3 (2005).

[26]Bulgakov, *The Lamb of God*, 219.

[27]Ibid., 220.

[28]See Bulgakov, *The Lamb of God*, 221; 224.

For Bulgakov, Christ does not abandon the divine nature, but rather the divine glory or life: 'While preserving his divine nature, the Second hypostasis thus abandons the divine life.'[29]

Although Bulgakov's Christology has not attracted as much criticism as his sophiology, Vladimir Lossky, for one, targets Bulgakov's Christology in his 1936 critique of sophiology (*Spor o Sofii*): 'Fr. Bulgakov's Christology bleeds into a cosmic panchristism, which absorbs both the Holy Spirit and the church.' More specifically, Lossky accuses Bulgakov of 'neo-Apollinarianism' for teaching that

> the Logos-spirit replaces the human spirit in Christ. As a spirit which is simultaneously both divine and human, the Logos is turned into some sort of intermediary nature – a single spiritual centre gathered into a new union – not only hypostatic union, but a natural union as well – divinity and humanity.[30]

Lossky is in effect accusing Bulgakov of conceiving Christ as a fusion of divinity and humanity, which would be contrary to Chalcedonian Christology. Bulgakov's Christology certainly raises doctrinal questions, such as his assertion that in 'becoming man', the 'hypostasis of the Logos, ceasing to be a divine hypostasis for himself while remaining such in his objective being, becomes a *human hypostasis*'.[31] Prima facie, this language appears to diverge from typical Chalcedonian Christological terminology, which does not refer to a human hypostasis in Christ, nor of the one Person of Christ as both divine and human, but rather speaks of the one divine Person of Christ in two natures. For Bulgakov, this is an aspect of the kenosis of the Son: 'The Second Hypostasis empties himself of his divinity. He abandons his divinity – not as a source of intratrinitarian interhypostatic life, but as the source of his personal divine being.'[32] Bulgakov is attempting to transcend a lingering tendency to assign 'divine' and 'human' characteristics to one or the other of Christ's *natures,* rather than to the one *Person* of Christ. Despite potential ambiguities in his language, by his strict adherence to the notion of the one Person of Christ, Bulgakov cannot be faulted for proto-Nestorianism.

The suffering of God

While Russian theology and spirituality highlight the humility of God, they do not linger on Christ's passion as such, because Christ's passion and death on the cross are always associated with the Resurrection. It is more the idea that God should lower himself to the status of a creature and identify himself with the poor and the suffering that attracts the Russian spirit. This duality is clear in the icons of the Crucifixion: the Body of Christ on the Cross is not a corpse, but is already spiritualized, filled with the promise of the Resurrection, and is often accompanied by ministering

---

[29]Bulgakov, *The Lamb of God*, 225.
[30]Vladimir Lossky, *Spor o sofii* (The Dispute about Sophia) (1935) (Moskva: Izdatel'stvo Sviato-Vladimirskogo Bratstva, 1996). Unpublished translation by William Kevin Fisher, *The Sophia Controversy: Protopriest S. Bulgakov's 'Report' and the Meaning of the Decree of the Moscow Patriarchate.*
[31]Bulgakov, *The Lamb of God*, 229.
[32]Ibid.

angels astonished to see their God stretched out on a Cross. The identification of Christ, the God-man, with the poor and the suffering – both in a broad sense of humanity as a whole, in exile from the 'house of the Father', and more specifically with the poor – found a sympathetic ear among the religious philosophers eager to establish their credentials with the Russian lower classes, and was reflected in the art and literature of the Russian religious renaissance.

A theme related to divine kenosis, furthered among Russian intellectuals in exile, is the notion of the suffering of God. This raises philosophical and theological issues: While Christ can and did suffer in his human nature, does God suffer in his divinity? Do human actions cause God to suffer? Does God suffer with suffering humanity? The starting point of theological reflections on God's suffering is the philosophical notion of divine unchangeability or impassibility, a notion prominent in dogmatic theology as inherited from Greek philosophy. Yet at the same time the Old Testament contains numerous references to divine affliction in the face of human failings and suffering.[33] These have often been interpreted as a sort of residual anthropomorphism, which is trumped by the doctrines of divine transcendence, immutability, impassibility and perfection. In this light, God cannot suffer in his divinity, because suffering implies physical and psychological pain and emotion, which are the changing characteristics of material and sentient creatures but not of the transcendent and perfect God. Thus, it was often argued, Christ was subject to physical distress and suffering (he was hungry, thirsty, tired, etc.) and even psychological pain (he cries over Lazarus's death, sweats blood in Gethsemane) *in his humanity*, but this does not affect the impassibility of *his divine nature*, eternally united with the Father and the Holy Spirit in the bliss of perichoresis. John of Damascus summarizes this doctrine:

> God's Word himself, then, endured all things in his flesh, while his divine nature, which alone is impassible, remained unaffected. For, when the one Christ made up of both divinity and humanity suffered, the passible part of him suffered, because it was of its nature to suffer, but the impassible did not suffer with it. Thus, since the soul is passible, it does feel pain and suffer with the body when the body is hurt, although it itself is not hurt. The divinity, however, being impassible, does not suffer with the body.[34]

The idea of the 'suffering God' has been explored by modern Orthodox theologians. Bulgakov argues that Christ suffers not only in his humanity, but also in his divinity, notably during the Passion: 'The Divinity of the Lord Jesus Christ spiritually co-suffers in relation to the fleshly passion of the hypostatic Word, for the nature cannot fail to suffer if its hypostasis suffers.'[35] He grounds this contentious assertion on the unity of Person in Christ, and in particular on the Chalcedonian formula that Christ's two natures are united 'without confusion': there cannot be incoherence between Christ's human nature and his divine nature, nor for that matter between the suffering of the Son and the suffering of the Father and the Holy Spirit, because of the unity and 'connection of

---

[33]See references in Lev Gillet, 'Does God Suffer', *Sobornost*, 3, 15 (1954), 117; and Kallistos Ware, *The Orthodox Way*, rev. ed. (Crestwood, NY: St Vladimir's Seminary Press, 1995), 63.

[34]John of Damascus, *An Exact Exposition of the Orthodox Faith* (Washington, DC: Catholic University of America Press, 1958), III:26, 331.

[35]Bulgakov, *The Lamb of God*, 259.

love in the Holy Trinity'.[36] Bulgakov rejects the philosophical notion of divine impassibility as 'an abstraction' and erroneous, 'for in creating the world and providing for it, God interacts with the world and enters into a relation with the world process and with human freedom.'[37]

The theme of the 'suffering God' was taken up by several French converts in Bulgakov's entourage, especially Fr Lev Gillet (1893–1980) and Elisabeth Behr-Sigel (1907–2005), and later, by Metropolitan Kallistos Ware (b. 1934). Olivier Clément (1921-2009) refers to Lev Gillet as a 'great theologian of the Suffering God and Limitless Love'.[38] In the face of human suffering, Gillet, Behr-Sigel and Ware, pastors as well as theologians, boldly ask: Is the traditional notion of divine impassibility adequate in the light of human suffering on the one hand, and infinite divine love on the other? Is Christ's suffering limited in time to his physical presence on earth? Or is Christ the Lamb of God immolated from all eternity?[39]

The issue arises dramatically in the pastoral context: Is God indifferent to the real present suffering of his creation, especially men and women? Lev Gillet puts his finger on the pastoral dilemma: 'Do we have the right to say to the man or woman who is suffering: "God himself, *at this very moment*, is suffering what you suffer, and is overcoming it?"'[40] Gillet presents several arguments to support his contention of the Suffering God. First, God's knowledge of human suffering is more than an abstract awareness; rather, it is an intimate comprehension of this suffering. Secondly, divine immanence in creation places God at the heart of suffering. Thirdly, God suffers actively and voluntarily – an apparent breach in divine perfection, but one which does not compromise it: 'God's suffering is divine love *freely creating* its own burden.'[41] Gillet's last argument is derived from the notion of time, human and divine. Whereas our notion and experience of time is a series of successive events, in God 'there are neither events nor history. … God's eternity is a single point, in which everything is present. … an eternal present.' Gillet applies this reflection to Christ's passion and death: 'The crucifixion is more than an event in time. The cross transcends time. … Even though historically the Passion came before the Resurrection, yet Good Friday and Easter are but one in the eternity of the divine life. God triumphs over suffering *through* suffering.'[42] At the same time, Gillet recognizes the inadequacy of human language to refer to divine suffering: 'The suffering of God is a mystery about which we can only speak by analogy and approximation.' He continues:

> The statement 'God suffers' does not describe the same experience as the statement 'I suffer.'… The suffering of God is a reality, as much as and more than the suffering of man. … The assertion

---

[36]Ibid., 260.

[37]Ibid., 260–1.

[38]Olivier Clément, 'Le père Lev Gillet, Grand théologien du Dieu souffrant et de l'Amour sans limites' (Fr Lev Gillet, A Great Theologian of the Suffering God and Unlimited Love) in Un Moine de l'Église d'Orient (Lev Gillet), *Au Cœur de la fournaise* (In the Heart of the Furnace) (Paris: Le Sel de la Terre/Le Cerf, 1998), 9.

[39]See Bulgakov, *The Lamb of God*, 129, 171–2, 338 and passim; and Bulgakov, *The Comforter*, 219.

[40]Gillet, 'Does God Suffer', 112. Kallistos Ware picks up this exact question in *The Orthodox Way*, 63.

[41]Gillet, 'Does God Suffer', 118.

[42]Ibid., 119. The last sentence is a reformulation of part of the Pascal troparion: 'Christ is risen from the dead, trampling down death by death'.

> 'God suffers' is the only possible translation, though a miserably inadequate one, of something which exists in God – and which is God in God and not man in God.[43]

Orthodox thinking is divided on the subject of divine suffering. Metropolitan Kallistos Ware has been taken to task for expounding on the notion of the Suffering God. 'Our misery causes grief to God,' he writes, 'the tears of God are joined to those of man.'[44] The main critique is that Ware (and others), despite the qualification that we need to be wary of 'ascribing human feelings to God in a crude or unqualified way',[45] departs from mainstream patristic teaching which stresses divine impassibility. As Hieromonk Patapios, a critic of the idea of the suffering of God, observes, 'The attribution of human emotions to God, whether of a negative kind or borne of sympathy for human suffering, is foreign to Orthodox theology.'[46] At the same time, Patapios leaves the door open, unintentionally perhaps, to Gillet's apophatic approach to divine suffering: 'The impassive nature of the Godhead does not suggest insensitivity, of course, but moves us away from imagining that mere human emotions or sentimentality are adequate to grasp or express the expansive, transcendent aspects of the Godhead, including Divine Love.'[47]

Personhood

The theology of the human person or personalism, one of the richest notions in modern Orthodox theology, was a major intuition of the Russian religious renaissance and was fully appropriated in neopatristic theology. The theological notion of the person originates in the theology of the Greek Fathers of the fourth century. At that time, nascent Christian theology was grappling with the tension between the idea of God as the Absolute of Greek philosophy, immobile and unchanging and the biblical revelation of God as the Creator who acts in his creation, who is involved in human affairs, and who in the 'last days' sends his only Son to become incarnate in human flesh 'for the life of the world'. The Fathers were also faced with the dilemma of reconciling God as One (Greek philosophy and the Old Testament), yet at the same time as three: Father, Son and Holy Spirit (the New Testament). During the Trinitarian and Christological debates of the fourth and fifth centuries, the ancient Fathers distinguished 'nature' (*ousia* or *physis*, that which is shared or common to the Father, Son and Holy Spirit) from 'person' in God (*hypostasis*, that which distinguishes the Persons from each other). This crucial distinction provided the basis for affirming that Father, Son and Holy Spirit are distinct Persons of the Holy Trinity, of one and the same divine nature (*homoousios*), and that Christ is one divine Person in two natures, divine and human. But the Fathers did not apply

---

[43]Gillet, 'Does God Suffer', 119. See also Gillet's meditation on divine suffering in A Monk of the Eastern Church, *Jesus: A Dialogue with the Saviour* (New York: Desclée, 1963), 163–9.
[44]See Ware, *The Orthodox Way*, 63.
[45]Ware, *The Orthodox Way*, 63.
[46]Hieromonk Patapios (Center for Traditionalist Orthodox Studies, Etna, CA), review of Kallistos Ware, *The Orthodox Way*, in *Orthodox Tradition*, 16, 3–4 (1999). Online: http://orthodoxinfo.com/phronema/review_tow.aspx (27 March 2015).
[47]Patapios, review of Kallistos Ware, *The Orthodox Way*.

the idea of personhood to individual human beings – this was not a significant issue in classical patristic times. As Olivier Clément notes: 'Fully grounded in Biblical revelation, the theme of the person received its theological expression in the Fathers of the fourth century: but at the level of divine existence, not yet of human existence.'[48]

The notion of human beings as persons rose to the top of the philosophical-theological agenda in modern times as a result of the cumulative effect of several factors. These include first, the Renaissance, the Enlightenment and the charters of human rights of the American and French Revolutions, all of which appeared to favour individual existence; secondly, the rise of impersonalist philosophies and ideologies (Marxism, Nazism and other extreme forms of nationalism), which denigrate or deny the value of human person or which reduce the person to one aspect of human existence (typically social or economic class, race, ethnicity and/or religion); thirdly, the massive violations of human rights in the twentieth century (communism, Nazism and dictatorships and fundamentalist regimes of all sorts) and finally the growing fascination in the West and in Russia with Oriental philosophies which express the final end of human existence as the fusion of the individual with an impersonal divine principle – the dissolution of the human person.

The Russian religious philosophers vigorously applied the notion of 'person' to human existence. For them, as for later Orthodox theologians, the personal existence of every human is closely associated with the biblical and patristic teaching that humans are made in the image of God, Just as God exists as three Persons, so humanity exists as a multiplicity of persons. Olivier Clément writes: 'It is, it seems to me, to the honour of Russian theology and religious philosophy in the nineteenth and twentieth centuries to have realized this approach, by distancing themselves as much from individualism as from mystical and totalitarian fusions.'[49]

The development of personalism in modern Orthodox thought can be traced to the Slavophiles of the mid-nineteenth century. Alexis Khomiakov (1804–60) was primarily interested in the notion of the church as community (*sobornost'*), but his reflection also 'insisted on the person as freedom and love, love constituting the real content of freedom'.[50] Ivan Kireevsky (1806–56), in his 'Fragments', published after his death, outlines some of the main ideas underlying personalism, in contrast with a rationalistic approach to personhood:

> For rationalistic thinking the living personality[51] dissolves into abstract laws of self-development, or it is a product of incidental principles, and in both cases it loses its actual meaning. ... Rationalistic

[48]Olivier Clément, 'Aperçus sur la théologie de la personne dans la "diaspora" russe en France' (Overview of the theology of the person in the Russian 'diaspora' in France), *Mille Ans de christianisme russe 988-1988* (A Thousand Years of Russian Christianity) (Paris: YMCA-Press, 1989), 303.

[49]Clément, 'Aperçus sur la théologie de la personne', 303.

[50]Olivier Clément, 'Le personnalisme chrétien dans la pensée russe' (Christian personalism in Russian thought), *Contacts*, 40, 143 (1988), 209.

[51]The unfortunate use of the word 'personality' in many translations of Orthodox theologians creates confusion, in that 'personality' corresponds more with the psychological notion of the external 'mask' which partially conceals the true inner self of a person. In this sense, 'personality' is closer to the ancient meaning of the Greek *prosopon*, the actor's mask, than to the theological sense of *hypostasis* applied to the divine Persons. In most cases, 'personhood' (although abstract), or simply 'person', would be more accurate renderings of the intent of modern Orthodox writers than 'personality'.

> thinking is incapable of a consciousness of the living personality of the Godhead and this personality's living relationship with the human personality. Consciousness of the relationship between the living divine personality and the human personality serves as a foundation for faith – or, more correctly, faith *is* that very consciousness, more or less clear and unmediated.[52]

The main figures of the Russian religious renaissance, in particular Pavel Florensky (1882–1937), Sergius Bulgakov and Nicolas Berdyaev, went on to affirm the uniqueness and hence the absolute value of the human person, an extension of the theological understanding of the Divine Persons and of love as the basis of intra-Trinitarian relationships.[53] As we saw in Chapter 4, their personalism constituted a Christian response to the impersonal, positivist, reductionist and nihilist philosophies, especially Marxism, competing for the Russian soul prior to the revolution.

Personalist theology achieved a fuller expression in the work of the Russian thinkers in exile and in later leading representatives of Orthodox theology such as Christos Yannaras, John Zizioulas and Kallistos Ware. There is a remarkable continuity in the development of ideas on what it means philosophically and theologically to be a person. Olivier Clément (1921–2009), referring to Nicolas Berdyaev, Sergius Bulgakov and Vladimir Lossky, says: 'These men conflicted with each other on other subjects. But they concur entirely concerning the person. I would not dare say: *consensus patrum* – but perhaps one should, because the Spirit is not exhausted, especially in times of distress and of lucidity.'[54] Others, such as Simeon Frank, can be added to this trio. Frank writes, for example:

> The true meaning of the Christian faith … lies in the direct relation between the idea of God and that of the reality and absolute value of the human personality. Christianity is a personalistic and anthropological religion. In it man for the first time *finds himself*, finds rest and security for that which forms his inmost unutterable essence, inevitably homeless in the world where it finds no understanding, sympathy or mercy at the tribunal of reason and objective rationalistic morality.[55]

Among the leading members of the Russian religious renaissance, Berdyaev is the pre-eminent philosopher of the person. As Clément writes, 'From beginning to end Nicolas Berdyaev's thought is a thought of the person.'[56] Berdyaev writes: 'The entire world is nothing in comparison with human personality, with the unique person of a man, with his unique fate.'[57] He continues: 'If man were not a person … then he would be like other things in the world and there would be nothing unusual about him. … Personality is like nothing else in the world, there is nothing with which it

[52] Ivan Kireevsky, 'Fragments', in Boris Jakim and Robert Bird, eds., *On Spiritual Unity: A Slavophile Reader* (Hudson, NY: Lindisfarne Books, 1998), 284–5.

[53] For an overview of personalism in modern Russian thought, see the two articles by Olivier Clément cited above and Aristotle Papanikolaou, 'Personhood and Its Exponents in Twentieth-Century Orthodox Theology', in Mary Cunningham and Elizabeth Theokritoff, eds., *The Cambridge Companion to Orthodox Christian Theology* (Cambridge: Cambridge University Press, 2008). Clément also stresses the importance of Feodor Dostoyevsky and Victor Nesmelov, in addition to Florensky, Bulgakov and Berdyaev, in the development of Russian personalism.

[54] Clément, 'Aperçus sur la théologie de la personne', 304.

[55] Frank, *God With Us*, 140–1.

[56] Clément, 'Le personnalisme chrétien', 305.

[57] Nicolas Berdyaev, *Slavery and Freedom* (London: Geoffrey Bles, 1943), 20.

can be compared, nothing which can be placed on a level with it.'[58] For Berdyaev the uniqueness of human personhood and the human vocation is made visible in the human face:

> The face of man is the summit of the cosmic process, the greatest of its offspring, but it cannot be the offspring of cosmic forces only, it presupposes the action of a spiritual force, which raises it above the sphere of the forces of nature. The face of man is the most amazing thing in the life of the world; another world shines out through it. It is the entrance of personality into the world process, with its uniqueness, its singleness, its unrepeatability.[59]

Both Pavel Florensky and Sergius Bulgakov sought to express the basis of the uniqueness of the person, emphasizing in particular that the person is above any rational category, making the person philosophically 'incomprehensible', not irrational, but beyond rationality, in the realm of mystery. Florensky writes in *The Pillar and Ground of the Truth* (1914):

> The personal character of a person, this living unity of his self-building activity, the creative transcending of his self-enclosedness, constitutes his nonsubsumability in any concept, his 'incomprehensibility', and therefore his unacceptability for rationalism. It is the victory over the law of identity that raises a person above a lifeless thing and makes him a living centre of activity.[60]

Bulgakov writes along the same lines a few years later in *The Unfading Light* (1917):

> Humankind is transcendent to the world and in this sense is free of the world, is nonworld. It is not exhausted by any *what*, is not defined by any definition, but is, like God, an absolute *not-what*. It places outside itself and opposes to itself any worldly giveness as a certain *what*, while remaining free of it and transcendent to it. Moreover, *humankind is transcendent to its own s*elf in all of its empirical or psychological giveness, in every self-definition, which leaves the peace of its absoluteness unbroken and its depths not muddied.[61]

Bulgakov stresses the apophatic nature of human personhood:

> What is a person? What is the I? No answer can be given to this question other than with a gesture that points inward. *A person is indefinable*, for it is always being defined with everything, remaining however *above* all of its conditions or determinations. Person is the unknowable mystery inherent to each, an unfathomable abyss, an immeasurable depth.[62]

Berdyaev contrasts the natural understanding of the human individual with the philosophical-theological notion of the person:

> Man, the only man known to biology and sociology, man as a natural being and a social being, is the offspring of the world and of the processes which take place in the world. But personality, man as a person, is not a child of the world, he is of another origin. … Personality is not nature, it does not

[58]Berdyaev, *Slavery and Freedom*, 21
[59]Ibid., 31.
[60]Pavel Florensky, *The Pillar and Ground of the Truth: An Essay in Orthodox Theodicy in Twelve Letters* (1914) (Princeton, NJ: Princeton University Press, 1997), 59–60.
[61]Sergius Bulgakov, *Unfading Light: Contemplations and Speculations* (1917) (Grand Rapids, MI: Eerdmans, 2012), 287.
[62]Bulgakov, *Unfading Light*, 290.

> belong to the objective hierarchy of nature, as a subordinate part of it. … Man is a personality not by nature but by spirit. By nature he is only an individual.[63]

The distinction between person and individual is an essential aspect of a robust Orthodox theology of the human person. While in ordinary parlance 'person' and 'individual' are often synonymous, the theological distinction between them is a powerful affirmation of the uniqueness of the human person created in the image of the Persons of the Trinity. An individual, on the other hand, is simply one example among many of the same type or species, in scientific terminology. Individuals can be counted and classified on the basis of similar characteristics, but persons cannot be, because they are unique. The distinction between 'person' and 'individual' is an important feature of Berdyaev's thinking; the divine image is found in human personhood, not in individuality:

> Individuality is a naturalistic and biological category, while personality is a religious and spiritual one. … An individual is part of the species, it springs from the species although it can isolate itself and come into conflict with it. The individual is produced by the biological generic process; it is born and it dies. But personality is not generated, it is created by God. It is God's idea, God's conception, which springs up in eternity. … Personality is the image and likeness of God in man and this is why it rises above the natural life. … The value of personality is the highest hierarchical value in the world, a value of the spiritual order.[64]

What Florensky, Bulgakov and Berdyaev sought to characterize as the essence of personhood, Vladimir Lossky pithily articulated by appealing directly to the familiar patristic categories of nature and person, in a formula which may be summarized as 'the irreducibility of person to nature':

> It will be impossible for us to form a concept of the human person and we will have to content ourselves with saying: 'person' signifies the irreducibility of man to his nature – 'irreducibility' and not 'something irreducible' or 'something which makes man irreducible to his nature' precisely because it cannot be a question here of 'something' distinct from 'another nature' but of *someone* who is distinct from his own nature, of someone who goes beyond his nature while still containing it, who makes it exist as human nature by this overstepping and yet does not exist in himself beyond the nature which he 'enhypostasizes' and which he constantly exceeds.[65]

John Zizioulas reiterates this idea in his book *Being as Communion*: 'I have excluded every possibility of regarding the person as an expression or emanation of the substance or nature of man (or even of God himself as "nature").'[66] If nature does not determine or circumscribe the

---

[63]Berdyaev, *Slavery and Freedom*, 21.

[64]Nicolas Berdyaev, *The Destiny of Man* (1931) (London: Geoffrey Bles, 1937), 71–2.

[65]Vladimir Lossky, 'The Theological Notion of the Human Person', *In the Image and Likeness of God* (Crestwood, NY: St Vladimir's Seminary Press, 1974), 120. Lossky says much the same thing in *The Mystical Theology of the Eastern Church*: 'The idea of the person implies freedom vis-à-vis the nature. The person is free from its nature, is not determined by it.' *The Mystical Theology of the Eastern Church* (1944) (Crestwood, NY: St Vladimir's Seminary Press, 1976), 122.

[66]John Zizioulas, 'Personhood and Being', in *Being as Communion: Studies in Personhood and the Church* (Crestwood, NY: St Vladimir's Seminary Press, 1985), 59.

person, what or rather who a person is remains a mystery, akin to the mystery of the divine Persons of the Trinity, the model for human personhood. The ancient Fathers struggled hard to identify what in humans constitutes the divine image, coming up with various answers, such as rationality, the human spirit and freedom, but modern Orthodox anthropology would be inclined to say that human personhood is the highest aspect of the divine image in humanity, which Christos Yannaras aptly characterizes as the personal 'mode of existence' and 'being-as-person'.[67] The Father, Son and Holy Spirit *and* humans exist as persons, unique and irreplaceable. John Zizioulas writes: 'The perfect man is consequently only he who is authentically a person, that is, he who subsists, who possess a "mode of existence" which is constituted as being, *in precisely the manner in which God also subsists as being*.'[68]

Berdyaev and others see a dynamic aspect in the theological notion of person, modelled on the classic patristic distinction between the divine image and the divine likeness. According to Berdyaev, a person can only exist in relation to other persons: 'From the point of view of the individual, personality is a task to be achieved.'[69] Full personhood can only be accomplished in interaction with other persons and, as in the Trinity, love is the basis for true interpersonal relations, a notion emphasized by later Orthodox theologians. Yannaras also advocates the notion of relation to other persons as the key to the full achievement of personhood:

> The actualization of personal relation is made complete … only in the fact of interpersonal communion, only with reference to supreme (that is *essential*) otherness. … The person represents the unique power of approaching the *mode* of existence of beings, beyond any objective, i.e., conventional, determination.[70]

Zizioulas draws a parallel between divine and human personal existence precisely in terms of relationship:

> Both in the case of God and in that of human beings the identity of a person is recognized and posited clearly and unequivocally, but this is so only in and through a *relationship*, and not through an objective ontology in which this identity would be *isolated*, pointed at and described in itself. Personal identity is totally lost if isolated, for its ontological condition is relationship.[71]

While the Greek personalists and others such as Kallistos Ware stress the relational aspect of personhood, they also emphasize the uniqueness of each human person, as in Yannaras:

> We characterize as personal this mode of existence that becomes known to us 'by participation', primarily because it corresponds to the experience we have of human personal existence. We know each human personal hypothesis only by participating in the energies that reveal its existential otherness – in speech, in thought, in imagination, in judgement, in intention, in the capacity to

---

[67]See Christos Yannaras, *Person and Eros* (Brookline, MA: Holy Cross Orthodox Press, 2007), 19.
[68]Zizioulas, *Being as Communion*, 55.
[69]Berdyaev, *The Destiny of Man*, 71.
[70]Yannaras, *Person and Eros*, 18.
[71]John Zizioulas, 'On Being a Person: Towards and Ontology of Personhood', in *Communion and Otherness: Further Studies in Personhood and the Church* (London: T&T Clark, 2006), 112.

> create, to love, to be original etc. ... Each human being expresses himself, thinks, imagines, judges, wills, creates and loves in a unique way or mode, distinct and unparalleled.[72]

The return to Christ and to the church of key members of the Russian intelligentsia at the beginning of the twentieth century was a triumph of the affirmation of human freedom in the Christian tradition. They saw no inconsistency between their commitment to human freedom and their adherence to a church grounded on central dogmas and the idea of tradition, although, as we also saw in Chapter 4, some members of the 'new religious consciousness' were unwilling to return to the institutional church for these reasons. The affirmation of human freedom in the face of all forms of determinism is evident in the 1909 *Vekhi* collection of essays, as the Christian thinkers warned the intelligentsia of the dangers of rigid Marxist and revolutionary philosophies which had scant regard for freedom. Nicolas Zernov (1898–1980) writes in this regard: 'They [the converted Marxists] remained fearless fighters against hypocrisy, religious bigotry and intolerance. They firmly defended the dignity and significance of the individual and the importance of social justice.'[73]

Berdyaev's thought, as we saw, is largely dominated by the notion of the human being as person and its essential corollary, freedom, the power and possibility to choose, to make free decisions among alternatives. Berdyaev concurs with the description of him as 'the philosopher of freedom'.[74] In Christianity, the notion of freedom is founded on the biblical account of the creation of man, the Garden of Eden and the fall and exile of humanity: humans have the freedom to choose, either to associate with God, or to turn from God. The Russian thinkers added to this biblical foundation a revolt against all forms of determinism originating from the West – whether theological, as in Calvinist predestination, or philosophical, as in Marxist determinism. God is not determined by any contingency and he has granted an image of divine freedom to his creature endowed with consciousness and personhood. The Russian spirit oscillates between a fatalistic submission to authority and *volnitsa*, a spirit of revolt against authority, often reflected on a personal level as licentiousness. Against a long history of authoritarian rule to contain this spirit of revolt, the Russian religious philosophers affirm the importance of personal freedom, itself an aspect of the divine image in man. Feodor Dostoyevsky was the prophet of freedom and served as an inspiration for the religious philosophers and theologians. The fate of the main personalities in *The Brothers Karamazov*, for instance, as well as the tale of the Grand Inquisitor, points to the risks and the limits of freedom.

The question of freedom becomes delicate in terms of the church: What is the freedom of the children of God (cf. Rom. 8.21) within the church, for example, with respect to theological thought? Alexander Bukharev quickly discovered the limits of this freedom and sought to overcome ecclesial constraints by his rather clumsy return to lay status. A major case in point is the Sophia affair of the 1930s: What are the limits of freedom of theological thought within the church?

---

[72]Christos Yannaras, *On the Absence and Unknowability of God: Heidegger and the Aeropagite* (1967) (London: T&T Clark, 2005), 84–5. This is a revised version of Yannaras's doctoral thesis at the Sorbonne.
[73]Nicolas Zernov, *The Russian Religious Renaissance of the Twentieth Century* (London: Darton, Longman & Todd, 1963), 294.
[74]Berdyaev, *The Russian Idea*, 242.

This question becomes crucial in the context of the role of tradition within the church: Are tradition and freedom compatible? We saw some of the parameters of this discussion in Chapter 8, with the sparring between Sergius Bulgakov and Georges Florovsky over the legitimacy of a distinction between dogma and doctrine-theologoumena, accepted by Bulgakov but rejected by Florovsky. Paul Valliere casts this debate in terms of tension between tradition and 'intellectual freedom' or theological freedom. Weighing the relative strengths of the thinkers of the Russian religious renaissance and the neopatristic theologians on the issue of freedom in the church, he emphasizes that 'unfortunately for the neopatristic side, the Sophia affair must figure in the evidence.'[75] Certainly the condemnation of Bulgakov's sophiology in the 1930s was a messy, unedifying affair, but Valliere is perhaps according too much weight to the condemnations by the two branches of the Russian Church in conflict with Bulgakov's own jurisdiction under Metropolitan Evlogy. Evlogy's jurisdiction did not condemn his sophiology, even though the committee that Evlogy had appointed to look into the matter found weaknesses in it. In addition, other innovative aspects of Bulgakov's theology were not condemned. And the far more questionable aspects of the theologies of such prominent figures as Vladimir Soloviev and Pavel Florensky were never formally condemned by the church – it was Leo Tolstoy who incurred the wrath and formal condemnation of the Russian Orthodox Church (ROC).

Metropolitan Kallistos Ware is also a keen advocate of an Orthodox theology of the human person, building on the work of both the Russian and the Greek personalists.[76] Ware argues that, following a major concern for ecclesiology in twentieth-century Orthodox thought, the theology of the person should be the most important priority for Orthodox theology in the twenty-first century:

> The key question in Orthodoxy today is not only 'What is the church?', but also and more fundamentally 'What is the human person?' What does it imply to be a person-in-relation according to the image of God the Holy Trinity? What does it mean to attain 'deification' (theosis) through incorporation into Christ?[77]

Ware evokes three reasons for stressing the importance of personalism in the twenty-first century: urbanization, globalization and technological advance, which put the individual person 'in danger of being swallowed up in vast social units and dominated by machines'; the challenges posed to the theology of human person by ethical questions arising from genetic engineering, the breakdown of the institution of marriage and the growing rejection of traditional sexual morality, especially regarding homosexuality; and the ecological crisis which contradicts the human vocation as priests

---

[75]Valliere, *Modern Russian Theology*, 395.

[76]See notably Ware's essays 'The Human Person as an Icon of the Trinity', *Sobornost*, 8, 2 (1986); 'The Unity of the Human Person according to the Greek Fathers', in Arthur Peacocke and Grant Gillett, eds., *Persons and Personality: A Contemporary Inquiry* (Oxford: Basil Blackwell, 1987); and '"In the Image and Likeness": The Uniqueness of the Human Person', in John T. Chirban, ed., *Personhood: Orthodox Christianity and the Connection between Body, Mind, and Soul* (Westport, CT: Bergin & Garvey, 1996).

[77]Kallistos Ware, 'Orthodox Theology Today: Trends and Tasks', *International Journal for the Study of the Christian Church*, 12, 2 (2012), 116. Same text in Kallistos Ware, *Orthodox Theology in the Twenty-First Century* (Geneva: World Council of Churches, 2012). See also his address 'The Present and Future of Orthodox Theology' (New York, St Vladimir's Orthodox Seminary, 8 September 2011). http://www.ancientfaith.com/specials/2011_alban_and_sergius/metropolitan_kallistos_ware_the_present_and_future_of_orthodox_theology (12 September 2017).

of creation.[78] Ware advances three hallmarks for a rejuvenation of Orthodox anthropology: the necessity of articulating an 'apophatic anthropology' that would sufficiently appreciate the 'mystery of the human person'; the retention of the patristic notion of humans as created in the image and likeness of God and the affirmation of human creativity as an aspect of the divine image.[79] If anything, emerging trends in twenty-first century thought and technology that impinge on conventional notions of what it means to be human add to the urgency of Ware's appeal for the priority of the theology of the human person.

Critiques of personalist theology

In the early years of the new millennium there emerged a lively debate among Orthodox theologians over personalism, especially as advocated by John Zizioulas and, to a lesser degree, by Christos Yannaras. Some of the concerns raised are methodological; others are substantive. Leaders in the critique of personalism include Jean-Claude Larchet (b. 1949), Nikolaos Loudovikos (b. 1959) and Lucian Turcescu (b. 1966), with Zizioulas, the leading personalist of the early twenty-first century, as the main target.[80] Zizioulas has equally ardent supporters, such as Alan Brown, Aristotle Papanikolaou (b. 1967) and Norman Russell (b. 1942).[81]

The chief methodological critique of Zizioulas targets his attempts to find a theology of the human person, including the distinction and indeed opposition between 'person' and 'nature' or 'essence', and between 'person' and 'individual', in the ancient Fathers. Several of Zizioulas's opponents accuse him of misreading patristic sources to support his contention that his approach to personalism is fully justified by the Fathers.[82]

Zizioulas's desire to ground his theology of the human person in the Greek Fathers was not a concern for his personalist predecessors in the Russian religious renaissance. Even Vladimir Lossky, while endorsing the search for a doctrine of the human person in the early Fathers, was unable to come up with convincing patristic sources, as he recognized as early as 1951: 'I must

[78]Ware, 'Orthodox Theology Today', 117.

[79]Ibid., 117–18.

[80]See Jean-Claude Larchet, 'Personne et nature. Une critique orthodoxe des théories personnalistes de Christos Yannaras et de Jean Zizioulas' (Person and nature: An Orthodox critique of the personalist theories of Christos Yannaras and John Zizioulas) in *Personne et nature, La Trinité – Le Christ – L'homme. Contributions aux dialogues interorthodoxe et interchrétien contemporains* (Person and Nature, The Trinity – Christ – Man: Contributions to Contemporary Inter-Orthodox and Inter-Christian Dialogues) (Paris: Le Cerf, 2011); Nicholas Loudovikos, 'Person instead of Grace and Dictated Otherness: John Zizioulas's Final Theological Position', *The Heythrop Journal*, 52 (2011); and Lucian Turcescu, '"Person" versus "Individual", and Other Modern Misreadings of Gregory of Nyssa', *Modern Theology*, 18, 4 (2002). For a more sympathetic but nonetheless critical overview of Zizioulas's personalist theology, see Andrew Louth, *Modern Orthodox Thinkers: From the Philokalia to the Present* (London: SPCK, 2015), 219–20; 224–5.

[81]See Alan Brown, 'On the Criticism of *Being as Communion* in Anglophone Orthodox Theology', in Douglas Knight, ed., *The Theology of John Zizioulas: Personhood and the Church* (Aldershot: Ashgate, 2007); Aristotle Papanikolaou, 'Is John Zizioulas an Existentialist in Disguise? Response to Lucian Turcescu', *Modern Theology*, 20, 4 (2004); also his *Being with God: Trinity, Apophaticism, and Divine-Human Communion* (Notre Dame, IN: University of Notre Dame Press, 2006); and Norman Russell, *The Doctrine of Deification in the Greek Patristic Tradition* (Oxford: Oxford University Press, 2004).

[82]See the publications of Larchet, Loudovikos and Turcescu cited above.

admit that until now I have not found what one might call an elaborated doctrine of the human person in patristic theology, alongside its very precise teaching on divine persons or hypostases.'[83]

There is a risk of not seeing the forest for the trees in such a methodological debate. The real issue is not whether modern notions of the human person can or cannot be found in the Fathers of old, but how to enunciate a robust theology of the human person in the face of depersonalizing threats in modern times, even if this means 'going beyond the Fathers', in the sense of building on their theologies to address modern problems.

More serious than debates over patristic antecedents are substantive critiques levied against personalism. The major critique of Zizioulas's personalism is that he treats the person as the supreme ontological category, the carrier of freedom, to the detriment of nature or essence. The same critique can be levied against Yannaras, whose thinking on human existence has been characterized as 'a *prosopo-centric* ontology'.[84] As a result of an undue emphasis on the person, critics assert, nature becomes tainted because it is seen as subject to determinism and is associated with degenerate or fallen humanity, destined to return to dust, non-existence or hell. For his critics, Zizioulas artificially opposes person and nature, with the person emerging as the clear favourite based on the criteria of freedom versus determinism, or communion versus corruption. Another aspect of the person-nature debate is a tendency to cast complex philosophical and theological reflections into a simplified East versus West dichotomy, as in Christos Yannaras:

> The West was trapped in a polarized view of Being as either analogically absolute and ontic or else mystical. This came about as the inevitable consequence of the priority Westerners gave, even in the first Christian centuries, to the intellectual definition of essence over the historical and existential experience of personhood – in contrast to the Greek East, which always relied for its starting-point on the priority of person over essence.[85]

The assertion of the inherent superiority of person over nature is the launching pad for critiques of personalism. Basing himself to a considerable extent on Maximus the Confessor and also the Cappadocians, Nikolaos Loudovikos argues that nature, even human nature, is inherently good because it is created by God, with its true purpose to be achieved in communion with God. Nature is thus not intended to disappear in the eschaton, but to realize its ultimate fulfilment through participation in God. The personalism of John Zizioulas and Christos Yannaras, Loudovikos contends, is deficient because of an inherently negative view of nature, more characteristic of fallen nature or nature distorted by sin, than of human nature as created by God and as bearing the potential of divine-human communion, partially in this life and fully in the eschaton.[86] Yannaras

---

[83]Vladimir Lossky, 'The Theological Notion of the Human Person', in *In the Image and Likeness of God* (Crestwood, NY: St Vladimir's Seminary Press, 1974), 112. Lossky nonetheless states that Christian anthropology, both Eastern and Western, is 'clearly personalist'. Ibid.

[84]Sotiris Mitralexis, 'Modern Greek Theology', in Andrew Louth and Andreas Andreopoulos, eds., *Oxford Handbook of Orthodox Theology* (Oxford: Oxford University Press, forthcoming). This essay contains an excellent overview of personalism in Yannaras and Zizioulas.

[85]Yannaras, *Person and Eros*, 21. John Zizioulas says the same thing with greater nuance. See Zizioulas, *Being as Communion*, 55.

[86]Nicholas Loudovikos, 'Hell and Heaven, Nature and Person. Chr. Yannaras, D. Staniloae and Maximus the Confessor', *International Journal of Orthodox Theology*, 5, 1 (2014), 22–5.

attempts to resolve this problem by the notion of *ek-stasis*, a surpassing of nature in the affirmation of the freedom of the person.[87] But in Loudovikos's eyes, this is not satisfactory because heaven/paradise then becomes 'the kingdom of fully realized self-control and self-transcendence, i.e. a flight from nature through an "*ek-static*" relation'.[88] Loudovikos argues that this undue emphasis on the person to the detriment of nature does not correspond with patristic theology, neither the Cappadocians nor Maximus, who see nature as in need of transformation rather than of absolute denial or rejection, as Zizioulas and Yannaras appear to imply.

In a similar vein Jean-Claude Larchet writes:

> The negative conception that Yannaras and Zizioulas have of essence takes the form of deep loathing encountered at every turn of their thought, such that Professor S. Agourdis has characterised our two authors as *ousiamachi* (literally, those who struggle against essence). This attitude leads our two authors (Zizioulas even more than Yannaras) to minimise the reality, the place and the role of essence or nature in the fields of Triadology, Christology and anthropology, where we seem to be dealing with persons without essence or without nature and everything that takes place occurs without them, at the level of the person considered as the sole true reality, the sole object of 'ontology' that our two authors advance as a model of contemporary Orthodox theology.[89]

Larchet quotes favourably the 'brilliant critique' of the Romanian theologian Joan Ică Junior, who characterizes the personalism of Yannaras and Zizioulas as a departure 'from ontology to personology' and 'the reduction of existence to the person' – a tongue-in-cheek parody of Vladimir Lossky's well-known statement concerning the irreducibility of person to essence.[90] For Larchet, this line of thought has its origins in modern personalist and existential philosophies and is incapable of validation in patristic sources.[91] Similar to Loudovikos's critique of personalism, Larchet concludes that in this vision, the person is the only ontological reality, set against nature/essence, which becomes the source of determinism and alienation. In contrast, for Larchet patristic thought does not separate nature/essence from hypostasis: 'The being of a person is simultaneously his hypostasis and his essence or nature as it exists in this hypostasis, and ontology is attached to both, which form a whole, and not to the person alone.'[92]

Larchet also finds inadequate Zizioulas's notion that personhood is a task to be accomplished, as distinct from the idea that any human is a person simply by being – that is, personhood is an aspect of human nature per se. The emphasis in Zizioulas and others on interpersonal relations, with disinterested love as their supreme expression, as the key to achieving personhood accords priority to the collective, horizontal dimension of human existence, at the expense of individual or 'personal' aspects of spiritual life, including direct, vertical relations with God, which thereby are

[87]As summarized in Loudovikos, 'Hell and Heaven', 20–1.
[88]Loudovikos, 'Hell and Heaven', 25.
[89]Larchet, *Personne et nature*, 236.
[90]Ibid., 236.
[91]Ibid., 238; 258; 264.
[92]Ibid., 272.

'systematically considered egotistical forms of moralism and pietism, accompanied as well by a tendency to submit the person to the collectivity'.[93]

These are serious accusations against personalism, not only of the Zizioulian variety, but also as formulated by his Russian predecessors and Yannaras. The accusations are in part based on a misreading of Zizioulas, for example a simplification of Zizioulas's subtle thinking on the relations of person and nature contained in assertions that he identifies nature with necessity, and person with freedom.[94]

Nonetheless, a core of this critique, for example that Zizioulas, as his defender Alexis Torrance recognizes, 'underplays nature (and, it is true, he does)', remains unanswered.[95] This indeed suggests that Zizioulian personalism requires revisiting. One line of defence of the methodological problem involved in Zizioulas is that it is necessary to look beyond the theological and philosophical words used by the ancient Fathers (*ousia, prosopon, hypostasis*), to the patristic schema of human potential for participation in God, encapsulated in the idea of theosis. Norman Russell writes: '"personhood" becomes with Zizioulas a way of re-expressing what the Fathers meant by "participation". For in virtue of its relational nature, personhood implies difference from God without division, as well as communion with him without confusion.'[96] While this may absolve Zizioulas from the accusation of misreading his patristic sources, he nonetheless confuses the issue by not clearly explaining his understanding of the relationship between *ousia-prosopon-hypostasis* on the one hand and theosis on the other. The greatest risk of misreading Zizioulas is the temptation to analyse his personalism mostly or even exclusively through the lens of ontology and its associated terminology, rather than in the broader context of salvation, participation in Christ, the sacraments and the church and deification.

Metropolitan Hierotheos (Vlachos) of Nafpaktos (b. 1945) is another critic of modern Orthodox personalism, advancing two principal arguments. First, he argues, personalism is of Western origin and has no basis in Orthodox tradition. This contentious observation is founded on his principal argument: that the ancient Fathers did not refer to humans as 'persons' (*prosopoi*), but as 'human beings' (*anthrōpoi*). Rather, argues Vlachos, 'The holy Fathers used the term *prosopon* (person), first and foremost in referring to God, and particularly the three Persons of the Holy Trinity.'[97] Vlachos notes that from Basil the Great onwards, the notion of *prosopon* was identified with hypostasis ('the essence with the particular peculiarities') and 'takes on great value, losing its impersonal and abstract character and acquiring ontology'.[98] On the other hand, 'For man the holy Fathers mainly used the term *anthropos*. They did not speak so much about a person,

[93]Jean-Claude Larchet, review of Jean Zizioulas, *L'Église et ses institutions* (The Church and Her Institutions) (Paris: Le Cerf, 2011). http://orthodoxie.com/category/lire/recensions (23 March 2015). No longer at this URL (12 September 2017).

[94]See Alexis Torrance, 'Personhood and Patristics in Orthodox Theology: Reassessing the Debate', *Heythrop Journal*, 52 (2011), 702–4. Torrance accuses Loudovikos of misrepresenting and even misquoting Zizioulas on several other key points. For other counter-critiques of Larchet and Loudovikos, see reviews of Larchet's book *Personne et nature* by Peter Bouteneff in *St Vladimir's Theological Quarterly*, 56, 1 (2012), and by Andrew Louth in *Journal of Theological Studies*, 65, 1 (2014).

[95]Torrance, 'Personhood and Patristics in Orthodox Theology', 703.

[96]Russell, *The Doctrine of Deification*, 318. Also Torrance, 'Personhood and Patristics in Orthodox Theology', 701.

[97]Hierotheos Vlachos, *The Person in the Orthodox Tradition* (Levadia, GR: Birth of the Theotokos Monastery, 1998), 68.

[98]Vlachos, *The Person in the Orthodox Tradition*, 72.

but about man.'[99] But, as Vlachos reluctantly recognizes, the Fathers did occasionally refer to humans as 'persons' (*prosopoi*), 'of course this is by condescension, because they know that there is an enormous difference between God and man, between Creator and creature. God is uncreated, while man is created.'[100]

As an alternative to referring systematically to all humans as 'persons', Vlachos proposes that only humans who manifestly have attained a high spiritual level should be called 'persons':

> I think that we can use the term 'person' also for man with great care, when we make certain distinctions. One of these is that, as in the case of the term 'man', according to the Fathers we cannot simply apply it to all those who are living, but chiefly to those who partake of the purifying, illuminating and deifying energy of God, and so we can use the term 'person' to refer to those who are on their way towards deification by grace and are being deified. Just as 'in the image' is potentially likeness and 'in the likeness' is actually 'image', so also man by his biological existence is potentially man and person. He will become a real man when he partakes of the uncreated energy of God. As God is Person, it means that man becomes a person when he unites with God.[101]

On this basis, Vlachos criticizes Christos Yannaras and John Zizioulas for their application of the term 'person' to humans. Vlachos uses Zizioulas's definition of the principal characteristics of personhood (freedom, love and uniqueness) against him, asserting that 'even these three distinguishing features which constitute the person exist only in God, since only God is self-existent, has real love and is singular'.[102] In effect, Vlachos faults the Orthodox personalists for speaking of God and humans as 'persons' in the same breath; only a few humans, those who have achieved a high degree of theosis, truly deserve the title 'persons'. The rest of humanity are only 'human beings'. Contrary to patristic anthropology which sought to elevate human existence by emphasizing the divine image in humans, Vlachos diminishes human existence by stressing the gap between God and humanity and refusing to recognize personhood as an aspect of the inalienable divine image in all humans.

Vlachos brought his campaign against the systematic reference to humans as 'persons' into the Council of the Orthodox Church held in Crete in 2016.[103] He succeeded in convincing the Church of Greece to adopt his stance that all references in Council documents to humans as 'persons' should be deleted, and that humans should be referred to only as 'human beings'. In fact, many references in Council documents were so changed even prior to the Council. Vlachos had lively exchanges with Zizioulas and Metropolitan Kallistos Ware at the Council itself, but in the end the

---

[99]Ibid., 75.

[100]Ibid., 76–7.

[101]Ibid., 79. See also his further elaboration of the use of the word 'person' at 80–1.

[102]Vlachos, *The Person in the Orthodox Tradition*, 85. See John Zizioulas, *Being as Communion: Studies in Personhood and the Church* (Crestwood, NY: St Vladimir's Seminary Press), 42–9.

[103]See inter alia Metropolitan Hierotheos (Vlachos) of Nafpaktos, 'Texts of "The Holy and Great Council" Distinguished by "Creative Ambiguity" and Other Flaws September 30, 2016'. https://orthodoxethos.com/post/the-decisions-of-the-hierarchy-of-the-church-of-greece-on-the-holy-and-great-council-and-the-final-outcome (9 April 2017).

Church of Greece withdrew its request to change the few remaining references to 'human persons' in Council documents to 'human beings'.[104]

As we have seen, the origins of modern Orthodox personalism can be found in the Russian Slavophiles and their successors during the Russian religious renaissance. In developing a personalist anthropology, the Russian Orthodox thinkers were responding to decidedly anti-personalist philosophies which sought to reduce human existence to one aspect only, such as rationality, race or nationality, social or economic identification or mere physical existence. In challenging these philosophies, Russian thinkers appealed to the patristic notion of the human being as a creature composed of a material body and an immaterial soul, created in the divine image. To assert the uniqueness and irreplaceability of each human being, the Russians elaborated the notion of the person, as distinct from an individual, based indeed on patristic thinking on the Persons of the Trinity. This permitted the Russians and their Orthodox successors elsewhere to affirm the infinite value of each human being.

In his dense but provocative book *Yearning for the One*, the Greek philosopher Stelios Ramfos (b. 1939) challenges conventional Orthodox wisdom on the superiority of the person over the individual.[105] This wisdom sees the individual, taken to be dominant in Western thought, certainly from the Enlightenment onwards, as egocentric because an island unto himself or herself, a consequence of humanity's separation from God, the divine and sustaining source of existence. The person, on the other hand, exists in a positive relationship with other persons, modelled on the Persons of the Holy Trinity, thus anticipating the eschatological fulfilment of human existence. According to this model, as much as individual existence is negative if not diabolic, personal existence leads to the fulfilment of human potential, which can be achieved only by positive relations – love – with other persons, human or divine. This schema characterizes the personalism of Yannaras and Zizioulas, for example.

Ramfos challenges this standard narrative by pointing out that overstating the person-in-relation or the person-in-community entails losing the sense of the individual as having intrinsic dignity and value in himself or herself. The West, he argues, has come to the notion of the person through that of the individual, whereas modern Orthodox thought, while highlighting the ontological significance of person-as-relation, has an inadequately developed sense of individual existence, the sense of individual interiority. The individual risks being subsumed into the community, with no autonomous existence as such.[106] On a broader level, this is the dilemma of the relationship of the one and the many, the human person and the community of persons.

[104]See Maxim Vasiljevic, *Diary of the Council: Reflections from the Holy and Great Council at the Orthodox Academy in Crete, June 17-26, 2016* (Alhambra, CA: Sebastian Press, 2016), 48; and Paul Ladouceur, 'Human Beings or Human Persons?' *Public Orthodoxy* (6 June 2017). https://publicorthodoxy.org/2017/06/06/human-beings-or-persons (8 September 2017).

[105]Stelios Ramfos, *Yearning for the One: Chapters in the Inner Life of the Greeks* (2000) (Brookline MA: Holy Cross Orthodox Press, 2011). Ramfos's book is cast primarily in Greek terms, but he is conscious of the relationship between earlier Russian thought and later Greek thought on personhood. He focuses mainly on particular texts of Christos Yannaras, John Zizioulas, John Panagopoulos and Savvas Agouridis, which he then considers in relation to Greek thinking on the person from classical Greece onwards. See also a summary of Ramfos's approach to personalism in Louth, *Modern Orthodox Thinkers*, 259–62.

[106]Ramfos, *Yearning for the One*, passim, especially 296–320.

Ramfos makes a valuable point. The pendulum in Orthodox thought has perhaps swung too far in the direction of personhood defined largely or solely in a social or communitarian sense – communion or love – which appears to diminish or even to deny dignity or merit to the individual human as such. As in the person-nature debate, Ramfos seeks to bring the pendulum back closer to the centre. Inspired by the patristic notion of Christ's divine hypostasis or person 'enhypostatizing' his human nature, body and soul, as expressed especially by Leontius of Byzantium and Maximus the Confessor, Ramfos argues for an Orthodox theology of human personhood encompassing both the individual and the social or communal dimensions:

> The person cannot be identified wholly with the ego or be submerged in the group aspect of social relationship. The person is the active existence of the human being on the level of meaning and, as such, includes in a transformative manner both the relation and the individual.[107]

His underlying interpretation of the core of Christian anthropology is that 'If something is peculiar to the Christian person, it is its individual character.'[108] The Orthodox peoples, he writes, 'must develop a human being whose free atomic individuality is combined harmoniously with a loving sense of community'[109] – that is, personhood in the Zizioulian sense. And later:

> Personhood is the catholicity of a particular individual. ... Universality refers to the fullness everywhere of oneness, not to a kind of general presence of it. It signifies the whole within the part. ... The atomic individual can pursue catholicity in the 'becoming' of time and thus achieve its own personhood.[110]

Human rights

There is lively debate in Orthodox circles concerning human rights as enshrined in the Universal Declaration of Human Rights and in the constitutions and legal instruments of many Western countries. Orthodox were generally favourable towards human rights until the late twentieth century. Indeed, Orthodox benefited from early applications of human rights thinking in such key historic events as Greek independence and the dismembering of the Ottoman and Austro-Hungarian Empires after the First World War, which resulted in the independence of several countries of Orthodox tradition. A leading Orthodox philosopher, diplomat and statesman from Lebanon, Charles Habib Malik (1906–87) was closely associated with the development of the Universal Declaration of Human Rights, adopted in 1948. In a 1982 paper on human rights, Stanley Harakas (b. 1932) wrote enthusiastically that 'There is a natural and ready acceptance of human rights affirmations on the part of the Orthodox Church. ... The Orthodox have accepted

[107] Ramfos, *Yearning for the One*, 281.
[108] Ibid., 15.
[109] Ibid., 7.
[110] Ibid., 282.

with remarkable alacrity the 1948 Universal Declaration of Human Rights.'[111] But Harakas was too optimistic, as Orthodox philosophers, theologians and Orthodox churches subsequently advanced wide-ranging critiques of human rights. Prominent Orthodox critics are Christos Yannaras, Vigen Guroian (b. 1948) and the Russian Orthodox Church (ROC), while defenders of human rights include Archbishop Anastasios Yannoulatos of Albania (b. 1929), Stanley Harakas, John McGuckin (b. 1952), Pantelis Kalaitzidis (b. 1961) and Aristotle Papanikolaou.[112]

A common Orthodox criticism of human rights is that the notion originates in the Enlightenment, and is founded on a deistic, non-theistic or even atheistic philosophies, resulting from the alienation of church and state in Western Europe, the separation of 'sacred' and 'secular', of religion and society. The Enlightenment itself was a development of the Renaissance, with its revival of pre-Christian humanistic values derived from classical Greece and Rome. In the eyes of critics, the grounding of human rights in a non-theistic concept of 'natural right' rather than in theological or metaphysical notions results in the exaltation of an autonomous humanity which can attain its ultimate purpose without the need of a transcendent deity, a form of auto-deification. For Christos Yannaras and other critics of human rights, such a strictly humanistic pre-supposition to human rights is unacceptable in the light of the Orthodox tradition of divine creation and of humans as bearers of the divine image. Yannaras writes:

> The denial of metaphysics encouraged the absolute affirmation of nature (physics). The idea was that normative principles and rules of justice should not be deduced from the hypothetical 'law of God' which was arbitrarily handled by religious institutions, but by the logic of the laws of nature which was objective and controllable.[113]

In face of the secularization of modern industrial societies, the loss of a sense of the transcendental or 'metaphysical', human rights language replaces religious discourse. But it is thereby inadequate to combat ideologies and social and economic forces which threaten to subjugate and depersonalize human beings and constitutes a rejection of the Christian foundations of Western civilization.

---

[111]Stanley Harakas, 'Human Rights: An Eastern Orthodox Perspective', *Journal of Ecumenical Studies*, 19, 3 (1982), 19; 20.

[112]Christos Yannaras: 'Human Rights and the Orthodox Church', in Emanuel Clapsis, ed., *The Orthodox Churches in a Pluralistic World* (Geneva: WCC publications, 2004), 84; 'The Inhuman Character of Human Rights (A Synopsis of the Homonymous Book of Prof. Christos Yannaras)' at www.academia.edu/3624303 (17 April 2015). Yannaras's book, with its telling title, was published in Athens in 1998. Vigen Guroian: 'Human Rights and Modern Western Faith: An Orthodox Christian Assessment', *Journal of Religious Ethics*, 26, 2 (1998). Russian Orthodox Church (ROC): 'Basic Teaching on Human Dignity, Freedom and Human Rights' (adopted in June 2008). https://mospat.ru/en/documents/dignity-freedom-rights (20 April 2015). Also Hilarion Alfeyev, 'A Blessing or a Curse? Tradition and Liberal Values in the Debate between Christianity and Secularism', Part IV in his *Orthodox Witness Today* (Geneva: WCC Publications, 2006). Anastasios Yannoulatos, 'Orthodoxy and Human Rights', Chapter 2 of his *Facing the World: Orthodox Christian Essays on Global Concerns* (Crestwood, NY: St Vladimir's Seminary Press, 2003). John McGuckin, 'The Issue of Human Rights in Byzantium and the Orthodox Christian Tradition', in John Witte and Frank Alexander, eds., *Christianity and Human Rights: An Introduction* (Cambridge: Cambridge University Press, 2011), 173–90; and *The Ascent of Christian Law: Byzantine and Patristic Formulations of a New Civilization* (Yonkers, NY: St Vladimir's Seminary Press, 2012). Aristotle Papanikolaou, 'Personhood and Human Rights', Chapter 3 of *The Mystical as Political: Democracy and Non-Radical Orthodoxy* (Notre Dame, IN: University of Notre Dame Press, 2012). Pantelis Kalaitzidis and Nikos Ntontos, eds., *Orthodoxía kai Neoterikótita Prolegómena* (Orthodoxy and Modernity: An Introduction) (Athens: Indiktos, 2007). Pantelis Kalaitzidis, 'Individual Versus Collective Rights: The Theological Foundation of Human Rights. An Eastern Orthodox Approach'. Proceedings of the International Consultation on 'Orthodoxy and Human Rights' (Louvain-la-Neuve, 26–27 April 2013).

[113]Yannaras, 'Human Rights and the Orthodox Church', 84.

The second line of critique argues that the denial of a theological or metaphysical basis for human rights derives from a secular or even materialistic view of human existence, which encourages egocentric individualism, by setting no limits on the satisfaction of human desires other than when their satisfaction enters into conflict with the rights of others: 'When the tyranny of metaphysics was rejected, the aim of individual metaphysical salvation was replaced by the aim of secularized (legal) protection,' writes Christos Yannaras. 'The "paradigm" of modernity was grounded on the egocentrism of "human rights".'[114] The notion of an inherent moral code which exists over and above the limited notion of human rights is absent in human rights codes and discourse. This is contrary, it is argued, to Christian notions of law founded on morality derived from revelation and theology, as well as the modern understanding of human personhood. The ROC declares that 'The weakness of the human rights institution lies in the fact that, while defending the freedom of choice, it tends to increasingly ignore the moral dimension of life and the freedom from sin.'[115]

Thirdly, the separation of rights from morality leads to appeals to human rights to justify practices, often enshrined in legislation, which are morally unacceptable in the Orthodox tradition. For the ROC, 'Human rights protection is often used as a plea to realize ideas which in essence radically disagree with Christian teaching,' citing 'sexual lechery and perversions, the worship of profit and violence …, abortion, euthanasia, use of human embryos in medicine, experiments changing a person's nature, and the like'.[116] Patriarch Kirill of Moscow adds to this list 'mockery of sacred things', and he specifies homosexuality.[117] Other specific add-ons would include single-sex marriage, trans-genderism and many artificial techniques of human reproduction.

Hilarion Alfeyev puts his finger on the limits of humanistic morality arising from the Enlightenment and representing the spirit behind modern conceptions of human rights:

> The idea of responsibility is also present in humanism, but with the absence of absolute moral norms this principle simply denotes the limitation of one person's freedom by the freedom of other people. From the standpoint of atheistic humanism, the realization of the potential of freedom is nothing other than the person's unhindered realization of all his desires and aspirations, except for those which hinder the realization of similar desires of other people.[118]

From this analysis, Alfeyev turns the notion of human rights on its head and leaps to catastrophic conclusions arising from the widespread adoption of human rights: 'Humanists refuse to admit that the humanization of morality through the rejection of religious norms was the main cause of the monstrosities of the French revolutionaries and later of the Communists and Nazis.'[119]

Fourthly, the individualistic nature of human rights disregards other types of rights, especially rights of collectivities and rights derived from historical experience. This argument is forcefully

---

[114]Ibid., 87; 89.
[115]ROC, 'Basic Teaching on Human Dignity, Freedom and Human Rights', II:2.
[116]ROC, 'Basic Teaching on Human Dignity, Freedom and Human Rights', Introduction; III:3.
[117]Kirill (Patriarch of Moscow), *Freedom and Responsibility: A Search for Harmony – Human Rights and Personal Dignity* (London: Darton, Longman and Todd, 2011), 64.
[118]Alfeyev, 'A Blessing or a Curse?', 233.
[119]Ibid., 236.

advanced in countries of Orthodox tradition, such as Russia, Romania, Greece and Bulgaria. There, the national Orthodox churches, as the majority religious denominations and key agents in the formation of the nation, have had and expect to maintain privileged positions in society and political life not available to other Christian denominations and non-Christian religions. In Romania, this line of argument, associating the Orthodox Church with the formation of the Romanian people, evolves into an ethno-theology, as we saw in Chapter 7. A related conception of collective and historical rights also underpins the ROC's 'Basic Teaching on Human Dignity, Freedom and Human Rights.' This places the concept of 'one's homeland', together with the local community and the family, even above individual human rights: 'Human rights should not contradict love for one's homeland and neighbours. … One's human rights cannot be set against the values and interests of one's homeland, community and family.'[120] In this conception, collective rights are superior to individual rights.

Fifthly, declarations of human rights, it is argued, often define rights in isolation from obligations. The ROC links 'human dignity' (not entirely identical to human rights) to morality:

> 'In the Eastern Orthodox tradition, the notion of 'dignity' has first of all a moral meaning, while the ideas of what is dignified and what is not are bound up with the moral or amoral actions of a person and with the inner state of his soul. … The acknowledgement of individual rights should be balanced with the assertion of people's responsibility before one another.'[121]

Anastasios Yannoulatos, generally sympathetic to human rights, nonetheless makes a similar point: 'The separation of rights from their corresponding obligations threatens to destroy human rights themselves, because equilibrium has been lost … A one-sided emphasis on rights can result in an unhealthy individualism.'[122]

Sixthly, human rights, closely bound to Western philosophical and legal concepts of democracy, the neutrality of the state, the separation of church and state and the rule of law, contribute to the marginalization of religion in public life and the historical role of Christianity in developing the very foundations of Western civilization. In this context, religion and religious discourse become simply one political factor (and a progressively weaker one at that) among many others competing for attention in the public square.

A final critique is that human rights codes and legislation are of themselves inadequate and ineffective to prevent violations of human rights, even on a massive scale, such as in Nazi Germany, the Soviet Union and other communist regimes, and every other dictatorship imaginable. The nominal adherence of almost all members of the United Nations to the Universal Declaration of Human Rights is thus a patent travesty, since most countries, even Western democracies, routinely violate the human rights of their citizens. As we saw in the citation of Hilarion Alfeyev above, some critics even go so far as to suggest that the secular notion of human rights is responsible for violations of human rights.

---

[120]ROC, 'Basic Teaching on Human Dignity, Freedom and Human Rights', III:4.
[121]Ibid., I.2; III:4.
[122]Yannoulatos, *Facing the World*, 55.

Faced with this broadside of criticisms, some Orthodox defenders of human rights concede that there is merit in certain arguments that the critics advance while pointing to the limits and weaknesses of the arguments. Several recognize that it is true that the modern concept of human rights, arising in the Enlightenment, sets out to establish rights without recourse to a divine referent. On the other hand, while the appellation 'human rights' is indeed modern and owes its origin to Enlightenment philosophies, the notions that human rights embody can be traced to the origins of Christianity, in the Gospels, the Epistles and patristic theology. As Aristotle Papanikolaou points out, in fact it is not possible to ground human rights on the basis of 'the inherent, inviolable, non-utilitarian worth of a human being' other than theistically[123]; or, as Anastasios Yannoulatos summarizes, 'human rights documents presuppose the Christian legacy.'[124] Similarly, for John McGuckin, the philosophical and theological notion of person originated in Eastern Christian thought and 'both the civil and the ecclesiastical law of the Orthodox Church … recognized the principle of human rights long before the deists of the Enlightenment era.'[125] Harakas is able to write bluntly that 'One has rights and duties not because one does or does not do certain things, but because of who or what one is. … Rights are due a person simply and uniquely because he or she is a human being.'[126] These assertions are sustained by a theology that recognizes the uniqueness, irreplaceability and infinite value of every human being created in the divine image by a deliberate act of the divine will. Harakas's statement corresponds with the notion of natural law and natural rights common in Western social and legal thought since the early Middle Ages,[127] but little developed in Orthodoxy. Yet natural law is founded on the cornerstone of patristic anthropology and modern Orthodox theology of the human person, the ontological equality of all humans, who share the divine gift of a personal mode of existence in the image of the Persons of the Trinity.

The basic strategy of defenders of human rights is thus to demonstrate that human rights discourse and codes are implicitly founded on Scripture, patristic thought, the Byzantine tradition and modern Orthodox thinking on human personhood and are compatible with Orthodox theologies of creation, humanity, theosis and community, even if they are deficient when measured against the full expression of Orthodox theology. Papanikolaou writes:

> Structuring relations between humans in terms of rights fall short of all that humans are created to be. … Political communities are by their very nature deficiently sacramental, put in place because humans have fallen short of relating to each other as God relates to each one of them, but not necessarily devoid of God's presence. Christians, thus, should never expect a fully sacramentalized form of political community, one in which the community exists in relations of love and freedom that constitute persons as unique and irreducible.[128]

---

[123]Papanikolaou, *The Mystical as Political*, 116. Papanikolaou cites the work of Michael Perry and Nicholas Wolterstorff in support of this contention (see his notes 91–100 on pages 218–19).

[124]Yannoulatos, *Facing the World*, 53.

[125]McGuckin, 'The Issue of Human Rights in Byzantium', 179.

[126]Harakas, 'Human Rights: An Eastern Orthodox Perspective', 15.

[127]See Nicholas Wolterstorff, 'Christianity and Human Rights', in John Witte and Christian Green, eds., *Religion and Human Rights: An Introduction* (New York: Oxford University Press, 2012), 42; and 'Divine-Human Communion and the Common Good', ch. 4 of Papanikolaou's *The Mystical as Political*.

[128]Papanikolaou, *The Mystical as Political*, 125.

In this light, it is unrealistic in pluralistic societies and in the global context to expect that a universal expression of human dignity and rights will be explicitly grounded on overtly Christian notions such as the divine image, personhood, love and divine-human communion. Yannoulatos is keenly aware of this problem: 'In an era such as ours, in which there is a great diversity of ideological views, it will clearly be impossible to reach philosophical and religious agreement on these immense issues.'[129]

A secular expression of human rights is a second-best alternative for Christian theology. This became obvious in the post-Second World War negotiations leading to the adoption of the Universal Declaration of Human Rights. The commission which drafted the Declaration was chaired by Eleanor Roosevelt (1884–1962) (an American Episcopalian, wife of President Franklin D. Roosevelt), and included as members Jacques Maritain (1882–1973) (a French Thomist philosopher), René Cassin (1887–1976) (a French Jewish jurist), Peng-chun Chang (1892–1957) (a Chinese Confucian philosopher), John Humphrey (1905–95) (a Canadian jurist, who wrote the first draft of the Declaration) and Charles Malik from Lebanon. It proved impossible to reach agreement in the commission and with the member countries of the United Nations to ground the Declaration either in explicitly religious language or even in natural law. The final Declaration, affirming a broad range of rights, is thus an 'open-foundation document', 'amenable to any kind of substantiation, but [it] propounded no grounding of its own, either religious or non-religious.'[130]

Orthodox supporters of human rights such as Aristotle Papanikolaou and Anastasios Yannoulatos also consider human rights documents as incomplete because they do not regard society as 'an organic social whole made up of people who are complete personalities and whose relationships are based on love – not merely a form of coexistence shared by isolated individuals'.[131] While imperfect, often vague and ambiguous, declarations of human rights nonetheless 'constitute a starting point', writes Yannoulatos; they 'reflect hope and express a moral judgement', even while failing to safeguard 'human dignity from becoming enslaved to human egotism … nor do they safeguard human dignity from the complex factors that operate in our modern technological society's multiform and impersonal structures.'[132]

Although Papanikolaou grounds his defence of human rights on Orthodox personalism,[133] he acknowledges the limits of human rights, supporting a short list of 'the right to life, the right to moral equality, and the right to religious freedom', and suggesting that other rights, basically in the social and economic spheres, are less consensual: health care, food, shelter, employment and protection of the environment.[134] In his discussion of human rights, Papanikolaou recognizes that inherited and contemporary human rights language falls short of Orthodox thinking on human existence: 'Rights language does not adequately indicate all that it possible for the human in

---

[129]Yannoulatos, *Facing the World*, 57.

[130]Johannes Van der Ven, 'The Religious Scope of Human Rights', in Alfons Brüning and Evert van des Zweerde, eds., *Orthodox Christianity and Human Rights* (Leuven: Peeters, 2012), 24.

[131]Yannoulatos, *Facing the World*, 22.

[132]Ibid., 57.

[133]Papanikolaou, *The Mystical as Political*, ch. 3, 'Personhood and Human Rights', 87–130.

[134]Papanikolaou, *The Mystical as Political*, 127.

relationship with God.'[135] Papanikolaou's point is that this inadequacy does not mean that human rights should be rejected, but rather that rights have to be understood in terms more compatible with Orthodox thought, such as the divine image and the uniqueness of each human person.

Stanley Harakas, upbeat in his early article on human rights in an Orthodox perspective, does well to remind his readers that human rights are 'the reciprocal side of duties or moral responsibilities' of Christians, the concern that they should have 'with defending and justifying the rights of the weak the poor and oppressed ... based on the common, God-given humanity that all share.'[136] Such reflections are well grounded in Jesus' actions and teachings (such as the Beatitudes and the parable of the Last Judgement), those of Fathers of the Church such as Basil the Great and John Chrysostom, and of modern Orthodox social activists such as St Elizabeth of Russia and St Maria of Paris.

As we saw above, Stelios Ramfos challenges conventional Orthodox thinking on the relative merits of the notion of the human person in contrast with that of the individual. Ramfos's analysis clearly has implications for Orthodox attitudes towards human rights. Orthodox critics of human rights denounce what they perceive as the individualistic, egotistic basis of the modern conception of human rights – one individual against other individuals. Against this is set the notion of the person as existing in community, based on the model of the Holy Trinity. One difficulty with this schema is that it leaves those who for whatever reason do not have satisfactory interpersonal relations without a basis for protection against the community or the state, since they are not 'persons', only 'individuals'. This could include not only criminals and dictators of all sorts, but even mentally handicapped persons, many of whom do not have what is normally considered satisfactory interpersonal relations, or even infants and children. If human rights are ascribed only to 'persons' in this theological sense, rather than to 'individuals', rights then become a function of merit, something acquired, rather than being intrinsic to human existence. This is evident in the ambiguous statement in the ROC declaration on 'Human Dignity, Freedom and Human Rights', which affirms that 'dignity' (which the ROC prefers over human rights) 'has first of all a moral meaning'.[137] Lying behind such an approach is an attempt to deny rights to categories of persons – for example homosexuals and even unmarried heterosexual couples – who do not satisfy the criterion of morality, as judged by the church.

Making human rights contingent on merit is contrary to the mainstream of the thinking of the ancient Fathers on the difference between the divine image and the divine likeness: the former is inherent in human nature and cannot be lost, whereas the latter is acquired by collaboration with God in view of theosis. In this sense, human rights are based on the divine image in humans and a personal mode of existence, inherent to all humans from the moment of conception, rather than on likeness, which refers to a more developed stage of human existence, the complete fulfilment of human personhood.

Critics also often fail to recognize that human rights are not unlimited, in that the rights of one person are necessarily limited by the rights of others. Rights thus create corresponding obligations

---

[135]Ibid., 119.

[136]Harakas, 'Human Rights: An Eastern Orthodox Perspective', 14.

[137]ROC, 'Basic Teaching on Human Dignity, Freedom and Human Rights', I:2.

or responsibilities: my right to life creates a responsibility on the part of my neighbour not to take my life – and vice versa. The Universal Declaration of Human Rights extends this principle to include certain collective requirements: 'In the exercise of his rights and freedoms, everyone shall be subject only to such limitations as are determined by law solely for the purpose of securing due recognition and respect for the rights and freedoms of others and of meeting the just requirements of morality, public order and the general welfare in a democratic society.'[138]

Although Orthodox human rights critics are typically short on alternatives, the ROC comes up with a partial alternative, in asserting the priority of morality and of collective and historical rights over individual rights, as we pointed out above:

> The development and implementation of the human rights concept should be harmonized with the norms of morality, with the ethical principle laid down by God in human nature and discernible in the human conscience.
>
> The implementation of human rights should not come into conflict with God-established moral norms and traditional morality based on them. One's human rights cannot be set against the values and interests of one's homeland, community and family. The exercise of human rights should not be used to justify any encroachment on religious holy symbols [and] things, cultural values and the identity of a nation.[139]

Despite its cautious, even sceptical approach to human rights, the ROC declaration on 'Human Dignity, Freedom and Rights' represents a shift from an outright rejection of human rights to 'a cautious opening towards a post-secular type of debate'.[140] But the declaration describes rights with such conditions and qualifications as to empty rights of any significant content; the document is more an indirect statement of rights claimed by the ROC itself than an affirmation of human rights. In the Russian context, collective and historical rights are defined by the church itself and sanctioned by the state, and aim above all at preserving the pre-eminent place of the ROC in society and public life, over and against other Christian denominations, non-Christian religions and institutions which should be religiously neutral. Respect for the dignity, uniqueness and freedom of the other, which flows from the Orthodox theology of personhood, is trumped by institutional and national prerogatives.[141] Yet institutional and national prerogatives are far less solidly grounded in Orthodox theology than the theology of the person.

One of the documents adopted at the Holy and Great Council of the Orthodox Church in June 2016 concerns 'The Mission of the Orthodox Church in Today's World'.[142] The document is a sweeping overview of the need for Orthodoxy to make its voice heard across a wide range of modern issues, focusing on the dignity of the human person, freedom and responsibility, peace

---

[138] Universal Declaration of Human Rights, Article 29 (2).

[139] ROC, 'Basic Teaching on Human Dignity, Freedom and Human Rights', III:3; III:5.

[140] Kristina Stoeckl, *The Russian Orthodox Church and Human Rights* (London: Routledge, 2014), 128.

[141] The notion of responsibilities to the community, while less developed in human rights instruments than personal rights, is not totally absent. Article 29 (1) of the Universal Declaration of Human Rights reads 'Everyone has duties to the community in which alone the free and full development of his personality is possible.'

[142] Holy and Great Council of the Orthodox Church, 'The Mission of the Orthodox Church in Today's World' (The contribution of the Orthodox Church in realizing peace, justice, freedom, fraternity and love between peoples, and in the removal of racial and other discriminations) (Crete GR, 2016). https://www.holycouncil.org (23 January 2018).

and justice, the aversion of war and discrimination. Christian notions of social justice and morality underpin the document, which features an endorsement of fundamental human rights: 'The Orthodox Church confesses that every human being, regardless of skin colour, religion, race, sex, ethnicity, and language, is created in the image and likeness of God, and enjoys equal rights in society' (§ E.2).

Another Council document, the Encyclical, seeks to strike a balance between 'the arrogant apotheosis of the individual and his rights', and 'the humiliating debasement of the human person within the vast contemporary structures of economy, society, politics and communication'. But the emphasis is less on the endorsement of human rights than concern over 'the danger of individual rights falling into individualism and a culture of "rights"' and 'the elevation of the precarious identification of freedom with individual license into a "universal value" that undermines the foundations of social values, of the family, of religion, of the nation and threatens fundamental moral values'.[143] The only right which is endorsed unequivocally is religious freedom.

Despite the often outspoken denunciation of the non-theistic framing of human rights, some Orthodox critics nonetheless recognize that the very notion of personal rights has profound Christian roots: 'I am personally persuaded,' writes Vigen Guroian, 'that the deepest inspiration of the doctrine of human rights has roots in Christian convictions'.[144] Christos Yannaras refers to the protection of individual rights as 'a major success and a precious achievement' and human rights as 'an undisputable achievement', even if far from fully realized.[145]

In this light, the task of Orthodox theology is to build bridges between secular rights discourse and the Orthodox tradition, rather than to tear them down. Guroian himself offers a key to resolving Orthodox ambiguity towards human rights: 'Human rights thinking is alien to Orthodoxy; however, the notion that a normative human nature is concretely manifested in every human individual who comes into existence is central to Orthodox anthropology and theology.'[146] In a somewhat similar vein, Patriarch Kirill of Moscow has written that 'Orthodox people are willing to accept human rights and work toward strengthening them, but on the condition that these norms promote the perfection of the individual, not the justification of his sinful condition.'[147]

In this perspective, the idea of 'overlapping consensus' may help to overcome Orthodox hesitations about human rights.[148] Overlapping consensus characterizes a situation in which divergent moral and religious conceptions of the good converge on an agreed common ground. Thus Christians, including Orthodox, could agree with believers of other religions and agnostic or

---

[143]Holy and Great Council of the Orthodox Church, 'Encyclical of the Holy and Great Council of the Orthodox Church, Crete, June 2016' (Crete GR, 2016). https://www.holycouncil.org (23 January 2018), § 16.

[144]Guroian, 'Human Rights and Modern Western Faith', 243.

[145]Yannaras, 'Human Rights and the Orthodox Church', 88.

[146]Guroian, 'Human Rights and Modern Western Faith', 242.

[147]Kirill of Moscow, *Freedom and Responsibility*, 68.

[148]The notion of overlapping consensus is particularly associated with the leading American moral and political philosopher John Rawls (1921–2002), as developed especially in his books *A Theory of Justice* (1971; rev. 1999), *Political Liberalism* (1993) and *Justice as Fairness: A Restatement* (2001). For a discussion of Rawls's theory and its critics in an Orthodox perspective, see Athanase Giocas, *Le Bien justifié: Une lecture contemporaine de la synthèse philosophico-juridique de Vladimir Soloviev* (The Justification of the Good: A Contemporary Reading of Vladimir Soloviev's Philosophical-Juridical Synthesis) (Québec: Presses de l'Université Laval, 2016), 177–201.

atheistic humanists on the necessity of affirming fundamental human rights, each group for reasons grounded in its own tradition. For Orthodox, this would be Scripture, patristic anthropology and modern theology of the person. Other Christians and believers of other faiths can find justification from their own traditions for human rights and non-believers in an intuitive conviction of the equality and worth of every human. The notion of overlapping consensus may assuage Orthodox concerns about the incomplete nature of human rights documents. This contention rests in large part on the absence of a Christian or even theistic justification for human rights. But the provision of this justification, in the perspective of overlapping consensus, reposes with each group, including Orthodox, which affirms the principle of human rights. The development and adoption of the Universal Declaration of Human Rights is an example of overlapping consensus – all agreed on the content of the Declaration but were unable to articulate a common grounding or basis to justify the Declaration.

Conclusion

Neopatristic theology has been wary of employing the idea and vocabulary of divine-humanity or Godmanhood, in part because its origin in Russian religious thought is seen as too closely associated with the more problematic notions of all-unity and Divine Wisdom. Neopatristic theology is more comfortable with the traditional terminology of the Incarnation, the two natures of Christ and *theosis* than the unfamiliar and ambiguous expression divine-humanity. The awkward translations of the Russian *bogochelovechestvo* are also obstacles to a broad acceptance of the concept. There is some misunderstanding of what the term really means and a concern that it might be associated with an unacceptable Christology – for example if the term were understood to mean, as in some misreadings of Bulgakov, that in Christ there is a new divine-human nature formed from the fusion of the two natures in Christ, which suggests some form of moderate monophysism. This would be contrary to Chalcedonian and neo-Chalcedonian Christology, but such an interpretation of the term is incorrect: the major theologians of the Russian religious renaissance did not understand *bogochelovechestvo* in this fashion.

On the contrary, a positive aspect about the term 'divine-humanity' and its related reference to Christ as 'the God-man' is that it stresses the oneness of Christ, the one divine Person, in contrast with a lingering tendency in Orthodox theology, and even in liturgical services, to speak of the two natures of Christ as though two distinct subjects were acting, or as though the natures were acting independently of the one Person of Christ.[149] In an essay concerning 'Irenaeus on "Atonement"',

[149]Examples occur in the liturgical services for the feast of the resurrection of Lazarus: as man, Jesus inquires where Lazarus is buried and weeps over the death of his friend, but as God, Christ resurrects Lazarus from the dead, as in this sticharion from Lauds of Lazarus Saturday: 'O Christ, as you are the resurrection and the life of mankind, you came to the tomb of Lazarus, and demonstrated for us both of your essences, O longsuffering One; for from the pure Virgin you have come indeed as both God and man. As a mortal you inquired where he was buried, and as God with your life-bearing summons you resurrected him who had been four days dead.' E-Matins, www.omhksea.org/wp-content/uploads/2015/04/matinsengsatlaz.pdf (6 October 2017).

John Behr (b. 1966) writes: 'The liberation of the human being from the tyranny of the devil is effected by Christ, who as human, fought the enemy. … and who as God, set free the weak and gave salvation to his handiwork.'[150] While this and similar references in other modern Orthodox authors must be read in conformity with Chalcedonian Christology, they can also be interpreted in a Nestorian sense – as Oriental Orthodox (non-Chalcedonian) did in fact understand Chalcedonian Orthodox theology for many centuries. The language of divine-humanity affirms and emphasizes that it is indeed the one and same Person of Christ who weeps over Lazarus and who resurrects his friend, who suffers in Gethsemane and dies on the cross and who resurrects the third day. This avoids a separation of Christ's operations into those which are characteristic of human nature and those characteristic of divine nature, a distinction which can easily be misinterpreted.

Despite continuing doubts about divine-humanity, there is still considerable unrealized potential and promise in the notion. It would be necessary to revisit the notion in Bulgakov's theology to remove the sophiological veneer in which he cloaked it and to eliminate the possibility of interpretations inconsistent with Chalcedonian Christology.

For many neopatristic theologians, the notion of 'person' in human beings constitutes the essential basis of the divine image in humans: 'Humans are truly persons when they image the loving, perichoretic communion of the persons of the Trinity,' writes Aristotle Papanicolaou.[151] This extends the patristic conception of person from God to humans while maintaining the essential foundations of patristic anthropology. The Persons of the Trinity are the model and source of human personhood. Each person is unique and irreplaceable, and human personhood, while being a feature of human nature, surpasses nature as such. Nor is personhood merely a particular attribute of an individual. In modern Orthodox thought, personhood is defined mainly in experiential and apophatic terms. The person is seen in terms of relations with other persons. Although the person is ultimately unfathomable, inexpressible and unknowable in a rational sense, human persons, like the divine Persons, can be known and experienced through a loving relationship. The fundamental intuition that the image of God in humanity, so dear to the Fathers, found in the personal mode of existence of human beings, constitutes the essential basis for divine-human communion. The dynamics of intra-Trinitarian relations which reveal the distinctness of each divine Person and are characterized by love is then the model and the ideal for both divine-human and intra-human relations or communion. Persons truly exist in plenitude only in relationship with other persons, or, in Zizioulas's poignant expression 'being as communion', more precisely in and through Christ. Humans cannot achieve their full potential in isolation, where they can subsist only as lonely individuals.

Although the theology of the human person features prominently in the theologies of several neopatristic theologians, such as Vladimir Lossky and John Zizioulas, modern personalist theology originated in the thinking of the principal figures of the Russian religious renaissance, as emphasized by Olivier Clément and Aristotle Papanikolaou. Papanikolaou writes: 'The Russian Sophiologists

---

[150]John Behr, 'Irenaeus on "Atonement"', in Matthew Baker, Seraphim Danckaert and Nicholas Marinides, eds., *On the Tree of the Cross: Georges Florovsky and the Patristic Doctrine of Atonement* (Jordanville, NY: Holy Trinity Seminary Press, 2016), 55.
[151]Papanikolaou, 'Personhood and Its Exponents', 232.

of the late nineteenth and early twentieth centuries were the first to forge the link between Trinity and personhood.'[152] Unfortunately the role of the Russian religious renaissance in laying the groundwork for the mature Orthodox theology of the person later in the twentieth century is easily overlooked or minimized, with attention accorded mainly or exclusively to the neopatristic personalist theologians. Oliver Clément points to the continuity in personalist thought between the leaders of the Russian religious renaissance and Vladimir Lossky and Paul Evdokimov, and Aristotle Papanikolaou refers to the historical role of the early Russians, naming Soloviev, Florensky and Bulgakov (he does not mention Berdyaev).[153] In contrast with their predecessors, however, Lossky and Zizioulas sought to ground their personalism more solidly in patristic theology. Lossky, who is sometimes referred to as the 'theologian of the person', purged the notion of 'person' in the religious philosophers of any sophiological elements. In turn, Lossky's theology of the person influenced first Yannaras and, through him, Zizioulas.[154] The most prominent neopatristic theologians of the person are thus in continuity with their predecessors of the Russian religious renaissance. Personalism is a golden thread running through modern Orthodox theology, from Kireevsky to Soloviev and Frank, and from Florensky and Bulgakov to Lossky, Yannaras, Zizioulas and Ware.

An important issue in Orthodox personalism is the tension between personal existence as simultaneously unique and irreplaceable (hence individuality) and as necessarily relational to other persons. As Stelios Ramfos points out, the apparent conflict or dilemma between 'person' and 'individual' is in fact artificial. Personal uniqueness is individuality under another but more acceptable name. Humans are simultaneously persons and individuals; the context determines which notion is dominant. Thus, for the automated accounting system of my bank (or income tax department or any other automated system), clearly I am merely an individual, one among thousands or millions whose affairs are handled rationally and impersonally by 'the system'. But this does not diminish my unique personhood or individuality. And if I enter into a personal relationship with a human agent of this system, it is possible, though not always realized, to pass from being an individual to a person in this context. My role is to treat the agent as a person, created just as much in the divine image as myself, with the hope of being treated as a person in return.

The critiques of John Zizioulas's attempt to discern modern personalism in the ancient Fathers, especially the Cappadocians, appear well founded. Although Zizioulas's anachronistic reading of human personhood in the Fathers is certainly a methodological weakness, this does not per se invalidate the main thrust of his personalist theology, any more than that of other modern theologians who are not as insistent as Zizioulas in reading intimations of modern personalism in patristic writings. As some defenders of Zizioulas point out, one has to look more to the theology

[152]Papanikolaou, 'Personhood and Its Exponents', 232. One should nonetheless mention an early reference to personalism in Ivan Kireevsky, as we saw (240–1).

[153]Clément, 'Aperçus sur la théologie de la personne', and 'Le personnalisme chrétien'; and Papanikolaou, 'Personhood and Its Exponents'.

[154]Papanikolaou, 'Personhood and Its Exponents', 233.

of theosis or divine-human communion for the patristic basis of personalism than to patristic thinking on *ousia*, *hypostasis* and *prosopon*.

Indeed, the critiques of Zizioulas on this score raise an important issue for modern Orthodox theology as a whole: Is it absolutely necessary to find, retrospectively, new theological insights in the writings of the ancient Fathers? This is certainly not what Georges Florovsky had in mind in charting the contours of neopatristic theology. As early as his declaration at the 1936 conference of Orthodox theologians in Athens, Florovsky saw the 'return to the Fathers' as 'a further *development* of this patristic teaching … One has to grow older or to go further, but *in the same direction* or, better to say, *in the same type and spirit*.'[155] In this light, the application of the notion of person-hypostasis to human existence constitutes a 'further development' of the original use of the term by the Cappadocians to distinguish the multiplicity of divine Persons from the one divine nature. This modern extension of the notion of person is a legitimate application of the original patristic notion of *hypostasis* to modern problems which were not at issue in patristic times, and comes under Florovsky's call to move '*in the same direction*' and '*in the same type and spirit*' as the Fathers.

There is nonetheless a good basis in the often vocal but also often exaggerated critique of personalism by Orthodox theologians. This is especially the case concerning the opposition of person and nature/essence that critics find notably in Berdyaev, Yannaras and Zizioulas. We are in a sense witnessing swings of the pendulum between these two key notions in Christian thought: from a perceived and long-standing concentration on essence to the detriment of person, perhaps largely inherited from scholasticism, Orthodox personalists sought to swing the pendulum towards the other pole, exalting the person as the supreme ontological category while downplaying and even denigrating essence. By rehabilitating essence, critics such as Jean-Claude Larchet and Nikolaos Loudovikos prod Orthodox theology in the opposite direction, away from a perceived exaggerated attachment to person to a revived importance of nature/essence. Zizioulas's critics are correct to point out that Zizioulas paints himself into a corner by an almost single-minded identification of human existence with person as relationality ('communion and otherness'), but the critics themselves do not adequately spell out how personhood fits into their own basically polemical schemes.

The critics of personalism run the risk of so belittling the application of personhood to human existence as to discredit the idea altogether, throwing out the baby of personhood with the bathwater of anti-essentialism. The supposed 'ousiamachia' of Zizioulas and others must not be replaced by a new 'prosoponomachia', whose proponents include Metropolitan Hierotheos Vlachos, though for other reasons. The person is indeed, as Yannaras poignantly expresses it, the proper 'mode of being' of human existence (= nature), the agent or hypostasis who actualizes human nature, both in this life and in the next. Just as human nature without a human person cannot be actualized but must be relegated to the realm of Platonic ideas with no real substance, a human person detached (*ek-stasis*) from human nature is but an evanescent phantom, again with no real substance. Nature and

[155]Georges Florovsky, 'Patristics and Modern Theology' (1936), in Brandon Gallaher and Paul Ladouceur, eds., *The Patristic Witness of Georges Florovsky: Essential Theological Writings* (London: T&T Clark, 2019), 155–6. See also Ch. 5, 109–12.

person are inseparable companions: in perfect harmony in the Holy Trinity; in an uneasy and often conflictual relationship in humans, certainly in this life. Both are divinely created; both are aspects of the inalienable divine image in humans; both are destined for theosis, deification.

By seeking to restrict Orthodox thinking on humans solely to patristic language, Hierotheos Vlachos not only ignores the long evolution of Orthodox thought on the person, but also presents a reductionist view of human existence, playing into the hands of atheistic philosophies, which also prefer to speak of 'human beings' and steer clear of the philosophical and theological notion of the 'person'. The refusal to attribute personhood to human existence, to see personhood as inherent to human nature, *downgrades* humanity. This is not fidelity to the spirit of patristic anthropology, but rather its betrayal. The Fathers sought to *elevate* humanity by stressing that humans are created in the divine image, with the potential for union with God (theosis), and are not mere pawns subject to impersonal and implacable destiny or the gods. If the notion that all humans are 'persons' is not acceptable, still less acceptable would be the idea that humans are 'individuals' (*atoma*), since this gives rise to selfish individualism, contrary to the commandment of love. If humans are neither 'persons' nor 'individuals', they are mere *anthrōpoi*, interchangeable and expendable specimens of *Homo sapiens*. This reductionist view of humanity, which downgrades or dismisses personhood, can only gladden the hearts of contemporary secularists, for whom humans are nothing more than intelligent animals.

Orthodox defenders of human rights see rights as the best option available in a pluralistic and imperfect world, offering some safeguard not only for religious freedom, but more precisely to create conditions favourable for the free development of full personhood as understood in contemporary Orthodox theology. This is recognized even in the ROC document on human rights: 'The political and legal institution of human rights can promote the good goals of protecting human dignity and contribute to the spiritual and ethical development of the personality [*sic*].'[156]

Critics of human rights often fail to pursue their line of criticism to its logical conclusions. Yannaras's criticisms are based on an idealized interpretation of the pre-Christian Greek city-state (but Athens rather than Sparta) and of the Byzantine Empire, which are hardly relevant as potential models for modern industrial and post-industrial societies. Orthodox critics of human rights run the risk of finding themselves on the same side of the issue as other anti-human rights theories and ideologies. Orthodox would do well to remind themselves how much their predecessors and contemporaries suffered and continue to suffer under regimes which trample human rights, such as the Ottoman Empire, communist regimes and Islamic fundamentalists. The strongest defence against injustices perpetrated by such regimes is the invocation of human rights.

Orthodox are understandably upset by the invocation of human rights to support morally unacceptable practices such as abortion or same-sex marriage. But they should not allow their indignation over moral issues to lose sight of the wider importance of human rights in the protection of human life and dignity. The Universal Declaration of Human Rights of 1948 is one of the greatest triumphs of Christian culture. Even if it is far from universally honoured, it sets a very high standard for human behaviour.

---

[156]Russian Orthodox Church, 'Basic Teaching on Human Dignity, Freedom and Human Rights', III:5.

Admittedly, the classification of Orthodox thinkers on human rights into 'critics' and 'supporters' is too simplistic. The 'critics' recognize a certain validity of human rights, even if they want to circumscribe them, while the 'supporters' see weaknesses in the lack of philosophical and especially theological underpinnings and expressions of human rights. Modern Orthodox thinking neither canonizes human rights, nor does it endorse a Taliban philosophy of human rights. Both critics and supporters appeal to human rights to judge hardships and atrocities inflicted on the church and believers by hostile regimes, both historical (the Ottoman Empire, the communist regimes of Russia and Eastern Europe) and contemporary (Islamic fundamentalist movements).

Alternatives to human rights are mostly unpleasant and they usually involve discriminatory and oppressive measures against identifiable segments of the population, if not all citizens. Such measures run counter to major aspects of the Orthodox notion of the person, notably respect for the personhood, dignity and freedom of the other – even if this means accepting that the other may not conform to my notion of the truth, Christianity or the Orthodox tradition. Orthodox can view the purpose of human rights as to provide satisfactory conditions for the largest number of persons to achieve of full personhood – the divine likeness of patristic theology, theosis or divine-human communion – in an imperfect world.

Personalism has important linkages in other areas, notably in ecclesiology, as the Christian community brought together for communal celebration of the Eucharist; in social theology, the basis for the actualization of Christian love in the world, particularly to alleviate suffering; and in human rights, as a corollary of the inalienable divine image in all humans. Personalism, originating in religious philosophy and brought to the forefront in neopatristic theology, is not only an important feature of modern Orthodox thought, but is one of the most significant twentieth-century Orthodox contributions to modern thought. Modern Orthodox theologians have made important advances in the theology of the person, but much remains to be done – not the least to clarify Orthodox thinking on the relationship between men and women, before God, in society and in the church (see Chapter 16).

We noted previously that Metropolitan Kallistos Ware advances three reasons militating for attaching high priority to the theology of the person: urbanization, globalization and technological advance. We can add to this list issues arising from early twenty-first-century debates on gender identity, artificial forms of human reproduction and the 'transhumanism' movement, all of which challenge ancient and modern thinking on what it means to be human. In the face of the impersonalist and dehumanizing forces and ideas present in contemporary society, personalism will undoubtedly continue to be of major importance in Orthodox theology in the years to come.

11

The Church of Christ

Chapter Outline

Orthodox visions of the church

The ancient Fathers of the Church had clear notions of the church, but only one treatise devoted specifically to the church has come down to us, Cyprian of Cartage's short but influential work on the unity of the church, *De catholicae Ecclesiae unitate* (c. 251).[1] Cyprian and other early Fathers considered the nature of the church mostly in the context of specific issues such as the return to the church of Christians who had 'lapsed' in the face of pagan persecution, or who had been members of schismatic or heretical groups. The church emerged as a distinct and major subject in Orthodox theology only in modern times and indeed the first modern treatise of Orthodox theology, Alexei Khomiakov's 'The Church Is One', dealt with ecclesiology.[2] This short essay, written in the mid-1840s but only published in 1864, is the foundation of a great deal of subsequent Orthodox ecclesiology. That Orthodox theology has devoted so much attention to the church since the mid-nineteenth century is a consequence of increasing contact with Western Christianity and the need for Orthodoxy to define itself in relation to Catholic and Protestant forms of Christianity.

[1]For a recent English translation, see Allen Brent, *St Cyprian of Carthage: On the Church: Select Treatises* (Crestwood, NY: St Vladimir's Seminary Press, 2006).

[2]Aleksei Khomiakov, 'The Church Is One' (c. 1848), in Boris Jakim and Robert Bird, eds. and trans., *On Spiritual Unity: A Slavophile Reader* (Hudson, NY: Lindisfarne Books, 1998); also in W. J. Birkbeck, ed., *Russia and the English Church during the Last Fifty Years*, vol. 1 (London: Rivington, Percival & Co., 1895). See Ch. 3 for a fuller discussion of the significance of Khomiakov's essay in modern Orthodox theology.

Metropolitan Kallistos Ware has often stated that ecclesiology was the most important theme in Orthodox theology in the twentieth century and that it should continue to be an important subject in the twenty-first century.[3]

Modern Orthodox notions of the church oscillate between two major poles, the biblical and patristic notion of the church as the Body of Christ, and the perception of the church as a hierarchical institution, albeit a divine-human institution, with a history stretching across two millennia. The church as the Body of Christ lends itself to symbolic, mystical, liturgical and eschatological images and language, whereas the church as a historical and hierarchical entity often tends to be treated, especially by religious studies scholars, both Orthodox and non-Orthodox, as a specialized kind of human institution, subject to the strengths and weaknesses of human nature, with a past (and present) often less than edifying. These two fundamental approaches to the church are far from exclusive and may be in creative dialogue, with a certain degree of tension and ambiguity between them but may also be marked by outright conflict. In modern Orthodox thought, the more mystical approach to the church is exemplified by theologians such as Sergius Bulgakov, Georges Florovsky, Nicholas Afanasiev, Dumitru Staniloae and Boris Bobrinskoy, and the more historical and institutional view of the church by Hilarion Alfeyev and Jean-Claude Larchet.[4]

The church in Russian religious thought

The development of modern Orthodox ecclesiology was initially stimulated by personal contacts with Western Christianity in the nineteenth century, such as Alexei Khomiakov's important correspondence and meetings with leading Anglican personalities.[5] In the twentieth century,

---

[3]Kallistos Ware, 'Orthodox Theology Today: Trends and Tasks', *International Journal for the Study of the Christian Church*, 12, 2 (2012), 115–16.

[4]See in particular Sergius Bulgakov, *The Orthodox Church* (1935) (Yonkers, NY: St Vladimir's Seminary Press, 1988); Sergius Bulgakov, *The Bride of the Lamb* (1945) (Grand Rapids, MI: Erdmann, 2001); Georges Florovsky, essays on 'Ecclesiology and Ecumenism', in Brandon Gallaher and Paul Ladouceur, eds. *The Patristic Witness of Georges Florovsky: Essential Theological Writings* (London: T&T Clark, 2019); Georges Florovsky, 'Le Corps du Christ vivant: Une interprétation orthodoxe de l'Église' (The Body of the Living Christ: an Orthodox interpretation of the church) in Georges Florovsky, Franz-Jehan Leenhardt et al., *La Sainte Église universelle: Confrontation œcuménique* (The Holy Universal Church: Ecumenical Encounter) (Neuchâtel, CH: Delachaux & Niestlé, 1948); Nicholas Afanasiev, *The Church of the Holy Spirit* (1975) (Notre Dame, IN: University of Notre Dame Press, 2007); Dumitru Staniloae, *The Church: Communion in the Holy Spirit* (1978) (*Vol. 4: The Experience of God: Orthodox Dogmatic Theology*) (Brookline, MA: Holy Cross Orthodox Press, 2012); Boris Bobrinskoy, *The Mystery of the Church* (2003) (Yonkers, NY: St Vladimir's Seminary Press, 2012); Hilarion Alfeyev, *Orthodox Christianity. Vol. I: The History and Canonical Structure of the Orthodox Church* (Yonkers, NY: St Vladimir's Seminary Press, 2011), and *Vol. II: Doctrine and Teaching of the Orthodox Church* (Yonkers, NY: St Vladimir's Seminary Press, 2011), Part Five: 'The Church' (387–488); and Jean-Claude Larchet, *L'Église, Corps du Christ Vol. I. Nature et structure. Vol. II. Les relations entre les Églises* (The Church, Body of Christ. Vol. 1 Nature and Structure. Vol. 2 Relations among the Churches) (Paris: Le Cerf, 2012). The Alfeyev, Bobrinskoy and Larchet books are reviewed in our article 'Three Contemporary Orthodox Visions of the Church', *St Vladimir's Theological Quarterly*, 58, 2 (2014).

[5]See Khomiakov's correspondence with William Palmer and related documents in Birkbeck, ed., *Russia and the English Church*.

Orthodox contacts with other Christian denominations became increasingly institutional as the ecumenical movement gathered momentum, beginning with the World Missionary Conference held in Edinburgh in 1910, and reaching a high point with the establishment of the World Council of Churches (WCC) in 1948. The Orthodox (and Catholics, for that matter) were not invited to the Edinburgh Conference, but Greek hierarchs and Russian clergy and theologians in exile after the revolution of 1917 were in contact with Western churches and theologians, Roman Catholic, Anglican and Protestant, and the question of the Orthodox view of the church became an urgent necessity as Orthodox participants in ecumenical encounters beginning in 1920 sought to define Orthodoxy in relation to Western Christianity.

As we saw in Chapter 3, Alexei Khomiakov (1804–60) emphatically articulated an ecclesiology centred on the church as 'a spiritual organism', 'the living ark of the Divine Spirit which bears Christ, her Lord and Saviour ..., bound to him by a close and inner unity which neither human thought can grasp nor human words express.'[6] Khomiakov's vision of the church is essentially organic, mystical and eschatological. The church is sustained by four pillars: faith, love, unity and freedom. 'The church is the revelation of the Holy Spirit to the mutual love of Christians, and it is this love that leads them to the Father by his incarnate Word, Jesus, our Lord,' writes Khomiakov.[7] 'Love is the crown and glory of the church.'[8] The church is thus 'an essentially invisible reality, a union of persons on the basis of their common faith in and love of Christian God'.[9] Khomiakov argues that the church is one because God is One and that the unity of the church subsists despite the multiplicity of Christians and of Christian denominations – the church is both One and many:

> The unity of the church follows necessarily from the unity of God, for the church is not a multiplicity of persons in their personal separateness, but the unity of God's grace, living in the multitude of rational creatures who submit themselves to grace. ... The unity of the church ... is not illusory: it is not metaphorical but true and essential, like the unity of the numerous members of a living body. The church is one despite her seeming division for people who still yet live on the earth. Only with respect to humanity is it possible to accept the division of the church into visible and invisible; her unity, in contrast, is true and absolute.[10]

The unity of the church contained in the common faith in Christ and mutual love among Christians flows from freedom. Freedom is a God-granted characteristic of the church which is transmitted to Christians and manifested in common prayer: 'The blood of the church is mutual prayer, and her breath is the praise of God. We pray in a spirit of love and not utility, in the spirit of filial freedom, and not of mercenary law that asks for payment.'[11]

---

[6]Aleksei Khomiakov, 'On the Western Confessions of Faith', in Alexander Schmemann, *Ultimate Questions: An Anthology of Modern Russian Religious Thought* (Crestwood, NY: St Vladimir's Seminary Press, 1977), 53.
[7]Aleksei Khomiakov, 'Some More Remarks by an Orthodox Christian Concerning the Western Communions, on the Occasion of Several Latin and Protestant Religious Publications', in Jakim and Bird, *On Spiritual Unity*, 121.
[8]Khomiakov, 'The Church Is One', 34.
[9]Aidan Nichols, *Light from the East: Authors and Themes in Orthodox Theology* (London: Sheed & Ward, 1995), 121.
[10]Khomiakov, 'The Church Is One', 31.
[11]Ibid., 50.

Khomiakov summarized his views of the essential distinguishing characteristics of the Orthodox, Catholic and Protestant churches in terms of contrasts between freedom and authority, love and obedience, community and individual, unity and disharmony. In one well-known passage he writes:

> Three great voices can be heard in Europe. 'Obey, and believe in my decrees', says the voice of Rome. 'Be free, and try to construct for yourselves', says the voice of Protestantism. And the voice of the [Orthodox] Church says to her children: 'Let us love one another, that with one accord we may confess Father, Son and Holy Spirit' [from the liturgy of St John Chrysostom].[12]

If the Catholic Church is characterized by authority and obedience, and Protestantism by freedom and individualism, Orthodoxy reflects simultaneously freedom, love, community and unity: 'But we proclaim the church to be one and free – one without need for an official representative of its unity [Catholicism] and free without this freedom being manifested in the disunion of its members [Protestantism].'[13] Nicolas Zernov (1898–1980) aptly characterizes Khomiakov's thinking on Catholicism and Protestantism:

> The reaction at the time of the Reformation against the excessive claims of the popes went amiss, for it sprang from the wrong spirit. Protestantism was nothing more than papal individualism brought to its logical conclusion. Rome had imposed upon the Christian West unity without freedom; the Protestants achieved freedom, but at the expense of unity. Yet neither unity without freedom nor freedom without unity was of any use. They both meant the isolation of man, and his exclusion from the redeeming influence of true Christian fellowship. The West had rejected the fundamental teaching of love, on which the whole life of the church was based.[14]

In one form or another, this reductionist analysis persists as the *leitmotiv* concerning Western Christianity among many Orthodox.

Khomiakov's principal ecclesiological concern was to distinguish Orthodoxy from the 'Western confessions', Catholicism and Protestantism. At times he separated the Anglican Church from Protestantism, seeing in Anglicanism the closest image to Orthodox tradition in the West. His contacts with leading Anglicans, together with the strong personal interest of the Anglican theologian and liturgical scholar William Palmer (1803–85) with the Russian Church, laid the foundations for the long-standing friendship between Orthodoxy and Anglicanism.

Despite a great affection for the Anglican Church – he refers to Anglicanism as 'the most pure and antilogic (*antilogique*) of all the Western confessions'.[15] Khomiakov was not blind to a major

---

[12]Aleksei Khomiakov, *L'Église latine et le Protestantisme au point de vue de l'Eglise d'Orient* (The Latin Church and Protestantism from the Perspective of the Eastern Church) (Lausanne, 1872; Vevey CH: Xenia, 2006), 308.

[13]Aleksei Khomiakov, 'Some Remarks by an Orthodox Christian Concerning the Western Communions on the Occasion of a Letter Published by the Archbishop of Paris', in Jakim and Bird, *On Spiritual Unity*, 78; *L'Église latine et le Protestantisme*, 117–18.

[14]Nicolas Zernov, *Three Russian Prophets: Khomiakov, Dostoyevsky, Soloviev* (London: SCM Press, 1944), 67. Zernov's summary of Khomiakov's argument is based mainly on Khomiakov's essay 'Some Remarks by an Orthodox Christian Concerning the Western Communions' (in Jakim and Bird, eds., *On Spiritual Unity*); and 'Some More Remarks by an Orthodox Christian Concerning the Western Communions'. The observation about unity and freedom is not entirely original. In 1832 the German Liberal leader Karl von Rotteck cried out at a rally, 'Rather freedom without unity than unity without freedom'.

[15]Khomiakov, *L'Église latine et le Protestantisme*, 257–8.

weakness in Anglicanism: the Anglican Church reflects a unity of ritual but a diversity of beliefs. Palmer wrote to Khomiakov citing passages from Anglican sources which affirmed the same doctrine as Metropolitan Philaret (Drozov) of Moscow (1782–1867) in his *Longer Catechism*. In his reply, Khomiakov points out that he could produce an alternative volume, quoting other authoritative Anglican writers who contradict Philaret. Khomiakov continues:

> The Calvinist Usher[16] is an Anglican no less than the bishops (whom you quote) who hold quite Orthodox language. We may and do sympathise with the individuals; we cannot and dare not sympathise with a church which interpolates the Symbol [the Nicene Creed] and doubts her right to that interpolation, or which gives Communion to those *who declare* the Bread and Wine of the High Sacrifice to be mere bread and wine, as well as to those who declare it to be the Body and Blood of Christ.[17]

Underlying the Slavophile criticism of the West in general and Western Christianity in particular was an assessment that saw the West as deviating from the truth of Christianity by an exaggerated importance attached to human rationality – a common Orthodox critique of the West. Ivan Kireevsky (1806–56), another leading Slavophile, sees the root cause of the split between East and West in 'the Roman mind' which favours 'the predominance of superficial rationality over the inner essence of things'[18]:

> Rome prefers abstract syllogism [i.e. logic or deductive reasoning] over sacred tradition, which is the repository of the common consciousness of the whole Christian world and holds the Universal Church together in a living, indissoluble unity. This preference for syllogism over tradition was actually the only condition for the separate and independent rise of Rome. … [Rome] defected from [the Universal Church] only because it wished to introduce new dogmas into the faith, dogmas unknown to church tradition and born of the arbitrary deductions of the logic of Western peoples.[19]

The Slavophiles essentially saw the church as the community of the faithful, modelled on the Russian peasant community, the *obshchina* ('commune') or *mir* (here, 'society', also 'peace' and 'world'). To characterize the church as community, the Slavophiles coined the term *sobornost'*, translated typically as 'catholicity' or 'conciliarity', corresponding approximately with the third 'mark' of the church in the Nicene Creed ('Catholic'), with the sense of 'organic togetherness'.[20]

The Slavophiles' reductionist views of the West and Western Christianity easily contrasted with an idealized vision of Orthodoxy. Their simplifications of the complex nature of Western

---

[16]James Usher (1580–1656), Archbishop of Armagh and Primate of All Ireland between 1625 and 1656, had strong Calvinist leanings.

[17]Alexei Khomiakov, 'Third Letter to Mr Palmer' (28 November 1846), in Jakim and Bird, eds., *On Spiritual Unity*, 152.

[18]Ivan Kireevsky, 'On the Nature of European Culture and on Its Relationship to Russian Culture: Letter to Count E. E. Komarovsky' (1852), in Jakim and Bird, eds., *On Spiritual Unity*, 200. See a fuller account of Kireevsky's thought in Ch. 3, 51–2.

[19]Ivan Kireevsky, 'On the Necessity and Possibility of New Principles in Philosophy', in Jakim and Bird, eds., *On Spiritual Unity*, 236–7. The 'dogmas unknown to sacred tradition' are likely the *filioque* and papal supremacy.

[20]See V. V. Zenkovsky, *A History of Russian Philosophy*, vol. 1 (London: Routeledge & Kegan Paul, 1953), 204.

culture, thought and religious experience and their failure to take account of the reality of the Orthodox Church did not escape the leaders of the Russian religious renaissance a few decades later. The nature of the church was a practical issue at the end of the nineteenth century for many Russian intellectuals: how to reconcile a mystical or spiritual notion of the church, based on the New Testament and the Fathers and idealized in the Slavophile vision of the Orthodox Church, with the Russian Orthodox Church (ROC) as a powerful hierarchical institution, displaying obvious weaknesses and largely controlled by the state? After the failed revolution of 1905, the ROC itself grappled with this dilemma, as factions in the church debated the need for reform of the church structures and governance put in place by Peter the Great two centuries earlier. Despite considerable preparation for a council, internal opposition, including that of the imperial family, prevented the convocation of a council to address these issues prior to the First World War. The council was finally held in late 1917, after the fall of the monarchy in the revolution of February 1917.[21] Notions derived from *sobornost'* figured high on the agenda and in the spirit of the council, including its structure: lay persons and lower clergy accounted for a majority of the official delegates. But it was too late for effective reform. The council's sessions took place under the canons of the Bolshevik revolution and the Bolsheviks prevented the council from terminating its work.

The ecclesiology of Vladimir Soloviev (1853–1900), consistent with his commitment to all-unity as a philosophical principle, revolves around his conviction of the underlying unity of Christianity, despite the visible division of Christians into numerous communities. Although Soloviev adopts the Slavophile notion of *sobornost'* as a prime characteristic of the church, he repudiates Slavophile structural anti-Westernism and its search for the meaning of Orthodoxy solely in Russo-Byzantine particularism. Despite a certain universalist inclination, Khomiakov had argued against a broad view of the church. 'The church', he wrote, 'cannot be a harmony of discords; it cannot be a numerical sum of Orthodox, Latins [Catholics] and Protestants'.[22] Against this exclusivist view of the church, Soloviev and many of his successors envisioned the church as inclusive or universal, founded on the Incarnation of the Word of God, on the divine-humanity of the Logos: 'The basic truth of the church is the union of the divine and the human in the Word made Flesh, the recognition of the Son of Man as the Christ, the Son of the living God.' Soloviev agrees with the Slavophiles that the truth of the church is signified in love, but love seen in its broadest sense: 'The love which is to create the religious unity of the human race, or the Universal Church, must surpass the bounds of nationality and have for its object the sum total of mankind.'[23]

Disturbed by the nationalism and anti-Westernism of the ROC and its subordination to the state, Soloviev looked for a more universal expression of the Church of Christ. This he saw initially in the Catholic Church, which for him was a supranational entity, the basis of true Christian unity. Soloviev expressed these ideas most forcibly in his book *Russia and the Universal Church*, published

[21]For a study and key documents of the Council of 1917–1918 see Hyacinthe Destivelle, *The Moscow Council (1917-1918): The Creation of the Conciliar Institutions of the Russian Orthodox Church* (Notre Dame, IN: University of Notre Dame Press, 2015).
[22]Khomiakov, 'Third Letter to Mr Palmer', 69.
[23]Vladimir Soloviev, *Russia and the Universal Church* (1889) (London: Geoffrey Bles. The Centenary Press, 1948), 99; 100.

in French in 1889 because it could not be published in Russia. Echoing the concern expressed by Alexander Bukharev a generation earlier, Soloviev is critical of the isolation of the Orthodox Church from the concerns of the people, 'its solitary asceticism and its contemplative mysticism, its withdrawal from political life and from all the social problems which concern mankind as a whole.'[24] Yet Soloviev does not dismiss the focus of the Orthodox Church on individual salvation: 'The religious ideal of the separated Christian East is not false'; rather, 'it is incomplete.'[25] The Western Church, he argues, is more holistic:

> In Eastern Christendom for the last thousand years, religion has been identified with personal piety, and prayer has been regarded as the one and only religious activity. The Western Church, without disparaging individual piety as the true germ of all religion, seeks the development of this germ and its blossoming into a social activity organised for the glory of God and the universal good of mankind. The Eastern prays, the Western prays and labours.[26]

For Soloviev, the Universal Church unites both East and West and it is incumbent on Orthodoxy to recognize that it is 'an organic part of the great body of Christendom' and to affirm 'our spiritual solidarity with our Western brethren.'[27] He concludes:

> We must, above all, recognise the insufficiency of our traditional religious ideal, and make a sincere attempt to realise a more complete conception of Christianity. There is no need to invent or create anything new for this purpose. We merely have to restore to our religion its Catholic or universal character by recognizing our oneness with the active part of the Christian world, with the West centralised and organised for a universal activity and possessing all that we lack. We are not asked to change our nature as Easterns or to repudiate the specific character of our religious genius. We have only to recognise unreservedly the elementary truth that we of the East are but a part of the Universal Church, a part moreover which has not its centre within itself, and that therefore it behoves us to restore the link between our individual forces upon the circumference and the great universal centre which Providence has placed in the West.[28]

Whereas the Slavophiles idealized the Orthodox Church, in *Russia and the Universal Church* (1889), Soloviev has an idealized view of the Catholic Church, as in this passage:

> From the humblest priest up to the Pope, the servant of the servants of God, all are absolutely free, as far as their sacred ministry is concerned, from self-asserting egoism or isolated particularism; each one is simply a distinct organ of a united social whole, the Universal Church.[29]

Later Soloviev moved to a less idealistic notion of the Catholic Church, notably in the last work published in his lifetime, *War, Progress, and the End of History: Three Conversations, Including a Short Tale of the Antichrist* (1900). In the *Tale of the Antichrist*, the papacy, driven from Rome

---

[24]Soloviev, *Russia and the Universal Church*, 40.
[25]Ibid.
[26]Ibid.
[27]Ibid., 42.
[28]Ibid., 41–2.
[29]Ibid., 204.

under pressure from the 'Great Emperor', finds refuge in St Petersburg, where, writes Soloviev, 'it soon became greatly simplified. Leaving practically unchanged the number of its colleges and offices, it was obliged to infuse into their work a fervent spirit, and to cut down to the smallest limits its pompous ritual and ceremonial. Many strange and seductive customs, though not formally abolished, fell of themselves into disuse.' Soloviev also refers to 'all the abuses of the Papal authority known to history'.[30] In the end, Christianity is saved from the anti-Christ, not by Catholicism or Orthodoxy, but by Protestantism, represented in the *Tale* by Professor Pauli, a German Lutheran theologian.

Soloviev's immediate successors, especially Sergius Bulgakov (1871–1944), continued to develop aspects of his thinking on the church, a concern which became vitally urgent as the leaders of the Russian religious renaissance found themselves in exile as an Orthodox minority in Western Europe. Bulgakov's ecclesiology includes both a vision of the church in the light of sophiology and a more conventional treatment of the church. Thus, Divine Sophia is the heavenly church, while creaturely Sophia is the earthly church, creaturely hypostases united in Christ.[31] Bulgakov's ecclesiology is infused with a cosmic vision of the church: not only Orthodox, not only all Christians, but all humanity, indeed all creation, belong to the church. In his popular work *The Orthodox Church* (1935), Bulgakov focuses especially on the church as *sobornost'*, understood in the broad sense of catholicity or conciliarity, interpreting *sobornost'* as 'ecumenicity', a universalist conception of the church which 'includes all peoples and all parts of the earth'.[32]

In his more substantial treatment of the church in *The Bride of the Lamb* (1945), Bulgakov views the church both as the mystical Bride of Christ and as a sacramental and hierarchical organization.[33] The church is creation called to achieve its ultimate purpose in God, its deification according to the divine plan: 'All human beings belong to Christ's humanity. And if this human condition is the church as the body of Christ, then, in this sense, *all* humanity belongs to the church. … The whole universe belongs to the church. The universe is the periphery, the cosmic face of the church.'[34] This is the full realization of divine-humanity, the meaning of the Incarnation, 'the universal and all-human power of Christ's Incarnation'.[35]

In a way Bulgakov's cosmic ecclesiology represents the fulfilment of the quest of the Russian religious renaissance for all-unity, both in creation and between Creator and creation, even if he casts the church in a sophiological mould from which it is difficult to extract. In Bulgakov, the church is the symbol and the reality of the all-unity of all that exists, divine and human, material and immaterial, animate and inanimate. The weakness of this grandiose vision is that, despite Bulgakov's defences of his theology, it can be conceived as opening the door to pantheism and determinism, as we discussed in Chapter 9.

[30]Vladimir Soloviev, *War, Progress, and the End of History: Three Conversations, Including a Short Tale of the Antichrist* (1900) (London: University of London Press/Hodder & Stouton, 1915), 202; 219. Revised reprint: Hudson, NY: Lindisfarne Books, 1990.
[31]See Bulgakov, *The Bride of the Lamb*, 253–68.
[32]Bulgakov, *The Orthodox Church*, 61.
[33]Bulgakov, 'The Church', Ch. 5 of *The Bride of the Lamb*, 253–314.
[34]Bulgakov, *The Bride of the Lamb*, 266–7.
[35]Ibid., 266.

Georges Florovsky's ecclesiology

Georges Florovsky (1893-1979) was the leading Orthodox figure in the ecumenical movement from the late 1930s until the 1970s. Florovsky's ecclesiology represents both continuity with certain notions of his predecessors concerning the church, as well as a break with them. In his seminal if still contested 1933 article on 'The Limits of the Church', Florovsky examines the reception of heretics and schismatics in the early church without the requirement of a new baptism, seeing in this a recognition of divine grace even among those visibly separated from the main body of the church.[36] Florovsky follows Augustine's more open and charismatic approach to the church than Cyprian's narrower, canonical vision of the church. While agreeing with Cyprian that sacraments are valid only within the church, Florovsky, like Augustine, brings the debate to a different level, the identity of the church. For Cyprian, the canonical church was *the* church, but Florovsky concludes that the charismatic and sacramental activity of the church extends beyond the canonical boundaries of the Orthodox Church:

> As a mystical organism, as the sacramental Body of Christ, the church cannot be adequately described in canonical terms or categories alone. It is impossible to state or discern the true limits of the church simply by canonical signs or marks. … In her sacramental, mysterious being the church surpasses canonical measurements. For that reason a canonical cleavage does not immediately signify mystical impoverishment and desolation.[37]

In his 1933 essay, Florovsky explicitly rejects the 'economic' argument for the validity of sacraments outside the canonical church, that is, that such sacramental rites become efficacious only when the non-Orthodox person joins the Orthodox Church. His principal theological argument is that the church does not have 'the power and the right, as it were, to convert the has-not-been into the has-been, to change the meaningless into the valid' (that is, to change an invalid or inefficacious baptismal rite into a valid and efficacious one).[38] Florovsky concludes unequivocally:

> The 'economical' interpretation is not the teaching of the church. It is only a private 'theological opinion', very late and very controversial, having arisen in a period of theological confusion and decadence in a hasty endeavour to dissociate oneself as sharply as possible from Roman theology.[39]

What then distinguishes heretics and schismatics from the church? Florovsky identifies the nature of their separation by appealing to the difference between the 'unity of the Spirit', the continuing action of the Holy Spirit in the church, or grace, and the 'union of peace', love and fellowship among the faithful:

> The unity of the church is based on a twofold bond – the 'unity of the Spirit' and the 'union of peace' (cf. Eph 4:3). In sects and schisms the 'union of peace' is broken and torn apart, but the 'unity of the Spirit' in the sacraments is [not] terminated. This is the unique paradox of sectarian existence;

---

[36]Georges Florovsky, 'The Limits of the Church' (1933), in Brandon Gallaher and Paul Ladouceur, eds., *The Patristic Witness of Georges Florovsky: Essential Theological Writings* (London: T&T Clark, 2019), 247–56.
[37]Florovsky, 'The Limits of the Church', 248–9.
[38]Ibid., 251.
[39]Ibid., 253.

> the sect remains united with the church in the grace of the sacraments, and this becomes a condemnation once love and communal mutuality have withered.[40]

Here and elsewhere Florovsky retains as an aspect of the church the general Slavophile characterization of the church as unity in freedom and love – *sobornost'* – , while putting aside, like Soloviev and Bulgakov, the Slavophile identification of the model of the church in Russian peasant communal organization. And whereas Bulgakov and others boldly advance a cosmic and eschatological vision of the church, Florovsky more timidly but perhaps more soundly opens the door to a consideration of the church as more than only the canonical Orthodox Church.

The originality of Florovsky's contribution to Orthodox ecclesiology lies in his unflinching focus on Christ as the basis of the unity of the church, a line of thought developed from the Pauline notion of the church as the Body of Christ. Florovsky's longest and most developed writing on the church is in fact entitled 'Le Corps du Christ vivant' – 'The Body of the Living Christ', an expanded version of a paper prepared for the founding Assembly of the WCC in Amsterdam in 1948.[41] Distinguishing between the Incarnation of the Word of God and the role of the Holy Spirit, Florovsky argues that

> Christians are united not only among themselves, but first of all they *are one – in Christ*, and only this communion *with* Christ makes the communion of all men possible – *in* him. The centre of unity *is the Lord* and the power that effects and enacts the unity *is the Spirit*. ... The church, as a whole, has her *personal centre* only in Christ, she is not an incarnation of the Holy Spirit, nor is she merely a Spirit-bearing community, but precisely the Body of Christ, the Incarnate Lord.[42]

Florovsky asks: 'Should we start just with the fact of the church's being a "Community", and then investigate her "structure" and "notes"? Or should we rather start with Christ, God Incarnate, and investigate the implications of the total dogma of the Incarnation, including the glory of the Risen and Ascended Lord, who sitteth at the right hand of the Father?'[43] It is in this sense that Florovsky states that 'the theology of the church is but a chapter, indeed a crucial chapter, of Christology. And without this chapter Christology itself would be incomplete. It is in the context of Christology that the mystery of the church is announced in the New Testament. It was presented in a similar fashion by the Greek and Latin Fathers.'[44]

---

[40]Ibid.

[41]Georges Florovsky, 'Le Corps du Christ vivant'. The original, much shorter version of Florovsky's essay was published as 'The Church: Her Nature and Task', in World Council of Churches, *The Universal Church in God's Design* (London: Student Christian Movement Press, 1948). English translation of the full text forthcoming: *The Body of the Living Christ: An Orthodox Interpretation of the Church* (New York: The Wheel). Florovsky's Introduction to 'The Body of the Living Christ' is contained in Gallaher and Ladouceur, eds., *The Patristic Witness of Georges Florovsky*, 273–7.

[42]Florovsky, 'The Church: Her Nature and Task', 46; 53–4.

[43]From Matthew Baker, 'The Body of the Living Christ: Ecclesiology in the Thought of Father Georges Florovsky'. Paper at the symposium 'The Body of the Living Christ: The Patristic Doctrine of the Church', Princeton Theological Seminary, 10–11 February 2012. www.fellowshipofstmaximos.org/?p=78 (6 December 2015). Baker's short paper is a fine overview of the sources and content of Florovsky's ecclesiology.

[44]Florovsky, 'The Body of the Living Christ' (1984), in Gallaher and Ladouceur, eds., *The Patristic Witness of Georges Florovsky*, 277.

Faithful to the insight that divisions in the church arise from a break in love and fellowship, in 1956 Florovsky stated:

> The church cannot be divided, as Christ is never divided. But both individuals and groups can 'go astray', and fail to abide in the 'fullness'. Membership in the church is constituted by an active and faithful sharing of the 'fullness'. Church is ever One and 'Undivided', but there are 'schisms' in the Christendom. The main paradox of the 'Divided Christendom' is that there are 'separated Christians', which are in a sense 'outside of the church' and yet are still intimately, and, in a varying measure, effectively related to her.[45]

Despite his emphasis on the corporate unity of the church in Christ, Florovsky was disturbed by the possible depersonalization and determinism inherent in the notion of the church as an organism. As a corrective to even his own vision of the church, Florovsky also stresses the continuing singularity of human personhood, never fused into a vast ecclesial entity or into the divinity with a loss of personal identity:

> The idea of an organism, when used of the church, has its own limitations. On the one hand, the church is composed of human personalities, which never can be regarded merely as elements or cells of the whole, because each is in direct and immediate union with Christ and his Father – the personal is not to be sacrificed or dissolved in the corporate, Christian 'togetherness' must not degenerate into impersonalism. The idea of the organism must be supplemented by the idea of a symphony of personalities, in which the mystery of the Holy Trinity is reflected (cf. Jn 17:21 and 23), and this is the core of the conception of 'catholicity' (*sobornost'*).[46]

The final key element in Florovsky's ecclesiology is a firm eschatological perspective. Present on earth, the church will achieve its fullness only in the plenitude of the Kingdom of God. The church lives 'in two lives' – *in duas vitas* (from Augustine):

> The church is still *in statu viae* ['in a state of journeying'] and yet it is already *in statu patriae* ['in the place of the Father', the Kingdom of God].[47] It has, as it were, a double life, both in heaven and on earth.[48] The church is a visible historical society, and the same is the Body of Christ. It is both the church of the redeemed, and the church of the miserable sinners – both at once. On the historical level no *final* goal has yet been attained. But the *ultimate* reality has been disclosed and revealed. This ultimate reality is still at hand, is truly available, in spite of the historical imperfection, though but in provisional forms. For the church is a sacramental society. *Sacramental* means no less than '*eschatological*'. *To eschaton* does not mean primarily *final*, in the temporal series of events; it means rather *ultimate* (decisive); and the ultimate is being realized within the stress of historical happenings and events. … Yet the Spirit abides in the church. This constitutes the mystery of the church: a visible 'society' of frail men *is* an organism of the Divine Grace.[49]

---

[45]Unpublished notes from a Florovsky lecture in 1956 cited in Seraphim Danckaert, 'Orthodoxy and Inter-Christian Dialogue: 10 Principles from Fr. Georges Florovsky' (in 'The Sounding', 14 June 2014). http://myocn.net/florovsky-and-ecumenism (12 December 2015).
[46]Florovsky, 'The Church: Her Nature and Task', 53.
[47]The expressions are likely from Thomas Aquinas, *Summa theologiae*, 3a, 8.3.2 and 7.10.3.
[48]Florovsky's note: St Augustine in *Evang. Joannis tract*, 124, 5, ML, 35, 19f., 7.
[49]Florovsky, 'The Church: Her Nature and Task', 54.

Yet these 'two lives' of the church are intimately interwoven; they are, writes Florovsky 'united and interrelated in the identity of subject: unconfusedly, unchangeably, indivisibly, inseparably. There is but one church, "visible" and "invisible" at once, humiliated and glorious at once. The human condition is not abrogated by divine grace but only redeemed and transfigured.'[50]

Much of Florovsky's ecclesiology is summed up in Augustine's well-known adage which Florovsky cites repeatedly: *Totus Christus: Caput et Corpus* (The whole Christ: Head and Body). As Matthew Baker writes, for Florovsky, Augustine's expression 'inscribes a paradox of fullness and expectation, fulfilment and historical duration.'[51]

Eucharistic ecclesiology

From the initial Slavophile intuition of the church as *sobornost'* and as reworked by Soloviev and Bulgakov into a universal rather than a Russian concept, Fr Nicholas Afanasiev (1893–1966), followed by Metropolitan John Zizioulas (b. 1931) and others, eloquently developed what became known as Eucharistic ecclesiology. Like the Slavophiles, Afanasiev, who taught at the St Sergius Theological Institute from 1930 to 1940 and again from 1947 to 1966, begins his reflection on the church as community. But instead of looking as did the Slavophiles to the traditional Russian peasant community as the model of the church, he turns to the early Christian communities, which he sees as Eucharistic communities embodying the fullness of the church in a given locality. Afanasiev summarizes his basic thesis in a few sentences:

> As the Body of Christ, the church manifests herself in all her fullness in the eucharistic assembly of the local church, because Christ is present in the Eucharist in the fullness of his body. This is why the local church possesses all the fullness of the church.[52]

Afanasiev's ecclesiology raises a fundamental issue which lies at the centre of much subsequent Orthodox reflection on the church: What is the relationship between the local church embodying the fullness of the church and the universal church? Afanasiev felt that he had provided for this relationship by highlighting the essential role of the bishop in the Eucharistic community:

> According to its very nature, the eucharistic assembly could not exist without its president, or, according to the terminology established by usage, without the bishop. The foundation of the ministry of the bishop is the eucharistic assembly. … Consequently, when we speak of the eucharistic assembly, we are in fact speaking of the bishop.[53]

---

[50]Georges Florovsky, 'The Historical Problem of a Definition of the Church', in Richard S. Haugh, ed., *Ecumenism II: A Historical Approach*, Vol. XIV of *The Collected Works of Georges Florovsky* (Vaduz: Büchervertriebsanstalt, 1989), 31.

[51]Baker, 'The Body of the Living Christ: Ecclesiology in the Thought of Father Georges Florovsky'. Augustine's adage appears immediately after the title in Florovsky's 'Le Corps du Christ vivant'.

[52]Nicholas Afanasiev, 'Una sancta' (1963), in Michael Plekon, ed., *Tradition Alive: On the Church and the Christian Life in Our Time – Readings from the Eastern Church* (Lanham, MD: Rowman & Littlefield, 2003), 14.

[53]Afanasiev, 'Una sancta', 14.

Afanasiev's thinking on the church goes beyond Eucharistic ecclesiology in a narrow sense, to see 'the church of God in Christ' first and foremost as 'the church of the Holy Spirit', the title of his posthumous treatise exploring pneumatological or charismatic ecclesiology in depth. The church 'lives and acts by the Spirit' and Afanasiev quotes approvingly Irenaeus's formula 'Wherever the church is, there also is the Holy Spirit; but wherever the Holy Spirit is, there is the church and the fullness of grace.'[54] Afanasiev's emphasis on the role of the Holy Spirit in the church stands in contrast with Florovsky's Christological approach to the church, opening the door to debates on the roles of Christ and the Holy Spirit in the church.

Afanasiev also devotes considerable attention to the royal priesthood of all the faithful, conferred by baptism and chrismation, which makes of every Christian a priest of the New Testament: 'In the New Testament, the entire people constitutes the priesthood, therefore no part could be separated from the rest.'[55] While Afanasiev carefully identifies the roles of the priest and the bishop in the church, he asserts that 'there can be no non-charismatic members in the church, just as there can be no members who do not minister in it.' The difference between those who have particular ministries and those who do not 'is not ontological but functional'.[56] The main function of the bishop or priest is to preside at the Eucharistic assembly, as in the early church.[57] The ontological versus the functional nature of the priesthood remains a contested issue. John Zizioulas, for one, rejects the dichotomy ontology/function and instead views ordination in terms of relation:

> In the light of the *koinonia* of the Holy Spirit, ordination relates the ordained man so profoundly and existentially to the community that in his new state after ordination he cannot be any longer, as a minister, conceived in himself. In this state, existence is determined by communion which qualifies and defines both 'ontology' and 'communion.'[58]

As a practical ecumenical conclusion of his ecclesiology, Afanasiev considers that Eucharistic unity has always existed between the Orthodox Church and the Catholic Church since they celebrate the same Eucharist despite dogmatic differences, a point of view shared by Orthodox thinkers such as Vladimir Soloviev and Sergius Bulgakov,[59] but contested by others, notably Georges Florovsky.

Afanasiev's emphasis on the local Eucharistic assembly and his apparent minimization of the importance of dogmatic differences in an ecumenical context stimulated major critiques and revisions of his ecclesiology, especially by John Zizioulas. Zizioulas emphasizes the importance of unity of faith in the church and, considerably more than Afanasiev, the role of the bishop both in the local Eucharistic community and in the universal church. Zizioulas affirms the divine origin and nature of episcopal authority and from there, the essential place of the bishop, beyond the celebration of the Eucharist, in defining the church:

---

[54] Afanasiev, *The Church of the Holy Spirit*, 20, citing *Adv. Haer.*, 3, 24, 1.

[55] Afanasiev, *The Church of the Holy Spirit*, 14.

[56] Ibid., 16.

[57] Afanasiev, 'Those Who Preside in the Lord', *The Church of the Holy Spirit*, 133–47.

[58] John Zizioulas, *Being as Communion: Studies in Priesthood and the Church* (Yonkers, NY: St Vladimir's Seminary Press, 1985), 226.

[59] Bulgakov also believed that this Eucharistic unity existed with the Anglican Church, as was made clear in his proposal for limited intercommunion between Anglicans and Orthodox in the Fellowship of St Alban and St Sergius (see Ch. 12, 289–93).

> The unity of the church is not simply eucharistic, but because of the relation of the Bishop to the Eucharist it becomes hierarchical as well. … Whatever is accomplished in the church is valid only when it is approved by the Bishop. The Bishop is not from men or through men but from Christ. … The catholic church, as the whole church, is such by virtue of the fact that she has the whole Christ. *But the local church too is likewise catholic, because she has the whole Christ through the Divine Eucharist. The Bishop as being directly connected with the Divine Eucharist* represents the local church in the same way as the whole Christ represents the generic (*katholou*) or catholic church.[60]

Zizioulas's ecclesiology is not only Eucharistic and hierarchical, but also Trinitarian and personalist. Just as God's being is fundamentally communion or love among the three Persons of the Holy Trinity, so humans are called to realize the fullness of their existence, of their personhood, in communion with God and with each other, through Eucharistic communion in the church. Zizioulas calls this aspect of human existence in the church an 'ecclesial hypostasis', which is 'something different' from the mere 'biological hypostasis':

> The ecclesial hypostasis is the *faith* of man in his capacity to become a person and his *hope* that he will indeed become an authentic person. … The Eucharist is first of all an assembly (*synaxis*), a community, a network of relations, in which man 'subsists' in a manner different from the biological as a member of a body which transcends every exclusiveness of a biological or social kind. … Christ is 'parted but not divided' and every communicant is the whole Christ and the whole church. The ecclesial identity, consequently, in its historical realization is eucharistic.[61]

Eucharistic ecclesiology as developed by Nicholas Afanasiev and John Zizioulas rapidly became the pre-eminent vision of the church in Orthodox thought and indeed had a powerful impact in wide Christian circles, especially in the Catholic Church, which endorsed Eucharistic ecclesiology at the Second Vatican Council (1962–65).[62] Afanasiev was in fact a specially invited observer at the Council. But in the new millennium Zizioulas's star began to wane as his ecclesiology and other aspects of his theology came under severe criticism within Orthodoxy (see the critiques of Zizioulas's theology of personhood in Chapter 10).

The main criticisms levied against Zizioulas's Eucharistic ecclesiology are that he overemphasizes the importance of the liturgical role of the bishop in the constitution of the church, to the detriment of the entire people of God, the priesthood and indeed the pastoral and teaching roles not only of the bishop but of spiritual elders in Orthodoxy (*gerontes* or *startsi*), who are also channels of grace and sources of teaching in the church. Zizioulas seeks justification for the primacy of the bishop at the local level, of the primate of the local (autocephalous) Orthodox churches and of the universal primate (the patriarch of Constantinople) mainly in the monarchy of the Father in Trinitarian

---

[60]John Zizioulas, *Eucharist, Bishop, Church: The Unity of the Church in the Divine Eucharist and the Bishop during the First Three Centuries* (1965), (Brookline, MA: Holy Cross Orthodox Press, 2001), 116–17.

[61]Zizioulas, *Being as Communion*, 58; 60–1.

[62]There are numerous studies of Eucharistic ecclesiology within the Catholic Church. For résumés, see Joseph Ratzinger, 'The Ecclesiology of the Constitution of the Church, Vatican II, Lumen Gentium', Rome (2000). www.ewtn.com/library/CURIA/CDFECCL.HTM; and 'The Ecclesiology of Vatican II', (Aversa IT, 2001). https://www.ewtn.com/library/CURIA/CDFECCV2.HTM (5 December 2015). For a longer treatment, see Jean-Marie Roger Tillard, *Église d'Églises. L'ecclésiologie de communion* (The Church of the Churches: Communion Ecclesiology) (Paris: Le Cerf, 1987).

theology, in Christology (Christ as the Head of the Church) and in Eucharistic ecclesiology (the bishop as the presider of the Eucharistic assembly).[63] Zizioulas is taken to task for ignoring the historical and canonical dimensions for the rise of hierarchy in the church.

Fr Cyril Hovorun traces the incrustation of the hierarchical principle in the church mainly to the models provided by the social and political hierarchies of the Roman world, and to the popularity of the Dionysian corpus of writings (early sixth century), which provided a theological justification for hierarchy and primacy in the church.[64] In contrast, from the historical experience of the church, Hovorun concludes that 'the church is not hierarchical in nature. The hierarchical principle is not even its natural property. It was borrowed from outside the church and remains there as its scaffolding.'[65] While this argument undermines the 'superstructure' of Zizioulas's ecclesiology founded on hierarchy, it does not destroy Eucharistic ecclesiology, but it does leave unresolved the relationship of the local Eucharistic community to the universal church.

Other critiques of Zizioulas's ecclesiology are that he attaches an excessive importance to collective aspects of the church and of the sacraments, especially the Eucharist, downplaying the personal nature of church membership and individual relations with God, including communion as a direct relationship with Christ and not only a communal function, as well as spiritual practices such as personal prayer, reading of Scripture and fasting; that he neglects sacraments other than the Eucharist, especially baptism, as the initiation into the church, and confession as a recognition of personal weakness and restoration of full life in the church; that his theology, like that of Nicholas Afanasiev, contains an imbalance in favour of the Holy Spirit (pneumatology) over Christ (Christology) in the church and that he attaches excessive weight to primacy in the church (the role of the hierarchy) over conciliarity (*sobornost'*).[66] Some critiques of Zizioulas's ecclesiology are derived from a broader critique of his personalism and indeed of the entire Orthodox personalist school, critiques based on a perceived and exaggerated opposition between nature-necessity-individual and person-freedom-communion (see Chapter 10).

Fr Dumitru Staniloae (1903–93), in his *Orthodox Dogmatic Theology*, concentrates on what we call the mystical approach to the church. Staniloae sees the church above all as an eschatological and cosmic entity and as a 'theandric' entity, with a dual divine and human nature. 'The church is

[63]See notably John Zizioulas, 'Primacy in the Church: An Orthodox Approach', *Eastern Churches Journal*, 5, 2 (1998); also in James F. Puglisi, ed., *Petrine Ministry and the Unity of the Church: Toward a Patient and Fraternal Dialogue* (Collegeville, MI: Liturgical Press, 1999); and *Sourozh*, 84 (2001).

[64]See Cyril Hovorun, *Scaffolds of the Church: Towards Poststructural Ecclesiology* (Eugene, OR: Cascade Books, 2017), especially Ch. 5, 'Pyramids: Primacy', and Ch. 6, 'Strata: Ministry'.

[65]Hovorun, *Scaffolds of the Church*, 141.

[66]For critiques of Zizioulas's ecclesiology, see John Behr, 'The Trinitarian Being of the Church', *St Vladimir's Theological Quarterly*, 48, 1 (2004), 697–70; John Eriksson, 'The Church in Modern Orthodox Thought: Towards a Baptismal Ecclesiology', *International Journal for the Study of the Christian Church*, 11, 2–3 (2011); Jean-Claude Larchet, review of John Zizioulas, *L'Église et ses institutions* (The Church and Her Institutions) (Paris: Le Cerf, 2011). www.orthodoxie.com/lire/recensions/recensiion-metropolite-jean-zizioulas-de-pergame-leglise-et-ses-institutions (7 August 2014); Nikolaos Loudovikos, 'Person Instead of Grace and Dictated Otherness: John Zizioulas's Final Theological Position', *Heythrop Journal*, 52, 4 (2011); Andrey Shishkov, 'Metropolitan John Zizioulas on Primacy in the Church', *Internationale Kirchliche Zeitschrift*, 104 (2014); Miroslav Volf, 'Zizioulas: Communion, One and Many', *After Our Likeness. The Church as the Image of the Trinity* (Grand Rapids, MI: Eerdmans, 1998), and Kallistos Ware, 'Sobornost and Eucharistic Ecclesiology: Aleksei Khomiakov and His Successors', *International Journal for the Study of the Christian Church*, 11, 2–3 (2011).

the union of all that exists,' he writes, 'or, in other words, she is destined to encompass all that exists: God and creation.'[67] Yet in his discussion of the priesthood, Staniloae considers that the retention of the three levels of the 'serving priesthood' (deacon, priest and bishop) is an essential criterion defining the church: 'The priesthood with its three levels is so necessary to the church that without it she "cannot be called church".[68] In fact, without the threefold ministry of Christ continued through visible instruments, there is no church.'[69] This tension between a universal cosmic vision of the church and a much narrower institutional definition remains unresolved and it is unclear whether Staniloae regards non-Orthodox Christian ecclesial bodies as in or out of the church.

Staniloae, like Afanasiev and Evdokimov, refers the universal priesthood of all members of the church: 'All are priests and sacrifices in the church, all are teachers and guides toward their salvation and the salvation of other faithful who are close to them.'[70] Yet he emphasizes even more emphatically the divine origin of the ordained priesthood and its essential role of intercessor and even as intermediary between humanity and God: 'The priest symbolizes Christ as intercessor; he symbolizes the fact that the human being cannot enter by himself into the infinite, loving relationship with God. … The believer receives Christ through the mediation of a priest who received grace from Christ.'[71] Staniloae does not refer to the ontological versus functional debate over the nature of the priesthood, but rather uses the expression 'serving priesthood'.

Staniloae seeks to reconcile the tension between a Christological and a pneumatological approach to the church by constantly associating the Holy Spirit with Christ in the church: 'The church pneumatized by the Spirit of the Risen Christ.'[72] Staniloae refers to the 'pneumatization' of the members of the church as a process made possible in and through the church: Christ dwells 'within us by the Holy Spirit'; and: 'The members of the church advance toward their pneumatisation, and thereby they advance on the path toward their resurrection with Christ.'[73]

At the beginning of this chapter we postulated that Orthodox notions of the church oscillate between the biblical and patristic notion of the church as the Body of Christ, and the perception of the church primarily as a historical and hierarchical institution. These two fundamental visions of the church continued to be reflected in early twenty-first century writings on the church. Metropolitan Hilarion Alfeyev, in his *Doctrine and Teaching of the Orthodox Church*, deals with broad aspects of ecclesiology, along with other subjects typical of a *Dogmatica*. In both this volume and his *History and Canonical Structure of the Orthodox Church*, he focuses mainly on the historical and institutional aspects of the church, paying scant attention to more mystical notions of church other than the four attributes of the church from the Nicene Creed. The general title of Jean-Claude Larchet's series on the church, *The Church, the Body of Christ*, picks up the patristic notion of the

[67]Dumitru Staniloae, *The Church: Communion in the Holy Spirit*, Vol. 4 of *The Experience of God: Orthodox Dogmatic Theology* (Brookline, MA: Holy Cross Orthodox Press, 2012), 13.
[68]St John Chrysostom, *On the Priesthood* 3.5 (PG 48:642) (Staniloae's note).
[69]Staniloae, *The Church*, 52.
[70]Ibid., 38.
[71]Ibid., 39; 42.
[72]Ibid. 27–31.
[73]Ibid., 28.

church, but Larchet's interest is also in the more institutional aspects of the church.[74] Both Larchet and Alfeyev downplay, dismiss or simply ignore notions such as Eucharistic ecclesiology, the royal priesthood of the faithful and the participation of the laity that feature so largely in other modern Orthodox theologians.

Fr Boris Bobrinskoy (b. 1925), former professor of dogmatic theology and Dean of the St Sergius Institute of Orthodox Theology in Paris, offers a balanced and representative Orthodox vision of the church in *The Mystery of the Church* (2003).[75] Bobrinskoy devotes two-thirds of his book to topics such as the church in the Old and the New Testaments, the 'marks' of the church, the 'threefold ministry of the church', Eucharistic ecclesiology and the royal priesthood of believers. He emphasizes the governance of the church by conciliarity (*sobornost'*) – in this respect Bobrinskoy's ecclesiology is perhaps closer to that of Afanasiev than that of Zizioulas. Bobrinskoy is open to ecumenism while maintaining the virtually universal Orthodox view that the full truth of Christianity is found only in the Orthodox Church. Yet Bobrinskoy is far from triumphant about Orthodoxy, advocating a humble recognition of weaknesses in the Orthodox Church. He is painfully aware of the dilemma between a high ecclesiology contained in the writings of leading Orthodox theologians over the past century, and the reality of the Orthodox Church, often deeply divided and fractious, authoritarian, intolerant, nationalist and only too often compromised in countries of Orthodox tradition with the regime of the day, whether to the political right or the political left. He writes: 'We must not have any illusions, we teach an exceptionally beautiful theology of collegiality which, unfortunately, the reality of our situation often belies'; and: 'No Orthodox Church can boast of being in the truth. We need to exhibit a great deal of humility and to guard especially against any sort of triumphalism.'[76]

Conclusion

Ecclesiology has been the most prominent theme of Orthodox theology since the mid-nineteenth century. Indeed, the origins of modern Orthodox theology can be traced to Slavophile reflection on Orthodoxy and the Orthodox Church. Alexei Khomiakov's initial insight into the church as a community of the faithful bound together by faith, love and freedom, his emphasis on the unity of the church and his sharp contrasts between the Orthodoxy and Western Christianity set the stage for later development of Orthodox ecclesiology. But the Slavophiles were largely focused on Russia and the Russian Church, especially in their elaboration of the idea of *sobornost'* as reflected ideally in the Russian peasant commune, the *mir*. In addition, the simplicity of Khomiakov's idealized vision of the Orthodox Church was subsequently seen as inadequate in view of his failure

[74]Larchet, *L'Église, Corps du Christ Vol. I. Nature et structure. Vol. II. Les relations entre les Églises*. The third volume of Larchet's trilogy is devoted to the sacraments, liturgy, prayer and asceticism: *La Vie sacramentelle* (Paris: Le Cerf, 2014).

[75]Bobrinskoy, *The Mystery of the Church*. See our review article of the books on the church by Hilarion Alfeyev, Boris Bobrinskoy and Jean-Claude Larchet: Paul Ladouceur, 'Three Contemporary Orthodox Visions of the Church', *St Vladimir's Theological Quarterly*, 58, 2 (2014).

[76]Bobrinskoy, *The Mystery of the Church*, 219; 234.

to articulate more substantially the nature of the church, to account for divisions in the church and his almost total neglect of the institutional and hierarchal aspects of the church.[77]

In contrast with the Russian focus of the Slavophiles, Vladimir Soloviev advanced a universal image of the church, aptly portrayed in the title of his major ecclesiological work, *Russia and the Universal Church*. Soloviev's conception of the church constitutes a starting point for universalist ecclesiology in Orthodoxy: the church is not specifically Russian, nor even exclusively Orthodox, but encompasses all Christians. His successors, especially Sergius Bulgakov, more explicitly extended Soloviev's vision to include all of humanity and all of creation, bringing to forefront the fundamentally ineffable and eschatological nature of the church: the church becomes a synonym for the Kingdom of God, when 'God may be all in all' (1 Cor. 15.28). In addition to purging the notion of *sobornost'* of its narrow identification with Russia, leading figures of the Russian religious renaissance in exile further developed the notion of the church as the people of God, and added Christological and pneumatological dimensions: the unity of the church is inspired and sustained by the Holy Spirit, who shapes the church as the Body of Christ, with Christ as its Head, thus picking up key Pauline notions of the church. Despite its weaknesses, *sobornost'* formed the starting point for the subsequent development of Eucharistic or communion ecclesiology.

If the Slavophiles presented an idealized vision of the Orthodox Church, early in his career Vladimir Soloviev posited a similarly idealized vision of the Catholic Church. Neither approach held much sway among twentieth-century Orthodox theologians. But they nonetheless drew on elements of the ecclesiologies of both the Slavophiles and Soloviev in building their own visions of the church. The *sobornost'* idea of the Slavophiles and Soloviev's universalist vision of Christianity had a powerful impact among the leaders of the Russian religious renaissance, especially when they found themselves in exile, a minority of Orthodox in relation to the Western Christianity divided into many denominations. For Berdyaev, Bulgakov, Afanasiev, Lossky, Evdokimov and even Florovsky, the natural implication of Soloviev's universal ecclesiology was a commitment to the ecumenical movement, even if they did not follow Soloviev's early vision of Christian unity centred on Rome.

Although Georges Florovsky was deeply and painfully aware of the profound differences between Eastern and Western Christendom, and despite his rejection of much of Soloviev's legacy, he remained faithful to the notion of an underlying, if ineffable unity of all those who profess Christ. Florovsky shared this conviction with Sergius Bulgakov and others in the Russian community in exile, who remained much closer than Florovsky to Soloviev's thought across a range of other issues.

Nicholas Afanasiev was a bridging or transitional theologian between the Russian religious renaissance and neopatristic theology. He built on the insights of the early Slavophiles and his colleagues among the Russian theologians in exile to produce a robust modern Orthodox ecclesiology centred on the notion of the church as first and foremost a Eucharistic community, with the local church as the manifestation of the universal church. While Afanasiev's Eucharistic ecclesiology attracted wide support among Orthodox and non-Orthodox theologians, few Orthodox theologians have reiterated his strong emphasis on the royal priesthood of all believers

---

[77]See Paul Evdokimov, *Le Christ dans la pensée russe* (Christ in Russian Thought) (Paris: Le Cerf, 1970), 72.

and his refusal to recognize an ontological difference between ordained and non-ordained in the church. Many later Orthodox writers on the church, such as Hilarion Alfeyev, Jean-Claude Larchet and John Zizioulas, either downplay the theology of the royal priesthood or simply ignore it altogether. Paul Evdokimov and Boris Bobrinskoy are among those who highlight the importance of the royal priesthood for a balanced view of the church as an institution, a counterpart to a natural tendency to focus on the hierarchy as the essence of the church. Evdokimov is one of the few modern Orthodox theologians to develop what may be called a theology of the laity, with the royal priesthood of the faithful as one of its components (see Chapter 13).

John Zizioulas brings together two major strands of modern Orthodox thought, personalism and Eucharistic ecclesiology. Zizioulas felt that he compensated for what he perceived as a weakness in Afanasiev's Eucharistic ecclesiology to relate adequately the local church to the universal church by defining the local church as the bishop and the clergy and faithful under his omophore. Zizioulas ignores Afanasiev's insistence on the importance of the royal priesthood and instead promotes the essential place and role of the bishop in the constitution of the church. If Afanasiev leans more towards a mystical and eschatological notion of the church, Zizioulas's vision of the church is decidedly more institutional and hierarchical. The Pauline and patristic idea of the church as the Body of the Living Christ, so strongly put forward by Florovsky, seems lost in the later discussions of how the local church, whether parish or diocese, relates to the universal church.

Although aspects of Zizioulas's theology are sharply criticized in both Orthodox and non-Orthodox quarters, his contributions, like those of Afanasiev on which he built, to Orthodox ecclesiology are enormous. Eucharistic ecclesiology, a high point of neopatristic theology, is in fact one of the most important Orthodox contributions to Christian theology as a whole and has had considerable impact in non-Orthodox circles, especially on Roman Catholic ecclesiology.

Boris Bobrinskoy's call for Orthodox humility with respect to the church can be applied to Eucharistic ecclesiology itself. Despite the theological richness of Eucharistic ecclesiology, there is all too often a large gap between theory and practice, inasmuch as in many parts of Orthodoxy, church attendance is minimal and actual communion even less, with many Orthodox taking communion only once or a few times a year. 'We cannot rest satisfied', writes Kallistos Ware, 'with a "eucharistic ecclesiology" that remains simply a theory, a distant ideal, a set of ideas on paper debated by doctrinal specialists. … There is no genuine "eucharistic ecclesiology" that is not *lived out* in practice.'[78] Beyond weaknesses in Eucharistic ecclesiology as presented by its principal advocates, Nicholas Afanasiev and John Zizioulas, Eucharistic ecclesiology remains the principal Orthodox ecclesiology in the early twenty-first century, as Ware recognizes:

> I am convinced that the eucharistic 'model' still retains full validity in Orthodox ecclesiology. No other 'model' has emerged in the last fifty years that is able to replace it. … There is every reason to expect that the style of ecclesiology propounded by Nikolai Afanasiev and Metropolitan John will continue to prevail in Orthodox thought during the future.[79]

---

[78]Ware, 'Sobornost and Eucharistic Ecclesiology', 233.
[79]Ibid., 233–4.

12

Ecumenical Theology and Religious Diversity

Chapter Outline

Ecumenical theology

Orthodox have been formally engaged in the modern ecumenical movement since the 1920s, not without considerable internal tension and controversy. Two approaches to Orthodox thinking on ecumenism and participation in ecumenical endeavours appeared early on. One affirms the persistence of a fundamental underlying unity of the church obscured as a result of tragic splits over the centuries, and sees ecumenism as the quest to realize this underlying unity; the other emphasizes the importance of doctrinal differences among Christians and considers Orthodox participation in ecumenism primarily as witness or testimony, without realistic expectation of arriving at some form of significant unity in the foreseeable future. The first approach is consistent with the theological legacy of Vladimir Soloviev and his successors, while the latter is closer to the ecclesiology of the Slavophiles, purged of its slavo-centrism and manifested in neopatristic theology.

In the 1930s Sergius Bulgakov and Georges Florovsky personified these two visions of ecumenism. Both shared a deep commitment to the ecumenical movement, but their perspectives and approaches were different. For Bulgakov, following Soloviev, real unity exists among Christians and the ecumenical task consists in the rediscovery and affirmation of the unity of the church already present in the Body of Christ, vivified by the Holy Spirit. In a 1939 article, one of his last writings on ecumenism, Bulgakov states notably:

> Prophecy is the dynamic factor in the life of the church, while hierarchy is what makes it static. It is only the coming together of both which forms the *Una Sancta*, the Divine-humanity *in actu*. This life is not limited to the visible ecclesial organisation; its overflows its boundaries. ... There, at this depth, we meet and mutually recognise our unity in Christ and in the Holy Spirit, as children of the one heavenly Father.[1]

In his ecumenical theology, Bulgakov emphasizes the common values of Christians: the Trinity; the divinity and mission of Christ; recognition of Scripture as divinely inspired; acceptance of baptism as initiation into the church and the Eucharist as the principal Christian ritual. A total fidelity to the Orthodox tradition accompanies this opening to other Christians. Only the Orthodox Church possesses the fullness of truth: 'Orthodoxy is the Church of Christ on earth', he writes in the opening sentence of his book *The Orthodox Church* (1935).[2] Bulgakov's ecumenism, like his ecclesiology, is mystical, charismatic, sacramental, prophetic, inclusive and existential: The Kingdom of God is not only in the world to come, but is already present in the unity of Christians.

For Florovsky, divisions among the Christian churches are above all dogmatic. He imposes strict conditions on church reunification to the point that, as Antoine Arjakovsky writes, 'he himself admitted that he had little faith in "theologians' conferences" and transferred his hope to an "eschatological twilight", that is, to the end of history, the moment of the authentic coming together'.[3] In this light, Orthodox participation in the ecumenical movement is justified primarily by witness, to witness to other Christians that the truth of Christ subsists fully only in the Orthodox Church. There is little possibility of an authentic meeting of equals in the ecumenical movement, other than in the context of conversion to Orthodoxy. Highlighting what separates rather than what unites Christians, Florovsky's ecumenical perspective is dogmatic, historical, patristic, canonical, exclusive and eschatological. In 1964, towards the end of his ecumenical activities, Florovsky summarized his outlook:

> My personal concern, however, was always with dialogue and confrontation. ... It was becoming increasingly evident that in 'divided Christendom' there was actually no real agreement concerning the basic issue – the very 'nature', or true character, of that unity which Christians are bound and called to seek. It may be contended that 'divided Christians' are not yet ready for the true unity, and probably are not willing or prepared to proceed. ... The task is of an enormous complexity, although the promise is still great. Disagreements are manifold, inveterate, radical. And there is no room for any compromise. This must be faced frankly and courageously, without reticence or evasion, rather

[1] Sergius Bulgakov, '*Una sancta*: The Foundations of Ecumenism' (in Russian), *Put'*, 58 (1939), 12–13. Cited in Antoine Arjakovsky, *The Way: Religious Thinkers of the Russian Emigration in Paris and Their Journal, 1925-1940* (Notre Dame, IN: University of Notre Dame Press, 2013), 487.

[2] Sergius Bulgakov, *The Orthodox Church* (1935) (Crestwood, NY: St Vladimir's Seminary Press, 1988), 1. Intended for an ecumenical audience, the book was first published in French in 1932, in English in 1935 and only subsequently in Russian.

[3] Arjakovsky, *The Way: Religious Thinkers of the Russian Emigration*, 359, citing Florovsky's article 'The Question of Christian Unity' (in Russian), *Put'*, 37 (Supplement) (1933), 8–9.

with confidence and trust. The actual division is profound. Short cuts and easy ways must be avoided. One has to be bold enough to meet the challenge of Christian tragedy.[4]

The controversy over limited intercommunion

In 1928 Florovsky became a member of the Fellowship of St Alban and St Sergius, founded the previous year to promote dialogue and rapprochement between the Anglican and Orthodox churches. Although Bulgakov was the senior Orthodox representative in the Fellowship in the 1930s, Florovsky soon became as prominent as Bulgakov, thanks to his learning, his eloquence, his personal charm and a good command of English. The Anglicans greatly respected Bulgakov, but they never warmed to his speculative theology, especially sophiology, and were more attracted by Florovsky's biblical and patristic orientation.

The theological differences between Bulgakov and Florovsky over ecumenism reached a crisis over the question of intercommunion between Anglicans and Orthodox within the Fellowship.[5] This developed in parallel with a clash over the wider question of ecclesiology between the 'modernists' and the 'traditionalists' among the Russians, carried out largely in the journal *Put'* (*The Way*).[6] After six years of meetings between Anglicans and Orthodox, Bulgakov advanced a novel and audacious proposal for 'partial intercommunion' in the context of meetings of the Fellowship: with the blessing of Anglican and Orthodox bishops, Anglicans would take communion at the celebration of the Divine Liturgy by Orthodox clergy and vice versa. He challenged the participants at the Fellowship's annual meeting in June 1933:

> Our common prayer at these conferences is a revelation – we are people who have been separated from each other for ages, praying together. We are called by God to be together. It is spiritually dangerous to continue forever in mere discussion of differences. We have been led up to the high wall of partition and we cannot continue to stare at it. Having come to this point we face a personal responsibility for the work of reunion. We must do what we can in the present historical conditions. … God calls us to action here and now.[7]

For Bulgakov, there was a true Christian encounter among the Anglican and Orthodox members of the Fellowship, already a 'partial reunion' of the churches, which should be marked by

---

[4]Georges Florovsky, 'The Ecumenical Dialogue' (1964), in Brandon Gallaher and Paul Ladouceur, eds., *The Patristic Witness of Georges Florovsky: Essential Theological Writings* (London: T&T Clark, 2019), 305.

[5]On the 'limited intercommunion' dispute, see especially Brandon Gallaher, 'Bulgakov and Intercommunion', *Sobornost/ECR*, 24, 1 and 24, 2 (2002); and his essay '"Great and Full of Grace": Partial Intercommunion and Sophiology in Sergii Bulgakov', in William C. Mills, ed., *Church and World: Essays in Honor of Michael Plekon* (Rollinsford, NH: Orthodox Research Institute, 2013); Sergei Nikolaev, 'Spiritual Unity: The Role of Religious Authority in the Disputes between Sergii Bulgakov and G. Florovsky concerning Intercommunion', *St Vladimir's Theological Quarterly*, 49, 1–2 (2005); Arjakovsky, *The Way: Religious Thinkers of the Russian Emigration*, 368–71; and our article '"Aimons-nous les uns les autres": Serge Boulgakov et Georges Florovsky' (Let us love one another: Sergius Bulgakov and Georges Florovsky), *Contacts*, 64, 237 (2012).

[6]Antoine Arjakovsky refers to the leading authors of *Put'* as 'a generation of modernist intellectuals'. See *The Way: Religious Thinkers of the Russian Emigration*, 36–86.

[7]'Summary of Speech by Fr Sergius Bulgakov', in 'General Report of the Fellowship Conference, June 1933', *Journal of the Fellowship of St Alban & St Sergius*, 20 (1933), 12. The *Journal* was renamed *Sobornost* in 1935.

'partial intercommunion'. Without denying the relevance of canonical authority in Orthodoxy, Bulgakov appeals to another authority, that of spiritual experience, according to which, and with the approval of the canonical authorities – bishops of both churches – partial intercommunion in the context of the Fellowship should be permitted. Bulgakov saw partial intercommunion as a stage in the 'molecular process' of restoring unity between the churches: 'The final aim of intercommunion, however, is the achievement of full corporate reunion between the Orthodox and the Anglican Churches.'[8]

Bulgakov affirms on the one hand the reality of Eucharistic unity at the altar: 'the call to unity which springs from the eucharistic chalice itself'.[9] But at the same time he nonetheless recognizes the necessity of a 'dogmatic minimum': common accord on the Eucharistic dogma, recognition of 'the *real* (and not the symbolically-significatory or the subjectively-reminiscent) character of the Sacrament ... the true Body and Blood of Christ through the changing of the bread and wine'; 'the acceptance of all the Seven Ecumenical Councils in their fundamental *Christological* definitions' and 'the efficacy of the celebrators as of the hierarchy of the "apostolic succession"'.[10]

Bulgakov's proposal received the support of the modernist group among the Russians, notably Nicolas Berdyaev, George Fedotov, Anthony Kartashev, Leon Zander and Nicolas Zernov and, apparently, Metropolitan Evlogy (Georgiyevsky) (1868–1946), Bulgakov's ecclesiastical superior, while the 'traditionalists', especially Georges Florovsky and Nicholas Arseniev, opposed it.[11] There was opposition on the Anglican side as well, but in the end the Anglican bishops gave their approval.

Florovsky questioned whether the points of doctrinal agreement that Bulgakov suggested were sufficient justification for intercommunion and he doubted that partial intercommunion would effectively lead to church reunion. Behind Florovsky's specific critiques of the proposal was the conviction that the only basis of church unity lay in global dogmatic agreement. Bulgakov, thought Florovsky, was playing on the positive psychological tone of the Fellowship meetings to seek support for his proposal, to the detriment of dogmatic and canonical norms.[12] Because significant dogmatic differences separate the Orthodox and Anglican churches, there can be no question of intercommunion. For Florovsky, full dogmatic agreement (and not merely a 'dogmatic minimum' as Bulgakov proposed) must take precedence over the experience of unity before the altar, over common prayer shared in the Fellowship; 'unity in truth' (that is, dogma) and canonical authority are more important than 'unity in love' and the shared experience of worship. Florovsky also objected that neither the Anglican nor the Orthodox members of the Fellowship were formally appointed representatives of their churches, and that communion cannot be 'partial' because,

---

[8]Nicolas Zernov, 'Some Explanations of Fr Sergius Bulgakov's Scheme for Intercommunion', Fellowship of St Alban and Saint Sergius Archives, cited by Nikolaev, 'Spiritual Unity', 111.

[9]Sergius Bulgakov, 'Ways to Church Reunion', *Sobornost*, 1, 2 (1935); reprinted in *Father Sergius Bulgakov 1871–1944. A Collection of Articles by Fr. Bulgakov* (London: Fellowship of St. Alban and St. Sergius, 1969), 23.

[10]Bulgakov, 'Ways to Church Reunion', 24.

[11]Arjakovsky, *The Way: Religious Thinkers of the Russian Emigration*, 368–71; Sergei V. Nikolaev, 'Church and Reunion in the Theology of Sergii Bulgakov and Georges Florovsky' (Ph.D. Thesis, Southern Methodist University, 2007) (Ann Arbor, MI: ProQuest, 2008), 250–2.

[12]See Georges Florovsky, 'Confessional Loyalty in the Ecumenical Movement' (1950), and 'Letter to William Nicholls' (1950), in Gallaher and Ladouceur, eds., *The Patristic Witness of Georges Florovsky*, 279–88.

as Arjakovsky puts it, 'communion is a catholic, not a private act'[13] – either churches are in communion or they are not. Florovsky also appealed to the therapeutic role of the absence of intercommunion, which serves as a painful reminder of the fragmentation of Christianity and an incentive towards the healing of rifts.[14]

Reminiscing in 1950 about the intercommunion controversy, Florovsky outlined the principal thrust of his argument:

> My main argument was that only a 'catholic action' is permissible in the Holy Catholic Church, that nothing partial and 'exceptional' can ever lead to a true integration. Or, in other words, we have to seek not the satisfaction of our dreams and hopes, as glorious and inspiring as they may be or seem to be, but solely the common revival of spiritual life in existing communities. The unity can only grow out of a 'molecular action', which is to be then integrated. An occasional intercommunion, or that by a special dispensation, will ultimately hinder the work of reunion. The immediate task is the recovery of common mind and sound theology.[15]

The Fellowship debated Bulgakov's proposal for two years after the 1933 conference. Bulgakov and Florovsky engaged in oral and literary duels in Russian and English, in Paris and England. The Fellowship discussed the intercommunion proposal at length at its annual meeting in June 1934, with Florovsky and Derwas Chitty (1901–71), an Anglican priest and writer on early Christian spirituality, leading the opposition.[16] In response to requests for clarification for the 1935 meeting of the Fellowship, Bulgakov prepared a more detailed proposal for a mutual 'episcopal blessing' to allow clergy and laypersons to take communion at both Anglican and Orthodox liturgies.[17]

In the literary duel, Bulgakov fired the first shot with his essay 'By Jacob's Well – John 4:23 (On the Actual Unity of the Divided Church in Faith, Prayer and Sacraments)' (1933).[18] Taking as his point of departure Jesus' statement to the Samaritan woman at the well that worship should be 'in spirit and in truth' (Jn 4.24), Bulgakov presents an essentially universalist and mystical vision of the church founded on faith in Christ and animated by mutual love, drawing on themes from both the Slavophiles and Vladimir Soloviev. Against a view that stresses 'our dogmatic disagreements much more than our common Christian heritage' (a characterization of Florovsky's

---

[13]Arjakovsky, *The Way: Religious Thinkers of the Russian Emigration*, 369.

[14]See Florovsky, 'Confessional Loyalty in the Ecumenical Movement', 282–4; and 'Letter to William Nicolls', 287–8.

[15]Florovsky, 'Letter to William Nicholls', 288. Editors' note in *The Patristic Witness of Georges Florovsky*: 'Both of the phrases, "catholic action" and "molecular action", were terms used frequently in the limited intercommunion controversy from 1933 to 1935. Both critics of the proposal (mainly Florovsky and many Anglican divines) and its main proponent (Bulgakov) used the term "catholic action," common in Anglo-Catholic and Roman Catholic circles of the 1920s and 1930s, to signify ecclesial engagement with the world, both political and sacramental. The term "molecular action", referring to the reintegration of the churches, was associated closely with those favouring limited intercommunion. Its use here is ironic, since Florovsky, as a critic of intercommunion, is appropriating it from his theological opponents'.

[16]For a summary of the discussion, see 'Report of Conference held at High Leigh June 26–28, 1934 on "The Healing of Schism"' (Fellowship archives – see Gallaher, 'Great and Full of Grace', 79, n. 27). An abbreviated version appeared in the Fellowship's *Journal* in September 1934, as 'The Healing of Schism', 3–7.

[17]Sergius Bulgakov, 'Partial Intercommunion (Notes and Comments by Fr. S. Bulgakov for Advisory Committee and Fellowship Executive)' 3.V.1935. Appendix to Gallaher, 'Great and Full of Grace', 118–21; summary and discussion, 91–102.

[18]Sergius Bulgakov, 'By Jacob's Well – John 4:23 (On the Actual Unity of the Divided Church in Faith, Prayer and Sacraments)', *Journal of the Fellowship of St Alban and St Sergius*, 22 (1933). Reprinted in Michael Plekon, ed., *Tradition Alive: On the Church and the Christian Life in Our Time-Readings from the Eastern Church* (Lanham, MD: Sheed & Ward, 2003).

position), Bulgakov argues that 'a mystical intercommunion has always existed among Christians.'[19] Christian unity is based on common prayer:

> The way toward the reunion of East and West does not lie through tournaments between theologians of the East and West, but through a reunion before the altar. The priesthood of the East and the West must realise itself as one priesthood, celebrating the one Eucharist; if the minds of the priests could become aflame with this idea, all barriers would fall. For in response to this, dogmatic unity will be achieved, or rather, a mutual understanding of one another in our distinctive features.[20]

In his article 'The Limits of the Church', Florovsky employs historical, dogmatic and canonical arguments based on patristic teachings concerning heretics and schismatics and the practices of the early church in reintegrating the 'lapsed', the 'lost sheep', into the fold of the church.[21] He does not accept the view of Cyprian of Carthage that there is no grace outside the (Orthodox) Church, but follows Augustine in recognizing that the Holy Spirit acts outside the canonical limits of the church. Despite this theological opening to non-Orthodox, Florovsky steadfastly maintained that acceptance of the full truth in the Orthodox Church is the only way to reunion, and hence the notions of 'partial union' and 'partial intercommunion' are unacceptable.[22]

Faced with Orthodox opposition and Anglican hesitations, Bulgakov retreated. At the 1933 Fellowship conference, Walter Frere (1863–1938), Bishop of Truro and one of the leading Anglican participants in the Fellowship, stated that there already existed 'spiritual communion at our Eucharists' and 'common worship and a very real, though not fully sacramental, communion with each other'.[23] In an article in the Fellowship's journal *Sobornost'* in September 1935, the Anglican divine Charles S. Gillett suggested that the Anglicans should make a 'spiritual communion' during the celebration of the Orthodox liturgy, and vice versa, as a solemn expression 'of a common contrition, a common purpose and a common eagerness for the fulfilment of that common purpose in all its sacramental completeness'.[24] In response, Bulgakov recognized that his proposal for intercommunion had floundered: 'Opinion was sharply divided, but I would say that, on the whole, conviction prevailed (a conviction which sprang not so much from the voice of a loving heart, as from the arguments of 'sober reason'!) that the time was not yet ripe for my suggestion.'[25] Bulgakov rallied to the minimalist notion of 'spiritual intercommunion', which represented Florovsky's view:

> Though we are deprived of *communio in sacris*, we are, nevertheless, already in a state of *spiritual communion* (or intercommunion). … The principle of *spiritual intercommunion* which has now been born in our fellowship and which gives expression to its nature is certainly novel from a dogmatic point of view. It originates at this particular 'historical hour' in the development of the Ecumenical Movement. It represents an inevitable attempt to appraise the worth of a new religious experience closely associated

[19] Bulgakov, 'By Jacob's Well', in Plekon, ed., *Tradition Alive*, 60.
[20] Ibid., 64–5.
[21] Georges Florovsky, 'The Limits of the Church' (1933), in Gallaher and Ladouceur, eds., *The Patristic Witness of Georges Florovsky*, 247–56.
[22] Georges Florovsky, 'Confessional Loyalty in the Ecumenical Movement', 282–4; and 'Letter to William Nicholls', 287–8.
[23] Walter Frere, in 'The Nature of Catholic Action', *Sobornost*, 2, 3 (1935), 24.
[24] C. S. Gillett, 'Intercommunion', *Sobornost'*, 2, 3 (1935), 22–3. Rev. Charles S. Gillett is not to be confused with Fr Lev Gillet (1893–1980), a French Orthodox priest also very active in the Fellowship of St Alban and Saint Sergius.
[25] Sergius Bulgakov, 'Spiritual Intercommunion', *Sobornost*, 4 (1935), 3; reprinted in *Father Sergius Bulgakov 1871–1944*. 29.

> with this movement. In this experience, confessional limitations are overcome in spite of the walls which separate the confessions from one another. One feels and discerns a true life, a 'standing before the face of God', a unity in Christ, which simply cannot be overcome by confessional division.[26]

Even Bulgakov's faith, prophetic vision and zeal were unable to overcome the objections to his proposal for partial intercommunion. Beginning in 1935, fallout from the sophiological controversy, with Bulgakov again at the centre of the storm, cast a long shadow over the Fellowship's activities. The possibility of some form of unity between the Anglican and Orthodox churches vanished from the agenda; the *kairos*, the moment to act, passed and would not return. At the end of the 1930s and after the Second World War, the broader ecumenical movement, dominated by Reformation churches and communities, eclipsed the Fellowship to some extent, as attention turned to the establishment of the World Council of Churches (WCC), which took place in 1948.

In his 1950 article 'Confessional Loyalty in the Ecumenical Movement', Florovsky spells out the more restrictive aspects of his ecumenical theology, beginning with his objections to open communion and intercommunion. Consistent with his stance in the partial intercommunion dispute fifteen years earlier, he argues that intercommunion compromises ecumenism because 'it would be to pretend falsely that Christendom has already been reunited. ... Tension remains, compelling us to move on. For that reason we still have only an ecumenical movement and not a united Christendom.'[27] The core of this article is a statement of faith:

> As a member and priest of the Orthodox Church, I believe that the church in which I was baptised and brought up is in very truth *the church*, i.e. *the true* church and the *only* true church. I believe that for many reasons: by personal conviction and by the inner testimony of the Spirit which breathes in the sacraments of the church and by all that I could learn from Scripture and from the universal tradition of the church. I am compelled therefore to regard all other Christian churches as deficient, and in many cases I can identify these deficiencies accurately enough. Therefore, for me, Christian reunion is just universal conversion to Orthodoxy. I have no confessional loyalty; my loyalty belongs solely to the *Una sancta*. ... It does not mean that everything in the past or present state of the Orthodox Church is to be equated with the truth of God. Many things are obviously changeable; indeed many things need improvement. The *true* church is not yet the *perfect* church.[28]

In spite of his insistence on the importance of dogmatic differences and the Orthodox Church as the true church, in an exchange of letters with an Anglican stimulated by Florovsky's article, Florovsky nonetheless recognizes an abiding unity in the church, a recognition which resembles Bulgakov's position:

> As everything in the church, unity is at once both given and required, has been given and is to be achieved. Schisms are failures of men to respond to the divine call to unity. Yet the given unity never disappears. After all, we all are united in and by the redeeming love and purpose of God. And that unity we discover in spite of all our disagreements, when we dig deep enough.[29]

---

[26]Sergius Bulgakov, 'Spiritual Intercommunion', in *Father Sergius Bulgakov 1871–1944. A Collection of Articles*, 29–30.

[27]Florovsky, 'Confessional Loyalty in the Ecumenical Movement', 284.

[28]Idem., 285.

[29]Florovsky, 'Open Letter to William Nicholls', 286.

Opposition to ecumenism

Orthodox involvement in the modern ecumenical movement has been criticized by various Orthodox groups since the 1920 encyclical of the Patriarchate of Constantinople on Christian unity and the ecumenical movement,[30] which opened the door to Orthodox participation in ecumenical undertakings, and since the first Orthodox contacts and dialogues with non-Orthodox in Western Europe by Greek and Russian clergy and hierarchs in the 1920s. The Holy and Great Council of the Orthodox Church held in Crete from 16 to 26 June 2016 brought to the forefront the long-smouldering controversy in Orthodox circles between ecumenists and anti-ecumenists. Already prior to the Council, there was serious opposition within several Orthodox churches to some formulations in the document. This opposition has to be seen in the light of long-standing criticism, especially since about 1970, of the involvement of the Orthodox Church in the ecumenical movement, which goes back to the 1920s.

Orthodox opposition to ecumenism is closely associated with a conservative tendency in Orthodoxy, whose adherents are variously referred to as 'fundamentalists', 'rigorists', 'zealots' and 'sectarians'.[31] For our part, we prefer to call this tendency in Orthodoxy neo-traditionalism.[32]

The main sources of neo-traditionalism in Orthodoxy, including anti-ecumenism, over the last half-century have been the conservative faction in the Russian Orthodox Church (ROC) in exile after the revolution, represented especially by the Russian Orthodox Church Outside of Russia (ROCOR)[33]; Greek 'neo-calendarists', who oppose the use of the Gregorian or 'new' calendar for the celebration of liturgical feasts falling on fixed days of the year; certain monastic figures, especially some, but not all, of the monasteries and important personalities of Mount Athos and individual hierarchs, clergy and theologians.[34] By the late 1990s, the Holy Synods of the Orthodox churches of Bulgaria and Georgia had rallied to the anti-ecumenical camp.

The starting point of neo-traditionalism is typically a systematic or even strident anti-Westernism, highlighting the historical, cultural, theological and socio-political factors which distinguish 'the

---

[30]'Encyclical of the Ecumenical Patriarch, 1920: "Unto the Churches of Christ Everywhere"', in Gennadios Limouris, ed., *Orthodox Visions of Ecumenism: Statements, Messages and Reports on the Ecumenical Movement, 1902-1992* (Geneva: WCC Publications, 1994).

[31]Two documents of the HGC refer to 'fundamentalism', the 'Message' (§ 4) and the 'Encyclical' (§ 17). In addition, the document on ecumenism ('Relations of the Orthodox Church with the Rest of the Christian World') contains this statement: 'The Orthodox Church considers all efforts to break the unity of the Church, undertaken by individuals or groups under the pretext of maintaining or allegedly defending true Orthodoxy, as being worthy of condemnation' (§ 22).

[32]The appellation 'traditionalist' is inappropriate because all Orthodox appeal to tradition, whereas 'neo-traditional' implies a novel approach to tradition, which is in tension with long-standing approaches to tradition. See Paul Ladouceur, 'Ecumenoclasm: Anti-Ecumenism in Orthodox Theology', *St Vladimir's Theological Quarterly*, 61, 3 (2017), 324.

[33]In May 2007 ROCA became a self-governing body within the Russian Orthodox Church. ROCOR has had to moderate its former strident opposition to ecumenism now that it is integrated into the ROC, an active participant in ecumenism.

[34]For more detailed overviews of the origins of modern anti-ecumenism in Orthodoxy, 'Neo-Traditionalism in Contemporary Orthodoxy'; see also Pantelis Kalaitzidis, 'Theological, Historical and Cultural Reasons for Anti-Ecumenical Movements in Eastern Orthodoxy', in Pantelis Kalaitzidis et al., *Orthodox Handbook on Ecumenism: Resources for Theological Education* (Volos, GR: Volos Academy Publications, with WCC Publications and Regnum Books International, 2014); and Vasilios Makrides, 'Orthodox Christian Rigorism: Attempting to Delineate a Multifaceted Phenomenon', *Interdisciplinary Journal for Religion and Transformation in Contemporary Society*, 3 (2016).

East' and 'the West', and Eastern and Western Christianity while typically ignoring factors which East and West share in common, and which distinguish the 'Christian world' from the non-Christian world. The usual conclusion of this historiographic and theological perspective is that Orthodoxy should minimize its contacts with the West, lest it be further affected by unhealthy Western values, including secularism, materialism, philosophical, theological and ethical relativism and of course ecumenism.[35]

Western converts to Orthodoxy typically take one of two attitudes vis-à-vis Western Christianity and ecumenism. Many prominent Western converts to Orthodoxy maintained an open attitude towards Western Christianity, recognizing both its strengths and its weaknesses, and were and are often active participants in the ecumenical movement. Examples include Fr Lev Gillet (1893–1980), Elisabeth Behr-Sigel (1907–2005), Olivier Clément (1923–2009), Metropolitan Kallistos Ware (b. 1934) and Fr Andrew Louth (b. 1944). But many converts to Orthodoxy are found at the other pole, characterized by an unrelenting critique of Western Christianity and a rejection of Orthodox participation in the ecumenical movement. Fr Seraphim Rose (1934–82) and Fr Peter Heers are representatives of this attitude, while the French theologian Jean-Claude Larchet (b. 1949) represents a more moderate view, who nonetheless shares much of the anti-ecumenical sentiment, if not its frequently extreme rhetoric.

Early anti-ecumenical literature was often characterized by denunciatory rhetoric, conspiracy theories and apocalyptic visions of evils that would befall Orthodoxy as a result of ecumenism, with a paucity of sound theology. This is evident in the 1967 report on ecumenism by Archbishop Vitaly (Ustinov) (1910–2006), primate of ROCOR, to the assembly of bishops. The report is singularly lacking in theological argumentation against ecumenism but abounds in accusations and denunciations, including the characterization of ecumenism as the 'heresy of heresies':

> Ecumenism is the heresy of heresies, because until now every separate heresy in the history of the church has striven itself to stand in the place of the true church, while the ecumenical movement, having united all heresies, invites them all together to honor themselves as the one true church. Here ancient Arianism, Monophysitism, Monothelitism, Iconoclasm, Pelagianism, and simply every possible superstition of the contemporary sects under completely different names, have united and charge to assault the church.[36]

---

[35]This perspective finds its fullest expression in the writings of Justin Popovich and of Greek Old Calendarists and, with more nuances, in John Romanides and Christos Yannaras. See Justin Popovitch, *The Orthodox Church and Ecumenism* (Birmingham: Lazarica Press, 2000); Chrysostomos of Etna and Auxentios of Photiki, *The Roman West and the Byzantine East* (Etna, CA: Center for Orthodox Traditionalist Studies, 2002); John Romanides, *Franks, Romans, Feudalism, and Doctrine: An Interplay Between Theology and Society* (Brookline, MA: Holy Cross Orthodox Press, 1981); Christos Yannaras, *Orthodoxy and the West: Hellenic Self-Identity in the Modern Age* (Brookline, MA: Holy Cross Orthodox Press, 2006).

[36]Archbishop Vitaly of Montreal and Canada, 'Report to the Sobor of Bishops of the Russian Orthodox Church Outside of Russi' (1967–8). http://www.roca-sobor.org/eng/ecumenism---a-report (4 October 2014). In a similar vein, see Metropolitan Philaret, 'The First Sorrowful Epistle of Metropolitan Philaret' (1969). http://orthodoxinfo.com/ecumenism/sorrow.aspx (4 October 2014). For a more ample and strident ROCOR anti-ecumenical perspective, see Ludmilla Perepiolkina, *Ecumenism – A Path to Perdition* (Saint Petersburg: Self publication, 1999). http://ecumenizm.tripod.com/ECUMENIZM/index.html (30 November 2016).

In this light, truth is present only in those Orthodox churches which reject the heresy of ecumenism. As for other religions and other Christian churches (and by implication Orthodox churches which participate in ecumenical endeavours):

> All other religions, so-called Christian, monotheistic or pagan, all without the slightest exception, whether it be Catholicism, Protestantism, Islam or Buddhism – all are obstacles placed by the devil as his traps between the Church of Christ and the whole human race ... in principle they all without exception belong to falsehood, having nothing in common with truth.[37]

Objections to ecumenism from the monasteries of Mount Athos are typically more reserved in tone and contain more historical and theological substance than statements from ROCOR or the Old Calendrists. One of the earliest anti-ecumenical actions originating from Mount Athos occurred in 1980, when the Joint International Commission for Theological Dialogue between the Catholic Church and the Orthodox Church was getting under way. A conference of the Sacred Community on Mount Athos (which brings together the superiors of the twenty sovereign Athonite monasteries) issued a statement which, while not openly objecting to Orthodox-Catholic theological discussions, saw these in a narrow context of witness with an aim towards conversion to Orthodoxy:

> Dialogue with the heterodox is not reprehensible from the Orthodox point of view if its goal is to inform them of the Orthodox faith and, thus, make it possible for them thereby to return to Orthodoxy when they receive divine enlightenment and their eyes are opened.[38]

Despite a generally more moderate tone, the Athonites, like ROCOR and the Old Calendrists, also have recourse to conspiracy theories and apocalyptic rhetoric in their anti-ecumenical statements: 'A Fifth Crusade is unfolding before our very eyes, the goal of which is a new conquest of the Orthodox peoples.'[39]

The principal bones of contention raised by anti-ecumenical Orthodox groups are an apparent acceptance of the 'two lung' theory of the church advanced by Pope John Paul II, or the related 'branch theory' of the church; implicit recognition of the presence of divine grace in other churches, capable of granting salvation; a perceived weakening of Orthodox opposition to the Greek Catholic churches established in the Ukraine and elsewhere (and especially Orthodox acceptance of communiqué of the June 1993 Balamand Conference of the Orthodox-Catholic Joint Commission)[40]; theological objections to the 1989 and 1990 Agreed Statements with the Oriental Orthodox churches, with recommendations for the lifting of the historic anathemas and the re-establishment

[37]Archbishop Vitaly of Montreal and Canada, 'Report to the Sobor of Bishops'.

[38]'Announcement of the Extraordinary Joint Conference of the Sacred Community of the Holy Mount Athos (April 9/22, 1980)'. http://orthodoxinfo.com/ecumenism/athos.aspx (21 November 2016).

[39]'Open letter from the Athonite Monks to Ecumenical Patriarch Bartholomew' (11 May 1999). http://orthodoxinfo.com/ecumenism/athonite_bartholomew.aspx (9 October 2016).

[40]See the 'Communiqué of the Seventh Plenary Session of the Joint International Commission for Theological Dialogue between the Catholic Church and the Orthodox Church' (Balamand, Lebanon, 17–24 June 1993). www.vatican.va/roman_curia/pontifical_councils/chrstuni/ch_orthodox_docs/rc_pc_chrstuni_doc_19930624_lebanon_en.html (31 March 2015).

of communion between the two families of churches[41]; visits of the ecumenical patriarch to Rome and of the pope and other Vatican representatives to Constantinople and other countries of Orthodox tradition (which appear to treat the two churches as equal in status, thereby, it is thought, undermining the Orthodox position on deficiencies in the Catholic Church) and Orthodox participation in common prayers with non-Orthodox and even with non-Christians.

The main theological focus of neo-traditionalist thinking is ecclesiology, especially ecumenism, with important ramifications in sacramental theology and soteriology, typically set in generalized anti-modernism and anti-Westernism. The main line of neo-traditionalist ecclesiology runs something like this:

> The Orthodox Church is *exclusively* the One, Holy, Catholic and Apostolic Church of Christ on earth. Since there is but One Christ and One Church, there can be no other church and those Christian bodies which call themselves 'church' are in fact not church at all. Having separated themselves from the Orthodox Church by heresy or schism, these bodies no longer possess the sacraments, which subsist only in the Orthodox Church. Thus the rituals carried out by non-Orthodox in imitation of true sacraments are without grace or effect, or (following Augustine) at best they may be valid but not effective, that is, they are not rendered instruments of grace by the action of the Holy Spirit. Thus the baptism administered by non-Orthodox is an empty ritual and does not make its recipients members of the One, Holy, Catholic and Apostolic Church, but instead signifies their membership in some sect or pseudo-church. Their eucharistic rituals may mimic Jesus' Last Supper with his Holy apostles, but the bread and wine are not changed into the Body and Blood of Christ, so there is no communion with the risen Lord.
>
> Outside the Orthodox Church, there are only heresies and schisms. The Orthodox Church has never united herself with heresies and schisms but condemns them and prays for the repentance and conversion of heretics and schismatics. Thus the only valid objective of Orthodox contacts with non-Orthodox is to urge them to recognize their errors, to repent and to return to the true Church of Christ, the Holy Orthodox Church.
>
> Christian unity has never been broken, nor could it, because Christ is the one Head of the Church and his Body, the Orthodox Church, cannot be divided. The Orthodox Church has always remained united with her Head, Jesus Christ, as his Body, in keeping with the teachings of the Holy Fathers, the ecumenical councils, the sacred canons and the saints throughout all ages. Thus there is no question of seeking a 'lost' unity of the church, only the return of heretics and schismatics to the Orthodox Church.[42]

---

[41]See the 'Second Agreed Statement' (1990), 'Recommendations on Pastoral Issues' (1990), and 'Proposals for Lifting Anathema' (1993) of the Joint Commission of the Theological Dialogue between the Orthodox Church and the Oriental Orthodox churches at: https://orthodoxjointcommission.wordpress.com (31 March 2015). See also our article 'Orthodox Critiques of the Agreed Statements between the Orthodox and the Oriental Orthodox Churches', *St Vladimir's Theological Quarterly*, 60, 3 (2016), 333–68.

[42]As examples of this line of argumentation, see the pre-conciliar letters of Metropolitan Hierotheos Vlachos: '[First] Letter to the Holy Synod of the Church of Greece on the texts proposed for approval by the upcoming Great and Holy Council of the Orthodox Church' (18 January 2016). www.pravoslavie.ru/english/90896.htm (5 September 2016); '[Second] Letter to the Holy Synod of Greece Concerning Preparations for the Upcoming Great and Holy Council' (20 January 2016). www.pravoslavie.ru/english/90812.htm (5 September 2016); '[Third] Letter to the Holy Synod of Greece Concerning the Draft Documents Prepared for the Upcoming Pan-Orthodox Council' (5 March 2016). www.pravoslavie.ru/english/91319.htm (5 September 2016). And also: Met. Athanasios of Limassol: 'What unity are we talking about? Those who departed from the Church are heretics and schismatics' (11 February 2016). www.pravoslavie.ru/english/90619.htm (5 September 2016); 'Open letter of the Holy Mount Athos Kinot to

Few neo-traditionalists carry their thinking to its logical conclusion, although a meeting of Bulgarian clergy and monastics in February 2016 did carry the argument this far:

> Since non-Orthodox (including of course non-Christians) are not members of the church, and only the church possesses and transmits the means of salvation, non-Orthodox are deprived of the means of salvation and thus they cannot enter the Kingdom of God, but are destined for hell unless they join the One, Holy Orthodox Church.[43]

This neo-traditionalist ecclesiology is usually presented with sufficient scriptural and patristic proof texts to convince many Orthodox and, as became obvious, the Holy Synods of several local Orthodox churches, to the point that they not only criticized the pre-conciliar documents, but also refused to attend the Holy and Great Council of the Orthodox Church held in Crete in June 2016, on the grounds that the documents, especially ecumenism document, did not contain their views grounded in neo-traditionalist theology.[44]

Until the strength of the neo-traditionalist, anti-ecumenical movement became clear in the conflicts surrounding the Council of 2016, many Orthodox theologians did not take the movement very seriously, with the result that neo-traditionalist theology went largely unstudied and unchallenged.[45]

Orthodoxy and religious diversity

Early Christian thinking on non-Christian religions was conditioned by the pagan polytheism of the Roman Empire, religious aspects of Greek philosophy and links between Christianity and Judaism, including the incorporation, not without some hesitation, of the Jewish sacred books into the Christian Bible. Some early Christian thinkers, especially St Justin Martyr (c.100–c.165) had a cautiously positive view concerning the existence of elements of truth among pagan philosophers

the Patriarch of Constantinople Bartholomew I' (25 May 2016). http://katehon.com/article/open-letter-holy-mount-athos-kinot-patriarch-constantinople-bartholomew-i (3 September 2016); Peter Heers, '*The Mystery of Baptism* and the Unity of the Church: The Idea of "Baptismal Unity" and its Acceptance by Orthodox Ecumenists' (2004). http://orthodoxinfo.com/ecumenism/ea_ecclesiology.aspx (5 October 2016); and Peter Heers's book *The Ecclesiological Renovation of Vatican II: An Orthodox Examination of Rome's Ecumenical Theology Regarding Baptism and the Church* (Simpsonville, SC: Uncut Mountain Press, 2015).

[43]See 'Des prêtres et moines de l'Église orthodoxe bulgare, soutenus par des laïcs, ont fait part au patriarche de Bulgarie Néophyte de leurs inquiétudes au sujet du document préconciliaire concernant les "Relations des Églises orthodoxes avec l'ensemble du monde chrétien"' (Priests and monks of the Bulgarian Orthodox Church, with the support of laity, have brought to the attention of Bulgarian Patriarch Neophyte their concerns over the pre-conciliar document 'Relations of the Orthodox Church with the Rest of the Christian World'), posted 23 February 2016 at: http://orthodoxie.com/category/actualites/relations-oecumeniques/ (5 September 2016).

[44]For an overview of the Council of 2016, see Paul Ladouceur, 'The Holy and Great Council of the Orthodox Church (June 2016)', *Oecuménisme/Ecumenism* (Montreal), 51, 198–9 (2016).

[45]Our article 'On Ecumenoclasm: Anti-Ecumenical Theology in Orthodoxy' critiques major aspects of neo-traditional ecclesiology and anti-ecumenical theology, including neo-traditionalist soteriology, ecclesiology and its views on Christian unity, common prayer among Christians and ecumenism as heresy. This article is a revised and expanded version of posts under the heading 'Ecumenoclasm' on the *Public Orthodoxy* website. https://publicorthodoxy.org/tag/paul-ladouceur/ (4 October 2016).

and Jewish sages, while Tertullian (c.155–c.240) represented a less tolerant view, which became more dominant in later Christian thinking. Later in history, Orthodoxy had extensive historical experience, not entirely negative, of life as a religious and cultural minority under non-Christian regimes in Persia, the Arabic Middle East and the Ottoman Empire. For long centuries, Christian communities were in a survival mode under Muslim rule in these areas, which made theological reflection on the meaning of religious diversity in God's plan for salvation difficult. Only in recent times have Orthodox theologians begun to reflect more systematically on religious diversity, especially as Orthodoxy is increasingly confronted with this reality both in countries of Orthodox immigration in Western Europe and North America, and increasingly in countries of Orthodox tradition. Contemporary Orthodox attitudes towards religious diversity are often linked with thinking on secularism, human rights and the religious policy of the state.

Several notions concerning non-Christian religions which have come down to us from the ancient Fathers are still relevant. The most important is no doubt from Justin Martyr, who applies the Hellenistic notion of the 'seeds of the Logos' (*logos spermatikos*) in a Christian sense.[46] Although there is some question of what exactly Justin meant by the term, his writings suggest that he was referring to those aspects of Christian truth present in the philosophers. Michel Fédou defines Justin's doctrine of the *logos spermatikos* as 'a universal divine communication in the world of the nations, in the expectation of the full revelation of the Logos of God at the moment of the Incarnation.'[47] Justin recognizes that the pagan philosophers, especially Socrates and Plato, had a degree of knowledge of truth, but that the fullness of truth resides only in Christian revelation. He even goes so far as to refer to certain Greek philosophers and various Jewish figures as Christians:

> We have been taught that Christ is the First-born of God, and we have suggested … that he is the *logos* of whom every race of men and women were partakers. And they who lived with the *logos* are Christians, even though they have been thought atheists; as, among the Greeks, Socrates and Heraclitus, and people like them; and among the barbarians,[48] Abraham, and Ananias, and Asarias, and Misael, and Elias.[49]
>
> For whatever either lawgivers or philosophers uttered well, they elaborated according to their share of *logos* by invention and contemplation. But since they did not know all that concerns *logos*, who is Christ, they often contradicted themselves.[50]

In his polemical treatise *Against the Heathen*, St Athanasius of Alexandria (c.296–373) recognizes, like Justin before him, the possibility that pagans can rise to knowledge of truth. Possessing a rational soul and free will, pagans can abandon idolatry and return to the true God:

> Just as they turned away from God with their mind and invented gods from nonexistent entities, so they can rise towards God with the mind of their soul and again turn back towards him. They can

---

[46]See Justin Martyr, *First Apology*, 32, 44 and 46; and especially the *Second Apology*, 8, 10 and 13. The citations below are from Justin Martyr, *The First and Second Apologies* (New York: Paulist Press, 1997).

[47]See Michel Fédou, 'La doctrine du Logos chez Justin: Enjeux philosophiques et théologiques' (The doctrine of the Logos in Justin: Philosophical and theological issues), *Kentron*, 25 (2009), 154.

[48]Justin is writing between 155 and 157 to the Emperor Antoninus (ruled 138 to 161). The 'barbarians' here are the Jews.

[49] Justin Martyr, *First Apology*, 46.

[50]Ibid., 10.

> turn back if they cast off the stain of all desire which they have put on, and wash themselves until they have eliminated every addition foreign to the soul and show it unadulterated, as it was made, in order that in this way they may be able to contemplate therewith the Word of the Father, in whose image they were made in the beginning.[51]

Other early Christian thinkers who recognized the existence of goodness and elements of truth in pagan religions and especially in the philosophers include Clement of Alexandria (c.150–c.215), Origen (c.184–c.253), Basil the Great (329–379), Gregory Nazianzus (329–390) and Augustine (354–430).[52]

But a critical evaluation of other religions, inheriting the negative attitude towards pagan idolatry in both the Old Testament and the New Testament, also found support in early Christianity. Tertullian represents the more conservative strain of early Christian thought, seeing in other religions only the work of demons, and more specifically considering that pagan gods are demons. In his *Apology*, Tertullian sets out to demonstrate to his pagan addressee that the pagan gods and demons are the same beings under different appellations, "that the nature (*qualitas*) of both terms is the same."[53]

Tertullian acknowledges that some philosophers openly attack pagan superstitions and have the same teachings on morality and virtue as Christians. Yet he criticizes the philosophers, for instance, Socrates, for corrupting truth by offering sacrifices to false gods and by ranking demons next to gods. These corruptions of the truth, according to Tertullian, ensure that the philosophers are tolerated in the Roman Empire, while Christians – who uphold the truth in all respects – suffer persecution.[54]

Byzantine thinking on non-Christian religions was strongly influenced by shifting attitudes towards Judaism and, later, towards Islam. From the more tolerant and open early approaches of Justin, Clement and others, subsequent writings on non-Christian religions moved to a more hostile and intolerant approach. Islam was first seen as a Christian heresy because of its rejection of the divinity of Christ, notably by St John of Damascus (676–749).[55] But subsequent Byzantine attitudes varied from anti-Jewish and anti-Islamic polemics to attempts at theological dialogue, such as in the writing of St Gregory Palamas (1296–1359) during his captivity by the Turks in 1354–1355 before he was finally released for a ransom.[56]

---

[51]Athanasius, *Against the Heathen*, 34. From Athanasius, *Contra Gentes and De Incarnatione* (Oxford: Clarendon Press, 1971), 95.

[52]For overviews of early Christian thinking on other religions and philosophies, see Anastasios Giannoulatos (Yannoulatos), *Various Christian Approaches to Other Religions (A Historical Outline)* (Athens: Poreuthentes, 1971), 13–31; Philip Sherrard, *Christianity: Lineaments of a Sacred Tradition* (Brookline, MA: Holy Cross Orthodox Press, 1998), 55–61; and John Garvey, *Seeds of the Word* (Yonkers, NY: St Vladimir's Seminary Press, 2005), 79–98.

[53]Tertullian, *Apology*, 23, 4. Citations from Tertullian, *Apologetical Works and Minucius Felix Octavius* (Washington: Catholic University of America Press, 1950).

[54]Tertullian, *Apology*, 46.

[55]Islam features as 'Heresy 101' under the title 'Against the Ishmaelites' in *Against Heresies*, a contested work attributed to John of Damascus. Another work by the Damascene is 'Disputation between a Christian and a Saracen'. For the Greek text of the former and selections from the latter, with English translations, see Daniel J. Janosik, *John of Damascus, First Apologist to the Muslims* (Eugene: Pickwick Publications, 2016). See also earlier references in Yannoulatos, *Various Christian Approaches to Other Religions*, 34, n. 54.

[56]On this episode and the resulting writings of Palamas, see G. Georgiades, Arnakis, 'Gregory Palamas among the Turks and Documents of His Captivity as Historical Sources', *Speculum*, 26, 1; and Nazar Sloboda, 'The Conversations of Gregory Palamas

These two strands of ancient Christian thinking about non-Christian religions and especially Greek philosophy – that they contain elements of truth and can somehow be assimilated to Christianity, and that they are works of demons intended to lead Christians astray – have come down to modern times.

Modern Orthodox thought on religious diversity

Orthodox ecclesiology since the mid-nineteenth century has devoted considerable attention to Orthodoxy in relation to other Christian churches and confessions, but very little to non-Christian religions. Nonetheless, several theologians have written significantly on the question. We shall focus here on the main lines of thought of Orthodox figures representing a range of approaches to religious diversity. Their writings on non-Christian religions are not extensive, consisting mainly of articles, essays and chapters in books, but they nonetheless sketch out basic elements of Orthodox thinking, both positive and negative, on non-Christian religions.

One of the earliest modern presentations of an Orthodox position on non-Christian religions was an address by Metropolitan Georges Khodr of Mount Lebanon (b. 1923) at the Central Committee of the WCC in Addis Ababa in 1971, under the title 'Christianity in a Pluralistic World – The Economy of the Holy Spirit'.[57] Khodr, a leading Orthodox ecumenist and promoter of dialogue between Christianity and Islam, argues for a vision of the church as 'the instrument of the mystery of the salvation of the nations' by appeals to the Noahic covenant, divine freedom and kenosis, the universality of the economy of Christ and especially the Resurrection and the mysterious, unbounded presence of the Holy Spirit. 'The church's task is to perceive … even in the world of the religions', writes Khodr, 'the God who is hidden within it, in anticipation of the final concrete manifestation of the Mystery'.[58] Khodr's bold thinking culminates in a universal and eschatological vision of world religions:

> Christ is hidden everywhere in the mystery of his self-abasement. Any reading of religions is a reading in Christ. It is Christ alone who is received as light when grace visits a Brahmin, a Buddhist or a Moslem reading his scriptures. … All who are visited by the Spirit are the people of God. The church represents the first-fruits of all humanity called to salvation. … The main task is

---

during His Ottoman Captivity'. www.academia.edu/12253003/ (3 March 2017).

[57]Georges Khodre, 'Le Christianisme dans un monde pluraliste: l'économie du Saint-Esprit', *Irénikon*, 44, 2 (1971). Translation: Georges Khodr, 'Christianity in a Pluralistic World: The Economy of the Holy Spirit', *The Ecumenical Review*, 23, 2 (1971). Reprinted in *Sobornost'* (Summer 1971); *Sourozh*, 53 (1993), 9–18; and in Michael Kinnamon and Brian Cope, eds., *The Ecumenical Movement: An Anthology of Key Texts and Voices* (Geneva: WCC Publications, 1997); and elsewhere. A later, shorter text contains many of the same ideas: 'An Orthodox Perspective of Interreligious Dialogue', *Current Dialogue* (WCC), 19 (1991).

[58]Khodr, 'Le Christianisme dans un monde pluraliste', 197.

> to identify all the Christic values in other religions, to show Christ as their bond and his love as their fulfilment.[59]

Elsewhere Khodr emphasizes that Christ's salvific mission is not limited to the visible Christian Church. 'Is the church exclusively those who are baptized', writes Khodr, 'or is it the Body of Christ – the Body of Christ in the sense that it extends to wherever he wishes it to extend? ... The church organization joins Christians together but does not limit Christ.'[60]

But in his enthusiasm Khodr does perhaps go too far in one statement: 'Every martyr for truth, every man persecuted for what he believes to be justice, dies in union with Christ.'[61] This sweeping hypothesis requires a deeper exploration, since extremists of all sorts may be persecuted and die for what they believe to be right.

Together with Georges Khodr, Archbishop Anastasios Yannoulatos (b. 1929) is another leading figure in Orthodox thought concerning religious diversity. Yannoulatos studied theology and world religions in Athens and in Germany and served as archbishop in East Africa from 1981 to 1991, before becoming primate of the Orthodox Church of Albania in 1992. As early as 1971 he published a survey of the evolution of Christian thinking on non-Christian religions from the early church to the Second Vatican Council, including patristic, Byzantine, Protestant and Roman Catholic approaches over the centuries.[62] In a 1974 essay, Yannoulatos grounds an Orthodox approach to non-Christian religions in the theology of the human person and the need for humans to exist in communion with other persons, a 'communion [*koinonia*] of love', which takes as its point of departure and model the communion among the divine Persons of the Holy Trinity. Yannoulatos has no hesitation in showing his colours: 'The universality of the church does not mean exclusivity; it means all-inclusiveness.'[63] And later in the same essay he writes: 'People who have different beliefs never lose the basic attributes of their spiritual identity: they never cease to be "children of God", created in "in God's image", and hence our brothers and sisters. God is the Father of us all.'[64] While this approach reiterates the ontological equality of all humans regardless of religion or even non-religion, it does not, as Yannoulatos recognizes, deal with the more specific issue of a theological understanding of non-Christian religions: 'An analysis of Christian theories on how to understand other religions will not be undertaken here. I believe that a satisfactory solution to this problem has not yet been found. We are still looking.'[65]

In a 1989 paper Yannoulatos tackles head-on the issue of the theological significance of non-Christian religions. Yannoulatos classifies Christian theories and attitudes towards other religions into six categories, covering the full gamut from Tertullian's view that non-Christian

---

[59] Ibid., 198, 200, 202.

[60] Georges Khodr, 'Will the Non-Christian Be Saved?' *An-Nahar* (in Arabic) (Beirut, 22 June 2002). Translation https://orthodoxyindialogue.com/2017/11/23/ (14 December 2017).

[61] Khodr, 'Le Christianisme dans un monde pluraliste', 198.

[62] Giannoulatos (Yannoulatos), *Various Christian Approaches to Other Religions.*

[63] Anastasios Yannoulatos, 'Toward a Global Community: Resources and Responsibilities' (1974), in *Facing the World: Orthodox Christian Essays on Global Concerns* (Crestwood, NY: WCC/St Vladimir's Seminary Press, 2003), 29.

[64] Yannoulatos, 'Toward a Global Community', 43.

[65] Ibid.

religions are the work of the devil, to relativism and syncretism.[66] Building on his earlier Trinitarian foundation of human relations, he postulates three key concepts for an Orthodox theology of religions. First, the 'universal radiance of God's glory': There is but one God, even if people have widely diverging conceptions about God; hence, 'God's glory pervades all of heaven and earth and every shape and form of life.'[67] The second principle is founded on the ontological equality of all humans, who thus have a common origin and destiny, extended to include universal divine revelation: 'The universal character of divine revelation to humanity is related to our innate religious sense.'[68] Yannoulatos's third principle is universal divine providence, God constantly providing for creation and humanity: 'God has never stopped caring for the whole world that he created.'[69] Yannoulatos refers to God's covenants with Adam and Eve (Gen. 2.16-17) and with Noah (Gen. 9:8-17). Like Khodr before him, Yannoulatos considers that the Noahic covenant is universal, permanent and all-pervasive, not only between God and Noah, but to all Noah's descendants, 'all flesh that is on the earth' (Gen. 9.16). 'All human beings', he concludes, 'are in a relationship with God through some previous covenant to which he himself set his own seal'.[70]

These fundamental principles serve as the underpinning of a Christological basis of an Orthodox understanding of other religions, not in an exclusivist sense of barring those who do not know or acknowledge Christ from salvation, but to affirm, with Justin Martyr and other early Christian writers, that Christ, the Logos of God, is 'the true Light which gives light to every man coming into the world' (Jn 1.8). But Yannoulatos also ventures into more perilous territory by affirming that it is the constant activity of the Holy Spirit which assures 'the manifestation of the Trinitarian God's presence – everywhere in the world, throughout time and for all eternity', and 'continues to act for the salvation of every person and the fulfillment and completion of the entire world'.[71] Yannoulatos appears to subscribe here to the theory of a twofold divine economy, attributed to Vladimir Lossky, whereby Christ is active primarily among Christians and the Holy Spirit among non-Christians. In his book *The Mystical Theology of the Eastern Church* (1944), Lossky devotes a chapter to 'The Economy of the Son' and another to 'The Economy of the Holy Spirit'. This suggests a real distinction in the economies of the Second and Third Persons of the Holy Trinity, assumed to be respectively within Christianity and beyond the boundaries of Christianity. Although Lossky does not actually assert distinct 'economies' of the Son and the Holy Spirit in the world, he is criticized for implying this.[72]

[66]Ibid., 132–5.
[67]Ibid., 139–40.
[68]Ibid., 141.
[69]Ibid.
[70]Ibid., 141–2.
[71]Ibid., 149.
[72]For criticisms of Lossky's *Mystical Theology*, see the references above, 108, n. 45.

While Yannoulatos does not clarify the respective roles of Christ and Holy Spirit in world religions, he affirms that 'the criterion by which Christians evaluate and accept different religious ideas and principles is Jesus Christ, the Word of God and incarnation of God's love.'[73]

Aware of this potential difficulty, some Orthodox theologians, such as Fr Emmanuel Clapsis, consciously seek to affirm the simultaneous presence and action of Christ and the Holy Spirit beyond Christianity:

> The Holy Spirit either precedes Christ preparing and moving all towards their eschatological fulfilment or follows Christ sustaining and continuing his mission in the world. … The recognition of the presence of God's Spirit in the world, outside of the distinctive boundaries of the church, must not be disassociated from Christ. … [The Spirit's] presence in the world is not separate from Christ's, since both, in their distinctive but interdependent missions, disclose the active love of God the Father.[74]

Philip Sherrard (1922–95) was an English scholar, author and translator who contributed greatly to increasing awareness of modern Greek culture and literature, especially poetry. Sherrard also wrote on a wide range of philosophical and theological themes. In his book *Christianity: Lineaments of a Sacred Tradition* (1998), he presents one of the most open views of religious diversity of any Orthodox writer. For Sherrard, the world's great spiritual traditions (primarily Christian, Jewish, Muslim, Hindu, Buddhist and Taoist) possess three essential features: a body of doctrine which 'enshrines the knowledge imparted by God through revelation, often in the form of a Holy Book or of Holy Books, and interpreted by the inspired spiritual masters of the tradition concerned'; the transmission of this spiritual influence 'by means of a ritual, sacramental or liturgical act, or of ritual acts"; and the existence of "a sacred or hieratic order', instituted by 'a divine or semi-divine being', and which receives the sacred tradition and transmits it to others.[75] Sherrard emphasizes the need 'to affiliate ourselves to an authentic sacred tradition' and he calls on the church to renounce 'the claim that the Christian revelation constitutes the sole and universal revelation of the universal Truth.'[76] He enunciates initially an inclusivist position regarding world religions, paraphrasing Georges Khodr: 'Any deep reading of another religion is a reading of the Logos, of Christ. It is the Logos who is received in the spiritual illumination of a Brahmin, a Buddhist, or a Moslem.'[77] But he goes further, affirming the validity and apparent equality of authentic spiritual traditions: 'Sacred traditions other than their own [Christians'] are divinely-instituted ways of spiritual realization. … There may be as many ways to God as there are individual human beings. … Since God is infinite,

---

[73]Yannoulatos, 'Toward a Global Community', 152.

[74]Emmanuel Clapsis, 'Theology of Religions as Concern for Ecumenical Dialogue of Orthodox Theologians', in Pantelis Kalaitzidis et al. eds., *Orthodox Handbook on Ecumenism: Resources for Theological Education* (Volos, GR: Volos Academy Publications; Oxford: Regnum Books; Geneva: World Council of Churches, 2013), 709; 710; 713. See also Gennadios Limouris, 'Come Holy Spirit – Renew the Whole Creation: Pneumatology in Symphony with Christology', in Gennadios Limouris, ed., *Come, Holy Spirit, Renew the Whole Creation: An Orthodox Approach for the Seventh Assembly of the World Council of Churches, Canberra, Australia, 6-21 February 1991* (Brookline, MA: Holy Cross Orthodox Press, 1990).

[75]Sherrard, *Christianity: Lineaments of a Sacred Tradition*, 15; 20; 21.

[76]Ibid., 21; 53.

[77]Ibid., 62.

there is nothing to prevent him from choosing to reveal himself in an infinite number of limited forms, all of which he himself, in his non-manifest nature, infinitely transcends.'[78]

The foundation of Sherrard's position is a conviction of a unity of truth, 'an underlying metaphysical order, a series of timeless and universal principles from which all derives and on which all depends … the essential unity of the unchanging, non-manifest, and timeless principles themselves'.[79] Sherrard is expressing here the central teaching of the traditionalist or perennialist school of thought. This school, following its principal modern architects the philosophers René Guénon (1886–1951) and Aldous Huxley (1894–1963), emphasizes the existence of primordial and universal truths upon which all major world religions draw as their prime source. 'There is the Truth', writes Sherrard, 'as it is "laid up in heaven" in its preformal and purely metaphysical state; and there is this Truth as it is when translated into the various doctrines and symbolic languages of the human race.'[80] Sherrard leaves open the possibility that one religious tradition may more fully express metaphysical Truth than others: 'Certain forms' in which God reveals himself may 'enshrine his reality more fully than others'; one religious tradition rooted in true revelation may 'express God's wisdom and knowledge more fully than others'.[81] But Sherrard, whose commitment to Orthodoxy is unwavering, stops short here of claiming that Christianity, let alone Orthodoxy, is precisely the tradition which most fully and accurately reflects divine reality or the transcendent Truth of which he writes.[82]

Nicholas Arseniev (1888–1977) taught Orthodox theology in Russia until 1920, then in Königsburg and Warsaw until 1939 and after the Second World War at St Vladimir's Seminary in New York. In his book *Revelation of Life Eternal* (1960), Arseniev sketches an outline of a Christian attitude towards the religious quests and beliefs of humanity beyond Judeo-Christian revelation, based on the premise 'that there is a certain knowledge of God or a yearning and craving and searching after him given to all'.[83] Arseniev explores this theme from the perspective of the simultaneous existence in religious traditions of both 'a higher conception or rather a higher experience of God' and 'the rubbish and trash of often morally repulsive and even ludicrous polytheistic and polydemonistic conceptions'.[84] But even in animistic religions dominated by the latter, there may occur a 'breaking through' of a higher conception of divinity, such as the notion of a 'merciful Supreme Father'. Arseniev gives several examples, from the Bushmen of South Africa, the Hinayâna Buddhist notion of nirvana, the Aztecs of Mexico and the Pygmies of Africa. He challenges a long-held view that there has been an evolution in the history of religion from lower to higher forms. Citing examples from anthropological studies of religious beliefs and practices in

[78]Ibid., 63; 70.
[79]Ibid., 62; 63.
[80]Ibid., 64.
[81]Ibid., 70; 73–4.
[82]Kallistos Ware writes that Sherrard was 'firm in his loyalty to the Orthodox Church', and that his spiritual vision 'extended at the same time beyond Orthodoxy and indeed beyond the Christian faith'. Kallistos Ware, 'Foreword' to *Christianity: Lineaments of a Sacred Tradition*, xvi.
[83]Nicholas Arseniev, *Revelation of Life Eternal: An Introduction to the Christian Message* (Crestwood, NY: St Vladimir's Seminary Press, 1982), 41.
[84]Arseniev, *Revelation of Life Eternal*, 47.

premodern societies, Arseniev argues that 'in many cases [there] seems to be an evolution of descent, of religious deterioration.'[85] Arseniev's perspective on non-Christian religions is decidedly committed: The values represented in the Judeo-Christian tradition are the standard against which he measures other religious traditions and practices.

Fr Lev Gillet (1893–1980) was engaged in interreligious dialogue long before the modern interreligious movement. Gillet, better known under his pen name 'A Monk of the Eastern Church', was a French Catholic priest and monk who joined the Orthodox Church in Paris in 1928.[86] In 1938 he moved to England, where he was closely associated with Fellowship of St Alban and Saint Sergius. Engaged in Jewish-Christian relations, in his first years in England he was chaplain for a hostel occupied by young Jews and Jewish Christian refugees from Germany and Austria until the British authorities interned its occupants as 'enemy aliens' in early 1940. The Religious Society of Friends (Quakers) then provided Gillet a fellowship to study Jewish theology and Jewish-Christian relations, the result of which was a pioneering book, *Communion in the Messiah*, published in 1942 at the height of the Second World War.[87] Going beyond advocating Christian solidarity with persecuted Jews in Hitler's Europe, Gillet sets out to identify points of convergence between Jewish and Christian theology, spirituality and religious practices. He focuses, as the title of book indicates, on the notion of the Messiah, and also other common theological insights such as the Jewish *shekinah*, the divine Presence or indwelling.[88]

After the war, Gillet worked for many years for the Union for the Study of Great Religions based in London, preparing 'book lists' for the Union's journal – in effect, reviews of publications relevant to interreligious understanding. Gillet was also secretary of the World Congress of Faiths devoted to interreligious dialogue for five years (1961–65). One of his responsibilities was to prepare meetings of the Congress, including acting as resource person for interfaith services – no small challenge. Gillet never wrote explicitly about his interreligious experience, but it is likely out of these activities that he published a unique series of meditations focused on the notion of Supreme Being as 'limitless love'.[89]

Most of the writings of Fr Alexander Men (1935–90) are pastoral, but for much of his adult life he was engaged in writing a comprehensive history of religion. The six-volume work was initially published in Brussels under the general title *The History of Religion: In Search of the Way, the Truth and the Life*, and copies were smuggled into the Soviet Union. Volume I, *The Wellsprings of Religion*, which examines the nature and origins of religion, has been published in translation.[90]

---

[85]Ibid., 47–51; 53–8; 56.

[86]See Elisabeth Behr-Sigel's masterly biography, *Un Moine de l'Église d'Orient, le père Lev Gillet: Un libre croyant universaliste, évangélique et mystique* (Paris: Le Cerf, 1993). English version: *Lev Gillet: A Monk of the Eastern Church, Fr. Lev Gillet* (London: Fellowship of Saint Alban and Saint Sergius, 1999). The subtitle of the French is missing in the English.

[87]Lev Gillet, *Communion in the Messiah: Studies in the Relationship between Judaism and Christianity* (London: Lutterworth, 1942; James Clarke, 2003; Eugene, OR: Wipf & Stock, 2013).

[88]On the *Shekinah*, see Gillet, *Communion in the Messiah*, 80–7; 138; 228–9.

[89]Un Moine de l'Église d'Orient (Lev Gillet), *L'Amour sans limites* (Unlimited Love) (Chevetogne, BE: Éditions de Chevetogne, 1971); translation in Lev Gillet, *In Thy Presence* (London: Mowbray, 1977; Crestwood, NY: St Vladimir's Seminary Press, 1977). See the summary and discussion of this work in Behr-Sigel, *Un Moine de l'Église d'Orient*, 515–19 and 556–8.

[90]Alexander Men, *History of Religion: In Search of the Way, the Truth and the Life* 5 vols. (in Russian) (Brussels, 1970–83). English translation of Vol. 1: *The Wellsprings of Religion* (Yonkers, NY: St Vladimir's Seminary Press, 2017).

Men's major objective in the *History of Religion* is to oppose communist anti-religious ideology. Throughout the study, he demonstrates from historical evidence that religious expression is the natural reflection of the deepest human longings and aspirations, whatever variations and divergences it may take. In the first volume, he challenges the communist contention that science and religion are incompatible, hence a chapter devoted to evolution, one of the first serious Orthodox theological reflections on the subject. Men points out that in ancient times religion was the source of science, and that science and religion, far from being incompatible, are complementary and autonomous, with different methodologies, but intimately connected to each other as expressions of one divine Truth.

In the multi-volume work, Men sees divine action in the truths of non-Christian religions, but also deviations from truth, especially in what he calls magic, attempts to know and control the world without God – the second volume is devoted to magic and monotheism in ancient religions. Divine providence is at work in ancient religions, which are not only of historical interest, but 'in them there is something eternal, real and pressing in any generation.'[91] It is in this sense that they may be included in the mystery of divine presence beyond the visible limits of Christianity. Even atheists are not really without faith; they have merely erected in the place of God other objects of faith: 'Anti-religious doctrines are often connected with inner religious impulses of a mystical character; the narrative or myth that goes with ideology, taken on board as faith, is in fact inverted religion.'[92] Thus in the place of God we find the 'overman' (*Übermensch*) (Friedrich Nietzsche; 1844–1900), human moral freedom (Albert Camus; 1913–60), reason and nature (the Enlightenment), humanity (Auguste Comte; 1798–1857), the creative energy of evolution (Julian Huxley; 1887–1975), the 'people' (communism) or biological racism (Nazism).[93] Men sets growing secularization against a universal tendency for humans to seek explanation and purpose for existence beyond themselves, a yearning reflected in many paths, some of which are dead ends, but may nonetheless contain elements of eternal Truth. Despite the historical diversity of religions, Men writes of a 'kind of kinship of religions', which arises from a common human nature and 'the similarity of the experiences that evoke in humanity a sense of the Sublime and ideas about it'.[94] Underlying Men's sweeping portrayal of human religiosity is a conviction of universal divine presence and providence.

A sharp contrast with the Orthodox personalities that we have considered so far is Fr Seraphim (Eugene) Rose (1934–82), an American convert to Orthodoxy. In the 1960s Rose studied Chinese philosophy under Gi-ming Shien, a remarkable Taoist philosopher installed in California, focusing on the *Tao Te Ching*, a classic Taoist work attributed to a likely mythical figure called Lao Tzu (sixth to fourth century BC).[95] Out of these studies Rose produced a master's thesis on '"Emptiness" and

---

[91]Men, *The Wellsprings of Religion*, 28.

[92]Ibid.

[93]See Men, *The Wellsprings of Religion*, 28–32.

[94]Men, *The Wellsprings of Religion*, 28, 97.

[95]For accounts of Rose's study of Chinese philosophy, see Hieromonk Damascene (John Christensen), *Christ the Eternal Tao* (Platina, CA: Valaam Books, 2004), 36–9; and Hieromonk Damascene (John Christensen), *Father Seraphim Rose: His Life and Works* (Platina, CA: St Herman of Alaska Brotherhood, 2005), 69–78 and 112–18.

"Fullness" in the Lao Tzu'.[96] After becoming Orthodox in 1962, Rose became an ardent critic of Western culture and ecumenism, espousing a neo-traditionalist approach to Orthodoxy. Rose's main concern in his book *Orthodoxy and the Religion of the Future* (1975) is to expose and denounce forms of religious and quasi-religious beliefs and spirituality which became widespread in the United States after the Second World War, including Islam, Hinduism, yoga, zen, transcendental meditation, Hare Krishna, Maharaj-ji, the charismatic revival, the New Age, personal sects and Unidentified Flying Objects (UFOs) – the components, one surmises, of 'the religion of the future'. Rose's objective is to warn Orthodox believers about the dangers of straying from the Orthodox faith inherent in these movements, but the book suffers from categorical language, inadequate knowledge of some its targets and weak theological justification. Rose goes on to condemn Orthodox participation in the ecumenical movement and in interreligious dialogue, casting the entire book in an anti-ecumenical, denunciatory, conspiratorial and apocalyptic vision of exotic religious movements threatening Orthodoxy.

Rose writes that dialogue with non-Christian religions is the product 'of a diabolical "suggestion" that can capture only those who have already departed so far from Christianity as to be virtual pagans: worshippers of the god of this world, Satan (2 Cor. 4.4), and followers of whatever intellectual fashion this powerful god is capable of inspiring.'[97] His main Orthodox target here is none other than Georges Khodr, severely taken to task for his January 1971 address to the Central Committee of the WCC. Rose accuses Khodr of leading 'the avant-garde of Orthodox apostates' who 'speak of the "spiritual riches" and "authentic spiritual life" of the non-Christian religions'.[98] Rose raises several serious theological objections to Khodr, including Khodr's 'projections' of Christ into non-Christian religions, the problem of Khodr's statement about martyrs for truth dying in communion with Christ and Khodr's apparent separation of the economy of the Holy Spirit from the economy of Christ.[99] Rose misrepresents the last point as: 'It is the "Holy Spirit", conceived as totally independent of Christ and his church, that is really the common denominator of all the world's religions.'[100] For Rose, this is a heresy because it 'denies the very nature of the Holy Trinity' with 'no aim but to undermine and destroy the whole idea and reality of the Church of Christ'.[101] Stripping away the impetuous language, Rose raises but does not resolve the major theological issue concerning the respective roles of Christ and the Holy Spirit beyond the visible boundaries of the church, especially in non-Christian religions, and indeed in people of good faith without religious belief.

---

[96]Eugene Dennis Rose, '"Emptiness" and "Fullness" in the Lao Tzu', M.A. thesis, University of California, 19 July 1961.
[97]Seraphim Rose, 'Introduction', *Orthodoxy and the Religion of the Future* (Platina, CA: St. Herman of Alaska Brotherhood, 1975; 4th ed., 1996), xxix.
[98]Rose, *Orthodoxy and the Religion of the Future*, xxix–xxx.
[99]Ibid., xxx–xxxi.
[100]Ibid., xxxi.
[101]Ibid.

Although in *Orthodoxy and the Religion of the Future*, Rose appears to inherit the Tertullian strand of intolerant early Christian thinking concerning non-Christian religions, even to the end of his life he maintained a respectful attitude towards Chinese thought.[102]

Following in the footsteps of Fr Lev Gillet, others have published works comparing Orthodoxy with other religious traditions. The book *Christ the Eternal Tao* by Hieromonk Damascene (John Christensen) (b. 1961) ranks among the most unusual books written by an Orthodox Christian in recent times. The author seeks to make linkages between Christianity and Taoism, in the context of the 'acculturation' of Christianity to Chinese culture. Damascene casts the ancient Chinese sage known as Lao Tzu and the *Tao Te Ching*, the great classic work of Taoism, as precursors to Christ, just as was Greek philosophy, stressing an analogy between the Logos of Greek philosophy and the Tao of Chinese philosophy. In fact, Chinese translations of the Gospel of John use the word 'Tao' to translate Logos; thus a reverse translation of the Prologue of John begins, 'In the beginning was the Tao...'.[103] The book contains an attempt to recast the *Tao Te Ching* in anticipation of Christian revelation, the unfolding of the revelation of the Tao in a comparison between hesychastic and Taoist spirituality and ascetic practices. Hieromonk Damascene presents a defence of the anticipated accusation of religious syncretism in the book. But he defines 'modern syncretism' as advocating 'all paths as possessing equal truth simultaneously',[104] a definition which accords more closely with religious pluralism than with syncretism defined as the combining or blending of religious beliefs and practices of different origins. While some aspects of *Christ the Eternal Tao* might be considered syncretic, Damascene sees his work as in the tradition of ancient Christian teachers who 'understood that there was an *unfolding* of wisdom throughout the ages', seeing in the writings of pre-Christian sages 'a preparation for Christ as the apogee of revelation', and in 'the ancient apologetic tradition'.[105]

The book *Buddhist-Christian Dialogue as Theological Exchange by* Ernest Valea discusses Mahayana Buddhism in Japan in relation to Orthodoxy in several perspectives, including the theology of Fr Dumitru Staniloae. Valea focuses in particular on the thinking of three leading twentieth-century Japanese Buddhist philosophers, highlighting a number of major areas in which Buddhist and Orthodox thinking converge and diverge. Among positive points of comparison feature compassion, prayer and the role of faith. But these seem outweighed by points of incompatibility with Christianity, such as the emphasis on the impermanence of existence in Buddhism (vs. the permanency of God as Ultimate Reality); the search for the abandonment of personal existence (vs. the permanence of individual or permanent existence) and the vision of human perfection as individual Enlightenment or Buddhahood (vs. deification/union with God).[106]

In *The Human Icon*, Christine Mangala Frost (b. 1945), a Hindu convert to Orthodoxy, compares Hindu and Orthodox beliefs and practices in five key areas: divinization or deification; devotional

[102]Fr Seraphim Rose, 'The Chinese Mind' (transcript of an oral teaching, 1981). https://sites.google.com/site/phoenixlxineohp2/thechinesemind (1 December 2017).

[103]Hieromonk Damascene (John Christensen), *Christ the Eternal Tao* (Platina, CA: Valaam Books, 2004), 8, with the Chinese on 10.

[104]Damascene, *Christ the Eternal Tao*, 40.

[105]Ibid., 40–1.

[106]Ernest M. Valea, *Buddhist-Christian Dialogue as Theological Exchange: An Orthodox Contribution to Comparative Theology* (Eugene, OR: Wipf and Stock, 2015), passim.

love; suffering and evil; asceticism; and spiritual elders and holy persons.[107] Although Mangala Frost's constant concern is to seek areas of convergence between Hinduism and Orthodox Christianity – and she identifies many – she does not hesitate to point to major areas of divergence between Christianity and Hinduism, such as the powerful (but not exclusive) impersonalist approach to divinity in Hinduism; the eternal and cyclical nature of existence in Hinduism; karma and reincarnation and the dissolution of the self in the impersonal divinity in *advaita* Vedanta. Despite these areas of incompatibility, Mangala Frost remains optimistic concerning prospects of mutual understanding, appreciation and dialogue between Orthodox and Hindus.[108]

Orthodoxy and theologies of religious diversity

The thinking of ancient Fathers and of modern Orthodox theologians on non-Christian religions can be considered in the light of typologies of interreligious theology. In 1983, the Anglican theologian Alan Race (b. 1951) put forward a threefold typology of Christian attitudes to non-Christian religions based on the possibility of salvation outside of Christianity.[109] An *exclusivist* position is based on the imperative and universal finality of divine revelation in Christ. It considers that non-Christian religions are globally 'excluded' from the history of salvation, as summarized by Marianne Moyaert (b. 1979) expressing the exclusivist position: 'The divine incarnation in Christ is … *ontologically* constitutive for salvation. But not all are redeemed: only those who recognise Jesus Christ as their personal Saviour sent by God can be redeemed.'[110] Christians are those who are called to salvation in Christ; non-Christian religions cannot offer salvation, leaving non-Christians beyond salvation. Tertullian is considered the pre-eminent exponent of exclusivism among the ancient Fathers.

The *inclusivist* position considers that other religions carry certain truths and values of Christianity, despite their errors, and can thus be considered as somehow 'included' in the mystery of Christ and the mission of the Holy Spirit among the nations: 'Salvation is still Christological', writes Moyaert, 'but in an ontological rather than epistemological sense: one can be saved even without knowing Christ at all.'[111] Justin Martyr, Clement and Origen reflect this inclusivism.

Religious pluralism goes further than inclusivism by considering that all great religious traditions are of divine origin and are equally valid paths to God and to salvation, however this may be defined. Religious traditions, Christianity included, 'constitute different ways of experiencing,

---

[107]Christine Mangala Frost, *The Human Icon: A Comparative Study of Hindu and Orthodox Christian Beliefs* (Cambridge: James Clarke, 2017).

[108]Frost, *The Human Icon*, especially 1–3; 315–19.

[109]See Alan Race, *Christians and Religious Pluralism: Patterns in the Christian Theology of Religions* (London: SCM Press, 1993).

[110]Marianne Moyaert expressing the exclusivist position, 'Recent Developments in the Theology of Interreligious Dialogue: From Soteriological Openness to Hermeneutical Openness' *Modern Theology*, 28, 1 (2012), 27.

[111]Moyaert, 'Recent Developments in the Theology of Interreligious Dialogue', 30.

conceiving and living in relation to a transcendent divine Reality which transcends all our varied visions of it'.[112]

Both exclusivism and inclusivism are essentially faith-based theologies which agree on the universality of Christ and the Christian message. Religious pluralism, while compatible with Christianity, takes a more restrictive view of the significance of Christ and Christianity by considering Christianity as one religion among many possible paths to God. In contrast, the ancient Fathers did not consider Christianity to be simply one path to God among others, but inherently superior because of its divine origin and divine Founder and Head. Eminent modern representatives of these three theologies of religious diversity are often said to be the Protestant theologian Karl Barth (1886–1968) (exclusivism); the Catholic theologian Karl Rahner (1904–84) (inclusivism) and the Anglo-American philosopher of religion and theologian John Hick (1922–2012) (religious pluralism).[113]

In addition to types of Christian attitudes towards non-Christian religions, a slightly different polarity is based on the extent of Christian claims in the face of other religions. *Absolutism* considers that only Christianity is absolute or universal, in that Christianity alone has the fullness of truth and thus the universal claims of other religions are false. Both exclusivism and inclusivism are forms of absolutism or universalism. At the opposite pole, *relativism* accords the same value to all religions. Christianity is seen as one religion among others, with no stronger claim to truth than other religions, or to no religion for that matter. A form of relativism lies at the theoretical base of religious pluralism and of the modern, secular, religiously neutral state – even if the state itself incorporates certain Christian notions.

Pushed to an extreme, exclusivism and absolutism can lead to religious *fundamentalism*, often characterized by intolerance, to the point of hostility and violence against other religions and their followers. At the other end of the spectrum, religious pluralism, carried to extreme limits, can open the door to *syncretism*, attempts to associate in one religious vision beliefs and practices from different traditions, which may or may not be inherently irreconcilable – such as attempts to incorporate reincarnation into Christianity.[114]

Although Race's threefold typology quickly became commonplace in interreligious studies, it has been under increasing criticism since the late 1990s and has undergone a process of refinement, with sub-categories of each basic approach identified.[115] The main critique is that it is based on Christian soteriology – who can be saved in terms of Christ's salvific mission – and thus does not allow non-Christian religions to be themselves as human responses to the fundamental questions of the existence of the world and the meaning of life.

---

[112]John Hick, *An Interpretation of Religion: Human Responses to the Transcendent* (Basingstoke UK: MacMillan, 1989; Yale University Press, 2004), 235–6.

[113]Foundational writings include notably Emil Brunner and Karl Barth, *Natural Theology* (London: Geoffrey Bles/Centenary Press, 1946); Karl Rahner, 'Christianity and the Non-Christian Religions', in *Theological Investigations*, Vol. 5 (London: Darton, Longman & Todd, 1966), 115–34; John Hick, *God and the Universe of Faiths* (London: Macmillan, 1973).

[114]See Paul Ladouceur, 'Christianisme et réincarnation' (Christianity and reincarnation), *Contacts*, 58, 214 (2006).

[115]For critiques of the soteriological typology, see Marianne Moyaert, 'Recent Developments in the Theology of Interreligious Dialogue'; and Gavin D'Costa, *Christianity and World Religions: Disputed Questions in the Theology of Religions* (Chichester UK: Wiley-Blackwell, 2009), especially 1–54.

Other models have come forward in response to critiques of soteriological typology. Against a Christocentric view of world religions is *particularism*, which emphasizes distinctiveness and differences among world religions. Particularism, founded on a cultural-linguistic outlook, argues that 'religions are thought of primarily as different idioms for construing reality, expressing experience and ordering life', writes a leading advocate of particularism, George Lindbeck (b. 1923–2018), an American Lutheran theologian.[116] This approach proposes no common framework for comparing religions, but rather irreducible differences 'that cannot be traced back to a common ground or universal structure'[117]; and that different religions 'may have incommensurable notions of truth, of experience and of categorical adequacy, and therefore also of what it would mean for something to be most important (i.e., 'God')'.[118]

The *comparative theology* approach also seeks to understand religions in themselves, but goes beyond this to identify points of congruence and divergence among religions. Like particularism, comparative theology discards a priori interpretative schemes (such as Christian soteriology) and 'a global meta-perspective on religion', but instead 'sets out to understanding the meaning of the Christian tradition by exploring it in the light of the teachings of other religious traditions'.[119] Comparative theology allows religions to speak for themselves – there is considerable emphasis on the study of primary sacred texts – but at the same time considers them from a Christian standpoint, not as a neutral bystander. It aims at bringing views of different religious traditions 'into dialogue and even argument', writes the American Jesuit Francis Clooney (b. 1950), a leading advocate of comparative theology, 'and thus promote a new, more integral conversation wherein traditions can remain distinct although their theologies are no longer separable. A religion may be unique, but its theology is not'.[120]

In comparison with the diversity and maturity of Orthodox thinking on the church, and indeed on ecumenical theology, modern Orthodox theological reflection on religious diversity is still in its formative stages. Metropolitan Georges Khodr and Archbishop Anastasios Yannoulatos are pioneers in the field, despite the small number of their writings devoted to the subject. In the soteriological model, Khodr and Yannoulatos represent *inclusivist* theological positions concerning non-Christian religions, with a cautiously positive outlook on religious diversity while upholding the universality of Orthodoxy's claims. Nicholas Arseniev also represents an inclusivist approach, with perhaps some elements of comparative theology, but without hesitating to critique cruder aspects of non-Christian religious practices, which he assimilates to lower religious manifestations.[121]

[116]George Lindbeck, *The Nature of Doctrine: Religion and Theology in a Postliberal Age* (London: SPCK, 1984), 47.
[117]Moyaert, 'Recent Developments in the Theology of Interreligious Dialogue', 35.
[118]Lindbeck, *The Nature of Doctrine*, 49.
[119]Moyaert, 'Recent Developments in the Theology of Interreligious Dialogue', 39.
[120]Francis Clooney, *Hindu God, Christian God: How Reason Helps Break Down the Boundaries between Religions* (New York: Oxford University Press, 2001), 8.
[121]Other Orthodox who endorse an inclusivist approach include Ioannis Karmiris, 'The Universality of Salvation in Christ', *Praktiká tis Akadimías Athinón*, 55 (1981), 261–89; and in *Theologia*, 52 (1981); Demetrios J. Constantelos, 'The Attitude of Orthodox Christians Toward Non-Christians' (Brookline, MA: Holy Cross Orthodox Press, 1992); also in Leonard Swidler and Paul Mojzes, eds., *Attitudes* of *Religions* and *Ideologies Toward* the *Outsider* (Lewiston, NY: Edward Melon, 1990); and George Papademetriou, 'An Orthodox Christian View of Non-Christian Religions'. www.goarch.org/ourfaith/ourfaith8089 (28 October 2016).

Fr Seraphim Rose, highly critical of both Orthodox involvement in ecumenism and interreligious dialogue, represents an Orthodox *exclusivist* position, spilling into fundamentalism (but not to the point of advocating physical violence against non-conformists). Opponents of an inclusivist approach to religious pluralism typically make no attempt to reconcile an entirely negative view of other religions with divine goodness and providence, a theology of the universal import of Christ's salvific mission, nor the philosophical problem of reconciling divine goodness with the creation of a large portion of humanity with no opportunity to accede to Christianity and hence, according to exclusivist theology, beyond salvation. The question of religious diversity has not featured on the agenda of Orthodox neo-traditionalists, other than Seraphim Rose. They have largely focused their energies on attacking ecumenism and Orthodox engaged in ecumenical endeavours. Nonetheless the logic of the neo-traditionalist approach to non-Orthodox Christians suggests that the neo-traditionalists would rally to the exclusivist camp – if their theology excludes non-Orthodox Christians from salvation, to be consistent they would also exclude all non-Christians as well.

Philip Sherrard could perhaps be identified with *religious pluralism* as defined above. Although Sherrard vacillates between inclusivism and religious pluralism, many statements in his book *Christianity: Lineaments of Sacred Tradition* point in the latter direction. Religious pluralism in the strict sense is unlikely to appeal to many Orthodox theologians since it appears to entail a surrender of the universal claims of Christian revelation and the missions of Christ and the Holy Spirit, in favour of a relativistic approach to religious diversity. The main line of Orthodox thought would emphasize that Christ himself is the perennial philosophy who shines forth, however obscurely at times, in non-Christian religions: 'I am the Way and the Truth and the Life' (Jn 14.6).

Fr Lev Gillet's approach to Judaism in his book *Communion in the Messiah* and, as far as we are aware, in his work for the Union for the Study of Great Religions and the World Congress of Faiths, makes him an Orthodox pioneer in *comparative theology*. Parallel with his commitment to building bridges between Orthodox and other Christians, Gillet sought to highlight what religious traditions share in common, rather than focus on fundamental differences. Yet he certainly never lost or diluted his commitment to Orthodoxy. Unfortunately, he never wrote a reflective piece on his approach to religious diversity, and even Elisabeth Behr-Sigel says little about this aspect of his life in her biography of Fr Lev. Many decades after Fr Lev's groundbreaking study of Jewish and Christian theology, several other Orthodox authors entered the field of comparative theology. The works of Hieromonk Damascene, Ernest Valea and Christine Mangala Frost represent very different approaches to the delicate task of understanding the theological significance of other religions traditions in terms of Orthodoxy.

The Holy and Great Council of the Orthodox Church held in Crete in June 2016 did not pronounce itself on religious diversity as such, but several Council documents contain positive statements on religious diversity. The document 'The Mission of the Orthodox Church in Today's World' endorses Orthodox involvement in promoting interreligious harmony: 'The various local Orthodox Churches can contribute to interreligious understanding and co-operation for the peaceful co-existence and harmonious living together in society, without this involving any religious syncretism.'[122] The Council's Encyclical and the Message state that 'Honest interfaith dialogue contributes to the development of mutual trust and to the promotion of peace and reconciliation.' The only other reference in the Council's decisions to non-Christians is a restatement of the long-standing Orthodox practice of refusing marriages between Orthodox and non-Christians: 'Marriage between Orthodox and non-Christians is categorically forbidden in accordance with canonical *akribeia*.'[123]

Ecumenical Patriarchs Athenagoras I (Kokkinakis) (1886–1972; patriarch 1948–72) and Bartholomew I (Archontonis) (b. 1940) (patriarch since 1991) manifest an open yet discerning attitude towards non-Christian religions. In conversations with the French theologian Olivier Clément, Athenagoras I refers to similarities between Orthodox and Islamic practices of the invocation of the Name of God and the practice of 'fools for God', to the important place that Jesus occupies in Islam. He is confident that 'the old suspicions [between Muslims and Christians] are subsiding and will continue to subside'[124] – this was in 1968, before the rise of Islamic radicalism. In a similar vein, Bartholomew I makes positive remarks about Judaism, Islam, Hinduism and Buddhism – and even the New Age Movement – as partial reflections, even if distorted, of the Logos of God.[125] Bartholomew sees points of convergence between Orthodox and Jewish theology in such as primacy of the person divine energies and divine presence in creation, wisdom, divine kenosis and aspects of spirituality. At the same time he is realistic in recognizing that there are also fundamental divergences and even contradictions on essential questions among major religions, as in his critique of the absence of a notion of a subsisting human person in Hinduism and Buddhism,[126] and in his address to the Conference on Interreligious Dialogue held in Istanbul in March 1998.[127]

Conclusion

There are three principal Orthodox approaches to the modern ecumenical movement. The first can be characterized as the *mystical-charismatic* approach. This focuses on points of communality among the Christian confessions, inspired by the notion that 'Church is One', despite evident institutional divisions among Christians. If the Church is indeed One in Christ, how then is this unity reflected in the face of Christian divisions? Dogmatic differences within Christianity are not ignored or glossed over, but the unity of the church subsists despite these differences; what unites

[122]Holy and Great Council of the Orthodox Church, 'The Mission of the Orthodox Church in Today's World' (Crete, June 2016), § A.3. www.holycouncil.org (7 May 2017).

[123]Holy and Great Council of the Orthodox Church, 'The Sacrament of Marriage and its Impediments' (Crete, June 2016), § II, 5, iii. www.holycouncil.org (23 December 2016).

[124]Olivier Clément, *Dialogues avec le patriarche Athénagoras* (Dialogues with Patriarch Athenagoras) (Paris: Fayard, 1969), 176.

[125]See Olivier Clément, *Conversations with Ecumenical Patriarch Bartholomew I* (St Vladimir's Seminary Press, 1997), 197–226.

[126]Clément, *Conversations with Ecumenical Patriarch Bartholomew I*, 222–4.

[127]Bartholomew I, 'Greeting' (Conference on Interreligious Dialogue), *Orthodoxia*, Second Period, 5. I (January–March 1998), 103–7 (in Greek). See also Metropolitan Emmanuel of France, 'Keynote Address' (International Council of Christians and Jews) (Istanbul, June 2010). www.ccjr.us/dialogika-resources/documents-and-statements/e-orthodox/1013-emmanuel2010june22 (28 December 2016).

Christians is more significant that what separates them. Many of the early Orthodox proponents of this approach sincerely believed that Christian unity, understood as the re-establishment of communion among Christian confessions (but not institutional reunification), was possible between the Orthodox Church and at least some Christian denominations, such as the Anglican Church, the Oriental Orthodox churches, the Old Catholic Church and possibly even the Roman Catholic Church.

This approach to ecumenism is mystical, because the ecclesiological point of departure is the church as the Body of Christ to which all those who profess Christ belong in some fashion; and it is charismatic, because it discerns the Holy Spirit revealing Christ outside the canonical limits of the Orthodox Church. Sergius Bulgakov, together with many of his entourage in interwar Paris, is the most eminent representative of this ecumenical theology, and later Orthodox theologians, such as Boris Bobrinskoy, are also favourably inclined to this approach.[128] This ecumenical vision was evident in Bulgakov's ill-fated proposal for limited intercommunion in the context of the Fellowship of St Alban and St Sergius and in writings such as his essay 'By Jacob's Well'.

The *dogmatic-canonical* approach stresses differences in faith which separate Christian churches and communities. The approach is dogmatic because doctrinal differences are considered to be unavoidable obstacles to visible union, and must be resolved before the re-establishment of communion, which would be the outcome of the resolution of dogmatic issues, not a step towards achieving unity. It is canonical because the canonical boundary between Orthodox and other Christian confessions is seen as sharp and determinative, even if there is acceptance of some underlying unity among Christians. Since dogmatic unity is difficult if not impossible, the main objective of Orthodox participation in the ecumenical movement is not so much to restore Christian unity as to witness to the fullness of Christian truth that is present only in the Orthodox Church. Georges Florovsky is the most eminent representative of the dogmatic approach, as can be seen in his opposition to Bulgakov's limited intercommunion proposal and his article 'Confessional Loyalty in the Ecumenical Movement'.

These two theologies of ecumenism are not entirely mutually exclusive and in fact there is overlap between them. Representatives of both tendencies agree on certain fundamental matters, for example, that the Orthodox Church alone, despite its weaknesses and failings, has preserved the fullness of the Christian faith, as taught by Jesus and transmitted by the apostles and their successors, and all other Christian denominations are deficient to a greater or lesser degree with respect to the fullness of the Christian faith.[129] Despite their differences, both Bulgakov and Florovsky believed that Christian unity was possible only by a return of all Christians to Orthodoxy. Bulgakov nonetheless considered that the restoration of a form of visible Christian unity, signified by intercommunion, was possible without full dogmatic agreement and institutional integration. But for Florovsky, 'partial intercommunion', in the absence of full

[128]See Bobrinskoy, *The Mystery of the Church*, and our review essay 'Three Contemporary Orthodox Visions of the Church'.

[129]The Roman Catholic Church has basically the same ecumenical theology – except that the fullness of truth lies only in the Catholic Church and all other churches are deficient to varying degrees with respect to this fullness of the truth present in the Catholic Church.

doctrinal agreement, was impossible, and the absence of intercommunion is then a painful reminder of Christian division.

Florovsky's vision of Orthodox involvement in the ecumenical movement primarily as witness to the truth of Orthodoxy has largely dominated the participation of Orthodox churches in ecumenical endeavours, especially in national and regional councils of churches and the World Council of Churches. This is perhaps less the case in bilateral ecumenical dialogues, especially the Orthodox-Oriental Orthodox dialogue, the Orthodox-Anglican dialogue or even the Orthodox-Roman Catholic dialogue, where there is some real, if distant, hope of re-establishing communion. The achievement of agreed statements on major theological issues in these three bilateral dialogues is sign that progress in mutual understanding is possible, even though the re-establishment of communion remains an elusive goal.[130]

There is also some erosion of canonical separation between the Orthodox Church and other Christian churches at the margins, in the form of local agreements, typically arising from pastoral needs, which transcend strict canonical boundaries, even in the absence of overall dogmatic agreement. Examples include pastoral agreements between the Orthodox patriarchates of Antioch and Alexandria and the Syriac and Coptic churches respectively, and mutual recognition of baptism among Christian denominations, such as in Australia, Germany, Switzerland and elsewhere.[131]

The third Orthodox approach to ecumenism, which may be termed 'exclusivist', consists in a radical rejection of ecumenism and all forms of Orthodox participation in ecumenical undertakings.[132] This approach considers non-Orthodox as heretics who certainly deserve prayers for their repentance and conversion to Orthodoxy and condemnation of their deviant beliefs. Ecumenism is labelled a 'heresy' or even the 'pan-heresy'. This exclusivism is an extreme form of the dogmatic approach: Since all non-Orthodox Christian communities are deficient with respect to the fullness of the faith, they are in effect heretics and there is no room for compromise with heresy. In this perspective, there is no point discussing with other Christians about theological and other matters; they have only to become Orthodox themselves. Ecumenical endeavours are

[130]The major statements and other documents, as well as scholarly studies relating to the Orthodox-Oriental dialogue, are contained in Christine Chaillot, ed., *The Dialogue between the Eastern Orthodox and the Oriental Orthodox Churches* (Volos, GR: Volos Academy Publications, 2016). See also Paul Ladouceur, 'Orthodox Critiques of the Agreed Statements between the Orthodox and the Oriental Orthodox Churches', *St Vladimir's Theological Quarterly*, 60, 3 (2016). For the statements arising from the Orthodox-Anglican dialogue, see www.anglicancommunion.org/relationships/ecumenical-dialogues/orthodox.aspx (6 May 2017). For the Orthodox-Catholic statements see www.vatican.va/roman_curia/pontifical_councils/chrstuni/sub-index/index_orthodox-ch.htm (6 May 2017). Also the Agreed Statement of the North American Orthodox-Catholic Consultation 'The Filioque: A Church Dividing Issue?' (October 2003). www.usccb.org/beliefs-and-teachings/ecumenical-and-interreligious/ecumenical/orthodox/filioque-church-dividing-issue-english.cfm (6 May 2017).

[131]See the joint declaration of the patriarchs of the Orthodox Church of Antioch and those of the Syrian Orthodox Church of Antioch signed in November 1991, and the 'Pastoral Agreement between the Coptic Orthodox and Greek Orthodox Patriarchates of Alexandria' signed in April 2001, in Chaillot, *The Dialogue between the Eastern Orthodox and the Oriental Orthodox Churches*. On mutual recognition of baptism, see 'Australian Churches Covenanting Together'. https://ecumenism.net/archive/docu/2010_australian_covenant.pdf (6 May 2017); in Germany: www.oekumene-ack.de/fileadmin/user_upload/Themen/Taufanerkennung2007.pdf (2 April 2015); in Switzerland: www.kirchenbund.ch/sites/default/files/08_agck_taufanerkennung.pdf (2 April 2015).

[132]We have also termed this approach to ecumenism 'ecumenoclasm'. See Ladouceur, 'On Ecumenoclasm: Anti-Ecumenism in Orthodox Theology'.

therefore useless and even harmful, since they could lead to a weakening of faith in the truth of Orthodoxy.

There is considerable antipathy towards ecumenism in some countries of Orthodox tradition, and even among Orthodox in the West, including converts. Anti-ecumenism is usually associated with a neo-traditionalist or fundamentalist approach to Orthodoxy, in the context of generalized anti-Westernism and anti-modernism. Orthodox anti-ecumenism has some impact, most notably in Bulgaria and Georgia, signified by the withdrawal of the respective Orthodox churches from the WCC in 1997 and 1998 respectively, in the failure of most local Orthodox churches to ratify the agreed statements arising from the Orthodox-Oriental Orthodox dialogue, and in the conflict over ecumenism surrounding the Holy and Great Council of the Orthodox Church of June 2016. Yet despite anti-ecumenical sentiments in certain Orthodox quarters, especially in Greece, Russia and Serbia, in addition to Bulgaria and Georgia, the Ecumenical Patriarchate and most other canonical Orthodox churches remain firmly committed to ecumenism.

In our survey of modern Orthodox thinking on religious diversity, religious inclusivism, in the sense that non-Christians are mysteriously included in Christ's salvific mission, emerges as the preferred Orthodox theology of religious diversity, with Georges Khodr and Anastasios Yannoulatos as the leading representatives, together with Ecumenical Patriarchs Athenagoras I and Bartholomew I. In authors such as Nicholas Arseniev and Lev Gillet, upholding the universal claims of Christianity opens to a comparative theological approach to world religions. This places Orthodox inclusivists in a comparable attitude towards non-Christian religions and philosophies as Justin Martyr, Clément and other early Fathers of the Church who looked favourably on elements of Christian truth found in non-Christian philosophies and religious beliefs. Seraphim Rose appears to inherit the exclusivist theology of Tertullian, while Philip Sherrard seems to advocate religious pluralism based on perennialist philosophy. There are no representatives of the particularist approach in our survey – in fact, only a few Orthodox are academic scholars of non-Christian religions, with Georges Khodr (Islam) and Lev Gillet (Judaism) as leading pioneers. With his book *Communion in the Messiah* (1942), Gillet can be considered a pioneer of comparative theology. Comparative theology lends itself to interreligious contact and dialogue, in which were engaged both Khodr and Gillet. Later Orthodox scholars, such as Hieromonk Damascene, Ernest Valea and Christina Mangala Frost, follow in Gillet's footsteps with their studies comparing Orthodox theology and practice with Taoism, Buddhism and Hinduism respectively.

Despite an Orthodox preference for inclusivist and comparative theology approaches to non-Christian religions, there are still major unresolved questions. These include the extent of Christ's salvific mission, divine inspiration in other religious traditions and their sacred writings, non-Christian religions as paths to God and salvation, the relationship of Christ and the Holy Spirit in world religions and the status of non-Christians with respect to the church. The arrival of large numbers of non-Christian migrants and refugees from the Middle East, Africa and Asia to Western Europe and North America and, to a much more limited extent, in countries of Orthodox tradition, should stimulate greater attention to the development of a robust Orthodox theology of religious diversity.

13

The Christification of Life

Chapter Outline

The churching of life and the Christification of life

The Russian term *tserkovnost'* (also *otserkovlenie*) can be rendered as 'churching' or 'churchification', a spirit of thinking, being and acting in the church.[1] For Russian ecclesiastical leaders of the nineteenth century, this implied docile obedience or submission of the faithful to the church, but for the principal personalities of the Slavophile movement and the Russian religious renaissance, such a narrow interpretation was antinomic with Christian liberty. Rather, they saw *tserkovnost'* as a consciousness of being a member of the church, of the 'union of all' in the church (from the Divine Liturgy), the Christian transformation of the life of the believer, as well the partaking of the means of achieving union with God. In this sense, both the Slavophile notion of *sobornost'* and Alexander Bukharev's programme of engagement with contemporary society, allowing the light of Christ to shine in the world, can be seen as manifestations of the idea of *tserkovnost'*. As the basic thrust of Bukharev's mission, *tserkovnost'* involves the bringing of all aspects of life into the church as the Body of Christ, the sanctification of the totality of human existence, under the sign of the freedom of the children of God, who consciously choose to follow Christ.

[1]See the discussion about *tserkovnost'* in Vera Shevzov, 'Letting the People into Church: Reflections on Orthodoxy and Community in Late Imperial Russia', in Valerie Kivelson and Robert Greene, eds, *Orthodox Russia: Belief and Practice Under the Tsars* (University Park, PE: Pennsylvania State University Press, 2003), 66–70.

Alexis Kniazeff (1913–91), rector and long-time professor of Old Testament and canon law at the St Sergius Orthodox Theological Institute in Paris, offers this definition of *tserkovnost'*:

> The Russian word that we are attempting to render by 'churchification' or 'churching' designates initiatives in a nominally Christian society intended to make life conform as closely as possible to the canonical and spiritual norms advocated by the church, or, expressed otherwise and definitively, to the teaching of Jesus Christ. These initiatives are directed towards both personal life and also liturgical life, and even to all activities in the cultural, social and political spheres.[2]

Mother Maria Skobtsov (St Maria of Paris) (1891–1944) prefers the expression *Khristovlenie*, the 'Christification' of life.[3] For her, the Christification of life is the true evangelical life, flowing from Paul's words, 'It is no longer I who live, but Christ who lives in me' (Gal. 2.20), and love is the measure of Christification, love of God inseparable from love of neighbour, the 'two commandments, which contain within themselves the totality of Christ's "Good News"'.[4] The 'churching of life' does not mean attending all church services or hanging an icon on every wall, but rather 'the sense of the whole world as one church, adorned with icons that should be venerated, that should be honoured and loved, because these icons are true images of God that have the holiness of the Living God upon them'.[5] The icons in question here are, of course, other human beings.

Tserkovnost' emerged as an important concept among Russian exiles in Western Europe in the early 1920s and became a rallying point of two major exile religious organizations, the Russian Student Christian Movement (better known from its French acronym, ACER, *Action chrétienne des étudiants russes*) and the St Sergius Institute (*Institut de théologie orthodoxe Saint-Serge*). The 'churching of life' was one of the main inspirations for the foundation of ACER in 1923 and is one of its two objectives, together with the preservation and promotion of Russian culture. If the St Sergius Institute became the principal focal point of the intellectual and academic life of the Russian Christian community in exile, ACER was its active arm, encouraging a personal commitment to Christ and the church, fostered by such means as publications, summer camps for children, retreats, seminars and annual meetings. Mother Maria Skobstov worked for about seven years as ACER 'travelling secretary' with the mission of reaching out to the isolated Russian communities scattered throughout France. Her mandate was both to bring the exiles into the orbit of the church and to foster Russian culture, but she quickly realized that concrete measures to alleviate poverty, alienation and despair of poor and uneducated exiles had to take priority over religious and cultural information and admonitions. This was the background of her decision to become a nun in 1932 and devote herself to social action among the poor.[6]

---

[2]Alexis Kniazeff, 'L'Ecclésialisation de la vie' (The Churching of life), *La Pensée orthodoxe*, Vol. 4 (Paris: L'Âge d'homme, 1987), 108.

[3]Mother Maria Skobtsova, 'Types of Religious Life', in *Mother Maria, Essential Writings* (Maryknoll, NY: Orbis Books, 2003), 174.

[4]Skobtsova, 'Types of Religious Life', 175.

[5]Mother Maria Skobtsova, 'The Mysticism of Human Communion', in *Mother Maria, Essential Writings*, 81.

[6]See Mother Maria's essays 'The Second Gospel Commandment', 'The Mysticism of Human Communion' and 'Towards a New Monasticism' in *Essential Writings*; and the essays on 'L'Évangile sociale' (The social Gospel) in Sainte Marie de Paris (Mère Marie

The twofold objectives of ACER, the promotion of religious life and of Russian culture, involved a certain tension which resulted in major conflicts both within the organization and in the wider exile community, between a universal, pan-Orthodox objective – the churching or Christification of life in the Orthodox tradition – and a particular national objective – the promotion of Russian culture. With the passage of time and the maturation of second- and third-generation children of exiles, the universal aspect of *tserkovnost'* became more prominent. A symbol of the acculturation of the Russian exile community was the change in the language of instruction from Russian to French after the Second World War at the St Sergius Institute. This opened the door to non-Russian instructors (such as Olivier Clément and Elisabeth Behr-Sigel) and students, and allowed the Institute to become a pan-Orthodox locus of theological education. In 1974 Orthodox from different ethnic backgrounds and ecclesial jurisdictions established the *Fraternité orthodoxe en Europe occidentale*, with the objective of inculcating an Orthodox culture among its members in an explicitly pan-Orthodox and ecumenical content. The *Fraternité orthodoxe* became a pan-Orthodox version of ACER, without the burden of a residual commitment to Russian culture.

ACER, the *Fraternité orthodoxe* and similar organizations in other countries, such as Zoe and other religious movements in Greece, and the *Mouvement de jeunesse orthodoxe* (MJO, Orthodox Youth Movement) in Lebanon and Syria are all manifestations of a desire to employ innovative organizational structures and activities to foster Christian piety and action among the Orthodox faithful. Their explicit theological, spiritual and ecclesial orientations vary considerably, as indeed their relative success and survival, but all can be seen under the broad umbrella of *tserkovnost'*.[7] The idea of the 'churching of life' constitutes a framework for Christian life in the modern world. In addition to the creation of a number of Orthodox institutions since the early twentieth century, modern Orthodox thinking has focused on four major areas as appropriate loci for the realization of *tserkovnost'*: liturgical theology, the theology of the laity, social theology and political theology (these latter will be considered in Chapter 14).

The Greek theologian Panayiotis Nellas (1936–86) also uses the expression Christification, in his book *Deification in Christ* (1979).[8] Nellas presents the spiritual life in the light of Nicholas Cabasilas's classic fourteenth-century work *The Life in Christ*[9] as a process of Christification through the progressive realization of the full implications and benefits of the three principal sacraments (baptism, chrismation and the Eucharist). He refers to the Christification of 'man's being' through baptism, of 'movement' through chrismation and of 'life' through the Eucharist, completed by the Christification of the mind and the will. Nellas concludes:

> Communion with Christ renews man. His new being, his new activity, life, knowledge and will, the whole transformed Christlike organism with the spiritual senses and graces of the Spirit which constitute his new mode of functioning, make up the new man in Christ.[10]

Skobtsov, 1891–1945), *Le Jour du Saint-Esprit*, Paul Ladouceur, ed. (Paris: Le Cerf, 2011), 327–94.

[7]For a comparative study of several such movements and institutions, see Paul Ladouceur, 'In My Father's House There Are Many Mansions (Jn 14:2): New Institutions in Modern Orthodox Spirituality', *St Vladimir's Theological Quarterly*, 55, 4 (2011).

[8]Panayiotis Nellas, *Deification in Christ: Orthodox Perspectives on the Nature of the Human Person* (1979) (Crestwood, NY: St Vladimir's Seminary Press, 1987).

[9]Nicholas Cabasilas, *The Life in Christ* (Crestwood, NY: St Vladimir's Seminary Press, 1974).

[10]Nellas, *Deification in Christ*, 139.

Liturgical theology and liturgical piety

Modern Orthodox liturgical theology is especially associated with Fr Alexander Schmemann (1921–83), who is credited with promoting liturgical theology both as an academic discipline and as a major if not pre-eminent focus of community and personal spiritual life. Liturgical theology is thus the study of the theological basis of the Orthodox liturgy, and of the Orthodox liturgy as a source of theology – and as a source and fulfilment of Orthodox piety and spirituality. But Schmemann is not the only Orthodox theologian who studied Orthodox liturgy methodically in the twentieth century and indeed Schmemann had predecessors among earlier generations of Russian theologians. These include Vladimir Ilyin (1891–1974), who wrote several works on the liturgical cycle and who taught at the St Sergius Institute from 1925 to 1940, and Schmemann's own professor of liturgical theology at the St Sergius Institute, Fr Cyprian Kern (1899-1960). Schmemann also benefited from a wide movement of liturgical renewal in other Christian churches, especially in the Catholic Church, leading up to the reforms of the Vatican II Council.[11] Other important modern Orthodox authors who have written on the liturgy are Fr Lev Gillet (1893–1980), who published works on the divine liturgy and the liturgical year; Constantine Andronikof (1916–97), one of Bulgakov's successors and his translator into French, who wrote on the divine liturgy and on the principal feasts of the liturgical calendar and Fr Thomas Hopko (1939–2015), who authored works on Great Lent and the Nativity.[12]

Modern Orthodox liturgical theology can be seen in the line of a long tradition in the church, extending back to the first centuries, when catechumens received instruction on Christian rituals, especially baptism, chrismation and the Eucharist. In a similar vein, Lev Gillet emphasizes the liturgical foundations of the Christian spiritual life:

> There exists, within the Orthodox tradition, a properly 'liturgical' line of thought and piety. A whole school of saints and doctors have conceived the entire Christian life according to a liturgical type and rhythm; it is in the church ritual that they seek and find the successive stages of the normal development of the Christian soul.[13]

The most well-known mystagogical teachings of the fourth century that have come down to us are those of St Cyril of Jerusalem, St John Chrysostom and Theodore of Mopsuestia; later writings, more speculative and symbolic, include *The Celestial Hierarchy* of the Pseudo-Dionysius and the

---

[11]For an overview of the pan-Christian movement of liturgical reform, see Andrew Louth, *Modern Orthodox Thinkers: From the Philokalia to the Present* (London: SPCK, 2015), 195–7.

[12]A Monk of the Eastern Church [Lev Gillet]: *The Year of Grace of the Lord: A Scriptural and Liturgical Commentary on the Calendar of the Orthodox Church* (Crestwood, NY: St Vladimir's Seminary Press, 1989); 'Our Life in the Liturgy' and 'Be My Priest', in *Serve the Lord With Gladness* (Crestwood, NY: St Vladimir's Seminary Press, 1990); Constantine Andronikof: *Le Sens des fêtes: t. 1. Le cycle fixe* (The Meaning of the Feasts. vol. 1: The Fixed Feasts) (Paris: Cerf, 1970); *Le Sens des fêtes: t. 2. Le Cycle pascal* (The Meaning of the Feasts. vol. 2: The Pascal Cyle) (Lausanne: L'Âge d'homme, 1985); *Le Sens de la Liturgie: La relation entre Dieu et l'homme* (The Meaning of the Liturgy: The Relationship between God and Man), (Paris: Cerf, 1988). Thomas Hopko: *The Lenten Spring* (Crestwood, NY: St Vladimir's Seminary Press, 1983); *The Winter Pascha* (Crestwood, NY: St Vladimir's Seminary Press, 1984).

[13]A Monk of the Eastern Church [Lev Gillet], *Orthodox Spirituality: An Outline of the Orthodox Ascetical and Mystical Tradition* (Crestwood, NY: St Vladimir's Seminary Press, 1987), 16.

Mystagogy of St Maximus the Confessor. The greatest of the Byzantine liturgical theologians was St Nicholas Cabasilas (fourteenth century), whose two major writings, *The Interpretation of the Divine Liturgy* and *The Life in Christ*, continue to be significant works of Orthodox liturgical spirituality.[14] Like Cabasilas, Lev Gillet structures the main portion of his masterly summary of Orthodox spirituality around the sacraments of baptism, chrismation and Eucharist: 'The Baptising Christ' (Chapter III); 'Christ the Sender of the Spirit' (Chapter IV) and 'Christ our Passover' (Chapter V).

Contemporary liturgical theology can thus be seen as a modern development of the more explicitly catechetic tradition of the early church, especially its mystagogical expression, centred on the major sacraments. The basic intent of both is similar: to make the rich liturgical tradition of Orthodoxy meaningful for the faithful as a fundamental pillar of the spiritual life. This is perhaps all the more essential in the light of modern hyper-rationality, which often makes it difficult to seize the symbolic sense of liturgical ritual and language. It is in this context that modern Orthodox liturgical theology is associated with a sacramental understanding of creation – 'the world as sacrament', an expression associated with one of Schmemann's popular books[15] (see Chapter 9). Three of Alexander Schmemann's books focus on the sacraments: *For the Life of the World: Sacraments and Orthodoxy* (first edition, 1963); *Of Water and the Spirit* (1974) and *The Eucharist* (1988). Schmemann's book *Great Lent: Journey to Pascha* (1969) has become a standard exploration of the liturgical and spiritual signification of Great Lent, a work partly completed by a much shorter piece on Holy Week.[16]

Alexander Schmemann's liturgical theology seeks to revitalize the Byzantine rite, not by a reform of the liturgy or sacramental rituals as such, but rather by a clearer understanding of the theological and spiritual foundations of the liturgy and the restoration of the sense of the Christian community in worship through the liturgy. For Schmemann, this includes greater participation of the laity in the celebration of the liturgy, especially the Eucharist, with the priest doing his part – for example, by the audible recitation of prayers often said silently by the clergy, including the epiclesis – , by more frequent communion, by a greater understanding of liturgical texts and in general by the promotion of liturgical piety, grounded in the Christian community, as an essential if not primordial component of the Christian spiritual life.

---

[14]Nicholas Cabasilas, *The Interpretation of the Divine Liturgy* (Crestwood, NY: St Vladimir's Seminary Press, 1997); and *The Life in Christ* (Crestwood, NY: St Vladimir's Seminary Press, 1997).

[15]Alexander Schmemann, *The World as Sacrament* (London: Darton, Longman & Todd, 1966). Revised edition published as *For the Life of the World: Sacraments and Orthodoxy* (Crestwood, NY: St Vladimir's Seminary Press, 1973). The expression 'the world as sacrament' does not actually occur in the book.

[16]Schmemann's major works on liturgical theology are *Holy Week: A Liturgical Explanation for the Days of Holy Week* (1961); *Sacraments and Orthodoxy* (1965) (subsequently *For the Life of the World: Sacraments and Orthodoxy*); *Great Lent: Journey to Pascha* (1969); *Introduction to Liturgical Theology*, (1966); *Of Water and the Spirit: A Liturgical Study of Baptism* (1974); *The Eucharist: Sacrament of the Kingdom* (1988) and essays in *Liturgy and Tradition: Theological Reflections of Alexander Schmemann*, (1997). All were published or re-issued by St Vladimir's Seminary Press, where Schmemann served as dean from 1962 to 1983. His short essay 'A Liturgical Explanation of Holy Week' is available as a monograph: (www.stnicholasdc.org/files/Holy%20Week/A-Liturgical-Explanation-of-Holy-Week.pdf) (20 November 2017). The French version is combined with an essay by Olivier Clément on Pascha: Alexandre Schmemann and Olivier Clément, *Le Mystère pascal: Commentaires liturgiques* (The Pascal Mystery: Liturgical Commentaries) (Bégrolles en Mauges, FR: Abbaye de Bellefontaine, 1975).

At the same time, Schmemann was sceptical and even overtly critical of personal forms of piety or, even worse, 'spirituality', outside the context of the Orthodox liturgy, especially the Eucharist. Schmemann's distaste for personal piety extends to individualistic approaches to liturgical worship, a critique akin to Orthodox criticism of pietism as manifested notably in the Greek religious fraternities, especially Zoe (see Chapter 6)[17]. Schmemann's well-known distaste for monasticism is another manifestation of this sentiment, but has other complex historical roots in the Russian émigré community in Western Europe.[18] In broad terms, Schmemann's negative attitude to personal as distinct from communal participation in the church arise from his interpretation of these as withdrawal not only from 'the world', the common human experience, but even from the church, into a cosy individualistic nook, as in this entry for his *Journals*:

> The monastic trend of the church is that the parish, community, etc., give this world only an opposition, while departure from this world is shown as the Orthodox answer and the true Orthodox way. The monastic trend, as strange as it may seem, considers the church as part of the world, so that one must leave not only the world but the church.[19]

Andrew Louth characterizes Schmemann's disdain for 'mysteriological piety' as 'almost a kind of blind spot, which shuts him off from a whole dimension of the Byzantine liturgical tradition'.[20] For Louth, this means that Schmemann dismisses the value of ancient writings on the liturgy by Pseudo-Dionysius, Maximus the Confessor, Nicholas Cabasilas and others, not to mention the writings of monastic non-monastic spiritual elders.[21] The alternative view, as we suggested, is to consider Schmemann's approach to liturgical theology as a modern expression of the church's long catechetical and liturgical tradition, despite his dislike of individual forms of piety, to which he assimilates, rather ineptly, monasticism.

Ioannis Foundalis (1927–2007) is a theologian well known in Greece for his writings on liturgical theology, especially the five-volume collection *Answers to Liturgical Problems* published between 1967 and 2003.[22] Foundalis deals with a wide range of issues concerning the liturgy, emphasizing, like Nicholas Cabasilas in his *Interpretation of the Divine Liturgy* long before him, the symbolic and theological import of liturgical gestures and language.[23]

Archimandrite Vasileios (Gondidakis) (b. 1936) is one of the leaders of the renaissance of Athonite monasticism in the second half of the twentieth century. He was igumen of Stavronikita Monastery, then of Iviron Monastery. His book *Hymn of Entry* (1974) owes its origin as an explanation for Athonite opposition to ecumenism (see Chapter 12), but it is more an extended meditation on the unity of the Orthodox tradition than an anti-ecumenical tract. For Fr Vasileios,

---

[17]See the discussion of this theme in Louth, *Modern Orthodox Thinkers*, 207–8.

[18]See Vassa Larin, 'Fr Alexander Schmemann and Monasticism', *St Vladimir's Theological Quarterly*, 53, (2009).

[19]Alexander Schmemann, *The Journals of Father Alexander Schmemann, 1973-1983* (Crestwood, NY: St Vladimir's Seminary Press, 2000), 269 (entry for Thursday, 2 October 1980).

[20]Louth, *Modern Orthodox Thinkers*, 208.

[21]See Louth, *Modern Orthodox Thinkers*, 207–8.

[22]Ioannis Foundoulis, *Apantíseis eis Leitourgikás Aporías* (Answers to Liturgical Problems), 5 vols. (Athens: Apostoliki Diakonia, 1967–2003).

[23]See Louth, *Modern Orthodox Thinkers*, 209–11.

the divine liturgy is the most profound expression of this unity, which brings together scripture, theology, personal and ecclesial prayer, spirituality, asceticism and icons into a harmonious image of the Holy Trinity. Liturgical theology is thus a vision of the entire Orthodox tradition in the light of the Transfiguration: 'Outside the framework of the divine liturgy, where God manifests his glory by the offering and self-emptying of his Son, and the faithful confess the Trinitarian truth by their love for one another, it is impossible to understand Orthodox faith and theology.'[24] Since Orthodoxy manifests an organic unity, celebrated above in the divine liturgy, it is clear that 'in the Orthodox faith there is no room for one jot of anything alien, belonging to a different understanding or of a different quality.'[25] It is in this context that Archimandrite Vasileios explicitly criticizes the prospects of dialogue or even the re-establishment of communion with the Catholic Church. The papacy and infallibility mark 'the acme of human self-assurance and alienation from the mystery of the church of the Incarnate Word', and intercommunion 'without unity of faith and the communion of the Holy Spirit, is merely a mechanical action, an act of magic'.[26] At the same time, Vasileios refers to Roman Catholics as 'brethren who are in need', 'deserving of our sympathy today because they are suffering and struggling'.[27]

Theology of the laity

Orthodox spirituality was initially developed primarily in a monastic context and indeed most early spiritual writings were written by monks and were intended primarily for monastics. Yet as St John Chrysostom reminded his flock as early as the fourth century:

> You certainly deceive yourself and are greatly mistaken if you think that there is one set of requirements for the person in the world and another for the monk. The difference between them is that one is married and the other is not. In all other respects they will have to render the same account.[28]

One of the major challenges to Orthodoxy in the modern era is to transmit the ancient treasure of Orthodox spirituality such that it is meaningful and accessible to those living 'in the world', in complex and increasingly secularized and de-Christianized societies. Early efforts in this direction in modern times were the publications of St Nicodemus the Athonite (1748–1809), not only the collection of ascetic writings gathered in *Philokalia* (1782), but also several other writings, including his book on frequent communion and an adaptation of *The Spiritual Combat and Path to Paradise* of Lorenzo Scupoli (1530–1610), under the title *Unseen Warfare*.[29] The vast movement of spiritual

---

[24]Vasileios Gondidakis, *Hymn of Entry: Liturgy and Life in the Orthodox Church* (1974) (Crestwood, NY: St Vladimir's Seminary Press, 1984), 30.
[25]Gondidakis, *Hymn of Entry*, 30.
[26]Ibid., 99; 31.
[27]Ibid., 56.
[28]John Chrysostom, 'To the Christian Parent', *Against the Opponents of the Monastic Life*, III:14. *A Comparison Between a King and a Monk/Against the Opponents of the Monastic Life* (Lewiston, NY: Edwin Mellen Press, 1988), 156.
[29]G. E. H. Palmer, Philip Sherrard and Kallistos Ware, trans., *The Philokalia: The Complete Text*, Vols 1–4 (London: Faber and Faber, 1979–95) (fifth volume forthcoming); St Nicodemus the Hagiorite, *Concerning Frequent Communion of the Immaculate*

renewal sparked by the *Philokalia*, especially the publication of Slavonic and Russian versions in the nineteenth century, and more recently translations of the *Philokalia* in Western European languages, reached large sectors of the Orthodox population and even many non-Orthodox.

Among modern Orthodox theologians, Nicholas Afanasiev (1888–1977) and Paul Evdokimov (1900–70) devote considerable attention to the elaboration of a theology of the laity. Afanasiev develops the role of laity in the context of the royal priesthood, the ministry of the laity in the church.[30] He takes his cue from 1 Peter: 'Like living stones be yourselves built into a spiritual house, to be a royal priesthood, to offer spiritual sacrifices acceptable to God through Jesus Christ. ... You are a chosen race, a royal priesthood, a holy nation, God's own people' (1 Pet. 2.5; 9). Afanasiev's basic argument for the notion of the royal priesthood is that all Christians are *laos theou* – the people of God. All are 'lay' (from *laos*) and constitute the priesthood in the spiritual house and offer spiritual sacrifices; hence all are 'clerics'. All receive the gifts of the Holy Spirit, but there is a diversity of ministries (see 1 Cor. 12.4-11). For Afanasiev, the key point is that the diversity of ministries is functional, not ontological.[31] As we noted above in the discussion of Eucharistic ecclesiology, one such ministry is that of the presider of the Christian Assembly; there is a *liturgical distinction* between the presider and those who do not preside, but this does not create an *ontological distinction*.

Afanasiev's assertion of the functional nature of ordained ministry is not without its critics. John Zizioulas, for one, contests Afanasiev's view on the distinction between the functional and the ontological nature of ordination, arguing that ordination surpasses the functional-ontological dilemma and must be considered as 'relational (= a place *in* the community) and at the same time strictly *specific* and personal (no eucharistic community without this *particular* order and *no confusion of orders*)'.[32] Zizioulas writes:

> In the light of the *koinonia* of the Holy Spirit, ordination relates the ordained man so profoundly and so existentially to the community that in his new state after ordination, he cannot be any longer, as a minister, conceived in himself. In this state, existence is determined by *communion* which qualifies and defines both 'ontology' and 'function'. Thus it becomes impossible in this state to say that one simply 'functions' without implying that his being is deeply and decisively affected by what he does.[33]

In Afanasiev's analysis, the liturgical or functional distinction between the clerics and the people unfortunately came to be seen an ontological distinction, with consecration or ordination as the seal of the separation of the church into two groups. Thus the priesthood of all the faithful came to be considered, falsely, as somehow in opposition to ordained priesthood:

Mysteries of Christ (1777) (Thessalonica, GR: Uncut Mountain Press, 2006); *Unseen Warfare: The Spiritual Combat and Path to Paradise of Lorenzo Scupoli*, edited by Nicodemus of the Holy Mountain and revised by Theophan the Recluse (London: Faber & Faber, 1963; Crestwood, NY: St Vladimir's Seminary Press, 1997).

[30]The first part of Afanasiev's classic work, *The Church of the Holy Spirit* (1971) (Notre Dame, IN: Notre Dame University Press, 2007), is devoted to the priesthood or ministry of all Christians (Chapters 1–4), the other to the consecrated priesthood (Chapters 5–8). See also his article 'Ministry of the Laity', *The Ecumenical Review* 10, 3 (1958).

[31]Afanasiev, *The Church of the Holy Spirit*, 16; 84; 96.

[32]John Zizioulas, 'Ministry and Communion', in *Being as Communion* (Yonkers, NY: St Vladimir's Seminary Press, 1985), 231–2.

[33]Zizioulas, *Being as Communion*, 226.

> The priesthood of God's people does not exclude the priesthood of the church hierarchy. On the contrary, the priesthood of the church hierarchy … is derived from the royal priesthood. The one priesthood cannot contradict the other, if one does not understand priesthood solely in terms of consecration, as scholastic theology does.[34]

Paul Evdokimov argues much the same position concerning the universal priesthood of the laity in his work *The Ages of the Spiritual Life*.[35] Afanasiev and Evdokimov were colleagues at the St Sergius Institute and Evdokimov's brief prior treatment of this subject may have influenced Afanasiev.

The notion of the royal priesthood of all believers is one of the pillars on which Alexander Schmemann builds his liturgical theology. Schmemann and Afanasiev taught at the St Sergius Institute in the late 1940s, until Schmemann's departure for New York in 1951. Schmemann unites Afanasiev's approach to the royal priesthood with the broader idea of humans as priests of creation. In his foundational text *For the Life of the World: Sacraments and Orthodoxy* (1963), Schmemann writes:

> All rational, spiritual and other qualities of man distinguishing him from other creatures have their focus and ultimate fulfilment in this capacity to bless God, to know, so to speak, the meaning of the thirst and hunger that constitute his life. *Homo Sapiens, Homo Faber* … yes, but first of all, *Homo adorans*. The first, the basic definition of man is that he is the priest. He stands in the centre of the world and unifies it in his act of blessing God, of both receiving the world from God and offering it to God – and by filling the world with this Eucharist, he transforms his life, the one that he receives from the world, into life in God, into communion with him.[36]

The royal priesthood is then a vital characteristic of the church herself:

> If there are priests in the church, if there is a priestly vocation in it, it is precisely in order to reveal to each its vocation, its priestly essence, to make the whole life of men the liturgy of the kingdom, to reveal the church as the royal priesthood of the redeemed world. It is, in other terms, not a vocation 'apart', but the expression of love for man's vocation as son of God and for the world as the sacrament of the Kingdom.[37]

Even in this cosmic context, Schmemann links the priestly vocation of the church in relation to Christ's priesthood, expressed succinctly in his last writing *The Eucharist: Sacrament of the Kingdom*, where he writes that the church '*is herself priesthood, offering and sacrifice*'. Expanding on this idea, he writes:

> The 'royal' or 'universal' priesthood in the church does not consist in her being a society of priests – for there are both priests and 'laymen' in her – but in the fact that she as a whole, as the body of

[34]Afanasiev, *The Church of the Holy Spirit*, 20.
[35]See Paul Evdokimov, 'The Universal Priesthood of the Laity', in *The Ages of the Spiritual Life* (1964) (Crestwood, NY: St Vladimir's Seminary Press, 1998), 227–43.
[36]Alexander Schmemann, *For the Life of the World: Sacraments and Orthodoxy* (1963) (Crestwood, NY: St Vladimir's Seminary Press, 1973), 15.
[37]Schmemann, *For The Life Of The World*, 93.

> Christ, has a priestly ministry in relation to the world, she fulfils the priesthood and intercession of the Lord himself.[38]

Like Afanasiev, Schmemann also insists on the validity of the distinction between the royal priesthood and the ordained priesthood as ministry in the church:

> As to the early church, she firmly held and affirmed both the institutional priesthood *in* the church and the 'royal priesthood' *of* the church as the two essential and complementary dimensions of her very life: *essential* as stemming from her experience both of Christ and of his unique priesthood, *complementary* as revealing in their mutual correlation each other's place and significance in the life and work of the church.[39]

In his book *The Mystery of the Church* (2003), Boris Bobrinskoy (b. 1925), former professor of dogmatic theology and Dean of the St Sergius Institute, takes up much of the Afanasiev-Evdokimov-Schmemann approach to the role of the laity in the church and the royal priesthood.[40] But this is far from the case for other Orthodox theologians. Jean-Claude Larchet (b. 1949), a French Orthodox theologian, downplays the significance of the royal priesthood, especially with respect to the liturgy. He chastises Afanasiev, Evdokimov and Schmemann for going too far in promoting the royal priesthood, notably for seeing an association between the royal priesthood and the liturgical priesthood of the ordained clergy, and for 'confusing' the two priesthoods, even speaking of the clergy and laity as 'co-liturgists': 'Their error is, however, to place the "royal priesthood", attributed to the laity, in parallel with the "priesthood of orders" (or ministerial priesthood) applicable to the clergy, thereby placing the two types of priesthood on an equal footing.'[41] This critique is based on a misreading of the authors in question. Larchet attributes the royal priesthood to the laity (in the narrow sense of the non-ordained) and the ministerial priesthood to the ordained clergy, whereas the writers in question, and Bobrinskoy following them, are consistent in considering that all the faithful constitute a royal priesthood, of whom some are called to exercise a ministerial priesthood on behalf of the Christian community as a whole and not apart from it.

Critics of the royal priesthood typically consider that there is an ontological instead of only a functional difference between the two types of priesthood, while some simply ignore altogether the concept of the royal priesthood of all believers. Metropolitan Hilarion Alfeyev (b. 1966) almost forgets the laity in his presentation of the church, which is strongly focused on the clergy and hierarchy. Although he cites the passage from 1 Peter referring to 'a royal priesthood', he does not elaborate and quickly passes to other subjects.[42]

---

[38]Alexander Schmemann, *The Eucharist: Sacrament of the Kingdom* (Crestwood, NY: St Vladimir's Seminary Press, 1987), 92.

[39]Alexander Schmemann, *Of Water and Spirit: A Liturgical Study of Baptism* (Canage Yonhers to Crestwood, NY: St Vladimir's Seminary Press, 1974), 94–5.

[40]Boris Bobrinskoy, *The Mystery of the Church* (2003) (Yonkers, NY: St Vladimir's Seminary Press, 2012). See especially pages 202–5 and 216–21.

[41]Jean-Claude Larchet, *L'Église, Corps du Christ. Vol. I: Nature et structure* (The Church, the Body of Christ. Vol. 1: Nature and Structure) (Paris: Le Cerf, 2012), 243.

[42]Hilarion Alfeyev, *Orthodox Christianity. Vol. I: The History and Canonical Structure of the Orthodox Church*; and 'The Church', Part Five of Vol. II: *Doctrine and Teaching of the Orthodox Church* (both volumes: Yonkers, NY: St Vladimir's Seminary Press,

Paul Evdokimov develops other aspects of a theology of the laity. He illustrates, for example, the applicability of traditional 'monastic' spirituality to lay persons in the modern societies. His starting point, echoing the statement of John Chrysostom quoted above, is that: 'It is its total demand that the Gospel addresses itself to everyone, everywhere.'[43] This is the traditional Orthodox perspective on spirituality, a restatement of the *tserkovnost'* principle, which admits no distinction between 'evangelical commandments', applicable to all, and 'evangelical precepts', which apply only to those of the 'consecrated life'. To render a spirituality largely developed in monastic settings meaningful to Christians 'in the world', Evdokimov employs such notions as the 'interiorized monasticism' of those living in the world based on the three traditional monastic vows (poverty, chastity and obedience): the domestic church; the royal priesthood of the faithful; marriage as a spiritual path; and the priesthood of marriage.[44] In addition to considering the spiritual sense of marriage, Evdokimov also sets out to define a place in the church of a social group that is often forgotten in Orthodox spiritual literature, unmarried lay persons.[45]

Other issues related to the role of the laity in Orthodoxy have come up in modern times. As we discussed in Chapter 2, the 1848 Encyclical of the Oriental Patriarchs advanced the principle that the preservation of faith resides in the total body of the church, that is to say, in the people itself.[46] Orthodox theologians later expanded on this insight by formulating this doctrine as the infallibility of the church. Archbishop Stylianos Hariankis of Australia (b. 1935) forcibly argues this in his book *The Infallibility of the Church in Orthodox Theology*: 'the bearer of the infallibility of the church should be considered to include all members collectively.'[47] In somewhat less categorical terms, Boris Bobrinskoy emphasizes 'the collegial responsibility of the people of God in receiving the faith, and in defending the faith and piety'. This collegial responsibility acquired 'a certain canonical authority' in the 1848 Encyclical of the Eastern Patriarchs.[48]

The basic argument is that the church is herself infallible in matters of dogma – not any one person nor a group of persons (not a council nor even an ecumenical council), as distinct from Roman Catholic doctrine, which assigns infallibility to one person, the pope of Rome. The argument is founded in part on the notion of the reception – or the non-reception – of the doctrinal proclamations of councils of bishops, with several well-known historical cases often cited as prominent examples, especially the Second Council of Ephesus in 449 and the Union Council of

---

2011). See pages 412 and 435 of Vol. II. See our review article on the Alfeyev, Bobrinskoy and Larchet books: 'Three Orthodox Visions of the Church', *St Vladimir's Theological Quarterly*, 58, 2 (2014).

[43]Evdokimov, *The Ages of the Spiritual Life*, 136.

[44]In addition to Evdokimov's *The Ages of the Spiritual Life*, see also his book *The Sacrament of Love: The Nuptial Mystery in the Light of the Orthodox Tradition* (1944) (Crestwood, NY: St Vladimir's Seminary Press, 1985); and his essay 'Ecclesia Domestica' in Paul Evdokimov, *La Nouveauté de l'Esprit: Études de spiritualité* (The Novelty of the Spirit: Studies in Spirituality) (Bégrolles en Mauge, FR: Éditions de l'Abbaye de Bellefontaine, 1977); and in Suzannah Herzel, *A Voice for Women* (Geneva: World Council of Churches, 1981).

[45]See 'Non-Monastic Celibacy' in Evdokimov, *The Sacrament of Love*.

[46]Text of the Encyclical in Jaroslav Pelikan and Valerie Hotchkiss, eds., *Creeds and Confessions of Faith in the Christian Tradition* Vol. III (New Haven, CN: Yale University Press, 2003), 266–88.

[47]Stylianos Hariankis, *The Infallibility of the Church in Orthodox Theology* (Adelaide: ATF Press & Sydney: St. Andrew's Orthodox Press, 2008), 124.

[48]Bobrinskoy, *The Mystery of the Church*, 219. On the 1848 Encyclical of the Eastern Patriarchs, see above 27–8 and 48.

Florence-Ferrare of 1438–39, as well as other seemingly canonical councils which fell by the wayside, such as the iconoclast councils of Hieria in 754 and St Sophia in 815. The council of 449 supported monophysite Christology, but its pronouncements were not received by the people or the majority of the hierarchy, and its decisions were formally overturned by the Fourth Ecumenical Council held in Chalcedon in 451. In a similar vein, the Orthodox Church rejected the results of the Council of Florence-Ferrare, by which the Orthodox Church would have accepted Latin positions on the *filioque*, the status of the pope and other matters, in exchange for promises of Western assistance against the Turks. From these historical examples, it is argued that the veracity of doctrinal pronouncements of councils requires the favourable reception by the entire body of the church, thus giving an important role to all the faithful, even on matters of dogma. Even the decisions of an ecumenical council must be received by the entire church before they can be considered truly valid. Hilarion Alfeyev writes: 'The reception of an ecumenical council presupposed not only the official promulgation of its teaching by church authorities but also its acceptance by theologians, monks, and lay persons. The whole of the church community was involved in this process.'[49]

Another sensitive question concerns the role of the laity in the governance of the church. Boris Bobrinskoy sets out the basic rationale for the participation of the people in the governance of the church:

> The discernment of the people regarding the royal, pastoral and hierarchical function in its governance is essential. It implies a perpetual conciliarity within the local church, at every level. Without this conciliarity, the bishop is cut off from his church, he does know his sheep, and can neither intercede for them, nor nourish them, nor serve as their conciliar representative.[50]

Bobrinskoy refers favourably to the Moscow Council of 1917–18 as having established 'the principle and modes of lay representation at every level of the life of the Russian Church', but he does not elaborate further on lay participation in church structures. Other Orthodox writers are much less favourably inclined towards lay involvement in church governance. For Hilarion Alfeyev, the 'conciliarity' of the church concerns only the hierarchy, and although he mentions the substantial role played by laymen in the Council of 1917–18, he quickly dismisses this as 'an innovation', pointing out that the laity played no role in ancient councils (except the emperor and possibly functionaries).[51]

The local Orthodox churches have generally been very reluctant to allow non-ordained faithful a meaningful role in the governance of the church, except at the parish level, where parish councils typically have a majority of lay members, together with the parish clergy. The practice at higher levels, the diocese and the national church, varies considerably. The Council of 1917–18 of the

---

[49]Hilarion Alfeyev, 'The Reception of the Ecumenical Councils in the Early Church', *St Vladimir's Theological Quarterly*, 47, 3–4 (2003), 416.

[50]Bobrinskoy, *The Mystery of the Church*, 220.

[51]Hilarion Alfeyev, *Orthodox Christianity. Vol. II: Doctrine and Teaching of the Orthodox Church* (Yonkers, NY: St Vladimir's Seminary Press, 2011), 435.

Russian Orthodox Church (ROC) set a modern beacon standard for lay participation in church administration, which in practice has rarely been followed.

The Council approved a structure for church governance that gave a prominent role to lay persons at the parish, deanery, diocesan and national levels. Deanery and diocesan assemblies were to have an equal number of clergy and lay members, while the number of lay persons on parish councils cannot be less than the number of clergy. At the national level, the Holy Synod, whose authority extends 'to matters of a hierarchical and pastoral nature that especially concern the inner life of the church' was to be composed exclusively of hierarchs, chaired by the patriarch. Of the fifteen members of the Supreme Council of the church, responsible for 'social-ecclesiastical matters, principally concerning the external aspect of the life of the church', six were to have been lay persons. The structure of the Local Council of the ROC was such that it was possible for a majority of delegates to be lay persons, which was the case at the Council of 1917–18.[52]

With the exception of the restoration of the patriarchate and the election of Patriarch Tikhon, the Bolshevik revolution prevented the Russian Church from implementing most of the decisions of the Council of 1917–18. The church structures approved by the Council remain a model for clergy-lay involvement in the governance of church affairs, rarely implemented in practice, not even by the ROC since the fall of communism. Some Orthodox jurisdictions in the West, such as the Orthodox Church in America and the Archdiocese of Russian Orthodox Parishes in Western Europe, have established structures based on those approved by the Russian Council, but in practice, the synod of bishops typically remains the ultimate authority over most if not all decisions.

Conclusion

The 'churching' (*tserkovnost'*) or Christification of life signifies that Christianity calls for a total commitment to a Christian way of life in whatever circumstances a person may be. Modern Orthodoxy faces a major challenge in rendering its ancient theological, spiritual and liturgical traditions into an 'orthopraxis' relevant in contemporary societies, both in countries of Orthodox tradition, increasingly secularized, and in the largely de-Christianized countries of Orthodox immigration, where Orthodox are a decided minority among Western Christians, believers of other faiths, atheists and the indifferent. In response to this challenge, the notion of *tserkovnost'* as developed in émigré communities after the Russian Revolution sustained the establishment of new institutions intended to stimulate and to support Orthodox faithful in their efforts to live an Orthodox way of life in the new surroundings. Organizations such as the ACER and the *Fraternité orthodoxe en Europe occidentale*, and similar movements such as the religious fraternities in Greece (see Chapter 6) and the Orthodox Youth Movement (MJO) in Lebanon and Syria, developed

[52]The definitions and decrees of the All-Russian Council of 1917–18, as well as the Statute of the Local Council itself, are included as Appendices to Hyacinthe Destivelle's study, *The Moscow Council (1917-1918): The Creation of Conciliar Institutions of the Russian Orthodox Church* (Notre Dame, IN: University of Notre Dame Press, 2015), 191–351.

activities in cooperation with or at times in competition with the local Orthodox churches, to foster religious engagement of the Orthodox faithful.[53]

Simultaneous with the emergence of innovative institutional forms fostering Orthodox spiritual life has been the development of a theological base to sustain them. These include notably the flowering of liturgical theology and accompanying calls for liturgical reform and the evolution of thinking on the role of the non-ordained faithful or laity in the church. Fr Alexander Schmemann, Fr Lev Gillet, Archimandrite Vasileios (Gondidakis) and others in their stead can be seen as modern successors to the mystagogical tradition of the early centuries.[54] While Gillet and Gondidakis aspire to situate themselves in this tradition, Schmemann takes his distance from it by his opposition to what he calls the 'mysteriological' tradition represented by Pseudo-Dionysius in particular, and by his hostility towards monasticism. Despite this caveat, Schmemann's own writings on the sacraments in general, on baptism and chrismation, and on the Eucharist, together with his works on Great Lent and Pascha, place him in a broad liturgical approach to the Christian life, a key component of *tserkovnost'*, providing a link between individual asceticism and piety and participation in the communal life of worship and prayer in the church. Gillet and Gondidakis, on the other hand, seek to reconcile a liturgically based spirituality with the traditional ascetically based spirituality extending forward from the Desert Fathers and the establishment of Christian monasticism in the fourth century. Although Schmemann's approach to liturgical theology was influential in both Orthodox and non-Orthodox circles, his dislike of the mystagogical-mysteriological tradition and monasticism remains a puzzling but minor feature of his overall contributions to modern Orthodoxy.

Fr Lev Gillet and Mother Maria Skobtsova (St Maria of Paris), with whom Gillet collaborated in the 1930s, also represent another unaccustomed phenomenon in Orthodoxy, monastics living in the world rather than in monasteries. The monk or nun 'in the city' is not an institution, but rather a practice which varies according to the needs, situation and potential of individual monks and nuns who neither live in a monastery nor are hermits, the two main traditional forms of monastic life. Examples can be cited from other countries, such as Fr André Scrima of Romania, Mother Gabriella Papayannis of Greece (1897–1992) and several other modern Greek elders who were either monks or lived monastic-type lives in urban settings.[55]

In addition to the development of liturgical theology, major thrusts directed towards an Orthodox theology of the laity revolve around the theology of the royal priesthood of all believers, the interpretation or translation of an essentially monastic spirituality for non-monastics and the role of the laity in the governance of the church. To these should be added the role of women in the

[53]For an overview and assessment of the Greek religious fraternities and the *Mouvement de jeunesse orthodoxe*, see Ladouceur, 'New Institutions in Modern Orthodox Spirituality', 441–7; and 456–62.

[54]There are several studies of Schmemann's liturgical theology. For an insightful résumé, see Louth, *Modern Orthodox Thinkers*, 198–206.

[55]On André Scrima, see Ch. 7, 175–6. On Gavrilia Papayannis, see Sister Gavrilia, *Mother Gavrilia, The Ascetic of Love* (Athens: Eptalophos, 2000). For other Greek elders, see Herman A. Middleton, *Precious Vessels of the Holy Spirit, The Lives and Counsels of Contemporary Elders of Greece* (Thessalonica, GR & Asheville NC: Protecting Veil Press, 2004), especially concerning St Porphyrios (Bairaktaris) the Kapsokalyvite (1906–91), St Iakovos (Tsalikis) of Euboea (1920–91), and Elders Philotheos (Zervakos) of Paros (1884–1980), and Epiphanios (Theodoropoulos) of Athens (1930–89).

church, especially liturgical roles, which will be considered in Chapter 16. The notion of royal priesthood, associated especially with Nicholas Afanasiev, Paul Evdokimov and Alexander Schmemann, has provoked critiques within Orthodoxy, because of a perceived confusion and conflict with the ordained ministry in the church. This friction arises in the encounter of two visions of the church, one which emphasizes the mystery of the church as the Body of Christ, unbounded by the frailty of human institutions, the other which stresses the historical, institutional and hierarchical aspects of the church. A gauge of these two divergent but far from incompatible approaches to the church is the nature of the governance of the church, characterized by a wide diversity in modern times. While the institutional-hierarchical model has clearly dominated the Orthodox scene, the Council of 1917–18 of the Russian Orthodox Church represents a model, in practice and in theory, which recognizes the non-ordained as full members of the church, reflected in their involvement in the governance of the church at all levels. This remains an ideal little implemented in the various local Orthodox churches.

In a revealing entry in his *Journal* towards the end of his life, Fr Alexander Schmemann expresses the fundamental issue concerning the role of the laity in the church. Whereas in the early church all were 'lay' in Afanasiev's sense, with the installation of 'a Christian epoch', the laity 'appeared as new form of Christian life', no longer those who were outside the church, but those who were not clerics, who live 'in the world'. The positive side of this development is that the lay person

> illumines it [the world] with knowledge, prayer etc. Sanctifies the world by another-worldly faith, time by eschatology, and the earth by heaven. The church sanctifies the lay person by making him a communicant of the Kingdom of God and sanctifies his life in the world by showing him – be it ideally – the meaning of life.[56]

This ministry of the laity was transformed as the church, writes Schmemann, 'in a way', 'did away with the laity', on the one hand, 'by transforming them into "customers" of the clerics, and clerics servicing their spiritual needs'; and on the other hand, by 'demanding religious activism from the laity, made them into members of a church organization, servicing the needs of the church'.[57] Even if jurisdictions implement often elaborate structures for the participation of all members of the church in the governing of the church, often the synod of bishops retains the last word on governance and can trump decisions made by joint lay-clergy assemblies. Typically, the participation of the laity (and indeed parish clergy) in the governance of the church remains more an ideal than a reality. Theologies such as the royal priesthood of the faithful and the infallibility of the church as the Body of Christ, perhaps not as fully developed as they should be, together with initiatives to define a theology of the laity and modes of lay participation in the governance of the church, remain bright beacons illuminating the temptation to view the church as a specialized human institution, and Christianity as narrowly defined religious belief detached from the complexities of modern life.

---

[56]Alexander Schmemann, *The Journals of Father Alexander Schmemann 1973-1983* (Crestwood, NY: St Vladimir's Seminary Press, 2002) (entry for 30 April 1982), 328.
[57]Schmemann, *The Journals*, 328.

14

Social and Political Theology

Chapter Outline

Sergius Bulgakov (1871–1944), in his essay 'Dogma and Dogmatic Theology' in the 1937 *Living Tradition* collection, presents a list of issues which he considers are open to investigation because they do not fall within the scope of 'undisputed dogmas of the church'. In addition to typically theological issues (the world, the human person, God's will and predestination, the church, grace and the sacraments, Eucharistic theology, history and eschatology and pneumatology), he adds issues relating to 'the problems of life', Christian culture, social Christianity, church and state, and ecumenism, questions which, as Bulgakov writes, 'knock at the Christian heart and request a dogmatic consciousness'.[1] Although Bulgakov and other leaders of the Russian religious renaissance were deeply engaged in social and political issues, later Orthodox thinkers had more difficulty in coming to grips with such 'problems of life', such as social and politcal issues, until the late twentieth century and the beginning of the twenty-first century.

Social and political thought in the Russian religious renaissance

Contrasting attitudes towards social and political issues are often said to be reflected in the principal theological streams of the twentieth century, the Russian religious renaissance and neopatristic

[1]Sergius Bulgakov, 'Dogma and Dogmatic Theology' (1937), in Michael Plekon, ed., *Tradition Alive: On the Church and the Christian Life in Our Time* (Lanham, MA: Rowan & Littlefield, 2003), 68; 73; 77.

theology, and to have been conditioned by personal, social and political circumstances of the leading Orthodox thinkers associated with each stream. Alexander Schmemann (1921–83), in his review of Russian theology up to the early 1970s, writes that 'research for a living and "applied" Orthodoxy was from the beginning one of the mainsprings of the more free "religious philosophy".'[2] He remarks that the former members of the revolutionary intelligentsia who returned to the church both before and after the revolution 'kept the radical zeal of their former world'. Schmemann cites a number of authors associated with the religious renaissance who wrote on social issues, but the sole representative of the neopatristic approach that he cites is Paul Evdokimov, with his works on woman and marriage.[3]

The fundamental issue in social and political theology is to define the relationship among God, the individual person and the collectivity or the society. Seeking to reconcile these in a coherent vision, the Russian Christian thinkers of the late nineteenth and early twentieth centuries were caught on the horns of a dilemma. Following on their Slavophile predecessors, they wished to define a Christian path for Russian social and political development without embracing either the unacceptable secularism and individualism that they perceived in Western liberalism, or the determinism, atheism and anti-religious aspects of Marxist philosophy, despite their attraction to the desirable goals of socialism. As we saw in Chapter 4, several prominent leaders of the Christian intelligentsia, among them notably Nicolas Berdyaev (1874–1948) and Sergius Bulgakov, returned to Christianity from Marxism, retaining a high level of social conscience, which they now redefined in Christianity terms. The acceptable economic and social objectives of Marxism which attracted leading members of the Russian religious renaissance include the fundamental equality of all members of society, the responsibility of society for all its members, the redistribution of wealth, the right to equitable remuneration for work and universal social programmes in education, health and other domains. The unacceptable aspects of Marxism are of course its inherent materialism and atheism, its view of humans solely as social and economic entities, a dialectical view of history interpreted as class struggle, and, especially evident in Lenin's Bolshevism, the use of violence as a means to achieve social and political objectives, the 'dictatorship of the proletariat' (which in practice meant the rule of communist leaders), the suppression of opposition and freedom of expression and the seizure of property without compensation.

In the mid-nineteenth century Alexander Bukharev (1829–71) sketched the contours of Orthodox engagement with modernity, but, as we saw in Chapter 3, he did not elaborate a comprehensive theology of modernity, including social and political theology. Although many early leaders of the Russian religious renaissance, including the novelists Fyodor Dostoyevsky (1821–81) and Leon Tolstoy (1828–1910) (see Chapter 4), were imbued with a sensitive social conscience, Vladimir Soloviev (1853–1900) was the principal architect who laid solid foundations

---

[2]Alexander Schmemann, 'Russian Theology 1920-1972: An Introductory Survey', *St Vladimir's Theological Quarterly*, 16, 4 (1972), 188.

[3]Schmemann, 'Russian Theology 1920-1972', 189.

for the emergence of modern Orthodox social and political thought. Soloviev's central political idea early in his career is summed up in the expression 'free theocracy'. For Soloviev, free theocracy was not theocracy in the normal sense of political rule by religious leaders. He referred to this notion of theocracy as 'false theocracy',[4] as typified in Roman Catholic and Orthodox clericalism in the Catholic Church and the Byzantine and Russian empires. Soloviev's free theocracy is rather 'the actualization of the divine principle in the world',[5] a principle visible in the first instance in the church, whose organization is neither aristocratic nor democratic, but 'it is, in fact, definitely *theocratic*, ruled by God'.[6] On the level of the state, the sense of the somewhat nebulous concept of free theocracy is that the religious aspirations of the population must be reflected in the goals of the state (hence 'theocracy') and must be freely realized, not imposed by state or religious power (hence 'free' theocracy).

Soloviev's theocracy is a social application of the notions of all-unity (*vseedinstvo*), the fundamental solidarity of all things: 'the connecting of all functions and institutions in society to the love of God', in Paul Valliere's words, and of Godmanhood (*bogochelovechestvo*), the cosmic implications of the Incarnation of the Logos.[7] Soloviev, like many of his contemporaries and successors in the religious renaissance, struggled to balance personal freedom and the needs of the community, leading to 'the ideal of a free community',[8] a system of governance characterized by autonomy of key spheres of modern societies, such as commerce, law, science and culture. Soloviev places a high value on the value, dignity and freedom of the human person, and thus he favours the separation of church and state, reflected in the expression 'a free church in a free state',[9] as well as the protection of human rights, including freedom of belief.

Later in his all too-short career, Soloviev shied away from the easily misunderstood expression free theocracy, but he developed in more detail the idea of social and economic justice, especially in his late work *The Justification of the Good* (1897). Here he seeks a Christian middle way between capitalist exploitation of the poor and radical socialist egalitarianism by advocating the necessity of providing the minimum material means for a 'dignified existence'. Soloviev sees the religious and the political spheres as working in harmony, each with distinct goals and motivation, with the church envisioned as '*collectively-organized piety*' and the state as '*collectively-organized pity*' (Soloviev's emphasis) – 'pity' in the sense of mercifulness, empathy or 'loving-kindness'.[10] The state

---

[4]Vladimir Soloviev, *Kritika otvlechennykh nachal* (The Critique of Abstract Principles) (Soloviev's doctoral thesis, 1880) (in Russian), 161. Cited by Paul Valliere in *Modern Russian Theology: Bukharev, Soloviev, Bulgakov: Orthodox Theology in a New Key* (Grand Rapids, MI: Eerdmans, 2000), 131.

[5]Vladimir Soloviev, *The Spiritual Foundations of Life*, *GW II*, 107, cited in Marin Terpstra, '"God's Case on Earth": Notes on Theocracy and the Political Theology of Vladimir Soloviev', in Wil van den Bercken et al., eds., *Soloviev, Reconciler and Polemicist* (Leuven, BE: Peeters, 2000), 421.

[6]Vladimir Soloviev, *God, Man and the Church: The Spiritual Foundations of Life* (1885), (Cambridge: James Clarke, 1974), 153.

[7]Valliere, *Modern Russian Theology*, 130.

[8]Soloviev, *Kritika*, 166, cited in Valliere, *Modern Russian Theology*, 127.

[9]Ibid., 132.

[10]Vladimir Soloviev, *Justification of the Good: An Essay on Moral Philosophy* (1897), Thomas Nemeth, ed. (Cham, CH: Springer International Publishing, 2015), 399. The unfortunate English word 'pity' fails to convey the full strength of the idea of

is responsible for the elevation of the principle of mercifulness 'from the level of an impotent and strictly limited feeling and gives it reality, its broad application and development', permitting the provision of '*pity, i.e., provide help and protection,* to tens and hundreds of millions of people, instead of to tens and at most hundreds of individuals'[11] – 'hundreds of individuals' being the practical limits of personal action.

Soloviev defines 'pity' as the correct relation among humans; thus pity is linked with moral truth and justice:

> The true essence of pity is not a simple identification of oneself with another, but the recognition of the other's own (proper) significance. … This idea of pity, taken as universal and as independent of the subjective mental states connected with it (i.e., taken logically and not psychologically), is connected with *moral truth* and *justice*. It is true that other creatures are similar to me, and it is right that I treat them as I do myself.

Pity in this sense is thus close to the Christian ideal of altruistic love, *agape*, and is therefore truth, whereas egoism is untruth:

> Altruism as corresponding to moral truth, or to what is, and egoism as presupposing an untruth, or what is not, since the individual self does not in fact have the exclusive and central significance that it ascribes to itself in egoism. Although the extension of personal egoism to the family, the nation, the state and religion expresses the historical achievements of morality, it does not eliminate the fundamental lie of egoism, which is refuted by the unconditional truth of the altruistic principle.[12]

In his social and political thought, Soloviev thus articulates a profoundly Christian philosophical and theological foundation for modern social legislation, which incorporates the idea of collective responsibility for the provision of the means for 'minimum human dignity' for all members of the polity, and indeed in a broad sense for all humanity – the theological foundation for international development assistance. For the Christian, the state and social and economic structures create opportunities for the evangelical love of neighbour, so vividly portrayed in Christ's parable of the Good Samaritan (Lk. 10.25-37).

Soloviev remained realistic about the acceptability of his political theology. In a letter to his French friend the philosopher of religion Eugène Tavernier (1854–1928), Soloviev wrote:

> If it is clear that the truth will only be definitively accepted by a small and likely persecuted minority, we must once and for all abandon the idea of the power and external grandeur of theocracy as the

unconditional love, *agape*, which lies behind Soloviev's notion of 'pity'. The Russian word translated as 'pity' is *zhalost'*, but the Russian sense is much more than pity in normal English usage: '*Zhalost'* differs from *pity* … in the presence of "loving" feelings toward the unfortunate target person … and in its absence of potentially invidious comparisons with other people … Unlike *pity, zhalost'* is, potentially, a feeling that can embrace all living creatures, just as *love* can' (Anna Wierzbicka, *Semantics, Culture, and Cognition* (New York: Oxford University Press, 1992), 168). Wierzbicka points out that Soloviev calls *zhalost'* 'the root of an ethical attitude towards … other human beings and towards living creatures in general'. In a theological perspective, *zhalost'* is close to the Slavonic *milost'*, the Greek *eleos* and the Latin *misericordia*, for which there are no equivalent English words, although the expression 'loving-kindness' is often used in translations.

[11]Soloviev, *Justification of the Good*, 399.

[12]Ibid., xiv. Both citations are from Soloviev's 'Table of Contents'. For the full development of these points, see Ch. 3 in the book 'Pity and Altruism', VII, 63–5.

direct and immediate goal of Christian politics. Its goal is justice, and glory is only a consequence which will come on its own.[13]

Despite the occasional complexity and ambiguity of his ideas, Soloviev's notions of free theocracy, autonomous social spheres and collective responsibility for all members of a society remained powerful attractions for his contemporaries and successors in the Russian religious renaissance. Soloviev was long identified with political conservatism, but recent scholarship stresses his liberal views,[14] even though he departs from classical Western European liberalism in deriving his political and social principles from a Christian vision of relations between God and humanity, characterized above all by mutual love, rather than from typically humanist foundations originating in the Renaissance and the Enlightenment. Aristotle Papanikolaou refers to Soloviev's thought as 'Christian liberalism' 'grounded in the love of God', a kind of Christian secularism which grants autonomy to various spheres of society, as the key to sound Orthodox political theology.[15] Soloviev's political theology can also be considered an extension of the notions of all-unity and Godmanhood, more problematic ideas which largely disappeared from Orthodox thought after the Second World War, as we saw in Chapters 9 and 10. But his political theology does not rely directly on these difficult notions.

Several former Marxists who retained their social commitment after their conversion or return to Orthodoxy set out to justify acceptable social goals for Christian action by grounding Christian social thought more explicitly than Soloviev in the New Testament and the social thought of the early Fathers. The task was not easy, because social and political thought in Russia at the beginning of the twentieth century had coalesced around two poles, the autocracy and authoritarianism of the decaying imperial regime, with the Russian Orthodox Church (ROC) as its ally, and radical atheistic humanism, embodied in political movements bent on the violent overthrow of the monarchy, the aristocracy and the capitalist regime and their replacement by an imposed socialist society. Socially concerned Christians were thus caught between autocratic imperialism and atheistic humanism. There was no Christian middle ground for them to occupy, but it had to be created, under the inspiration of the social and political thought of Soloviev and reflected in such popular writings as the novels of Feodor Dostoyevsky.

In a key text published in September 1905 at the height of the aborted revolution, Sergius Bulgakov (1871–1944) proposes to resolve the dilemma by defining a Christian approach to social and political issues. 'An Urgent Task' is an attempt to recoup what can be salvaged from humanist and Marxist socialism in a Christian perspective, a passionate plea for Christian politics and specifically Christian socialism.[16] Bulgakov wrote this article after he had broken with Marxism

---

[13]Vladimir Soloviev, *La Sophia et les autres écrits français* (Sophia and Other Writings in French) (Lausanne: L'Âge d'Homme, 1978), 338.

[14]See Andrzej Walicki, 'Vladimir Soloviev: Religious Philosophy and the Emergence of the "New Liberalism,"' Chapter III of Walicki's *Legal Philosophies of Russian Liberalism* (Oxford: Clarendon Press, 1987); and Greg Gaut 'A Practical Unity: Vladimir Solov'ev and Russian Liberalism', *Canadian Slavonic Papers*, 42, 3 (2000), 295.

[15]Aristotle Papanikolaou, *The Mystical as Political: Democracy and Non-Radical Orthodoxy* (Notre Dame, IN: University of Notre Dame Press, 2012), 34–5.

[16]'An Urgent Task' was first published in *Voprosy zhizni* (Problems of Life), an intelligentsia journal edited by Nicolas Berdyaev. Translation in Bernice Glatzer Rosenthal and Martha Bohachevsky-Chomiak, eds., *A Revolution of the Spirit: Crisis of Value in*

and embraced Christianity philosophically, but before his active return to the church, which occurred a few years later, around 1908. He was still very much distraught by the unholy alliance of the ROC and the imperial regime and the article contains bitter denunciations of church bureaucracy and the subservience of the church to the government.[17] In places Bulgakov's language is quasi-Marxist, coming very close to endorsing the Marxist notion of class struggle.[18]

Bulgakov's theological argument for Christian politics and Christian socialism reposes on three pillars: first, the Incarnation of Christ and history as 'the process of God-Man, wherein a united mankind, "the body of Christ"' is assembled and organized'; secondly, Christ's precept of love of neighbour, which 'must be extended not only to inner feelings but to outer or social and political relations as well'; and finally the 'absolute dignity of the human person, who bears God's image'.[19] Bulgakov is in the line of Alexander Bukharev and *tserkovnost'* when he writes: 'Christianity extends its sphere of interests and influence over all realms of life; it determines all human life, according to its own idea, from the first cry to the last.' Against the argument that personal charity satisfies Christian social obligations, Bulgakov contends that personal morality must extend to 'social morality, that is, politics'. It is in this theological context that Bulgakov endorses typically humanist ideals such as 'the emancipation of all humanity, universal freedom, for which there can be no distinction among nationalities, religions or denominations', 'the human person's natural and sacred rights to freedom of speech, freedom of conscience, freedom of association', separation of church and state, 'complex social techniques of social legislation, workers' organizations, strikes and the cooperative movement' and even such measures as increasing direct taxes and introducing progressive income tax (implemented in Russia in 1916, during the First World War).

Bulgakov's views here are thus similar to Soloviev's, as expressed in *The Justification of the Good*, but Bulgakov more explicitly endorses typically liberal social and political objectives. His article is both a theological treatise and a manifesto for Christian politics and ends with a call for the establishment of a Union of Christian Politics, devoted to 'the cultivation of Christian community'.[20] Bulgakov was one of the founders of the Union of Liberation in 1902, which became the Constitutional Democratic ('Kadet') Party. He did in fact found a Union of Christian Politics and was elected to the short-lived Second Duma (February to June 1907) as an independent Christian socialist. But the experience of the fractious and ineffective Duma left him disillusioned and he never returned to active politics.[21]

Beginning with *The Unfading Light* (1917), Sergius Bulgakov's first properly theological work, and for the rest of his life, the great theologian was primarily concerned with typically dogmatic

---

Russia, 1890-1924 (New York: Fordham University Press, 1990).

[17]For examples, see Bulgakov, 'An Urgent Task', 139–40; 144.

[18]Referring to the existence of 'struggling classes', Bulgakov writes that 'One cannot stand above this social struggle; rather, one must intervene in it actively and consciously'. 'An Urgent Task', 147.

[19]This and subsequent quotations in this paragraph from Bulgakov, 'An Urgent Task', passim 142–50.

[20]Bulgakov, 'An Urgent Task', 158. For a study of the development of Bulgakov's social and political thought in this period, see especially Catherine Evtuhov, *The Cross & the Sickle: Sergei Bulgakov and the Fate of Russian Religious Philosophy* (Ithaca, NY: Cornell University Press, 1997), particularly Ch. 7, 'Christian Socialism'.

[21]See Rowan Williams, ed., *Sergii Bulgakov: Towards a Russian Political Economy* (Edinburgh: T&T Clark, 1999), 55–61; Evtuhov, *The Cross & the Sickle*, 115–26.

theological questions, especially the elaboration and defence of his doctrines of Godmanhood and sophiology. Although disheartened by the perverse nature of Russia's socialist revolution, of which he was himself a victim (loss of his teaching posts and exile), he did not abandon completely his earlier preoccupation with social, economic and political issues, which are reflected in a number of publications in the early and mid-1930s. In 1932 Bulgakov published an important essay on 'The Soul of Socialism' in the periodical *Novyi grad* (The New City).[22] Closely associated with *Novyi grad* were Ilya Fondaminski (1880–1942) and Mother Maria Skobtsov (St Maria of Paris) (1891–1945) and it is likely that they influenced Bulgakov's return to social themes in the early 1930s – Bulgakov was Mother Maria's spiritual father and he supported her social, intellectual and cultural undertakings and her wish to become a nun.

The spirit of Bulgakov's 'The Soul of Socialism' is markedly different from 'An Urgent Task', as three decades of turmoil and conflict left its marks on the author. Gone is the enthusiasm for Christian socialism, its place taken by a certain pessimism about socialism, arising from the bitter experience of the Russian Revolution. Socialism is now seen almost exclusively as communism, a 'materialist economism', inexorably connected with fatalism and revolution: 'Socialism has soul of its own – a *soul* that is admittedly wholly pagan – and a *spirit* which has so far been decidedly hostile to God.'[23] This is a far cry from Christian notions of a religious interpretation of economics: 'The Christian ideal of the Kingdom of God is realized historically in a whole series of alternating historical tasks: at the present time, one of these is the attainment of social justice along with personal liberty.'[24] But Bulgakov fails to see his way to a Christian socialism, or even to support for a secular, humanist welfare or socialist movement purged of communist, atheist and anti-religious baggage.

In the autumn of 1934 Bulgakov visited Canada and the United States, where he delivered a lecture at the Seabury-Western Theological Seminary (Evanston, IL) 'Social Teaching in Modern Russian Orthodox Theology'.[25] In his analysis of the history of social concern in Orthodoxy, Bulgakov stresses, like others of his time, that the concern for personal salvation and asceticism resulted in a flight from the world on the part of both individuals and the church and a corresponding neglect of social issues, with the result that 'the vacuum created by the absence of social leadership on the part of Christianity was filled in by a new paganism or by atheistic humanism.'[26] Bulgakov ties social theology to ecclesiology, arguing that 'the task of the church includes not only ways of personal salvation but of the transfiguration of the world' and he posits Christian humanism as an answer to the question of 'false, atheistic humanism' put to the church, the 'opposite of the godless

[22]Sergius Bulgakov, 'The Soul of Socialism' (*Novyi grad* 3, 1932) in Williams, ed., *Sergii Bulgakov: Towards a Russian Political Economy*. *Novyi grad* (New City), edited notably by the historian Georges Fedotov and published by YMCA-Press between 1932 and 1939, was more socially and politically oriented than *Put'* (The Way), the leading philosophical-theological periodical of the Russian religious intelligentsia in the interwar period, edited by Nicolas Berdyaev.

[23]Bulgakov, 'The Soul of Socialism', 239.

[24]Ibid., 248.

[25]Sergius Bulgakov, *Social Teaching in Modern Russian Orthodox Theology: The Twentieth Annual Hale Memorial Sermon* (Evanston, IL: Seabury-Western Theological Seminary, 1934). Reprinted in Williams, ed., *Sergii Bulgakov: Towards a Russian Political Theology*.

[26]Bulgakov, *Social Teaching in Modern Russian Orthodox Theology*, 10.

humanism of modern times': 'All these creative efforts must be made in the name of Jesus Christ; being inspired by the Holy Ghost, Pentecost is continued.'[27] Love is the foundation of Christian social and political engagement: 'Social life is to be organized according to the postulates of Christian love, so also the whole of political life.'[28] The weaknesses of Bulgakov's analysis lies in his failure to account adequately for social teachings and undertakings in the early church and in the history of monasticism, and in casting humanism into two 'opposite streams of thought', atheistic humanism, identified almost entirely with 'materialistic socialism, especially communism', and Christian humanism.[29] Despite a more positive tone than in 'The Soul of Socialism' two years earlier, Bulgakov does not admit the possibility of non-religious liberal humanism free of militant communist atheism, with which Christian humanism could collaborate in the edification of a modern state reflecting Christian values.

Bulgakov takes a more conciliatory position in his book *The Orthodox Church* (1935), intended for a non-Orthodox audience, which contains chapters on 'Orthodoxy and the State' and 'Orthodoxy and Economic Life'. 'Orthodoxy should not oppose socialism', writes Bulgakov, 'if the latter recognizes individual liberty; quite the contrary, for socialism is the realization in social life of the commandment of love.'[30]

Taken as a whole, Bulgakov's late social and political thought is very much in the line of Alexander Bukharev – the full engagement of Christianity with society:

> We must seek for a state of things in which the church may penetrate as with inward power the whole of human life. The separation of the church from life must be overcome, and all sides of the natural existence of men – certainly excluding sin – are to be included in the grace-abounding life of the church.[31]

There was a certain tension concerning differing approaches to social and political issues between the older generation of Russian theologians of the religious renaissance and the younger generation who had not participated in pre-revolutionary debates about the future of Russia and was more attuned to neopatristic theology. In his typical brash manner, Nicolas Berdyaev (1874–1948) takes Georges Florovsky (1893–1979) to task for the failure to recognize tyranny and the struggle against oppression in Florovsky's *The Ways of Russian Theology*:

> [Florovsky] does not understand the theme of moral indignation against the wronging and oppression of man. He considers it appropriate to deprecate Vladimir Soloviev for seeking social justice and the realization of Christian justice in society. ... Fr. G. Florovsky ignores the anguish of the Russian soul in the face of the terrible evil of serfdom, the debasement of man by the autocracy, and the impact that this had on all Russian thought. ... Fr. G. Florovsky evidently considers moral feelings and

---

[27]Ibid., 15; 16.
[28]Ibid., 17.
[29]Ibid., 20.
[30]Sergius Bulgakov, *The Orthodox Church* (1935) (Yonkers, NY: St Vladimir's Seminary Press, 1988), 173.
[31]Bulgakov, *Social Teaching in Modern Russian Orthodox Theology*, 17.

> heightened consciousness as utopianism and he struggles not only against romanticism, but also against utopianism.[32]

Berdyaev's reference here to 'utopianism' is the search for a more just social order which was, as we have seen, the major preoccupation of the pre-revolutionary Russian intelligentsia. Berdyaev goes on to speculate that Byzantine theology itself may provide an explanation for the apparent neglect of social justice in Florovsky's book:

> This might perhaps be explained by the failure of Byzantine Orthodoxy to be authentically involved with man. When man is seen exclusively as a sinful being in need of salvation, the abasement of man and affronts against his dignity are ignored.

Berdyaev has of course inadequately characterized 'Byzantine Orthodoxy' as concerned exclusively with salvation, ignoring the social concerns reflected in the Gospels and the epistles and the social initiatives of St Basil the Great and St John Chrysostom and other early Fathers. But he does nonetheless have a point: a strong focus on more narrowly 'theological', 'metaphysical' or 'spiritual' issues has led to a relative neglect of questions of social justice in Orthodox thought. This critique is often associated with a related criticism, that the strong emphasis on personal salvation and ascetic practices frequently found in Orthodoxy can too easily result in a debasing of material concerns, social and political issues and even the human body. Orthodox monasticism is sometimes criticized for the same reasons.[33] In his 1905 essay 'An Urgent Task', Bulgakov places among the 'antisocial forms of Christianity' 'that medieval monastic Christianity that denies all earthly tasks and teaches us to look above the God-forsaken sinful earth'.[34] While this critique could apply to both Eastern and Western Christianity, again it overlooks the social undertakings of monasteries in health, education, hospitality and famine relief.

The commitment to social ideals did not remain purely theoretical for a number of Russian intellectuals, both prior to the revolution and in exile. There are several important examples of personal commitment to the improvement of the well-being of the disadvantaged. These include two women who engaged in social activities, both of whom were martyred and both now canonized, St Elizabeth (Feodorovna) of Russia (1864–1918) and St Maria of Paris. They had very different personalities, but were united in one conviction, that love of God must be manifested in love of neighbour, not in an abstract sense, but in actual social commitment. Both founded social undertakings, Elizabeth in pre-revolutionary Moscow and Mother Maria in interwar Paris. Elizabeth Feodorovna established the Mission of Martha and Mary, a religious order of women

---

[32]Nicolas Berdyaev, 'Ortodoksiya i chelovechnost' (Ortodoxia and Humanness), *Put'*, 53 (1937), 53–65. Translation by Steven Janos: www.berdyaev.com/Berdyaev/berd_lib/1937_424.html (5 April 2015).

[33]Fr Alexander Schmemann was known for his disregard for monasticism. In the entry in his Journal for 20 January 1981, he writes: 'More and more often it seems to me that revising the monasticism that everybody so ecstatically talks about – or at least trying to revive it – can be done only by liquidating first of all the monastic institution itself, i.e. the whole vaudeville of *klobuks*, cowls, stylization, etc.' *The Journals of Father Alexander Schmemann 1973-1983* (Crestwood, NY: St Vladimir's Seminary Press, 2002), 284. See the discussion and references in Andrew Louth, *Modern Orthodox Thinkers: From the Philokalia to the Present* (London: SPCK, 2015), 208.

[34]Bulgakov, 'An Urgent Task', 150.

devoted to social action, like Roman Catholic and Lutheran social religious communities. It was successful but was closed by the Bolsheviks in 1919, after Elizabeth herself had suffered martyrdom in 1918 as a member of the Russian imperial family.[35]

During the revolution, Mother Maria, then Elizabeth Kuzmin-Karavaev, was actively involved both in national politics as a member of the Socialist Revolutionary Party, in competition with Lenin's Bolsheviks, and in local politics, as deputy mayor and then mayor of her hometown municipality of Anapa on the Black Sea. In the 1930s she established charitable institutions in Paris. She enjoyed not only the support of Sergius Bulgakov and Metropolitan Evlogy (Georgievsky) (1868–1946), but also the active collaboration in her undertakings of intellectuals such as Nicolas Berdyaev, Fr Lev Gillet ('A Monk of the Eastern church'; 1893–1980), art critic and writer Constantin Motchulski (1892–1948) and writer and publisher Ilya Fondaminski (1880–1942). After Mother Maria's arrest by the Gestapo in 1943 and her deportation and death in a German concentration camp in 1945, her charitable works ceased.[36] Both Elizabeth of Russia and Maria of Paris have become inspirations for similar undertakings. Elizabeth of Russia's community was revived in Saint Petersburg after the fall of communism in Russia, and inspired a sister community in Minsk, Byelorussia.

Mother Maria's social theology revolved around the idea that a Christian social conscience in the modern world is an imperative necessity flowing from the gospel commandments, love of God and love of neighbour, since one cannot be separated from the other, and a vision of the world as a prolongation of the liturgy:

> The 'liturgy outside the church' is our sacrificial ministry in the church of the world, adorned with living icons of God, our common ministry, an all-human sacrificial offering of love. ... In this liturgical communion with people, we partake of a communion with God; we really become one flock and one Shepherd, one body, of which the inalienable head is Christ.[37]

In her classic essay 'The Second Gospel Commandment' (1939), Mother Maria argues from Scripture, the liturgy, the Church Fathers and even the ascetic texts in the *Philokalia*, for the essential unity of religious life and social commitment, in a holistic caring for the other: 'Christian love teaches us to give to our brother not only material but also spiritual gifts.'[38] Mother Maria refers even to the need 'to give one's soul for one's neighbours',[39] a human solidarity which reflects both sincere empathy for the plight and sufferings of another and a caring for the psychological and spiritual well-being of all. The final stages of her own life were, of course, an example of such a

---

[35]Grand Duchess Elizabeth (Feodorovna) of Russia, a granddaughter of Queen Victoria, was a German princess married to Grand Duke Sergei Alexandrovich (1857–1905), son of Alexander II. She was both aunt to Nicholas II by her own marriage, and his sister-in-law by the marriage of her sister Alexandra to Nicholas. On the Mission of Martha and Mary, see Paul Ladouceur, 'New Institutions in Modern Orthodox Spirituality', *St Vladimir's Theological Quarterly*, 55, 4 (2011), 447–56.

[36]See Ladouceur, 'New Institutions in Modern Orthodox Spirituality', 471–4.

[37]Mother Maria Skobtsova, 'The Mysticism of Human Communion', in *Mother Maria, Essential Writings* (Maryknoll, NY: Orbis Books, 2003), 81.

[38]Skobtsova, 'The Second Gospel Commandment', 54.

[39]Ibid., 59.

total commitment and she remains, as she wrote in one of her many poems, a 'calling' to her fellow Christians rather than merely a 'memory'.[40]

Social and political thought in neopatristic theology

In his Introduction to the book *The Teachings of Modern Orthodox Christianity on Law, Politics, and Human Nature*, Paul Valliere seeks to account for a perceived weakness of neopatristic theology with respect to social and political theology:

> The construction of ethical systems reflects the West's 'scholastic' approach to theology, that is, the interpretation and application of mysteries of faith by means of discursive reasoning. The procedure is supposedly alien to Orthodoxy, which prefers to set theology in a liturgical and mystical context. Orthodox theologians, so the argument goes, do not seek general principles but focus on personal experience.[41]

Valliere puts forward two important caveats to this explanation. The first is that a number of modern Orthodox thinkers have in fact engaged in such reflection. He cites Soloviev and Berdyaev, and he could have added Sergius Bulgakov (absent from the Orthodox thinkers presented in the book) and Mother Maria Skobtsov (who features in the book). The Russian religious thinkers retained their 'sense of social responsibility and social conscience'[42] in their situation of forced exile, as they sought to understand the social, economic and religious factors which led to the Revolution.[43] Some, notably Berdyaev and Mother Maria, also reflected on the social, economic and political situation of their countries of adoption, especially in the light of the desperate plight of many poor Russian émigrés, the economic problems of the 1930s and the rise of Nazism and fascism.[44]

Valliere's second caveat is relevant to the situation of the younger Russian neopatristic theologians. Like their elders from the pre-revolution religious renaissance, they were intellectuals in exile, many having left revolutionary Russia as children or young adults with their parents.

[40]'I do not want to be a memory. I shall be for you a calling.' Cited in Hélène Arjakovsky-Klépinine, 'La Joie du don' (The joy of giving) in Mère Marie Skobtsov, *Le Sacrement du frère* (The Sacrament of the Brother) (Paris: Le Cerf, 2001), 69. See the entire poem in Paul Ladouceur, 'The Social and Political Theology of Love in St Maria of Paris', *Sobornost*, 40, 1 (2018), 74.

[41]Paul Valliere, 'Introduction to the Modern Orthodox Tradition', in John Witte Jr. and Frank S. Alexander, eds., *The Teachings of Modern Orthodox Christianity on Law, Politics, and Human Nature* (New York: Columbia University Press, 2007), 4.

[42]Leonid Kishkovsky, 'Russian Theology after Totalitarianism', in Mary Cunningham and Elizabeth Theokritoff, eds., *The Cambridge Companion to Orthodox Christian Theology* (Cambridge University Press, 2009). *Orthodox Christian Theology*, 262.

[43]See notably Berdyaev's *The Russian Revolution* (London: Sheed and Ward, 1931), which contains the articles 'Russian Religious Psychology and Communistic Atheism' and 'The Religion of Communism'. Also Berdyaev's *The Origin of Russian Communism* (London: G. Bles, 1937).

[44]See Mother Maria's essays 'Under the Sign of Our Time', 'Insight in Wartime' in *Mother Maria Skobtsova, Essential Writings*; and her essays under the heading 'L'Évangile social' (The social gospel) and the essays 'Les sentinelles de la liberté' (The guardians of freedom) (on the role of the Western churches in defending liberty against fascism) and 'Quatre portraits' (Four portraits) (a Christian view of the European political situation just prior to the Second World War) in Sainte Marie de Paris (Mère Marie Skobtsova 1891–1945), *Le Jour du Saint-Esprit* (The Day of the Holy Spirit), Paul Ladouceur, ed. (Paris: Éditions du Cerf, 2011).

But unlike their predecessors in pre-revolutionary Russia, the younger generation, such as Georges Florovsky, Vladimir Lossky (1903–58), Paul Evdokimov (1901–70), Alexander Schmemann and others, conducted theology in a foreign context divorced from the problems, needs and aspirations of their homeland, as we emphasized in Chapter 4. Valliere writes that 'Except in Greece, Orthodox theologians worked in contexts where they had virtually no access to social or political power and bore no responsibility for its management. It is no wonder that they regarded theological reflection on law, society, and politics to be disconnected from reality – scholastic in the pejorative sense.'[45]

Valliere accuses the early neopatristic theologians of having a limited view of theology which effectively marginalized social and political questions:

> Lossky, Florovsky, and other first-generation neopatristic thinkers embraced a rigorously mystical and apophatic view of theology that effectively discouraged the theological interpretation of legal, social, and political questions. Mystical or apophatic theology is an effective means of contemplating the mystery of God as experienced in the depths of personal being. It is not a useful tool for fashioning a theory of the state, evaluating a system of positive law, forging an interpretation of history, or other tasks normally involved in the construction of a social and political ethic.[46]

Valliere, in general strongly critical of neopatristic theology, concludes that neopatristic thinkers 'stopped looking for an Orthodox legal, social, and political doctrine. They did not address issues of law, society, and politics in any of their major works.'[47] While Valliere's interpretation is overly categorical, it does point to a major weakness in neopatristic theology as it was practised in the second half of the twentieth century. The theological priorities of early neopatristic theologians were clearly centred, with good reason as we argued in Chapter 5, on major doctrinal questions, such as apophatism, the divine energies, the procession of the Holy Spirit (the *Filioque*), deification, the church and relations with non-Orthodox Christianity. It was necessary to restore or to establish authentic Orthodox theology in these areas after centuries of distortion or even *oubli* in the face of scholasticism and other Western influences on Orthodox theology – to reverse the pseudomorphism denounced by Georges Florovsky. This already full theological agenda left little room for addressing social and political issues. This was reinforced, as Valliere points out, by the social situation of the émigré communities, since Orthodox in countries of immigration were a small minority with little possibility of exerting much influence on public policy. And with the passage of time, the deep involvement of Christian thinkers in pre-revolutionary Russia in social and political issues became an increasingly distant historical memory.

Nonetheless, the development of social and political theology and concern among neopatristic theologians, while limited, was not entirely absent. For example, many of Fr Dumitru Staniloae's early writings in the *Telegraful Roman* in Sibiu between 1929 and 1946 expressed an Orthodox perspective on contemporary national and cultural questions. But as we noted in Chapter 7, his foray into religious-ethnic nationalism in the 1930s and after the fall of communism constitutes an

---

[45] Valliere, 'Introduction to the Modern Orthodox Tradition', 4–5.
[46] Ibid., 14.
[47] Ibid.

unfortunate distraction from his major theological contributions, in which religious-ethnic nationalism does not feature.

Among the younger generation of Orthodox theologians who turned to patristic roots for inspiration, Paul Evdokimov (1900–70) was deeply socially engaged. Even while pursuing his theological interests, he was employed for many years by the French Protestant social organization, Cimade (*Comité inter-mouvements auprès des évacués*), and he was responsible for a Cimade hostel for displaced persons from 1946 to 1968.[48] Evdokimov is an important exception to the generally minor role of social and political thought and concern among neopatristic theologians. Even though he wrote little about social theology as such, in 1967 he published a major essay on 'The Church and Society'.[49] Like Mother Maria before him, Evdokimov appeals to the Gospel, the Fathers of the Church, the history of the church and the leaders of the Russian religious renaissance to support his central argument that concern for the other is an essential component of the Christian life, and is reflected in the social activities of major Fathers such as Basil the Great and in the charitable undertakings of monasteries. 'The social teaching of the church contains the very essence of Christianity,' he writes. Evdokimov seeks to bridge the apparent gap between concern for personal salvation and social engagement: 'In every effort towards perfection, personal holiness is inseparable from the social dimension.'[50] Like many religious philosophers, he argues that despite the hostility of socialism to religious elements, 'in its origins, socialism is Christian.'[51] At the same time he repeats several times the notion that 'no social arrangement can be "dogmatized" or "canonized".'[52] Recalling the thinking of his predecessors in the Russian religious renaissance, Evdokimov considers that only Christian personalism offers a solution to the polarities of capitalist individualism versus Marxist collectivism, both of which are 'anti-personalist and anti-communitarian for they deal not with unique persons but with a world where anonymity rules.'[53] Personalism aims not at 'the empty terms "happiness" or "good fortune"', but rather 'the flourishing of the adult person in the adult community'.[54]

Although Evdokimov mounts a formidable array of arguments for the social engagement of Christians and of the church, he does not fully clarify whether personal action – 'charity' – is sufficient, or whether the Christian conscience must go further, to engage the weight of the modern state to favour Christian social goals. It is perhaps this timidity which distinguishes Evdokimov from his predecessors and mentors among the great figures of the Russian religious renaissance, beginning with Soloviev and extending to Bulgakov and Mother Maria. For them, the employment of the apparatus of the state in the achievement of social objectives was a necessary extension of

[48]Paul Evdokimov gives a brief account of his social service in his autobiographical essay 'Some Landmarks on Life's Journey' (1981), in Michael Plekon and Alexis Vinogradov, eds., *In the World, Of the Church: A Paul Evdokimov Reader* (Crestwood, NY: St Vladimir's Seminary Press, 2000).
[49]Paul Evdokimov, 'The Church and Society: The Social Dimension of Orthodox Ecclesiology' (1967) in Michael Plekon and Alexis Vinogradov, eds., *In the World, Of the Church: A Paul Evdokimov Reader* (Crestwood, NY: St Vladimir's Seminary Press, 2000).
[50]Evdokimov, 'The Church and Society', 62; 63–4.
[51]Ibid., 71.
[52]Ibid., 64.
[53]Ibid., 72.
[54]Ibid., 76.

personal social commitment and action. Evdokimov limits himself to saying that the reflection of the Fathers on a Christian social order 'surpasses by far individual acts of charity and demands profound, radical social reform',[55] without indicating what this means in complex modern societies.

If Paul Evdokimov stands out among his contemporaries for his social engagement, other neopatristic theologians, including Georges Florovsky, were certainly aware of social issues. In 1950 Florovsky published an article on 'The Social Problem in the Eastern Orthodox Church'.[56] Florovsky begins his article with a startling assertion (for Florovsky): 'Christianity is essentially a social religion.'[57] He points to the 'social and corporate' nature of Christian existence, including the sacraments, the church as 'New Society', the social responsibilities and roles of monasticism, early Fathers of the Church and the social aspects of the teachings of the Slavophiles, Dostoyevsky and Berdyaev. Even Florovsky's principal bête noire among the religious philosophers, Vladimir Soloviev, receives a favourable mention: 'All his life Soloviev firmly believed in the social mission of Christianity and of the church.'[58] Florovsky asks 'why then was there so little social action in the East and the whole richness of social ideas left without an adequate embodiment?'[59] He seeks an answer in the social actions of the state, especially of course in the Soviet Union, but does not explore, as others have done, explanations which point to a certain mystical and eschatological orientation in Orthodoxy itself, which some interpret as leading to a neglect of material concerns, the principal objective of social and political activities.

If neopatristic theologians such as Florovsky were aware of social issues, this did not feature prominently in their thinking, unlike their predecessors in the Russian religious renaissance, nor result in social engagement such as that of Mother Maria and Paul Evdokimov. The mitigated response of neopatristic theologians to social and political theology and issues became a central theme for many younger Orthodox theologians in the early twenty-first century.

Political theology for the twenty-first century

In the late twentieth century and the early twenty-first century, political theology became a prominent issue both among Orthodox in Western democracies and in countries of Orthodox tradition. The urgency of developing Orthodox political theology was galvanized by the fall of communism in Russia and Eastern Europe, religiously motivated politics in some Western democracies, global migration, both organized and spontaneous, the Arab Spring of 2011, radical Islamic movements and regimes and the rise of conservative nationalist parties and governments in the United States, Great Britain, other Western European countries and Russia. The dilemma facing Orthodox in

---

[55] Ibid., 84.

[56] Georges Florovsky, 'The Social Problem in the Eastern Orthodox Church' (1950), in Georges Florovsky, *Christianity and Culture*, Vol. 2 of *The Collected Works of Georges Florovsky* (Belmont, MA: Nordland, 1974).

[57] Ibid., 131.

[58] Ibid., 138.

[59] Ibid.

liberal democracies at the beginning of the twenty-first century was not dissimilar to that facing Christian thinkers in late imperial Russia: How to support commendable social programmes and goals, and the noble ideals (if often ignored in practice) of democratic states without approving the secular philosophies which lay behind them.

One of the upshots of social and political tendencies of the early twenty-first century was the emergence of a wide range of thinking in Orthodox circles about the relationship of Orthodoxy to the political sphere, or to civil society in general, under the broader umbrella of Orthodox thinking on modernity. This is well illustrated in the diversity of views expressed by Orthodox scholars in the book *Political Theologies in Orthodox Christianity: Common Challenges – Divergent Positions* (2017).[60] The editors (Kristina Stoeckl, Ingeborg Gabriel and Aristotle Papanikolaou) group the essays under two broad categories: those representing 'church-centered perspectives, considering which politics, if any, the church supports' and those representing 'world-centered perspectives, seeing the church as related to the political, as part of civil society or as an institutional partner with the state'.[61] The first category contains theologies grouped under the headings of 'prophetic' and 'ecclesial', and the second, under the headings of 'civic and symphonic'. But even the wide range of views among the contributors to this volume does not exhaust the full range of approaches to political theology represented in early twenty-first-century theology. By and large, all the authors share a modernist viewpoint to church-state relations, even when they analyse more conservative or neo-traditional thinkers in Bulgaria, Romania, Russia and Serbia.[62] One must look elsewhere for voices advocating, for example, more authoritarian and ethically dominated politics under the guidance of the national Orthodox Church.

Most Orthodox thinking on modernity falls into two broad categories. First, a neo-traditionalist maximalism which denounces and rejects modernity in all its ramifications because of its perceived anti-religious if not atheistic origins, notably in the Enlightenment, and its rationalistic perspective, which evacuates the mystical or the transcendental, resulting in a de facto positivist view of the world, the relegation of religion to the private domain, a secular state and an individualism which prizes the subjugation of the world, including the human body, to the satisfaction of desires. This ethos is seen as incompatible if not openly hostile to Orthodox thinking and practice, notably in personal and social ethics in such areas as sexuality, especially homosexuality, gender theory and practice, human reproduction and abortion and the end of life. Neo-traditionalist proponents of anti-modernism are often hard put to propose viable alternatives to living in the modern world as we find it, although an alternative appears to be emerging in post-Communist Russia under Vladimir Putin (b. 1952). In Greece, Christos Yannaras (b.1935) is often assimilated to an anti-modernist stance (although this is a partial distortion of his thinking), as are neo-traditionalists

[60]Kristina Stoeckl, Ingeborg Gabriel and Aristotle Papanikolaou, eds., *Political Theologies in Orthodox Christianity: Common Challenges – Divergent Positions* (London: T&T Clark, 2017). The introduction by the editors and the essay by Kristina Stoeckl ('Modernity and Political Theologies') relate the range of approaches to political theology to attitudes towards modernity.

[61]Stoeckl, Gabriel and Papanikolaou, eds., *Political Theologies in Orthodox Christianity*, 7.

[62]For discussions on church-state relations, see Stoeckl, Gabriel and Papanikolaou, eds., *Political Theologies in Orthodox Christianity*, Chs. 10 and 15 (Russia); 11 (Serbia); 16 (Romania) and 17 (Bulgaria).

such as Father Seraphim Rose (1934–82) and Metropolitan Hierotheos (Vlachos) of Nafpaktos (b. 1945). In Russia, the official stance of the ROC is also anti-modernist.[63]

Political theology in this perspective consists in seeking to encompass the political within the religious, as a bulwark against the disruptive forces of modernity, with the state becoming an agent for the promotion of religious objectives. It seeks to preserve or to re-connect, as Kristina Stoeckl expresses it, the religious context of the individual and the society with the wider cultural context, often by idealizing a past, such as the Byzantine and the Russian empires, when religion and culture/society supposedly coincided. Such political theologies typically endeavour to preserve a privileged role of the local Orthodox Church in society and public affairs, often limiting the rights of other religious bodies, and to impose religious ethical norms on the entire society.[64]

The second approach to modernity recognizes most of the weaknesses of modernity identified by the proponents of neo-traditionalism. But it also discerns that modernity nonetheless reflects certain Christian and Orthodox values and that it provides an environment in which Orthodoxy, Christianity and religion, in general, can not only survive but perhaps even flourish. This inclusive approach accepts the reality of modernity, for better and for worse, and seeks, not surrender or compromise of fundamental beliefs and principles, but a nuanced relationship to particular aspects of modernity, identifying the divine presence wherever it is to be found, and illuminating with the light of Christ where it is weak or absent. This prophetic and eschatological realism is a fulfilment of the vision of Alexander Bukharev, in direct line with the social and political thinking of Vladimir Soloviev, Nicolas Berdyaev and Sergius Bulgakov, as we discussed above.

Political theologies based on this assessment of modernity accept that the modern state is religiously neutral but nonetheless includes, or should include, certain values and practices which allow religious actors such as churches to have a voice in determining state policy and programmes. In this light, religious freedom, as an essential component of human rights, is not inimical to Christianity or to Orthodoxy, but rather an assurance that believers may continue to exercise their religious convictions and practices, even as a minority in largely non-religious societies, and to make their voices heard as alternatives to a dominant secular culture.

Our discussion here focuses primarily on two Orthodox theologians whose thinking embodies, in different ways, a prophetic and eschatological or ecclesial approach to modernity, consistent with Orthodox thinking on the 'churching' or 'Christification' of life presented in Chapter 13. Pantelis Kalaitzidis (b. 1961) and Aristotle Papanikolaou (b. 1967) are among Orthodox theologians coming to maturity at the beginning of the twenty-first century. Well aware of the inadequate

---

[63]See the discussion on Christos Yannaras in Ch. 6, 141–4. Also for Greece, see Pantelis Kalaitzidis and Nikos Ntontos, eds., *Orthodoxía kai neoterikótita* (Orthodox Christianity and Modernity) (Athens: Indiktos Publications, 2007); and the separately published Introduction by Pantelis Kalaitzidis: *Orthodoxía kai neoterikótita: Prolegómena* (Orthodoxy and Modernity: An Introduction) (Athens: Indiktos Publications, 2007); Trine Stauning Willert, *New Voices in Greek Orthodox Thought: Untying the Bond between Nation and Religion* (Farnham, Surrey: Ashgate, 2014), 72; Vasilios N. Makrides, '"The Barbarian West": A Form of Orthodox Christian Anti-Western Critique,' in Andrii Krawchuk and Thomas Bremer, eds., *Eastern Orthodox Encounters of Identity and Otherness: Values, Self-Reflection, Dialogue* (New York: Palgrave Macmillan, 2014). For Russia, see especially Kristina Stoeckl, *The Russian Orthodox Church and Human Rights* (London: Routedge, 2014).

[64]See Stoeckl, 'Modernity and Political Theologies', 19–23.

treatment of social and political issues in neopatristic theology, they have ventured boldly into the minefield of political theology. To these should be added notably Athanasios N. Papathanasiou (b. 1959), less well known outside Greece, whose liberation political theology we considered in Chapter 6.

In *Orthodoxy and Political Theology* (2012), Pantelis Kalaitzidis argues that the heavy weight of past relations between the Orthodox Church and political regimes prevented the emergence of a political or 'liberation' theology.[65] Orthodoxy's close association with the imperial regimes in Byzantium and tsarist Russia resulted in an integration of church and state, with the detrimental effect that the church lost sight of its fundamentally eschatological nature and mission, focusing instead on its role in the state; the 'not-yet' became subordinate to the 'already' in the proclamation of the Good News of the New Testament. The political responsibility of the Orthodox Church for Christians in the Ottoman Empire actually re-enforced tendencies to confound the church with the power structure of the day. Later, as the peoples of Orthodox tradition sought to free themselves from Ottoman domination, Orthodoxy became identified as an important element, if not the key component of ethnic national identity, whether in Greece, Serbia, Romania, Bulgaria and, in a different context, even in Russia, especially in post-Communist era. In this situation, argues Kalaitzidis, the Christian identity 'does not refer to participation in the Eucharistic and eschatological community which is the church', but rather to

> a pre-determined collective reality whose borders are co-extensive with borders of the nation and in which the label 'Christian' does not necessarily include any criteria or ecclesiological requirements for personal or social life, but is connected with traditional cultural and historical designations.[66]

Thus on the one hand, Orthodoxy is marked by a 'flight from history' (Kalaitzidis is especially critical of Christos Yannaras and John Zizioulas (b. 1931) in this respect), in the sense of a refusal to recognize the realities of the Byzantine and Russian empires, and yet simultaneously by an entrapment 'in a purely ethnocentric dimension operating exclusively within history'. The result is 'the identification of the religious with the national and ethnic identity with Christian identity'.[67]

Kalaitzidis enmeshes neopatristic theology in this conundrum: the focus in neopatristic theology on a 'return to the Fathers' and the effort to 'de-westernize' Orthodox theology, 'overshadowed all other theological questions, as well as challenges the modern world had posed – and continues to pose – to Orthodox theology'.[68] Kalaitzidis advances the proposition that the failure of Orthodox theology to develop a meaningful political theology, and the accompanying inadequate response to modernity and social issues, is 'the lack of a democratic ethos and a culture

---

[65]Pantelis Kalaitzidis, *Orthodoxy and Political Theology* (Geneva: WCC Publications, 2012), passim, especially Chapter 3, 'Why Has Orthodoxy Not Developed a Political or Liberation Theology?', 65–80.

[66]Kalaitzidis, *Orthodoxy and Political Theology*, 69.

[67]Ibid., 68.

[68]Ibid., 75–6. See also 89–90. Kalaitzidis excuses Georges Florovsky from this critique of neopatristic theology (89), but he does not specify which neopatristic theologians he is criticizing. See also Kalaitzidis's article 'From the "Return To The Fathers" To the Need For a Modern Orthodox Theology', *St Vladimir's Theological Quarterly*, 54, 1 (2010), especially 5–10.

of dialogue and deliberation'.[69] Tradition became conservatism, bound up in nostalgia for the Orthodox past of Byzantium, Russia, Romania or Serbia, with the result that 'Orthodox are thus usually unable to engage in serious theological reflection and to participate equally and creatively in the contemporary world.'[70]

Kalaitzidis does not marshal adequate evidence to sustain his often blunt and sweeping conclusions concerning the unfortunate association of Orthodoxy and religious and ethnic nationalism. Relevant evidence is nonetheless abundant, especially in case studies on the often unhealthy relationships between local Orthodox churches and national political regimes, whether of the right or the left, in major countries of Orthodox tradition, especially Greece, Romania and Russia.[71]

For Kalaitzidis, the solution to this nexus of problems in contemporary Orthodox thought is the re-affirmation of eschatology at the heart of Orthodox theology and ecclesiology: The church's mission is to promote the Kingdom of God, which can only be partially attained in this world and is certainly not identified with any particular political regime nor fused with an ethnic or national identity. The full achievement of the church will be in the Kingdom of God to come, the eschatological accomplishment of the church as the Body of Christ. Thus, major manifestations of the Orthodox tradition such as the Eucharist and iconography are profoundly eschatological, 'a foretaste and proleptic manifestation of the *eschaton*'.[72] He sees Orthodox involvement in politics largely in social terms, the promotion of a threefold 'way of love, freedom and charismatic service', as 'a foretaste, glimpse and witness of and to another life', the transformation of politics with the eschatological perspective of the church.[73] This is contrasted with 'the way of power', characterized by force, domination and legal or institutional coercion, ideas to which the church is exposed and all too often falls prey. Kalaitzidis somewhat timidly here states that Orthodoxy must acknowledge and accept 'the achievements of Western modernity and the reality of multicultural societies'.[74]

In some ways Aristotle Papanikolaou's book *The Mystical as Political* (2012) carries on where Pantelis Kalaitzidis leaves off. Papanikolaou shows his colours from the outset, unequivocally endorsing 'a political community that is democratic in a way that structures itself around the modern liberal principles of freedom of choice, religious freedom …, the protection of human rights … and church-state separation'.[75] Papanikolaou grounds his endorsement of liberal

---

[69]Kalaitzidis, *Orthodoxy and Political Theology*, 54.

[70]Ibid., 90.

[71]Prominent are studies of the relationship between the local Orthodox churches and political regimes during and after the communist period, especially in Romania and in Russia. Notable examples include Lucian Leustan, *Orthodoxy and the Cold War: Religion and Political Power in Romania* (Basingstoke: Palgrove Macmillan, 2009); Lavinia Stan and Lucian Turcescu, *Religion and Politics in Post-Communist Romania* (Oxford: Oxford University Press, 2007); Kristina Stoeckl, *The Russian Orthodox Church and Human Rights* and Katya Tolstaya, *Orthodox Paradoxes: Heterogeneities and Complexities in Contemporary Russian Orthodoxy* (Brill: Leiden & Boston: Brill, 2014). On Greece see the references in Ch. 6, n. 95, 153.

[72]Kalaitzidis, *Orthodoxy and Political Theology*, 102.

[73]Ibid., 119; 135. The triad love-freedom-service recurs at 123, 125, 127, 128 and 135.

[74]Kalaitzidis, *Orthodoxy and Political Theology*, 136.

[75]Aristotle Papanikolaou, *The Mystical as Political: Democracy and Non-Radical Orthodoxy* (Notre Dame, IN: University of Notre Dame Press, 2012), 12.

democracy on traditional Orthodox thinking on theosis and modern Orthodox theologies of personhood and Eucharistic ecclesiology. But rather than use the always-problematic translations of theosis as 'deification' or 'divinization', Papanikolaou hinges his argument on theosis defined as 'divine-human communion'.[76] This definition immediately gets him into hot water for seemingly downplaying the more maximalist and eschatological connotations typically associated with theosis, closer to Kalaitzidis's thinking.

Papanikolaou's book is set in the context of mistrust and critique, even denunciation, in many Christian ecclesial and intellectual circles, especially among Orthodox neo-traditionalists, of liberal democracy and the related notion of human rights. The main critiques are typically that these ideas, arising from the Renaissance and more especially the Enlightenment, represent a denial of divine creation, human dependency on God and divine providence and that they promote individualism and the evacuation of religion from public life (see Chapter 10). In short, they are an attempt to erect humanity as the measure of all things, not the God-man of the Incarnation, but the man-god of a sinful humanity attempting to achieve divine status without God – the 'Godless Theosis' of Vigen Gurorian's scathing review of *The Mystical as Political*.[77]

Papanikolaou's daring thesis is that theosis defined as divine-human communion and Eucharistic ecclesiology is best achieved in a liberal democratic state:

> As Christians progress to realize the divine in their lives, then the inevitable result would be a liberal democratic form of political community.
>
> The logic of divine-human communion leads to the formation of a liberal democratic political community with a good internal to itself.[78]

Papanikolaou recognizes the limits from a Christian perspective of strictly humanistic arguments for democracy and human rights. He rejects the conclusion that this means an incompatibility or 'mutual exclusivity' between 'modern liberal notions of human rights and a theological anthropology based on the principle of divine-human communion'.[79]

While most of the book is devoted to critiques of the Christian detractors, both Orthodox and non-Orthodox, of liberal democracy and of human rights, Papanikolaou does not adequately demonstrate why theosis, however defined, should lead inevitably to liberal democracy as the most suitable political form for its realization. Yet such arguments are not lacking. As we saw in Chapter 13 and earlier in this chapter, Mother Maria (Skobtsova) anchors her advocacy of a Christian social theology squarely in Jesus' teachings, especially on the second Gospel commandment, and patristic

---

[76]See the discussion on theosis in Georges Florovsky, 'St Gregory Palamas and the Tradition of the Fathers' (1960), in Brandon Gallaher and Paul Ladouceur, eds., *The Patristic Witness of Georges Florovsky: Essential Theological Writings* (London: T&T Clark, 2019). Florovsky notably writes: 'Only the word *theosis* can render adequately the uniqueness of the promise and offer. The term *theosis* is indeed quite embarrassing, if we would think in "ontological" categories. … It is that intimate intercourse of man with God, in which the whole of human existence is, as it were, permeated by the Divine Presence.' Florovsky, 'St Gregory Palamas', 229.
[77]Vigen Gurorian, 'Godless Theosis: A Review of *The Mystical as Political*', *First Things* (April 2014). www.firstthings.com/article/2014/04/godless-theosis (5 February 2017). For a more balanced review of *The Mystical as Political*, see Athanasios Giocas, 'Christian Practice as the Foundation for Modern Political Theology', *Journal of Law and Religion*, 30, 1 (2015).
[78]Papanikolaou, *The Mystical as Political*, 80, 144. See also his earlier article 'Byzantium, Orthodoxy and Democracy', *Journal of the American Academy of Religion*, 71, 1 (2003).
[79]Papanikolaou, *The Mystical as Political*, 87.

teachings on social justice and charity towards others. From patristic theology of the divine image in humanity and divine and human freedom, together with modern Orthodox thought on human personal existence, can be constructed powerful arguments for liberal democracy and human rights. At the same time, it must be recognized that Christianity survived and even flourished under the most improbable political regimes, including the pagan Roman Empire, the ancient Persian Empire, the Muslim Ottoman Empire and atheist Soviet Union and communist Eastern Europe. The witness of saints and martyrs in these regimes as the achievement of theosis or divine-human communion attests to the possibility of holiness even in the absence of modern notions of liberal democracy.

In his critique of *The Mystical as Political*, Vigen Guroian (b. 1948) brings to light several important weaknesses in Papanikolaou's central ideas, beginning with Papanikolaou's definition of theosis as 'divine-human communion'. For Guroian, this divorces theosis from 'its ecclesial and sacramental matrix' and from baptism in particular. While Guroian's critique is pertinent, behind it appears to lay the questionable assumption that theosis – or salvation for that matter – is only for Christians, and that we cannot say anything about the ultimate fate of non-Christians, but it certainly would not be theosis as perceived in Orthodox thinking. Papanikolaou's definition departs from the typical Orthodox attachment of the term to the expression in 2 Pet. 1.4, that Christians are called 'to become partakers of the divine nature', and to the patristic adage 'God became man so that man might become God.'[80] Certainly the very idea of theosis is problematic not only for non-Orthodox, but for many Orthodox as well. Perhaps a more fundamental problem with 'divine-human communion' is that on the surface it can be seen as reducing both the powerful spiritual impact of the idea of deification and its ultimate eschatological fulfilment to a more 'here-and-now' application.

Guroian's main critique, though, is that Papanikolaou has in effect sold the soul of Orthodoxy to liberal democracy and culture, offering, instead of Orthodox soteriology, 'the claptrack of diversity and political correctness', the 'secular battering rams' of the 'new ideology of "diversity and cultural difference".' Guroian is voicing a neo-traditionalist critique of Orthodox attempts to find an acceptable modus vivendi with Western liberal, secular, democratic and pluralist societies. Furthermore, argues Guroian, the witness of the Orthodox Church is 'to the eschatological kingdom of God ..., not one or another form of political regime' – a distant echo of Kalaitzidis's emphasis on eschatology.

The document of the Holy and Great Council of the Orthodox Church in June 2016 on 'The Mission of the Orthodox Church in Today's World' enumerates a broad range of modern issues which should fall within the purview of the church, and it includes a mild endorsement of human rights, an endorsement which is qualified by statements in the Council's Encyclical (see Chapter 10).[81] The Council documents are timid responses to the challenges of modernity, and

---

[80]The idea first occurs in St Irenaeus of Lyons (*Adv. haer.* V, Pref.): 'Our Lord Jesus Christ, who did, through his transcendent love, become what we are, that he might bring us to be even what he is himself.' But it is in the succinct formulation by St Athanasius of Alexandria in *On the Incarnation* (54:3) as quoted above that the adage is most well known.

[81]Holy and Great Council of the Orthodox Church, 'The Mission of the Orthodox Church in Today's World' and 'Encyclical of the Holy and Great Council of the Orthodox Church', (Crete GR, 2016). https://www.holycouncil.org (23 January 2018).

are replete with denunciations of secularism, consumerism and a host of specific evils which beset modern societies.[82] The Encyclical does nonetheless recognize a political aspect to the church's role in society: 'Her witness, however, is essentially political insofar as it expresses concern for man and his spiritual freedom.' It calls on local Orthodox churches 'to promote a new constructive synergy with the secular state and its rule of law within the new framework of international relations' (§ 16). This synergy must, however, 'preserve the specific identity of both church and state', a principle which appears to be compromised in the cases of established churches and where the church acts as a de factor agent of the state in promoting unquestioningly the state's domestic and international agendas.

A new symphonia?

In traditional Orthodox thinking, arising from the Byzantine Empire, the political theology of *symphonia* is characterized by the existence of two autonomous but interrelated sources of authority, the church and the empire. While each has its proper sphere and mode of activity, they overlap and collaborate for the furtherance of the Gospel and the Kingdom, yet without merging one with the other. Neither is subordinate to the other; the church does not absorb the state, nor the state the church. Historically this ideal situation was never fully achieved and was constantly put to the test, both in Byzantium and later in the Russian Empire. Although ecclesial leaders from time to time interfered inappropriately in matters of state, more typically ambitious rulers sought to co-opt the church as an agent of the state. In a classic case, after the clumsy attempt of Patriarch Nikon of Russia (1605–81) to meddle in state affairs in the mid-seventeenth century, Peter the Great (1672–1725) subsequently hobbled the ROC such that it could no longer do so (see Chapter 3). Peter's much-decried *Spiritual Regulation* abolished the patriarchate and established a state-appointed Holy Synod to govern the church. The resulting subordination of the church to the state was a *pseudo-symphonia*, a clear departure from the Byzantine ideal of two autonomous yet interrelated and cooperating centres of authority.

A somewhat similar situation occurred during the communist periods in Russia and Eastern Europe. The church no longer operated as an autonomous agent, but was subject to state control on matters of internal and external state policy and church governance, for example in terms of the appointment of senior hierarchs, the discipline of dissident and recalcitrant clergy and control of monasticism and theological education.

[82]Paragraph B.2 of 'The Mission of the Orthodox Church in Today's World' mentions 'secularism; violence; moral laxity; detrimental phenomena such as the use of addictive substances and other addictions especially in the lives of certain youth; racism; the arms race and wars, as well as the resulting social catastrophes; the oppression of certain social groups, religious communities, and entire peoples; social inequality; the restriction of human rights in the field of freedom of conscience – in particular religious freedom; the misinformation and manipulation of public opinion; economic misery; the disproportionate redistribution of vital resources or complete lack thereof; the hunger of millions of people; forced migration of populations and human trafficking; the refugee crisis; the destruction of the environment; and the unrestrained use of genetic biotechnology and biomedicine at the beginning, duration, and end of human life'.

Russia under the rule of Vladimir Putin bears examination in this light. Vladimir Putin rose through the ranks of the Soviet secret police, the notorious KGB, and through the civil administrations of Leningrad and Moscow to become President of Russia in 2000. After the constitutional two four-year terms, Putin stepped into the shadows as Prime Minister from 2008 to 2012, only to return to the presidency for six-year terms beginning in 2012 and 2018. From 2000 onwards he exercised virtually unlimited powers over the executive, the legislature, the judiciary and the media, with only token criticism and opposition permitted. Putin has played the nationalist card, a mild pan-Slavism in the case of Russian support for Serbia during the Kosovo independence crisis and NATO bombing of Serbia (1999). But a powerful Great Russian ethnic nationalism emerged in Russia, fanned by the Putin regime, in the Russo-Georgian crisis over South Ossetia and Abkhazia (2008), the Russian annexation of the Crimea (2014) and support for pro-Russian separatists in Eastern Ukraine (2014). Barely hidden is the ambition to restore the now-independent former Soviet republics to renewed Russian domination and rule.

In parallel with the political and economic turmoil that followed the fall of communism and the rise of Putin to supreme power, the ROC shook off the remaining constraints of seven decades of communist rule. The 1988 celebration of the millennium of the baptism of ancient *Rus'* in 988 marked the end of Soviet persecution of the church. The ROC rapidly revived, strengthened by millions of converts, the reopening of churches and monasteries and the construction of new ones. From the initial heady days of the 'springtime of the faith'[83] in the early 1990s, the church found itself confronted with a society still deeply infected with the wounds imposed by the long communist rule, increasing Western social and cultural influence, and a catastrophic economic situation, until prosperity began to return after 2000, thanks to high energy prices. Senior church officials quickly realized that a weakened Russian society was threatened not only by the heritage of communist atheism but also by Western influences in the form of liberalism, secularism, consumerism, bound up in a non-theistic humanist philosophy typified especially in human rights, democracy and the religious neutrality of the state. In response, the ROC posed itself as the champion of traditional religious, social and national values against these unwanted Western influences.

Church officials, led by Patriarch Kirill (Gundaev) (b. 1946, patriarch since 2009) and Metropolitan Hilarion Alfeyev (b. 1966) see the global geo-political-religious scene as a clash between 'liberalism or "militant secularism" with tradition or traditionalism and the search for a harmonization of human rights (which are often simply identified with secularism) with "traditional" and "eternal" Christian values'.[84] The discourse of anti-modernism, anti-secularism, anti-Westernism and anti-human rights (as understood in the West), and the replacement of these perceived dubious or outright evil values by Orthodox values, is accompanied by heavy doses of

---

[83]See the sympathetic account of the resurrection of the Russian church in Irène Semenoff-Tian-Chansky, *Printemps de la foi en Russie: Les chrétiens de Gorbatchev à Poutine* (The Springtime of Faith in Russia: Christians from Gorbachev to Putin) (Paris: Éditions St-Paul, 2000).

[84]Brandon Gallaher, 'A Tale of Two Speeches: Secularism and Primacy in Contemporary Roman Catholicism and Russian Orthodoxy', in John Chryssavgis, ed., *Primacy in the Church: The Office of Primate and the Authority of Councils*, vol. 2 (Yonkers, NY: St Vladimir's Seminary Press, 2016), 816.

selective moralism[85] and Russian nationalism. Both church and state function to restore Russia to its former greatness during the imperial era and under communism, and to radiate Russian influence throughout the Orthodoxy and in the world. The principal obstacles which stand in the way of this Russian crusade are 'the West', Western Europe and the United States, and the Orthodox churches which look to the Ecumenical Patriarch as the Orthodox centre of gravity. Other obstacles include immigrants of Russian descent in the West who prefer to keep their distance from the current stance of the ROC – especially the Archdiocese of ROC in Western Europe (under the Patriarchate of Constantinople).[86]

An important vehicle of the new Russian church-state ideology is the foundation *Russkii mir'* (Russian World), which Putin established in 2008. On the surface, *Russkii mir'* can be compared with similar Western institutions such as the British Council, the *Goethe Institut* (Germany) and the *Alliance française* (France). These are often described as 'soft power' institutions, intended to promote abroad the national language and culture of the sponsoring country. *Russkii mir'* has an explicit ideology, articulated by senior church officials, geared to extending the worldwide influence of both Russia and the ROC.[87] Not far beneath the surface of this thinking is the notion of Moscow as the Third Rome, the leader of the Orthodox world, an idea which first appeared in the sixteenth century (see Chapter 3).

Accompanying and in some ways underpinning the promotion of a 'new symphonia *à la russe*' has been a revival and expansion of Eurasian philosophy originally developed by Russian exiles in Eastern Europe in the 1920s.[88] The core of Eurasian philosophy is that Russia belongs neither to the West nor to the East, but is a unique divine-human civilization situated between and above East and West and as such has a divine vocation to promote Orthodox and Russian values, and indeed hegemony, throughout the world. The geographic core of neo-Eurasianism is Russia, the Ukraine and Byelorussia, but also includes all the former Soviet Union. Alexander Dugin (b. 1962), a leading Eurasian ideologue, sees Russia as leading a veritable crusade against the decadent West, with the United States as the prime target and Western Europe as a potential vassal.[89] Russia is called to exercise global leadership to replace Western-style liberal democracy and human rights which have resulted in moral degradation and cultural decline with traditional Orthodox communal values and moral principles. Although the Russian church and government distance themselves from Dugin's more extreme views (which include 'national bolshevism', war against the Ukraine and calls for the destruction of American liberalism), the core of Dugin's Eurasian thinking has

---

[85]The ROC's moralism focuses on certain issues, especially sexual morality. The ROC is silent about other major moral questions in Russia such as the muzzling of opposition by any means including violence, political corruption and economic exploitation by Russia's oligarchs.

[86]This jurisdiction, based in Paris, placed itself under Constantinople in 1931, during the tenure of Metropolitan Evlogy (Georgiyevsky) (1868–1946). See Ch. 4, 90.

[87]For a discussion on *Russkii mir*, see Gallaher, 'A Tale of Two Speeches', especially 819–24.

[88]Georges Florovsky was associated with the Eurasian movement from 1920 to about 1925, but he subsequently broke with it. See Paul Gavrilyuk, *Georges Florovsky and the Russian Religious Renaissance* (Oxford: Oxford University Press, 2013), especially Ch. 4, 'The Eurasian Temptation', 60–79.

[89]See Anton Barbashin and Hannah Thoburn, 'Putin's Brain: Alexander Dugin and the Philosophy Behind Putin's Invasion of Crimea', Council on Foreign Relations (31 March 2014). www.foreignaffairs.com/articles/russia-fsu/2014-03-31/putins-brain (8 February 2016).

found its way into mainstream Russian ecclesial and state rhetoric, characterized as 'authoritarian in essence, traditional, anti-American, and anti-European', valuing religion and public submission and expansionist in outlook.[90]

According to the 'Bases of the Social Concept of the Russian Orthodox Church' (2000), the ROC does not accept an absolute separation of church and state, but rather mutual non-interference and collaboration:

> In the contemporary world, state is normally secular and not bound by any religious commitments. Its co-operation with the church is limited to several areas and based on mutual non-interference into each other's affairs. However, the state is aware as a rule that earthly well-being is unthinkable without respect for certain moral norms – the norms which are also essential for the eternal salvation of man. Therefore, the tasks and work of the church and the state may coincide not only in seeking purely earthly welfare, but also in the fulfilment of the salvific mission of the church.[91]

This mild expression of a minimal separation of church and state must be weighed against the unlimited and unconditional support of the ROC for the Putin regime and the Kremlin's unqualified support of the ROC both in Russia (for example, vis-à-vis other Christian denominations) and abroad (support for the ROC in its rivalry with the Ecumenical Patriarchate and the Archdiocese of ROC of Western Europe). Going beyond a simple superficial symphonia-like vision of church-state relations, Fr Vsevolod Chaplin (b. 1968), then head of the ROC's Synodal Department for the Cooperation of Church and State, sees a complementarity bordering on fusion, not separation, between church and state: 'The religious neutrality of the state is a fiction,' he stated in a 2012 interview. 'It has no basis in reality. I think the West made a mistake when it tried to completely separate these spheres. They are completely inseparable. The same people act in the sphere of politics and the sphere of religion.'[92] While there is no formal incorporation of the church into the state as during the Synodal period (from Peter the Great to the Russian Revolution), under Kirill and Putin the ROC is so intimately integrated into the state that the church appears to have lost its ability (and its willingness) to speak or act independently of state policy. The ROC is increasingly viewed as an integral part of a Russian propaganda offensive against the West, Putin's 'secret weapon': 'One of the Kremlin's most important new "soft-power" instruments is the Russian Orthodox Church,' writes one analyst, with a mission to undermine Western values, particularly universal human rights, democracy and freedom of expression, and to assume global leadership of the Orthodox Church.[93]

---

[90]Barbashin and Thoburn, 'Putin's Brain: Alexander Dugin'. See also Valentyna Hlushak, 'Alexander Dugin: "American Liberalism Must be Destroyed"'. www.uapost.us/blog/-american-liberalism-must-be-destroyed-alexander-dugin/ (15 February 2017).

[91]'Bases of the Social Concept of the Russian Orthodox Church' § III.3. www.mospat.ru/en/documents/social-concept (14 August 2015).

[92]Simon Shuster, 'The Priest Who Beat Pussy Riot: The Orthodox Point Man with the Kremlin' (*Time Magazine*, 20 August 2012). http://world.time.com/2012/08/20/the-priest-who-beat-pussy-riot-the-orthodox-point-man-with-the-kremlin (15 February 2017). See also Miriam Elder, 'God Is Judging Pussy Riot, Says Russian Church Leader' (*The Guardian*, 31 July 2012). www.guardian.co.uk/world/2012/jul/31/god-is-judging-pussy-riot (15 February 2017). Chaplin rose in Department for External Church Relations of the Moscow Patriarchate between 1990 and 2009, serving as vice-president from 2001 to 2009. Chaplin, an ultra-conservative, was dismissed from his ROC positions in December 2015 and he began criticizing Patriarch Kirill.

[93]Marcel Van Herpen, *Putin's Propaganda Machine: Soft Power and Russian Foreign Policy* (Lanham, MD: Rowman & Littlefield, 2016), 11. Part II of Van Herpen's book deals with the foreign policy role of the ROC: 'Creating a New Missionary Ideology: The Role of the Russian Orthodox Church', 127–75.

The ROC Bases of the Social Concept refers to the universal nature of the church (last paragraph, § II.1); the emphasis is clearly on the value of nation, ethnicity and the state (§ II.2 and II.3), with fulsome praise for 'Christian patriotism': 'The Orthodox Christian is called to love his fatherland, which has a territorial dimension, and his brothers by blood who live everywhere in the world' (§ II.3). The ideal state is 'an Orthodox nation': 'When a nation, civil or ethnic, represents fully or predominantly a monoconfessional Orthodox community, it can in a certain sense be regarded as the one community of faith – an Orthodox nation' (§ II.3). In the Russian context, this vision leaves little or no more room for non-ethnic Russians or non-Orthodox, and proves a basis for ROC criticism of Western pluralistic and religiously neutral democracies and its support for Russian to weaken them. Although the ROC document warns against 'national sentiments can cause such sinful phenomena as aggressive nationalism, xenophobia, national exclusiveness and inter-ethnic enmity' (§ II.4), there is little evidence of this attitude among the leadership of the Russian Church under Putin.

During the Soviet period, the upper echelons of the ROC were by and large unwilling mouthpieces of Soviet domestic and foreign policy, especially abroad, but in Putin's Russia, there is widespread voluntary submission of the hierarchy and large sectors of the clergy, monastics and the faithful to the state, with strong support for authoritarian rule centred on one person with unlimited power, subjugation of all sectors of society, especially the media, leading industries, the judiciary and even sport, to government control, all impregnated with generous doses of Russian nationalism. This is a break with the ideal of the Byzantine model of church-state relations and constitutes, not a new symphonia, but rather an example of a false symphonia.

Conclusion

The relationship of faith and the church to civil power structures has been on the agenda of Christianity since its origins, even in Jesus' teachings – 'Render unto Caesar the things that are Caesar's, and unto God the things that are God's' (Mt. 22.21). From earliest times the Fathers of the Church reflected on issues of church and society, church and state. Yet the very term 'political theology' requires elucidation – it is foreign to ancient Christian writings, and indeed to conventional textbooks of Orthodox dogmatic theology. A book on Orthodox political thought in the early twenty-first century offers these definitions of political theology: 'a theological approach to the political'; and 'the ways theologians conceive of the relationship of the church and the church's mission to bring about salvation in relation to the political sphere as a system of power and institutions'.[94] Thus political theology provides a framework or explanation to conceive of how the church relates to the state, ecclesial existence to non-ecclesial existence.

Much of modern Orthodox thought concerning social and political questions vacillates around three basic orientations. First, a profound engagement with contemporary social and political

[94]Stoeckl, Gabriel and Papanikolaou, eds., *Political Theologies in Orthodox Christianity*, 2.

issues; secondly, a detached and laissez-faire attitude which leaves many observers puzzled, dismayed or even outraged; and thirdly, a nostalgic wistfulness for a romanticized past typically identified with the Byzantine and Russian empires, overshadowed by the notion of *symphonia*, the ideal, never really achieved in practice, of the harmonious governance of a Christian ruler and the Orthodox Church over a Christian people in a Christian state.

A Christian perspective on social and political issues was one of the major themes of the Russian religious renaissance. The leading figures of this movement grappled with the problem of defining a Christian alternative to the immobility of the autocratic and authoritarian Russian state and its supporters in the upper echelons of the Russian Orthodox Church on the one hand, and atheistic and anti-religious philosophies which called for the overthrow of the imperial regime, and the church with it, and its replacement by a revolutionary regime, on the other hand. In Vladimir Soloviev and his successors, especially Nicolas Berdyeav and Sergius Bulkakov, we find the basis of a social and political theology consistent with evangelical precepts and the social and political thinking and actions of the early Fathers of the Church, especially St John Chrysostom and St Basil the Great. Although the leading philosopher-theologians of the religious renaissance did not always couch their thinking in explicitly Christian terms, their social and political thought flows from such fundamental theological and spiritual principles as the ontological equality of all human beings, the evangelical imperative of love of neighbour as a reflection of love of God, the uniqueness of the human person, and freedom as an aspect of the divine image in humanity. The leaders of the religious renaissance in exile after the Russian Revolution and the civil war deepened their reflection on these themes. Despite the bitter experiences of the revolution and exile, the most prominent of this group, especially Berdyaev, Bulgakov and Mother Maria Skobtsova, sought to accommodate their thinking to the new personal circumstances in which they found themselves, as a minority in Western states dominated by an ethos of state neutrality in religious matters and growing commitments to large-scale social programmes under state auspices.

A younger generation of Orthodox theologians, led by Georges Florovsky and Vladimir Lossky, had a different agenda from their predecessors. Their energies were directed first and foremost to defining Orthodoxy in relation to Western Christianity, which meant recovering those aspects of authentic patristic and Orthodox thought which had weakened or disappeared over the centuries since the fall of Constantinople in 1453, as a result of a wide range of Western influences. Fundamental theological issues such as the apophatism, divine energies, theosis, ecclesiology, pneumatology (the *filioque*) and anthropology dominated the neopatristic theological agenda, leaving little room for social and political issues, with some exceptions, such as Paul Evdokimov. Evdokimov had a foot in both the religious renaissance and neopatristic theology, and, like Mother Maria, he gave flesh to his social thinking by personal commitment and direct social action.

Attempts to formulate an Orthodox social and political theology in Romania, rather isolated from vibrant Orthodox thinking in Western Europe and North America, proved disappointing. Fr Dumitru Staniloae certainly ranks as one of the leading Orthodox theologians of the modern times, but his social and political thinking dipped dangerously into ethnic-religious nationalism, especially prior to the Second World War and after the fall of communism in Romania. The 'social apostolate', promoted by the Romanian Orthodox Church after the imposition of communist rule in 1948, was an attempt to blend evangelical and patristic reflection on church and state with Marxist ideology, a project destined for failure by its very premises (see Chapter 7).

With the onset of a new millennium, the weaknesses of neopatristic theology became increasingly evident, including its adequate attention to social and political issues. The neopatristic focus on core doctrinal issues appeared increasingly out of step with rapid technological changes and the growing social, ethnic and religious complexity of modern industrial and post-industrial societies. Large-scale trends such as secularization, the marginalization of religion, threats to security, growing social and economic inequalities and the erosion of civil liberties now appeared far more important than metaphysical doctrinal questions, which consumed much of Orthodox theological energy in the second half of the twentieth century. Younger Orthodox theologians turned increasingly to these issues as they explored new approaches to social and political theology.

The initial results of these trusts, in such figures as Pantelis Kalaitzidis, Aristotle Papanikolaou and Athanasios Papathanasiou, reflect bold thinking. Defence of liberal democracy, a theology of liberation and human rights, rank high on their agenda, with mixed results. In the Orthodox context, Papanikolaou goes out on a limb in opting so determinedly for liberal democracy as the best means of achieving what he refers to as divine-human communion (a new definition, inadequate for some, of the traditional notion of theosis). Since Orthodoxy has survived under a wide range of political regimes, one would be hard pressed to demonstrate that one regime has been more favourable than others to the furthering of salvation, the church's prime objective. Rather than attempting to prove that the logic of theosis 'leads to the formation of a liberal democratic political community',[95] a more modest ambition would be to demonstrate that liberal democracy and human rights are compatible with and indeed conducive to the goals of Orthodox theology and spirituality.

Orthodox defenders of human rights see rights as the best option available in a pluralistic and imperfect world, offering some safeguards not only for religious freedom, but more precisely for creating conditions favourable for the free development of full personhood as understood in contemporary Orthodox theology. This is recognized even in the ROC document on human rights: 'The political and legal institution of human rights can promote the good goals of protecting human dignity and contribute to the spiritual and ethical development of the personality [personhood].'[96]

Orthodox critics of democracy and human rights are noticeably short on alternatives – other than a romantic nostalgia for a largely mythical golden age of Byzantium or the Russian Empire. Indeed, a modern version of the Byzantine *symphonia* turns out to be the Russia of Vladimir Putin, characterized by authoritarianism, pseudo-democracy, ethno-nationalism and imperialist expansionism, garnished with a coating of Orthodox traditionalism. It is unlikely that even the most Orthodox of political regimes will successfully turn back the tide of secularization and accompanying depersonalization. Whatever the inadequacies and failings of Western-style

---

[95]Papanikolaou, *The Mystical as Political*, 80.
[96]Russian Orthodox Church, 'Basic Teaching on Human Dignity, Freedom and Human Rights', § III.5.

democracy and human rights, these must be weighed against the undesirable features of ideologies and regimes offered as alternatives.

Orthodox social and political theology is still in its infancy. The important legacy of the social and political thought of the Russian religious renaissance is half-forgotten, but still offers precious insights for Orthodox thinking in the early twenty-first century. Orthodox advocates of dialogue with Western-style liberal democratic philosophies find themselves under fire from within Orthodoxy by thinkers and even national Orthodox churches attracted by the notion of an Orthodox state standing in opposition to a Western ethos of secularism, separation of church and state and unrestricted human rights. In this atmosphere, the elaboration of a viable alternative vision of Orthodox social and political thinking featuring recognition of the social, ethnic and religious other as a child of God created in the divine image is an uphill battle.

As the church prays in the Divine Liturgy of St Basil:

> Remember, Lord, this country and all those in public service whom you have allowed to govern on earth. … Grant them profound and lasting peace. Speak to their hearts good things concerning your church and all your people that through the faithful conduct of their duties we may live peaceful and serene lives in all piety and holiness.[97]

[97]Greek Orthodox Archdiocese of North America, 'Liturgical Texts of the Orthodox Church'. https://www.goarch.org/chapel/texts/ (10 December 2018).

15

Onomatodoxy: The Name-of-God Conflict

Chapter Outline

Conflict on Mount Athos and in Russia over the Name of God

On Mount Athos and in Russia prior to the First World War, a major theological conflict took place over a doctrine known as 'Name-praising' or 'Name-glorification' (*onomatodoxy*, from the Greek; in Russian, *imenoslavie*). The Name-of-God conflict has its origins in 1907 with the publication of the book in Russia *Na Gorakh Kavkaza* (On the Mountains of the Caucasus), by Archimandrite Hilarion (Domratchev) (1845–1916).[1] The publication of the first edition of Schemamonk Hilarion's

[1]The full title of the book is *On the Mountains of the Caucasus. Discussions between Two Hermits on the Inner Union with the Lord of Our Hearts by the Prayer of Jesus Christ, or the Spiritual Practice of Contemporary Hermits. Composed by a Hermit of the Mountains, Forests and Canyons of the Caucasus.* The book has not been translated into English. French translation: Hieromonk Hilarion (Domratchev), *Sur les Monts du Caucase: Dialogue de deux Solitaires sur la Prière de Jésus* (On the Mountains of the Caucasus: Dialogue of Two Hermits on the Jesus Prayer) (Paris: Éditions des Syrtes, 2016). For a summary of the little that is known about Archimandrite Hilarion and a résumé of *Na Gorakh Kavkaza*, see G. M. Hamburg, 'The Origins of "Heresy" on Mount Athos: Ilarion's *Na Gorakh Kavkaza* (1907)', *Occasional Papers on Religion in Eastern Europe*, 23, 2 (2003); and the Preface by Metropolitan Hilarion (Alfeyev) to Hieromonk Hilarion, *Sur les Monts du Caucase*, 7–11.

book was financed by Grand Duchess Elizabeth Feodorovna (St Elizabeth of Russia, 1845–1918), aunt and sister-in-law of Tsar Nicolas II. The book was reprinted in 1910 and 1912 and reissued in Russia in 1998.

Archimandrite Hilarion's unsystematic book includes spiritual dialogues with his Elder, Desiderius, concerning mostly prayer, especially the Jesus Prayer; Hilarion's own development of related themes; descriptions of the Caucasus Mountains and their mystical significance; citations supporting Hilarion's assertions; meditations on the Gospel and selected spiritual correspondence. Like the popular anonymous *Pilgrim's Tale* (the 'Russian pilgrim' 1884), the book is in the Russian mystical and hesychastic tradition and its main subject is the Jesus Prayer: 'Lord Jesus Christ, Son of God, have mercy on me, a sinner.' Hilarion's teaching on Jesus Prayer corresponds to the Eastern Christian ascetic tradition, following closely teachings on the Jesus Prayer in the *Philokalia* (1782) and complementary presentations by St Ignatius Briantchaninov (1807–67) and St Theophanes the Recluse (1815–94).

It is Hilarion's audacious statements on the Name of God, a secondary theme in the book, which triggered the 'quarrel of the Name'. The main thesis of onomatodoxy is expressed in an abrupt and provocative formula borrowed from the popular pastor St John of Kronstadt (1829–1908), whom Hilarion cites: 'The Name of the Lord is the Lord himself … the Name of God the Almighty is God himself, the Spirit everywhere present and infinitely simple.'[2]

Hilarion writes:

> God is present in his holy Name with his whole being and his infinite properties. … For every faithful servant of Christ, loving his Master and Lord, praying fervently and bearing his Name piously and lovingly in his heart, this Name worthy of worship and all-powerful is what he is himself, namely the Lord Almighty, God and our very dear Redeemer Jesus Christ, born of the Father before all ages, consubstantial and equal to him in everything. … The Lord is a spiritual being, who must be contemplated in an immaterial fashion, and his Name as well. … It is impossible to separate the Name of our Lord Jesus Christ from his holy person. … We can only reside in him through prayer, by uniting our spirit and our heart to his most holy Name, in which he himself is present.[3]

---

[2]Cited by Hieromonk Hilarion, *Sur les Monts du Caucase*, 45. The citation is from John of Kronstadt's *My Life in Christ*. See *My Life in Christ: Extracts from the Diary of St John of Kronstadt* (London: Cassell & Co, 1897; Jordanville, NY: Holy Trinity Russian Orthodox Monastery, 1957), 430.

[3]Schemamonk Hilarion, *Na Gorakh Kavkaza*, cited in Hilarion Alfeyev, *Le Mystère sacré de l'Église. Introduction à l'histoire et à la problématique des débats athonites sur la vénération du nom de Dieu* (The Sacred Mystery: Introduction to the History and Problem of the Athonite Debates on the Veneration of the Name of God) (Fribourg, CH: Academic Press, 2007), 21. Alfeyev's study of the Name of God (Saint Petersburg, 2002) is translated into French in two volumes: *Le Nom grand et glorieux, La Vénération du Nom de Dieu et la prière de Jésus dans la tradition orthodoxe* (The Great and Glorious Name: The Veneration of the Name of God and the Jesus Prayer in the Orthodox Tradition) (Paris: Cerf, 2007), a general study of the divine Name in the Judeo-Christian tradition, and *Le Mystère sacré de l'Église*, which deals more specifically with the Athonite quarrel. Tom E. Dykstra's unpublished Master's thesis 'Heresy on Mt. Athos: Conflict over the Name of God among Russian Monks and Hierarchs, 1912-1914' (St Vladimir's Seminary, 1988) is a useful history of the conflict. For an examination of the Name of God in the context of a philosophy of names, see Helena Gourko, *Divine Onomatology: Name of God in Imyaslavie, Symbolism, and Deconstruction* (VDM Verlag: Saarbrucken/DE, 2009).

Hilarion developed no theological or philosophical arguments to support his statements; rather, for him, confirmation of the presence of God in his Name is based on the experience of ascetics after long years of practice of the Jesus Prayer.

Initially, the book received an enthusiastic welcome in both Russian monastic communities and among the Christian intelligentsia, even in some ecclesiastical circles. But two years later a controversy broke out on Mount Athos concerning Hilarion's statements on the Name of God, especially the statement 'the Name of God is God himself.' A negative review of Hilarion's book by a monk of the Russian skete of St Elijah on Mount Athos unleashed a storm of indignation among the Russian monks of Athos, who divided into two camps, the *imiaslavtsy*, favourable to Hilarion's teachings, and his opponents, called *imiabortsy* ('those who fight against the Name').[4] Hilarion's opponents considered his assertions idolatrous, bordering on pantheism and magic, as they seemed to deify the syllables and letters of the name of God, especially the name Jesus. They argued that the names of God are created realities, distinct from God, and therefore cannot be identified with God.

In 1912 the conflict spread to Russia, with both sides publishing articles and books in defence of their positions. Soon the supporters of Hilarion's ideas had rallied against them the Holy Synod of the Orthodox Church of Russia, the Russian government, most Russian media, which publicized only the texts of their opponents, the Holy Community of Mount Athos (which governs Mount Athos) and the Ecumenical Patriarchate. In April 1913, the Holy Synod of the Russian Orthodox Church (ROC) heard three reports on the issue, all negative to the doctrine. Proponents of the 'hard line' against the *imiaslavtsy*, led by Archbishop Antony (Khrapovitsky) (1864–1936), prevailed in Russia. In May 1913, the Holy Synod sent a pastoral letter to the *imiaslavtsy*, rejecting their doctrine, which it equated with 'magicism', endorsing the decision of the Ecumenical Patriarchate condemning the new doctrine as heretical and blasphemous, and calling on the *imiaslavtsy* to abandon the 'false wisdom' and to submit themselves humbly to Mother Church. A Synod delegation to Mount Athos, supported by Russian soldiers and a warship, obliged monks who declared themselves for onomatodoxy to board a steamship. The *imiaslavtsy* of the St Panteleimon monastery refused, offering passive resistance, which received a forceful response resulting in injuries and possibly even deaths. Some 833 monks were deported to Russia and subsequently other Russian monks voluntarily left the Holy Mountain; estimates range up to 1,500 monks in all, about half the Russian monks on Athos at the time.[5]

After 1913, the 'quarrel of the Name' was conducted entirely in Russia. The monks expelled from Athos were distributed in various dioceses, which extended the dissent throughout Russia. They were persecuted by religious and civil authorities, barred from communion and celebration of the sacraments, and most were stripped of their monastic robes and reduced to civil status. The harsh treatment meted out to the recalcitrant monks resulted in widespread public support and their cause was taken up in the press and specialized publications by a number of prominent Orthodox intellectuals, including Nicolas Berdyaev (1874–1948), Sergius Bulgakov (1871–1944),

---

[4]These are the names used by the supporters of the doctrine. *Imiabortsy* (*onamatomachi* in Greek) is derogatory. Archimandrite Hilarion was still alive when the storm broke, but no one, neither the Holy Synod nor the supporters of onomatodoxy, thought of asking him to elaborate on his ideas and his book. He died in 1916.

[5]See Hilarion Alfeyev, *Le Nom grand et glorieux*, 293.

Vladimir Ern (1881–1915), Pavel Florensky (1882–1937), Anton Kartashev (1875–1960), Alexei Losev (1893–1988) and Mikhail Novesolov (1864–1938).

Faced with evident sympathy of Nicholas II and other members of the royal family for the monks and the public uproar, the Holy Synod had no choice but to backtrack: the condemnations for heresy were abrogated and in May 1914 the Synod lifted excommunication for monks who signified that they accepted the dogmas of the Holy Church, and it referred the theological issue to a future Council. Onomatodoxy was on the agenda of the Council of the ROC which met in 1917–18 and a sub-commission of the Council, composed mostly of persons favourable to onomatodoxy, including Sergius Bulgakov, was appointed to deal with matter. The sub-commission had several meetings but did not complete its deliberations before the Council adjourned in September 1918, never to reconvene.

Several philosophers and theologians continued to reflect on the matter in the 1920s. An 'Onomatodoxy Circle' had a number of meetings in Moscow until 1925, when such gatherings became too dangerous and many participants had been arrested. Papers discussed at the meetings explored the linguistic, philosophical and theological aspects of onomatodoxy.

The inability of the Church Council of 1917–18 to deal with onomatodoxy resulted in a relative 'freezing' of the positions of the church hierarchy towards the *imiaslavtsy*, most of whom were never fully reintegrated into the church. Many *imiaslavtsy* were deported to or took refuge in the Caucasian Mountains, where they played an important role in maintaining the faith in certain villages and valleys. The Communists dealt with onomatodoxy in their fashion: they deemed the doctrine a subversive ideology and fabricated a vast 'clerical-monarchist conspiracy' aimed at overthrowing the Soviet government and restoring the monarchy, in which 'counter-revolutionary onomatodoxy' supposedly played a lead role. Between 1929 and 1931 many *imiaslavtsy* were rounded up in the Caucasus, their monasteries closed and they were deported or executed. In 1930, 148 'worshipers of the Name' interned at the Solovki concentration camp on an island in the White Sea, perhaps monks deported from Mount Athos, refused to work or even give their name. They were shot, hands bound behind their backs to prevent them from making the Sign of the Cross.[6]

The Soviets also persecuted the intellectual supporters of onomatodoxy still in Russia, including Alexei Losev and Mikhail Novesolov, who were sentenced in September 1931 to ten years in the camps and eight years imprisonment respectively. Pavel Florensky, arrested first in 1928 and released after a few years in exile, was sent to the camps in 1933, initially to the Urals then to Solovki. Losev was released in 1933 and continued his philosophical activities for the rest of his life, discreetly concealing his religious commitment. Some of his fellows from the 'Moscow Circle' of the early 1920s did not fare as well: Florensky was executed on 8 December 1937, and Novesolov sometime after January 1938.

The arrests, deportations and executions of many of the *imiaslavtsy* and their intellectual supporters in the late 1920s and 1930s effectively put an end to the quarrel of the Name in the Soviet Union, but philosophical and theological reflection on the issues raised during the quarrel continued in the exiled Russian intellectual community. Serious consideration of onomatodoxy,

---

[6]Pierre Pascal, *La Religion du people russe* (The Religion of the Russian People) (Lausanne: L'Âge d'homme, 1973), 128.

begun in the heat of the action in the years 1913–18, reached maturity in works of the 'Moscow Circle' of the early 1920s and in writings of Russian theologians in exile, notably Sergius Bulgakov and Archimandrite Sophrony (Sakharov) (1896–1993).

Theology of the Name

The quarrel of the Name was clearly more than a tempest in a theological pot of tea. In addition to the tragic human consequences on Mount Athos and in Russia before and after the First World War, major theological and canonical issues are involved. Archimandrite Hilarion, author of *On the Mountains of the Caucasus*, and his principal defender, Hieromonk Antony Bulatovitch (1870–1919), were ill-equipped to deal with the profound philosophical and theological issues at stake, as indeed were the opponents of the doctrine, who saw the matter primarily in terms of scholastically inspired academic theology and ecclesial authority and discipline. From Hilarion's emphasis on spiritual authority of the elders, the *startsy*, and his apparent disregard of the institutional church, ecclesial authorities could feel threatened in their role as consecrated official leaders of Orthodoxy.[7] It was thus the members of the religious intelligentsia who identified the underlying issues and worked towards possible solutions.

We shall consider the thinking of four leading intellectuals, philosopher-theologians, who reflected in depth on the onomatodoxy controversy: Pavel Florensky, Alexei Losev, Sergius Bulgakov and Archimandrite Sophrony (Sakharov). Florensky and Bulgakov were married priests, Losev a lay philosopher, Sophrony a priest-monk who spent twenty years on Mount Athos. Florensky, Losev and Bulgakov were leading members of the Russian religious renaissance of the early twentieth century and they were direct participants in the debates on onomatodoxy in the 1910s. Their mature reflections on the issue date from the 1920s. Bulgakov's reflections on onomatodoxy were written in 1920–22, just prior to his expulsion from the Soviet Union, but they were only published posthumously in 1953, under the title *The Philosophy of the Name*.[8] Sophrony, although influenced by the religious philosophers, was closer to the Orthodox ascetic-mystic tradition than they were and his thinking on the Name of God was published in 1977, in the context of broad reflections on Orthodox spiritual life, especially prayer.[9]

Archimandrite Sophrony was not directly involved in the quarrel, but he heard a great deal about it after his arrival at the St Panteleimon Monastery in 1925. Sophrony was the disciple and biographer of St Silouan the Athonite (1866–1937), the most illustrious Russian monk of the Holy

[7]See Hamburg, 'The Origins of "Heresy" on Mount Athos', 33.

[8]Sergius Bulgakov, *Filosofiya imeni* (The Philosophy of the Name) (Paris: YMCA-Press, 1953). French translation: *La Philosophie du Verbe et du Nom* (The Philosophy of the Verb and the Name) (Lausanne: L'Âge d'homme, 1991). The Conclusion of this book is included in Sergius Bulgakov, *Icons and the Name of God* (Grand Rapids, MI: Eerdmans, 2012), together with a 'Post Scriptum to the Name of God: A Sophiological Interpretation of the Dogma of the Name of Jesus'.

[9]See Archimandrite Sophrony, *His Life Is Mine* (Crestwood, NY: St Vladimir's Seminary Press, 1977). The French version is not identical: *Sa Vie est la mienne* (Paris: Le Cerf, 1981). The original Russian text with additional material was published in Paris in 1990 under the title *O molitve* (On Prayer).

Mountain in modern times. Sophrony writes that the 'time of troubles' over onomatodoxy was a period in Silouan's life during which he engaged in a relentless struggle against vainglory and pride. Although Silouan 'carried constantly in his heart the most sweet Name of Christ – the Jesus Prayer never ceased its action in him – he notwithstanding distanced himself from all argument concerning the nature of this Name.'[10] Sophrony also states that Silouan, who lived at that time at Old Russikon (former site of the St Panteleimon Monastery), narrowly escaped being beaten by a fanatical supporter of onomatodoxy. From this incident, we can infer that Silouan was not favourable to the doctrine – although, as Hilarion Alfeyev points out, it is not possible to conclude that Silouan actively opposed the movement.[11] That Silouan was not deported to Russia in 1913 indicates that either he declared himself opposed to onomatodoxy, or he simply stayed out of sight during the troubles.

We will consider theological reflections on onomatodoxy under three major concepts or approaches: the Name as word, symbol, image and icon; the relevance of the distinction between divine essence and divine energies to the theology of the Name of God and the Name of God in religious experience. Although there are important differences among the thinkers in their use and application of these approaches to onomatodoxy, we shall present here a broad overview of their reflections.

The Name of God as word, symbol, image and icon

Several religious philosophers begin their consideration of onomatodoxy with an appeal to linguistics and semantics or the philosophy of language. Typically, this takes the form of an exploration of the relationship between the subject and the predicate in the key postulate of onomatodoxy, 'the Name of God is God himself.' It is in the context of a philosophy of the Name that Alexei Losev and Sergius Bulgakov elaborated their reflections on onomatodoxy. For example, Bulgakov notes that the word 'God' in the formula is a predicate, not an indication of a 'substantial identity' between the Being of God and the Name of God, but in the sense that 'the Name of God enters into the domain of the divine Being, that it is imbued with power, that it manifests what the Constantinopolitan Fathers called divine energy.'[12]

This is an important initial qualification, but a more fruitful approach focuses on the Name as symbol. A symbol is more than just a conventional sign (like a 'STOP' sign); it signifies or points to another reality which it invokes by means of a physical medium. The function of a symbol is thus to unite the perceiver of the symbol with that which is symbolized. Pavel Florensky sees the symbol as the 'union of two beings, two strata, one inferior, the other superior, a union in which the inferior

[10]Archimandrite Sophrony, *St Silouan the Athonite* (Crestwood, NY: St Vladimir's Seminary Press, 1991), 93.
[11]Alfeyev, *Le Mystère sacré de l'Église*, 84–5.
[12]Bulgakov, *La Philosophie du Verbe et du Nom*, 206.

encloses the superior within itself, allows itself to be penetrated by it, to become imbued with it.'[13] Thus the Name of God in some fashion, but not in an absolute sense, 'encloses' God within itself; it is penetrated and imbued by God.

Alexei Losev advances a philosophy which he called 'absolute symbolism', situated between 'absolute apophatism' (God is absolutely unknowable and does not reveal himself) and 'religious rationalism' (God reveals himself entirely, thus evacuating the divine Mystery). The Names of God are symbolic, 'revealing the infinite essence of God … living symbols of God who manifests himself, or in other words, God himself in his manifestations to his creation'.[14] Bulgakov adds: 'The sacred Name of God is a very holy verbal symbol. It is precisely from this idea of symbol and the symbolic nature of speech that we can seize the significance of the Name of God and the fact of the real presence of divine power in it.'[15] For Bulgakov it is not humans who name God but rather God names himself in human language. Like Florensky, Bulgakov considers that the Name of God is the product of divine-human synergy.

The Name of God is thus a symbol pointing to God himself and uniting the believer with God. The syllables and sounds of the Name are only the external 'envelope' of the symbol, which is contained in the *sense* or referent of the syllables and sounds, not in syllables and sounds themselves. That which a symbol invokes is somehow present in the symbol itself: hence God is mysteriously present in his Name, without being identified with it.

Bulgakov advances two other patristic notions to elucidate the nature of the Name of God, the image of God in humanity and the icon. He attaches considerable importance to the human facility to name things, a facility of divine origin (see Gen. 1.19-20):

> This onomato-poetic facility … represents an aspect of the divine image in humanity, which it possesses by essence. We can thus understand why humans have and create names, why they give a name to each and every thing and why they have names themselves. … Name in general (and the ability to name) reaches an ontological level inaccessible to the critique of psychology: the image of God in humanity, a component of its nature.[16]

Bulgakov develops extensively the idea that the Name of God is a verbal icon: 'The Name of God conceals itself at the same time that it reveals itself in speech, in our human parlance, in sound, which becomes a kind of icon of the Name, fearsome, incomprehensible and transcendental, of the "I" of God.'[17] The icon is 'developed Name' and just as there are many icons depicting Christ, there are many names of God, each of which represents 'the seal of the Name of God in speech'. Similar to icons, the names of God are the result of divine-human synergy: 'As in an icon, divine power and human speech join [in the names of God] without division and without confusion. Humans speak and name, but that which is named is given, it is revealed.'[18] For Bulgakov, the Name of God is

[13]Pavel Florensky, 'The Name of God' (July 1921), cited by Hilarion Alfeyev, *Le Mystère sacré de l'Église*, 316.
[14]Cited by Alfeyev, *Le Mystère sacré de l'Église*, 324; 328.
[15]Bulgakov, *La Philosophie du Verbe et du Nom*, 186.
[16]Ibid., 196.
[17]Ibid., 184.
[18]Ibid., 179.

superior to the icon because, as in the Eucharist, the Name is transformed, the natural is absorbed by the divine, whereas the icon remains external to the divine nature.

Archimandrite Sophrony picks up the idea that the revealed Names of God have a special quality: 'We know that not only the Name "Jesus" but also all the other Names revealed to us are ontologically linked with God. And we know this by experience in the church.'[19] Like Bulgakov, Sophrony points out that the sacraments, and in fact all Christian worship, are carried out by the invocation of the divine Names, above all that of the Holy Trinity. He also affirms the existence of the name Jesus prior to creation, contrary to the *imiabortsy*, who claim that it is a human creation: 'The Name "Jesus" was given by revelation from on high. It originates in the divine and eternal sphere and is in no way the product of human intelligence, even though it is expressed by a created word.'[20]

The concept of symbol or icon applied to the Name of God is certainly helpful, a starting point in a doctrine of the Name of God. But nonetheless it is limited, in that to consider a symbol itself divine is to run the risk of slipping into idolatry. A further refinement is necessary to eliminate this possibility. Thus the idea of symbol easily spills over into the distinction between the divine essence and the divine energies, to which all the religious thinkers on onomatodoxy appeal.

The Name of God as divine energy

The religious philosophers were quick to realize that the distinction between the divine essence and the divine energies is a crucial theological key to understanding onomatodoxy. Although this distinction is found in the Cappadocian Fathers in the fourth century, it was only fully developed by St Gregory Palamas in the fourteenth century during the quarrel over hesychasm. The Palamite theology of the divine energies was enshrined in decisions of councils of the Church of Constantinople between 1341 and 1351, but in subsequent centuries it was quietly 'forgotten' in Russian and Greek academic theology, which fell under the influence of Western theology, especially scholasticism. The doctrine of the divine energies, together with its concomitant doctrines, apophatism and divinization (theosis), was only revived in Orthodox theology beginning in the 1920s (see Chapter 5). The essence-energies distinction did not feature as basic theological elements of the *imiabortsy*, trained in the formal theology of the Russian academies.

The doctrine of the divine energies states that the divine essence, God-in-himself, is unknowable to any creature, whereas God makes himself known in creation by his divine energies, which are inseparable from the divine essence yet distinct from it. Humans know and experience God through his energies. The unknowability of the divine essence is the foundation of apophatic theology, while the experience of the divine energies, revelation and the Incarnation of the Logos of God are the basis not only of positive theology, but of all experience of God. There is a crucial

[19]Archimandrite Sophrony, *Sa Vie est la mienne*, 133. The English version is somewhat different. Compare Archimandrite Sophrony, *His Life Is Mine*, 108ff.

[20]Archimandrite Sophrony, *Sa Vie est la mienne*, 137.

corollary: divine energies are not created, they are God himself, 'operation, self-disclosure, self-revelation of the Divinity', in Florensky's words.[21] Energies are indeed God, but God is more than his energies.

It is in this context that supporters of onomatodoxy asserted that the Name of God is a divine energy. Florensky, for example, considers that the Name of God functions as a symbol and becomes the locus of a synergetic encounter between God and humans, the co-penetration of two energies, divine and human. He writes:

> The Name of God is God, but God is not name. God's essence is superior to his energy, even though this energy expresses the essence of the Name of God. ... The Name of God appears as a reality disclosing and manifesting the divine being. The Name of God is therefore superior to itself, it is divine and is thus God himself. ... Just as God is knowable, God is not limited by the knowledge that humans have of him, God is not name and his nature is not the nature of name.[22]

Losev's 'absolute symbolism' has characteristics typical of the essence-energies distinction, which encompass the experience and doctrine of noetic light of the Eastern mystics, and the Jesus Prayer, a prime locus of divine-human encounter. Building on a formula first put forward by Florensky, Losev advances these propositions: 'The Name of God is divine energy, inseparable from the very essence of God and is therefore God himself. However, God is other than his energies and his Name. God is neither his Name, nor name in general.'[23]

The notion that the divine energies are at once distinct from the divine essence yet inseparable from it is critical to understanding the application of the doctrine to onomatodoxy. Losev drives home his point by referring to several characteristic divine energies:

> The Light of God is inseparable from the divine essence, the Power of God is inseparable from the divine essence, the Perfection of God is inseparable from the divine essence, [hence] the energy of the divine essence is inseparable from God himself and is God himself; the Name of God is inseparable from the divine essence and is therefore God himself.[24]

The use of the Palamite essence-energy distinction with respect to the Name of God raises a subtle point: Is the Name of God *a divine energy as such* or *a manifestation of divine energy*, which remains transcendent to the Name? While some of our authors do not make this distinction, others merge the two notions or alternate between them. Bulgakov writes:

> The actions of God in the world and notably in humans reveal themselves as divine names (as shown by the wisdom of the Aeropagite [Pseudo-Dionysius]); these are manifestations of his energy. ... [The] 'attribution' of names is a manifestation of the energy of God and a human response. However, this manifestation is distinct from the energy while being at the same time inseparable from it. Distinct because it actualizes itself in humans and by human means; inseparable because, in keeping

[21]Cited by Alfeyev, *Le Mystère sacré de l'Église*, 316.
[22]Ibid., 317–19.
[23]Ibid., 325.
[24]Ibid., 327.

with the general nature of speech, a divine energy speaks of its own in humans, reveals itself by a word, and this, as a Name of God, is like its incarnation.[25]

Archimandrite Sophrony also appeals to the essence-energy distinction as the key to understanding the significance of the Name of God, especially the Name Jesus:

> As a vehicle of meaning and knowledge, as an 'energy' of God in his relation with the world and as his proper Name, the Name 'Jesus' is ontologically linked with him. … For us it is a bridge which unites us to him; it is channel by which we receive divine strength. Coming from the Holy God, it is holy and sanctifies us when we invoke it. … God is present in this Name as in a receptacle, as in a precious vase filled with perfume. Through it, the Transcendental becomes perceptibly immanent. As divine energy, it proceeds from the divine Essence and is itself divine.[26]

The Name of God as religious experience

Like Archimandrite Hilarion of the Caucasus, Archimandrite Sophrony writes of prayer, the Jesus Prayer in particular, and the Name of God from the perspective of a long monastic life devoted to prayer. Sophrony begins his consideration of the Jesus Prayer by citing Jesus' words, 'Until now you have asked nothing in my Name. … Most assuredly, I say to you, whatever you ask the Father in my Name he will give you' (Jn 15.24; 23).[27] Sophrony's main interest, like that of Hilarion six decades earlier, is to give a teaching on the Jesus Prayer, not specifically to expound a theology of the Name of God. Yet Sophrony's approach to the Jesus Prayer is certainly conditioned by the theology of the Name of God. His sympathies are clearly with onomatodoxy and he presents a theology of the Name very much in keeping with that of the religious philosophers. Sophrony was familiar with Bulgakov's *Philosophy of the Name* and, although he does not name Bulgakov, he draws on several themes and ideas from Bulgakov that contribute to his approach to the Name of God, particularly the Name Jesus, in the context of the spiritual experience of practitioners of the Jesus Prayer.

The religious experience of onomatodoxy arises from the invocation of the name of Jesus, which occupies a unique place among the names of God. Bulgakov in particular examines the name Jesus, which, just as the name Jevovah-Yahve was revealed to Moses (Exod 3.14), is a name revealed to the Virgin Mary (Lk. 2.31). But there is a radical difference between the two names, a difference which forms the basis of the invocation of the name of Jesus:

> If, in the Old Testament, the Name of God is terrifying and mysterious, that of Jesus is 'very sweet', while still full of power: by it we communicate with the love of God, we taste the grace of the divine Name. … For the Jew of old, the Name of God was like the summit of Sinai, surrounded by dark clouds and lightening, which only Moses approached; any invocation of the Name, other than in the formal rite fixed by the Law, was in error and sinful. The Name of Jesus is given 'at all times and at

---

[25]Bulgakov, *La Philosophie du Verbe et du Nom*, 173.
[26]Sophrony, *Sa Vie est la mienne*, 132–3.
[27]Ibid., 120.

> every hour' (concluding prayer of canonical Hours). We must be very conscious of this difference, this opposition, between the Name of the transcendent Divinity, distant and terrifying. ... and the Name of Jesus, of which every human heart is the temple, of which every member of the faithful is the priest.[28]

The Name Jesus is a divine-human Name, not the external 'envelope' of the Name, which can also be a simple human name, but only when it refers to Jesus the incarnate Logos. Just as the Logos 'became flesh and dwelt among us' (Jn 1.14), so also the pre-existent Name of Jesus became incarnate in Jesus the Christ. For Bulgakov, just as Christ is the universal human being, so also the Name Jesus is the universal Name, 'the Name of all names'.[29]

One of the crucial questions which arose in the onomatodoxy quarrel touched on the nature of prayer and more particularly on the efficacy of the invocation of the Name of God, especially the name Jesus, the heart of the Jesus Prayer. The *imiabortsy* argued that the efficacy of the invocation was contingent on the state of the person invoking the Name, on the fervour or personal disposition of the person praying. Bulgakov and others are strongly critical of this 'psychologism' or subjectivism as applied to prayer, arguing that God is present in his Name independently of the psychological or subjective dispositions of the person praying. The supporters of onomatodoxy apply an objective realism to the invocation of the Name of God and draw a parallel with the invocation of the Name of God in sacraments, especially the Eucharist: 'Just as the Holy Eucharistic Species are invariably Body and Blood of Christ, be this "for salvation" for some or "for judgement and condemnation" ... for others, so the Name of God is a divine energy, regardless of our attitude, pious or sacrilegious.'[30]

The issue penetrates to the very nature of prayer, the central act of all religion:

> Prayer becomes prayer to God, it acquires its objective value as the union of the human being with God precisely because of the presence of God in prayer, due to the indwelling, simultaneously transcendental and immanent, of the Name of God. This is the ontological foundation, the substance, the virtue, the significance of prayer. ... All prayer is miracle, if we mean a rupture into the immanent and a piercing of the transcendental. This miracle is the Name of God , which is the Divinity.[31]

Hence liturgy is characterized by ontological objectivity; it is not dependent on the 'disposition of the spirit' of the celebrants, but is accomplished 'in the Name of God', Father, Son and Holy Spirit, 'not as a metaphor, as the *imiabortsy* think, but as a mystical reality'.[32] More specifically, the formula of John of Kronstadt picked up by Archimandrite Hilarion

> simply signifies that the Name is divine, that it participates in the domain of the energies of God ... The Lord is present by his energy, by his 'simplicity', by the indivisibility of his natures. ... The presence of [the Divinity One] ... manifests the eternal and inaccessible mystery of the divine

[28]Bulgakov, *La Philosophie du Verbe et du Nom*, 200–1.
[29]Ibid., 197–8.
[30]Ibid., 202.
[31]Ibid.
[32]Ibid., 203.

Incarnation and condescendence, the mystery of the presence of God in his Name, confirmed by the sacrament of prayer.[33]

Archimandrite Sophrony is more cautious about dismissing entirely the psychological or personal aspect of prayer. A *starets* (spiritual father) himself, Sophrony, like his religious philosophy predecessors, distances himself from any hint of attributing magical power to the words themselves of prayer, including the Jesus Prayer, but he nonetheless stresses the importance of the attitude of the devotee in prayer:

> When pray conscious of what we have just said, our prayer becomes a formidable act, and at the same time a triumphant one. … We do not attribute magical power to the words [of the divine Names] as such, as audible phenomena, but when they are pronounced as a true confession of faith and in a state of fear of God, reverence and love, then in truth we have God together with his Names.[34]

Sophrony speaks of the power of the Name from personal experience that can only be termed mystical; at times he is circumspect, at times more direct:

> Now that the most profound sense of all divine Names has been unveiled by Christ's coming, we also should tremble – as this happens to numerous ascetes among whom I had the possibility of living – when we pronounce the holy Name of Jesus. An invocation of the divine Name fills our entire being with the presence of God, transports our intellect to other spheres, communicates a special energy and a new life to us. A divine light, of which it is not easy to speak, accompanies this Name.[35]
>
> I remember starting the Lord's prayer, 'Our Father', and my soul swooned in blissful awe. I could not continue. My mind stopped, everything in me fell silent. … Only once did it happen to me with such force. … Some time afterwards, something similar happened to me when I was invoking the Name of Jesus Christ. I was obliged to stop pronouncing his Name: the effect was too much for me: my soul, without word, without thought, trembled at the nearness of God. … The following day I celebrated the Liturgy and Christ-God was in me and with me and outside of me and in the holy sacraments of his Body and Blood. And the divine Name and the words of the liturgical texts issued from my mouth like a flame. I continued in this state for three days.[36]

As a general remark it should be stressed that onomatodoxy is not a dogmatic pronouncement of the Orthodox Church, and should not be examined under a theological microscope as dogma or heresy. Rather, it is an attempt, no doubt feeble and inadequate, as is any endeavour to put words on ineffable mystical experience, to express the experience of invocation of the Name of God and more particularly the Name Jesus in the life of prayer. As pre-revolutionary theologian Eugene Troubetskoy (1863–1920) wrote in 1913 after reading Bulatovitch's *Apology*:

---

[33]Ibid., 206.
[34]Sophrony, *Sa Vie est la mienne*, 133.
[35]Ibid.
[36]Archimandrite Sophrony, *On Prayer* (Crestwood, NY: St Vladimir's Seminary Press, 1998), 47.

> I read Bulatovitch's book and am increasingly persuaded that the key to the problem lies not in this weak and clumsy theology, but in life, which is profound and elevated and does not reduce itself to this theology. One has only to draw near to feel the warmth and joy that radiates from it.[37]

Conclusion

The 'quarrel of the Name' was a tragic confrontation between two visions of the Christian life, two modes of spirituality, two theologies, two traditions in the Russian Orthodox Church: the academic-moral tradition, to which belonged most of the church hierarchy, characterized by a rational approach to theology inherited from Western scholasticism; and the ascetic-mystical tradition, which traces its pedigree back to the Desert Fathers, through the long history of Orthodox spirituality and monasticism, resurfacing dramatically in the 'Philokalic revival' in Orthodox spirituality, stimulated by the publication of the *Philokalia* in 1782, which reached deep into the Russian soul in the nineteenth century. Throughout most of the nineteenth century these two groups maintained a state of peaceful coexistence, but Archimandrite Hilarion's book *On the Mountains of the Caucasus* struck a sensitive chord and ultimately represented a challenge that some hierarchs could not ignore, both for personal reasons and for the prestige and authority of the ROC.

The conflict between the two groups brought to light another fundamental division that developed in the second half of the nineteenth century, between the church hierarchy and the intelligentsia. Large segments of the Russian nobility, the upper classes and the intelligentsia had deserted the church by the end of the nineteenth century. The basic programme of the intelligentsia, the overthrow of the imperial regime, put it at odds with the church, closely identified with the detested monarchy. The late nineteenth century nonetheless saw the flowering of a remarkable religious renaissance among leading members of the intelligentsia, as we discussed in Chapter 4, but the church was even unable to see eye to eye with this true Christian intelligentsia. It was members of this group, Pavel Florensky, Sergius Bulgakov, Alexei Losev and others who flew to the rescue of the beleaguered *imiaslavtsy*, unable to express adequately the philosophical and theological underpinnings of their spiritual experience concerning the Name of God.

The conflict over the Name of God recalls the great fourteenth-century quarrel over hesychasm, in which Mount Athos was also the centre of the storm. The issue then was not dissimilar to that of the early twentieth century: the claim of the hesychasts who asserted that they had a real experience of God in their prayer life, experience sealed by visions of Divine Light, was confronted by a theology inspired by the humanism of the early Renaissance, which denied that it was possible for humans to have a real experience of God, who is unknowable. In the fourteenth century, St Gregory Palamas, himself an Athonite, became the articulate spokesman of the hesychasts, especially by developing the idea latent in Eastern Christian theology since the Cappadocian Fathers, the

[37] Cited by Alfeyev, *Le Mystère sacré de l'Église*, 382.

distinction between the divine essence and the divine energies. But the twentieth-century hesychasts had no Gregory Palamas in their midst and it was their supporters among the Christian intelligentsia who took up the challenge of formulating the profound philosophical and theological issues underlying onomatodoxy.

The *imiabortsy* had an erroneous point of departure for their critique of onomatodoxy: an attempt to assess religious experience, the life of prayer, both liturgical and personal, in terms of scholastically inspired dogmatic theology, which largely evacuates the mystical and the transcendental which lay at the core of true prayer. The real tragedy occurred when ambitious hierarchs, nourished on a formalistic approach to religion and religious experience, seized on the Athonite critique of Archimandrite Hilarion's book and cast the issue as doctrinal, conflicting with the accepted wisdom of the official church, and seemingly threatening its authority. Even faced with the origin of the formula 'the Name of God is God' in John of Kronstadt, an eminent and beloved pastor, they were unable to approach onomatodoxy in the context of prayer and liturgy.

Although the defenders of onomatodoxy among the Christian intelligentsia were pre-eminent thinkers, philosophers and theologians, ironically they were far more attuned to the experiential, mystical dimension of the faith and the church than the hierarchs who made up the chief opposition to onomatodoxy and who must be held responsible for the tragic dénouement of the 'Athonite affair'. It was this handful of intellectuals who stood up to be counted, both in heat of the action and afterwards, even at the risk of their lives.

Archimandrite Sophrony places the doctrine of the Name of God squarely in the ascetical-mystical tradition of the Orthodox Church, as did the author of *On the Mountains of the Caucasus*. Sophrony considers onomatodoxy in the light of the life of prayer, in the context of 'our spiritual growth',[38] rather than from the perspective of abstract theology remote from *praxis*. Sophrony and the religious philosophers were imbibed with a keen sense of the continuity between the spiritual life, and ultimately mystical experience, and Orthodox theology, what Vladimir Lossky characterized as 'the mystical theology of the Eastern Church'.[39] Nonetheless, Sophrony was more theologically inclined than his monastic predecessor of the early twentieth century, Archimandrite Hilarion, and he had the benefit of the mature reflections of Bulgakov and others on the subject.

It is in this light that we should see Hilarion Alfeyev's positive contemporary assessments of the contributions of Bulgakov and Sophrony to the evolution of Orthodox reflection on the theology of the Name. Alfeyev considers that the doctrine of Sergius Bulgakov on the Name of God contained in *The Philosophy of the Name* is 'the most complete and the most relevant expression of the onomatodoxy doctrine of the Name of God', while that of Archimandrite Sophrony appears as 'the most accurate, the most concise, at the same time the most sound theologically', and it 'completes the process of maturation of the doctrine of the Name of God in Russian theology'.[40]

[38]Sophrony, *Sa Vie est la mienne*, 136.
[39]Vladimir Lossky, *The Mystical Theology of the Eastern Church* (1944) (Crestwood, NY: St Vladimir's Seminary Press, 1976).
[40]Alfeyev, *Le Mystère sacré de l'Église*, 385.

Bulgakov's consideration of onomatodoxy is more philosophically based and more robust and exhaustive theologically, while that of Sophrony is more biblically and liturgically based, and it integrates more thoroughly spiritual and existential aspects of the Name of God in prayer with theological considerations. This is more a matter of personal disposition and emphasis than a reflection of fundamental differences. Sophrony is perhaps more cautious than Bulgakov in his theological reflections and language, for example he does not use the contested 'onomatodoxy formula' ('the Name of God is God'), nor does he consider the Name of God to be superior to the icon, as does Bulgakov.

In turn, Hilarion Alfeyev is more cautious still than the principal supporters of onomatodoxy. For example, he rejects the 'onomatodoxy formula' on the grounds that we cannot affirm the identity of God with his Name (assuming that the verb 'to be' in the formula is understood in the sense of identification), that we believe that God can be named and that the Names of God can adequately express the divine essence. The formula is nonetheless useful, he finds, if it is understood along the lines that 'God is present in his Name' or that 'God resides in his Name.' Similarly, he rejects the straightforward contention that the Name of God is a divine energy, 'if the term energy is used in a Palamite sense and thus designates an energy co-eternal with God, inseparable from his nature, independently of the existence of the created world.'[41]

In his caution, Alfeyev cites approvingly the only text that we have from Vladimir Lossky on onomatodoxy, remarks contained in a letter written in 1938. For Lossky, the dogmatic question of the Name of God is as important as that of icons and just as the dogmatic expression concerning icons resulted in the 'triumph of Orthodoxy' in the ninth century, so the Orthodox doctrine of the Names 'should provoke a new triumph of Orthodoxy, the manifestation of new beatifying and sanctifying forces'. Lossky rejects both the rationalist modern-day iconoclasts of the Name, typified by Antony Khrapovitsky, and the radical 'worshippers of the Name', who divinize the sounds of the divine Name. Lossky points instead to the theology of Gregory Palamas and to spirituality as the basis of a solution. He cites a formula of Archbishop Theophanes (Bystrov) of Poltava (1873–1940): 'The Divinity resides in the Name of God,' and comments: 'When this formula will be clear, filled with spiritual experience and spiritually obvious, many questions will automatically fall by the wayside and many difficulties will then appear childish.'[42]

Writing in the 1930s, Georges Florovsky, in his monumental *The Ways of Russian Theology*, makes only a few general remarks on onomatodoxy. But in these few remarks he puts his finger on the heart of both the historical and the theological aspects of the controversy:

> In the history of Russian theology one detects a creative confusion. Most harmful has proven the gulf separating theology and piety, theological learning and devotional prayer, the theology of the schools and the life of the church. A split or schism between the 'intelligentsia' and the 'people' occurred

[41]See Hilarion Alfeyev's theological conclusions in *Le Mystère sacré de l'Église*, 381–8.
[42]Cited by Alfeyev in *Le Mystère sacré de l'Église*, 387–8.

> within the church itself. … This is so characteristically expressed in the 1912-1913 'Athos controversy' concerning the names of God and the Jesus Prayer.[43]

In a footnote Florovsky says about the 'onomatodoxy formula': 'It would seem that this was not so much a theological assertion as much as it was simply a description of the reality of the prayer. But even this reality seemed too daring. Psychologism in the explanation of prayer appeared to many safer, more humble and more pious.'[44]

Neither Lossky nor Florovsky refer to the thinking of the religious philosophers on onomatodoxy. Although both lived in Paris in the 1930s, they were on opposite sides of the theological fence from Sergius Bulgakov, yet quite possibly both would have found Bulgakov's 'theology of the Name' quite satisfactory as an Orthodox approach to the issue.

The failure of the Council of the ROC of 1917–18 to deal with onomatodoxy means that it is still an open question and the issue has resurfaced in post-communist Russia. In 2000 the Theological Commission of the ROC proposed as a future task a theological analysis of *imiaslavie*. While Hilarion Alfeyev's study is no doubt the most thorough exploration of the historical and theological aspects of the quarrel of the Name, many contemporary Orthodox neo-traditionalist and monastically orientated writers criticize the 'Name-Worshippers' as heretics, using much the same arguments as those advanced by the opponents of *imiaslavie* in the years before the First World War. Surprisingly though, the conservative and traditional Russian Bishop Diomid (Dzyuban) supports the *imiaslavtsy* doctrines, vehemently denouncing their detractors as 'heretics'.[45] Moderate opposition to onomatodoxy comes from the important Orthodox thinker Sergei Khoruzhii (b. 1941), who considers that the 'Name-Glorifiers' and their supporters misunderstand and misuse the Palamite theology of the divine energies. His basic argument is that in generalizing from an experiential or existentialist understanding of the presence of the divine energies in the Name of God during prayer to a universal principle of divine presence, the *imiaslavtsy* depart from the synergy between God and humans necessary to the actualization of the divine presence in the Name – in other words, transforming an existentialist approach to energy into an essentialist one.[46] The weakness in Khoruzhii's argument is that the divine energies thereby become dependent on human response, reciprocity or synergy, without which God, through the divine energies, is not present in creation. The broader theological question left dangling is divine presence in creation in the absence of human contemplation (see Chapter 9).

In a lengthy paper, Vladimir (Anthony) Moss (b. 1949), an English convert to Orthodoxy, attacks the arguments of the Hieromonk Antony (Bulatovitch), the main Athonite proponent of *imiaslavie* in the 1910s, and the contemporary Russian monk Gregory (Lourié), referring to 'the

---

[43]Georges Florovsky, *The Ways of Russian Theology* (1937) in *The Collected Works of Georges Florovsky*, Vol. VI (Vaduz: Buchervertriebsanstalt, 1972), 290.

[44]Florovsky, *The Ways of Russian Theology*, 376.

[45]See Scott Kenworthy, 'Debating the Theology of the Name in Post-Soviet Russia: Metropolitan Ilarion Alfeev and Sergei Khoruzhii', in Katya Tolstaya, ed., *Orthodox Paradoxes: Heterogeneities and Complexities in Contemporary Russian Orthodoxy* (Leiden & Boston, 2014), 249–53.

[46]For a summary of Khoruzhii's analysis of onomatodoxy, see Kenworthy, 'Debating the Theology of the Name in Post-Soviet Russia', 253–6.

Name-Worshipping Heresy of Fr. A. Bulatovich and Fr. G. Louri'.[47] But Moss does not criticize directly Archimandrite Hilarion or the book *On the Mountains of the Caucasus*, nor does he address the philosophical and theological arguments of Florensky, Bulgakov and Losev and other early twentieth-century supporters of the *imiaslavtsy*.

Should onomatodoxy/*imiaslavie* again be considered in an ecclesiastical context, at a century's interval from the tragic events of the 1910s, there is now a solid philosophical and theological base to work towards more measured doctrinal and canonical conclusions than was the case then. Any reconsideration of the issue has to be based on a holistic vision of the Orthodox tradition: theology, spirituality and liturgy cannot be separated. The expression 'the Name of the Lord' occurs frequently in Orthodox liturgy, almost invariably referring to or invoking the Name of God as identical to referring to or invoking God. At the end of the Liturgy of St John Chrysostom, the choir and the people sing: 'Blessed be the Name of the Lord both now and forever.' The experience of the divine Name in prayer, especially the Jesus Prayer, must remain the inspiration and base of a theology of the Name of God.

[47]Vladimir Moss, 'On the Name of God: Against the Name-Worshipping Heresy of Fr. A. Bulatovich and Fr. G. Louri' (2007). www.orthodoxchristianbooks.com/books/ (11 April 2016). See also 'Dialogue on Name-Worshipping between Hieromonk Gregory (Lourié) and Vladimir Moss' (in Russian). http://imiaslav.narod.ru/dialogue/dialogue.htm (16 April 2016).

16

The Ordination of Women

Chapter Outline

Women in the Orthodox Church

The role of women in the church has been on the Orthodox agenda since the 1960s. If the broad issue concerns the place that women should have in the Orthodox Church, the narrower issue is the ordination of women to ministerial office. While it is generally accepted that women should do more than organize parish social events and clean the church, liturgical roles for women are contentious. Most Orthodox consider that it is proper for women to sing in the church choir and even direct the choir, lead catechism for children (and perhaps even adults), serve as members of the parish council, carry out charitable acts undertaken by the community and assume other responsibilities in the administration of the parish. Some of these activities are already liturgical or pastoral roles, such as directing the choir and leading catechetical activities, and in some parishes women read the prescribed texts during services, for example during vespers and the epistle during the Divine Liturgy. Women are not, however, ordained or formally blessed to carry out these activities – typically they simply do them, generally at the request of the local priest. Strictly speaking, though, those who read in church services should be readers, the first level in the Orthodox ecclesiastical hierarchy (readers are not members of the clergy). The more substantive question is thus: What liturgical role should women have in the Orthodox Church? Or more directly: Should women be admitted to ordained ministry in the Orthodox Church?

The ordination of women became an issue in Orthodoxy as a result of Orthodox participation in the ecumenical movement. In the 1960s and 1970s, the Anglican Church and many Protestant communities were debating the ordination of women to ministerial office and it was inevitable that Orthodox participants in ecumenical meetings should be asked to express the point of view of the Orthodox Church. The Anglican Church and many Protestant churches decided after long and frequently acrimonious debate to ordain women to the priesthood or to ministry. The weight of modern Orthodox thinking has generally been against the ordination of women, although there have been some prominent Orthodox voices, such as those of Elisabeth Behr-Sigel (1907–2005) and, less visibly, Metropolitan Anthony Bloom (1914–2003), favouring the ordination of women.[1] Despite Behr-Sigel's commitment to the ordination of women, she was well aware of the sensitivity of the issue in Orthodoxy, and she generally proceeded cautiously, preferring to speak of the need to re-examine the role of women in the church, than to tackle directly the inflammatory issue of ordination. Many Orthodox women who have written on the issue have opposed the ordination of women.[2] Metropolitan Kallistos Ware (b. 1934), another prominent Orthodox figure who has addressed the question of the ordination of women, initially opposed the ordination of women, but by the late 1990s he considered that the ordination of women should be 'an open question' for the Orthodox Church, to be approached 'with an open mind and an open heart'.[3]

Important intra-Orthodox meetings held in 1976 and 1988 focused on the role of women in the church. A Consultation of Orthodox Women took place at the women's monastery in Agapia, Romania, in September 1976. Sponsored by the World Council of Churches to foster the voices of Orthodox women in discussions on the role of women in church, including the issue of ordination, the meeting brought together women from both the Eastern Orthodox (Chalcedonian) and Oriental Orthodox (pre- or non-Chalcedonian) churches. Elisabeth Behr-Sigel gave the keynote address, her first involvement in the question of women in the church. The issue of the ordination of women did not feature prominently in the discussions and the meeting expressed the need for women to become more involved in theological education, administration and decision-making in all levels of church life, social service and religious and spiritual education. The final statement, entitled 'Our Concerns', modestly called for study and consideration of the 'reactivation' of the office of deaconess where this could be necessary, carefully affirming that the 'form and content' of the office of deaconess 'is that of service and does not have the character of a liturgical-sacramental

---

[1]See Elisabeth Behr-Sigel, *The Ministry of Women in the Church* (1987) (Crestwood, NY: St Vladimir's Seminary Press, 1999); Elisabeth Behr-Sigel and Kallistos Ware, *The Ordination of Women in the Orthodox Church* (Geneva: WCC Publications, 2000); and Elisabeth Behr-Sigel, *Discerning the Signs of the Times. The Vision of Elisabeth Behr-Sigel* (Crestwood, NY: St Vladimir's Seminary Press, 2001). Metropolitan Anthony Bloom's Preface to Behr-Sigel's 1987 book advances arguments for the ontological equality of men and women but does not explicitly endorse the ordination of women. See *The Ministry of Women in the Church*, xiii-xiv.

[2]Examples are the essays written by women in Thomas Hopko, ed., *Women and the Priesthood* (Crestwood, NY: St Vladimir's Seminary Press, 1983): Kyriaki Karidoyanes FitzGerald, 'The Nature and Characteristics of the Order of Deaconess'; and Deborah Malacky Belonik, 'Testing the Spirits'; together with the additional essay in the revised 1999 edition: Nonna Verna Harrison, 'Orthodox Arguments Against the Ordination of Women as Priests'.

[3]Kallistos Ware, 'Man, Woman and the Priesthood of Christ', in Thomas Hopko, ed., *Women and the Priesthood* (Crestwood, NY: St Vladimir's Seminary Press, 1983; revised edition, 1999), 7; 52 (1999 edition).

function ... nor can it be considered as a "first step" to the ordained priesthood.'[4] Somewhat ironically, it was the senior Orthodox hierarch at the meeting, Metropolitan Emilianos Timiadis (1916–2008), head of the Geneva office of the Ecumenical Patriarchate, who unequivocally advocated that women 'should be admitted to the minor orders, as readers and acolytes', and for 'a restoration of the diaconate for women and of the orders of virgins, widows and *didascaloi* (teachers)'.[5] Prior to the Agapia meeting, Timiadis had encouraged Elisabeth Behr-Sigel to become involved in the question of women in the Orthodox Church and to attend the meeting at Agapia.

The closest that the Orthodox Church has come to adapting a formal position on the ordination of women was at an inter-Orthodox symposium organized by the Ecumenical Patriarchate in Rhodes in 1988. The meeting was attended by a large number of Orthodox hierarchs, clergy, monastics and lay theologians, but its outcome had been predetermined. As the editor of the proceedings states candidly in his Introduction, 'Through this volume it is shown beyond doubt that the Orthodox Tradition leaves no room for the ordination of women to the priesthood.'[6] The purpose of the meeting was not to explore the theological dimensions involved in the question of the ordination of women, but rather to articulate the reasons for Orthodox opposition to the ordination of women. Unlike the Agapia meeting, an overwhelming majority of participants were men, either clerics or lay theologians. Elisabeth Behr-Sigel participated in the symposium but was not invited to present a paper. There were no dissenting voices among the papers presented nor were any reflected in the 'Conclusions of the Consultation', although a wider range of points of view was expressed at the symposium itself. In her report and comments on the meeting, Behr-Sigel points out that the diversity of views expressed on the question of the ordination of women is not reflected in the Conclusions: 'The revelation of pluralism, particularly in relation to the problem of the ordination of women, surprised and frightened some of the bishops and theologians. And this hardly appears in the official text of the conclusions. … The official text of the conclusion was unable or unwilling to take account of this pluralism.'[7] She later wrote that the conclusions contain 'inconsistencies and contradictions'.[8]

The most prominent Orthodox opposition to the ordination of women is the book edited by Fr Thomas Hopko (1939–2015), *Women and the Priesthood*. All six contributors to the first edition in 1983, together with Fr Alexander Schmemann (1921–83), who provided the Preface, oppose the ordination of women. Elisabeth Behr-Sigel was apparently not invited to contribute to this volume, which thus reflects only the strand of Orthodox thought opposing the ordination of women.

---

[4]Constance J. Tarasar and Irina Kirillova, eds., *Orthodox Women: Their Role and Participation in the Orthodox Church. Report on the Consultation of Orthodox Women September 11-17, 1976, Agapia, Romania* (Geneva: World Council of Churches, 1977), 50.

[5]Emilianos Timiadis, 'The Concern for Women in the Orthodox Tradition: New Challenges', in Tarasar and Kirillova, eds., *Orthodox Women*, 35.

[6]Gennadios Limouris, ed., *The Place of Woman in the Orthodox Church and the Question of the Ordination of Women. Inter-Orthodox Symposium, Rhodos, Greece, 30 October-7 November 1988* (Katerini, GR: Ecumenical Patriarchate and Tertios Publications, 1992), 15.

[7]Elisabeth Behr-Sigel, 'La consultation interorthodoxe de Rhodes: Présentation et essai d'évaluation' (The inter-Orthodox consultation in Rhodes: Presentation and evaluation), *Contacts*, 41 (1989), 86.

[8]Behr-Sigel and Ware, *The Ordination of Women in the Orthodox Church*, 31.

Most of the discussion among Orthodox on the subject of the ordination of women has taken place around the arguments *against* the ordination of women, rather than arguments *favouring* ordination. Indeed, those favouring ordination of women have devoted more attention to finding weaknesses in arguments opposed to the ordination than they have to developing arguments supporting ordination, while those opposed to ordination typically ignore arguments favouring ordination and carry on as if there were no objections or weaknesses in their own arguments. As a result, the arguments against ordination and the critiques of these arguments are far more developed than those favouring ordination. A major exception to this pattern is Kallistos Ware in the revised 1999 version of his essay 'Man, Woman and the Priesthood of Christ', first published in 1983.

Arguments against the ordination of women

Between the early 1960s and the late 1980s, Orthodox theologians advanced a number of arguments against the ordination of women to the priesthood – in fact, to any clerical office. Many of the arguments against the ordination of women were originally developed from an a priori assumption that women should not be ordained, and that it was simply a matter of expressing the theological reasons for this foregone conclusion.[9]

Almost all opposition to the ordination of women can be assimilated to one of six major arguments, which we will consider in turn.

Ritual impurity

Ritual purity means freedom of flaws or uncleanness which would bar one from contact with holy objects or places, especially from contact with the holy presence of God in worship. Ritual impurity is associated with contact with objects, places or persons considered impure, and includes the loss of body fluids, notably blood. God is the ideal of purity, and those who are to come in contact with God's presence are also to be pure. The Old Testament contains other sources of ritual impurity, such as contact with a corpse or with idols; and, as we see in the recital of Christ's crucifixion, too close a contact with pagans, such as entry into Pilate's house prior to Pascha (cf. Jn 18.28).

The argument with respect to the ordination of women is that a woman's loss of blood during menstruation renders her impure and hence unfit for the celebration of the Eucharist and other sacraments. This argument was first advanced by Professor Nicolae Chitescu (1904–91) of the Faculty of Theology of Bucharest at the Fourth World Conference on Faith and Order in Montreal in 1963. In his summary of thinking in the early church and ancient canons bearing on the role of women in the church, he refers to

[9]See Valerie Karras, 'Theological Presuppositions and Logical Fallacies in much of the Contemporary Discussion on the Ordination of Women', in Petros Vassiliadis, Niki Papageorgiou, and Eleni Kasselouri-Hatzivassiliadi, eds, *Deaconesses, the Ordination of Women and Orthodox Theology* (Cambridge: Cambridge Scholars Publishing, 2017), 89.

> the period during which women are 'impure', stressed in the Old Testament (see Le 12 and 15: 19sq.), during which according to certain canons women were not permitted to receive baptism. During this period women could not carry out priestly duties [*sic*]. There is a special canon prohibiting women priests, based on this point of view.[10]

The rather simplistic argument of women's ritual impurity is based more on archaic taboos typical of prehistoric religious and social beliefs and practices, reflected in the Old Testament, than on a Christian vision of women. Kallistos Ware dismisses the argument of ritual impurity by pointing out that Christ's teachings and the decisions of the Apostolic Council (Acts 15) make it 'abundantly clear ... that the Old Testament prohibitions concerning ritual impurity are not applicable within the New Covenant of the Church'.[11] The argument soon vanished from official Orthodox discourse on the ordination of women, although it still resurfaces from time to time, especially in countries of Orthodox tradition such as Russia and Greece. The notion of ritual impurity subsists in the continuing practice in some Orthodox jurisdictions of not allowing women to receive communion during menstruation or even not allowing them into the church.[12] There is also an echo of the prehistoric view of the ritual impurity of women in the service of the 'purification' of the mother after childbirth.[13]

The natural hierarchy or order between man and woman

The basic argument underlying the 'natural hierarchy' between men and women is that men are inherently superior to women, and hence women are unsuited to clerical office. At its crudest level, this hierarchy of the sexes was based in the first instance on size and physical strength: men are generally bigger and stronger than women. This rather primitive view of a hierarchy of the sexes has nonetheless had a profound impact on the human collective unconscious. The modern theological argument is far more sophisticated and is generally based on Scripture. The second account of creation in Genesis is often interpreted as putting woman in an inferior position to man,

---

[10]Nicolae Chitescu, 'The Ordination of Women: A Comment on the Attitude of the Orthodox Church', World Council of Churches Commission on Faith and Order & Department on the Cooperation of Men and Women in Church, Family, and Society, *Concerning the Ordination of Women* (Geneva: World Council of Churches, 1964), 58.

[11]Ware, 'Man, Woman and the Priesthood of Christ' (1999), 35.

[12]Boris Bobrinskoy refers obliquely to 'female physiology during her participation in the sacramental life' (*The Mystery of the Church* (Yonkers, NY: St Vladimir's Seminary Press, 2012), 229). Lawrence Farley reviews the history and theology of the practice of denying communion to menstruating women and concludes that there is no basis to maintain this practice, on the grounds that 'Christianity is not a religion', since 'in Christ we transcend religion with all its categories'. See Lawrence Farley, *Feminism and Tradition: Quiet Reflections on Ordination and Communion* (Yonkers, NY: St Vladimir's Seminary Press, 2012), 176–7.

[13]Elisabeth Behr-Sigel interprets this ritual in a way that serves to elevate the woman that has given birth rather than denigrate her for ritual impurity because of the blood associated with childbirth: the woman who has given birth has had a direct experience of the sacred cosmic order by cooperating intimately with God in the creation of life, and the ritual signifies her return to the normal mode of participation in the Kingdom of God. See Elisabeth Behr-Sigel and Nicole Maillard, 'Orthodoxy and Women in France', in Jeanne Becher, ed., *Women, Religion and Sexuality: Studies on the Impact of Religious Teachings on Women* (Geneva: WCC Publications, 1990), 189–90.

since man was created first and since the woman is drawn from Adam (his rib) and not vice versa (Gen. 2.21-22). Furthermore, the argument goes, God says to Eve after the transgression: 'He [Adam] shall rule over you' (Gen. 3.16). Paul invokes this reading of Genesis when he writes: 'For the man is not of the woman; but the woman of the man. Neither was the man created for the woman; but the woman for the man' (1 Cor. 11.8-9). In biblical exegesis, Eve is often accused of having brought about the fall of Adam; woman is the 'temptress' and man is the 'tempted'. Most patristic exegesis does not focus on this interpretation of Genesis but rather highlights that the God's pact was with Adam and that it was his disobedience, not Eve's, that led to the fall. Paul's admonitions concerning women in the Christian community are also cited in support of the natural hierarchy hypothesis: Paul requires that women cover their heads in the assembly, but not men (1 Cor. 11.3-13); women should not speak in the assembly (1 Cor. 14.33-34) and wives should be subject to their husbands (Eph. 5.22-24). These and other passages seem to support the contention of biblical support for a natural hierarchy between men and women, and more particularly, the submission of wives to husbands.

The logical argument based on the second Genesis account of creation is that since man (*aner*, *vir*) was created before woman and woman was created from man, therefore man is superior to woman and hence a man can be a priest but not a woman. However we may interpret the biblical passages which seem to suggest a hierarchy between men and women – male superiority over women – there is no direct logical link between the sequence of the creation of the sexes, a hierarchy between men and women and the ordination of women. Even if we admit the premise of male superiority, it simply does not follow from the affirmation that 'Men are superior to women,' that 'Therefore women should not be priests.' The accession of women to positions of leadership in most spheres of contemporary life undermines the premise of inherent or ontological or natural male superiority over women, so the basis of a 'natural hierarchy' must be sought elsewhere.

Fr Lawrence Farley (b. 1954), in his book *Feminism and Tradition* (2012), grounds his position against the ordination of women largely on the natural hierarchy argument. Farley concedes the ontological equality of men and women, but insists that the biblical record, the Fathers and the practice of the church all demonstrate the subordination of women to men.[14] For Farley, the historical fact that Christ did not choose a woman to be an apostle shows that Christ 'recognized their [women's] subordination'.[15] This is an interpretation of the significance of Christ's action, not a logical conclusion – it is a non sequitur. It is certainly much easier to support the contention of women as subordinate to men from the Pauline epistles than from the Gospels, where Jesus treats men and women as equally in need of teaching, healing and forgiveness. Farley goes on to argue that the Fathers and the church steadfastly maintain the teaching of 'equality but subordination' and hence 'since the pastoral office involves exercising authority over men in the church ... this is inconsistent with women's subordination.'[16]

[14]Lawrence Farley, *Feminism and Tradition: Quiet Reflections on Ordination and Communion* (Yonkers, NY: St Vladimir's Seminary Press, 2012), 30, 37, 66–7, 89–91. See our review of this book in *St Vladimir's Theological Quarterly*, 60, 3 (2016).
[15]Farley, *Feminism and Tradition*, 66.
[16]Ibid., 69.

Farley's argument leaves several questions dangling. One is the relationship between equality and subordination. Since he seems to say that women's subordination to men is built into God's intention in creation and is therefore ontological, he does not reconcile two seemingly opposing ontological principles, equality and subordination. He tries to get around this problem by referring to the 'loving and voluntary subordination of an ontological equal' (the woman to the man), but this looks more like wishful thinking than reality. Another question left dangling is whether this 'subordination' implies that all women are subordinate to all men, or, as the biblical and patristic witnesses mostly stress, wives to husbands? It is not clear where this leaves unmarried women: to which men are they to be subordinate? In any case Farley does not explain what this subordination really entails, other than excluding women from leadership roles in the family and the church. Since Farley concedes that women can exercise leadership over men in all domains except the church and the family,[17] this concession alone undermines ontological subordination. Nonetheless, for Farley as for other Orthodox theologians, in the family and the church, sexual differentiation, which includes women's subordination to men, takes precedence over ontological equality.

Commenting on the biblical passages relating to men and women, Kallistos Ware recognizes that while the Pauline texts in particular suggest a certain hierarchy between men and women, such a hierarchy 'is not the same as subordination', using as a comparison the 'order' (*taxis*) or hierarchy ascribed to the Persons of the Holy Trinity, which does not mean subordination.[18] He similarly qualifies patristic strictures against women occupying leadership roles in the family, the church and public life, questioning whether 'we can treat every patristic statement as embodying eternal truth, while ignoring the structures of the society in which the Fathers were living.'[19] Ware raises here the complex question of the impact of social and cultural values on both the Bible and patristic writings, which we will consider below.

The priest as icon of Christ

One of the major arguments against the ordination of women is based on the symbolic significance of Christ's maleness. This argument was first advanced by Fr Georges Khodre (subsequently Metropolitan) (b. 1923) in 1964 and was developed by Fr Thomas Hopko (1939–2015) of St Vladimir's Theological Seminary and several other Orthodox theologians. Stripped to its essentials, the argument runs like this:

> Christ was incarnate as a male.
> The bishop or the priest acting for the bishop is the living image or icon of Christ.
> Therefore to be an accurate icon of Christ, the priest must be a male.
> Therefore women cannot be priests.

[17]Ibid., 109.
[18]Ware, 'Man, Woman and the Priesthood of Christ' (1999), 36.
[19]Ibid.

Khodre first presented the argument on the basis of the role of the bishop in the church and the Pauline image of the church as the Bride of Christ:

> He [the bishop] is the living image of the Lord, his sacrament, the head which renews the members. The church is the Bride of Christ. The bishop carries out the functions of the Bridegroom toward the church. … It is therefore normal that the charisma of representing Christ in relation to the church (the Bride) should be borne by a man.[20]

Fr Alexander Schmemann puts the argument more directly: 'If the bearer, the icon and the fulfiller of that unique priesthood [Christ's] is *man* and not woman, it is because Christ is *man* and not woman.'[21] Kallistos Ware, in the original 1983 version of his essay, is more subtle: 'The priest is an icon of Christ; and since the incarnate Christ became not only man but a male – since furthermore, in the order of nature the roles of male and female are not interchangeable – it is necessary that the priest should be a male.'[22]

Thomas Hopko summarizes the entire argument:

> The specific ministry of being the presbyterial/episcopal head of the sacramental community … is the specific ministry of imaging the person and effecting the ministry of the Son and Word of God incarnate in human form, in his specifically 'masculine' being and activity. The sacramental priest is not the image of God or divinity in general. He is certainly not the image of the Trinity or of the Holy Spirit. He is the image of Jesus Christ. … And this 'image' can only be actualized and effected by certain male members of the church, who are called and equipped for this ministry.[23]

Hopko attempts to distance himself from a simplistic argument of 'natural resemblance' of a human male to Jesus by adding other characteristics necessary for a priest: 'a sound Christian, whole in body and soul, without scandal and of good reputation'. These are, of course, applicable equally to men and women. But two of his additional criteria are masculine: 'a once-married or celibate man … a masculine person capable of heading the body (of the faithful) with the compassionate wisdom and sacrificial love of a husband and father'.[24] Expressed in this fashion, the argument is circular: a woman cannot be a priest because only men can be priests.

The iconic argument is further buttressed by other secondary arguments, based for example on the image of Christ as Bridegroom (a woman cannot be the 'bridegroom') and the church as the Bride (from St Paul). In this argument, the entire church is seen in a feminine relation to Christ. The priest, as the image or icon of Christ, and associated with his priestly ministry, stands in

---

[20]Georges Khodre, 'The Ordination of Women: A Comment', *Concerning the Ordination of Women*, 63.

[21]Alexander Schmemann, 'Concerning Women's Ordination: Letter to an Episcopal Friend', *St Vladimir's Theological Quarterly*, 17, 3 (1973), 242.

[22]Ware, 'Man, Woman and the Priesthood of Christ' (1983), 27.

[23]Thomas Hopko, 'Women and the Priesthood: Reflections on the Debate – 1983', in Hopko, ed., *Women and the Priesthood* (1999), 241. See also his substantive assay in the same volume 'Presbyter/Bishop: A Masculine Ministry' and his addition to the 1999 edition, 'The Debate Continues – 1998'.

[24]Hopko, 'Reflections on the Debate – 1983', 243.

relation to the church as Christ: that is, as the Bridegroom to the Bride, a reflection well represented in the Fathers. Hence, the argument goes, the priest must be a male.[25]

Other related secondary arguments are that Mary, the Mother of God, was not a priest, although she, above all women, was eminently worthy of association with Christ's priesthood. A further argument is that the priest is the 'father' of the community of the faithful and a woman qua woman cannot be the father of the community – only a male can.

There are several major problems with the iconic argument. First, it has no basis in Scripture nor in the Fathers, even if some Fathers, following Paul, speak of the church in allegorical terms as the Bride of Christ. On the contrary, the ancient Fathers focused on the Incarnation of the Son of God as human (*anthropos*; *homos*) and had only passing interest in the fact that he was male (*anir*; *vir*), a point reflected in the Nicene Creed – the Creed refers to Christ becoming *anthropos*, not *anir*.[26] It is the Incarnation, the taking on of human nature (*physis*) which deifies human nature, not the fact that Christ was male, which would suggest that only males can be redeemed or sanctified. As Valerie Karras points out, 'If Christ's maleness is somehow not simply a particular characteristic of his hypostasization of human nature but an ontologically essential element of his person, then he has not assumed *female* humanity.'[27] The position that Christ assumes only male humanity is, of course, theologically untenable.

In philosophical terms and in Christian anthropology, male and female are not different natures; there is one human nature, expressed in one of two forms, male or female. In the second creation account in Genesis, God says, 'Let us make man in our image, according to our likeness' (Gen. 1.26). Again, the Greek word (LXX) is *anthropos*, not *anir* – humanity, not a male.

The fact that a theological argument has no firm basis or none at all in Scripture or in the Fathers does not automatically dismiss the argument, but it raises a warning flag and suggests additional prudence in assessing its theological import.

Secondly, the iconic argument is an argument from analogy, which is at best a weak basis for establishing a theological doctrine. An analogy is just that: an analogy only partially reflects or parallels the original; they are not exactly identical in all respects, which would make the analogy a clone or identical copy. An ordained priest is not an identical copy or clone of Christ. To derive a doctrine solely from analogy is to transform an essentially symbolic or poetic expression of a reality that remains a mystery, or is a didactic device, into an ontological reality. In other words, it equates the symbol with the reality that the symbol is intended to evocate. It is legitimate to say that the priest may be an icon or symbol of Christ – but he is not Christ. Similarly, Christ can be compared to the Bridegroom in relation to the church as the Bride, a symbol or analogy from human marriage. But this is a symbolic expression, not the reality itself of the relationship between Christ and the church or God and humanity or creation. By confounding image or symbol and reality, an argument from analogy stretches the intent of the analogy far beyond its true significance, in support of

[25]A variant of this argument is that all humanity, indeed all creation, is in a feminine relationship with God, as the active, creative force, since humanity and the rest of creation are passive and receive existence from God, who has the active role in the relationship.
[26]See Ware, 'Man, Woman and the Priesthood of Christ' (1999), 50.
[27]Karras, 'Theological Presuppositions and Logical Fallacies', 96.

conclusions which are not sustained by the image or symbol itself. The symbol becomes distorted and interpreted for programmatic or ideological purposes.

In his discussion of the iconic argument, Kallistos Ware agrees that there is a sense in which the priest represents Christ, but he also emphasizes that during the Eucharistic anaphora, and indeed in most of the Divine Liturgy, the priest 'speaks not *in persona Christi* but *in persona Ecclesiae*, as the representative not of Christ but of the church'.[28] Thus the priest represents the church, the Bride, in supplication before God and in offering praise, adoration and thanksgiving. Ware turns the iconic argument on its head: 'If men can represent the church and the Bride, why cannot women represent Christ as Bridegroom?'[29] The notion of the priest as Christ's icon does not 'in itself exclude women from the priesthood', he writes.[30]

In a similar vein, John H. Erickson (b. 1943), in a paper at the Orthodox Symposium in Rhodes in 1988, points out that for the Fathers, a priest is not only *hiereus* (priest in a strict sense), but also presider, superior, teacher, initiator into mysteries and physician of souls.[31] Elisabeth Behr-Sigel remarks that a one-sided insistence on the priest as symbol of Christ in the Eucharist 'diverts attention from other important aspects of the presbyteral ministry which were abundantly developed by the Church Fathers'.[32] In this context Behr-Sigel, referring to John Chrysostom's expression that the priest 'lends his tongue and supplies his hand' pointing 'to the invisible, spiritual presence – in and by the Holy Spirit – of the one High priest, Christ', asks why these hands and this tongue could not be those of a baptized Christian woman 'who has received chrismation and communion, is made Christ-like, according to the profound meaning of the Orthodox rites of Christian initiation, by her communion with him who is the Anointed One, Christ?'[33]

The basic iconic argument also contains a logical fallacy, a non sequitur: from the fact that Christ was a male, it does not follow logically that a priest necessarily has to be a male. This is an inference or interpretation, not a logical necessity.

Although the iconic argument featured prominently in Orthodox discourse on the ordination of women in the late twentieth century, it began to fade in subsequent years. Lawrence Farley agrees with Ware's critiques of the original iconic argument of the priest as icon of Christ, but he immediately recasts the iconic argument in a new form. For him, the priest 'functions as an icon of God', and since God is revealed as 'masculine' (but not 'male'), it follows that to image 'this masculine God', the priest must be a male.[34] There are, of course, considerable scriptural, patristic, liturgical and historical references supporting a masculine image of God. But to say that God is 'masculine' yet not 'male' sounds more like a semantic sleight of hand than good theology. The conventional (but not exclusive) use of masculine language to refer to God has to be weighed in the light of Christian theology that God transcends sexual differentiation and is

[28]Ware, 'Man, Woman and the Priesthood of Christ' (1999), 47.

[29]Ibid., 51.

[30]Ibid., 49.

[31]John H. Erickson, 'The Priesthood in Patristic Teaching', in Limouris, ed., *The Place of Woman in the Orthodox Church*, 113.

[32]Behr-Sigel, 'The Ordination of Women', 42.

[33]Elisabeth Behr-Sigel, 'The Ordination of Women: Also a Question for the Orthodox Churches', in Behr-Sigel and Ware, *The Ordination of Women in the Orthodox Church*, 42. Cited by Ware in 'Man, Woman and the Priesthood of Christ' (1999), 49.

[34]Farley, *Feminism and Tradition*, 89–91.

neither male nor female, masculine nor feminine, even if human language typically obliges us to use the masculine (or occasionally the feminine) gender to refer to God. It is incorrect to sublimate admittedly imperfect human language into an ontological principle. An apophatic approach which recognizes the mystery of divine being and the limits of human language is sounder. In resorting, necessarily, to anthropomorphic language with reference to God, then it should always be clear that this gender-based language does not say something about God's ontological reality and that by analogy only is God both 'masculine' and 'feminine', not solely masculine. The recast of the iconic argument into the priest as an 'icon of God' is even shaker than the original model of the priest as 'icon of Christ', where at least one can point to the unquestioned maleness of Jesus.

The different charisms of men and women

A subtle argument against the ordination of women seeks to establish that there are significant differences between qualities or charisms particular to men and charisms particular to women, which make women unsuitable for priesthood. Paul Evdokimov (1901–70) powerfully develops this argument in his book *Woman and the Salvation of the World* (1958).[35] The charisms argument was subsequently taken up by Thomas Hopko and by Kallistos Ware, in the 1983 version of his essay 'Woman and the Priesthood of Christ'. In the early years of Elisabeth Behr-Sigel's involvement in the question of women in the church, she also subscribed to the charism theory advanced by her close friend Paul Evdokimov, but she gradually abandoned his approach to the role of men and women in the church, with the final break occurring between 1981 and 1984.[36]

Evdokimov's principal concern was to develop a theology of the sexes, woman in particular, which would affirm simultaneously the ontological equality and ontological differences of men and women. Beginning with the principle of the natural or ontological equality of man and woman, he argues that sexual differentiation is also ontological and archetypical and not merely physical or a consequence or an anticipation of a primeval fall of humanity from communion with God. He then goes on to assert that men and women have different roles or vocations in life, apart from the obvious physical roles of paternity and maternity. Men and women are not potential substitutes for each other in the essential roles which reflect their ontological differences; to attempt to do so involves a loss, a degradation of their own masculine or feminine nature. The crux of the argument lies in the detailing of masculine and feminine charisms. In Evdokimov and later writers, male charisms are typically those of initiative, activity, creativity and rationality, with which the male penetrates and sanctifies the world. In contrast, female charisms are the reception, vivification,

[35]Paul Evdokimov, *Woman and the Salvation of the World: A Christian Anthropology on the Charisms of Women* (1958; revised 1983) (Crestwood, NY: St Vladimir's Seminary Press, 1994).

[36]For an assessment of Behr-Sigel's thinking on Evdokimov's theory late in her life, see her essay 'Women in the Orthodox Church', in Elisabeth Behr-Sigel and Kallistos Ware, *The Ordination of Women in the Orthodox Church* (Geneva: WCC Publications, 2000), 16–19. For a presentation of Evdokimov's theology of woman in relation to the thought of Elisabeth Behr-Sigel, see Sarah Hinlicky Wilson, *Woman, Women, and the Priesthood in the Trinitarian Theology of Elisabeth Behr-Sigel* (London: T&T Clark, 2013), especially 11–18; 29–32; 38–41; 50–1; 57–61.

safeguarding and protection of the very holiness of being brought about the actions of the man.[37] Evdokimov writes:

> While man extends himself in the world by means of tools, woman does so by her gift of herself. It is through this *gift* that every *woman* is potentially a mother, and carries the *world's* treasure in her soul. While man's aim to act, women's is to be, which is the pre-eminent religious category … This is woman's vocation: to protect the world of humans as mother, and to save it as a virgin, by giving to the world a soul, her soul.[38]

Key words typically used to describe the role of women include maternity, service, self-effacement, modesty, 'the daily service of the most humble, in silence, hearing the Word, inwardly receiving the whole deposit of the faith in adoration and in praise'.[39] The implication of this line of thought is that priesthood is an actualization of male charisms but not of female charisms. Even before the accession of women to the priesthood became an issue in Orthodoxy, Evdokimov drew the basic conclusions of his doctrine:

> The question of the priesthood of woman finds its solution at the very precise level of charisms. … The priesthood of orders lies in the masculine *function* of witnessing. … But the ministry of woman does not lie in 'functions'; it resides in her nature. The ministry of orders does not belong to her charisms; that would be a betrayal of her being. … 'Man the Overseer' sacramentally penetrates the elements of this world, in order to consecrate them and transform them into the Kingdom. 'Man the Witness' acts through his virile energy; by means of his priestly powers he pierces the flesh of the world. …, Woman is Eve – ('Life') who safeguards, vivifies and protects every part of the masculine creation. … A woman cannot be a priest without betraying herself. It is through her being, her nature, that she is called to fulfil her royal priesthood in conformity with her charismatic state.[40]

Evdokimov extends his line of thought concerning ontological differences between men and women even further, by positing the existence of 'an ontic affinity between the masculine and Word' and 'an ontic affinity between the feminine and the Holy Spirit'.[41] The inspiration for this audacious doctrine likely comes from Sergius Bulgakov (1871–1944), under whom Evdokimov studied at the Saint Sergius Institute in the late 1920s. In his cosmology and his Trinitarian theology, Bulgakov develops a theology of the sexes in which the Logos is associated with men because of Christ's Incarnation 'in the male image' and the Holy Spirit with women, because of the role of the Holy Spirit in the Incarnation with the 'Spirit-bearer, the Ever-Virgin Mary', 'the most perfect manifestation of the Holy Spirit'.[42] Bulgakov explains further:

> All humankind in the male image is the one hypostasis of Christ, is Christ; it finds its hypostases in Christ's hypostasis, reflects and is reflected in his hypostasis. All humankind in the female image is

---

[37]See Evdokimov, *Woman and the Salvation of the World*, 185; 215–16; 222–4.
[38]Evdokimov, *Woman and the Salvation of the World*, 184.
[39]Boris Bobrinskoy, referring to the myrrh-bearing women at Christ's tomb in particular, *The Mystery of the Church*, 226.
[40]Evdokimov, *Woman and the Salvation of the World*, 214–16.
[41]Ibid., 27.
[42]Sergius Bulgakov, *The Comforter* (1936) (Grand Rapids, MI: Eerdmans, 2004), 187.

> the hypostasis of the Holy Spirit, which is revealed, becomes transparent, in the image of the Mother of God and, in this sense, is manifested in her hypostasis.[43]

In his own similar reflections, Evdokimov goes to some length to demonstrate the 'maternal' function of the Holy Spirit, reflected in womanhood:

> Time and time again the Spirit sanctifies, fashions, and brings forth; at the end of his activity, some form of the Incarnation appears. ... It is the Spirit who 'forms' Christ, brings him forth in the soul of each believer; and he prepares the eschatological birth of the age of the Kingdom. The charismatic vocation of woman is most explicit here; it is spiritual motherhood that brings forth Christ in every human being through the power of the Holy Spirit.[44]

Again the conclusion is drawn that women should not be ordained. Thus we have a series of associations or analogous relationships:

PERSONS OF THE TRINITY	GENDER ASSOCIATION	HUMANITY	PRIESTHOOD
Son of God/Christ	Masculine	Men	Priest
Holy Spirit	Feminine	Women	Non-priest

The idea of men and women as 'equal but different' in nature or essence found its way into much Orthodox discourse on the roles of men and women in the church and especially as ground for excluding women from the priesthood, although few follow Evdokimov into his more speculative association of men with Christ and women with the Holy Spirit. This extended speculation treads on dangerous theological ground, since it extends some sort of sexual differentiation into the Trinity, which brings to mind the male and female goddess of ancient religions. As such, the argument is fundamentally anthropomorphic, not theological.

Lawrence Farley dismisses the notion of male and female charisms extended to a connection between men and Christ and women and the Holy Spirit. This is dangerous anthropology and theology and Farley does a good job attacking it.[45] It is a bit of straw man, though, since Farley retains Evdokimov's point that men have certain characteristics (charisms) that render them apt for leadership in the church, while women's charisms are suited to non-liturgical and subordinate roles. Yet while Farley readily ascribes 'masculine' roles to priests in the church (ruling, fathering, governing, defining, protecting), he is unwilling to assign 'feminine' roles to women only ('birth-giving, nurturing and beautifying'), arguing that these belong to the entire church community and to ministries of both genders in the community.[46] For him, men have distinctive and unique roles in the church, but women do not.

---

[43]Sergius Bulgakov, *The Bride of the Lamb* (1945) (Grand Rapids, MI: Eerdmans, 2002), 97. Bulgakov points in this direction but is much less explicit in *Sophia: The Wisdom of God. An Outline of Sophiology* (1935) (Hudson, NY: Lindisfarne Press, 1993), 80.
[44]Evdokimov, *Woman and the Salvation of the World*, 222.
[45]Farley, *Feminism and Tradition*, 124–35.
[46]Ibid., 102; 121–2.

Nonna Verna Harrison, who opposes the ordination of women based on the argument from the tradition of the church and the 'iconic' argument, nonetheless dismisses both the subordination argument and the charisms argument and its extension in the association of men with Christ and women with the Holy Spirit:

> The attempt to base women's non-ordination to the priesthood on a universal subordination of women to men or a global designation of some human tasks as masculine and others as feminine thus has far-reaching, and in my view devastating, social implications which would affect all men and women, not only those interested in ordained ministry.[47]

In the 1999 revision of his essay on 'Man, Woman and the Priesthood of Christ', Kallistos Ware raises red flags concerning the charisms argument: Is there any support in Scripture or the Fathers, he asks? Should we not think primarily of men and women in terms of shared humanity? Are there not dangers in generalizing about 'woman' in the abstract? And he concludes: 'Even if women do indeed possess, as a sex, distinctive spiritual gifts, it does not therefore follow that they cannot performs the same tasks as men; we are only justified in concluding that they will perform these tasks in a different way.'[48]

The absence of women apostles

The strongest historical argument against the ordination of women is that Christ did not choose a woman to be an apostle, neither among the twelve nor among the seventy, thereby giving by example the course that the church must follow. He could have chosen a woman, the argument goes, but he did not. This argument is often closely related to the next argument, a broader appeal to tradition, not only the biblical witness, but also the actual practice of the church.

Supporters of the ordination of women typically advance two major lines of objection against this argument. One is that the church has not limited ordination to other characteristics of the initial apostles: that they were all Jewish, Caucasian and Palestinian. Why, then, the supporters of ordination ask, should their biological sex be privileged as a cause for denying ordination to women over the other social characteristics of the apostles? The reply to this objection is also historical: the church expanded Christian discipleship and ministry beyond its Jewish-Caucasian-Palestinian origins from the beginning, as is clear in the Acts of the apostles. But it never admitted women to the priesthood. As Kallistos Ware points out, 'The difference between the two cases is immediately apparent, and it is enormous.'[49]

The second line of objection is that Jesus was conforming to the social and cultural values of the time, when women were considered and were treated as inherently inferior to men. While it would have been unthinkable at that time for Jesus to have both men and women in the apostolic college,

---

[47]Harrison, 'Orthodox Arguments against the Ordination of Women as Priests', 172. See her study of patristic views on gender in 'Male and Female in Cappadocian Theology', *Journal of Theological Studies*, 41 (1990), and a summary in 'Orthodox Arguments against the Ordination of Women as Priests', 173–9.

[48]Ware, 'Man, Woman and the Priesthood of Christ' (1999), 23.

[49]Ibid., 29.

the argument is that the social and cultural context has changed radically since New Testament times, so that today the presence of men and women in the college of apostles would be not only acceptable, but expected. Thomas Hopko's counterargument is that the church advocated many 'foolish and scandalous teachings' in relation to the intellectual and cultural norms of the societies in which the early church developed and that therefore there must have been 'sound reasons' for limiting priesthood to men.[50] Behind his argumentation lies the unstated assumption that the early church was unaffected by the social and cultural norms governing relations between men and women and their social status.

Those who advance the argument from Jesus' choice of apostles focus only on the fact that Jesus did not select a woman as an apostle, neglecting or downplaying the full range of Jesus' dealings with women. Jesus' relations with women are always personal; he never speaks with women as a separate group. As Elisabeth Behr-Sigel points out, 'Jesus is not interested in woman, but rather in women, in each of them as he meets her personally.'[51] The range of Jesus' encounters with women is extremely broad, from brief healing episodes (such as the woman with the issue of blood), to profound discourses (the Samaritan women), to sinful women (the woman caught in adultery), to physical contact (the woman who anoints Jesus' feet and wipes them with her hair), to close friends (Martha and Mary). For Jesus, women, like men, are equally in need of spiritual and physical healing, comforting and instruction.

The broader question is whether Christ's example in not selecting a woman as apostle must be seen as mandatory for the church. Was the fact that none of the apostles was a woman a reflection of the social and cultural reality of the time, or was Christ saying something about women which would prevent them from being ordained? Fr Boris Bobrinskoy hints at this broader message to the church when he writes: 'It was not out of disdain for the female gender, nor for sociological reasons that women were not called to the apostolate of the Twelve and to a ministerial priesthood.'[52]

Yet one cannot but be left with the impression that those who see in Christ's actions an implicit command to the church not to ordain women themselves see women as less than men. Opponents of the invocation of Jesus' example in not selecting woman apostles object that this is an argument from silence. Jesus did not select a woman as apostle, but neither did he instruct his followers not to allow women to occupy positions of responsibility and authority in the church, including sacramental and liturgical functions. An argument from silence is at best a weak argument.[53] In practice, this argument is often linked with an argument from the history of the church, which will be considered below.

The Orthodox Church has not always followed Christ's explicit teachings to the letter – for example, with respect to divorce and remarriage. Christ's teachings on marriage seem clearly to exclude divorce 'except for the cause of fornication', and the possibility of remarriage (Mt. 5. 32; also Mt. 19.9 and Mk 10.11-12) But the Orthodox Church permits, reluctantly, divorce and remarriage.

---

[50]Thomas Hopko, 'Presbyter/Bishop: A Masculine Ministry', in Hopko, ed., *Women and the Priesthood*, 140–1.

[51]See Elisabeth Behr-Sigel, 'Jesus and Women', in Michael Plekon and Sarah Hinlicky, eds., *Discerning the Signs of the Times: The Vision of Elisabeth Behr-Sigel* (Yonkers, NY: St Vladimir's Seminary Press, 2010), 96.

[52]Bobrinskoy, *The Mystery of the Church*, 227.

[53]See Ware, 'Man, Woman and the Priesthood of Christ' (1999), 30.

Kallistos Ware writes: 'In theory the canons only permit divorce in cases of adultery, but in practice it is sometimes granted for other reasons as well.'[54] In the case of the ordination of women, we are looking at Jesus' example, not an explicit teaching. And whereas divorce and remarriage raise ethical issues, the ordination of women does not. One could seek to understand why Christ did not select a woman as an apostle, but this quest for understanding would likely lead one less to theological reasons than to psychological, social and cultural reasons related to the position and roles of women in traditional societies.

The tradition of the Orthodox Church

Since the beginning the Orthodox Church has not ordained women to the priesthood and there are a number of ancient canons and patristic writings opposing the ordination of women.[55] Opponents to the ordination of women point out that some schismatic groups in the early centuries had women priests and bishops, which reinforced their separateness from the Catholic Church. In the early centuries, there were women deacons, but the liturgical role of women deacons, other than assisting women during baptism, is open to question (see later in this chapter). From the historical absence of women priests in Orthodoxy, the opponents of the ordination of women conclude that nearly two millennia of tradition cannot be wrong and to change this would destroy the integrity of the church. For Fr John Meyendorff, the experience of the early church, with the absence of women priests, 'must determine the life of the church today'. The reason, he argues, is that 'the very "historical conditioning" which characterizes the Gospel of Christ is, in a sense, *normative for us*.'[56] Fr Alexander Schmemann ascribes apocalyptic consequences to the eventual ordination of women to the priesthood, arguing that this would be 'tantamount to a radical and irreparable mutilation of the entire faith, the rejection of the whole Scripture'.[57] Farley concludes from his examination of patristic material on men and women that 'the Fathers grasped the essential scriptural teachings, that women were equal to women and also called to a subordinate position, especially in the Christian *synaxis*'.[58]

The main difficulty with the appeal to tradition against the ordination of women is that it views Orthodox tradition as rigid and immutable: whatever has been done in the past, especially on a continuous basis, must be divinely ordained and therefore must be absolutely correct and forever repeated in the future. Modern Orthodox theologians tend to view tradition as more dynamic than the mere repetition of the past, seeing it rather as 'living tradition', or, in the poignant expression of Vladimir Lossky, as 'the life of the Holy Spirit in the church, communicating to each member of the Body of Christ the faculty of hearing, of receiving, of knowing the Truth in the Light which belongs

---

[54]Timothy (Kallistos) Ware, *The Orthodox Church: An Introduction to Eastern Christianity* (London: Penguin, 3rd ed, 2015), 288.

[55]For an overview of patristic writings and canons against the ordination of women, see Ware, 'Man, Woman and the Priesthood of Christ' (1999), 31–2; and Farley, *Feminism and Tradition*, 71–83.

[56]John Meyendorff, 'The Orthodox Churches', in Michael Hamilton and Nancy Montgomery, *The Ordination of Women: Pro and Con* (New York: Morehouse-Barlow, 1975), 130.

[57]Schmemann, 'Concerning Women's Ordination', 239.

[58]Farley, *Feminism and Tradition*, 81.

to it'.[59] This vibrant rather than static view of tradition does not preclude change in non-dogmatic elements of Orthodoxy. An example is the adoption by some Orthodox churches of the Gregorian or New Calendar in the 1920s, despite the fact that the liturgical use of the Julian calendar was approved by the First Ecumenical Council in 325. The calendar is not a dogmatic question (an essential truth of Christianity); neither is it a moral issue (there is no ethically right or wrong in the calendar). Rather, the calendar is a matter of church organization or discipline. Similarly, it is argued that the non-ordination of women priests in the past is not an insurmountable obstacle to a change in the church's practice. As Kallistos Ware writes:

> Obedience to Tradition must not be seen as a kind of dead fundamentalism. It does not mean that nothing can ever be done for the first time. Holy Tradition, rightly understood, is dynamic, not static and inert. It is received and lived by each new generation in its own way, tested and enriched by the fresh experience that the church is continually gaining.[60]

From a theological perspective, Schmemann's reference to the ordination of women (not only in Orthodoxy) as 'mutilation of the entire faith' and 'the rejection of the whole Scripture' is an exaggerated reaction to the discussion then engaged in the Anglican/Episcopalian Church on the ordination of women. John Erickson concludes his essay on 'The Priesthood in Patristic Teaching' prepared for the Rhodes meeting in 1988 by admitting 'quite simply' that 'while the Fathers have blessed us with a multifaceted yet coherent teaching on the priesthood, they have not given us a complete and altogether satisfactory answer to the question of the ordination of women.'[61] A dynamic view of tradition leaves the possibility, as Kallistos Ware puts it, of the ordination of women as 'an open question'.

Arguments in favour of the ordination of women

The ontological equality of men and women

The strongest theological argument favouring the ordination of women is the ontological equality of men and women, a doctrine firmly based on Scripture and patristic anthropology. Metropolitan Anthony Bloom, in his preface to Behr-Sigel's *The Ministry of Women in the Church*, referring to the secondary place of women in society and in the church, alludes to the equality argument:

> We forget, is it a Freudian slip, the creation of the total Man, undifferentiated, which contains all masculinity and all femininity. In this unique Man (*anthropos*), masculinity and femininity attain a maturity that requires for its perfect development and fulfilment the separation into two entities at

[59]Vladimir Lossky, 'Tradition and Traditions', *In the Image and Likeness of God* (St Vladimir's Seminary Press, 1974), 152.
[60]Ware, 'Man, Woman and the Priesthood of Christ' (1999), 25.
[61]Eriksson, 'The Priesthood in Patristic Teaching', 115.

the moment of Eve's birth. We too easily forget that God created Eve for Adam so that she would be a 'partner', not a subordinate. She was to be his 'half'.[62]

Men and women partake of the same human nature and are thus naturally equal; they are both divinely created in the image of God; both are children of God. In this ontological argument, sexual differentiation is relativized, men and women are not different 'natures', one inferior or subordinate to the other, and is secondary 'to the unity of men and women in their nature, destiny and vocation'.[63] The sexual differentiation of male and female is a biological fact, a feature that humans share with most animals and plants. But in philosophy and theology, there is no 'female nature' or 'male nature', there is only human nature, in two expressions, male and female. Men's nature and women's nature may exist in secular psychology and popular literature, but not in Christian theology. The closest that Orthodox thinking has come to trying to establish men's nature and women's nature has been the charisms argument that we discussed above, with all its weaknesses. Even the proponents of this doctrine never go so far as to attempt to establish that there are two 'human natures'. Hence to treat sexual differentiation as primary to natural equality attacks patristic anthropology, which is based on the primacy of human nature as created by God. In effect, the Fathers favour the first Genesis account of human creation over the second account, which, as we saw, can be interpreted as suggesting the ontological inferiority of women to men – hence leading to the idea of the inferiority or subordination of women to men. Patristic teaching on the ontological unity and equality of men and women is summarized in the well-known words of St Gregory of Nazianzus: 'The same creator for man and for woman, both made from the same dust, the same image, the same law, the same death, the same resurrection.'[64] As Elisabeth Behr-Sigel succinctly sums up the argument: 'The image of God is present in women just as much as in their male partners, transcending sexual difference without denying or obscuring it.'[65]

Most opponents of the ordination of women concede the ontological equality of men and women and are hence obliged to rely on other arguments to support their perspective. As we saw above, Lawrence Farley argues that the Fathers affirm both ontological quality and the subordination of women to men. Emphasis on differences between men and women, or the 'charisms' or vocations specific to men or women, now becomes paramount. Kyriaki FitzGerald reflects this ambiguity:

> Human nature is dimorphic. Both male and female human persons are fully and equally human, yet they each express their common humanity in different modes. … The difference between them includes, but is not limited to, the physical domain. Rather, it is a difference of being which is rooted in the very essence of creation and manifested in the particular expression of personhood.[66]

---

[62]Anthony Bloom, 'Preface to the French Edition', Behr-Sigel, *The Ministry of Women in the Church*, xiii.

[63]Behr-Sigel, 'The Ordination of Women: Also a Question for the Orthodox Churches', in Behr-Sigel and Ware, *The Ordination of Women in the Orthodox Church*, 38–9.

[64]Gregory of Nazianzus, *Discourse 37*, 6. Grégoire de Nazianze, *Discours 32-37* (SC 318) (Paris: Éditions du Cerf, 1985), 285.

[65]Behr-Sigel, 'The Ordination of Women', 36.

[66]Kyriaki FitzGerald, 'An Orthodox Assessment of Modern Feminist Theology', in Limouris, ed., *The Place of Woman in the Orthodox Church*, 305.

The expressions 'difference of being' and 'the very essence of creation' suggest an ontological difference between men and women, but the author does not elaborate further. Kallistos Ware questions 'how far this viewpoint can claim explicit corroboration from the Greek patristic tradition,' since, he writes, 'there is much evidence to support the view that, for Fathers such as the three Cappadocians and St Maximus the Confessor, sexual differentiation is not a central theological concept.'[67]

The argument in favour of ordination of women poses as premise the ontological equality of men and women, and from this concludes that both men and women *can* be priests. But from the ontological equality of men and women, it does not follow that therefore women *should* be ordained; it simply demonstrates that there is no *ontological* reason for not ordaining women – but there may be reasons of a different order.

Christ defies human nature

Christ does not save just men by his masculinity or maleness (*anir – vir*); rather, by his humanity (*anthropos – homo*), Christ saves both men and women. Men and women are one in Christ, as St Paul asserts (Gal. 3.28), and the Fathers of the Church developed the theology of the Incarnation and salvation on the basis of Christ as human (*anthropos*) rather than as male. Thus Christ by his Incarnation as human, his life and teachings, his passion and death and his resurrection redeems human nature, both in its male form and its female form: 'The Word, in becoming flesh', writes Elisabeth Behr-Sigel, 'took on the whole of humanity in order to save the whole of humanity'.[68] Anthony Bloom criticizes a tendency to focus on Christ's maleness:

> The churches that call themselves 'Traditional' never cease referring to the fact that in Christ God showed himself as man (*anir*, male), and they forget that he is the total and perfect Man (*anthropos*), who contains and reveals the totality of the human being and not just the 'virile', for 'what he did not assume, he did not save'.[69]

While the argument that Christ saves both men and women and deifies human nature is sound theology, we cannot conclude from this that therefore women should be ordained. The argument only establishes that Christ saves all humans, both men and women, and that there is no soteriological reason for not ordaining women.

Spiritual gifts are accorded to both men and women

In all the passages where St Paul writes of ministries within the church and gifts and fruits of the Holy Spirit, he does not distinguish between ministries, gifts and fruits associated with men or with women. He writes about ministries in the church (apostles, prophets, evangelists, pastors

[67] Ware, 'Men, Women and the Priesthood of Christ' (1999), 39.
[68] Behr-Sigel, 'The Ordination of Women', 36.
[69] Bloom in Behr-Sigel, *The Ministry of Women in the Church*, xiii.

and teachers) (Eph. 4.11-14), and about 'the varieties of gifts' (wisdom, knowledge, faith, gifts of healing, miracles, prophecy, tongues and the interpretation of tongues) (1 Cor. 12.4-11), the working 'of the same Spirit' and 'the same Lord', but he does not attribute different ministries and gifts to men and to women.[70] Elisabeth Behr-Sigel stresses that gifts of the Spirit are given, 'not to a group defined by their sex, but to persons, unique persons', a 'mysterious uniqueness' which 'cannot be reduced to any male/female cultural stereotype'.[71]

This approach to ministry and service in the church stands in opposition to the 'charisms' argument. Citing St Paul, Kallistos Ware warns against 'associating certain charisms or ministries primarily or exclusively with women, and others primarily or exclusively with men', but urges rather that we should think 'in terms of our shared humanity'.[72] As we noted above, even if we were to admit that women possess distinctive spiritual gifts, he argues that this does not exclude women from performing the same tasks as men, but only that they will perform these tasks differently.[73]

The royal priesthood of the faithful

The equality of all faithful as members of the church, the Body of Christ, is reflected in the doctrine of the royal priesthood of all, clergy and laity, men and women, monastics and those 'in the world': all share in the one priesthood of Christ, the sole High Priest of the New Testament.[74] While all baptized Christians are called to bear witness to Christ and to serve the community in different ways, some are called to serve more especially in the ministry of the consecrated priesthood. The Orthodox tradition accepts the royal priesthood of believers, although many members of the clergy tend to accord it scant attention, because it can be misunderstood and seems to downplay the importance and role of the ordained priesthood or result in confusion between the two types of priesthood.

Kallistos Ware discusses Paul's famous expressions in Galatians, that 'in Christ Jesus you are all sons of God, through faith. For as many of you as were baptized into Christ have put on Christ. There is neither Jew nor Greek, there is neither slave nor free, there is neither male nor female; for you are all one in Christ Jesus' (Gal. 3.26-28). For Ware, the reference to baptism clearly refers to the equality of all in the royal priesthood of all believers, not to the ministerial priesthood.[75]

If men and women are equal as members of the royal priesthood, the argument goes, they should also be equal in terms of accessibility to the ordained priesthood. Again, this argument does not determine that women should be priests; it only affirms that both men and women, as members

---

[70]See also 1 Cor. 12.28-31 (ministries in the Church); and Gal. 5.22-23 (the fruit of the Spirit).

[71]Behr-Sigel, 'The Ordination of Women', 36.

[72]Ware, 'Men, Women and the Priesthood of Christ' (1999), 23.

[73]Ibid.

[74]See Ch. 11, 280; 284. Major references are Nicholas Afanasiev, 'The Royal Priesthood', in his *The Church of the Holy Spirit* (Notre Dame, IN: University of Notre Dame Press, 2007); Boris Bobrinskoy, *The Mystery of the Church* (Crestwood, NY: St Vladimir's Seminary Press, 2012), 202–12; 216–20; Paul Evdokimov, 'The Universal Priesthood of the Laity', in his *The Ages of the Spiritual Life* (Crestwood, NY: St Vladimir's Seminary Press, 1998).

[75]Ware, 'Men, Women and the Priesthood of Christ' (1999), 42–3.

of the Body of Christ, the church, participate in the royal priesthood of all believers and hence on this basis can be considered equally eligible for ministerial priesthood.

The church as a communion of persons

This argument is based to some extent on Paul in Galatians (Gal. 3.26-28, as cited above), the equality of all the faithful in Christ, and it also relies on the *sobornost'* ecclesiology, the church as a community of those who follow Christ, of the Slavophiles and their successors (see Chapter 11). It draws more particularly on Eucharistic ecclesiology: the church is actualized in a particular location and at a particular time by the celebration of the Eucharist and the participation of all the faithful in the one communion with Christ. Behr-Sigel writes that the church is 'essentially a communion, a *koinonia*, of persons, a communion in Christ by the Holy Spirit which rules out any discrimination based on race, class or sex (Gal 3:28)'.[76] Thus within this community of ontological equals under the headship of Christ, there is no justification for restricting access to ministries based solely on a distinction of sex.

Women as 'equal to the apostles'

The Orthodox tradition bestows the title 'equal-to-the-apostles' (*isapóstolos*) to certain saints in recognition of their outstanding service in the spreading and assertion of Christianity, comparable to that of the original apostles. These include many women, such as Mary Magdalene and the other Myrrh-bearing Women; Photina, the Samaritan Woman at Jacob's Well; Thekla, follower of Paul the Apostle; Helena, mother of Constantine the Great (ca. 250–ca. 330); Nino of Georgia (ca. 296–ca. 338 or 340), who preached Christianity in Georgia; and Olga of Kiev (ca. 890–969), the first Rus' ruler to convert to Christianity, either in 945 or in 957. In this light it is argued, that, since the church considers such women as indeed 'equal to the apostles', why could not women also be eligible for the priesthood?

Women and the mission of the church

Another line of thought favouring the ordination of women to the priesthood is more pastorally oriented than most arguments. This sees ordination to clerical office in terms of assisting the church in the fulfilment of its mission. Teva Regule advances several ways in which the opening of the ministry of the priesthood to women would assist the church in carrying out its liturgical and pastoral functions: ordaining women to the priesthood images the fullness of humanity more than an exclusively male priesthood; the ordination of women models the eschatological reality of the reign of God and the Eucharist that we are celebrating; ordaining women to the priesthood

[76]Behr-Sigel, 'The Ordination of Women', 36.

would have positive pastoral implications for many women (and indeed men) in the community, as was the case in the early centuries of women's diaconate; it models leadership for the community, especially for young girls ('seeing' people exercise ministry is important for our own understanding of what is possible for ourselves); finally, the gifts of the particular person for ministry would be reinforced, without consideration of biological sex.[77]

Women deacons

From the Rhodes Symposium in 1988 onwards, there have been repeated calls for the full restoration of the ancient order of deaconess. The office of deaconess was never formally abolished in the Orthodox Church, although it gradually decreased in importance and virtually disappeared towards the end of the first millennium. There are several references in the New Testament to women deacons, notably to Phoebe, whom St Paul names as 'a deacon [*diaconon*] of the church of Cenchreae' (Rom. 16.1). Women deacons were a feature of the early church, although there was no uniformity concerning the status and roles of deaconesses. The main responsibilities of deaconesses related to women in the community, such as assisting in the baptism of women, exchanging the kiss of peace with women during the liturgy, overseeing women in the congregation, providing instruction for women on the Christian life and performing works of charity and ministering to Christian women.[78] There are no indications that deaconesses in the early church carried out liturgical roles comparable to those later exercised by deacons, or that they substituted for deacons if necessary. The reasons for the gradual disappearance of deaconesses are also unclear, although the rise of infant baptism and the growth of minor orders of male clergy (readers and sub-deacons) are usually seen as the principal causes. In the later Byzantine period, the office survived primarily in women's monasteries.

In modern times there has been skirmishing over the nature and significance of the ritual of consecration of deaconesses. Some consider that deaconesses were installed by appointment or blessing (*cheirothesia*) in the nave of the church, like holders of minor orders, thus minimizing the stature of the office. But the weight of modern scholarship, especially the work of Professor Evangelos Theodorou (b. 1921) of the Faculty of Theology at Athens, indicates that deaconesses received an ordination (*cheirotonia*), fully comparable to that of deacons, and in fact the historical ritual for the ordination of deaconesses differed little from that of deacons and was performed at the altar during the Divine Liturgy, like those of male clergy (deacon, priest and bishop).[79]

---

[77]Private communication from Teva Regule, 22 September 2015.

[78]FitzGerald, 'The Nature and Characteristics of the Order of Deaconess', 102–3.

[79]Ibid., 108–18. Evangelos Theodorou, the principal proponent of the installation of deaconesses by ordination based on ancient practice, wrote two books on the subject: *Heroines of Love: Deaconesses through the Ages* (in Greek) (Athens: Apostlika Diakonia, 1949); and *The Ordination or Appointment of Deaconesses* (in Greek) (Athens, 1954). See his papers for the Agapia and Rhodes meetings, 'The Ministry of Deaconess in the Greek Orthodox Church', in Tarasar and Kirillova, eds., *Orthodox Women*; and 'The Institution of Deaconess in the Orthodox Church and the Possibility of Its Restoration', in Limouris, *The Place of Woman in the Orthodox Church*.

There were several initiatives in Russia and Greece to revive the institution of deaconess in the nineteenth and early twentieth centuries.[80] After the assassination of her husband Grand Duke Serge Alexandrovitch in 1905, Grand Duchess Elizaveta Feodorovna (St Elizabeth of Russia) (1864–1918), aunt and sister-in-law to Tsar Nicholas II, proposed the creation of a religious order whose members would be called deaconesses, devoted to works of charity. In 1910 and 1911 the Holy Synod of the Russian Orthodox Church (ROC) approved her proposed rule for the Convent of Martha and Mary in Moscow, but declined definitive approval of the title of deaconess, pending a formal decision for the restoration of the order of deaconesses in the ROC.[81] The convent was later closed by the Bolsheviks, who executed Elizaveta Feodorovna, head of the convent, as a member of the imperial family. In Greece in 1911, St Nectarius of Aegina (1846–1920) ordained as deaconesses two nuns of the women's monastery that he founded, explaining that the monastery needed their ministry. In the early 1950s, the Church of Greece established a school of deaconesses, subsequently absorbed into the School of Social Work of the University of Athens. In 1986 Metropolitan Christodoulos of Dimitriados (Volos) (1939–2008) (future primate of the Church of Greece) ordained as deaconess the abbess of a women's monastery. In October, 2004, the Holy Synod of the Church of Greece approved a limited restoration of the deaconate for women monastics, authorizing local bishops to institute abbesses in remote monasteries as deaconesses.

As mentioned above, the Consultation of Orthodox Women held at the monastery of Agapia, Romania, in 1976 called for study of the 'reactivation' of the office of deaconess, but less equivocal support came from the Inter-Orthodox Symposium in Rhodes in 1988. No doubt as a counterpart to the rejection of the idea of women priests, the Symposium strongly called for the revival of the 'apostolic order of the deaconess', with support for the ordination of deaconesses in the sanctuary during the Divine Liturgy. The Symposium also asked whether it would not be 'possible and desirable to allow women to enter the "lower orders" … sub-deacon, reader, cantor, teacher', calling for further study of this question.[82] Additional endorsements for the restoration of the order of deaconess occurred at Orthodox consultations and conferences held in January 1990 (Crete), November 1994 (Levadia, Greece), January 1996 (Addis Ababa), October 1996 (Damascus), May 1997 (Istanbul), May 1998 (Cambridge and New York) and June 1998 (Nairobi).[83]

Modern views envisage a women's diaconate largely as a service function, especially the provision of social services, religious education and other charitable undertakings, similar to the social and educational religious orders for women in the Catholic Church, while minimizing possible liturgical functions that women deacons could play. Even strong proponents of ordination of women to higher orders are careful to limit possible role of women deacons to social rather

---

[80]See FitzGerald, *Women Deacons in the Orthodox Church*, 149–60; and FitzGerald, 'The Nature and Characteristics of the Order of Deaconess', 123–8.

[81]See André Posternak, 'De la question de l'attribution du titre de "diaconesses" aux sœurs de la Demeure de miséricorde' (On the question of the attribution of the title 'deaconnesses' to the sisters of the House of Mercy), in Anne Khoudokormoff-Kotschoubey and Sister Elisabeth, *Élisabeth de Russie: Moniale, martyre et sainte* (Elizabeth of Russia: Nun, Martyr and Saint) (Brussels: Lessius, 2010), 200–1; and Elizabeth N. Grygo, *The Deaconess Movement in the Russian Orthodox Church, 1860-1917* (Seattle, WA: University of Washington, 1990).

[82]'Conclusions of the Consultation', in Limouris, *The Place of Woman in the Orthodox Church*, 31–2.

[83]See FitzGerald, *Women Deacons in the Orthodox Church*, 166–73.

than liturgical functions. Teva Regule lists four areas where women deacons could benefit the church: strengthening the pastoral care of the faithful and enhancing this care through the sacramental life of the church, for example in serving as chaplains in hospitals and hospices, bringing solace to the sick and dying, offering Holy Communion to the faithful and providing spiritual guidance; 'recapturing the philanthropic dimension of liturgy' – the 'liturgy after the liturgy' in ministering to the poor and the homeless; focusing on the Word of God, especially by women who have studied scripture; and connecting the pastoral, social and liturgical dimensions of the diaconate more fully.[84]

Going somewhat further, Kyriaki FitzGerald opens the door to reflection on liturgical roles for women:

> It is important to remember that in the past women deacons did have important responsibilities in the Eucharist assembly as well as in the administration of baptism, in praying with and for those in need, and in bringing Holy Communion to those unable to attend the Eucharist. ...Today, these expressions of ministry can certainly continue. At the same time, we also need to examine how women deacons can participate in the Eucharist and other liturgical services in a manner which is expressive of the living Tradition of the church and which is not defined by cultural norms of another time.[85]

The restoration of the women's diaconate solely for community functions, leaving liturgical functions exclusively to male deacons, would perpetuate a distinction based only on sex; for Regule, this constitutes a 'distortion of the office'.[86]

While supporting the revival of the order of deaconess and the equality of male and female deacons, Kallistos Ware emphasizes the fundamental difference between the orders of deacon and priest, especially with respect to the performance of sacraments.[87] In the absence of significant discussion on the possibility of the ordination of women to the priesthood, there is in fact greater emphasis on seeing the diaconate as a ministry in its right, and not merely as a stepping stone to the priesthood.

In February 2016, the Holy Synod of the Orthodox Patriarchate of Alexandria, whose jurisdiction covers all of Africa, approved the restoration of the ministry of deaconesses as an aid in the Orthodox mission field. During a pastoral visit to Kolwezi, Republic of Congo, Patriarch Theodoros II consecrated several African women as 'Deaconess of the Missions' of the Metropolis of Katanga and read the prayer for those entering the 'ecclesiastic ministry' for three nuns and two catechists. The announcement of this event created considerable excitement in Orthodox circles that at last an Orthodox jurisdiction had actually restored the women's diaconate. But a closer examination of the rite and the description of the responsibilities of the women makes it clear that, despite the title of deaconess, the ancient ritual for the ordination of deaconess was not used,

---

[84]Teva Regule, 'Rejuvenating the Diaconate: Opportunities, Challenges, and Steps', paper at the St Phoebe Conference 'Women and Diaconal Ministry: Past, Present, and Future' (6 June 2014), 7–12. https://orthodoxdeaconess.org/wp-content/uploads/2015/02/StPhoebeConfDiacTalk-Fin2b.pdf (1 August 2017).
[85]FitzGerald, *Women Deacons in the Orthodox Church*, 197.
[86]Regule, 'Rejuvenating the Diaconate', 12.
[87]Ware, 'Man, Woman and the Priesthood of Christ', 17.

but rather a ritual akin to the consecration of sub-deacons. The responsibilities of the women are pastoral functions related to the missionary effort of the metropolis, particularly with respect to baptisms of adults and marriages, and in the catechetical department of the metropolis. It appears therefore that this was not a restoration of the women's diaconate, but rather the use of the title of deaconess, with the rite of ordination similar to that for minor orders, for women engaged in well-defined pastoral roles.[88]

Conclusion

Although there was considerable interest in Orthodox circles in the 1980s concerning the ordination of women, by the end of the 1990s discussion appeared to have come full circle, resulting in apparent immobility. Only the question of the revival of the order of deaconess remained on the table, yet even here, there was no significant movement until the Patriarchate of Alexandria ordained several women as 'Deaconess of Missions' in the Congo in 2016 – although the significance of these ordinations remains ambiguous. The publication of Lawrence Farley's book *Feminism and Tradition* in 2012 seemed to seal the debate for the foreseeable future, even if the theology concerning the ordination of women is far from decisive, either for or against.

None of the arguments either in favour of or opposed to the ordination of women is conclusive in itself, nor can arguments be accumulated in order to confirm one position or the other as definitive. The arguments in favour of ordination of women eliminate potential obstacles to ordination, but do not determine that women must be ordained to the priesthood. Kallistos Ware concludes his review of the arguments for and against ordination in the same vein: 'Perhaps there is no conclusive argument *against* the ordination of women, but is there any conclusive argument in *favour* of it?'[89] As a summation of her involvement in the question of the ordination of women in the Orthodox Church, Elisabeth Behr-Sigel drew a cautious conclusion: 'I venture to express the opinion, not without having had to overcome my own prejudices, that there is no strictly theological reason against it'[90] – without affirming that there is an imperative reason supporting the ordination of women.

Arguments in favour of the ordination of women are in general not particularly well developed, strong or convincing and certainly do not create a compelling obligation on the Orthodox Church to ordain women to the priesthood. As Kallistos Ware wrote in 1999: 'I am far from convinced by many of the arguments advanced in favour of women priests; but at the same time a number of the arguments urged on the other side now appear to me a great deal less conclusive than they did twenty years ago.'[91] Many of the arguments advanced in favour of the ordination of women suffer from some

[88]See 'The Orthodox Christians of Kolwezi Wished the Missionary Patriarch for His Nameday' (18 February 2016). www.patriarchateofalexandria.com/index.php?module=news&action=details&id=1242 (1 August 2017); and 'Patriarch Theodoros of Alexandria Performs First Consecration of Deaconesses' (22 February 2016). http://basilica.ro/en/patriarch-theodoros-of-alexandria-performs-first-consecration-of-deaconesses (1 August 2017).

[89]Ware, 'Man, Woman and the Priesthood of Christ' (1999), 33.

[90]Behr-Sigel, 'Women in the Orthodox Church', 36.

[91]Ware, 'Man, Woman and the Priesthood of Christ' (1999), 7.

of the same logical fallacies as the arguments against the ordination of women, most notably non sequiturs – the obligation to ordain women does not flow logically from the stated premises.

While the charge against the ordination of women has been led by men, especially Georges Khodr, Paul Evdokimov, Alexander Schmemann, Thomas Hopko and more recently Lawrence Farley and Chad Hatfield, many Orthodox women theologians have written against the ordination of women, more or less repeating the arguments advanced by their male colleagues, especially the 'iconic' thesis.

There is a final argument against the ordination of women in the Orthodox Church, at least at this time and possibly for a long time, perhaps the strongest argument of all: most local Orthodox communities are simply not ready for such a step. Elisabeth Behr-Sigel was well aware of this and for this reason she generally proceeded cautiously, arguing mainly for a revision in the Orthodox view of women and their role in the church as a whole, rather than advancing only the highly inflammable issue of priesthood. She poked holes in the arguments against ordination, leaving readers to draw their own conclusions. She was aware that the issue of the ordination of women does not 'just concern the thinking of the faith in the clear light of the divine Logos', but 'it also touches the darker and very powerful regions of the emotions, the unconscious, and cultural archetypes.'[92] 'In its present state any decision to ordain women to the priesthood would almost inevitably give rise to schism in the Orthodox Church,' she writes. 'In view of this risk, we must be patiently impatient.'[93] This is where the matter stands at the beginning of the twenty-first century: the ordination of women remains a dormant issue.

Until the breach opened by the institution of women deaconesses by the Patriarchate of Alexandria in Africa in 2016, little happened in the way of formal reinstatement of the deaconesses – despite greater awareness of the ancient practice, modern precedents, the absence of canonical obstacles and numerous endorsements for the restoration of the order of deaconesses by pan-Orthodox gatherings. The reasons for this lay no doubt partly in institutional inertia, and perhaps partly as well in concerns among local Orthodox churches that the restoration of the women's deaconate may reopen the Pandora's Box of debate over the ordination of women to the priesthood. Those favourable to the restoration of the female diaconate but opposed to women priests may hope that women deacons may dispel any move towards women priests, especially if the functions of women deacons are defined mainly in terms of social and educational activities, rather than liturgical functions. Those opposed to both women's diaconate and priesthood consider the women's diaconate a Trojan horse, or the 'thin edge of the wedge', which would increase the pressure for women to be admitted to the priesthood as well.[94] This is not a theological argument; it is a psychological argument and a logical fallacy.[95]

---

[92]Behr-Sigel, *The Ministry of Women in the Church*, 179.

[93]Behr-Sigel, 'The Ordination of Women', 44.

[94]See Chad Hatfield and Lawrence Farley, 'Deaconesses' (Transcript of an interview, 3 December 2014). http://www.ancientfaith.com/podcasts/svsvoices/deaconesses (2014) (8 November 2017); and Lawrence Farley, 'A Second Look at the Rejuvenation of the Ministry of the Ordained Deaconess' (4 December 2014). http://myocn.net/second-look-rejuvenation-ministry-ordained-deaconess/ (7 November 2017). Farley's main reason for opposing the restoration of the women's deaconate is fear that this will lead inexorably to the ordination of women priests.

[95]See Paul Ladouceur, 'Review, Lawrence Farley, *Feminism and Tradition: Quiet Reflections on Ordination and Communion*', *St Vladimir's Theological Quarterly*, 60, no. 3 (2016): 415–21; and 'Christ, the Fathers and Feminism: Dialogue with Fr Lawrence

Since none of the theological arguments either for or against ordination is conclusive, can it be that it is not a theological question at all? In this perspective, the ordination of women can best be seen as a pastoral or 'economic' question, a question of church organization or structure and church discipline. Yet even if the body of the Orthodox Church is far from ready for such a step, Orthodox should, in the words of Kallistos Ware, 'have the courage to approach the question of women's ministry in the church with an open mind and an open heart'.[96] When the time comes, when 'it is time to act for the Lord,' then the church should proceed, knowing that there are no theological obstacles to such a step.

Farley', *St Vladimir's Theological Quarterly*, 62, no. 3 (2018): 287–95.

[96]Ware, 'Man, Woman and the Priesthood of Christ' (1999), 52.

Part III

Assessments and Conclusions

17

Light and Shadows in Modern Orthodox Theology

Chapter Outline

The Russian religious renaissance in the spotlight

The most favourable assessment of the Russian religious renaissance is perhaps that of Nicolas Zernov (1898–1980) in his classic study *The Russian Religious Renaissance of the Twentieth Century* (1963).[1] Zernov was himself an important actor on the Orthodox theological scene in the mid-twentieth century, a leading ecumenical figure, and he knew personally almost all the major Russian religious figures in exile. From 1947 to 1966, he was Spalding Lecturer in Eastern

[1]Nicolas Zernov, *The Russian Religious Renaissance of the Twentieth Century* (New York: Harper & Row, 1963). This work remains, over a half-century after its original publication in 1963, the best historical study of the Russian religious renaissance.

Orthodox Studies at Oxford University (a position subsequently held by Bishop Kallistos Ware). In his book, Zernov goes well beyond theology as such and he places the Russian religious renaissance in the broad setting of the social, political, intellectual and cultural ferment of late imperial Russia. This contextual assessment of the Russian religious renaissance distinguishes Zernov's approach from that of his contemporary, Georges Florovsky, the major critic of religious philosophy, in his *Ways of Russian Theology* (1937), who focuses largely on ideas and little on the context in which the ideas developed.[2]

Zernov sees the religious renaissance as a Christian perspective, a return to the church, of a leading segment of the Russian intelligentsia which had almost entirely abandoned Christianity in favour of secular and often anti-religious philosophies and ideologies. Zernov can be faulted for an overly schematic presentation of the intelligentsia as virtually a separate class in Russian society. He refers to the intelligentsia as an 'Order', which suggests a degree of organization and even a 'membership' which the intelligentsia certainly did not have.[3]

In his brief summary of the main features of 'The Legacy of the Russian Intelligentsia' (the title of his conclusion), Zernov highlights the accomplishments of the religious renaissance in its social, political and ecclesial context:

> It produced a convincing exposition of traditional Orthodoxy, formulated in terms intelligible to modern educated people. It preserved the continuity of Russian Christian culture at a time when it was being systematically destroyed by the Communists; it enriched the Ecumenical Movement at an important period of its initial development by familiarizing it with Eastern theology; finally it demonstrated once more that God sends his servants and prophets to those who are in distress and in special need of comfort and consolation.[4]

In retrospect, surely Zernov is too modest in his assessment of the significance of the Russian religious renaissance for modern Orthodox theology as a whole. He does not mention the enduring theological legacy of the Russian theologians and philosophers of the first decades of the twentieth century, especially their impact on neopatristic theology. In the early 1960s, when Zernov was writing his book, the appeal of religious philosophy had already waned considerably, and there appeared to be more conflict than continuity between religious philosophy and emerging neopatristic theology. It was only at the beginning of the twenty-first century that it became clear that the origins of neopatristic theology must be seen as a prolongation of the Russian religious renaissance in another mode, rather than standing diametrically opposed to it.

Other favourable assessments of the Russian religious renaissance, such as those of Antoine Arjakovsky, Michael Plekon and Paul Valliere, focus on its principal ideas, either in their own right,

---

[2]Georges Florovsky, *Puti russkogo bogosloviia* (Paris: YMCA-Press, 1937; 1983). In English: *The Ways of Russian Theology*, in *The Collected Works of Georges Florovsky*, Vols. V and VI (Belmont, MA: Nordland, 1979).

[3]Zernov adopts the notion of the intelligentsia as an 'Order' from the comparison that several members of the intelligentsia themselves made to religious orders. See *The Russian Religious Renaissance*, 2–3. By page 17, Zernov capitalizes Order when referring to the intelligentsia. See our discussion of the intelligentsia as an 'Order' in Ch. 4, 61.

[4]Zernov, *The Russian Religious Renaissance*, 329–30.

or as predecessors to their fuller development in neopatristic theology.[5] Arjakovsky is an ardent advocate of Bulgakov's theology,[6] while Plekon sees a continuation of the Russian religious renaissance in such figures as Nicholas Afanasiev, Paul Evdokimov, John Meyendorff and Alexander Schmemann, but he considers that the theologies of Georges Florovsky and Vladimir Lossky constitute a deviation from the main line of the religious renaissance.[7]

In his study *Modern Russian Theology*, Paul Valliere identifies the principal contributions of the 'Russian school' to dogmatic theology as:

> the thematization of the humanity of God (*bogochelovechestvo*); the concept of the whole of things (*vseedinstvo*); the idea of Cosmodicy; the greatly expanded doctrine of kenosis; sophiology; the theory of the Trinitarian Dyad; the relational logic of church-and-world dogmatics; dogmatic applications of the idea of pan-humanity (*vsechelovechestvo*); the dogmatic case for a humane church (the divine-human imperative).[8]

Most of these ideas, at least the way that the religious philosophers expressed them, were discarded in subsequent patristic-based Orthodox theology. On the other hand, other major themes of the religious renaissance which Valliere does not mention, such as the theology of the human person, the church as community or the conciliarity of the church (*sobornost'*) and the 'churching' or 'Christification' of life, with its ramifications in social and political theology, found their way into the mainstream of neopatristic theology.

Accounts of Russian thought after Florovsky's severe critiques in *The Ways of Russian Theology* (1937) are also generally more favourable to the religious renaissance. The histories of Russian philosophy by Nicolas Lossky and Basil Zenkovsky, both important figures of the religious renaissance in their own right, focus on the leading figures of the renaissance, rather than on general assessments of the religious renaissance as such. Nonetheless, in his concluding remarks on Pavel Florensky, Lossky, well aware of the critiques of Florensky's theology, seeks to situate Florensky, especially his *The Pillar and Ground of the Truth*, within the broader context of the times:

> The diseases of modern civilization – the loss of the idea of absolute value of personality, of the idea of state based upon justice, of the ideal of free spiritual creativeness – are due in the first instance to the fact that the intellectuals, and, following them, the masses, have forsaken Christianity and become non-religious. The main task of our epoch is to bring, first, the intellectuals and through them, the masses, back to Christianity and consequently to Christian humanism. That purpose may be particularly well served by religiously philosophic works, written in the new, more or less secular

---

[5]See Antoine Arjakovsky, *The Way: Religious Thinkers of the Russian Emigration in Paris and their Journal* (University of Notre Dame Press, 2013); Michael Plekon, *Living Icons: Persons of Faith in the Eastern Church* (Notre Dame, IN: University of Notre Dame Press, 2002) and Paul Valliere, *Modern Russian Theology: Bukharev, Soloviev, Bulgakov: Orthodox Theology in a New Key* (Grand Rapids, MI: Eerdmans, 2000).

[6]See Antoine Arjakovsky, *Essai sur le père Serge Boulgakov, philosophe et théologien chrétien* (Essay on Fr Sergius Bulgakov, Christian Philosopher and Theologian), (Paris: Parole et silence, 2006).

[7]Michael Plekon, 'The Russian Religious Renaissance and Its Theological Legacy', in Mary B. Cunningham and Elizabeth Theokritoff, eds., *The Cambridge Companion to Orthodox Christian Theology* (Cambridge: Cambridge University Press, 2009).

[8]Valliere, *Modern Russian Theology*, 388.

> style, connecting religious problems with modern science and metaphysical investigations of the higher realms of being which transcend the human world. Florensky's works belong to this category and therefore are highly valuable, whatever defects they may have from the point of view of the traditional style and content of Orthodox theological literature.[9]

Lossky summarizes here the general programme or intent of the Russian religious renaissance. His remark about the defects of Florensky's work in terms of 'the traditional style and content' of Orthodox theology could be directed against Florovsky in particular, whose theological judgement is based mainly on the degree of Western influence in an author and on conformity to or deviation from patristic theology. Lossky's approach, seeing the religious renaissance within its general social and political context, anticipates Zernov's later *The Russian Religious Renaissance of the Twentieth Century.*

In a similar vein, Basil Zenkovsky, in his brief concluding remarks to his *History of Russian Philosophy*, expresses his firm conviction that Russian philosophy has a 'special path' in contrast with the rationalism and secularism typical of modern Western philosophy. The path of Russian philosophy 'is opened to us by the Orthodox view of culture and life, of man and nature'; that, in essence, in the mainstream of Russian thought, 'there has been no foundation for a rejection of ecclesiastical truth as a matter of principle.' It is this which defines the 'valuational' element in his own historiosophical scheme, founded, as he writes, on 'Christianity as the basic creative force of Russian culture'.[10]

In one of his final books, *The Russian Idea* (1946), Nicolas Berdyaev refers to himself as 'the extreme left in the Russian religious philosophy of the time of the [religious] Renaissance'.[11] He identifies the prime focus of the religious renaissance as the relation of Creator and creation:

> The basic theme of Russian thought at the beginning of the twentieth century is the theme of the divine in the cosmos, of cosmic divine transfiguration, of the energies of the Creator in creation. It is the theme of the divine in man, of the creative vocation of man and the meaning of culture. It is an eschatological theme of the philosophy of history. The Russians meditated upon all problems in their essential nature, as if they were standing face to face with the mystery of being.[12]

As we saw in Chapter 4, Berdyaev's main criticism of the Russian religious renaissance prior to the Revolutions of 1917 is its failure to reach beyond a highly cultured elite concentrated in Saint Petersburg:

> There was a breach between the interests of the higher cultural classes of the Renaissance, and the interests of the revolutionary social movement among the people and in the left Intelligentsia, which had not yet passed through the intellectual and spiritual crisis. They lived at different levels of culture, almost in different centuries.[13]

---

[9]Nicolas Lossky, *History of Russian Philosophy* (New York: International Universities Press, 1951; London: George Allen & Unwin, 1952), 191.

[10]V. V. Zenkovsky, *A History of Russian Philosophy* (1950) (London: Routledge & Kegan Paul and New York: Columbia University Press, 1953), II: 923–4.

[11]Nicolas Berdyaev, *The Russian Idea* (New York: Macmillan, 1948), 244.

[12]Berdyaev, *The Russian Idea*, 245.

[13]Ibid., 246.

In another essay, he wrote: 'The weakness of the Russian spiritual renaissance was in its absence of a broad social base'.[14]

Paul Evdokimov considers that Russian religious philosophy stood in opposition both to Kant's denial of metaphysics and to Hegel's logical monism by positing 'immediate experience in a very wide sense' in contrast to all systems of abstract thought.[15] The religious philosophers were certainly influenced by Western philosophies, writes Evdokimov, but they maintained their originality and major figures such as Vladimir Soloviev, Symeon Franck, Nicolas Lossky and Nicolas Berdyaev did not construct philosophical systems.[16] Evdokimov, while recognizing that sophiology and other ideas of religious philosophy are indeed problematic, goes so far as to say that Russian philosophy 'can serve as an excellent introduction to the essentially religious reflection on being and existence'; the problems investigated by the Russians 'are never theoretical but eminently practical and their complete vision of existence is constructed in the light of the dogmas'.[17] Evdokimov approves Nicolas Lossky's characterization of the common principle of religious philosophy as 'concrete ideal-realism', 'the inseparable unity of the ideal and the real aspects of the nature of the world, and also the unity of abstract thought and contemplative intuition'[18] – an implicit validation, even if only as a goal, of the concept of all-unity.

As we saw in Chapter 4, a major factor which favoured the flowering of the religious renaissance was the inability of the Russian Orthodox Church (ROC) and official theology to respond adequately to the religious and philosophical issues and queries of late imperial Russia. Many church leaders did not consider that a dialogue with cultural and intellectual figures outside the church could lead to anything productive. Until the Revolution, only Fr Pavel Florensky among the leading personalities of the religious renaissance was within the formal structure of the ROC. The combined effect of the religious renaissance and the Revolution was the marginalization of academic theology in Russian religious thought. Some academic theologians, such as Anton Kartashev (1875–1960), became major figures in exile, moving close to the religious renaissance, while the spirit of Russian academic theology was perpetuated mainly in conservative exile circles, especially in the Russian Orthodox Church Outside of Russia (ROCOR), and in translations or adaptations of Russian theological textbooks in other Orthodox countries such as Greece and Romania (see Chapters 6 and 7). For many decades Fr Michael Pomazansky (1888–1988), professor of dogmatic theology from 1949 until 1980 at ROCOR's Holy Trinity Orthodox Seminary in Jordanville, New York, was the most prominent descendent of pre-revolutionary academic theology.[19]

---

[14]Nicolas Berdyaev, 'The Russian Spiritual Renaissance of the Beginning of the XXth Century and the Journal *Put'* (For the Tenth Anniversary of *Put'*)', *Put'*, 49 (1935) (in Russian). www.chebucto.ns.ca/Philosophy/Sui-Generis/Berdyaev/essays/rsr.htm (13 March 2017).

[15]Paul Evdokimov, *Le Christ dans la pensée russe* (Christ in Russian Thought) (Paris: Le Cerf, 1970), 147. The scope of Evdokimov's underrated book is broader than the title suggests as it encompasses Russian religious thought in general.

[16]Nonetheless, sophiology, beginning with Soloviev and reaching its fullest expression in Bulgakov, as an integration of philosophy and theology into a coherent mode of thought, can indeed be considered a 'system'.

[17]Evdokimov, *Le Christ dans la pensée russe*, 147.

[18]Ibid., 147–8.

[19]Pomazansky's most important work is his textbook *Orthodox Dogmatic Theology: A Concise Exposition* (1963), (Platina, CA: St. Herman of Alaska Brotherhood Press, 1984).

Critiques of Russian religious thought

The dialogue of Russian Christian thinkers with contemporary philosophy, the arts and society prior to the Revolution recalls the encounter between the early church and Greek philosophy in the first centuries of the church. Just as early Christian thinkers sought out and adapted religious elements in ancient Greek culture, so the leaders of the religious renaissance in Russia drew on religious and more especially Christian elements in modern thought and culture. Justin the Philosopher (mid-second century) was one of the first to attempt to bridge the gap, but another two centuries after Justin would pass before an appropriate synthesis was made between divine revelation and Greek philosophy, in the work of the great Fathers of the Church of the fourth and fifth centuries, an encounter which produced Christian theology. The Russian religious philosophers thought that they were also effecting just such a synthesis, not with ancient Greek philosophy but with modern philosophy. But for the critics of the religious renaissance, Georges Florovsky and Vladimir Lossky in particular, the starting point of the religious renaissance was wrong. Whereas in the early centuries, the basis of theology was first and foremost revelation and the experience of church, which served as the basis for the interpretation and appropriation of elements of Greek philosophy, for the critics, the religious philosophers sought to understand Christian truths in the light of modern philosophy. For them, modern philosophies are unacceptable as a basis for expressing Christian truth, which can only be satisfactorily articulated in the concepts and language of the ancient Fathers of the Church.

In the late 1920s and early 1930s, when Georges Florovsky was formulating his neopatristic project, both he and Sergius Bulgakov were professors at the Saint Sergius Institute of Orthodox Theology in Paris – in fact, Bulgakov was instrumental in the invitation to Florovsky to join the staff of newly founded Institute in 1926. Despite the close working association between the two leading Orthodox theologians, and their disagreement on crucial theological issues, especially sophiology, Florovsky studiously avoided direct criticism, at least in print, of the senior theologian or of his theology, even though he regarded sophiology as 'near-paganism.'[20] Instead, Florovsky chose to attack the historical and theological premises on which sophiology rested, such as its appeal to certain Fathers of the Church and to representations of Divine Wisdom in the iconographic tradition. Despite theological differences, personal relations between Bulgakov and Florovsky remained friendly until Bulgakov's death in 1944.[21]

As we saw previously, it was in part in reaction to what Florovsky considered the excesses and errors of the theology of the religious renaissance that he launched his appeal for a 'return to the Fathers' – although the neo-scholastic theology of the academies and the ROC loomed just as large as a target of his critiques. In his theological method, Florovsky's interest

---

[20]Andrew Louth, 'The Patristic Revival and Its Protagonists', in Cunningham and Theokritoff, *The Cambridge Companion to Orthodox Christian Theology*, 189. Mary B. Cunningham and Elizabeth Theokritoff, eds., *The Cambridge Companion to Orthodox Christian Theology* (Cambridge University Press, 2009), 189.

[21]See Paul Ladouceur, 'Aimons-nous les uns les autres: Serge Boulgakov et Georges Florovsky' ('Let us love another': Sergius Bulgakov and Georges Florovsky), *Contacts*, 64, 237, (2012).

is mainly in ideas, their origin, their nature and their relationship with the teachings and history of the Church. Despite his historical outlook, in his *Ways of Russian Theology* he pays scant attention to the particular circumstances in which Christian thought developed and flourished and its unique role in the last decades of the Russian Empire. Florovsky was primarily a historian of ideas and he accorded little importance to the social and political context in which ideas developed.

In *The Ways of Russian Theology*, Florovsky characterizes religious philosophy as 'a return to German idealism and German mysticism', marked, like all 'Western romanticism, especially the German variety', by the 'substitution of "religious philosophy" for theology'.[22] For Florovsky, religious philosophy is inherently inadequate as an expression of the Orthodox tradition because it deviates from scripturally based patristic thought. The religious renaissance is imbued with 'neo-Westernism', specifically Kantianism and romanticism, idealist metaphysics, relativism, psychologism, 'unhistorical utopianism' and 'pseudo-apocalyptism'; it is infused with 'historicism', tinged with fatalism and even predestination. Echoing Berdyaev's self-criticism, Florovsky also rebukes the religious renaissance for being an elite movement with no broad social base.[23] While many of these points have some substance, Florovsky creates a caricature of the religious renaissance, painting a dark portrait with broad brush strokes of unqualified generalizations, without providing substantiation for most of his negative characterizations.

Nonetheless, Florovsky gives passing marks to some religious philosophers. Vladimir Ern (1879–1917) is credited with struggling 'against psychologism and for ontology', that is, against personal experience often marked with romantic emotionalism as distinct from ontological reality as the basis for theology. Personal experience ranked high on the scale of values of many figures of the religious renaissance, as indeed it did in many earlier phases of Christianity, such as the hesychastic quarrel of the fourteenth century. Florovsky's unease with religious experience is as much a reflection of his own personality as it is a theological statement. Nicolas Berdyaev and even Sergius Bulgakov also come out relatively well in Florovsky's book, but only inasmuch as they focus on history, which leads 'to the acceptance of the "historical" church'.[24] As we saw in Chapter 4, acceptance of the Orthodox Church was problematic for many figures of the religious renaissance, especially those associated with the 'new religious consciousness'. On the other hand, Florovsky considers that some of Berdyaev's thinking abandons historical Christianity and the patristic tradition for esoteric speculative mysticism. Florovsky does not consider the full range of Bulgakov's theology, since *The Ways of Russian Theology*, even though it was published in 1937, covers the period only up to the beginning of the First World War, and thus excludes Bulgakov's major theological works published in the late 1920s and 1930s.

Florovsky reserves his most severe criticism for the theology of Fr Pavel Florensky, who in some ways is a stand-in for Bulgakov. Florovsky had only a very limited personal contact with Florensky. Florovsky's criticism of Florensky goes well beyond a dispassionate and objective critique of

---

[22]Florovsky, *The Ways of Russian Theology*, II:275.
[23]Ibid., II:271–5.
[24]Ibid., II:274.

Florensky's ideas, to a personal attack. Florensky was an easy target, since he remained in the Soviet Union after the triumph of the Bolsheviks and could not defend himself. Florovsky writes that Florensky 'always lived in a secluded, cosy nook' and that he 'escaped from the tragic crossroads of life and concealed himself in a confined but comfortable cell'.[25] For most of the 1930s, Florensky was indeed in a 'confined cell', but not a comfortable one nor one of his own choosing – he was in communist prison camps in Siberia and at the Solovki Monastery in northern Russia converted to a prison. In 1937, the year of publication of Florovsky's book, Florensky was brought before a communist 'troika' tribunal, condemned to death and executed by firing squad. It was Florovsky who escaped from the 'tragic crossroads of life' by leaving Russia in the early 1920s; Florensky stayed at the crossroads and suffered the consequences. If Florovsky had known of Florensky's fate, he would undoubtedly have written something quite different; in the mid-1930s, it was known in Paris only that Florensky had disappeared into the prison camps.

Modern writers, both Orthodox and non-Orthodox, have been kinder to Pavel Florensky while not endorsing all aspects of his theology, especially sophiology. Nicolas Lossky recalls warmly two meetings with Florensky and he writes that in 1913 Florensky sent him a copy of *The Pillar and Ground of the Truth*, which 'furthered my gradual return to the church, which finally took place in 1918'.[26] Lossky's presentation of Florensky's theology is generally sympathetic, even Florensky's sophiology, and, as we saw at the beginning of this chapter, Lossky defends Florensky against Florovsky's broad critique of Florensky's thinking and personality, considering that 'Florensky's works "are highly valuable"'.[27] Paul Evdokimov's assessment of Florensky also stands in sharp contrast with Florovsky's. Evdokimov describes Florensky as a 'genius' and a 'martyr', even before Florensky's exact fate became known.[28] Comparing the treatment accorded to Florensky by Florovsky on the one hand, and by Lossky and Evdokimov on the other, one has some difficulty realizing that they are writing about the same person and his thinking.

Basil Zenkovsky is also kinder to Florensky than Florovsky, praising him for 'his strong emphasis on the living unity of the cosmos', but nonetheless faulting Florensky for 'pretentiousness in expounding his *own* ideas as firm ecclesiastical truth', for placing too much emphasis on personal religious experience (which Zenkovsky also refers to as psychologism), for introducing 'many extra-ecclesiastical ideas', for 'dilettante excursions into the field of philology' and more generally for 'banishing' rather than resolving philosophical difficulties, especially concerning Florensky's

---

[25]Ibid., II: 277. Florovsky's text on Florensky (nearly half the section on religious philosophy) is a slightly revised version of his review of *The Pillar and Ground of Truth*, published in 1930: 'The Weariness of the Spirit: On Florensky's *The Pillar and Confirmation of Truth*', in *Philosophy, Philosophical Problems and Movements* (*The Collected Works of Georges Florovsky*, Vol. XII) (Vaduz 1989).

[26]Lossky, *History of Russian Philosophy*, 177.

[27]Ibid., 191.

[28]Evdokimov, *Le Christ dans la pensée russe*, 178. During the Second World War the Soviets propagated the story that Florensky died in 1943 – hence Bulgakov's eulogy of Florensky in 1944. In the 1950s, Soviet propaganda revised his death to 1948, the year that Paul Evdokimov, writing in 1970, uses in his book. Florensky's execution in 1937 was discovered when the NKVD archives were opened after the fall of communism. See Vitali Chentalinski, 'Un Leonardo russe: Le dossier KGB de Pavel Florensky' (A Russian Leonardo: Pavel Florensky's KGB file), in *La Parole ressuscitée: Dans les archives littéraires du KGB* (The Resurrection of the Word: In the KGB's Documentary Files) (Paris: Robert Laffont, 1994).

attempt to establish cosmic total-unity.[29] Other biographies and assessments of Florensky are also generally sympathetic towards him while not endorsing all aspects of this theology.[30]

A frequent critique of the Russian religious thought is that it is tainted by a cosmic determinism, directing humanity inevitably towards an all-unity embracing God, humanity and the cosmos. Basil Zenkovsky traces the origin of this determinism to Vladimir Soloviev's notion of the 'the triumph of the good', ineluctably guided by divine Sophia. Soloviev made an effort to reconcile cosmic all-unity with human freedom and Christian dogma, but for some critics he was unsuccessful. Zenkovsky writes of determinism in Soloviev:

> The 'end of history' is the Kingdom of God, i.e. the complete union of the 'Absolute in the process of becoming' with the First Principle. This sophiological determinism echoes the Enlightenment faith in progress, just as it echoes another determinism which was being formulated during Soloviev's lifetime – the historical determinism of Marxism. Soloviev's profound faith in the triumph of the good was internally connected with his historiosophical determinism. … The 'salvation' of the world, i.e. the re-integration of the cosmos with the Absolute, is proceeding undeviatingly in the womb of the cosmos, and pre-eminently in man.[31]

Zenkovsky quotes Bulgakov, who also expresses a sophio-historical determinism: 'Sophia directs history, as its objective conformity to law; the sophiological quality of history is the sole *guarantee* that something will issue from it.'[32] But this perceived determinism clashes with another fundamental doctrine of the religious renaissance, human freedom. Zenkovsky remarks that this problem constantly preoccupied Bulgakov, but that Bulgakov was 'unable to break the spell of the metaphysics of total-unity', falling into 'a sophiological monism'.[33] In a similar vein, in the heat of the sophiological controversy of the mid-1930s, Vladimir Lossky saw in Bulgakov's teaching on apocatastasis a 'sophianic-natural determinism' 'which destroys human freedom'.[34] Berdyaev, the most ardent apostle of freedom among the religious philosophers, thought that he resolved the problem by rejecting sophiology altogether.[35] However the mechanism of the inevitable harmonious union of God and creation is described, the final outcome of God's relation with the creation is in effect a revival of the ancient doctrine of universal salvation or apocatastasis, towards

---

[29]Zenkovsky, *A History of Russian Philosophy*, II:875–90, passim.

[30]See the biographies by Avril Pyman, *Pavel Florensky: A Quiet Genius: The Tragic and Extraordinary Life of Russia's Unknown da Vinci* (Continuum, 2010); Robert Slesinski, *Pavel Florensky: A Metaphysics of Love* (Yonkers, NY: St Vladimir's Seminary Press, 1984) and Milan Zust, *À la recherche de la vérité vivante. L'expérience religieuse de Pavel A. Florenskij (1882-1937)* (In Search of the Living Truth: The Religious Experience of Pavel A. Florensky (1882–1937)) (Rome: Lipa, 2002).

[31]Zenkovsky, *A History of Russian Philosophy*, II:525–6. For a more detailed but broadly similar analysis of determinism in Soloviev and Bulgakov, see Brandon Gallaher, 'Antinomism, Trinity and the Challenge of Solovëvan Pantheism in the Theology of Sergij Bulgakov', *Studies in East European Thought*, 64 (2012).

[32]From Bulgakov's *The Philosophy of Economy*, quoted by Zenkovsky, *A History of Russian Philosophy*, II:910.

[33]Zenkovsky, *A History of Russian Philosophy*, II:916; 915.

[34]See Vladimir Lossky, *The Sophia Controversy: Protopriest S. Bulgakov's 'Report' and the Meaning of the Decree of the Moscow Patriarchate* (in Russian) (Paris, 1936). Unpublished translation by William Kevin Fisher (2004), sections 8 to 10; and the summary in Part III.

[35]See Berdyaev, *The Russian Idea*, 241: 'I do not myself share the views of the sophiological school, but I place a high value on Bulgakov's line of thought in Orthodoxy and upon his statement of new problems.'

which both Florensky and Bulgakov were sympathetic.[36] The religious philosophers did not see their way to the possibility of reconciling divine providence and human freedom as a hope rather than a certainty of universal salvation within the boundaries of church dogmas.[37]

The generally favourable assessments of Russian religious renaissance by Nicolas Lossky, Basil Zenkovsky and Paul Evdokimov are a far cry from Georges Florovsky's single-minded focus on Western influence as the basis of his near-universal condemnation of religious philosophy. Florovsky did not see himself as a beneficiary of the religious thought of the pre-revolutionary period – even though his own religious awakening as a teenager was a direct result of his early contacts with the writings of the religious philosophers, especially Soloviev.[38] As we suggested above, he had difficulty reconciling theological enunciations and religious experience, dogma and intuition, Scripture and mysticism. His own predilection was largely noetic: the truth of Christianity is expressed in ideas, forever enshrined in the language of the Greek Fathers. He had little faith in personal experience, however exalted and ecclesial it may be, as the basis for religious truth. Although the religious renaissance provided his first exposure to philosophy and theology, he soon moved away from the renaissance and became its most ardent critic. Uncompromising in his intellectual integrity, Florovsky even criticized aspects of Vladimir Lossky's theology while holding up Lossky's *The Mystical Theology of the Eastern Church* as a prime example of neopatristic theology.[39]

Other critiques of the Russian religious renaissance come from more conservative Orthodox theologians, such as Fr Michael Pomazansky. Pomazansky's main target is Soloviev, whom he accuses, together with his followers Bulgakov and Berdyaev, of neo-Gnosticism.[40] He specifically criticizes Soloviev for a host of teachings which 'are most evidently distinct from, and even directly depart from the teachings of the faith confessed by the church'.[41] These doctrines include dogmatic development and sophiology. He dismisses the attempt of the Russian religious renaissance to join philosophy and theology: 'It is essential there be a precise distinction between dogmatic theology and Christian philosophy, and every attempt to turn dogmatics into Christian philosophy must be decisively rejected.'[42] It does not occur to Pomazansky that for the Fathers of old a distinction between Christian philosophy and dogmatic theology would have made no sense and it is perhaps for this reason that his radar fails to detect neopatristic theology.

---

[36]See Pavel Florensky's chapter on eschatology, 'Letter Eight: Gehenna', in *The Pillar and Ground of the Truth: An Essay in Orthodox Theodicy in Twelve Letters* (Princeton, NJ: Princeton University Press, 1997); and Sergius Bulgakov, 'On the Question of the Apocatastasis of the Fallen Spirits', in *Apocatastasis and Transfiguration* (New Haven, CT: Variable Press, 1995).

[37]As an alternative which preserves divine and human freedom to a deterministic view of apocatastasis, see Kallistos Ware, 'Dare We Hope for the Salvation of All?' *Theology Digest*, 45, 4 (1998). Reprinted in *The Inner Kingdom* (Crestwood, NY: St Vladimir's Seminary Press, 2001).

[38]See Paul Gavrilyuk, *Georges Florovsky and the Russian Religious Renaissance* (Oxford: Oxford University Press, 2013), 32–41.

[39]See Florovsky's review of the English translation of Lossky's *The Mystical Theology of the Eastern Church*, in *The Journal of Religion*, 38 (1958).

[40]Michael Pomazansky, *Orthodox Dogmatic Theology: A Concise Exposition* (1963) (Platina, CA: St. Herman of Alaska Brotherhood Press, 1994), 366, n. 2. Pomazansky entitles Appendix I of his work 'On New Currents in Russian Philosophico-Theological Thought from the Point of View of the Dogmas of the Orthodox Christian Faith'. The 'New Currents' in question are the Russian religious renaissance; neopatristic theology does not feature in his book.

[41]Pomazansky, *Orthodox Dogmatic Theology*, 366.

[42]Ibid., 365.

Pomazansky's critique of sophiology is based principally on an analysis of Wisdom in Scripture and he concludes: 'There are no grounds for seeing in a direct sense any personal spiritual being, distinct from God himself, a soul of the world or idea of the world.'[43] Despite Pomazansky's zealous defence of traditional Orthodox dogmatic theology against claims from secular philosophy, he does not dismiss religious philosophy entirely and indeed accurately expresses the dilemma of the Christian philosopher:

> Christian religious philosophy has a difficult path: to bring together freedom of thought, as a principle of philosophy, with faithfulness to the dogmas and the whole teaching of the church. 'Go by the free way, wherever the free mind draws you,' says the duty of the thinker; 'be faithful to Divine Truth,' whispers to him the duty of the Christian. Therefore, one might always expect that in practical realization the compilers of the systems of Christian philosophy will be forced to sacrifice, willingly or unwillingly, the principles of one sphere in favour of the other. The church consciousness welcomes sincere attempts at creating a harmonious, philosophical Christian world view; but the church views them as private, personal creations, and does not sanction them with its authority.[44]

Taken at face value, this would place sophiology as a *theologumena*, which is likely how Florensky and Bulgakov considered it, a personal teaching open to questioning, not a doctrine or dogma of the church. Even if Pomazansky awkwardly dismisses the religious renaissance, his concluding statement concerning the relationship of philosophy and theology would strike a sympathetic chord among many Orthodox thinkers.

The broad scope and manifold expressions of the Russian religious renaissance argue for a nuanced approach to its enduring value, attentive to personalities and themes. From a certain perspective, the renaissance was indeed too audacious in its approach, and too uncritical in its appropriation of certain ideas of Western philosophy, especially German idealism, which led to deviations from traditional Orthodox thought. It is important to distinguish among the different generations and tendencies within the religious renaissance. Some important figures, such as Leon Tolstoy, Basil Rozanov, Dimitri Merezhkovsky, Zinaida Hippius and in some ways even Vladimir Soloviev, remained on the margins of the church, and their ideas frequently strayed from major Christian doctrines. On the other hand, it is difficult to fault the principal philosopher-theologians, especially Pavel Florensky and Sergius Bulgakov, for ignoring the Fathers of the Church or for departing consciously from church dogmas. Both were deeply committed Christians, both were priests and both paid dearly for their faith, Florensky with his life and Bulgakov with the loss of employment and with exile. Both had a wide knowledge of the Fathers, evident in their writings, especially in Florensky's *The Pillar and the Foundation of the Truth* and in Bulgakov's major and minor theological trilogies. Both Florensky and Bulgakov, especially the latter, introduced important correctives to the bold but frequently non-Christian thinking of Soloviev, as is evidenced by the evolution of the notion of the Sophia from Soloviev to Bulgakov. Berdyaev was perhaps the most independent and audacious major figure of the renaissance, but after his return to Orthodoxy,

[43]Ibid., 371.
[44]Ibid., 365.

he remained a faithful son of the church, even if he continued to rebel against any attempt of church authorities to stifle free religious thought.

Beyond criticism of Russian religious philosophy as an extension of Western philosophical and social currents, especially idealism and romanticism and the label of 'neo-Gnosticism', and the more positive assessments by Nicolas Lossky, Basil Zenkovsky and Paul Evdokimov, there remains to be undertaken a dispassionate assessment of the achievements, strengths and weaknesses of Russian religious philosophy, which would elucidate more thoroughly than this book the 'breaks and links' between the thinking of the Russian religious renaissance and subsequent Orthodox thought.

Neopatristic theology and its critics

As we saw in Chapters 5 and 8, the achievements of neopatristic theology are considerable and by the late twentieth century, few Orthodox theologians identified themselves with any other general theological approach – despite difficulties in defining with any degree of precision what constitutes neopatristic theology. Neopatristic theology so dominated the Orthodox theological scene in the second half of the twentieth century that for many decades it had few critics. The new millennium ushered in a period of reassessment of neopatristic theology by both Orthodox and non-Orthodox who question the virtual monopoly in Orthodox theology that the neopatristic approach enjoyed for half a century.

Initially, critiques of the neopatristic approach to theology were directed towards aspects of Georges Florovsky's theology and especially his book *The Ways of Russian Philosophy*. Florovsky's book is a broadly based indictment of virtually all Russian philosophy and theology up to the First World War. He sees Russian religious thought as dominated for centuries by Western ideas, estranged from and often conflicting with authentic Orthodox thinking represented by patristic theology. Florovsky's book implies that most Russian theology should in effect be razed to the ground and that a new theological edifice, solidly grounded on authentic Orthodox foundations, namely Greek-Byzantine patristic theology, be erected in its place.

Nicolas Berdyaev fired the first shot at Florovsky's project of a return to the Fathers, which Florovsky later called 'neopatristic synthesis', in the form of a scathing review of Florovsky's *The Ways of Russian Philosophy*.[45] Although Berdyaev was taking aim specifically at this book, many of his critiques were prophetic and are relevant to a general assessment of neopatristic theology. Berdyaev's review is often a clumsy and overdrawn emotional response to Florovsky's book, but nonetheless frequently true to the mark. For several decades after Berdyaev's review, criticism of the neopatristic approach was largely indirect, notably in form of studies of Russian philosophy which serve as correctives to Florovsky's unrelenting critique of Russian thought. As we saw,

[45]Nicolas Berdyaev, 'Orthdoksiya i chelvechnost', (Ortodoksia and Humanness) *Put'*, 53 (Paris, 1937), 53–65. Review of Georges Florovsky, *The Ways of Russian Theology* (Paris: YMCA-Press, 1937). Unpublished translation by Stephen Janos. www.berdyaev.com/Berdyaev/berd_lib/1937_424.html (13 May 2015).

important achievements along these lines are histories of Russian philosophy by two of its principal representatives still active after the Second World War, Basil Zenkovsky and Nicolas Lossky.[46] Their *Histories of Russian Philosophy* (1950 and 1951 respectively), together with the later books of Nicolas Zernov (*The Russian Religious Renaissance of the Twentieth Century*, 1963) and Paul Evdokimov (*Le Christ dans la pensée russe* [Christ in Russian Thought], 1970), serve as antidotes to Florovsky's *The Ways of Russian Theology*. These books open the door to seeing continuity and not only conflict between the two major strands of modern Orthodox theology.

We will review a wide range of critiques of neopatristic theology that have been advanced since the 1930s.

'Hellenism' and 'Byzantinism'

One of the most important critiques levied against neopatristic theology, especially as defined by Georges Florovsky, is that it is too narrowly conceived in terms of Hellenism or the Greek-Byzantine theological tradition. Berdyaev first articulated this problem in his review of *The Ways of Russian Theology*:

> The Hellenism of Fr G. Florovsky seeks to make absolute the categories of Greek thought, to acknowledge them as eternal. … Patristic thought is steeped in elements taken from Greek philosophy. And this is the question, whether the Greek intellectualism of the Fathers is eternal and immutable; this Greek intellectualism issues from man and not from God.[47]

John Meyendorff, a great Byzantine scholar and a major figure of neopatristic theology, in his introduction to the 1983 reprint of the Russian edition of *The Ways of Russian Theology*, reiterates, more articulately, the point made by Berdyaev in 1937:

> Without denying the intelligence, the talent or the abilities of certain writers and always sketching a lively portrait of each epoch, Fr Georges applies to each and to all the patristic or Byzantine criterion, which he has definitively adopted and which is for him the only one which is Orthodox. … An Orthodox theologian certainly has the right to ask himself if Florovsky does not consider the tradition of the Fathers too narrowly. If we wish to criticize Russian Orthodoxy in the name of 'Byzantinism', would it not also be appropriate to critique Byzantinism itself? Is it equivalent to Holy Tradition as such?[48]

By questioning whether the Greek-Byzantine theological tradition is the sole valid Christian theological tradition, Berdyaev and Meyendorff raise doubts concerning a major cornerstone

[46]Paul Valliere describes Zenkovsky's *History of Russian Philosophy* as both 'the most impressive work of the Russian school after Bulgakov's death' and 'a response to Florovsky's *Ways of Russian Theology*'. Valliere, *Modern Russian Theology*, 374. For an assessment of the two *Histories of Russian Philosophy*, see Kare Johan Mjor, *Reformulating Russia: The Cultural and Intellectual Historiography of Russian First-Wave Émigré Writers* (Leiden and Boston: Brill, 2011), 253–6.
[47]Berdyaev, 'Ortodoksia and Humanness'.
[48]John Meyendorff, 'Preface' to Georges Florovsky, *Puti russkogo bogosloviia* (Paris: YMCA-Press, 3rd ed., 1983), 4.

of Florovsky's call for a return to the Fathers. Following Florovsky, many of the practitioners of neopatristic theology tended to define, in practice if not in theory, the Fathers of the Church almost exclusively in Greek-Byzantine terms, leaving little or no room for non-Byzantine Fathers and expressions of the faith – whether Latin, Syriac, Russian, Coptic or Armenian. This outlook also implies that the patristic age ended with the Byzantine Empire in 1453 and that there can be no more Fathers of the Church, either in the intervening centuries, now or in the future.

Borys Gudziak (b. 1960), head of the Ukrainian Greek Catholic Eparchy of Paris and former rector and president of the Ukrainian Catholic University in Lviv, addresses this aspect of Florovsky's theological method in the context of 'inculturation'. Gudziak asks why it should be considered appropriate for the early Fathers to effect a synthesis of Jewish and Christian revelation with elements of Greek philosophy to produce Christian theology, but it is not acceptable for modern theologians to attempt to produce a synthesis of modern philosophy and revelation: 'If the Fathers' achievement', he asks, 'was one of inculturation then is not a new inculturation in the categories of each age a possibility and even a requirement?'[49] He cites Berdyaev:

> The teachers of the church employed the thought categories of Greek philosophy, the only philosophy of their time, and without its services could not have progressed in their theologizing, even in the elaboration of the dogmatic statements themselves. … The teachers of the church were no less dependent upon philosophy in their thought than Russian religious thinkers of the nineteenth and twentieth centuries. The philosophy of the 'pagans', Plato and Aristotle, was no more Christian than the philosophy of Hegel and Schelling, which is, after all, permeated by Christian elements. There has never been a theology completely independent of philosophy nor will there ever be. Theology is not religious revelation. Theology is the reaction of human thought to revelation, and this reaction is dependent on categories of philosophical thought. The Hellenism of Fr G. Florovsky seeks to make absolute the categories of Greek thought, to acknowledge them as eternal. His 'objectivism' is nowhere substantiated, it is simply imposed as a dogma, as a sign of orthodoxy.[50]

Other commentators pick up this point. Metropolitan Hilarion Alfeyev, quoting both Berdyaev and Meyendorff, states unequivocally that 'one cannot, for instance, judge Syriac, Latin or Russian patristics from a Byzantine perspective'[51] – which is what Florovsky does in *The Ways of Russian Theology* and other writings. The alternative to Florovsky's limited view of what constitutes the basis of Orthodox tradition is to recognize the legitimacy of non-Byzantine expressions of Christianity. This requires nonetheless a discriminating approach, since it is then necessary to discern in other traditions elements which fall outside the boundaries of fundamental Christian dogmas.

Florovsky exhibited a certain ambiguity about Western theological influence. Augustine was one of his preferred patristic authors, even though Augustine was and still is often considered in many Orthodox circles as the prime source of many Western deviations from authentic (read Greek-Byzantine) patristic theology – everything from the transmission of original sin and

---

[49]Borys Gudziak, 'Towards an Analysis of the Neo-patristic Synthesis of Georges Florovsky', *Logos*, 41–2 (2000–1), 229.

[50]Berdyaev, 'Ortodoksia and Humanness', cited in Gudziak, 'The Neo-Patristic Synthesis of Georges Florovsky', 230–1.

[51]Cited in Hilarion Alfeyev, 'The Patristic Heritage and Modernity', in *Orthodox Witness Today* (Geneva: World Council of Churches, 2006), 156. Alfeyev makes the same point in his article 'The Patristic Background of the Orthodox Faith and the Study of the Fathers on the Threshold of the 21st Century', *St Vladimir's Theological Quarterly*, 51, 4 (2007), 384–5.

predestination to essentialism and the *Filioque*.[52] Florovsky tries to get around this difficulty by asserting that, after all, Augustine was *really* a Greek Father, 'a *Father* of the Church Universal'.[53] 'Christian Hellenism is much wider than one is prepared to realize. St Augustine and even St Jerome were no less Hellenistic than St Gregory of Nyssa and St [John] Chrysostom,' he wrote in 1939.[54]

Towards the end of his life, Florovsky stated that he struggled against 'two fronts': 'the belated revival of Hebraism and all attempts to reformulate dogmas in categories of modern philosophies, whether German, Danish, or French (Hegel, Heidegger, Kierkegaard, Bergson, Teilhard de Chardin) and of alleged Slavic mentality'.[55] By 'Hebraism', Florovsky likely meant any form of the Oriental Orthodox tradition, notably its Coptic and Syriac expressions. Alfeyev writes that Florovsky 'lost the war he wished to wager' against 'Hebraism', with the recognition of the existence of a *Patrologia Orientalis*, 'the thriving world of "Oriental" theological traditions, deeply authentic in form and content'.[56]

Later readings of Florovsky seek to exculpate him from the accusation of an undue Greek-Byzantine bias and broader anti-Westernism by pointing to his break with structurally anti-Western Eurasianism, his engagement with Catholic patristic scholarship, his frequent approving references to Cyprian of Carthage, Vincent of Lérins, Hilary of Poitiers and especially Augustine in his writings – 'indeed, Augustine is the main patristic source for his ecclesiology,' writes Matthew Baker.[57] But whether it is Augustine, Cyprian or even Thomas Aquinas or Cardinal Newman, for Florovsky these Western theologians are acceptable to the extent that their theology is fundamentally Byzantine: 'the Fathers, both Greek and Latin, were interpreting the Apostolic message, the original Good News, in Greek categories.'[58]

Florovsky's struggle against the use of modern philosophies to express Christian theology is another matter. Alfeyev agrees with Florovsky that 'it is indeed dangerous to attempt to "reformulate" dogmas in the categories of contemporary philosophical tendencies.' At the same time, Alfeyev speaks favourably of existentialism (he mentions Heidegger and Kierkegaard), as do other modern Orthodox intellectuals, such as Christos Yannaras, seeing in existentialism a departure of Western thought from Renaissance anthropomorphism and Enlightenment rationalism, and advancing the idea that existentialism may serve as a 'pedagogue' towards Christ, echoing the language of early

---

[52]For studies of the wide range of early and modern Orthodox views on Augustine, see Aristotle Papanikolaou and George. E. Demacopoulos eds., *Orthodox Readings of Augustine* (Crestwood, NY: St Vladimir's Seminary Press, 2008).

[53]Georges Florovsky, 'St Cyprian and Saint Augustine on Schism', in *Ecumenism II: A Historical Approach*, Vol. 14 of *The Collected Works of Georges Florovsky* (Vaduz: Büchervertriebanstalt, 1989), 50. See George E. Demacopoulos and Aristotle Papanikolaou, 'Augustine and the Orthodox: "The West" in the East', in Demacopoulos and Papanikolaou, eds., *Orthodox Readings of Augustine*, 26–7.

[54]Georges Florovsky, 'Preface to *In Ligno Crucis*' (1939), in Brandon Gallaher and Paul Ladouceur, eds., *The Patristic Witness of Georges Florovsky: Essential Theological Writings* (London: T&T Clark, 2019), 67.

[55]Cited in Andrew Blane, ed., *Georges Florovsky, Russian Intellectual, Orthodox Churchman* (Crestwood, NY: St Vladimir's Seminary Press, 1993), 152.

[56]Alfeyev, 'The Patristic Heritage and Modernity', 157.

[57]Matthew Baker, 'Neopatristic Synthesis and Ecumenism: Towards the "Reintegration" of Christian Tradition', in Andrii Krawchuk and Thomas Bremer, eds., *Eastern Orthodox Encounters of Identity and Otherness: Values, Self-Reflection, Dialogue* (New York: Palgrave MacMillan, 2014), 239. Baker refers to Florovsky's 'profound veneration for St Augustine'.

[58]Georges Florovsky, 'The Eastern Orthodox Church and the Ecumenical Movement', *Theology Today*, 7, 1 (1950), 74.

Fathers with respect to Greek philosophy.[59] Florovsky rejected existentialism as a means of expressing Christian truth just as firmly as he did German idealism, an important source of inspiration for a considerable portion of Russian religious philosophy.

One can also question whether the charge of 'Byzantinism', directed against Florovsky in particular, can be applied to neopatristic theology as a whole. Several observations are in order. First, it is clear that many Orthodox neopatristic theologians are often far more familiar with the Greek Fathers than with Latin or Oriental Fathers. And while the works of Latin Fathers are widely available in translation, this is not the case for the Oriental Fathers, with a few notable exceptions, such as Ephrem the Syrian and Isaac the Syrian – who are to all intents and purposes generally assimilated to Greek-Byzantine theology and spirituality. Secondly, neopatristic scholars are simply more at ease with the thinking of the Greek Fathers, much of which can be fit into a coherent and continuous intellectual stream, at least up to Gregory Palamas.[60] Finally, even if neopatristic scholars recognize the legitimacy of non-Byzantine theology, they will usually accord more weight and credibility to Greek sources. Often they will refer to Latin Fathers such as Augustine and Aquinas either to criticize them from a Byzantine perspective or, like Florovsky, to buttress arguments conceived essentially in Greek-Byzantine terms.

Anti-Westernism

As we saw in Chapter 5, the major premise underlying Georges Florovsky's *The Ways of Russian Theology*, and indeed much of his theology as a whole,[61] is that Western influences over the centuries, especially after the fall of Constantinople in 1453, corrupted Orthodox and especially Russian thought, producing a 'Western captivity' of Orthodoxy theology, a phenomenon which Florovsky designated as 'pseudomorphism'. Underlying Florovsky's thesis is the sense that Western influence, to the extent that it deviates from Greek/Byzantine models and thought, is inherently dangerous and destructive to authentic Orthodox tradition. Berdyaev attacks this fundamental premise on several fronts. For Berdyaev, Florovsky sets up an irreconcilable opposition between 'East' and 'West', which allows Florovsky to attack 'Russianism', as sort of sub-species of Westernism. Berdyaev writes:

> [Florovsky] holds to a completely mistaken and antiquated opposition of Russia and the West. He borrows this opposition from Russian thought of the nineteenth century, but with the original twist that he regards in a negative light not only the West, but also Russia, since it has succumbed to Western influence. He sets the Byzantine East in opposition to the West, reacting both critically and negatively towards Russian Christianity and Russian theology on the grounds that he sees Western influence in it. … Fr. G. Florovsky reacts far more negatively towards the West than either the

[59]Alfeyev, 'The Patristic Heritage and Modernity', 158.

[60]The extreme expression of this is the idea of *consensus patrum* – see the discussion below.

[61]For an overview of polemicism and anti-Westernism in Florovsky, see Brandon Gallaher, '"Waiting for the Barbarians": Identity and Polemicism in the Neo-Patristic Synthesis of Georges Florovsky', *Modern Theology*, 27, 4 (2011).

> Slavophiles or Dostoevsky or K. Leontev. … For him even the Slavophiles were too Western and he denounces them for their Europeanism and romanticism.[62]

Criticism of aspects of Western theology is typical of a great deal of modern Orthodox thought. It can be argued that much of Orthodox theology from the hesychastic quarrel of the fourteenth century onwards has been stimulated by the need to defend Orthodoxy against ideas stemming from Western Europe, beginning with Frankish theology of the Trinity (the *Filioque*), authority in the church (the papacy), the possibility of knowing and experiencing God (Barlaam versus Palamas), extending through scholasticism, the Reformation, the Counter-Reformation, to the Enlightenment and German philosophies. Behind this anti-Westernism is the assumption that secularism, individualism and rationalism and their noxious offspring (such as Marxism and consumerism), arising in the West and conveyed by Western culture, have not only falsified Western Christianity, but threaten to overwhelm Eastern Christianity.

An important distinction must be made among the strands of anti-Westernism in modern Orthodox thought. For many Orthodox theologians, the clash with West theology remains at the level of ideas: certain theologies found in the West simply do not correspond with Orthodox tradition and must therefore be identified, and, if they have found their way into Orthodox thought, be replaced with authentic Orthodox doctrines. Florovsky's call for a return to the Fathers was based on a perception that Orthodox theology had fallen prey to Western ideas and it was necessary to restore the Greek/Byzantine roots of Orthodoxy. A major aspect of this restoration movement, as we saw, was the revival of the interrelated doctrines of apophatism, the divine energies and theosis. It also includes generalized Orthodox opposition to rationalism, individualism, legalism and scholasticism, reflected in Orthodox critiques of a number of specific Western doctrines. Anti-Westernism can also be found in Orthodox opposition to certain ecclesiastical doctrines, from papal supremacy in the Catholic Church to Protestant congregationalism.

Yet theologians such as Sergius Bulgakov, Georges Florovsky, Vladimir Lossky, John Meyendorff and Alexander Schmemann, often critical of certain Western doctrines, are not perceived as fundamentally anti-Western. They and many other leading Orthodox theologians of the twentieth century were deeply committed to ecumenism and participated actively in the ecumenical movement from the late 1920s onwards. They saw no inconsistency between criticism of certain Western theologies and ecumenism.

On the other hand, as we saw in Chapter 6, several modern Greek theologians, John Romanides and Christos Yannaras in particular, have a reputation for a broadly based or systematic anti-Westernism. Indeed, Yannaras, in his Preface to the English edition of *Orthodoxy and West*, felt the need to explain that he is not attacking 'an external Western adversary' but is engaging in self-criticism as 'a Western person searching for answers to the problems tormenting Western people today', searching for what is right in 'a society radically and unhappily westernized'.[63] Small but

---

[62]Berdyaev, 'Ortodoksia and Humanness'.

[63]Christos Yannaras, *Orthodoxy and the West, Hellenic Self-Identity in the Modern Age* (Brookline, MA: Holy Cross Orthodox Press, 2006), viii–ix.

vocal anti-Western ecclesiastics and groups have been characteristic of contemporary Greek Orthodoxy for several decades.[64]

Is systematic anti-Westernism built into the very structure of neopatristic theology, as some critics affirm?[65] Even though the tone of Florovsky's *The Ways of Russian Theology* suggests that any form of Western influence is inherently destructive to Orthodoxy, this broad thematic cannot be sustained in the light of Florovsky's overall corpus. The main thrust of Orthodox theology since the 1930s has, it is true, focused on the return to traditional, patristically based doctrines in such areas as apophatism, the divine energies, theosis and sacramental theology. Our study of Orthodox neopatristic theology suggests that, with some notable exceptions (such as Romanides), Orthodox theologians have been critical of counterpart Western teaching in these areas, without resorting to a structural anti-Westernism which rejects Western theology a priori, and for that matter, all forms of Western culture. Issue-oriented critique of specific Western theological doctrines is more characteristic of modern Orthodox theology than systematic anti-Westernism.

Consensus patrum

Another key critique of neopatristic theology is a tendency to treat 'the Fathers' as reflecting a unified system of thought, or at least one that evolved coherently and consistently over the centuries. Berdyaev first pointed to this problem with a casual remark in his review of Florovsky's *The Ways of Russian Theology* to the effect that 'the teachers of the church wrangled much amongst themselves',[66] while Borys Gudziak highlights more explicitly the problem of divergences among the Fathers:

> These differences exist among the Greek, Latin, Syriac and Coptic patristic traditions but also within each of them. There are numerous explicit contradictions in the corpus of literature constituting what Florovsky calls the normative legacy of sacred Hellenism.[67]

Patristic thought in the Greek-Byzantine tradition developed over a period of some thirteen centuries, if we consider Christian Hellenistic thought as beginning with the apologists such as Justin Martyr and Irenaeus of Lyons in the second century, and stretching to Gregory Palamas in

---

[64]On anti-Westernism in Greek Orthodoxy, see for example Vasilios N. Makrides and Dirk Uffelmann, 'Studying Eastern Orthodox Anti-Westernism: The Need for a Comparative Research Agenda' in Jonathan Sutton and William Peter van den Bercken, eds., *Orthodox Christianity and Contemporary Europe* (Leuven: Peeters, 2003); Vasilios N. Makrides and Lina Molokotos-Liederman, 'Orthodoxy in Greece Today' (*Social Compass*, 51, 4, 2004); Vasilios N. Makrides, 'L'autre orthodoxie: courants du rigorisme orthodoxe grec' (The other Orthodoxy: Currents of Greek Orthodox rigourism), *Social Compass*, 51, 4 (2004).

[65]See for example the critique of neopatristic theology in Ivana Noble, Kateterina Bauerova, Tim Noble and Parush Parushev, *Wrestling with the Mind of the Fathers* (Yonkers, NY: St Vladimir's Seminary Press, 2015), especially the Introduction and Ch. 1, 'The Neo-Patristic Synthesis', 9–78. See also our review of this book (together with Andrew Louth, *Modern Orthodox Thinkers: From the Philokalia to the Present* (London: SPCK & Downers Grove, IL: InterVarsity Press, 2015)), in 'Scenes from Modern Orthodox Theology', *St Vladimir's Theological Quarterly*, 60, 4 (2016).

[66]Berdyaev, 'Ortodoksia and Humanness'.

[67]Gudziak, 'Towards an Analysis of the Neo-Patristic Synthesis of Georges Florovsky', 234.

the fourteenth century and Mark of Ephesus in the fifteenth century. It is inevitable that language and concerns evolve over such a long period of time. Yet despite variations, not only in expression, but in emphasis and in doctrine, among various Fathers, it is nonetheless legitimate to speak of a *consensus patrum*, at least from the fourth century onwards, on a limited number of major Christian dogmas, especially the Trinity and the two natures of the incarnate Son of God, consecrated in the dogmatic formulations of the ecumenical councils. But this is certainly not the case for many other theological issues, nor even for the manner in which various Fathers expressed essential Christian dogmas. This is amply (and tragically) illustrated in the Christological debates of the fifth century, which constitute the most important example of an attempt to recognize only one theological expression as the sole normative statement of the faith. This resulted in the first major schism in the Christian Church, the split between the 'Byzantine' churches and the 'Oriental' churches.

Other critics have picked up the fundamental problem of a 'flat' approach to patristic theology in neopatristic thought. Already in 1937 Sergius Bulgakov pointed to a methodological problem in Florovsky's approach to the Fathers:

> Here it becomes clear to anyone who happens upon patristic writing that even in the realm of one and the same question, there is rarely a single patristic tradition. These often contradictory (or at least different) opinions therefore force us to make a choice, to give preference to one or the other patristic tradition, as is in fact done. This means that the Holy Fathers' writings in themselves cannot be considered dogmatically infallible. They are authoritative witnesses but they cannot by any means be transformed into unerring texts.[68]

Hilarion Alfeyev and Andrew Louth recognize that this is indeed a problem in neopatristic theology. Alfeyev writes:

> Many are accustomed to speaking of the holy Fathers as a group of persons working together and writing approximately the same things. The Fathers of the Church, of course, lived in different eras: they related their writings to distinct cultural, historical, ecclesial and theological contexts, and were not infrequently engaged in controversy with one another. … Besides, some Fathers have expressed so-called private theological opinions (*theologoumena*), not adopted by the fullness of the church. In this light, one may reasonably ask: Is it at all acceptable to speak of the teaching of the holy Fathers as a unique and coherent theological system, or, should the expression 'patristic theology' be used only as a generic term (in the way that, for instance, we speak of 'Greek philosophy')?[69]

Andrew Louth raises the same concern:

> There is a tendency in Orthodox theology to represent the teaching of the various Fathers of the Church in a rather flat way, as if they had all lived at the same time, so historical considerations are scarcely necessary. In this respect, such Orthodox theology recalls older ways of presenting the history of doctrine in the West. It has been remarked of several of the older histories of dogma (I

---

[68]Sergius Bulgakov, 'Dogma and Dogmatic Theology' (1937), in Michael Plekon, ed., *Tradition Alive: On the Church and the Christian Life in Our Time* (Lanham, MA: Rowan & Littlefield, 2003), 70.
[69]Alfeyev, 'The Patristic Heritage and Modernity', 148–9.

won't single any one out) that so far as any sense of historical, political, and/or social context is concerned, the whole story of Christian doctrine might well have taken place on the moon.[70]

Louth goes on to speak of 'a tendency in Orthodox theology to give an account of historical doctrine that tends to be unhistorical or ahistorical', and he warns against the risk of 'glossing' 'one Father with another and so lose a sense of their individuality and historical context'.

Recognizing this problem, Alfeyev and Louth offer a possible solution, a contextual reading of the Fathers – seeing the individual Fathers in terms of their own times and places, with different cultural, social, political, ecclesial and theological contexts and problems that they addressed.[71] The upshot, concludes Alfeyev, is the possibility – even the necessity – of different acceptable expressions of the faith: 'One and the same truth may be articulated in different terminological expressions.' He cites as an example the Christological doctrines of the Third and the Fourth Ecumenical Councils, the one reflecting the Alexandrian tradition and the other the Antiochene tradition, concluding that indeed 'one and the same truth was expressed differently by two theological traditions, with both expressions proven to be essentially "orthodox"'.[72]

There are nonetheless limits beyond which different expressions of the faith can be considered unacceptable in an Orthodox perspective. The prime example is the *Filioque*, if interpreted in the typical Latin-Western manner as applying to the divine essence, the eternal procession of the Holy Spirit from the Father *and* the Son. In Orthodox thought from the tenth century onwards, this was not considered 'one and the same truth expressed differently by two theological traditions'; it was seen as an *unacceptable* expression of the faith.[73]

An equally thorny issue is the two Christologies which emerged from the Fourth Ecumenical Council held in Chalcedon in 431. For centuries, it was thought on both sides of the Chalcedonian divide that the theology of the other party was an unacceptable expression of the faith, with mutual anathemas marking the scene. The modern dialogue between the Chalcedonian (or Eastern or Byzantine) Orthodox churches and the non-Chalcedonian (or Oriental) Orthodox churches concluded that the fundamental problem was one of terminology and that Christology of the

---

[70] Andrew Louth, 'Is Development of Doctrine a Valid Category for Orthodox Theology?' in Valerie Hotchkiss and Patrick Henry, eds., *Orthodoxy and Western Culture, A Collection of Essays Honoring Jaroslav Pelikan on His Eightieth Birthday* (Crestwood, NY: St Vladimir's Seminary Press, 2006), 44–5.

[71] Alfeyev, 'The Patristic Heritage and Modernity', 153–4 and 158–60; and 'The Patristic Background of the Orthodox Faith and the Study of the Fathers on the Threshold of the 21st Century', *St Vladimir's Theological Quarterly*, 51, 4 (2007), 379–91; and Andrew Louth, 'Is Development of Doctrine a Valid Category for Orthodox Theology?' 55. Alfeyev gives an example of the contextual method based on his research on St Symeon the New Theologian, 161–5. Alfeyev's argument for a contextual reading to the Fathers stands in contrast with his own *Orthodox Christianity, Vol. II, Doctrine and Teaching of the Orthodox Church* (Yonkers, NY: St Vladimir's Seminary Press, 2012). This is in effect a textbook of patristic dogmatic theology. See our review in *St Vladimir's Theological Quarterly*, 58, 4 (2014).

[72] Alfeyev, 'The Patristic Background of the Orthodox Faith', 378.

[73] Attempts in Orthodox-Catholic theological discussions in recent years to find common ground on this question have not fully resolved the problem. While there is an acceptable Orthodox reading of *Filioque* – the sending of the Holy Spirit on the apostles and the Church by the Father and the Son – this does not address the divine procession of the Holy Spirit, which is clearly meant by Latin theology. The most positive joint Catholic-Orthodox outlook on the *Filioque* has come from the North American Orthodox-Catholic Consultation: 'The Filioque: A Church Dividing Issue?: An Agreed Statement' (2003). www.usccb.org/beliefs-and-teachings/ecumenical-and-interreligious/ecumenical/orthodox/filioque-church-dividing-issue-english.cfm (9 March 2017).

families of Orthodox churches was basically the same. The outcome of the dialogue was Agreed Statements signed in 1989 and 1990 between representatives of the two parties.[74] But neither side formally ratified the Agreed Statements, which remained unimplemented, in large part because of criticisms levied against the Statements, and lingering suspicions that despite the dialogue, the Christology of the other is either monophysite or Nestorian, depending on one's standpoint. From the Byzantine perspective, the question remains whether the 'one nature' Christological language of the Oriental Orthodox is an acceptable expression of the faith.[75]

In the light of the difficulty of finding a *consensus patrum* on many issues, the simple invocation of this or that Father on this or that issue is insufficient to settle a problem in modern theology – despite the fact that the invocation of a supposed *consensus patrum* can become a convenient battle-axe to decapitate new ideas. This suggests to Hilarion Alfeyev and others that perhaps it is necessary to relativize the Fathers to some extent. Rather than considering them invariably as undisputable sources of authority on all subjects, the Fathers can be seen as offering informed and enlightened consideration on a wide range of issues, and as posing certain external limits on theological speculation. Alfeyev writes: 'Knowledge of the Fathers prevents Orthodox Christians from losing their way amid the multitude of currents in modern philosophy and world-views, from getting "carried away by strange teachings" [He 13:9].'[76] With this, we are close to Bulgakov's attitude expressed in his 1937 essay on 'Dogma and Dogmatic Theology' (see Chapter 8).

Intellectual freedom and creativity

In his presentation of Anton Kartashev's essay 'The Freedom of Scientific-Theological Research and Church Authority' in the 1937 *Living Tradition* anthology, Paul Valliere raises the question of the relative capacity of religious philosophy and of neopatristic theology to deal with the delicate matter of intellectual freedom in theology. Because of the constant appeal to tradition in Orthodoxy, the restriction of intellectual freedom in the name of 'tradition' is always a temptation, a temptation which at times Orthodox have difficulty resisting. The question that Valliere puts is: 'Which of the two schools had the clearer understanding of the concept of intellectual freedom and its implications for the life of the church?' He argues that the Sophia affair of the 1930s must weigh in the balance: 'Whatever one thinks of Bulgakov's sophiology, no one who values intellectual freedom will find it

[74]Most of the key dialogue documents are available in Christine Chaillot, ed., *The Theological Dialogue Between the Eastern Orthodox and Oriental Orthodox Churches* (Volos, GR: Volos Academy Publications, 2016); Thomas FitzGerald and Emmanuel J. Gratsias, eds., *Restoring the Unity in Faith: The Orthodox-Oriental Orthodox Theological Dialogue* (Brookline, MA: Holy Cross Orthodox Press, 2007); and Christine Chaillot and Alexander Belopopsky, eds., *Towards Unity: The Theological Dialogue Between the Orthodox Church and the Oriental Orthodox Churches* (Inter-Orthodox Dialogue, 1998).

[75]See a wide range of studies of the issue in Chaillot, *The Theological Dialogue*. We offer a possible resolution of the Christological issue in Paul Ladouceur 'Orthodox Critiques of the Agreed Statements between the Orthodox and the Oriental Orthodox Churches', *St Vladimir's Theological Quarterly*, 60, 3 (2016), 362–3.

[76]Alfeyev, 'The Patristic Heritage and Modernity', 169–70.

easy to admire the procedures employed by his opponents to attack it.' He goes on to enumerate the various infringements of 'due process' in the condemnation of Bulgakov's teachings.[77]

As we saw in Chapter 10, freedom was a key theme in Russian religious thought, arising from the theology of the human person, the infinite value of human personhood in the image of the Persons of the Holy Trinity. The emphasis on freedom in the Russian religious renaissance was a counterpoint to the heavy-handedness of the imperial regime, followed all too quickly by the persecution of dissent by the Bolshevik regime. Even though Berdyaev did not accept Bulgakov's sophiology, he rose to Bulgakov's defence in 1935, notably in a sharply worded essay following the condemnation of sophiology by the *ukaz* (decree) of Metropolitan Sergius (Stragorodsky), then the de facto head of the ROC. Berdyaev compares Metropolitan Sergius to the Grand Inquisitor in Dostoyevsky's *The Brothers Karamazov*.[78] Florovsky was aware of the anti-freedom tendency evident in the official structures of the Russian Church under the tsars as is made clear in his chapter in *The Ways of Russian Theology* on Constantine Pobedonostev (1827–1907). Pobedonostev, as *Oberprocurator* or secretary of the Holy Synod of the ROC, oversaw the church with an iron fist from 1880 to 1905.[79] In the heat of the controversy over sophiology, Florovsky, for all his disagreement with Sergius Bulgakov on theological issues, remained on good terms with the elder theologian and disapproved of the harassment of Bulgakov in the mid-1930s.[80]

Valliere's invocation of the 'trial of sophiology' in the 1930s is not entirely to the point, since sophiology fell prey to ecclesial politics among the Russian jurisdictions, as well as to the theological conservatism of the Moscow Patriarchate and the Synod of Russian Orthodox bishops in exile. In the historical context of the mid-1930s, it was not a victim of neopatristic theology as such. One would be hard put to find later Orthodox theologians who approve of the treatment that Bulgakov received in the 1930s, even if Orthodoxy has not received sophiology. While the Sophia affair may not be relevant, it is nonetheless difficult to escape Valliere's implied conclusion to his comments on Kartashev's 1937 article, that religious philosophy was inherently more open to intellectual freedom than neopatristic theology.

The question of intellectual freedom in theology and the church takes on a heightened importance depending on how one views the relationship between dogma and tradition: the more one 'dogmatizes' the content of tradition, the less room there is for intellectual freedom. As we discussed in Chapter 8, Orthodoxy has always had a tradition of *theologumena*, 'theological opinions', which may be 'doctrines', in the sense of teachings of individual theologians but which do not represent the dogmatic teaching of the church, even if advanced by a Father of the Church. Clearly, if everything is dogma, then *theologumena* are squeezed out of the picture. It is only a short step from there to the condemnation of any new idea, any innovation, as heretical – the Sophia

[77]Valliere, *Modern Russian Theology*, 395.

[78]Nicolas Berdyaev, 'The Spirit of the Grand Inquisitor (Regarding the Ukaz of Metropolitan Sergei Condemning the Theological Views of Fr S. Bulgakov)', *Put'* 1937 (in Russian). www.berdyaev.com/Berdyaev/berd_lib/1935_404.html (25 September 2015).

[79]See Georges Florovsky, *The Ways of Russian Theology*, in Florovsky, *Collected Works*, VI, 184–99. The original Russian title of the chapter is simply 'The Pobedonostev Epoch', but the editor's English title is more tellingly 'Prohibition of Questioning'.

[80]See Alexis Klimoff, 'Georges Florovsky and the Sophiological Controversy', *St Vladimir's Theological Quarterly*, 49, 1–2 (2005), 80; and Ladouceur, 'Aimons-nous les uns les autres', 78–83.

affair being a case in point – and to the use of heavy-handed procedures to suppress upstart ideas and their promoters. Examples in Christian history are numerous (the Inquisition being one extreme), but the case still fresh in the memories of Russian exiles in the 1930s was the suppression of the 'veneration of the Name of God' doctrine (onomatodoxy/*imiaslavie*) just prior to the First World War. Leading figures of the Russian religious renaissance defended the advocates of the veneration of the Name of God against attacks from the ROC and academic theologians (see Chapter 15).

Related to the question of freedom in the church is that of theological creativity: freedom is a basic requirement for creativity to flower. Valliere astutely points out that 'there cannot be a canon of creativity because creativity is not a *traditum*,'[81] something handed down. Bulgakov links creativity with prophecy: 'Creative inspiration represents a manifestation of the prophetic spirit, the absence of rules and the newness of the path correspond to the very spirit of prophecy, which is directed toward the new and the unknown. There cannot be a *Philokalia* of creativity, for the latter is outside of law and regularity.'[82] Religious philosophy had no monopoly on theological creativity, but then neither does neopatristic theology; both were remarkably creative in very different ways, as Valliere himself recognizes: 'The neopatristic turn sparked a remarkable outburst of creativity in Orthodox theology. … Both the Russian and the neopatristic schools were creative in their time.'[83]

There nonetheless is a tendency in neopatristic theology to have a limited view of creativity in theology, to consider creativity as the contemporary application of a notion already contained in tradition. While this interpretation of creativity has some merit, it can all too easily act as a constraint on intellectual freedom: if a new idea cannot somehow be 'justified' in terms of tradition – especially in terms of Greek-Byzantine thought – , it is at best questionable and should probably be abandoned. This line of thinking makes it difficult to deal with the theological implications of modern scientific discoveries and with changes in modern societies. It is not insurmountable, as many neopatristic scholars have shown, but it represents a hurdle to overcome.

Intellectualism

Berdyaev criticizes *The Ways of Russian Theology* for its 'intellectualist' bias, claiming that the book 'rather exaggerates the importance of theology and the intellectual element in religious life', to the neglect of spiritual elements: '[Florovsky] speaks very little about the spiritual life, about the saints, or about that which might be called Russian spirituality.' Berdyaev points out that Florovsky is critical even of some Russian saints:

> He does not spare even the saints. He sees Catholic influence in St Dimitri of Rostov and the influence of Arndt (*On the True Christianity*) and Western Christian humanism in St Tikhon of Zadonsk

[81]Valliere, *Modern Russian Theology*, 385.
[82]Sergius Bulgakov, *The Comforter* (1936) (Grand Rapids, MI: Eerdmans, 2004), 313.
[83]Valliere, *Modern Russian Theology*, 385.

(which is completely accurate). Even Ignatius Briantchaninov emerges as not at all Orthodox, while St Seraphim of Sarov is dispatched under the heading of the historical school.[84]

Borys Gudziak picks up this point, stating that Florovsky's theology 'remains largely on the ideological level' (that is, at the level of ideas). Gudziak, surveying Florovsky's work as a whole, concludes that 'there is surprisingly little integration into the conceptual framework of the centrality of the ascetic legacy, monastic spirituality and prayer'; Florovsky's thought consists of 'ideas about ideas'. Gudziak presents as further evidence to support this contention the fact that Florovsky not only neglected the connection between theology and the spiritual life, but displayed a 'curious lack of attention to the works, as opposed to words, of the "Holy Fathers".'[85]

Intellectualism remains a temptation in all theology, perhaps more acutely in neopatristic theology because of a certain built-in bias towards abstract issues. While the critique of undue intellectualism may indeed be levied against much of Florovsky's corpus, and perhaps of other neopatristic scholars, in their defence it must be said that one cannot expect everyone to cover the full range of Orthodox thought and life all the time. The initial agenda of neopatristic theology comprised largely dogmatic questions relating to the nature of theology (apophatism), the Trinity (the divine energies and the *Filioque*) and ecclesiology. But it is true, as we suggested above and in previous chapters, that neopatristic theology had more difficulty dealing with applied theology in such areas as social, political and economic questions.

Even Florovsky must be absolved in part of the accusation of intellectualism. Concern for salvation and the spiritual life underlay his theological endeavours. 'A theologian is called upon to bear witness in this world,' he wrote in the concluding paragraphs of *The Ways of Russian Theology*. 'Theology must articulate the Good News, the *kerygma*.'[86] Nor can we overlook Florovsky's work on the ascetic fathers, or his writings on spiritual and ascetic questions, even if these remained secondary among his intellectual concerns.[87] But certainly other neopatristic theologians have done better than Florovsky in this respect – Florovsky's fellow neo-patrologue Vladimir Lossky is a case in point. From the brilliant exposition of the main themes of dogmatic theology, Lossky's *Mystical Theology of the Eastern Church* leads directly into 'spiritual theology' – the 'mystical theology' of the title – the spiritual life, theosis, the 'divine light' and the 'feast of the Kingdom', the subject of the last three chapters of the book.[88] The same may be said of other leading neopatristic theologians, such as Dumitru Staniloae and Kallistos Ware, for whom theology is not an abstract intellectual undertaking but a framework for salvation and the spiritual life of the Christian. In addition, any relative weakness of neopatristic theology in this respect must be seen in the context

---

[84]Berdyaev, 'Ortodoksia and Humanness'.

[85]Gudziak, 'The Neo-patristic Synthesis of Georges Florovsky', 224; 235.

[86]Florovsky, 'Breaks and Links', Conclusion to *The Ways of Russian Philosophy*, in Gallaher and Ladouceur, eds., *The Patristic Witness of Georges Florovsky*, 177–8.

[87]See especially Georges Florovsky, *The Byzantine Ascetic and Spiritual Fathers*, Vol. X of *The Collected Works of Georges Florovsky* (Vaduz: Buchervertriebsanstalt, 1987).

[88]Vladimir Lossky, *The Mystical Theology of the Eastern Church* (1944) (Crestwood, NY: St Vladimir's Seminary Press, 1976), 196–249.

of the wealth of spiritual writings of modern Orthodox saints and elders (Greek, Romanian, Russian, Serbian, Orthodox elders in the West, etc.).

Biblical scholarship

It has long been obvious that, in comparison with Western theology, biblical scholarship remains one of the weakest areas of modern Orthodox theology. Alexander Schmemann wrote in the early 1970s: 'For the several reasons biblical studies represent the weakest area in modern Russian theology.'[89] Schmemann cites as partial explanations pre-revolutionary censorship of any attempt at a critical approach to Scripture and of course the impossibility of biblical scholarship in the Soviet Union after the Revolution. Neither factor applies to the religious renaissance in exile, nor to the neopatristic theologians.

Schmemann also mentions two more relevant factors:

> Orthodox theology has never felt 'at home' in modern biblical scholarship and has not accepted as its own the biblical problem as formulated within the Western theological development. … Orthodox theology implicitly rather than explicitly rejects the isolation of Scripture in a closed and self-sufficient field of study, yet firmly maintains the scriptural roots and 'dimensions' of every theological discipline: dogma, ecclesiology, moral theology.

These arguments are fundamental. Orthodoxy was never challenged by Reformation *sola scriptura* theology and Scripture is always seen within the tradition of the church, the most important aspect, complemented by other components of tradition, such as the dogmatic declarations of ecumenical councils, the teachings of the Fathers, including their extensive commentaries on Scripture, and the liturgy and icons.

Despite the difficulties inherent in Orthodox biblical scholarship mentioned by Schmemann, in recent decades Orthodox scholars such as Savas Agourides, Daniel Ayuch, John Breck, John McGuckin, Nicolas Abou Mrad, John Romanides, Theodore Stylianopoulos, Paul Tarazi and Petros Vassiliades have made significant progress in furthering modern Orthodox biblical studies.[90] In post-communist Russia, the achievements of modern biblical criticism are starting to make their way into theological circles, but the most urgent issue in Russia is the need for a contemporary translation of the Bible, since the translation still used, the 'Synodal' translation of the nineteenth century, is long outdated.[91]

---

[89]Alexander Schmemann, 'Russian Theology 1920-1972, An Introductory Survey', *St Vladimir's Theological Quarterly*, 16, 4 (1972), passim.

[90]For overviews of modern Orthodox biblical studies, see Theodore G. Stylianopoulos, 'Scripture and Tradition in the Church' and Nicolas Abou Mrad, 'The Witness of the Church in a Pluralistic World', in Cunningham and Theokritoff, *The Cambridge Companion to Orthodox Christian Theology*, especially pages 31–3 and 251–3.

[91]See Hilarion Alfeyev, 'Orthodox Theology on the Threshold of the 21st Century: Will There Be a Renaissance of Russian Theological Scholarship?' *Ecumenical Review*, 52, 3 (2000).

Although biblical studies have taken a greater importance in Orthodox theology, especially in Greece, biblical scholarship remains a weak area in Orthodoxy, but the reasons for this cannot be ascribed solely to the neopatristic approach. More important are fundamental attitudes in Orthodoxy, including, as mentioned by Alexander Schmemann, a continued resistance to biblical criticism, which many Orthodox still consider as yet another undesirable result of Enlightenment rationalism and intellectual scepticism and thus a threat to Orthodox faith. Orthodox theology is decidedly more at ease with dogmatic issues, patristics, liturgical studies, church history and spirituality than with biblical studies as such. As Schmemann indicates, Orthodox typically appeal to Scripture in all theological disciplines, rather than study the Bible independently of other aspects of tradition.

Revisionism in modern Orthodox thought

Neopatristic theology or the 'neopatristic synthesis' so dominated the Orthodox theological scene in the second half of the twentieth century that to many it became virtually synonymous with modern Orthodox theology, to the point that some critics even advance a sort of conspiracy theory on the part of neopatristic theologians to silence their opponents representing other perspectives.[92] Certainly, criticism of neopatristic theology mounted in the opening years of the twenty-first century and Orthodox theology has embarked on a period of introspection, a rethinking of the approach to Orthodox theology which predominated for the last half-century.[93] But before declaring that the neopatristic synthesis has 'not succeeded',[94] we must give due credit to the historical significance and the major accomplishments of neopatristic theology, and avoid repeating the summary dismissal of religious philosophy in the second half of the twentieth century. Its many valuable features, such as a broad Christian engagement with the modernity and contemporary issues, were discarded

---

[92]See in particular Ivana Noble, Kateterina Bauerova, Tim Noble and Parush Parushev, *The Ways of Orthodox Theology in the West* (Yonkers, NY: St Vladimir's Seminary Press, 2015) (e.g., 318 and 328) and their *Wrestling with the Mind of the Fathers* (Yonkers, NY: St Vladimir's Seminary Press, 2015) (e.g. 13), as well as our reviews of these books in *St Vladimir's Theological Quarterly*, 59, 4 (2015), and *St Vladimir's Theological Quarterly*, 60, 4 (2016) respectively.

[93]For critiques of neopatristic theology in general and of Georges Florovsky's project in particular, see Paul Valliere, 'The Limits of Tradition', conclusion to his *Modern Russian Theology: Bukharev, Soloviev, Bulgakov: Orthodox Theology in a New Key* (Grand Rapids, MI: Eerdmans, 2000); Borys Gudziak, 'Towards an Analysis of the Neo-patristic Synthesis of Georges Florovsky', *Logos* (Vol. 41–2, 2000–1); Hilarion Alfeyev, 'The Patristic Heritage and Modernity', in *Orthodox Witness Today* (Geneva: World Council of Churches, 2006); Hilarion Alfeyev, 'The Patristic Background of the Orthodox Faith and the Study of the Fathers on the Threshold of the 21st Century', *St Vladimir's Theological Quarterly*, 51, 4 (2007); Pantelis Kalaitzidis, 'From the "Return to the Fathers" to the Need for a Modern Orthodox Theology', *St Vladimir's Theological Quarterly*, 54, 1 (2010); Paul Gavrilyuk, 'Harnack's Hellenized Christianity or Florovsky's "Sacred Hellenism": Questioning Two Metanarratives of Early Christian Engagement With Late Antique Culture', *St Vladimir's Theological Quarterly*, 54, 3–4 (2010); Paul Gavrilyuk, 'Florovsky's Neopatristic Synthesis and the Future Ways of Orthodox Theology', in George Demacopoulos and Aristotle Papanikolaou, eds., *Orthodox Constructions of the West* (New York: Fordham University Press, 2013) and Brandon Gallaher, 'Waiting for the Barbarians: Identity and Polemicism in the Neo-Patristic Synthesis of George Florovsky', *Modern Theology*, 27, 4 (2011).

[94]Pantelis Kalaitzidis quotes approvingly Hilarion Alfeyev to the effect that the neopatristic synthesis has not 'succeeded' because 'in the twentieth century the time for such a synthesis had not yet come'. See Kalaitzidis, 'From the "Return to the Fathers" to the Need for a Modern Orthodox Theology', 33–4, quoting Alfeyev, 'The Patristic Heritage and Modernity', 153.

along with less desirable aspects, such as sophiology. And, for many, an overly speculative and personal approach to theology.

At a conference held at the Volos Academy for Theological Studies (Greece) from 3 to 6 July 2010 on the theme 'Patristic or "Post-Patristic" Theology: Can Orthodox Theology Be Contextual?', a number of speakers (notably John Behr, Paul Gavrilyuk, Pantelis Kalaitzidis, Aristotle Papanikolaou and Marcus Plested) aired wide-ranging critiques of neopatristic theology, voicing many of the criticisms discussed above.[95] The inflammatory and misleading expression 'post-patristic theology' of the Volos Conference provided a ready-made target for Orthodox neo-traditionalists. The Conference stimulated an equal and opposite reaction in the form of a symposium organized by Metropolitan Seraphim (Mentzelopoulos) of Piraeus (b. 1956) to denounce 'post-patristic theology' in general and the Volos Conference in particular. The symposium, held in Piraeus on 15 February 2012, brought together leading Greek neo-traditionalist hierarchs and theologians, notably Metropolitan Hierotheos (Vlachos) of Nafpaktos (b. 1945), Dimitrios Tselengidis and Fr Theodoros Zisis (University of Thessaloniki) (b. 1941) and Fr Georgios Metallinos (University of Athens) (b. 1940). Organizers boasted that some 1,500 people attended the event.[96]

The main target of the 2012 symposium was the idea of 'post-patristic theology', but neopatristic theology suffered collateral damage. The scholarship was weak but the rhetoric strong. Speakers saw most Orthodox theology from the Slavophiles to neopatristic theology, and Orthodox involvement in ecumenism as a vast modernist conspiracy against true Orthodoxy. In his paper Hierotheos Vlachos conflates the Slavophiles, the Russian religious renaissance and neopatristic theology into 'post-patristic theology'. He traces the origin of post-patristic thinking in Orthodoxy to the Slavophiles, especially Alexei Khomiakov, through the Russian émigré theologians of the Saint Sergius Institute in Paris, from whom it passed to Greece under the designation 'neo-Orthodoxy', notably in the thinking of Christos Yannaras, with Ramfos Stelios also featuring prominently. Relying heavily on Fr John Romanides (1927–2001), Vlachos criticizes in particular four principal theological tenets of post-patristic theology: the interpretation of ecclesiology and anthropology on the basis of Trinitarian theology rather than Christology; the 'ontology of the person', considered as the 'philosophy and thinking of heretics' as distinct from 'the experience of the revelation of the prophets, apostles and Fathers who saw God'; Eucharistic ecclesiology and 'over-emphasis on the resurrectional nature of the Orthodox Church, with an under-valuation of the life of the Cross', a separation of 'the mystery of the Cross from the vision of the glory of the Resurrection of Christ'.[97] While Georges Florovsky for one could agree with the first and last of

---

[95]See the conference proceedings in Pantelis Kalaitzidis and Nikolaos Asproulis, eds., *Neopaterikí sýnthesi í metapaterikí theología? To aítima tis theologías tis synáfeias* (Neopatristic Synthesis or Postpatristic Theology: Can Orthodox Theology Be Contextual?), (Volos, GR: Ekdotike Demetriados, 2018). English version forthcoming.

[96]An English translation of the main papers is available: 'Patristic Theology and Post-Patristic Heresy: Symposium of the Holy Metropolis of Piraeus' (Piraeus GR, 15 February 2012). https://fr.scribd.com/document/305700579/Patristic-Theology (14 August 2017).

[97]Hierotheos Vlachos, 'Post-Patristic Theology from a Church Perspective' in 'Patristic Theology and Post-Patristic Heresy', 117; 119–22; 123; 125. In his critique of post-patristic theology, Vlachos draws extensively on John Romanides and on Andrew Sopko, *Prophet of Roman Orthodoxy: The Theology of John Romanides* (Dewdney, BC: Synaxis Press, 1998).

these critiques, personalism and Eucharist theology are major elements of neopatristic theology (see Chapters 10 and 11), closely associated with Metropolitan John Zizioulas, Vlachos's unnamed principal target.

Vlachos sees post-patristic theology as a project aiming to formulate 'the word of Christ' in language 'other than that of the holy Fathers of the Church because today we have a different culture'.[98] For Vlachos, the fundamental mistake of post-patristic theology is linking theology with culture, focusing on 'questions posed by the particular culture of our age', while ignoring 'the reality of the struggle of Christians against the devil, sin and death', accompanied by an under-valuation or rejection of the neptic-hesychast tradition of the church, including the traditional threefold categorization of the spiritual life (purification, illumination and deification or perfection) – distinctions common to both Eastern and Western Christianity.[99]

While Russian religious philosophy would undoubtedly fall under the category of 'post-patristic theology', Vlachos is ambiguous in his approach to neopatristic theology. He speaks favourably of Georges Florovsky, because of 'the acceptance of the hesychast-neptic tradition',[100] yet he castigates two major themes of neopatristic theology, the theology of the person and Eucharistic ecclesiology, as principal elements of post-patristic theology. If Florovsky comes off reasonably well in Vlachos's paper, in another text he indirectly criticizes Florovsky's theological project of applying what Vlachos calls the 'spirit' of the Fathers to modern issues. 'This, despite the goodwill of some', writes Vlachos, 'is extremely dangerous, because in effect it undermines the entire patristic theology'.[101] Vlachos appears to be advocating here what Florovsky would no doubt call a 'theology of repetition' of the Fathers, rather than the creative application of 'the patristic mind' to contemporary problems, the heart of Florovsky's theological project.

Engaging the modern world

The relationship of Orthodoxy to the modern world – 'modern' in the sense of the world inhabited if not dominated by Western ideas and values – has been on the agenda of Orthodox theology at least since the fourteenth century. The conflict over hesychasm resulted in a clear expression of Orthodox thought on the possibility of knowing and experiencing God, supported by the Palamite theology of the divine energies. But after the fall of Constantinople and the end of the Byzantine Empire in 1453, Orthodoxy was poorly equipped to resist the constant stream of ideas arriving from the West. Higher learning in the Orthodox tradition was impossible in the Ottoman Empire, and the Russian theological academies were too imbued with Western models to convey adequately the fullness of the Orthodox tradition. The ROC was co-opted into the imperial regime

[98] Vlachos, 'Post-Patristic Theology', 108.
[99] Ibid., 107; 127.
[100] Ibid., 107.
[101] Cited in Cyril Hovorun, 'Patristics after Neo-Patristics', in Justin A. Mihoc and Leonard Aldea, eds., *A Celebration of Living Theology: A Festschrift in Honour of Andrew Louth* (London: T&T Clark, 2014), 205, n. 1.

and academic theology cut off from the wider society. Russian thinkers outside the church grappled with the question of the future of Russia, often drawing on Western theories and models. Alexander Bukharev, in both his writings and his personal life, restated the pressing need for Orthodoxy to relate effectively to the modern world: How can Orthodox Christianity express the truth of Christ, bear witness to Christ, in terms comprehensible to the modern world? Bukharev saw the need for the light of Christ to shine in all aspects of modern society, but his awkward personal attempt to apply this was too much for the Russian Church of his day.

Bukharev remained an isolated prophet and it was only after his death that leading Russian Christian thinkers began to engage the modern world in its philosophical, social, political and cultural expressions. By the late nineteenth century, the key figures of the Russian religious renaissance were deeply engaged in the clash of ideas that characterized the Russian intellectual scene up to the Bolshevik revolution. Whatever one might think of the specific expressions of the Russian religious renaissance, its intellectual and cultural figures asserted Christ's presence and a Christian perspective on society in the intellectual tumult of the time, sometimes, as we saw in Chapter 4, as an unheeded prophetic voice, as in the 1909 *Vekhi* (Signposts) collection of essays.

In contrast with the powerful engagement of religious philosophy with modernity, neopatristic theology is taken to task for its weak track record in dealing with the modern world and with new issues, unknown in patristic times.[102] Nicolas Berdyaev was the first to point to this problem in his critique of Florovsky's *The Ways of Russian Theology*. Although Berdyaev, as he often does, exaggerates his case, his basic intuition is not far off the mark:

> Mere repetition of the thoughts of the Greek and the Byzantine Fathers signifies a misunderstanding and negation of their theme. Humanity can have new experiences, new quests, and new horizons can open up. The experience of Byzantium had its limits, its horizons were constricted, and many issues had yet not been put before Christian consciousness.[103]

While neopatristic theology no doubt contributed to the poor engagement of Orthodoxy with modernity in the second half of the twentieth century, it served to re-enforce long-standing characteristics of the Orthodox world: the isolation of much of Orthodoxy from the major developments which marked the emergence of modernity in Western Europe, from the Renaissance and the Reformation to the Enlightenment; a slow transition from rural, agriculture-based societies to industrial and urban societies; lower standards of living; foreign rule, especially under the Ottoman Empire; the long decades of isolation under communist rule and a religious ethos which places great value on tradition and continuity. The fall of communism in Russia and Eastern Europe brought questions of modernity to the forefront as the newly liberated countries had to deal with major issues relating to the nature of their political regimes, the sudden access to Western culture, to political, economic and military alliances, and to relations with minority ethnic, social and religious groups. These questions had remained on the shelf for decades, in part because there was no pressing need to deal with them. When they suddenly rose to the top of national agendas,

---

[102]See for example Pantelis Kalaitzidis, 'From the "Return to the Fathers" to the Need for a Modern Orthodox Theology', *St Vladimir's Theological Quarterly*, 54, 1 (2010).
[103]Berdyaev, 'Ortodoksia and Humanness'.

Orthodox Church leaders and theologians were poorly equipped to deal with them. Scholastically based theological training still dominated theological education, the Russian religious renaissance was only a distant memory or largely unknown, and even neopatristic theology was regarded with suspicion as a potentially dangerous innovation. It was easier to fall back on the comfort of known past attitudes and practices, rather than to take to new paths. Where neopatristic theology was favourably received, it often served to reinforce conservative tendencies in Orthodoxy, the simple invocation of the words of the Fathers, rather than becoming a theological method to confront the complex issues of modernity with 'the mind of the Fathers' – how the Fathers conducted theology – as Georges Florovsky considered his theological approach.

One of the reasons for the difficulty of neopatristic theology to come to grips with issues arising from the nature of industrial and post-industrial societies is its fundamentally historical orientation. Many twentieth-century Orthodox theologians were more comfortable dealing with familiar patristic issues, especially those typically coming under the purview of dogmatic theology, and with the study of the Fathers, than they were in tackling unfamiliar questions of social and political theology, issues arising from psychology and medicine and science-based issues such as modern cosmology, evolution, genetic engineering and artificial intelligence. In these fields, theology encounters other disciplines often cast in non-theistic frameworks. Nonetheless, some contemporary problems have fared better than others in neopatristic theology, especially ethical issues raised by modern science and medicine in areas such as reproductive biology and euthanasia, as shown by the work of John Breck (b. 1939), H. Tristram Engelhardt (b. 1941), Vigen Guroian (b. 1948), Stanley Harakas (b. 1932) and others,[104] and issues relating to the environment.[105] But many other contemporary questions have not received sufficient attention in neopatristic theology, including issues relating to secularization, democracy, law, human rights, globalization, privacy and modern social organization (see Chapter 14).

Pantelis Kalaitzidis (b. 1961), one of the most ardent analysts of the failure of Orthodoxy to engage meaningfully with modernity, opens his discussion on Orthodoxy and modernity with the provocative question: 'Did Orthodoxy Come to a Halt before Modernity?'[106] He expresses the complex relationship between neopatristic theology and modernity in the form of questions:

---

[104]See inter alia John Breck, *The Sacred Gift of Life: Orthodox Christianity and Bioethics* (Crestwood, NY: St Vladimir's Seminary Press, 1999); H. Tristram Engelhardt, *The Foundations of Bioethics* (New York: Oxford University Press, 2nd ed., 1996) and *The Foundations of Christian Bioethics* (Exton, PA: Swets & Zeitlinger, 2000); Vigen Guroian, *Incarnate Love: Essays in Orthodox Ethics* (South Bend, IN: University of Notre Dame Press, 2nd ed., 2002) and *Life's Living Toward Dying: A Theological and Medical-Ethical Study* (Grand Rapids, MI: Eerdmans, 1996); Stanley Harakas, *Wholeness of Faith and Life: Orthodox Christian Ethics* (Brookline, MA: Holy Cross Orthodox Press, 2004); Dominique Beaufils, *Ta foi t'a sauvé: Approache orthodoxe de la maladie et de la mort* (Your Faith Has Saved You: An Orthodox Approach To Sickness and Death) (Paris: Desclée de Brouwer, 1996); Jean-Claude Larchet, *The Theology of Illness* (Crestwood, NY: St Vladimir's Seminary Press, 2002).

[105]See the essays in John Chryssavgis, John and Bruce V. Foltz, eds. *Toward an Ecology of Transfiguration: Orthodox Christian Perspectives on Environment, Nature, and Creation* (New York: Fordham University Press, 2013); Elizabeth Theokritoff, *Living in God's Creation: Orthodox Perspectives on Ecology* (Crestwood: St Vladimir's Seminary Press, 2010); and Ecumenical Patriarch Bartholomew, *On Earth as in Heaven: Ecological Vision and Initiatives of Ecumenical Patriarch Bartholomew* (New York: Fordham University Press, 2012).

[106]Pantelis Kalaitzidis, Ch. 6 of his 'Orthodoxy and Modernity: An Introduction'. Unpublished English translation by Elizabeth Theokritoff of *Orthodoxía kai Neoterikótita (Prolegómena)* (Athens: Indiktos Publications, 2007), 58–64. See also his unpublished papers at the Catholic University of Linz (15 May 2008) and in Trebinje, Herzegovina (11 February 2017).

> Has not the famous 'return to the Fathers', as it was understood and applied, served equally as a bulwark against modernity and the challenges it posed, despite itself and contrary to its programmatic aim of renewal? … Has it not contributed in its own way to making our entire church life a prisoner to pre-modern structures and practices and to a conservative mentality?[107]

In comparison with the cautious adherence, with important shades of difference, of Alfeyev, Louth and Ware to the continuing relevance of the patristic tradition to contemporary Orthodox theology, Kalaitzidis downplays and even rejects the relevance of patristic theology to contemporary issues:

> It is imperative, then, for Orthodox theology to examine the possibility of devising, through the Holy Spirit, new terms and new names ('to coin new names', in the words of St Gregory the Theologian), correlated to today's needs and challenges, just as the need for a new incarnation of the Word and the eternal truth of the Gospel is also urgently necessary. A theology of repetition, a theology that is satisfied simply with a 'return to the sources', or that relies on the 'return to the Fathers' and the neopatristic synthesis, cannot, by definition, respond to this need and the manifold challenges of the post-modern pluralistic world.[108]

Kalaitzidis pointed remarks reflect a malaise with how neopatristic theology has been conducted, especially the perceived failure to engage modern problems meaningfully and its underlying anti-Westernism, as manifested notably in John Romanides and Christos Yannaras.

Cyril Hovorun (b. 1974) refers to neopatristic synthesis as an 'introvert': 'It does not go much beyond patristic texts and contexts, did not open up to the world of modern ideas, does not open up to the world as such.'[109] Despite this sweeping oversimplification, Hovorun recognizes the possibility that initially – in Florovsky's original project – neopatristic theology was intended to be more open to the contemporary world. Thus the problem is not so much Florovsky's theological project as its implementation – and perhaps unintended side effects. Florovsky certainly had the right idea: it is necessary to acquire the 'mind of the Fathers' to deal with contemporary issues, just as the Fathers dealt with contemporary issues in their time. But neopatristic theology tended to focus on the intellectual concerns arising from the faith that preoccupied the Greek-Byzantine Fathers, including the restoration of neglected doctrines such as the essence-energies distinction. Yet some Fathers, notably John Chrysostom, addressed issues arising from their social milieu, but these were not foremost on the theological agenda of many of the ancient Fathers. The Fathers did not have to contend with issues arising from the complex nature of modern societies, or from modern science and technological advances, which are major sources of new issues that modern theology must face. In hindsight, there were aspects of ancient societies which merited attention, particularly those relating to social justice (slavery, serfdom, autocratic government, social classes, economic exploitation and inequalities) but by and large these were not major issues in patristic times.

[107]Kalaitzidis, 'Orthodoxy and Modernity: An Introduction', 59.

[108]Kalaitzidis, 'From the "Return to the Fathers"', 29.

[109]Cyril Hovorun, 'Patristics after Neo-Patristics', in Justin A. Mihoc and Leonard Aldea, eds., *A Celebration of Living Theology: A Festschrift in Honour of Andrew Louth* (London: T&T Clark, 2014), 209.

Many studies, especially concerning Russia and Romania, have documented the difficulty of post-communist Orthodoxy in dealing with issues of modernity.[110] Aspects of Western-style modernity which grate against the Orthodox ethos as expressed by Orthodox neo-traditionalists include: democratic political systems, marked by human rights, the separation of church and state, the religious neutrality of the state, the independence of the judiciary and the press; toleration of criticism on a very broad front; the liberalization of morals; philosophies which emphasize individual freedom and self-determination; recognition of minority rights, especially those of sexual, ethnic and religious minorities.[111] In contrast, leadership in countries of Orthodox tradition prefers authoritarian political regimes, with privileges for the local Orthodox Church, curtailment of criticism, enforcement of traditional morality, preference for social or community values over individual rights and restrictions on the rights of minorities. Even by the early twenty-first century, Orthodoxy had barely begun to focus creatively on such issues, although the document adopted at the Holy and Great Council of the Orthodox Church in June 2016 on 'The Mission of the Orthodox Church in Today's World' marks fresh, if timid, initiative in staking out a position of the Orthodox Church on a wide range of social and economic issues (see Chapter 14.)

---

[110]See, among other studies, Kristina Stoeckl, *Community after Totalitarianism: The Russian Orthodox Intellectual Tradition and the Philosophical Discourse of Political Modernity* (Frankfurt am Main: Peter Lang, 2008), and Lavinia Stan and Lucian Turcescu, *Religion and Politics in Post-Communist Romania* (Oxford: Oxford University Press, 2007).

[111]See Vasilios Makrides, 'Orthodox Christianity, Modernity and Postmodernity: Overview, Analysis and Assessment', *Religion, State and Society*, 40, 3–4 (2012), especially 260–2. This article is an excellent overview of Orthodoxy and modernity, with numerous references.

18

The Living Tradition of Orthodox Theology

Chapter Outline

Trends in modern Orthodox theology

Much of all modern Orthodox theology owes its origin, directly or indirectly, to Russian Christian thinkers, beginning with the Slavophiles of the middle of the nineteenth century, extending through the Russian religious renaissance of the early twentieth century, and to its sequels in exile after the Russian Revolution and the Civil War. Even if certain philosophical-theological constructs of the leaders of the Russian religious renaissance, especially those of Vladimir Soloviev, Pavel Florensky and Sergius Bulgakov, were largely relegated to the status of intellectual museum pieces in the second half of the twentieth century, it was their immediate successors associated with the neopatristic mode of theology who became the leaders of Orthodox thought after the Second World War. Paul Evdokimov, Georges Florovsky, Vladimir Lossky, John Meyendorff, Alexander Schmemann and others owed in large part their theological apprenticeship to the first generation of Russian exiles, especially those who founded and taught at the Saint Sergius Institute of Orthodox Theology in Paris in its early decades. From them, the neopatristic approach to theology spread to the Greek-speaking world and throughout Orthodoxy, slowly, but not entirely displacing scholastically inspired academic theology which dominated much of Orthodox theology in the nineteenth century and the first half of the twentieth century.

Neopatristic theology, which rapidly became the leading approach in Orthodox theology after the Second World War, represented a poised alternative to the often audacious theology of the earlier 'Russian School', characterized, so its critics considered, by speculations often only poorly connected with the roots of Orthodox theological tradition in the ancient Fathers of the Church. While this assessment has some validity, neopatristic theology had its origins in the very same renaissance of Russian religious thought as religious philosophy and indeed incorporated some of its critical insights while discarding others. Neopatristic theology is a child of Russian religious philosophy and theology – true, a fractious and rebellious child, – but its child nonetheless. An initial and still lingering line of analysis emphasizes a fundamental opposition between neopatristic theology and religious philosophy,[1] but this approach is far too reductionist to reflect the complex interrelationships among Orthodox approaches to theology and their indebtedness to each other. As we saw in this study, there are strong linkages and continuities of neopatristic theology with earlier religious thought in such areas as the theology of the person, Eucharistic ecclesiology and liturgical theology.

As a child of the Russian religious renaissance, neopatristic theology inherited important characteristics of its parents. These include a break with the stifling academic theology dominated by Western modes of thought and a return to patristic inspiration for Orthodox thought, with of course different outlooks on the significance of patristic teachings. Although Soloviev paid little attention to the early Fathers of the Church, Florensky and Bulgakov were well versed in patristic literature, even if they found it necessary to look also to other sources of thought for their engagement with modernity.

Another trait that neopatristic theology inherited from its parents, and indeed from late academic theology as well, is a high level of scholarship. Although academic theology too had achieved a high level of scholarship in pre-revolutionary Russia in such areas as patristics and biblical studies (other than biblical criticism), its scope was limited by its very premises and methods, which draw on Catholic and Protestant neo-scholasticism. The leaders of the Russian religious renaissance searched for inspiration from a wide range of both ancient and modern sources as they sought to bring a Christian perspective to bear on contemporary issues in an intellectual and socio-cultural scene dominated by non-Christian thinking. Neopatristic theology, while largely rejecting modern sources of inspiration for theology, achieved greater fidelity to patristic inspiration than religious thought, but at a price – in particular a difficulty, as we highlighted in Chapter 17, in coming to grips with modernity in all its facets. By the early twenty-first century, for many younger Orthodox theologians, this price was excessive, as Orthodox thought appeared increasingly ill-adapted to face the complex challenges imposed by rapid social, political, economic, scientific and technological change.

Academic theology features as a poor second cousin of religious philosophy and theology and neopatristic theology in this study. Yet academic theology was and remains a powerful force in Orthodoxy, especially in theological education, notably in seminaries and theological schools in

---

[1]For a fuller discussion of the 'standard narrative' of the 'two-school theory' and its critique, see Brandon Gallaher and Paul Ladouceur, 'Introduction: Georges Florovsky and the Mind of the Fathers', in Brandon Gallaher and Paul Ladouceur, eds., *The Patristic Witness of Georges Florovsky: Essential Theological Writings* (London: T&T Clark, 2019), 2–4, and n. 4 for additional references.

countries of Orthodox tradition, where manuals of theology in the old style are still popular. Orthodox academic theology continued to exercise a certain fascination in non-Orthodox circles long after it became *dépassée* in mainstream Orthodox thought. An example of the appeal of academic theology outside Orthodoxy is the French translation of Panayiotis Trembelas's *Dogmatica*, all 1,744 pages, a heroic labour of several years by Dom Pierre Dumont (1901–70), published by the Monastery of Chevetogne in Belgium in three volumes between 1966 and 1968.[2] In 1976 George Maloney (1924–2005), a noted American Roman Catholic theologian, published *A History of Orthodox Theology Since 1453*.[3] Despite the book's ambitious title, it is mostly a scholarly study of Orthodox *academic* theology. The Russian religious renaissance and neopatristic theology hardly receive more than passing nods,[4] and are certainly not seen as significantly different approaches to theology than 'school' theology. Maloney deals summarily with Russian theology in exile, but the religious renaissance prior to the Revolution of 1917 merits less than a page. The vibrant Greek 'theology of the '60s' is not signalled out – the author covers in some detail Christos Androutsos and Panayiotis Trembelas, but among the leaders of the theology of the 1960s, only John Romanides is mentioned, and then solely in connection with theological education in the United States.[5]

On the other hand, by the 1970s other non-Orthodox scholars were well aware of the creative ferment in modern Orthodox theology, especially as a result of the visibility of Orthodox theologians in the United Kingdom, France and elsewhere in Europe and in the United States, through translations of works of the major Russian theologians in exile, the revival of Palamite theology, especially the publication of the works of John Meyendorff and others (see Chapters 5 and 8) and the participation of Orthodox theologians in academic and ecumenical undertakings. Two general studies of Orthodox theology published in the 1990s signalled recognition by non-Orthodox scholars of the shift away from academic theology in Orthodoxy. Yannis Spiteris (b. 1940), a Catholic bishop, later cardinal, in his full-length study of modern Greek theology, *La Teologia ortodossa neo-greca* (Neo-Greek Orthodox Theology) (1992), devotes considerably more attention to the major personalities of the 'neo-Orthodox current' than to academic theology, focusing in particular on Panayiotis Nellas, John Romanides, Christos Yannaras, Nikos Nissiotis and John Zizioulas.[6] The Dominican Aidan Nichols (b. 1948), in his book *Light from the East* (1995), deals with eleven modern Russian and Greek theologians, with only Trembelas representing academic theology.[7]

[2]Panagiotis N. Trembelas, *Dogmatique de l'Église orthodoxe* (The Dogmatic Theology of the Orthodox Church) (Bruges, BE: Chevetogne/Desclée de Brouwer, 1966–8), 3 vols. See also the subtly worded review of this work by Metropolitan Kallistos Ware, 'Review of Panagiotis N. Trembelas, *Dogmatique de l'Église orthodoxe*', *Eastern Churches Review*, 3, 4 (1971). See also Ch. 6, 126–9.
[3]George A. Maloney, *A History of Orthodox Theology since 1453* (Belmont, MA: Nordland, 1976).
[4]See Maloney, *Orthodox Theology since 1453*, 73–8; 79–82.
[5]Ibid., 209–10.
[6]Yannis Spiteris, *La teologia ortodossa neo-greca* (Neo-Greek Orthodox Theology) (Bologna: Edizione Dehoniane, 1992), 255–416. Spiteris also covers major figures of the Faculty of Theology of Thessaloniki: Savvas Agourdis, Ioannis Fountoulis, Panayiotis Chrestou, George Mantzaridis and Nikos Matsoukas (417–54).
[7]Aidan Nichols, *Light from the East: Authors and Themes in Orthodox Theology* (London: Sheed & Ward, 1995).

The two principal approaches to modern Orthodox theology are sometimes characterized by different slogans: '*Back* to the Fathers' is supposed to embody the programme of neopatristic theology, while '*Beyond* the Fathers' is said to characterize the 'Russian school' or religious philosophy. Such reductionist slogans are, of course, gross oversimplifications which inaccurately depict the range of thinking in the two broad streams of twentieth-century Orthodox theology. Both were in fact grounded on the patristic foundation, but, as Paul Valliere aptly remarks, 'The issue concerns that which is added to the foundation.'[8]

From the mid-1930s onwards, it was increasingly clear to the Orthodox theologians in Paris that there were two broad approaches to Orthodox theology. This was amply demonstrated in the conflict over sophiology and the publication in 1937 of books reflecting the two theological perspectives, George Florovsky's *The Ways of Russian Theology* and the collection of eleven essays under the title *Living Tradition: Orthodoxy in the Modern World.*[9] *Living Tradition* demonstrated that the emerging patristic-based theology did not have a monopoly on Orthodox tradition, and that tradition must be seen as dynamic rather than static.[10] There was no doubt a polemical undercurrent in the motivation for the book, especially in the aftermath of the sophiology affair of the previous years.

While an aggressive tone marked Vladimir Lossky's critiques of Sergius Bulgakov's theology in the mid-1930s, personal relations between Bulgakov and Georges Florovsky, the two leading figures of modern Orthodox theology, remained respectful and even friendly, despite their widely divergent views on a range of theological issues.[11] Florovsky never criticized Bulgakov's theology directly in print, even if he did so in private conversation at the time and in public lectures towards the end of his academic career.[12] In *The Ways of Russian Theology*, Florovsky treats Bulgakov's pre-exile works with considerable circumspect,[13] leaving aside Bulgakov's great dogmatic works, several of which had appeared by the time that *Ways* was published.

An early treatment of modern Orthodox theology in terms of two opposing 'schools' is found in Fr Alexander Schmemann's short essay, 'Roll of Honour', written for George Florovsky's sixtieth birthday in 1953:

> Schematically, we should distinguish two main streams or trends, two different types of theological approach. One of these types had its roots in the tradition of Russian religious and philosophical

[8]Paul Valliere, *Modern Russian Theology: Bukharev, Soloviev, Bulgakov: Orthodox Theology in a New Key* (Grand Rapids, MI: Eerdmans, 2000), 376.

[9]Georges Florovsky, *The Ways of Russian Theology* (1937), Vols. V–VI of *The Collected Works of Georges Florovsky,* Richard Haugh, ed. (Belmont, MA: Nordland, 1979); *Zhivoe predanie: pravoslavie v sovremennosti* (Living Tradition: Orthodoxy in the Modern World) (Paris: YMCA-Press, 1937). The essays of Nicholas Afanasiev, Sergius Bulgakov, Cyprian Kern and Lev Zander are translated in Michael Plekon, ed., *Tradition Alive: On the Church and the Christian Life in Our Time* (Lanham, MA: Rowan & Littlefield, 2003).

[10]See Ch. 5, See Ch. 8, 179–186.

[11]See Paul Ladouceur, "Aimons-nous les uns les autres': Serge Boulgakov et Georges Florovsky' ('Let Us Love One Another': Sergius Bulgakov and Georges Florovsky), *Contacts,* 64, 237 (2012).

[12]See Georges Florovsky, 'The Renewal of Orthodox Theology – Florensky, Bulgakov and the Others: On the Way to a Christian Philosophy', unpublished paper at the symposium 'Idealist Philosophy in Russia', Aix-en-Provence, 25–29 March 1968. Transcription in the Georges Florovsky Papers (C0586), Manuscripts Division, Department of Rare Books and Special Collections, Princeton University Library.

[13]Florovsky, *The Ways of Russian Theology*, Vol. II, 274.

> thought of the nineteenth century, and was closely connected, although in different ways, with the names of Khomiakov, Vladimir Soloviev, Dostoevsky, Metropolitan Anthony Khrapovitsky, Nesmelov, Florensky and others. One may describe this school of thought as a 'Russian school', because of the importance which all its representatives, regardless of their mutual disagreements, attributed to the problems and ideas which constituted the main bulk of Russian religious thinking. They wanted to move further in the same direction.
>
> Against this background, Dr Florovsky's position has been in fact 'the opposite pole'. The struggle between the two movements, which in many respects conditioned the history of 'Parisian Theology', is much more important than personal difficulties which often complicated the issues and were experienced by those involved sometimes more acutely than the lasting values of the issues themselves.
>
> What was then the meaning and the actual content of the controversy? Without rejecting the achievements of the 'Russian religious thought', Father Florovsky has chosen as a cornerstone of the Orthodox theological revival not any modern traditions of the school, but the sacred Tradition of the Church. He called for a 'return to the Fathers', to the Fathers of the Church Universal – to that 'sacred Hellenism', which in his expression is an eternal and perennial category of historical Orthodoxy.[14]

Two decades later, Schmemann identifies two pre-revolutionary theological traditions in Russia: the 'academic', based in the theological academies; and the 'free', descended from the early Slavophiles and which formed the core of the religious renaissance at the end of the nineteenth century and the beginning of the twentieth century, outside the formal structures of the Russian Orthodox Church.[15] Schmemann writes that it is in the field of dogmatic theology in particular 'that one can clearly discern the two main trends or orientations whose correlation and mutual opposition constitute the main theme of modern Russian theology'. Both orientations agree that 'Orthodox theology must keep its patristic foundations.' But while the first 'trend', 'whose most typical and "complete" representative' was Sergius Bulgakov, considered that Orthodox theology must go 'beyond the Fathers', the theologians of the second 'trend', whose principal representatives were Georges Florovsky, Vladimir Lossky and Serge Verhovsky, emphasized the 'return to the Fathers', 'the permanent and eternal value of the Hellenic categories for Orthodox theological thought'.[16] Despite these fundamental differences in approach to tradition, Schmemann perceptively identified commonalities between the two modern modes of Orthodox thought: 'Representatives of both trends are indeed united in their criticism of the "Western captivity" of Russian theology, in their desire to root theology again in the traditional sources: the Fathers, the liturgy, the living spiritual experience of the church.'[17]

---

[14]Alexander Schmemann, 'Roll of Honour', *St Vladimir's Seminary Quarterly*, 3, 1 (1953), 6–7. The presence of Metropolitan Anthony (Khrapovitsky) (1863–1936) in the religious philosophy group is anomalous. In exile, Khrapovitsky was the head of the Russian Orthodox Church Outside of Russia (ROCOR), which condemned Bulgakov's sophiology in 1935. Paul Evdokimov situates Khrapovitsky in the 'moralist school', which Evdokimov equates with academic theology. See Paul Evdokimov, *Le Christ dans la pensée russe* (Christ in Russian Thought) (Paris: Le Cerf, 1970), 122–6.

[15]Alexander Schmemann, 'Russian Theology 1920-1972: An Introductory Survey', *St Vladimir's Theological Quarterly*, 16, 4 (1972), 175.

[16]Schmemann, 'Russian Theology 1920-1972', 178–81.

[17]Ibid., 178.

In his book *Le Christ dans la pensée russe* (Christ in Russian Thought), Paul Evdokimov also distinguishes sharply between the 'religious philosophy of Russian thinkers' (under this heading he places Simon Frank, Nicholas Lossky, Basil Zenkovsky, Boris Vicheslavtsev, Nicolas Berdyaev, Pavel Florensky and Sergius Bulgakov) and 'neopatristic theology' (Georges Florovsky, Vladimir Lossky, Olivier Clément, John Meyendorff, Alexander Schmemann, Anton Kartashev and Bishop Cassien Besobrasov).[18] Nonetheless, Evdokimov offers a generally serene view of modern Orthodox theology, highlighting positive aspects of all modes of theology. Evdokimov's book, together with the histories of Russian philosophy by Nicolas Lossky and Basil Zenkovsky,[19] are in a way 'antidotes' to Georges Florovsky's *The Ways of Russian Theology*. As much as Florovsky seeks to deconstruct almost all Russian theology up to the early twentieth century as contaminated by Western influences of various sorts, these three books rehabilitate Russian philosophy and theology with more balanced assessments than Florovsky's frequently impetuous and harsh judgements. Evdokimov, generally considered within the neopatristic tradition, also had strong ties with the Russian religious renaissance and, together with Olivier Clément, is a bridging figure between the two approaches to theology in his own thinking.

Modern Russian and Greek theology

The development of Russian and Greek theology since the mid-nineteenth century shows both important common elements and major differences. Most significantly, both Russian and Greek theology went through a long period of 'pseudomorphism', as Georges Florovsky referred to the imitation of Western modes of theology and the adoption of certain Western doctrines, and which others call the 'Western captivity' of Orthodox thought, and even the 'Babylonian captivity'.[20] Nonetheless, the historical experience of the two major centres of Orthodox thought differed in several important respects. In the first place, a renewal of theology began much earlier in Russia than in Greece. As we saw in Chapter 3, the first stirrings of a modern theological renewal occurred in the Russian Slavophiles in the mid-nineteenth century, at a time when Greece was struggling to emerge from centuries of Turkish rule. Theology in the newly independent Greece was cast in the mode of Western academic schools of theology, dominated by scholasticism and largely isolated from the life of the church, with the result that significant theological renewal in Greece dates only from the late 1950s and the 1960s.

---

[18]Evdokimov, *Le Christ dans la pensée russe*. The presence of Anton Kartashev among the 'neopatristic theologians' may be surprising. Former professor of church history at the St Petersburg Theological Academy and Minister of Church Affairs in the Provisional Government of 1917, Kartashev was later associated with the religious renaissance. He taught at the Saint Sergius Institute and was a contributor to the 1937 *Living Tradition* (*Zhivoe prendanie*) collection of essays by the leading religious renaissance theologians in exile. Evdokimov's own discussion of Kartashev's main themes places him in the religious philosophy tradition.

[19]V. V. (Basil) Zenkovsky, *A History of Russian Philosophy* (New York: Colombia University Press, 1953) and Nicolas Lossky, *A History of Russian Philosophy* (London: Allen and Unwin, 1952).

[20]See Ch. 5, 96, n.2; and Ch.17, 422–4.

Secondly, a patristic revival began already in the mid-nineteenth century in the Russian theological academies and, in the wake of the publication of the *Philokalia* and its Slavonic and Russian translations, in Russian monasteries, notably the Monastery of Optino. This patristic revival resulted in many translations of the works of the Fathers and studies of patristic thought. A similar movement occurred much later in Greece, again only in the second half of the twentieth century, typified by appeals to patristic theology in contemporary expositions of Orthodox theology, and signalled by John Romanides's doctoral thesis *Ancestral Sin* (1957)[21], Greek translations of works of Russian neopatristic theologians, and new editions of patristic works, most prominently the writings of St Gregory Palamas. Panayiotis Trembelas's somewhat pathetic attempt to invoke patristic citations to buttress the formalistic academic theology of his *Dogmatica* (1959–61) was only a pale shadow of a true patristic revival.

Thirdly, Greek theology has no equivalent of Russian religious philosophy, and in fact little of the thinking of the Russian religious philosophers and theologians is known in Greece, in part because there are few translations into Greek, with the exception of works of Nicolas Berdyaev and short extracts of others.[22] As a result, even by the early twenty-first century Greek theologians had not yet engaged seriously with Russian religious thought. Nonetheless, some efforts are being made to raise awareness in Greece of the heritage of Russian religious renaissance, notably by the philosopher Dimitrios Baltas (b. 1970), who has published several small books and numerous articles on Russian philosophers and theologians.[23] For the most part, however, given the importance of neopatristic theology among Greek theologians, Russian religious thought remains largely outside the purview of theology in Greece. Chronology provides a partial explanation. By the time that younger Greek theologians began to be aware of Orthodox theology outside Greece in the late 1950s and early 1960s, religious philosophy was in sharp decline and had already been largely superseded by the neopatristic approach to theology. No doubt too, the particularly Russian and philosophical context of religious thought had little attraction in Greece, whereas Greek theologians were more at ease with a theological approach which stressed Greek Fathers of the Church.

Another reason for the absence of religious philosophy in Greece is that while eighteenth- and nineteenth-century Western philosophy, especially German idealism, had a considerable impact on Russian religious thought, it did not significantly influence Greek academic theology, which remained deeply enmeshed in a scholastic approach to theology well into the second half of the twentieth century. On the other hand, some late twentieth-century Greek philosophers and theologians have been influenced by existentialists, especially Martin Heidegger (1889–1976) – Christos Yannaras in particular is identified as inclined to existentialism and John Zizioulas is

---

[21] John Romanides, *The Ancestral Sin* (1957) (Ridgewood, NJ: Zephyr, 2002). See Ch. 6, 136–7.

[22] An important part of the Berdyaev corpus has been published in Greek translation, beginning in the early 1950s. See a bibliography in Dimitrios Baltas, *Rósoi filósofoi 19os-20os aiónas* (Russian Philosophers of the 19th and 20th Centuries) (Athens: Savalas, 2002), 93–4.

[23] Baltas's anthology *Rósoi filósofoi 19os-20os aiónas* provides short translated extracts from Mikhail Bakunin, Alexander Herzen, Vladimir Soloviev, Peter Struve, Sergius Bulgakov, Evgeny Troubetskoy, Nicolas Berdyaev, Nicolas Lossky and Basil Zenkovsky. Other books by Baltas on Russian religious thought include *Thémata rossikís filosofías* (Issues in Russian Philosophy) (2004); *Stathmoí tis Róssikis filosofías* (Stations of Russian Philosophy) (2008); and *Tomés sti Róssiki sképsi* (Intersections in Russian Thought) (2009).

accused of being 'an existentialist in disguise'.[24] Among the Russians, Nicolas Berdyaev is referred to as a 'Christian existentialist'.[25]

Fourthly, theology and religious practice in Greece were strongly affected by movements inspired by European pietism, in the form of the Greek religious brotherhoods, especially Zoe, from the early twentieth century until the 1960s and 1970s (see Chapter 6). Although pietism had some impact in the Russian Church, there were no significant movements in Russia or among Russians in exile along the lines of the Greek religious brotherhoods. Thus, while the development of neopatristic theology in Russian circles in exile owes its origins primarily to a reaction against dry academic theology and the bold speculations of religious philosophy, the rise of neopatristic theology in Greece was a response to academic theology and to the pietistic moralism of the religious brotherhoods.

Fifthly, a major characteristic of both Russian and Greek modern theology is criticism of Western influence on Orthodox thought, a criticism exemplified in Georges Florovsky's book *Ways of Russian Theology* (1937), and Christos Yannaras's *Orthodoxy and the West* (1982). As we pointed out in Chapter 17, there is nonetheless a subtle difference in the nature of their criticism. Russian theologians such as Florovsky, Lossky, Meyendorff and Schmemann are rarely accused of being fundamentally anti-Western, whereas some Greek theologians, especially John Romanides and Christos Yannaras, have acquired a reputation, deserved or not, for being systematically anti-Western. This likely arises from their often explicit condemnations of the very basis of Western European civilization, which both trace mainly to the theology of St Augustine and to 'Frankish' theology.

Finally, one of the consequences of the 'exile of Russian theology' after 1917 was a sort of reconciliation of academic theologians with the leaders of the religious renaissance – as shown by the presence of several leading academic theologians, such as Anton Kartashev, among the teaching staff of the Saint Sergius Institute in Paris. No doubt the shared depravation of the exile situation of the Russian intellectuals contributed to this reconciliation. A parallel reconciliation between academic theology and neopatristic theology does not seem to have taken place in Greece.

Self-critique in modern Orthodox theology

A major feature of modern Orthodox thought is the critique of Orthodox theologians by other Orthodox theologians. In fact, with the exception of the attacks against neo-Palamite theology by non-Orthodox theologians, the most ardent critics of Orthodox theology have been other Orthodox. The most criticized Orthodox thinker of modern times has perhaps been Vladimir

---

[24]Andrew Louth refers to Yannaras's thought as 'personalist existentialism'. See Andrew Louth, 'Some Recent Works by Christos Yannaras in English Translation', *Modern Theology*, 25, 2 (2009), 336. See also Andrew Louth, *Modern Orthodox Thinkers: From the Philokalia to the Present* (London: SPCK, 2015), 254–6; and Aristotle Papanikolaou, 'Is John Zizioulas an Existentialist in Disguise? Response to Lucian Turcescu', *Modern Theology*, 20, 4 (2004).

[25]See Louth, *Modern Orthodox Thinkers*, 65.

Soloviev – despite, or perhaps because of his role as a leading figure, indeed the principal intellectual inspiration, of the Russian religious renaissance. Georges Florovsky led the charge against Soloviev, although in part his critique of Soloviev was also an indirect attack on Soloviev's successors, especially Pavel Florensky and Sergius Bulgakov.

Pavel Florensky has been another favourite target for some critics, because of the unusual nature of his theology, especially his major work, *The Pillar and Ground of the Truth* (1913), and because of major lapses such as the weakness or even absence of Christology in his theology and an uncritical acceptance of Soloviev's sophiology. In any overall assessment of Florensky, weaknesses in his theology have to be weighed against his unquestioning faithfulness to the Orthodox Church, his public Christian witness under communism and his martyrdom. Florensky and Mother Maria (Skobtsova) are the only major Orthodox theologians martyred for their faith and commitment to the church in the twentieth century. By canonizing all victims of communist persecution in 1981, the Russian Orthodox Church Outside of Russia indirectly canonized Florensky, whose theology it nonetheless disavows.[26] The Ecumenical Patriarchate canonized Mother Maria, together with her companions killed in German concentration camps, in 2004.

Sergius Bulgakov is also heavily criticized, beginning in the 1920s, especially for his sophiology, and for other aspects of his theology, as part of a general disavowal, articulated if only indirectly by Georges Florovsky and others, of the theological heritage of the Russian religious renaissance (see Chapters 5, 8, 9 and 12).

As we saw in Chapters 6 and 17, until the beginning of the twenty-first century, critique of neopatristic theologians was mild in comparison with attacks against Soloviev and his successors. More recently, among the major neopatristic theologians, John Zizioulas has been under heavy fire for several aspects of his theology (see Chapters 6, 10 and 11). Other founding fathers of neopatristic theology such as Georges Florovsky and Dumitru Staniloae have been much less criticized. Vladimir Lossky has been criticized, for example, for an overemphasis on apophatism in Eastern Christian thought and for unduly separating the missions of the Son and the Holy Spirit,[27] but such critiques are a far cry from the broader criticism and rejection of sophiology and other key ideas of the Russian religious renaissance. Criticism of neopatristic theology in the early twenty-first century has been directed less towards specific doctrines and more against neopatristic theology as a theological method, which virtually predetermined major neopatristic themes. While there are few critiques of Florovsky's theology as such, a major exception is Berdyaev's prophetic critique of Florovsky's project in his review of *The Ways of Russian Theology*. Many of the issues that Berdyaev raised in his 1937 review were subsequently identified as weaknesses in the actual practice of neopatristic theology (see Chapter 17).

Alexander Schmemann maintained a balanced attitude towards his teachers at the Saint Sergius Institute, especially Sergius Bulgakov. This is clear in Schmemann's 'three portraits' of Fr Sergius,

---

[26]Fr Pavel Florensky is named, together with numerous other victims of communism, on the icon painted for the glorification of the New Martyrs by ROCOR on 1 November 1981 – but he is not shown on the icon itself. ROCOR subsequently denied that it had thus canonized Florensky, claiming that the inclusion of his name on the icon was an error. See www.monachos.net/conversation/topic/5205-saint-pavlov-florensky (6 April 2017).

[27]See the references in Ch. 5, n. 45.

written in 1971, twenty-seven years after Bulgakov's death. Schmemann fondly recalls and praises Fr Sergius for the depth of his faith and his profound celebration of the Divine Liturgy, calling him 'one of the most remarkable men of this tragic half-century of Russian history', from whom he received 'his flame, his faith and his joy': 'He gave me to drink that which was best and most pure in Russian spirituality.'[28] At the same time Schmemann distances himself from Bulgakov's teachings, declaring at the outset that he never accepted sophiology. Schmemann recalls that some refer to Fr Sergius as a 'heretic' – but seeing Fr Sergius, 'I felt with all my being that this man was not a heretic but on the contrary he radiated all that was most important and most authentic in Orthodoxy.'[29]

Even Vladimir Lossky softened his attitude towards Bulgakov after his strident criticism of most of Bulgakov's principal ideas during Sophia dispute of the mid-1930s, especially in his 1936 book *Spor o Sofii* (The Dispute over Sophia) (see Chapter 4). Bulgakov and Lossky corresponded during the Second World War, and Bulgakov encouraged Lossky 'to turn his attention to constructive rather than controversial theological writing.'[30] In his classic *The Mystical Theology of the Eastern Church* (1944), Lossky mildly refers to Bulgakov's sophiology as an 'ecclesiology gone astray.'[31] And that same year, learning of Fr Sergius's death, Vladimir Lossky attended his funeral, even though this entailed a long walk from his home on the outskirts of Paris to the Russian cathedral on the *rue Daru* where the funeral service was held.

The revisionist trend of the early twenty-first century in contemporary Orthodox theology (see Chapters 6 and 17) can be interpreted not so much as a frontal attack on neopatristic theology, but rather as an attempt to correct its most obvious weaknesses. These weaknesses are typically identified as inherent anti-Westernism, often coupled with undue Hellenism and 'Byzantinism'; a difficulty in engaging with modernity, especially in social and political theology; a perceived over-exaltation of monastic spirituality and a minimizing of liturgical-based spirituality; and overemphasis on patristic studies, with a corresponding neglect of biblical scholarship. Correctives for these weaknesses are well within the scope of Georges Florovsky's call for the 'acquisition of the patristic mind' – not the repetition of the letter of patristic writings, but as the proper way of doing theology, theologizing as the Fathers theologized (see Chapter 5). The most significant departure from Florovsky's neopatristic vision would entail a relativization of the Greek-Byzantine patristic tradition by the recognition of the validity of other Christian theological traditions, notably the Latin and the Oriental – and the Russian, – as potential sources of inspiration for modern Orthodox theologizing.

The contemporary concern to engage issues of modernity from an Orthodox perspective can also be seen as a belated response to Alexander Bukharev's advocacy in the mid-nineteenth century

[28]Alexander Schmemann, 'Trois Images [du père Serge Boulgakov]' (Three portraits [of Fr Sergius Bulgakov]), *Le Messager orthodoxe*, 57 (1972), 2; 4.

[29]Schmemann, 'Trois Images', 5–6.

[30]Rowan Williams, 'The Theology of Vladimir Nikolaievich Lossky: An Exposition and Critique' (D. Phil. thesis, University of Oxford, 1975), 13.

[31]Vladimir Lossky, *The Mystical Theology of the Eastern Church* (1944) (Crestwood, NY: St Vladimir's Seminary Press, 1976), 112. For Lossky, Bulgakov's 'fundamental error' was 'to see in the energy of Wisdom (*Sofia*), which he identified with the essence, the very principle of the Godhead' (*The Mystical Theology*, 80).

of an Orthodoxy in dialogue with the modern world. It is also a continuation, in another form and context, of the deep involvement of the leaders of the Russian religious renaissance of the beginning of the twentieth century in the burning political, social and cultural issues tormenting pre-revolutionary Russia, an engagement which many Russian theologians continued in the changed circumstances of their exile situation (see Chapters 4, 10, 13 and 14).

In Chapter 17, we discussed theological weaknesses in the Russian religious renaissance. Despite these weaknesses, the Russian religious renaissance is the most striking example of the engagement of Orthodox thought with modern issues. The encounter of Russian Christian intellectuals with modernity at the end of the nineteenth century and the beginning of the twentieth century was brought to an abrupt halt in Russia itself after the Bolshevik revolution in 1917, although this encounter continued in the Russian thinkers in exile, especially Nicolas Berdyaev, whose most important works were in fact written in exile. Perhaps because there is no Greek equivalent to the Russian religious renaissance, it is easy to overlook the importance of the Russian religious renaissance as the most significant example of Orthodox engagement with the modern world. If the religious renaissance failed to have much impact on the course of events in Russia, its leaders cannot be faulted for not having done their utmost to bring a Christian perspective to bear on Russian society during the tragic decades prior to the First World War and the revolution.

The debt of modern Orthodox thinking, including neopatristic theology, to the Russian religious renaissance is enormous. In some cases, the development of thought from one period to another is direct and the links obvious, as in ecclesiology and the theology of the human person (see Chapters 10 and 11). In other areas, the thinkers of the Russian religious renaissance are more distant ancestors or predecessors, but contemporary Orthodox thought has in many cases arrived at the same point as the Russians, such as in social and political theology and human rights.

Although the roots of neopatristic theology have to be sought in the Russian religious renaissance, neopatristic theology spread far beyond the confines of the exiled Russian community, reaching throughout the Orthodox world, especially in Greece, but also in Romania and Serbia. Neopatristic theology in Romania had an independent source, in the writings of Fr Dumitru Staniloae (see Chapter 7). Independently of the Russians, Staniloae sought to revive patristic theology, especially the theology of the divine energies of Gregory Palamas. The importance of Staniloae's theological project is increasingly recognized as his major works, especially his *Dogmatica*, are being published in English translations.[32]

Neopatristic theology has been criticized for both 'historicism' and 'ahistoricism'. The critique of historicism reads much of neopatristic theology as 'traditionalism', according absolute value to the teachings of the Fathers of Church on all subjects, whether or not these touch essential dogmas; the writings of this or that Father on this or that subject become the principal if not sole legitimate criteria of truth.[33] Although Georges Florovsky constantly appeals to the Fathers in his theology,

---

[32]Staniloae's *Teologia dogmatică ortodoxă* (Orthodox Dogmatic Theology), originally published in three volumes in 1978, has been translated in six volumes under the general title *The Experience of God* (Brookline, MA: Holy Cross Orthodox Press, 2005–13).
[33]Nicolas Berdyaev accuses Florovsky of 'historicism', which others refer to as patristicism, patristic fundamentalism or even patristic heresy. See 'Tradition and the Nature of Theology', Ch. 8, 179–187.

he frequently warned against the dangers of a 'theology of repetition' and, late in life, referred to the Fathers as 'guides and witnesses, no more'.[34]

The critique of ahistoricism arises from the tendency to consider the teachings of the Fathers as abstract ideas, removed from the context in which they arose.[35] While there is some value in this critique, there are also limits. Appeals for a contextual approach to the theology of the ancient Fathers as a corrective for the removal of patristic ideas from their historical setting and a chronological levelling of patristic writings may be satisfactory for academic study of the Fathers, but how then do we draw on the Fathers as sources of inspiration to deal with new issues? In order for the Fathers to be relevant to the modern situation, it is necessary to understand both their approach to theology, which Florovsky called 'acquiring the mind of the Fathers', and to seek the continuing value of central patristic ideas which can be applied to modern problems.

There is unease and criticism in certain Orthodox quarters of the pronouncements of some leading monastic figures on contemporary issues such as modernism in general.[36] This arises not so much from a questioning of the importance of monasticism in the Orthodox tradition as from a sense that certain monastic figures have overstepped their role, advocating a narrow interpretation of Orthodox tradition and spirituality, and elevating the monastic life as the supreme criterion of Orthodox life. This vision of monasticism and Orthodox spirituality, founded on anti-Westernism and anti-modernism, does not correspond with the experience and circumstances of the large mass of Orthodox faithful living 'in the world'. But it is not the only possible vision of Orthodox spirituality. Writers such as Paul Evdokimov, Fr Lev Gillet, Fr Alexander Schmemann, Mother Maria Skobtsova and Metropolitan Kallistos Ware seek to build bridges between Orthodox theology and spirituality and life in contemporary society, rather than to erect barriers between them or place obstacles in the lives of Orthodox faithful.

Conclusion

Part I of this book dealt with the principal moments and movements of modern Orthodox theology from the fall of Constantinople in 1453 to the beginning of the twenty-first century, with emphasis on theology in Russia and among Russian exiles, and in Greece and Romania. Part II of the book examined major themes in modern Orthodox thought, focusing on issues on which there have been marked differences of views and, at least in some cases, a significant evolution in thought over the years. We have sought throughout to point to key relationships among the major strands of modern Orthodox thought after the mid-nineteenth century, slavophilism, the Russian religious

[34]Georges Florovsky, 'On the Authority of the Fathers', letter to A. F. Dobbie Bateman, 12 December 1963, in Gallaher and Ladouceur, eds., *The Patristic Witness of Georges Florovsky*, 237–40.

[35]See the critiques by Sergius Bulgakov, Hilarion Alfeyev and Andrew Louth in Ch. 17, 420; 425–6.

[36]See Pantelis Kalaitzidis, 'Theological, Historical and Cultural Reasons for Anti-Ecumenical Movements in Eastern Orthodoxy', in Pantelis Kalaitzidis et al., eds., *Orthodox Handbook on Ecumenism: Resources for Theological Education* (Volos, GR: Volos Academy Publications, WCC Publications & Regnum Books, 2014), 149–50. Kalaitzidis notably refers to monks who 'seek to be considered as the ultimate authority and the genuine voice of Orthodoxy' as 'Orthodox ayatollahs' (150).

renaissance, neopatristic theology and even academic theology. During this period, ideas and themes flowed from one period and mode of thought to the other; older ideas were refined, some were discarded and new concerns and concepts appeared. In Chapter 17, we reviewed the two major trusts in modern Orthodox theology, Russian religious thought and neopatristic theology, including critiques that have been levied against them over the years. This prepares the way for a consideration of the present state and future of Orthodox thought in an increasingly secular and global social, economic and political environment.

The Russian religious renaissance, represented by the theologians, philosophers and artistic and cultural figures who dominated Orthodox religious thought from the late nineteenth century to the middle of the twentieth century, has passed largely into the realm of intellectual and literary history. Yet the legacy of this remarkably fertile intellectual, spiritual and cultural movement had a powerful influence on the development of subsequent Orthodox thought, either by the appropriation and development of some of its ideas or in reaction against them. In a number of specific areas, such as the theology of the human person and ecclesiology, there has been a marked continuity in the development of Orthodox thought between the Russian religious renaissance and the neopatristic theology which flowered in the second half of the twentieth century. Neopatristic theology owes its origins and several of its most valuable insights to thinkers of the Russian religious renaissance, even if certain key notions of the religious philosophers, especially all-unity and sophiology, were summarily dismissed. An earlier view of the development of modern Orthodox theology considered that neopatristic theology represented a rejection of the religious renaissance and simply replaced or supplanted it, going off in a different direction, dominated by a revival of patristic thought as the sole authentic wellspring of Orthodox theology (see Chapters 5 and 8). A more balanced view sees neopatristic theology as a prolongation or extension of the Russian religious renaissance rather than as standing in steadfast opposition to it.

Possibly the greatest and most enduring achievement of neopatristic theology has been the restoration of Palamite theology of the essence and energies of God at the centre of Orthodox theology, and in its wake, the related doctrines of apophatism and theosis (see Chapters 5 and 9). The restoration of these doctrines to their rightful place in Orthodox was the most important aspect of the liberation of Orthodox theology from the shackles of neo-scholastically inspired academic theology and of its emergence as a theology faithful to the apostolic kerygma and to the tradition of the ancient Fathers.

The restoration of the three doctrines also enabled Orthodox thought to return to a greater equilibrium between theology as a system of thought manifested in precisely worded doctrines or dogmas, and theology as the living experience of God in Christ through the Holy Spirit - the inseparable links, as Vladimir Lossky emphasizes, between theology and mysticism, between belief in God and the experience of God in the liturgy, the sacraments, prayer and daily life.[37] Intuitions of these links are found in the thinkers of the Russian religious renaissance, but it is in neopatristic

[37]See Vladimir Lossky, *The Mystical Theology of the Eastern Church* (1944) (Crestwood, NY: St Vladimir's Seminary Press, 1976), especially Chs. 1, 10, 11 and 12.

theology that they were made explicit, not only in Vladimir Lossky and Dumitru Staniloae, but also in spiritual writers such as Archimandrite Sophrony and Fr Lev Gillet.

Neither of the two main approaches to Orthodox theology in the twentieth century, nor academic theology for that matter, has a monopoly on truth, nor is devoid of truth. Each approach to theology has strengths and weaknesses, as indicated in this study. Many of the major ideas of the Russian religious renaissance have a bad press in some Orthodox circles and certain ideas of the renaissance have not been received in Orthodoxy. This can easily lead to a categorical rejection of the entire movement. Yet this is to consider the leaders of religious renaissance apart from the particular context in which they lived, the twilight years of imperial Russia. It also overlooks the crucial role of the renaissance in the origins and development of neopatristic theology which succeeded religious philosophy, and which gave it several of its most important insights. The leaders of the Russian religious renaissance were Christian voices arrayed against the host of non-Christian and anti-Christian philosophies competing for the Russian soul. The genius of the religious renaissance was to have asked the right questions, but its Achilles's heel was, in several key areas, to have given the wrong answers. Certainly there is a need to explore further the intimate relationships between the two major strands of modern Orthodox thought, seeking the 'links' rather than focusing single-mindedly on the 'breaks'.[38]

A positive sign in this direction is a revival of interest in the early twenty-first century in Bulgakov's theology brought about in part by the publication in English translation of the most important of Bulgakov's theological writings. This revival is, however, largely restricted to academic milieus in the United States and the United Kingdom, and is stronger among non-Orthodox than Orthodox theologians. Few major Orthodox theologians can be described as a 'Bulgakovians'.[39] In addition, several publications seek to appropriate Bulgakov to particularist schools such as perennialist philosophy and feminism.[40] Such narrow readings of Bulgakov are likely to diminish his standing in more mainstream Orthodoxy.

The principal critics of neopatristic theology in the early twenty-first century rightly focus on some of the evident weaknesses in the way that this form of theology was carried out after the Second World War (see Chapter 17). But in this criticism there is some risk of throwing out the 'patristic baby' with the 'neopatristic bathwater'. By concentrating on the weaknesses of neopatristic theology, critics appear to question the continued relevance of patristic thought and to overlook the main thrust of Florovsky's project: the acquisition of the patristic way of doing theology – what

---

[38]From Georges Florovsky, 'Breaks and Links', conclusion to *The Ways of Russian Theology* (1937), in Gallaher and Ladouceur, eds., *The Patristic Witness of Georges Florovsky*, 159–83.

[39]Antoine Arjakovsky has been an ardent defender of Bulgakov's theology. See especially his study of the exiled Russian religious intelligentsia, centred on the periodical *Put'*, edited by Berdyaev between 1925 and 1939: *The Way: Religious Thinkers of the Russian Emigration in Paris and Their Journal* (Notre Dame, IN: University of Notre Dame Press, 2013); and his book. *Essai sur le père Serge Boulgakov, philosophe et théologien chrétien* (Essay on Fr Sergius Bulgakov, Christian Philosopher and Theologian) (Paris: Parole et Silence, 2006).

[40]Madonna Sophia Compton situates aspects of Bulgakov's theology in a feminist framework and Robert Thompson within perennialist philosophy. See Madonna Sophia Compton, *Sophia-Spirit-Mary: Sergius Bulgakov and the Patristic Roots of a Feminine Sprit* (Berkeley, CA, and Lawrence, KS: The Raphael Group, 2015); and Robert F. Thompson, *From Glory to Glory: The Sophianic Vision of Fr Sergius Bulgakov* (Memphis, TN: Perennials Study Group, 2016).

Florovsky calls 'the acquisition of the patristic mind'[41] – in order to address contemporary problems. Paul Evdokimov aptly characterizes the programme of neopatristic theology:

> a vast synthesis of the teaching of the Fathers and its ecumenical engagement with the modern world and its problems. To combat atheism, theology must elaborate an integrated system of Christian thought. This is not only erudition, but the acquisition and possession of patristic theology from the inside, by an experiential rediscovery; in short, a veritable 'patristic style'. To return to the Fathers means to advance constantly, never retreating nor imitating. It is a theology of kerygma and witness to contemplation, and not the justification of an idea.[42]

Orthodox theology can and indeed must deal with issues unknown in patristic times, and in this sense must go beyond the Fathers, but it can never become post-patristic if this is understood as abandoning the patristic approach to theology.

Even the most ardent critics of neopatristic theology fail to come up with a viable alternative. Florovsky argued in season and out of season that patristic theology is an eternal value in Christianity. But his own understanding of what constitutes patristic theology, like that of others such as Vladimir Lossky, was too narrowly restricted to Greek-Byzantine theology – even if Florovsky considered his favourite Father, Augustine, as a Greek Father. Latin theology in its fullness, Oriental theology, modern Russian, Greek and Romanian theology, and Orthodox theology outside of countries of Orthodox tradition, are all legitimate aspects of the Orthodox theological heritage – but not all theologies are born equal. The question is neither to reject a priori nor to accept blindly one or another approach to theology, but rather to exercise theological discernment – a theological *nepsis* (watchfulness),[43] – seeking truth in all forms of theology. The Holy Spirit is the Spirit of Truth (Jn 16.13; 1 Jn 5.6), and the theologian must be a seeker of Truth, the merchant whom Jesus singles out, seeking beautiful pearls, 'who, when he had found one pearl of great price, went and sold all that he had and bought it' (Mt. 13.45-46).

While the Greek-Byzantine Fathers of old certainly played a dominant role in the elaboration of Orthodox theology, Orthodoxy is broader than the Greek-Byzantine world and the notion of Fathers of the Church must be seen in a wide context, to include the Latin, Oriental and even modern Fathers and Mothers of the Church. Both Georges Florovsky and Kallistos Ware admit the possibility of modern Fathers of the Church: 'The church is still fully authoritative as she has been in the ages past', writes Florovsky, 'since the Spirit of Truth quickens her now no less effectively as in ancient times'.[44] But neither Florovsky nor Ware name any modern figures as Fathers and Mothers of the Church. Will future generations consider Elisabeth Behr-Sigel, Sergius Bulgakov, Olivier

---

[41]See Ch. 5, 113–4.

[42]Evdokimov, *Le Christ dans la pensée russe*, 194.

[43]In Orthodox ascetic literature, the word *nepsis* or *nipsis* is typically translated as watchfulness, alertness or vigilance: 'literally, the opposite to a state of drunken stupor; hence spiritual sobriety … It signifies an attitude of attentiveness (*prosochí*), whereby one keeps watch over one's inward thoughts and fantasies, maintaining guard over the heart and intellect'. G. E. H. Palmer, Philip Sherrard and Kallistos Ware, eds. and trans., *The Philokalia: The Complete Text Compiled by St Nikodimos of the Holy Mountain and St Makarios of Corinth*, vol. 1 (London: Faber and Faber, 1979), 379.

[44]Georges Florovsky, 'Saint Gregory Palamas and the Tradition of the Fathers', in Gallaher and Ladouceur, eds., *The Patristic Witness of Georges Florovsky*, 226. See Kallistos Ware, *The Orthodox Church* (London: Penguin Books, 2nd ed. 1993), 204.

Clément, Paul Evdokimov, Pavel Florensky, Georges Florovsky, Vladimir Lossky, John Meyendorff, Mother Maria of Paris, Alexander Schmemann, Dumitru Staniloae or other modern Orthodox theologians, even Alexei Khomiakov and Vladimir Soloviev, as Fathers and Mothers of the Church? Despite clear divergences in their theologies, they share a common commitment to Christ, the church and the Orthodox tradition. As in classical patristic times, modern Orthodox theology is characterized by a rich diversity of themes and expressions of the one continuing faith in Jesus Christ, a divine-human encounter in true synergy.

Selected Bibliography

References are separated into Primary Sources and Secondary Sources for most chapters, while in some chapters this distinction is not particularly meaningful. Items relevant to more than chapter may occur under several chapters, except for books in the General References, which are not repeated. Years in brackets after the title indicate the year of first publication. The literature for Christian theology from the beginnings to the fall of Constantinople in 1453 is vast; the bibliography for Chapter 1 is limited to selected works by modern Orthodox authors. The bibliography for Part III (Chapters 17 and 18) includes only works which do not already occur in the bibliographies of earlier chapters. Some works listed here appear only in footnotes in the main text and hence the authors and the titles of the works are not listed in the Index.

General References

Berdyaev, Nicolas. *The Russian Idea*. Trans. R. M. French. London: Geoffrey Bles and New York: Macmillan, 1947; Hudson, NY: Lindisfarne Press, 1992.

Evdokimov, Paul. *Le Christ dans la pensée russe* (Christ in Russian Thought). Paris: Le Cerf, 1970; 2011.

Florovsky, Georges. *The Ways of Russian Theology* (1937). Trans. Robert L. Nichols, in *The Collected Works of Georges Florovsky* (vols. 5–6). Belmont, MA: Nordland, 1979.

Lossky, Nicolas O. *A History of Russian Philosophy*. London: Allen and Unwin, 1952.

Louth, Andrew. *Modern Orthodox Thinkers: From the Philokalia to the Present*. London: SPCK; Downers Grove, IL: IVP Academic, 2015.

Špidlík, Tomáš. *L'Idée russe: Une autre vision de l'homme* (The Russian Idea: Another Vision of the World). Troyes, FR: Fates, 1994.

Ware, Timothy (Metropolitan Kallistos of Diokleia). *The Orthodox Church* (1963). London: Penguin Books, 1997; 2015.

Yannaras, Christos. *Orthodoxy and the West: Hellenic Self-Identity in the Modern Age* (1992). Trans. Peter Chamberas and Norman Russell. Brookline, MA: Holy Cross Orthodox Press, 2006.

Zenkovsky, Vasily V. (Basil). *A History of Russian Philosophy*, 2 vols. Trans. George L. Kline. New York: Colombia University Press, 1953.

Zernov, Nicolas. *The Russian Religious Renaissance of the Twentieth Century*. New York: Harper & Row, 1963.

1. Prolegomena to Modern Orthodox Theology

Behr, John. *The Way to Nicea*. Crestwood, NY: St Vladimir's Seminary Press, 2001.
Behr, John. *The Nicene Faith* (2 vols.). Crestwood, NY: St Vladimir's Seminary Press, 2004.
Erickson, John H. *The Challenge of Our Past: Studies in Orthodox Canon Law and Church History*. Crestwood, NY: St Vladimir's Seminary Press, 1991.
Kesich, Vaselin. *The Birth of the Church AD 33–200*. Crestwood, NY: St Vladimir's Seminary Press, 2007.
Louth, Andrew. *Greek East and Latin West: The Church 681–1071*. Crestwood, NY: St Vladimir's Seminary Press, 2007.
McGuckin, John Anthony. *The Path of Christianity: The First Thousand Years*. Downers Grove, IL: IVP Academic, 2017.
Meyendorff, John. *Byzantine Theology: Historical Trends and Doctrinal Themes*. New York: Fordham University Press, 1974.
Meyendorff, John. *Imperial Unity and Christian Divisions: The Church AD 450–680*. Crestwood, NY: St Vladimir's Seminary Press, 1989.
Meyendorff, John. *The Orthodox Church: Its Past and Its Role in the World Today* (1981). Crestwood, NY: St Vladimir's Seminary Press, 1996.
Meyendorff, John. *St Gregory Palamas and Orthodox Spirituality* (1965). Crestwood, NY: St Vladimir's Seminary Press, 1974; 1998.
Obolensky, Dimitri. *The Byzantine Commonwealth: Eastern Europe 500–1453*. London: Weidenfeld and Nicolson, 1971.
Papadakis, Aristeidis (with John Meyendorff). *The Christian East and the Rise of the Papacy: The Church AD 1071–1453*. Crestwood, NY: St Vladimir's Seminary Press, 1994.
Pelikan, Jaroslav. *The Emergence of the Catholic Tradition (100–600)*. Chicago and London: University of Chicago Press, 1971.
Pelikan, Jaroslav. *The Spirit of Eastern Christendom (600–1700)*. Chicago and London: University of Chicago Press, 1974.
Schmemann, Alexander. *The Historical Road of Orthodoxy*. New York: Holt, Rinehart and Winston, 1963; Crestwood, NY: St Vladimir's Seminary Press, 1997.
Sherrard, Philip. *The Greek East and the Latin West*. Oxford University Press, 1959; Athens: Denise Harvey, 1992.
Tatakis, Basil. *Byzantine Philosophy* (1949). Trans. Nicholas Moutafakis. Indianapolis, IN: Hackett, 2001.

PART I MODERN ORTHODOX THOUGHT IN HISTORICAL PERSPECTIVE

2. Theological Encounters with the West

Primary Sources

Cabasilas, Nicholas. *A Commentary on the Divine Liturgy*. Trans. J. M. Hussey and P. A. McNulty. London: SPCK, 1960; Crestwood, NY: St Vladimir's Seminary Press, 1960.
Cabasilas, Nicholas. *The Life in Christ*. Trans. Carmino J. de Catanzaro. Crestwood, NY: St Vladimir's Seminary Press, 1974.

Gregory Palamas. *The Triads*. Trans. John Meyendorff. Mahwah, NJ: Paulist Press, 1983.
Mastrantonis, George. *Augsburg and Constantinople: The Correspondence between the Tübingen Theologians and Patriarch Jeremiah II of Constantinople on the Augsburg Confession*. Brookline, MA: Holy Cross Orthodox Press, 1982.
Moghila, Peter. *The Orthodox Confession of the Catholic and Apostolic Eastern Church* (1772). Trans. Philip Lodvel. Ed. J. J. Overbeck. London: Thomas Baker, 1898.
[Nikodimos of the Holy Mountain and Makarios of Corinth] *The Philokalia: The Complete Text Compiled by St Nikodimos of the Holy Mountain and St Makarios of Corinth* (4 vols.). Trans. and eds. G. E. H. Palmer, Philip Sherrard and Kallistos Ware. London: Faber and Faber, 1979–95.
Pelikan, Jaroslav, and Valerie Hotchkiss, eds. *Creeds and Confessions of Faith in the Christian Tradition* (4 vols.). New Haven, CT: Yale University Press, 2003.
Robertson, J. N. W. B., trans. and ed. *The Acts and Decrees of the Synod of Jerusalem* [1672]. London: Thomas Baker, 1899. Revised trans. Dennis Bratcher (Confession of Dositheus). <www.crivoice.org/creeddositheus.html> (11 July 2018).

Secondary Sources

Bathrellos, Demetrios. 'Love, Purification, and Forgiveness versus Justice, Punishment, and Satisfaction: The Debates on Purgatory and the Forgiveness of Sins at the Council of Ferrara-Florence'. *Journal of Theological Studies* NS 65, no. 1 (2014): 78–121.
Bulgakov, Sergius. *The Orthodox Church* (1935). Trans. revised by Lydia Kesich. Crestwood, NY: St Vladimir's Seminary Press, 1988.
Chrysostomos (Archbishop of Etna). 'The Myth of the "Calvinist Patriarch"'. <http://orthodoxinfo.com/inquirers/ca4_loukaris.aspx> (28 May 2014).
Davey, Colin. *Pioneer for Unity: Metrophanes Kritopoulos 1589–1639 and Relations between the Orthodox, Roman Catholic and Reformed Churches*. London: British Council of Churches, 1987.
Florovsky, Georges. 'Patriarch Jeremiah II and the Lutheran Divines' ('An Early Ecumenical Correspondence') (1950); 'The Greek Version of the Augsburg Confession' (1959); and 'The Orthodox Churches and the Ecumenical Movement Prior to 1910' (1954). In *Christianity and Culture, The Collected Works of Georges Florovsky* (vol. 2). Belmont, MA: Nordland, 1974: 143–232.
Geanakoplos, Deno J. *Byzantine East and Latin West: Two Worlds of Christendom in Middle Ages and Renaissance*. Oxford: Basil Blackwell, 1966.
Langford, H. W. 'The Non-Jurors and the Eastern Orthodox', paper read to the Fellowship of St Alban and St Sergius Conference at Durham (26 June 1965). <http://anglicanhistory.org/nonjurors/langford1.html> (14 May 2014).
Maloney, George A. *A History of Orthodox Theology since 1453*. Belmont, MA: Nordland, 1976.
Meyendorff, John. *Orthodoxy and Catholicity*. New York: Sheed & Ward, 1966.
Meyendorff, John. *The Orthodox Church: Its Past and Its Role in the World Today* (1981). Crestwood, NY: St Vladimir's Seminary Press, 4th ed., 1996.
Michaelides, George P. 'The Greek Orthodox Position on the Confession of Cyril Lucaris'. *Church History* 12, no. 2 (1943): 118–29.
Paliouras, Athanasios. 'Cyril I Lucaris' <www.ec-patr.org/list/index.php?lang=en&id=202> (28 May 2014).
Pelikan, Jaroslav. *Credo: Historical and Theological Guide to Creeds and Confessions of Faith in the Christian Tradition*. New Haven, CT: Yale University Press, 2003.

Schmemann, Alexander. 'St Mark of Ephesus and the Theological Conflicts in Byzantium', *St Vladimir's Seminary Quarterly* 1, no. 1 (1957): 43–55.

Tsirpanlis, Constantine. *Mark Eugenicus and the Council of Florence: A Historical Re-evaluation of His Personality*. New York: Center for Byzantine Studies, 1979.

Ware, Kallistos (Timothy). *Eustratios Argenti: A Study of the Greek Church under Turkish Rule*. Oxford University Press, 1964; Eugene, OR: Wipf & Stock, 2013.

3. Theology in Imperial Russia

Primary Sources

Avvakum (Archpriest). *The Life Written by Himself: With the Study of V. V. Vinogradov*. Trans. Kenneth N. Brostrom. Ann Arbor, MI: University of Michigan Press, 1979.

Birkbeck, W. J., ed. *Russia and the English Church during the Last Fifty Years Containing Correspondence between Mr. William Palmer and M. Khomiakoff, in the Years 1844–1854*. London: Rivington, Percival & Co., 1895; Farnborough, UK: Gregg International, 1969.

Chaadaev, Peter. 'Letters on the Philosophy of History: First Letter'. In *Russian Intellectual History: An Anthology*, ed. Marc Raeff. New York: Harcourt, Brace & World, 1966: 160–73.

Goldfrank, David, trans. and ed. *The Monastic Rule of Iosif Volotsky*. Kalamazoo, MI: Cistercian Publications, 2000.

Goldfrank, David, trans. and ed. *Nil Sorsky: The Authentic Writings*. Kalamazoo, MI: Cistercian Publications, 2008.

Jakim, Boris, and Robert Bird, trans. and eds. *On Spiritual Unity: A Slavophile Reader*. Hudson, NY: Lindisfarne Books, 1998.

Khomiakov, Alexei. 'On the Western Confessions of Faith'. In *Ultimate Questions: An Anthology of Modern Russian Religious Thought*, ed. Alexander Schmemann. Crestwood, NY: St Vladimir's Seminary Press, 1977: 31–69.

Muller, Alexander V., trans. and ed. *The Spiritual Regulation of Peter the Great*. Seattle: University of Washington Press, 1972.

Philaret (Drozdov) (Metropolitan). *The Longer Catechism of the Orthodox, Catholic, Eastern Church*, ed. R. W. Blackmore. In *The Creeds of Christendom with a History and Critical Notes*, ed. Philip Schaff (3 vols.). New York: Harper, 1876. <www.ccel.org/s/schaff/creeds2> (30 May 2014).

Secondary Sources

Behr-Sigel, Élisabeth. *Alexandre Boukarev–Un théologien de l'Église orthodoxe russe en dialogue avec le monde moderne*. (Alexander Bukarev: A Theologian of the Russian Orthodox Church in Dialogue with the Modern World) Paris: Beauchesne, 1977.

Berdyaev, Nicolas. *Aleksei Stepanovitch Khomiakov* (excerpts). In *On Spiritual Unity: A Slavophile Reader*, trans. and ed. Boris Jakim and Robert Bird. Hudson, NY: Lindisfarne Books, 1998: 326–50.

Florensky, Pavel. 'Around Khomiakov' (excerpts). In *On Spiritual Unity: A Slavophile Reader*, trans. and ed. Boris Jakim and Robert Bird. Hudson, NY: Lindisfarne Books, 1998: 319–25.

Florovsky, Georges. 'Western Influences in Russian Theology'. In *The Patristic Witness of Georges Florovsky: Essential Theological Writings*, eds. Brandon Gallaher and Paul Ladouceur. London: T&T Clark, 2019: 129–51.

Horujy, Sergey. 'Slavophiles, Westernisers and the Birth of Russian Philosophical Humanism'. Trans. Patrick Lally Michelson. In *A History of Russian Philosophy 1830–1930: Faith, Reason and the Defense of Human Dignity*, eds. Gary M. Hamburg and Randall A. Poole. Cambridge: Cambridge University Press, 2010: 27–51.

Kline, George L. 'Russian Religious Thought.' In *Nineteenth-Century Religious Thought in the West* (vol. 2), eds. Ninian Smart, John Clayton, Patrick Sherry and Steven T. Katz. Cambridge: Cambridge University Press, 1985: 179–230.

Maloney, George. 'The Russian Church.' In *A History of Orthodox Theology since 1453*. Belmont, MA: Nordland Publishing, 1976: 11–87.

Meyendorff, Paul. *Russia, Ritual, and Reform: The Liturgical Reforms of Nikon in the 17th Century*. Crestwood, NY: St Vladimir's Seminary Press, 1991.

Nesmiyanova, Olga. 'Russian Theology'. In *The Blackwell Companion to Nineteenth-Century Theology*, ed. David Fergusson. Chichester, UK: John Wiley-Blackwell, 2010: 214–34.

Pospielovsky, Dimitry. *The Orthodox Church in the History of Russia*. Crestwood, NY: St Vladimir's Seminary Press, 1998.

Schmemann, Alexander. 'Russian Theology: 1920–1972: An Introductory Survey'. *St Vladimir's Theological Quarterly* 16, no. 4 (1972): 172–94.

Shevzov, Vera. *Russian Orthodoxy on the Eve of Revolution*. Oxford: Oxford University Press, 2004.

Shevzov, Vera. 'The Burdens of Tradition: Orthodox Constructions of the West in Russia Late 19th – Early 20th c.' In *Orthodox Constructions of the West*, eds. George Demacopoulos and Aristotle Papanikolaou. New York: Fordham University Press, 2013: 83–101.

Valliere, Paul. *Modern Russian Theology: Bukharev, Soloviev, Bulgakov: Orthodox Theology in a New Key*. Grand Rapids, MI: William B. Eerdmans, 2000.

Zenkovsky, Vasily V. *A History of Russian Philosophy* (2 vols.). Trans. George L. Kline. London: Routledge & Kegan Paul; New York: Columbia University Press, 1953.

4. The Russian Religious Renaissance

Primary Sources

Berdyaev, Nicolas. 'The Russian Spiritual Renaissance of the Beginning of the XXth Century and the Journal *Put'* For the Tenth Anniversary of *Put*." *Put'* 49 (1935). Trans. Stephen Janos. <www.chebucto.ns.ca/Philosophy/Sui-Generis/Berdyaev/essays/rsr.htm> (2 February 2017).

Berdyaev, Nicolas. *Dream and Reality: An Essay in Autobiography*. Trans. Katharine Lampert. London: Bles, 1950.

Berdyaev, Nicolas. *Christian Existentialism: A Berdyaev Anthology*, ed. Donald Lowrie. London: Allen & Unwin, 1965.

Berdyaev, Nicolas. *The Spiritual Crisis of the Intelligentsia: Articles on Societal and Religious Psychology (1907–1909)* (1910). Trans. Stephen Janos. Portsmouth, NH: Vilnius Press, 2014.

Bulgakov, Sergius. *The Wisdom of God: A Brief Summary of Sophiology*. Trans. O. Fielding Clarke, Patrick Thompson and Xenia Braikevitc. London: Williams & Norgate, 1937.

Bulgakov, Sergius. 'Autobiographical Notes.' In *A Bulgakov Anthology*, eds. James Pain and Nicolas Zernov. London: SPCK, 1976.

Bulgakov, Sergius. *Ma vie dans l'Orthodoxie: Notes autobiographiques* (My Life In Orthodoxy: Autobiographical Notes). Trans. Irène Rovere-Sova and Mireille Rovere-Tsivikis. Geneva: Syrtes, 2015.

Florensky, Pavel. *The Pillar and Ground of the Truth: An Essay in Orthodox Theodicy in Twelve Letters*. Trans. Boris Jakim. Princeton, NJ: Princeton University Press, 1997.

Gippius, Zinaida. *Between Paris and St. Petersburg: Selected Diaries of Zinaida Hippius*. Trans. and ed. Temira Pachmuss. Urbana, IL: University of Illinois Press, 1975.

Lossky, Vladimir. *Spor o Sofii: 'Dokladnaia' Zapiska prot. S. Bulgakova I smysl ukaza Moskovskoi Patriarkhii* (The Sophia Controversy: Protopriest S. Bulgakov's 'Report' and the Meaning of the Decree of the Moscow Patriarchate). Paris, 1936; Moscow: Izdatel'stvo Sviato-Vladimirskogo Bratstva, 1996. Unpublished trans. William Kevin Fisher.

Poole, Randall, trans. and ed. *Problems of Idealism: Essays in Russian Social Philosophy*. New Haven, CT: Yale University Press, 2003.

Rozanov, Vasily. *The Apocalypse of Our Time and Other Writings*. Trans. and ed. Robert Payne. New York: Praeger, 1977.

Rozanov, Vasily. *Four Faces of Rozanov: Christianity, Sex, Jews, and the Russian Revolution*. Trans. Spencer E. Roberts. New York: Philosophical Library, 1978.

[Russian Orthodox Church]. 'The Definitions and Decrees of the Sacred Council of the Russian Orthodoix Church of 1917–1918' and 'The Statute of the Local Council of the Orthodox Church of All Russia'. In *Hyacinthe Destivelle, The Moscow Council 1917–1918: The Creation of the Conciliar Institutions of the Russian Orthodox Church*. Trans. Jerry Ryan. Notre Dame, IN: University of Notre Dame Press, 2015: 191–351.

Schmemann, Alexander, trans. and ed. *Ultimate Questions: An Anthology of Modern Russian Religious Thought*. New York: Holt, Rinehart & Winston, 1965: Crestwood, NY: St Vladimir's Seminary Press, 1977.

Skobtsova, Maria. *Mother Maria Skobtsova: Essential Writings*. Trans. Richard Pevear and Larissa Volokhonsky. Maryknoll, NY: Orbis Books, 2003.

Shatz, Marshall S., and Judith E. Zimmerman, trans. and eds. *Vekhi: Landmarks: A Collection of Articles about the Russian Intelligentsia*. Armonk, NY: M. E. Sharpe, 1994.

Shragin, Boris, and Albert Todd, trans. and eds. *Landmarks: A Collection of Essays on the Russian Intelligentsia, 1909*. New York: Karz Howard, 1977.

Soloviev, Vladimir. *Lectures on Godmanhood* (Lectures on Divine Humanity) (1881). Trans. Peter Zouboff; revised and ed. Boris Jakim. Hudson, NY: Lindisfarne Press, 1995.

Woehrlin, William, trans. and ed. *Out of the Depths (De Profundis): A Collection of Articles on the Russian Revolution*. Irvine, CA: Charles Schlacks, 1986.

Secondary Sources

Aizlewood, Robin, and Ruth Coates, eds. *Landmarks Revisited: The Vekhi Symposium 100 Years On*. Boston: Academic Studies Press, 2013.

Antoine Arjakovsky. *Essai sur le père Serge Boulgakov* (Essay on Fr Sergius Bulgakov). Paris: Parole et Silence, 2006.

Arjakovsky, Antoine. *The Way: Religious Thinkers of the Russian Emigration in Paris and Their Journal*. Trans. Jerry Ryan. Notre Dame, IN: University of Notre Dame Press, 2013.
Destivelle, Hyacinthe. *The Moscow Council 1917–1918: The Creation of the Conciliar Institutions of the Russian Orthodox Church*. Trans. Jerry Ryan. Notre Dame, IN: University of Notre Dame Press, 2015.
Finkel, Stuart. *On the Ideological Front: The Russian Intelligentsia and the Making of the Soviet Public Sphere*. New Haven, CT: Yale University Press, 2007.
Hackel, Sergei. *Pearl of Great Price: The Life of Mother Maria Skobtsova, 1891–1945*. Crestwood, NY: St Vladimir's Seminary Press, 1981.
Kornblatt, Judith Deutsch, and Richard F. Gustafson, eds. *Russian Religious Thought*. Madison, WI: University of Wisconsin Press, 1996.
Lowrie, Donald A. *Rebellious Prophet: A Life of Nicolai Berdyaev*. London: Victor Gollanz, 1960.
Matich, Olga. *Erotic Utopia: The Decadent Imagination in Russia's Fin de Siècle*. Madison, WI: University of Wisconsin Press, 2005.
Mjor, Kare Johan. *Reformulating Russia: The Cultural and Intellectual Historiography of Russian First-Wave Émigré Writers*. Leiden and Boston: Brill, 2011.
Pachmuss, Temira. *Zinaida Hippius: An Intellectual Profile*. Carbondale, IL: Southern Illinois University Press, 1971.
Pipes, Richard, ed. *The Russian Intelligentsia*. New York: Columbia University Press, 1961.
Raeff, Marc. *Russia Abroad: A Cultural History of the Russian Emigration, 1919–1939*. New York: Oxford University Press, 1990.
Read, Christopher. *Religion, Revolution and the Russian Intelligentsia, 1900–1912: The Vekhi Debate and Its Intellectual Background*. London: Macmillan, 1979.
St Vladimir's Theological Quarterly 49, 1–2 (2005). [Special issue on Sergius Bulgakov with articles by Brandon Gallaher and Irina Kukota, Bryn Geffert, Alexis Klimoff, Sergei V. Nikolaev, Michael Plekon, Andrew Louth, Wendy Wiseman, Robert Slesinki Myroslaw Tataryn, and Antoine Arjakovsky.]
Schapiro, Leonard. 'The Vekhi Group and the Mystique of Revolution' (1955). In *Russian Studies*, ed. Ellen Dahrendorff. London: Collins Harvill, 1986.
Ure, Adam. *Vasilii Rozanov and the Creation: The Edenic Vision and the Rejection of Eschatology*. New York: Continuum, 2011.
Vallon, Michel A. *An Apostle of Freedom: Life and Teachings of Nicolas Berdyaev*. New York: Philosophical Library, 1960.
Zenkovsky, Vasily V. *A History of Russian Philosophy* (2 vols.). Trans. George L. Kline. New York: Columbia University Press; London: Routledge & Kegan Paul, 1953; 2003.
Zernov, Nicolas. *Three Russian Prophets: Khomiakov, Dostoevsky, Soloviev*. London: SCM Press, 1944.
Zernov, Nicolas. *The Russian Religious Renaissance of the Twentieth Century*. New York: Harper & Row, 1963.

5. The Origins and Nature of Neopatristic Theology

Primary Sources

Alivisatos, Hamilcar S., ed. *Procès-verbaux du premier Congrès de théologie orthodoxe à Athènes, 29 novembre-6 décembre 1936* (Minutes of the First Congress of Orthodox Theologians, Athens, 29 November–6 December 1936). Athens: Pyrsos, 1939.

Berdiaeff, Nicolas. *Essai de métaphysique eschatologique: Acte créateur et objectivation* (Essay on Eschatological Metaphysics: The Creative Act and Objectification). Trans. Maxime Herman. Paris: Aubier, 1946.

Bulgakov, Sergius. *Unfading Light: Contemplations and Speculations* (1917). Trans. T. Allan Smith. Grand Rapids, MI: Eerdmans, 2012.

Gallaher, Brandon, and Paul Ladouceur, eds. *The Patristic Witness of Georges Florovsky: Essential Theological Writings*. London: T&T Clark, 2019.

Guichardan, Sébastien. *Le Problème de la simplicité divine en Orient et en Occident aux XIVe etXve s.: Grégoire Palamas, Duns Scott, Georges Scholarios* (The Problem of Divine Simplicity in East and West in the 14th and 15th Centuries: Gregory Palamas, Duns Scotus and George Scholarios). Lyons: Legendre, 1933.

Jugie, Martin. 'Palamas Grégoire' and 'Palamite Controverse'. In *Dictionnaire de théologie catholique* (Dictionary of Catholic Theology) (vol. 11: 2). Paris: Letouzey et Ané, 1932: cols. 1735–76 and 1777–1818;

Kern, Cyprian. 'Spiritual Predecessors of St Gregory Palamas'. *Theological Thought* (1942).

Kern, Cyprian. 'Les éléments de la théologie de Grégoire Palamas' (Elements of the Theology of Gregory Palamas). *Irénikon* 20 (1947): 6–33; 164–93.

Krivoshein, Basil. 'The Ascetic and Theological Teaching of Gregory Palamas'. *Eastern Churches Quarterly* 3 (1938): 26–33; 71–84; 138–56; 193–214 (reprinted 1968).

Lossky, Vladimir. *The Mystical Theology of the Eastern Church* (1944). Trans. Fellowship of St Alban and St Sergius. London: J. Clarke, 1957; Crestwood, NY: St Vladimir's Seminary Press, 1976.

Lossky, Vladimir. *In the Image and Likeness of God*. Crestwood, NY: St Vladimir's Seminary Press, 1974.

Lossky, Vladimir. *The Vision of God*. Trans. Ashleigh Morrhouse. London: The Faith Press, 1963; Crestwood, NY: St Vladimir's Seminary Press, 1983.

[Nikodimos the Athonite and Makarios of Corinth, eds.]. *The Philokalia: The Complete Text* (4 vols.) (1782). Trans. Gerald E. H. Palmer, Philip Sherrard and Kallistos Ware. London: Faber and Faber, 1983–1995.

Nikodimos the Hagiorite. *The Philokalia: Writings of Holy Mystic Fathers* (1782). Trans. Constantine Cavarnos. Belmont, MA: Institute for Byzantine and Modern Greek Studies, 2008.

Plekon, Michael, ed. *Tradition Alive: On the Church and the Christian Life in Our Time*. Lanham, MD: Rowman and Littlefield, 2003.

Zizioulas, John. *Being as Communion: Studies in Personhood and the Church*. Crestwood, NY: St Vladimir's Seminary Press, 1985.

Secondary Sources

Baker, Matthew, Seraphim Danckaert, and Nicholas Marinides, eds. *On the Tree of the Cross: Georges Florovsky and the Patristic Doctrine of Atonement*. Jordanville, NY: Holy Trinity Seminary Press, 2016.

Berdyaev, Nicolas, 'Orthdoksiya I chelovechnost' (Orthodoksia and Humanness). Review of Georges Florovsky. *The Ways of Russian Theology*. Paris: YMCA-Press, 1937. *Put'* 53 (1937). Trans. Stephen Janos. <http://www.berdyaev.com/berdiaev/berd_lib/1937_424.html> (27 June 2018).

Blane, Andrew, ed. *Georges Florovsky: Russian Intellectual and Orthodox Churchman*. Crestwood, NY: St Vladimir's Seminary Press, 1993.

Cunningham, Mary B., and Elizabeth Theokritoff, eds. *The Cambridge Companion to Orthodox Christian Theology*. Cambridge: Cambridge University Press, 2008.

Gavrilyuk, Paul L. *Georges Florovsky and the Russian Religious Renaissance*. Oxford: Oxford University Press, 2013.

Valliere, Paul. *Modern Russian Theology: Bukharev, Soloviev, Bulgakov: Orthodox Theology in a New Key*. Grand Rapids, MI: Eerdmans, 2000.

Williams, George H. 'Georges Florovsky: His American Career 1948–1965'. *Greek Orthodox Theological Review* 11, no. 1 (1965): 7–107.

6. Theology New and Old in Greece

Primary Sources

Hadjinicolaou, John, ed. *Synaxis: An Anthology of the Most Significant Orthodox Theology in Greece Appearing in the Journal Synaxi from 1982 to 2002* (3 vols.). Montreal: Alexander Press, 2006.

Karmiris, Ioannis. *Ta Dogmatiká kai Symvoliká Mnimeía tis Orthodóxou Katholikís Ekklisías* (Dogmatic and Symbolic Monuments of the Orthodox Catholic Church) (2 vols.). Athens, 1952–1953; Graz, 1968.

Loudovikos, Nicholas. *A Eucharistic Ontology: Maximus the Confessor's Eschatological Ontology of Being as Dialogical Reciprocity*. Brookline, MA: Holy Cross Orthodox Press, 2010.

Loudovikos, Nicholas. *Church in the Making: An Apophatic Ecclesiology of Consubstantiality*. Yonkers, NY: St Vladimir's Seminary Press, 2016.

Mantzaridis, George. *The Deification of Man: St Gregory Palamas and the Orthodox Tradition*. Trans. Liadain Sherrard. Crestwood, NY: St Vladimir's Seminary Press, 1984.

Mastroyannopoulos, Elias. 'The Task of the Churches Today: Some Forgotten Obligations'. *Sobornost* 4, no. 8 (1963): 415–19.

Middleton, Herman. *Precious Vessels: The Lives and Counsels of Contemporary Elders of Greece*. Thessalonica and Ashville, NC: Protecting Veil Press, 2003.

Nellas, Panayiotis. *Deification in Christ: Orthodox Perspectives on the Nature of the Human Person*. Trans. Norman Russell. Yonkers, NY: St Vladimir's Seminary Press, 1987.

Papacostas, Seraphim. *Repentance*. Athens: Zoe Brotherhood of Theologians, 3rd ed., 1987.

Papathanasiou, Athanasios N. *I Ríxi Me to Midén: Sfinákia Politikís Theologías* (Rupture with Nothingness: Snippets of Political Theology). Athens: Armos Publications, 2015.

Ramfos, Stelios. *Yearning for the One: Chapters in the Inner Life of the Greeks* (2000). Trans. Norman Russell. Brookline, MA: Holy Cross Orthodox Press, 2011.

Romanides, John. *The Ancestral Sin*. Trans. George S. Gabriel. Ridgewood, NJ: Zephyr, 1957.

Romanides, John. *The Ancestral Sin*. Trans. George S. Gabriel. Ridgewood, NJ: Zephyr, 1957.
Romanides, John. *Franks, Romans, Feudalism, and Doctrine: An Interplay between Theology and Society*. Brookline, MA: Holy Cross Orthodox Press, 1981.
Trembelas, Panagiotis N. *Dogmatique de l'Église orthodoxe* (Dogmatica of the Orthodox Church) (2 vols.). Trans. Pierre Dumont. Bruges, BE: Chevetogne/Desclée de Brouwer. 1966–1968.
Yannaras, Christos. *Freedom of Morality*. Trans. Elizabeth Briere. Crestwood, NY: St Vladimir's Seminary Press, 1984.
Yannaras, Christos. *Alítheia kai Enótita tis Ekklisías* (1979). *Vérité et unité de l'Église* (Truth and Unity of the Church). Trans. Jean-Louis Palièrne. Grez-Doiceau, BE: Axios, 1989.
Yannaras, Christos. *Person and Eros*. Trans. Norman Russell. Brookline, MA: Holy Cross Orthodox Press, 2008.
Zizioulas, John. *Eucharist, Bishop, Church: The Unity of the Church in the Divine Eucharist and the Bishop during the First Three Centuries*. Trans. Elizabeth Theokritoff. Brookline, MA: Holy Cross Press, 2001.

Secondary Sources

Allchin, Arthur Macdonald. 'Some New Tendencies in Greek Theology.' *Sobornost* 4, no. 8 (1963): 455–63.
Argyriou, Astérios. *Spirituels Néo-Grecs, XVe–XXe siècles* (Neo-Greek Spiritual Figures, 15th-20th Centuries). Namur, BE: Soleil Levant, 1967.
Behr-Sigel, Elisabeth. 'Rencontre avec la Grèce chrétienne' (Encounter with Christian Greece). *Contacts, Revue française d'Orthodoxie* 16, no. 45 (1964): 56–62.
Constantelos, Demetrios J. 'The Zoe Movement in Greece.' *St Vladimir's Theological Quarterly* 3, no. 2 (1959): 11–25.
Jioultsis, Basil. 'Religious Brotherhoods: A Sociological View'. *Social Compass* 22, no. 1 (1975): 67–83.
Kalaitzidis, Pantelis. *Orthodoxía Kai Neoterikótita: Prolegomena* (Orthodoxy and Modernity: An Introduction). Athens: Indiktos Publications, 2007.
Kalaitzidis, Pantelis. *Hellenicity and Anti-Westernism in the Greek 'Theology of the '60s'* (in Greek). Ph.D. dissertation, Aristotle University of Thessalonika, 2008.
Kalaitzidis, Pantelis. 'New Trends in Greek Orthodox Theology: Challenges in the Movement towards a Genuine Renewal and Christian Unity'. *Scottish Journal of Theology* 67, no. 2 (2014): 127–64.
Makrides, Vasilios. 'The Brotherhoods of Theologians in Contemporary Greece'. *Greek Orthodox Theological Review* 33, no. 2 (1988): 167–87.
Makrides, Vasilios. 'Byzantium in Contemporary Greece: The Neo-Orthodox Current of Ideas'. In *Byzantium and the Modern Greek Identity*, eds. David Ricks and Paul Magdalino. Aldershot, UK: Ashgate, 1998: 141–53.
Maloney, George. 'The History of Orthodox Theology among Greek-Speaking Churches.' In Part II of his *History of Orthodox Theology since 1453*. Belmont, MA: Nordland, 1976: 89–210.
Meyendorff, Jean. 'Zoï'. *Le Messager orthodoxe* 5 (1959): 24–6.
Psilopoulos, Emmanuel. 'Le mouvement Zoï dans l'Église orthodoxe de Grèce'. (The Zoe Movement in the Orthodox Church of Greece). *Revue des sciences religieuses* 40, no. 3 (1966): 258–89.
Raudvere, Catharina, Krzysztof Stala, and Trine Stauning Willert, eds. *Rethinking the Space for Religion: New Actors in Central and Southeast Europe on Religion, Authenticity and Belonging*. Lund, SE: Nordic Academic Press, 2012.

Roudometof, Victor, and Vasilios N. Makrides, eds. *Orthodox Christianity in 21st Century Greece: The Role of Religion in Culture, Ethnicity and Politics*. Farnham: Ashgate, 2010.

Russell, Norman. 'Modern Greek Theologians and the Greek Fathers'. *Philosophy & Theology* 18, no. 1 (2006): 77–92.

Spiteris, Yannis. *La teologia ortodossa neo-greca* (Neo-Greek Orthodox Theology). Bologna: Edizione Dehoniane, 1992.

Vassiliadis, Petros. 'Greek Theology in the Making, Trends and Facts in the 80s – Vision for the 90s'. *St Vladimir's Theological Quarterly* 35, no. 1 (1991): 33–52.

Yannaras, Christos. 'Theology in Present-Day Greece'. *St Vladimir's Theological Quarterly* 17, no. 4 (1972): 195–214.

Ware, Kallistos, Christos Yannaras, Elias Mastroyannopoulos, and Arthur Macdonald Allchin. 'In Memoriam Demetrios Koutroubis'. *Sobornost* 6, no. 1 (1984): 67–77.

Willert, Trine Stauning. *New Voices in Greek Orthodox Thought: Untying the Bond between Nation and Religion*. Farnham, Surrey: Ashgate, 2014.

Willert, Trine Stauning, and Lina Molokotos-Liederman, eds. *Innovation in the Greek Orthodox Tradition? The Question of Change in Greek Orthodox Thought and Practice*. Farnham: Ashgate, 2012.

7. Theology in Romania

Primary Sources

Braga, Roman. *On the Way of Faith*. Rives Junction, MI: Dormition of the Mother of God Orthodox Monastery, 1997.

Braga, Roman. 'On Compromise in the Hierarchy during the Communist Yoke'. <www.orthodoxytoday.org/articles6/BragaChurch.php> (3 November 2014).

Bria, Ion. 'Évolution et originalité de l'Église locale de Roumanie' (Evolution and Originality of the Local Church of Romania). In *Autre visage de l'orthodoxie, Église de Roumanie* (Another Face of Orthodoxy: The Church of Romania). Geneva: Éditions du Centre orthodoxe, 1981.

Calciu, George. *Christ Is Calling You: A Course in Catacomb Pastorship*. Platina, CA: St. Herman of Alaska Brotherhood, 1997.

Calcui, George. *Father George Calciu: Interviews, Talks, and Homilies*. Platina, CA: St. Herman of Alaska Brotherhood, 2010.

Chiţescu, Nicolae, Isidor Todoran, I. Petreuţă, [and Dumitru Staniloae]. *Teologia Dogmatică şi Simbolică* (2 vols.) (Dogmatic and Symbolic Theology). Cluj-Napoca, RO: Editura Renaşterea, 2004.

Cleopa (Ilie). *The Truth of Our Faith: Discourses from Holy Scripture on the Tenets of Christian Orthodoxy*. Trans. Peter Heers. Thessalonica, GR: Uncut Mountain Press, 2001.

Plamadeala, Antonie. 'Biserica slujitoare în Sfânta Scriptură, Sfânta Tradiţie şi în teologia contemporană'. (The Servant Church in Holy Scripture: Holy Tradition and Contemporary Theology). *Studii Teologice* 14, no. 5–8 (1972): 325–641.

Plamadeala, Antonie. 'Church and State in Romania.' In *Church and State: Opening a New Ecumenical Discussion* (Faith and Order Paper 85). Geneva: WCC, 1978: 90–106.

[Scrima, André] Un Moine de l'Église orthodoxe de Roumanie. 'L'avènement philocalique dans l'Orthodoxie roumaine' (The Advent of the Philokalia in Romanian Orthodoxy). *Istina* 3 (1958): 295–328; *Istina* 4 (1958): 443–74.

Scrima, André. *Timpul rugului aprins: Maestrul spiritual în tradiția răsăriteană* (The Time of the Burning Bush: The Spiritual Master in the Eastern Tradition). Bucharest: Humanitas, 1996.

Staniloae, Dumitru. *Ortodoxie si românism* (Orthodoxy and Romanianism). Sibiu, 1939.

Staniloae, Dumitru. *Dieu est Amour* (God Is Love). Geneva: Labor et Fides, 1980.

Staniloae, Dumitru. *Prayer and Holiness: The Icon of Man Renewed in God*. Oxford: SLG Press, 1982.

Staniloae, Dumitru. *Prière de Jésus et expérience de l'Esprit Saint* (The Jesus Prayer and the Experience of the Holy Spirit). Paris: Desclée de Brouwer, 1991.

Staniloae, Dumitru. *Natiune si creşitinism* (Nation and Christianity). Bucharest: Elion Press, 2003.

Staniloae, Dumitru. *Orthodox Spirituality: A Practical Guide for the Faithful and a Definitive Manual for the Scholar*. Trans. Jerome Newville and Otilia Kloos. South Canaan, PA: St Tikhon's Seminary Press, 2003.

Staniloae, Dumitru. *The Experience of God. Orthodox Dogmatic Theology: The Experience of God.* Vol. 1: *Revelation and Knowledge of the Triune God*; Vol. 2: *The World: Creation and Deification*; Vol. 3: *The Person of Jesus Christ as God and Savior*; Vol. 4: *The Church: Communion in the Holy Spirit*; Vol. 5: *The Sanctifying Mysteries*; Vol. 6: *The Fulfillment of Creation*. Brookline, MA: Holy Cross Orthodox Press, 2005–2013.

Secondary Sources

Balan, Ioanichie. *Shepherd of Souls: The Life and Teachings of Elder Cleopa*. Platina, CA: St. Herman of Alaska Brotherhood, 2000.

Bielawski, Maciej. *The Philocalical Vision of the World in the Theology of Dumitru Staniloae*. Bydgoszcz, HU: Homini, 1997.

Biliuta, Ionita. 'The Afterlife of the 1930s Orthodoxism-Nationalism beyond Nichifor Crainic and Nae Ionescu.' *Anuarul Institutului de Cercetări Socio-Umane* (2009): 159–78.

Biliuta, Ionita. 'The Archangel's Consecrated Servants. An Inquiry in The Relationship Between the Romanian Orthodox Church and the Iron Guard (1930–1941)'. PhD dissertation, Central European University, Budapest, 2013.

Biliuta, Ionita. 'Between Orthodoxy and the Nation: Traditionalist Definitions of Romanianness in Interwar Romania'. MA thesis, Central European University, Budapest, 2013.

Clark, Roland. 'Nationalism, Ethnotheology, and Mysticism in Interwar Romania'. *The Carl Beck Papers in Russian & East European Studies*, No. 2002. Pittsburgh, OH: Center for Russian and East European Studies, 2009.

Clément, Olivier. 'L'Eglise orthodoxe roumaine et le Buisson Ardent.' (The Romanian Orthodox Church and the Burning Bush). *Réforme* 644 (Paris, 20 July 1957).

Gillet, Olivier. *Religion et nationalisme: L'Idéologie de l'Église orthodoxe roumaine sous le régime communiste* (Religion and Nationalism: The Ideology of the Romanian Orthodox Church during the Communist Regime). Bruxelles: Éditions de l'Université de Bruxelles, 1997.

Giocas, Athanasios, and Paul Ladouceur. 'The Burning Bush Group and Father André Scrima in Romanian Spirituality'. *Greek Orthodox Theological Review* 52, no. 1–4 (2007) (published in 2010): 37–62.

Joanta, Serafim. *Treasures of Romanian Christianity: Hesychastic Tradition and Culture.* Revised trans. Iulia Banica and Corina Hancianu Latis. Whitby, ON: Cross Meridian, 2013.

Johansen, Alf. *Theological Study in the Romanian Orthodox Church under Communist Rule*. London: Faith Press, 1961.

Leustan, Lucian. *Orthodoxy and the Cold War: Religion and Political Power in Romania.* Basingstoke: Palgrave Macmillan, 2009.

Neamtu, Mihail. 'Between the Gospel and the Nation: Dumitru Stăniloae's Ethno-Theology'. *Studia Archaeus* (Bucarest) 10, no. 3 (2006): 7–44.

Romocea, Cristian. *Church and State: Religious Nationalism and State Identification in Post-Communist Romania.* London: Continuum, 2011.

Stan, Lavinia, and Lucian Turcescu. *Religion and Politics in Post-Communist Romania.* Oxford: Oxford University Press, 2007.

8. Tradition and The Restoration of Patristic Thought

Alfeyev, Hilarion. 'The Patristic Heritage and Modernity'. In *Orthodox Witness Today*, Geneva: World Council of Churches, 2006: 146–72.

Bouteneff, Peter. *Sweeter than Honey: Orthodox Thinking on Dogma and Truth.* Yonkers, NY: St Vladimir's Seminary Press, 2006.

Brown, Alan. 'On the Criticism of *Being as Communion* in Anglophone Orthodox Theology.' In *The Theology of John Zizioulas: Personhood and the Church*, ed. Douglas Knight. Aldershot, UK: Ashgate, 2007: 35–78.

Bulgakov, Sergius. 'Dogma and Dogmatic Theology' (1937). In *Tradition Alive: On the Church and the Christian Life in Our Time*, ed. Michael Plekon. Lanham, MA: Rowan & Littlefield, 2003: 67–80.

Casiday, Augustine. *Remember the Days of Old: Orthodox Thinking on the Patristic Heritage.* Yonkers, NY: St Vladimir's Seminary Press, 2014.

Gallaher, Brandon, and Paul Ladouceur, eds. *The Patristic Witness of Georges Florovsky: Essential Theological Writings.* London: T&T Clark, 2019.

Hovorun, Cyril. 'Patristics after Neo-Patristics.' In *A Celebration of Living Theology: A Festschrift in Honour of Andrew Louth*, eds. Justin A. Mihoc and Leonard Aldea. London: T&T Clark, 2014: 205–213.

Kalaitzidis, Pantelis. 'From the "Return to the Fathers" to the Need for a Modern Orthodox Theology'. *St Vladimir's Theological Quarterly* 54, no. 1 (2010): 5–36.

Kalaitzidis, Pantelis, ed. *Neo-Patristic Synthesis or Post-Patristic Theology: Can Orthodox Theology be Contextual?* (Proceedings of a Conference held at Volos, Greece, 3–6 June 2010) (In Greek). Volos, GR: Volos Academy for Theological Studies, 2018. (English version forthcoming.)

Lossky, Vladimir. 'Tradition and Traditions' (1952). In *In the Image and Likeness of God.* Crestwood, NY: St Vladimir's Seminary Press, 1985: 141–68.

Louth, Andrew. 'Is Development of Doctrine a Valid Category for Orthodox Theology?' In *Orthodoxy and Western Culture, A Collection of Essays Honoring Jaroslav Pelikan on His Eightieth Birthday*, eds. Valerie Hotchkiss and Patrick Henry. Crestwood, NY: St Vladimir's Seminary Press, 2006: 45–63.

Louth, Andrew. 'The Patristic Revival and Its Protagonists'. In *The Cambridge Companion to Orthodox Christian Theology*, eds. Mary B. Cunningham and Elizabeth Theokritoff. Cambridge: Cambridge University Press, 2008: 188–202.

Meyendorff, John. *Living Tradition: Orthodox Witness in the Contemporary World.* Crestwood, NY: St Vladimir's Seminary Press, 1978.

Plekon, Michael, 'The Russian Religious Revival and Its Theological Legacy'. In *The Cambridge Companion to Orthodox Christian Theology*, eds. Mary B. Cunningham and Elizabeth Theokritoff. Cambridge: Cambridge University Press, 2008: 203–17.

Pomazansky, Michael. 'On the New Currents in Russian Philosophico-Theological Thought'. In his book *Orthodox Dogmatic Theology, A Concise Exposition*. Trans. Seraphim Rose. Platina, CA: St. Herman of Alaska Brotherhood, 1984: 357–72.

Valliere, Paul. 'Conclusion: The Limits of Tradition'. In his book *Modern Russian Theology: Bukharev, Soloviev, Bulgakov: Russian Theology in a New Key*. Edinburgh: T&T Clark, 2000: 373–403.

PART II THEMES AND CONFLICTS IN MODERN ORTHODOX THEOLOGY

9. God and Creation

Primary Sources

Bulgakov, Sergius. 'Le problème central de la sophiologie' (The Central Problem of Sophiology) (1936). Trans. Constantin Andronikof. *Le Messager orthodoxe* 98 (1985): 83–7.

Bulgakov, Sergius. *Sophia, The Wisdom of God: An Outline of Sophiology* (1937). Trans. Patrick Thompson, O. Fielding Clarke and Xenia Braikevitc. Hudson, NY: Lindisfarne Press, 1993.

Bulgakov, Sergius. *The Comforter* (1936). Trans. Boris Jakim. Grand Rapids, MI: Eerdmans, 2004.

Bulgakov, Sergius. 'Hypostasis and Hypostaticity: Scholia to The Unfading Light' (1925). Trans. Arthur F. Dobbie Bateman. *St Vladimir's Theological Quarterly* 49, no. 1–2 (2005): 17–46.

Bulgakov, Sergius. *The Lamb of God* (1933). Trans. Boris Jakim. Grand Rapids, MI: Eerdmans, 2008.

Bulgakov, Sergius. *Judas Iscarioth, L'Apôtre traître* (Judas Iscariot, The Perfidious Apostle) (1931). Trans. Michel Niqueux. Geneva: Syrtes, 2015.

Dostoyevsky, Fyodor. *The Brothers Karamazov* (1880). Trans. Constance Garnett. London: Heinemann, 1912.

Florensky, Pavel. *The Pillar and Ground of the Truth: An Essay in Orthodox Theodicy in Twelve Letters* (1914). Trans. Boris Jakim. Princeton University Press, 1997.

Florovsky, Georges. 'Creation and Createdness'. In *The Patristic Witness of Georges Florovsky: Essential Theological Writings*, eds. Brandon Gallaher and Paul Ladouceur. London: T&T Clark, 2019: 33–63.

Kallistos Ware, 'Through Creation to the Creator'. Third Marco Pallis Memorial Lecture, *Ecotheology*, 2 (London: Friends of the Centre, 1996).

Kornblatt, Judith Deutsch, trans. and ed. *Divine Sophia: The Wisdom Writings of Vladimir Solovyov*. Ithaca and London: Cornell University Press, 2009.

Lossky, Vladimir. *In the Image and Likeness of God* (1967), eds. John H. Erickson and Thomas E. Bird. London: Mowbrays; Crestwood, NY: St Vladimir's Seminary Press, 1974.

Lossky, Vladimir. *Spor o sofii* (The Dispute about Sophia) (1936). Moskva: Izdatel'stvo Sviato-Vladimirskogo Bratstva, 1996. (Unpublished translation by William Kevin Fisher: *The Sophia Controversy: Protopriest S. Bulgakov's "Report" and the Meaning of the Decree of the Moscow Patriarchate*. Paris, 2004.)

Meyendorff, John. *A Study of Gregory Palamas* (1959). London: Faith Press, 1964.

Meyendorff, John. *St Gregory Palamas and Orthodox Spirituality* (1959). Crestwood, NY: St Vladimir's Seminary Press, 1974.
Meyendorff, John. *Gregory Palamas: The Triads*. New York: Paulist Press, 1983.
Pain, James, and Nicolas Zernov, eds. *A Bulgakov Anthology*. London: SPCK, 1976.
Schmemann, Alexander. *For the Life of the World: Sacraments and Orthodoxy* (1963). Crestwood, NY: St Vladimir's Seminary Press, 2nd rev. ed., 1973.
Schmemann, Alexander. 'The World as Sacrament'. In *Church, World, Mission: Reflections on Orthodoxy in the West*. Crestwood, NY: St Vladimir's Seminary Press, 1979: 217–27.
Staniloae, Dumitru. *The Experience of God*. Trans. Ioan Ionita and Robert Barringer. Brookline, MA: Holy Cross Orthodox Press, 1994.
Staniloae, Dumitru. 'The Contemplation of God in Creation'. In *Orthodox Spirituality: A Practical Guide for the Faithful and a Definitive Manual for the Scholar*. Trans. Jerome Newville and Otilia Kloos. South Canaan, PA: St Tikhon's Seminary Press, 2002: 203–23.
Soloviev, Vladimir. *Russia and the Universal Church*. Trans. Herbert Rees. London: Geoffrey Bles-Centenary Press, 1948.
Soloviev, Vladimir. *Lectures on Godmanhood* (Lectures on Divine Humanity) (1881). Trans. Peter Zouboff; revised and ed. Boris Jakim. Hudson, NY: Lindisfarne Press, 1995.
Williams, Rowan, ed. *Sergii Bulgakov: Towards a Russian Political Theology*. Edinburgh: T&T Clark, 1999.
Wozniuk, Vladimir, trans. and ed. *The Heart of Reality: Essays on Beauty, Love and Ethics by V.S. Soloviev*. Notre Dame, IN: University of Notre Dame Press, 2003.
Yannaras, Christos. 'The Distinction between Essence and Energies and Its Importance for Theology'. Trans. Peter Chamberas. *St Vladimir's Theological Quarterly* 19, no. 4 (1975): 232–45.
Zizioulas, John. 'Man the Priest of Creation: A Response to the Ecological Problem'. In *Living Orthodoxy in the Modern World: Orthodox Christianity & Society*, eds. Andrew Walker and Costa Carras. Crestwood, NY: St Vladimir's Seminary Press, 1996: 178–216.
Zizioulas, John. 'Proprietors or Priests of Creation?' (2003). In *Toward an Ecology of Transfiguration: Orthodox Christian Perspectives on Environment, Nature, and Creation*, eds. John Chryssavgis and Bruce V. Foltz. New York: Fordham University Press, 2013: 163–71.

Secondary Sources

Arjakovsky, Antoine. *Essai sur le père Serge Boulgakov (1871–1944): Philosophe et théologien chrétien* (Essay on Fr Sergius Bulgakov: Christian Philosopher and Theologian). Paris: Parole et Silence, 2006.
Athanasopoulos, Constantinos, and Christoph Schneider, eds. *Divine Essence and Divine Energies: Ecumenical Reflections on the Presence of God in Eastern Orthodoxy*. Cambridge: James Clarke, 2013.
Barrois, Georges. 'Palamism Revisited'. *St Vladimir's Theological Quarterly* 19, no. 4 (1975): 211–31.
Behr-Sigel, Elisabeth. 'Réflexions sur la doctrine de Grégoire Palamas' (Reflections on the Doctrine of Gregory Palamas). *Contacts, Revue française d'Orthodoxie* 12 (1960): 118–24.
Clayton, Philip, and Arthur Peacocke, eds. *In Whom We Live and Move and Have Our Being: Panentheistic Reflections on God's Presence in a Scientific World*. Grand Rapids, MI: Eerdmans, 2004.
De Halleux, André. 'Palamisme et Tradition' (Palamism and Tradition). *Irénikon* 48 (1975): 479–93.
Eastern Churches Review 9 (1977). Special issue on 'Palamism Today'. Articles: George Mantzarides, 'Tradition and Renewal in the Theology of Saint Gregory Palamas'; Illtyd Trethowan, 'Irrationality in Theology and the Palamite Distinction'; Rowan Williams, 'The Philosophical Structures of

Palamism'; Kallistos Ware, 'The Debate about Palamism'; and Gabriel Patacsi, 'Palamism before Palamas.'

Gallaher, Brandon. 'Antinomism, Trinity and the Challenge of Solov'ëvan Pantheism in the Theology of Sergij Bulgakov'. *Studies in East European Thought* 64, no. 3–4 (2012): 205–25.

Gallaher, Brandon. *Freedom and Necessity in Modern Trinitarian Theology*. Oxford: Oxford University Press, 2016.

Karayiannis, Vasilios. *Maxime le Confesseur: Essence et énergies de Dieu* (Maximus the Confessor: The Essence and Energies of God). Paris: Beauchesne, 1993.

Romanides, John. 'Notes on the Palamite Controversy and Related Topics'. Part I, *Greek Orthodox Theological Review* 6, no. 2 (1960–1961): 186–205; Part II, *idem*. 9, no. 2 (1963–1964): 225–70.

Russell, Norman. 'The Reception of Palamas in the West Today'. *Theologia* (Athens) 83, no. 3 (2012): 7–21.

Theokritoff, Elizabeth. *Living in God's Creation: Orthodox Perspectives on Ecology*. Crestwood, NY: St Vladimir's Seminary Press, 2010.

Ware, Kallistos. 'God Hidden and Revealed: The Apophatic Way and the Essence-Energies Distinction'. *Eastern Churches Review* 7, no. 2 (1975): 125–36.

10. Divine-Humanity, Personhood and Human Rights

Primary Sources

Behr-Sigel, Elisabeth. 'The Kenotic, the Humble Christ'. In *Discerning the Signs of the Times: The Vision of Elisabeth Behr-Sigel*, eds. Michael Plekon and Sarah E. Hinlicky. Crestwood, NY: St Vladimir's Seminary Press, 2001: 29–40.

Berdyaev, Nicolas. *The Destiny of Man* (1931). Trans. Natalie Duddington. London: Geoffrey Bles, 1937.

Berdyaev, Nicolas. *Slavery and Freedom* (1939). Trans. Reginald M. French. London: Geoffrey Bles, 1943.

Bulgakov, Sergius. *The Lamb of God* (1933). Trans. Boris Jakim. Grand Rapids, MI: Eerdmans, 2008.

Bulgakov, Sergius. *Unfading Light: Contemplations and Speculations* (1917). Trans. T. Allan Smith. Grand Rapids, MI: Eerdmans, 2012.

Florensky, Pavel. *The Pillar and Ground of the Truth: An Essay in Orthodox Theodicy in Twelve Letters* (1914). Trans. Boris Jakim. Princeton: Princeton University Press, 1997.

Frank, Simeon. *God with Us: Three Mediations* (1942). London: Jonathan Cape, 1946.

Gillet, Lev. 'Does God Suffer'. *Sobornost* 3, no. 15 (1954): 112–20.

[Gillet, Lev]. 'A Monk of the Eastern Church. [On Divine Suffering]. *Jesus: A Dialogue with the Saviour*. New York: Desclée, 1963: 163–9.

Gorodetsky, Nadejda. *The Humiliated Christ in Russian Thought*. London: SPCK, 1938.

Guroian, Vigen. 'Human Rights and Modern Western Faith: An Orthodox Christian Assessment.' *Journal of Religious Ethics* 26, no. 2 (1998): 241–7.

Harakas, Stanley. 'Human Rights: An Eastern Orthodox Perspective'. *Journal of Ecumenical Studies* 19, no. 3 (1982): 13–24.

Holy and Great Council of the Orthodox Church. 'The Mission of the Orthodox Church in Today's World' (Crete GR, 2016). <https://www.holycouncil.org> (23 January 2018).
Holy and Great Council of the Orthodox Church. 'Encyclical of the Holy and Great Council of the Orthodox Church' (Crete GR, 2016). <https://www.holycouncil.org> (23 January 2018).
Kireevsky, Ivan. 'Fragments'. In *On Spiritual Unity: A Slavophile Reader*, trans. and eds. Boris Jakim and Robert Bird. Hudson, NY: Lindisfarne Books, 1998: 275–92.
Kirill (Patriarch of Moscow). *Freedom and Responsibility: A Search for Harmony – Human Rights and Personal Dignity*. Trans. Richard Chartres. London: Darton, Longman & Todd, 2011.
Lossky, Vladimir. 'The Theological Notion of the Human Person'. In *In the Image and Likeness of God*, eds. John H. Erickson and Thomas E. Bird. London: Mowbrays; Crestwood, NY: St Vladimir's Seminary Press, 1974: 111–24.
Ramfos, Stelios. *Yearning for the One: Chapters in the Inner Life of the Greeks* (2000). Trans. Norman Russell. Brookline, MA: Holy Cross Orthodox Press, 2011.
Russian Orthodox Church. 'Basic Teaching on Human Dignity, Freedom and Human Rights' (2008). <https://mospat.ru/en/documents/dignity-freedom-rights> (16 July 2018).
Vlachos, Hierotheos. *The Person in the Orthodox Tradition*. Trans. Esther Williams. Levadia, GR: Birth of the Theotokos Monastery, 1998.
Yannaras, Christos. 'Human Rights and the Orthodox Church'. In *The Orthodox Churches in a Pluralistic World*, ed. Emanuel Clapsis. Geneva: WCC publications, 2004: 83–9.
Yannaras, Christos. *On the Absence and Unknowability of God: Heidegger and the Aeropagite* (1967). Trans. Haralambos Ventis. London: T&T Clark, 2005.
Yannaras, Christos. *Person and Eros*. Trans. Norman Russell. Brookline, MA: Holy Cross Orthodox Press, 2007.
Yannaras, Christos. 'The Inhuman Character of Human Rights (A Synopsis of the Homonymous Book of Prof. Christos Yannaras)' (1998). Trans. and ed. Anastasia Byrou. <www.academia.edu/3624303> (17 April 2015).
Yannoulatos, Anastasios. 'Orthodoxy and Human Rights'. In *Facing the World: Orthodox Christian Essays on Global Concerns*, ed. Anastasios Yannoulatos. Crestwood, NY: St Vladimir's Seminary Press, 2003: 49–78.
Zizioulas, John. *Being as Communion: Studies in Personhood and the Church*. Crestwood, NY: St Vladimir's Seminary Press, 1985.
Zizioulas, John. *Communion and Otherness: Further Studies in Personhood and the Church*. London: T&T Clark, 2006.

Secondary Sources

Brown, Alan. 'On the Criticism of Being as Communion in Anglophone Orthodox Theology'. In *The Theology of John Zizioulas: Personhood and the Church*, ed. Douglas Knight. Aldershot: Ashgate, 2007: 35–78.
Clément, Olivier. 'Le personnalisme chrétien dans la pensée russe des 19e et 20e siècles: Quelques aperçus' (Christian Personalism in Russian Thought of the 19th and 20th Centuries: Some Overviews). *Contacts, Revue française d'Orthodoxie* 40, no. 143 (1988): 206–25.
Clément, Olivier. 'Aperçus sur la théologie de la personne dans la "diaspora" russe en France' (Overviews of the Theology of the Person in the Russian "Diaspora" in France). In *Mille Ans de*

christianisme russe 988–1988 (A Thousand Years of Russian Christianity 988–1988). Paris: YMCA-Press, 1989: 303–9.

Clément, Olivier. 'Le père Lev Gillet, Grand théologien du Dieu souffrant et de l'Amour sans limites' (Fr Lev Gillet, A Great Theologian of the Suffering God and Unlimited Love). In Un Moine de l'Église d'Orient (Lev Gillet). *Au Cœur de la fournaise* (In the Heart of the Furnace). Paris: Le Sel de la Terre/Le Cerf, 1998: 9–23.

Larchet, Jean-Claude. 'Personne et nature. Une critique orthodoxe des théories personnalistes de Christos Yannaras et de Jean Zizioulas' (Person and Nature: An Orthodox Critique of the Personalist Theories of Christos Yannaras and John Zizioulas). In *Personne et nature, La Trinité – Le Christ – L'homme. Contributions aux dialogues interorthodoxe et interchrétien contemporains* (Person and Nature, The Trinity – Christ – Man: Contributions to Contemporary Inter-Orthodox and Inter-Christian Dialogues). Paris: Le Cerf, 2011: 207–394.

Loudovikos, Nicholas. 'Person instead of Grace and Dictated Otherness: John Zizioulas's Final Theological Position'. *The Heythrop Journal* 52 (2011): 684–99.

Loudovikos, Nicholas. 'Hell and Heaven, Nature and Person. Chr. Yannaras, D. Staniloae and Maximus the Confessor'. *International Journal of Orthodox Theology* 5, no. 1 (2014): 9–32.

McGuckin, John. 'The Issue of Human Rights in Byzantium and the Orthodox Christian Tradition'. In *Christianity and Human Rights: An Introduction*, eds. John Witte and Frank Alexander. Cambridge: Cambridge University Press, 2011: 173–90.

McGuckin, John. *The Ascent of Christian Law: Byzantine and Patristic Formulations of a New Civilization*. Yonkers, NY: St Vladimir's Seminary Press, 2012.

Mitralexis, Sotiris. 'Modern Greek Theology'. In *Oxford Handbook of Orthodox Theology*, eds. Andrew Louth and Andreas Andreopoulos. Oxford: Oxford University Press, forthcoming 2019.

Papanikolaou, Aristotle. 'Is John Zizioulas an Existentialist in Disguise? Response to Lucian Turcescu'. *Modern Theology* 20, no. 4 (2004): 600–7.

Papanikolaou, Aristotle. *Being with God: Trinity, Apophaticism, and Divine-Human Communion*. Notre Dame, IN: University of Notre Dame Press, 2006.

Papanikolaou, Aristotle. 'Personhood and Its Exponents in Twentieth-Century Orthodox Theology'. In *The Cambridge Companion to Orthodox Christian Theology*, eds. Mary Cunningham and Elizabeth Theokritoff. Cambridge: Cambridge University Press, 2008: 232–45.

Papanikolaou, Aristotle. *The Mystical as Political: Democracy and Non-Radical Orthodoxy*. Notre Dame, IN: University of Notre Dame Press, 2012.

Stoeckl, Kristina. *The Russian Orthodox Church and Human Rights*. London: Routledge, 2014.

Torrance, Alexis. 'Personhood and Patristics in Orthodox Theology: Reassessing the Debate'. *Heythrop Journal* 52 (2011): 700–7.

Turcescu, Lucian. '"Person" versus "Individual", and Other Modern Misreadings of Gregory of Nyssa'. *Modern Theology* 18, no. 4 (2002): 527–39.

Valliere, Paul. *Modern Russian Theology: Bukharev, Soloviev, Bulgakov: Orthodox Theology in a New Key*. Grand Rapids, MI: Eerdmans, 2000.

Van der Ven, Johannes. 'The Religious Scope of Human Rights'. In *Orthodox Christianity and Human Rights*, eds. Alfons Brüning and Evert van der Zweerde. Leuven: Peeters, 2012: 19–34.

Ware, Kallistos. 'The Human Person as an Icon of the Trinity'. *Sobornost* 8, no. 2 (1986): 6–23.

Ware, Kallistos. 'The Unity of the Human Person according to the Greek Fathers'. In *Persons and Personality: A Contemporary Inquiry*, eds. Arthur Peacocke and Grant Gillett. Oxford: Basil Blackwell, 1987: 197–206.

Ware, Kallistos. '"In the Image and Likeness": The Uniqueness of the Human Person'. In *Personhood: Orthodox Christianity and the Connection between Body, Mind, and Soul*, ed. John T. Chirban. Westport, CT: Bergin & Garvey, 1996: 1–13.

Ware, Kallistos. *Orthodox Theology in the Twenty-First Century*. Geneva: World Council of Churches, 2012.

Wolterstorff, Nicholas. 'Christianity and Human Rights'. In *Religion and Human Rights: An Introduction*, eds. John Witte and Christian Green. New York: Oxford University Press, 2012: 42–55.

11. The Church of Christ

Primary Sources

Afanasiev, Nicholas. *The Church of the Holy Spirit* (1975). Trans. Vitaly Permiakov. Notre Dame, IN: University of Notre Dame Press, 2007.

Birkbeck, W. J., ed. *Russia and the English Church during the Last Fifty Years Containing Correspondence between Mr. William Palmer and M. Khomiakoff, in the Years 1844–1854*. London: Rivington, Percival & Co., 1895; Farnborough, UK: Gregg International, 1969.

Bulgakov, Sergius. *The Orthodox Church* (1935). Revised trans. Lydia Kesich. Crestwood, NY: St Vladimir's Seminary Press, 1988.

Bulgakov, Sergius. *The Bride of the Lamb* (1945). Trans. Boris Jakim. Grand Rapids, MI: Erdmann, 2001.

Florovsky, Georges. 'Le Corps du Christ vivant: Une interprétation orthodoxe de l'Église' (The Body of the Living Christ: An Orthodox Interpretation of the Church). In *La Sainte Église universelle: Confrontation œcuménique* (The Holy Universal Church: Ecumenical Encounter), eds. Georges Florovsky, Franz-Jehan Leenhardt et al. Neuchâtel, CH: Delachaux & Niestlé, 1948.

Gallaher, Brandon, and Paul Ladouceur, eds. *The Patristic Witness of Georges Florovsky: Essential Theological Writings*. London: T&T Clark, 2019.

Jakim, Boris, and Robert Bird, trans. and eds. *On Spiritual Unity: A Slavophile Reader*. Hudson, NY: Lindisfarne Books, 1998.

Khomiakov, Aleksei. 'On the Western Confessions of Faith'. In *Ultimate Questions: An Anthology of Modern Russian Religious Thought*, ed. Alexander Schmemann. Crestwood, NY: St Vladimir's Seminary Press, 1977.

Khomiakov, Aleksei. *L'Église latine et le Protestantisme au point de vue de l'Eglise d'Orient* (The Latin Church and Protestantism from the Perspective of the Eastern Church). Lausanne, 1872; Vevey, CH: Xenia, 2006.

Plekon, Michael, ed. *Tradition Alive: On the Church and the Christian Life in Our Time – Readings from the Eastern Church*. Lanham, MD: Rowman & Littlefield, 2003. [Selections by Afanasiev, Bulgakov, Evdokimov, Behr-Sigel].

Soloviev, Vladimir. *Russia and the Universal Church* (1895). Trans. Herbert Rees. London: Geoffrey Bles-Centenary Press, 1948.

Soloviev, Vladimir. *War, Progress, and the End of History: Three Conversations, Including a Short Tale of the Antichrist* (1900). Trans. Alexander Bakshy. London: University of London Press/Hodder & Stouton, 1915. Revised trans. Thomas R. Beyer, Jr. Hudson, NY: Lindisfarne Books, 1990.

Staniloae, Dumitru. *Theology and the Church*. Trans. Robert Barringer. Crestwood, NY: St Vladimir's Seminary Press, 1980.

Staniloae, Dumitru. *The Church: Communion in the Holy Spirit* (1978). Trans. Ioan Ionita. Brookline, MA: Holy Cross Orthodox Press, 2012.

Zizioulas, John. *Being as Communion: Studies in Personhood and the Church*. Crestwood, NY: St Vladimir's Seminary Press, 1985.

Zizioulas, John. *Eucharist, Bishop, Church: The Unity of the Church in the* Divine Eucharist *and the Bishop during the First Three Centuries* (1965). Trans. Elizabeth Theokritoff. Brookline, MA: Holy Cross Press, 2001.

Secondary Sources

Alfeyev, Hilarion. *Orthodox Christianity. Vol. I: The History and Canonical Structure of the Orthodox Church. Vol. II: Doctrine and Teaching of the Orthodox Church*. Trans. Basil Bush. Yonkers, NY: St Vladimir's Seminary Press, 2011.

Bobrinskoy, Boris. *The Mystery of the Church: A Course in Orthodox Dogmatic Theology* (2003). Trans. Michael Breck. Yonkers, NY: St Vladimir's Seminary Press, 2012.

Destivelle, Hyacinthe. *The Moscow Council 1917–1918: The Creation of the Conciliar Institutions of the Russian Orthodox Church*. Trans. Jerry Ryan. Notre Dame, IN: University of Notre Dame Press, 2015.

Erickson, John, 'The Church in Modern Orthodox Thought: Towards a Baptismal Ecclesiology'. *International Journal for the Study of the Christian Church* 11, no. 2–3 (2011): 137–51.

Ladouceur, Paul. 'Three Contemporary Orthodox Visions of the Church'. *St Vladimir's Theological Quarterly* 58, no. 2 (2014): 217–34.

Larchet, Jean-Claude. *L'Église, Corps du Christ Vol. I. Nature et structure. Vol. II. Les relations entre les Églises* (The Church, Body of Christ. Vol. 1 Nature and Structure. Vol. 2 Relations among the Churches). Paris: Le Cerf, 2012.

Loudovikos, Nikolaos, 'Person Instead of Grace and Dictated Otherness: John Zizioulas's Final Theological Position'. *Heythrop Journal* 52, no. 4 (2011): 684–99.

Ware, Kallistos. 'Sobornost and Eucharistic Ecclesiology: Aleksei Khomiakov and His Successors'. *International Journal for the Study of the Christian Church* 11, no. 2–3 (2011): 216–35.

Zernov, Nicolas. *Three Russian Prophets: Khomiakov, Dostoyevsky, Soloviev*. London: SCM Press, 1944.

12. Ecumenical Theology and Religious Diversity

Primary Sources

Bulgakov, Sergius. 'Ways to Church Reunion' (1935) and 'Spiritual Intercommunion' (1935). In *Father Sergius Bulgakov 1871–1944. A Collection of Articles by Fr. Bulgakov*. London: Fellowship of St. Alban and St. Sergius, 1969: 22–28; 29–32.

Bulgakov, Sergius. 'By Jacob's Well—John 4:23 (On the Actual Unity of the Divided Church in Faith, Prayer and Sacraments)' (1933). In *Tradition Alive: On the Church and the Christian Life in Our*

Time-Readings from the Eastern Church, ed. Michael Plekon. Lanham, MD: Sheed & Ward, 2003: 55–65.

Chaillot, Christine, ed. *The Dialogue between the Eastern Orthodox and the Oriental Orthodox Churches*. Volos, GR: Volos Academy Publications, 2016. [Contains dialogue documents and studies.]

Damascene (Hieromonk) (John Christensen). *Christ the Eternal Tao*. Platina, CA: Valaam Books, 2004.

Frost, Christine Mangala. *The Human Icon: A Comparative Study of Hindu and Orthodox Christian Beliefs*. Cambridge: James Clarke, 2017.

Gallaher, Brandon, and Paul Ladouceur, eds. *The Patristic Witness of Georges Florovsky: Essential Theological Writings*. London: T&T Clark, 2019.

Gillet, Lev. *In Thy Presence*. London: Mowbray: Crestwood, NY: St Vladimir's Seminary Press, 1977.

Gillet, Lev. *Communion in the Messiah: Studies in the Relationship between Judaism and Christianity* (1942). Eugene, OR: Wipf & Stock, 2013.

Holy and Great Council of the Orthodox Church. 'The Mission of the Orthodox Church in Today's World' (Crete, June 2016). <www.holycouncil.org> (7 May 2017).

Justin Martyr, *The First and Second Apologies*. Trans. Leslie W. Barnard. New York: Paulist Press, 1997.

Khodr, Georges. 'Christianity in a Pluralistic World: The Economy of the Holy Spirit'. *The Ecumenical Review* 23, no. 2 (1971): 118–28.

Limouris, Gennadios, ed. *Orthodox Visions of Ecumenism: Statements, Messages and Reports on the Ecumenical Movement, 1902–1992*. Geneva: WCC Publications, 1994.

Men, Alexander. *The History of Religion: In Search of the Way, the Truth and the Life* (in Russian) (5 vols.). Brussels (1970–1983). Vol. 1: *The Wellsprings of Religion*. Trans. Alasdair Macnaughton. Yonkers, NY: St Vladimir's Seminary Press, 2017.

Popovitch, Justin. *The Orthodox Church and Ecumenism*. Trans. Benjamin E. Stanley. Birmingham: Lazarica Press, 2000.

Rose, Seraphim. *Orthodoxy and the Religion of the Future* (1975). Platina, CA: St. Herman of Alaska Brotherhood, 1996.

Sherrard, Philip. *Christianity: Lineaments of a Sacred Tradition*. Brookline, MA: Holy Cross Orthodox Press, 1998.

Ustinov, Vitaly (Archbishop). 'Report to the Sobor of Bishops of the Russian Orthodox Church Outside of Russia' (1967–1968). <orthodoxinfo.com/ecumenism/vitaly.aspx> (15 July 2018).

Voznesensky, Philaret (Metropolitan). 'The First Sorrowful Epistle of Metropolitan Philaret' (1969). <http://orthodoxinfo.com/ecumenism/sorrow.aspx> (4 August 2014).

[Yannoulatos], Anastasios (Giannoulatos), *Various Christian Approaches to Other Religions* (*A Historical Outline*). Athens: Poreuthentes, 1971.

Yannoulatos, Anastasios. 'Toward a Global Community: Resources and Responsibilities' (1974); and 'A Theological Approach to Understanding Other Religions'. In *Facing the World: Orthodox Christian Essays on Global Concerns*, ed. Anastasios Yannoulatos. Crestwood, NY: WCC/St Vladimir's Seminary Press, 2003: 15–48; 127–54.

Secondary Sources

Arseniev, Nicholas. *Revelation of Life Eternal: An Introduction to the Christian Message*. Yonkers, NY: St Vladimir's Seminary Press, 1982.

Clapsis, Emmanuel, 'Theology of Religions as Concern for Ecumenical Dialogue of Orthodox Theologians'. In *Orthodox Handbook on Ecumenism: Resources for Theological Education*, eds. Pantelis Kalaitzidis, Thomas Fitzgerald, Cyril Hovorun, Aikaterini, Nikolaos Asproulis, Dietrich Werner and Guy Liagre. Volos, GR: Volos Academy Publications; Oxford: Regnum Books; Geneva: World Council of Churches, 2013: 706–13.

Constantelos, Demetrios J. *The Attitude of Orthodox Christians toward Non-Christians*. Brookline, MA: Holy Cross Orthodox Press, 1992.

Gallaher, Brandon. 'Bulgakov and Intercommunion'. *Sobornost/ECR* 24, no. 2 (2002): 9–28.

Gallaher, Brandon. '"Great and Full of Grace": Partial Intercommunion and Sophiology in Sergii Bulgakov'. In *Church and World: Essays in Honor of Michael Plekon*, ed. William C. Mills. Rollinsford, NH: Orthodox Research Institute, 2013: 69–121.

Fédou, Michel. 'La doctrine du Logos chez Justin: Enjeux philosophiques et théologiques' (The Doctrine of the Logos in Justin: Philosophical and Theological Issues). *Kentron* 25 (2009): 145–58.

Garvey, John. *Seeds of the Word*. Yonkers, NY: St Vladimir's Seminary Press, 2005.

Heers, Peter. 'The Mystery of Baptism and the Unity of the Church: The Idea of "Baptismal Unity" and its Acceptance by Orthodox Ecumenists' (2004). <http://orthodoxinfo.com/ecumenism/ea_ecclesiology.aspx> (5 October 2016).

Heers, Peter. *The Ecclesiological Renovation of Vatican II: An Orthodox Examination of Rome's Ecumenical Theology Regarding Baptism and the Church*. Simpsonville, SC: Uncut Mountain Press, 2015.

Kalaitzidis, Pantelis. 'Theological, Historical and Cultural Reasons for Anti-Ecumenical Movements in Eastern Orthodoxy'. In *Orthodox Handbook on Ecumenism: Resources for Theological Education*, eds. Pantelis Kalaitzidis, Thomas Fitzgerald, Cyril Hovorun et al. Volos, GR: Volos Academy Publications; Oxford: Regnum Books; Geneva: World Council of Churches, 2013: 134–52.

Karmiris, Ioannis. 'The Universality of Salvation in Christ' (in Greek). *Theologia* 51 (1980): 645–91; *Theologia* 52 (1981): 14–45.

Ladouceur, Paul. 'Christianisme et réincarnation' (Christianity and Reincarnation), *Contacts, Revue française d'orthodoxie* 58, no. 214 (2006): 238–56.

Ladouceur, Paul. '"Aimons-nous les uns les autres": Serge Boulgakov et Georges Florovsky' (Let Us Love One Another: Sergius Bulgakov and Georges Florovsky). *Contacts, Revue française d'Orthodoxie* 64, no. 237 (2012): 56–87.

Ladouceur, Paul. 'The Holy and Great Council of the Orthodox Church (June 2016)'. *Oecuménisme/Ecumenism* (Montreal) 51, no. 198–9 (2016): 18–39.

Ladouceur, Paul. 'Orthodox Critiques of the Agreed Statements between the Orthodox and the Oriental Orthodox Churches', *St Vladimir's Theological Quarterly* 60, no. 3 (2016): 333–68.

Ladouceur, Paul. 'On Ecumenoclasm: Anti-Ecumenism in Orthodox Theology'. *St Vladimir's Theological Quarterly* 61, no. 3 (2017): 323–56.

Ladouceur, Paul. 'Religious Diversity in Modern Orthodox Thought'. *Religions* 8 (5), no. 77 (2017). <www.mdpi.com/journal/religions/special_issues/orthodox_churches> (7 May 2017). Also in: John

Jillions, ed., *Inward Being and Outward Identity: The Orthodox Churches in the 21st Century*. Basel, CH: MDPI, 2018: 44–56.
Makrides, Vasilios. 'Orthodox Christian Rigorism: Attempting to Delineate a Multifaceted Phenomenon'. *Interdisciplinary Journal for Religion and Transformation in Contemporary Society* 3 (2016): 216–52.
Moyaert, Marianne. 'Recent Developments in the Theology of Interreligious Dialogue: From Soteriological Openness to Hermeneutical Openness'. *Modern Theology* 28, no. 1 (2012): 25–52.
Nikolaev, Sergei. 'Spiritual Unity: The Role of Religious Authority in the Disputes between Sergii Bulgakov and G. Florovsky concerning Intercommunion'. *St Vladimir's Theological Quarterly* 49, no. 1–2 (2005): 101–24.
Papademetriou, George. 'An Orthodox Christian View of Non-Christian Religions'. <www.goarch.org/ourfaith/ourfaith8089> (28 October 2016).
Perepiolkina, Ludmilla. *Ecumenism – A Path to Perdition*. Saint Petersburg: Self Publication, 1999. <http://ecumenizm.tripod.com/ECUMENIZM/index.html> (30 November 2016).
Valea, Ernest M. *Buddhist-Christian Dialogue as Theological Exchange: An Orthodox Contribution to Comparative Theology*. Eugene, OR: Wipf and Stock, 2015.

13. The Christification of Life

Afanasiev, Nicholas. 'Ministry of the Laity'. *The Ecumenical Review* 10, no. 3 (1958): 255–63.
Afanasiev, Nicholas. *The Church of the Holy Spirit* (1975). Trans. Vitaly Permiakov. Notre Dame, IN: University of Notre Dame Press, 2007.
Andronikof, Constantine. *Le Sens des fêtes: t. 1. Le cycle fixe* (The Meaning of the Feasts: v.1. The Fixed Feasts). Paris: Cerf, 1970; *Le Sens des fêtes: t. 2. Le Cycle pascal* (The Meaning of the Feasts: v.2. The Paschal Cycle). Lausanne: L'Âge d'homme, 1985.
Andronikof, Constantine. *Le Sens de la Liturgie: La relation entre Dieu et l'homme* (The Meaning of the Liturgy: Relations between God and Humans). Paris: Le Cerf, 1988.
Bobrinskoy, Boris. *The Mystery of the Church* (2003). Trans. Michael Breck. Yonkers, NY: St Vladimir's Seminary Press, 2012.
Cabasilas, Nicholas (St). *The Life in Christ*. Trans. Carmino J. De Catanzaro. Crestwood, NY: St Vladimir's Seminary Press, 1974.
Cabasilas, Nicholas (St). *The Interpretation of the Divine Liturgy*. Trans. Joan M. Hussey and P. A. McNulty. Crestwood, NY: St Vladimir's Seminary Press, 1997.
Evdokimov, Paul. 'Ecclesia Domestica' (1962). In *A Voice for Women*, ed. Suzannah Herzel. Geneva: World Council of Churches, 1981: 174–83.
Evdokimov, Paul. *The Sacrament of Love: The Nuptial Mystery in the Light of the Orthodox Tradition* (1944). Trans. Anthony P. Gythiel and Victoria Steadman. Crestwood, NY: St Vladimir's Seminary Press, 1985.
Evdokimov, Paul. *The Ages of the Spiritual Life* (1964). Trans. Sister Gertrude, Michael Plekon and Alexis Vinogradov. Crestwood, NY: St Vladimir's Seminary Press, 1998.
Gavrilia (Nun). *Mother Gavrilia, The Ascetic of Love*. Trans. Helen Anthony. Athens: Eptalophos, 2000.
[Gillet, Lev]. A Monk of the Eastern Church. *Orthodox Spirituality: An Outline of the Orthodox Ascetical and Mystical Tradition* (1944). Crestwood, NY: St Vladimir's Seminary Press, 1987.

[Gillet, Lev]. A Monk of the Eastern Church. *The Year of Grace of the Lord: A Scriptural and Liturgical Commentary on the Calendar of the Orthodox Church*. Trans. Deborah Cowen. Crestwood, NY: St Vladimir's Seminary Press, 1989.

[Gillet, Lev]. A Monk of the Eastern Church. *Serve the Lord With Gladness: Basic Reflections on the Eucharist and the Priesthood*. Trans. John Breck. Crestwood, NY: St Vladimir's Seminary Press, 1990.

Gondidakis, Vasileios. *Hymn of Entry: Liturgy and Life in the Orthodox Church* (1974). Trans. Elizabeth Briere. Crestwood, NY: St Vladimir's Seminary Press, 1984.

Hariankis, Stylianos. *The Infallibility of the Church in Orthodox Theology*. Adelaide: ATF Press; Sydney: St. Andrew's Orthodox Press, 2008.

Hopko, Thomas. *The Lenten Spring*. Crestwood, NY: St Vladimir's Seminary Press, 1983.

Hopko, Thomas. *The Winter Pascha*. Crestwood, NY: St Vladimir's Seminary Press, 1984.

Kniazeff, Alexis. 'L'Ecclésialisation de la vie' (The Churchification of Life). *La Pensée orthodoxe*, no. 4. Paris: L'Âge d'homme, 1987: 108–35.

Ladouceur, Paul. 'In My Father's House There Are Many Mansions (Jn 14:2): New Institutions in Modern Orthodox Spirituality'. *St Vladimir's Theological Quarterly* 55, no. 4 (2011): 439–83.

Larin, Vassa, 'Fr Alexander Schmemann and Monasticism'. *St Vladimir's Theological Quarterly* 53, no. (2009): 5–26.

Middleton, Herman A. *Precious Vessels of the Holy Spirit, The Lives and Counsels of Contemporary Elders of Greece*. Thessalonica, GR and Asheville, NC: Protecting Veil Press, 2004.

Nellas, Panayiotis. *Deification in Christ: Orthodox Perspectives on the Nature of the Human Person* (1979). Trans. Norman Russell. Crestwood, NY: St Vladimir's Seminary Press, 1987.

Nikodemos the Hagiorite (Saint), trans. and ed. *Unseen Warfare: The Spiritual Combat and Path to Paradise of Lorenzo Scupoli*. Revised by Theophan the Recluse (Saint). Trans. Eugenic Kadloubovsky and Gerald E. H. Palmer. London: Faber & Faber, 1952; Crestwood, NY: St Vladimir's Seminary Press, 1997.

Nikodemos the Hagiorite (Saint). *Concerning Frequent Communion of the Immaculate Mysteries of Christ* (1777). Trans. George Dokos. Thessalonica, GR: Uncut Mountain Press, 2006.

Schmemann, Alexander. *Introduction to Liturgical Theology*. Crestwood, NY: St Vladimir's Seminary Press, 1966.

Schmemann, Alexander. *Great Lent: Journey to Pascha*. Crestwood, NY: St Vladimir's Seminary Press, 1969.

Schmemann, Alexander. *For the Life of the World: Sacraments and Orthodoxy* (1965). Crestwood, NY: St Vladimir's Seminary Press, 1973.

Schmemann, Alexander. *Of Water and Spirit: A Liturgical Study of Baptism*. Crestwood, NY: St Vladimir's Seminary Press, 1974.

Schmemann, Alexander. *The Eucharist: Sacrament of the Kingdom*. Crestwood, NY: St Vladimir's Seminary Press, 1987.

Schmemann, Alexander. *The Journals of Father Alexander Schmemann 1973–1983*. Trans. and ed. Juliana Schmemann. Crestwood, NY: St Vladimir's Seminary Press, 2002.

Schmemann, Alexander. 'A Liturgical Explanation of Holy Week'. <www.stnicholasdc.org/files/Holy%20Week/A-Liturgical-Explanation-of-Holy-Week.pdf> (20 November 2017).

Shevzov, Vera. 'Letting the People into Church: Reflections on Orthodoxy and Community in Late Imperial Russia'. In *Orthodox Russia: Belief and Practice under the Tsars*, eds. Valerie Kivelson and Robert Greene. University Park, PE: Pennsylvania State University Press, 2003: 59–77.

Skobtsova, Maria (Mother). 'Types of Religious Life'. In *Mother Maria, Essential Writings*. Maryknoll, NY: Orbis Books, 2003: 140–86.

Skobtsova, Maria (Mother). 'L'Évangile sociale' (The Social Gospel). In Sainte Marie de Paris (Mère Marie Skobtsov, 1891–1945), *Le Jour du Saint-Esprit*, ed. Paul Ladouceur. Paris: Le Cerf, 2011: 327–94.

14. Social and Political Theology

Primary Sources

Berdyaev, Nicolas. *The Russian Revolution*. Trans. D. Attwater. London: Sheed and Ward, 1931.

Berdyaev, Nicolas. *The Origin of Russian Communism*. Trans. Reginald M. French. London: G. Bles, 1937.

Berdyaev, Nicolas. 'Ortodoksiya I chelovechnost' (Ortodoxia and Humanness). *Put'* 53 (1937). Trans. Steven Janos. <www.berdyaev.com/Berdyaev/berd_lib/1937_424.html> (5 April 2015).

Bulgakov, Sergius. 'An Urgent Task' (1905). In *A Revolution of the Spirit: Crisis of Value in Russia, 1890–1924*. Trans. and eds. Bernice Glatzer Rosenthal and Martha Bohachevsky-Chomiak. New York: Fordham University Press, 1990: 137–59.

Bulgakov, Sergius. 'The Soul of Socialism' (1932) and 'Social Teaching in Modern Russian Orthodox Theology' (1934). In *Sergii Bulgakov: Towards a Russian Political Economy*, ed. Rowan Williams. Edinburgh: T&T Clark, 1999: 229–68; 269–92.

Bulgakov, Sergius. 'Dogma and Dogmatic Theology' (1937). In *Tradition Alive: On the Church and the Christian Life in Our Time*, ed. Michael Plekon. Lanham, MA: Rowan & Littlefield, 2003: 67–80.

Evdokimov, Paul. 'Some Landmarks on Life's Journey' (1981); and 'The Church and Society: The Social Dimension of Orthodox Ecclesiology' (1967). In *In the World, Of the Church: A Paul Evdokimov Reader*, eds. Michael Plekon and Alexis Vinogradov. Crestwood, NY: St Vladimir's Seminary Press, 2000: 37–47; 61–94.

Florovsky, Georges. 'The Social Problem in the Eastern Orthodox Church'. *The Journal of Religious Thought* 8, no. 1 (1950–1951): 41–51. Also in Georges Florovsky, *Christianity and Culture*, Vol. 2 of *The Collected Works of Georges Florovsky* (Belmont, MA: Nordland, 1974): 131–42.

Holy and Great Council of the Orthodox Church. 'The Mission of the Orthodox Church in Today's World' and 'Encyclical of the Holy and Great Council of the Orthodox Church' (Crete GR, 2016). <https://www.holycouncil.org> (23 January 2018).

Kalaitzidis, Pantelis. *Orthodoxía kai neoterikótita: Prolegómena* (Orthodoxy and Modernity: An Introduction). Athens: Indiktos Publications, 2007.

Kalaitzidis, Pantelis. *Orthodoxy and Political Theology*. Geneva: WCC Publications, 2012.

Papanikolaou, Aristotle. *The Mystical as Political: Democracy and Non-Radical Orthodoxy*. Notre Dame, IN: University of Notre Dame Press, 2012.

Russian Orthodox Church. 'Basis of the Social Concept of the Russian Orthodox Church' (2001). <www.mospat.ru/en/documents/social-concept> (16 July 2018).

Russian Orthodox Church. 'Basic Teaching on Human Dignity, Freedom and Human Rights' (2008). <https://mospat.ru/en/documents/dignity-freedom-rights> (16 July 2018).

Skobtsova, Maria (Mother). *Mother Maria, Essential Writings*. Maryknoll, NY: Orbis Books, 2003.

Skobtsova, Maria (Mother). 'L'Évangile sociale' (The Social Gospel) In Sainte Marie de Paris (Mère Marie Skobtsov, 1891–1945), *Le Jour du Saint-Esprit*, ed. Paul Ladouceur. Paris: Le Cerf, 2011: 327–94.

Soloviev, Vladimir. *La Sophia et les autres écrits français* (Sophia and Other Writings in French), ed. François Rouleau. Lausanne: L'Âge d'Homme, 1978.

Soloviev, Vladimir. *Justification of the Good: An Essay on Moral Philosophy* (1897). Trans. and ed., Thomas Nemeth. Cham, CH: Springer International Publishing, 2015.

Secondary Sources

Evtuhov, Catherine. *The Cross & the Sickle: Sergei Bulgakov and the Fate of Russian Religious Philosophy*. Ithaca, NY: Cornell University Press, 1997.

Gaut, Greg. 'A Practical Unity: Vladimir Solov'ev and Russian Liberalism'. *Canadian Slavonic Papers* 42, no. 3 (2000): 295–314.

Giocas, Athanasios. 'Christian Practice as the Foundation for Modern Political Theology'. *Journal of Law and Religion* 30, no. 1 (2015): 161–9.

Gurorian, Vigen. 'Godless Theosis: A Review of *The Mystical as Political*'. *First Things* (April 2014). <www.firstthings.com/article/2014/04/godless-theosis> (5 February 2017).

Kishkovsky, Leonid. 'Russian Theology after Totalitarianism'. In *The Cambridge Companion to Orthodox Christian Theology*, eds. Mary Cunningham and Elizabeth Theokritoff. Cambridge: Cambridge University Press, 2009: 261–75.

Ladouceur, Paul. 'In My Father's House There Are Many Mansions (Jn 14:2): New Institutions in Modern Orthodox Spirituality'. *St Vladimir's Theological Quarterly* 55, no. 4 (2011): 439–83.

Ladouceur, Paul. 'The Social and Political Theology of Love in St Maria of Paris'. *Sobornost* 40, no. 1 (2018): 60–74.

Makrides, Vasilios N. '"The Barbarian West": A Form of Orthodox Christian Anti-Western Critique'. In *Eastern Orthodox Encounters of Identity and Otherness: Values, Self-Reflection, Dialogue*, eds. Andrii Krawchuk and Thomas Bremer. New York: Palgrave Macmillan, 2014: 141–58.

Stoeckl, Kristina. *The Russian Orthodox Church and Human Rights*. London: Routledge, 2014.

Stoeckl, Kristina, Ingeborg Gabriel and Aristotle Papanikolaou, eds. *Political Theologies in Orthodox Christianity: Common Challenges – Divergent Positions*. London: T&T Clark, 2017.

Terpstra, Marin. '"God's Case on Earth": Notes on Theocracy and the Political Theology of Vladimir Soloviev'. In *Soloviev, Reconciler and Polemicist*, eds. Wil van den Bercken, Manon de Courten and Evert van der Zweerde. Leuven, BE: Peeters, 2000: 411–29.

Valliere, Paul. *Modern Russian Theology: Bukharev, Soloviev, Bulgakov: Orthodox Theology in a New Key*. Grand Rapids, MI: Eerdmans, 2000.

Valliere, Paul. 'Introduction to the Modern Orthodox Tradition'. In *The Teachings of Modern Orthodox Christianity on Law, Politics, and Human Nature*, eds. John Witte Jr. and Frank S. Alexander. New York: Columbia University Press, 2007.

Van Herpen, Marcel. *Putin's Propaganda Machine: Soft Power and Russian Foreign Policy*. Lanham, MD: Rowman & Littlefield, 2016.

Walicki, Andrzej. *Legal Philosophies of Russian Liberalism*. Oxford: Clarendon Press, 1987.

Willert, Trine Stauning. *New Voices in Greek Orthodox Thought: Untying the Bond between Nation and Religion*. Farnham, Surrey: Ashgate, 2014.

15. Otomatodoxy: The Name-of-God Conflict

Primary Sources

Bulgakov, Sergius. *La Philosophie du Verbe et du Nom* (The Philosophy of the Verb and the Name) (1953). Trans. Constantin Andronikof. Lausanne: L'Âge d'homme, 1991.

Bulgakov, Sergius. *Icons and the Name of God* (1931; 1953). Trans. Boris Jakim. Grand Rapids, MI: Eerdmans, 2012.

Florensky, Pavel. 'Imiaslavie kak filosofskaia predposilka' (Name-Worshipping as Philosophical Presupposition) (1918). In Pavel Florensky, *Sochineniya c chetireh tomah* (Works in Four Volumes) (vol. 3), 1. (Moscow, 1999): 252–86.

Hilarion (Domratchev) (Hieromonk). *Sur les Monts du Caucase: Dialogue de deux Solitaires sur la Prière de Jésus* (On the Mountains of the Caucasus: Dialogue of Two Hermits on the Jesus Prayer) [Translation of *Na Gorakh Kavkaza* (1907)]. Trans. André Louf. Paris: Éditions des Syrtes, 2016.

John of Kronstadt (Ivan Ilyich Sergiev). *My Life in Christ: Extracts from the Diary of St John of Kronstadt*. Trans E. E. Goulaeff. London: Cassell, 1897; Jordanville, NY: Holy Trinity Russian Orthodox Monastery, 1957.

Sophrony (Sakharov) (Archimandrite). *His Life Is Mine*. Trans. Rosemary Edmonds. Crestwood, NY: St Vladimir's Seminary Press, 1977.

Sophrony (Sakharov) (Archimandrite). *Sa Vie est la mienne* (His Life Is Mine). Trans. Claude Lopez and Hieromonk Symeon. Paris: Le Cerf, 1981.

Sophrony (Sakharov) (Archimandrite). *St Silouan the Athonite*. Trans. Rosemary Edmonds. Crestwood, NY: St Vladimir's Seminary Press, 1991.

Sophrony (Sakharov) (Archimandrite). *On Prayer*. Trans. Rosemary Edmonds. Crestwood, NY: St Vladimir's Seminary Press, 1998.

Secondary Sources

Alfeyev, Hilarion. *Le Mystère sacré de l'Église. Introduction à l'histoire et à la problématique des débats athonites sur la vénération du nom de Dieu* (The Sacred Mystery: Introduction to the History and Problem of the Athonite Debates on the Veneration of the Name of God). Trans. Claire Jounievy and Alexandre Siniakov. Fribourg, CH: Academic Press, 2007.

Alfeyev, Hilarion. *Le Nom grand et glorieux, La Vénération du Nom de Dieu et la prière de Jésus dans la tradition orthodoxe* (The Great and Glorious Name: The Veneration of the Name of God and the Jesus Prayer in the Orthodox Tradition). Trans. Claire Jounievy, Alexandre Siniakov and André Louf. Paris: Cerf, 2007.

Dykstra, Tom E. 'Heresy on Mt. Athos: Conflict over the Name of God among Russian Monks and Hierarchs, 1912–1914'. M.Div. thesis, St Vladimir's Orthodox Theological Seminary, 1988. <http://www.pravoslav.de/imiaslavie/english/dykstra/dikstra.htm> (16 July 2018).

Gourko, Helena. *Divine Onomatology: Name of God in Imyaslavie, Symbolism, and Deconstruction*. Saarbrucken, DE: VDM Verlag, 2009.

Hamburg, Gary M. 'The Origins of "Heresy" on Mount Athos: Ilarion's *Na Gorakh Kavkaza* (1907)'. *Occasional Papers on Religion in Eastern Europe* 23, no. 2 (2003): 16–47.

Kenworthy, Scott. 'Debating the Theology of the Name in Post-Soviet Russia: Metropolitan Ilarion Alfeev and Sergei Khoruzhii'. In *Orthodox Paradoxes: Heterogeneities and Complexities in Contemporary Russian Orthodoxy*, ed. Katya Tolstaya. Leiden and Boston: Brill, 2014: 250–64.

Ladouceur, Paul. 'The Name-of-God Conflict in Orthodox Theology'. *St Vladimir's Theological Quarterly* 56, no. 4 (2012): 415–36.
Moss, Vladimir. 'On the Name of God: Against the Name-Worshipping Heresy of Fr A. Bulatovich and Fr G. Louri' (Y). <www.orthodoxchristianbooks.com/books/> (11 April 2016).
Pascal, Pierre. *La Religion du people russe* (The Religion of the Russian People). Lausanne: L'Âge d'homme, 1973.

16. The Ordination of Women

Afanasiev, Nicholas. *The Church of the Holy Spirit* (1975). Trans. Vitaly Permiakov. Notre Dame, IN: University of Notre Dame Press, 2007.
Behr-Sigel, Elisabeth. 'La consultation interorthodoxe de Rhodes: Présentation et essai d'évaluation' (The Interorthodox Consultation in Rhodes: Presentation and Preliminary Assessment). *Contacts, Revue française d'Orthodoxie* 41, no. 146 (1989): 81–93.
Behr-Sigel, Elisabeth, and Nicole Maillard. 'Orthodoxy and Women in France'. In *Women, Religion and Sexuality: Studies on the Impact of Religious Teachings on Women*, ed. Jeanne Becher. Geneva: WCC Publications, 1990: 184–91.
Behr-Sigel, Elisabeth. *The Ministry of Women in the Church* (1987). Trans. Steven Bigham. Crestwood, NY: St Vladimir's Seminary Press, 1999.
Behr-Sigel, Elisabeth, and Kallistos Ware, *The Ordination of Women in the Orthodox Church*. Geneva: WCC Publications, 2000.
Behr-Sigel, Elisabeth. *Discerning the Signs of the Times: The Vision of Elisabeth Behr-Sigel*, eds. Michael Plekon and Sarah Hinlicky. Crestwood, NY: St Vladimir's Seminary Press, 2001.
Bobrinskoy, Boris. *The Mystery of the Church: A Course in Orthodox Dogmatic Theology* (2003). Trans. Michael Breck. Yonkers, NY: St Vladimir's Seminary Press, 2012.
Bulgakov, Sergius. *The Bride of the Lamb* (1945). Trans. Boris Jakim. Grand Rapids, MI: Eerdmanns, 2001.
Bulgakov, Sergius. *The Comforter* (1936). Trans. Boris Jakim. Grand Rapids, MI: Eerdmans, 2004.
Evdokimov, Paul. *Woman and the Salvation of the World: A Christian Anthropology on the Charisms of Women* (1958; revised 1983). Trans. Anthony P. Gythiel. Crestwood, NY: St Vladimir's Seminary Press, 1994.
Evdokimov, Paul. *The Ages of the Spiritual Life* (1964). Trans. Sister Gertrude, Michael Plekon and Alexis Vinogradov. Crestwood, NY: St Vladimir's Seminary Press, 1998.
Farley, Lawrence. *Feminism and Tradition: Quiet Reflections on Ordination and Communion*. Yonkers, NY: St Vladimir's Seminary Press, 2012.
Farley, Lawrence. 'Rejoinder to Dr Ladouceur'. *St Vladimir's Theological Quarterly* 62, no. 1 (2018): 87–93.
Grygo, Elizabeth N. *The Deaconess Movement in the Russian Orthodox Church, 1860–1917*. Seattle, WA: University of Washington, 1990.
Harrison, Valerie. 'Male and Female in Cappadocian Theology'. *Journal of Theological Studies* 41, no. 2 (1990): 441–71.
Hopko, Thomas, ed. *Women and the Priesthood*. Crestwood, NY: St Vladimir's Seminary Press (1983). Revised edition (1999).

Ladouceur, Paul. Book Review: 'Lawrence Farley, *Feminism and Tradition: Quiet Reflections on Ordination and Communion* (2012)'. *St Vladimir's Theological Quarterly* 60, no. 3 (2016): 415–21.

Ladouceur, Paul. 'Christ, the Fathers and Feminism: Dialogue with Fr. Lawrence Farley'. *St Vladimir's Theological Quarterly* 62, no. 3 (2018): 287–95.

Limouris, Gennadios, ed. *The Place of Woman in the Orthodox Church and the Question of the Ordination of Women. Inter-Orthodox Symposium, Rhodos, Greece, 30 October-7 November 1988.* Katerini, GR: Ecumenical Patriarchate and Tertios Publications, 1992.

Meyendorff, John. 'The Orthodox Churches'. In *The Ordination of Women: Pro and Con*, eds. Michael Hamilton and Nancy Montgomery. New York: Morehouse-Barlow, 1975: 128–35.

Patriarchate of Alexandria. 'Patriarch Theodoros of Alexandria Performs First Consecration of Deaconesses' (22 February 2016) <http://basilica.ro/en/patriarch-theodoros-of-alexandria-performs-first-consecration-of-deaconesses> (1 August 2017).

Regule, Teva. 'Rejuvenating the Diaconate: Opportunities, Challenges, and Steps'. St Phoebe Conference 'Women and Diaconal Ministry: Past, Present, and Future' (6 June 2014). <https://orthodoxdeaconess.org/wp-content/uploads/2015/02/StPhoebeConfDiacTalk-Fin2b.pdf> (1 August 2017).

Schmemann, Alexander. 'Concerning Women's Ordination: Letter to an Episcopal Friend'. *St Vladimir's Theological Quarterly* 17, no. 3 (1973): 239–43.

Tarasar, Constance J., and Irina Kirillova, eds. *Orthodox Women: Their Role and Participation in the Orthodox Church. Report on the Consultation of Orthodox Women September 11–17, 1976, Agapia, Romania.* Geneva: World Council of Churches, 1977.

Theodorou, Evangelos. *Iroides tis Christianikis Agapis* (Heroines of Christian Love). (Deaconesses through the Ages). Athens: Apostlika Diakonia, 1949.

Theodorou, Evangelos. 'I 'cheirotonia', i 'cheirothesia' ton diakonisson' (The Ordination or Appointment of Deaconesses), *Theologia* 25 (Athens) (1954): 430–69; 596–601; 26 (1955): 57–76.

Vassiliadis, Petros, Niki Papageorgiou and Eleni Kasselouri-Hatzivassiliadi, eds. *Deaconesses, the Ordination of Women and Orthodox Theology*. Cambridge: Cambridge Scholars Publishing, 2017.

World Council of Churches, Commission on Faith and Order & Department on the Cooperation of Men and Women in Church, Family, and Society. *Concerning the Ordination of Women*. Geneva: World Council of Churches, 1964. [Contains Nicolae Chitescu, 'The Ordination of Women: A Comment on the Attitude of the Orthodox Church' and Georges Khodre, 'The Ordination of Women: A Comment'].

PART III ASSESSMENTS AND CONCLUSIONS

17. Light and Shadows in Modern Orthodox Theology

and

18. The Living Tradition of Orthodox Theology

Alfeyev, Hilarion. 'Orthodox Theology on the Threshold of the 21st Century: Will There Be a Renaissance of Russian Theological Scholarship?' *Ecumenical Review* 52, no. 3 (2000): 309–25.

Baker, Matthew. 'Neopatristic Synthesis and Ecumenism: Towards the "Reintegration" of Christian Tradition'. In *Eastern Orthodox Encounters of Identity and Otherness: Values, Self-Reflection, Dialogue*, eds. Andrii Krawchuk and Thomas Bremer. New York: Palgrave MacMillan, 2014: 235–60.

Berdyaev, Nicolas. 'The Spirit of the Grand Inquisitor (Regarding the Ukaz of Met. Sergei Condemning the Theological Views of Fr S. Bulgakov)' (in Russian). *Put'* 49 (1937): 72–81. Trans. Stephen Janos. <www.berdyaev.com/Berdyaev/berd_lib/1935_404.html> (10 July 2018).

Bulgakov, Sergius. *Apocatastasis and Transfiguration*. Trans. Boris Jakim. New Haven, CT: Variable Press, 1995.

Compton, Madonna Sophia, *Sophia-Spirit-Mary: Sergius Bulgakov and the Patristic Roots of a Feminine Sprit*. Berkeley, CA, and Lawrence, KS: The Raphael Group, 2015.

Demacopoulos, George, and Aristotle Papanikolaou, eds. *Orthodox Constructions of the West*. New York: Fordham University Press, 2013.

Florovsky, Georges. *The Byzantine Ascetic and Spiritual Fathers* (1933). Vol. 10 of *The Collected Works of Georges Florovsky*. Vaduz: Buchervertriebsanstalt, 1987.

Florovsky, Georges. 'Russian Philosophy at the Turn of the Century' and 'The Renewal of Orthodox Theology – Florensky, Bulgakov and the Others: On the Way to a Christian Philosophy'. Oral remarks at the symposium 'Idealist Philosophy in Russia,' Aix-en-Provence, 25–29 March 1968. Transcriptions in the Georges Florovsky Papers (C0586), Manuscripts Division, Department of Rare Books and Special Collections, Princeton University Library.

Gallaher, Brandon. '"Waiting for the Barbarians": Identity and Polemicism in the Neo-Patristic Synthesis of Georges Florovsky'. *Modern Theology* 27, no. 4 (2011): 659–91.

Gavrilyuk, Paul. 'Harnack's Hellenized Christianity or Florovsky's "Sacred Hellenism": Questioning Two Metanarratives of Early Christian Engagement With Late Antique Culture'. *St Vladimir's Theological Quarterly* 54, no. 3–4 (2010): 323–44.

Gudziak, Borys. 'Towards an Analysis of the Neo-patristic Synthesis of Georges Florovsky'. *Logos* 41–2 (2000–2001): 197–238.

Kalaitzidis, Pantelis, and Nikolaos Asproulis, eds. *Neopaterikí sýnthesi í metapaterikí theología? To aítima tis theologías tis synáfeias* (Neopatristic Synthesis or Postpatristic Theology: Can Orthodox Theology Be Contextual?). Trans. Nikolaos Asproulis. Volos, GR: Ekdotike Demetriados, 2018. (English version forthcoming.)

Klimoff, Alexis. 'Georges Florovsky and the Sophiological Controversy'. *St Vladimir's Theological Quarterly* 49, no. 1–2 (2005): 67–100.

Ladouceur, Paul. 'Treasures New and Old: Landmarks of Orthodox Neopatristic Theology'. *St Vladimir's Theological Quarterly* 56, no. 2 (2012): 191–228.

Ladouceur, Paul. 'The Ways of Orthodox Theology in the West'. (Review of Ivana Noble, Kateterina Bauerova, Tim Noble and Parush Parushev, *The Ways of Orthodox Theology in the West*. (Yonkers, NY: St Vladimir's Seminary Press, 2015)). *St Vladimir's Theological Quarterly* 59, no. 4 (2015): 475–84.

Ladouceur, Paul. 'Scenes from Modern Orthodox Theology'. (Review of Ivana Noble, Kateterina Bauerova, Tim Noble and Parush Parushev, *Wrestling with the Mind of the Fathers*. Yonkers, NY: St Vladimir's Seminary Press, 2015; and Andrew Louth, *Modern Orthodox Thinkers: From the Philokalia to the Present*. London: SPCK Press, 2015). *St Vladimir's Theological Quarterly* 60, no. 4 (2016): 505–20.

Louth, Andrew, 'Some Recent Works by Christos Yannaras in English Translation'. *Modern Theology* 25, no. 2 (2009): 329–40.

Makrides, Vasilios. 'Orthodox Christianity, Modernity and Postmodernity: Overview, Analysis and Assessment'. *Religion, State and Society* 40, no. 3–4 (2012): 248–85,

[Metropolis of Piraeus (GR)]. 'Patristic Theology and Post-Patristic Heresy: Symposium of the Holy Metropolis of Piraeus'. Piraeus, GR: 2012. <https://fr.scribd.com/document/305700579/Patristic-Theology> (17 July 2018).

Mjør, Kåre Johan. 'Vasilii Zenkovskii and the History of Russian Philosophy'. *Reformulating Russia: The Cultural and Intellectual Historiography of Russian First-Wave Émigré Writers*. Leiden and Boston: Brill, 2011: 251–6.

Nichols, Aidan. *Light from the East: Authors and Themes in Orthodox Theology*. London: Sheed & Ward, 1995.

Nichols, Aidan. *Mystical Theologian: The Work of Vladimir Lossky*. Leominster, UK: Gracewing, 2017.

Noble, Ivana, Kateterina Bauerova, Tim Noble and Parush Parushev, *The Ways of Orthodox Theology in the West*. Yonkers, NY: St Vladimir's Seminary Press, 2015.

Noble, Ivana, Kateterina Bauerova, Tim Noble and Parush Parushev. *Wrestling with the Mind of the Fathers*. Yonkers, NY: St Vladimir's Seminary Press, 2015.

Papanikolaou, Aristotle, and George. E. Demacopoulos, eds. *Orthodox Readings of Augustine*. Crestwood, NY: St Vladimir's Seminary Press, 2008.

Plekon, Michael. *Living Icons: Persons of Faith in the Eastern Church*. Notre Dame, IN: University of Notre Dame Press, 2002.

Plekon, Michael. 'The Russian Religious Renaissance and Its Theological Legacy'. In *The Cambridge Companion to Orthodox Christian Theology*, eds. Mary B. Cunningham and Elizabeth Theokritoff. Cambridge: Cambridge University Press, 2008: 203–17.

Pyman, Avril. *Pavel Florensky: A Quiet Genius: The Tragic and Extraordinary Life of Russia's Unknown da Vinci*. London: Continuum, 2010.

Schmemann, Alexander. 'Roll of Honour'. *St Vladimir's Seminary Quarterly* 3, no. 1 (1953): 5–11.

Schmemann, Alexander. 'Trois images' [du père Serge Boulgakov] (Three Portraits [of Fr Sergius Bulgakov]). *Le Messager orthodoxe* 57 (1972): 2–21.

Slesinski, Robert. *Pavel Florensky: A Metaphysics of Love*. Crestwood, NY: St Vladimir's Seminary Press, 1984.

Slesinski, Robert. *The Theology of Sergius Bulgakov*. Yonkers, NY: St Vladimir's Seminary Press, 2017.

Stan, Lavinia, and Lucian Turcescu, *Religion and Politics in Post-Communist Romania*. Oxford: Oxford University Press, 2007.

[St Sergius Orthodox Theological Institute (Paris)]. *Zhivoe predanie: pravoslavie v sovremennosti* (Living Tradition: Orthodoxy in the Modern World). Paris: YMCA-Press, 1937.

Stoeckl, Kristina. *Community after Totalitarianism: The Russian Orthodox Intellectual Tradition and the Philosophical Discourse of Political Modernity*. Frankfurt am Main: Peter Lang, 2008.

Stylianopoulos, Theodore G. 'Scripture and Tradition in the Church'. In *The Cambridge Companion to Orthodox Christian Theology*, eds. Mary B. Cunningham and Elizabeth Theokritoff. Cambridge: Cambridge University Press, 2008: 21–34.

Thompson, Robert F. *From Glory to Glory: The Sophianic Vision of Fr Sergius Bulgakov*. Memphis, TN: Perennials Study Group, 2016.

Ware, Kallistos. 'Review of Panagiotis N. Trembelas, *Dogmatique de l'Église orthodoxe*'. *Eastern Churches Review* 3, no. 4 (1971): 477–80.

Ware, Kallistos. 'Dare We Hope for the Salvation of All?' In *The Inner Kingdom*. Crestwood, NY: St Vladimir's Seminary Press, 2001: 193–216.

Williams, Rowan. 'The Theology of Vladimir Nikolaievich Lossky: An Exposition and Critique'. D. Phil. thesis, University of Oxford, 1975.

Zust, Milan. *À la recherche de la vérité vivante. L'expérience religieuse de Pavel A. Florenskij (1882–1937)* (In Search of the Living Truth: The Religious Experience of Pavel A. Florensky). Rome: Lipa, 2002.

Recommended Readings

The Recommended Readings are extracts from essential works intended to illustrate key themes for each chapter. Only selections available in English are given, with an emphasis on primary sources. No selections are repeated in the Recommended Readings.

1. Prolegomena to Modern Orthodox Theology

John Behr, 'The Tradition and the Canon of the Gospel According to the Scriptures'. In *The Way to Nicea* (Crestwood, NY: St Vladimir's Seminary Press, 2001): 17–48.

John Anthony McGuckin, 'The Arian Crisis and Its Resolution', 'The Cappadocian Theological Resolution', and 'The Councils of Constantinople of 381 and 382'. In *The Path of Christianity: The First Thousand Years* (Downers Grove, IL: IVP Academic, 2017): 282–336.

John Meyendorff, 'The Christological Issue'. In *Byzantine Theology: Historical Trends and Doctrinal Themes* (New York: Fordham University Press, 1974): 32–41.

Jaroslav Pelikan, 'The Authority of the Fathers'. In *The Spirit of Eastern Christendom (600–1700)* (Chicago and London: University of Chicago Press, 1974): 8–36.

Alexander Schmemann, 'Byzantium'. In *The Historical Road of Orthodoxy* (1963) (Crestwood, NY: St Vladimir's Seminary Press, 1997): 198–270.

Philip Sherrard, 'The Breach in Christendom'. In *The Greek East and the Latin West* (1959) (Athens: Denise Harvey, 1992): 48–72.

PART I MODERN ORTHODOX THOUGHT IN HISTORICAL PERSPECTIVE

2. Theological Encounters with the West

Patriarch Jeremiah II, [Letters to the Lutheran Theologians of Tübingen, 1576–1581]. In *Augsburg and Constantinople*, trans. and ed. George Mastrantonis (Brookline, MA: Holy Cross Orthodox Press, 1982). Letter I. Sent to Tubingen [May 15] 1576 (Introduction; §§ 18; 20; 29; 30): 31; 78–81; 83–90; 102–3. Letter II. Sent to Tubingen [May 1579] ('Concerning the Procession of the Holy Spirit'; §§ 1; 4–5; 13–16; 42; Conclusion): 151–4; 162–4; 173–4; 210. Letter III. Sent to Tubingen [6 June 1581] (Introduction; §§ A; C-E): 289–90; 305–6.

Jaroslav Pelikan and Valerie Hotchkiss, eds. *Creeds and Confessions of Faith in the Christian Tradition* (New Haven, CT: Yale University Press, 2003).

Vol. 1: The *Confession* of Mark of Ephesus (1439): 380–4. The *Confession* of Cyril Lucaris (1629): 551–8. The *Confession* of Peter Moghila (1640) (QQ. 24; 102; 107): 573; 602; 604–6. The *Confession* of Dositheus (1672) (§§ 2; 3; 13; 14; 18): 615–7; 623–4; 631–5. Vol. 3: Eastern Orthodox Patriarchs, 'Response to Pope Pius IX'. *Encyclical of the Oriental Patriarchs* (1848) (§§ 1–5; 17): 266–71; 281–3.

3. Theology in Imperial Russia

Alexei Khomiakov, 'The Church Is One' (§§ 1–8) and 'Third Letter to William Palmer'. In *On Spiritual Unity: A Slavophile Reader*, eds. Boris Jakim and Robert Bird (Hudson, NY: Lindisfarne Books, 1998): 31–40; 143–53.

Ivan Kireevsky, 'New Principles in Philosophy' (extract), and 'Fragments'. In *On Spiritual Unity*, eds. Jakim and Bird: 262–73; 276–91.

Philaret of Russia (Saint), *The Longer Catechism of the Orthodox, Catholic, Eastern Church* (1830). In Philip Schaff, ed., *The Creeds of Christendom with a History and Critical Notes*, 3 Vols. (New York: Harper, 1876) (QQ. 84–6; 238–42; 252–61; 338–40; 372–7). CCEL Online Edition (http://www.ccel.org/s/schaff/creeds2) [20 September 2018]): 447–8; 466; 468–9; 479–80; 484–5.

Paul Valliere, 'Orthodoxy and the Modern World'. In *Modern Russian Theology: Bukharev, Soloviev, Bulgakov: Orthodox Theology in a New Key*, ed. Paul Valliere (Grand Rapids, MI: William B. Eerdmans, 2000): 37–72. [In the absence of English translations of the writings of Alexander Bukharev, we recommend Paul Valliere's summary and commentary of Bukharev's *On Orthodoxy in Relation to the Modern World* (1860).]

4. The Russian Religious Renaissance

Nicolas Berdyaev, 'The Russian Spiritual Renaissance at the Beginning of the 20th Century and the Journal *Put'*. For the Tenth Anniversary of *Put"*. *Put'* no. 49 (1935) (in Russian). Trans. Fr. Stephen Janos. <www.chebucto.ns.ca/Philosophy/Sui-Generis/Berdyaev/essays/rsr.htm> (13 July 2018).

Sergius Bulgakov, 'My Conversion' and 'Hagia Sophia'. In *Autobiographical Notes* (in Russian) (Paris: YMCA-Press, 1946). In *A Bulgakov Anthology*, eds. James Pain and Lev Zander (London: SPCK, 1976): 10–12; 13–14.

Sergius Bulgakov, 'A Summary of Sophiology' (c. 1936), *St Vladimir's Theological Quarterly* 49, no. 1–2 (2005): 43–6.

Fyodor Dostoyevsky, 'The Legend of the Grand Inquisitor'. In *The Brothers Karamazov* (V, 5) (1880), trans. Constance Garnett (1912) (Gutenberg EBook edition, 2009): 309–33.

Pavel Florensky, 'To the Reader' and 'Letter Six: Contradiction'. In *The Pillar and Ground of Truth* (1913), trans. Boris Jakim (Princeton, NJ: Princeton University Press, 1997): 5–9; 106–23.

Vladimir Soloviev, 'A Short Story of the Anti-Christ'. In *War, Progress, and the End of History: Three Conversations, Including a Short Story of the Anti-Christ* (1900), trans. Alexander Bakshy, rev. Thomas R. Berger (London: Hodder & Stoughton, 1915; Lindisfarne Books, 1990): 159–94.

Vladimir Soloviev, 'Lectures 11 and 12'. In *Lectures on Godmanhood* [Lectures on Divine-Humanity] (1878–1881), trans. Peter Zouboff; revised and ed. Boris Jakim. (Hudson, NY: Lindisfarne Press, 1995): 192–207.

Peter Struve, 'The Intelligentsia and the Revolution'. In Nicholas Berdyaev et al., *Vekhi / Landmarks: A Collection of Articles about the Russian Intelligentsia* (1909), eds. Marshall S. Shatz and Judith E. Zimmerman (Armonk, NY: M. E. Sharpe, 1994): 115–29.

5. The Origins and Nature of Neopatristic Theology

Nicolas Berdyaev, 'Ortodoksia and Humanness'. *Put'*, no. 53, 1937 (Review of Georges Florovsky, *The Ways of Russian Theology* (in Russian) (Paris: YMCA-Press, 1937)). Trans. Fr Steven Janos <http://www.berdyaev.com/berdiaev/berd_lib/1937_424.html> (13 July 2018).

Georges Florovsky, 'Western Influences in Russian Theology' (1936); 'Patristics and Modern Theology' (1936); 'Breaks and Links' (1937); 'The Legacy and the Task of Orthodox Theology' (1949). In *The Patristic Witness of Georges Florovsky: Essential Theological Writings*, eds. Brandon Gallaher and Paul Ladouceur ((London: T&T Clark, 2019): 129–52; 153–6; 185–92.

Vladimir Lossky, 'Introduction: Theology and Mysticism in the Tradition of the Eastern Church', and 'The Divine Darkness'. In *The Mystical Theology of the Eastern Church* (1944) (Crestwood, NY: St Vladimir's Seminary Press, 1976): 7–43.

Alexander Schmemann, 'Russian Theology 1920–1972: An Introductory Survey'. *St Vladimir's Theological Quarterly* 16, no. 4 (1972): 172–94.

6. Theology New and Old in Greece

Pantelis Kalaitzidis, 'New Trends in Greek Orthodox Theology: Challenges in the Movement towards a Genuine Renewal and Christian Unity'. *Scottish Journal of Theology* 67, no. 2 (2014): 127–64.

John Romanides, 'The Ancestral Sin'. In *The Ancestral Sin* (1965) (Ridgewood, NJ: Zephyr, 2002): 155–69.

Norman Russell, 'Modern Greek Theologians and the Greek Fathers'. *Philosophy & Theology* 18, no. 1 (2006): 77–91.

Petros Vassiliadis, 'Greek Theology in the Making, Trends and Facts in the 80s – Vision for the 90s'. *St Vladimir's Theological Quarterly* 35, no. 1 (1991): 33–52.

Christos Yannaras, 'Theology in Present-Day Greece'. *St Vladimir's Theological Quarterly* 17, no. 4 (1972): 195–214.

John Zizioulas, 'From Mask to Person: The Birth of an Ontology of Personhood'. In *Being and Communion: Studies in Personhood and the Church* (Crestwood, NY: St Vladimir's Seminary Press, 1984): 27–48.

7. Theology in Romania

Athanasios Giocas and Paul Ladouceur, 'The Burning Bush Group and Father André Scrima in Romanian Spirituality'. *Greek Orthodox Theological Review* 52, no. 1–4 (2007) (published in 2010): 37–62.

Serafim Joanta, 'Romanian Hesychasm of the 20th Century'. In *Treasures of Romanian Christianity: Hesychastic Tradition and Culture* (Toronto, ON: Cross Meridian, 2013): 247–76.

Dumitru Staniloae, 'Natural Revelation'. In *The Experience of God: Orthodox Dogmatic Theology*, (vol. 1) (Brookline, MA: Holy Cross Press, 2000): 1–14.

Dumitru Staniloae, 'Creation: The Visible World'. In *The World: Creation and Deification* (Vol. 2 of *The Experience of God*) (Brookline, MA: Holy Cross Press, 2002): 1–20.

8. Tradition and the Restoration of Patristic Thought

Sergius Bulgakov, 'Dogma and Dogmatic Theology' (1937). In *Tradition Alive: On the Church and the Christian Life in Our Time*, ed. Michael Plekon (Lanham, MA: Rowan & Littlefield, 2003): 67–80.

Pantelis Kalaitzidis, 'From the "Return to the Fathers" to the Need for a Modern Orthodox Theology'. *St Vladimir's Theological Quarterly* 54, no. 1 (2010): 5–36.

Vladimir Lossky, 'Tradition and Traditions' (1952). In *In the Image and Likeness of God* (Yonkers, NY: St Vladimir's Seminary Press, 1985): 141–68.

Andrew Louth, 'Is Development of Doctrine a Valid Category for Orthodox Theology?' In *Orthodoxy and Western Culture, A Collection of Essays Honoring Jaroslav Pelikan on His Eightieth Birthday*, eds. Valerie Hotchkiss and Patrick Henry (Crestwood, NY: St Vladimir's Seminary Press, 2006): 45–63.

Andrew Louth, 'What Is Theology? What Is Orthodox Theology?' *St Vladimir's Theological Quarterly* 51, no. 4 (2007): 435–44.

Paul Valliere, 'The Limits of Tradition'. In *Modern Russian Theology: Bukharev, Soloviev, Bulgakov: Orthodox Theology in a New Key* (Grand Rapids, MI: Eerdmans, 2000): 373–403.

Kallistos Ware, 'Orthodox Theology Today: Trends and Tasks'. *International Journal for the Study of the Christian Church* 12, no. 2 (2012): 105–21.

PART II THEMES AND CONFLICTS IN MODERN ORTHODOX THEOLOGY

9. God and Creation

Sergius Bulgakov, 'The Divine and the Creaturely Sophia'. In *Sophia, The Wisdom of God: An Outline of Sophiology* (1937) (Hudson, NY: Lindisfarne Press, 1993): 54–81.

Fyodor Dostoyevsky, [Zossima and the Peasant Boy] 'In my youth, long ago, I travelled…' (VI, 2, b); [After the Duel] '"Gentlemen", I cried suddenly…' (VI, 2, c); [Alyosha and the

Starry Night] 'Something glowed in Alyosha's heart...' VII, 4). *The Brothers Karamazov* (1880), trans. Constance Garnett (1912) (Gutenberg EBook edition, 2009): 371–2; 379; 461–3.

Pavel Florensky, 'Letter 10: Sophia'. In *The Pillar and Ground of the Truth: An Essay in Orthodox Theodicy in Twelve Letters* (1914) (Princeton: Princeton University Press, 1997): 231–83.

Georges Florovsky, 'Creation and Createdness' (1928). In *The Patristic Witness of Georges Florovsky: Essential Theological Writings*, eds. Brandon Gallaher and Paul Ladouceur (London: T&T Clark, 2019): 33–63.

John Meyendorff, 'An Existential Theology: Essence and Energy'. In *A Study of Gregory Palamas* (1959) (London: Faith Press, 1964): 202–27.

Alexander Schmemann, 'The World as Sacrament'. In *Church, World, Mission: Reflections on Orthodoxy in the West* (Crestwood, NY: St Vladimir's Seminary Press, 1979): 217–27.

Vladimir Soloviev, 'The Trinitarian Principle and Its Social Application' (extracts from *Russia and the Universal Church* [1889]); and 'Three Encounters' (1898). In *Divine Sophia: The Wisdom Writings of Vladimir Solovyov*, trans. and ed. Judith Deutsch Kornblatt (Ithaca and London: Cornell University Press, 2009): 192–210; 264–72.

Dumitru Staniloae, 'The Contemplation of God in Creation'. In *Orthodox Spirituality: A Practical Guide for the Faithful and a Definitive Manual for the Scholar* (South Canaan, PA: St Tikhon's Seminary Press, 2002): 203–23.

Kallistos Ware, 'God Hidden and Revealed: The Apophatic Way and the Essence-Energies Distinction'. *Eastern Churches Review* 7, no. 2 (1975): 125–36.

Kallistos Ware, 'Through Creation to the Creator'. *Ecotheology*, 2 (London: Friends of the Centre, 1996): 18–26.

John Zizioulas, 'Man the Priest of Creation: A Response to the Ecological Problem'. In *Living Orthodoxy in the Modern World: Orthodox Christianity & Society*, eds. Andrew Walker and Costa Carras (Crestwood, NY: St Vladimir's Seminary Press, 1996): 178–216.

10. Divine-Humanity, Personhood and Human Rights

Nicolas Berdyaev, 'Man'. In *The Destiny of Man* (London: Geoffrey Bles, 1937): 45–50.

Nicolas Berdyaev, 'Personality'. In *Slavery and Freedom* (London: Geoffrey Bles, 1943): 20–37.

Sergius Bulgakov, 'The Image of God in the Human Being' and 'The Likeness of God in the Human Being'. In *Unfading Light – Compilations and Speculations* (1917) (Grand Rapids, MI: Eerdmans, 2012): 285–94; 315–18.

Pavel Florensky, ['Person and Thing']. From 'Letter 4: The Light of the Truth'. In *The Pillar and the Ground of Truth* (1913) (Princeton, NJ: Princeton University Press, 1997): 58–62.

Vigen Guroian, 'Human Rights and Modern Western Faith: An Orthodox Christian Assessment'. *Journal of Religious Ethics* 26, no. 2 (1998): 241–7.

Stanley Harakas, 'Human Rights: An Eastern Orthodox Perspective'. *Journal of Ecumenical Studies* 19, no. 3 (1982): 13–24.

Vladimir Lossky, 'The Theological Notion of the Human Person'. In *In the Image and Likeness of God* (Crestwood, NY: St Vladimir's Seminary Press, 1974): 111–23.

Stelios Ramfos, 'The Person and Relation' and 'Collective Identity and the Person'. In *Yearning for the One: Chapters in the Inner Life of the Greeks* (2000) (Brookline, MA: Holy Cross Orthodox Press, 2011): 296–320.

Russian Orthodox Church, 'Basic Teaching on Human Dignity, Freedom and Human Rights' (2008). <https://mospat.ru/en/documents/dignity-freedom-rights> (16 July 2018).

Kallistos Ware, '"In the Image and Likeness": The Uniqueness of the Human Person'. In *Personhood. Orthodox Christianity and the Connection between Body, Mind and Soul*, ed. J. B. Chirban (London: Bergin & Garvey, 1996): 1–13.

Christos Yannaras, 'The Masks of Morality and the Ethos of the Person'. In *The Freedom of Morality* (Crestwood, NY: St Vladimir's Seminary Press, 1984): 13–24.

Christos Yannaras, 'Human Rights and the Orthodox Church'. In *The Orthodox Churches in a Pluralistic World*, ed. Emanuel Clapsis (Geneva: WCC, 2004): 83–9.

Christos Yannaras, 'The Ecstatic Character of Personhood'. In *Person and Eros* (Brookline, MA: Holy Cross Orthodox Press, 2007): 5–23; 295–300.

Anastasios Yannoulatos, 'Orthodoxy and Human Rights'. In *Facing the World: Orthodox Christian Essays on Global Concerns* (Crestwood, NY: St Vladimir's Seminary Press, 2003): 49–78.

John Zizioulas, 'On Being a Person: Towards an Ontology of Personhood'. In *Communion and Otherness: Further Studies in Personhood and the Church* (London: T&T Clark, 2007): 99–112.

11. The Church of Christ

Nicholas Afanasiev, ['Conclusion'], 'The Church Which Presides In Love' (1963). In *The Primacy of Peter: Essays in Ecclesiology and the Early Church*, ed. John Meyendorff (Crestwood, NY: St Vladimir's Seminary Press, 1992): 140–3.

Nicholas Afanasiev, 'The Royal Priesthood' and 'Those Who Preside in the Lord'. In *The Church of the Holy Spirit* (1971) (Notre Dame, IN: University of Notre Dame Press, 2007): 9–21; 133–47.

Sergius Bulgakov, 'The Church' and 'The Nature of Church Tradition'. *The Orthodox Church* (1935) (Crestwood, NY: St Vladimir's Seminary Press, 1988): 1–8; 26–35.

Paul Evdokimov, 'The Universal Priesthood of the Laity in the Eastern Church Tradition'. In *The Ages of the Spiritual Life* (Crestwood, NY: St Vladimir's Seminary Press, 1998): 227–43.

Paul Evdokimov, 'The Church and Society: The Social Dimension of Orthodox Ecclesiology'. In *In the World, of the Church: A Paul Evdokimov Reader* (Crestwood, NY: St Vladimir's Seminary Press, 2001): 61–94.

Georges Florovsky, 'The Limits of the Church' (1933); 'Sobornost: The Catholicity of the Church' (1934); and 'The Body of the Living Christ: An Orthodox Interpretation of the Church' (1948). In *The Patristic Witness of Georges Florovsky: Essential Theological Writings*, eds. Brandon Gallaher and Paul Ladouceur (London: T&T Clark, 2019): 247–56; 257–71; 273–77.

Alexei Khomiakov, 'The Church Is One' [c. 1850]. In *On Spiritual Unity: A Slavophile Reader*, trans. and eds. Boris Jakim and Robert Bird (Hudson, NY: Lindisfarne Books, 1998): 31–53.

John Meyendorff, 'Ecclesiastical Regionalism: Structures of Communion or Cover for Separatism?' In *The Byzantine Legacy in the Orthodox Church* (Crestwood, NY: St Vladimir's Seminary Press, 1982): 217–33.

John Meyendorff, 'One Bishop in One City'. In *Catholicity and the Church* (Crestwood, NY: St Vladimir's Seminary Press, 1983): 107–18.

Alexander Schmemann, 'The Underlying Question' and 'Freedom in the Church'. In *Church, World, Mission: Reflections on Orthodox in the West* (Crestwood, NY: St Vladimir's Seminary Press, 1979): 7–24; 179–91.

Vladimir Soloviev, 'The Church as a Universal Society'. In *Russia and the Universal Church* (1888) (London: Geoffrey Bles/Centenary Press, 1948): 99–108.

John Zizioulas, 'The Local Church in a Perspective of Communion'. In *Being as Communion: Studies in Personhood and the Church* (Crestwood, NY: St Vladimir's Seminary Press, 1985): 247–60.

12. Ecumenical Theology and Religious Diversity

Sergius Bulgakov, 'St Peter and St John' (1926). In *A Bulgakov Anthology*, eds James Pain and Nicolas Zernov (London: SPCK, 1976): 79–85.

Sergius Bulgakov, 'By Jacob's Well – John 4:23 (On the Actual Unity of the Divided Church in Faith, Prayer and Sacraments)' (1933). In *Tradition Alive: On the Church and the Christian Life in Our Time-Readings from the Eastern Church*, ed. Michael Plekon (Lanham, MD: Sheed & Ward, 2003): 55–65.

Ecumenical Patriarchate, 'Encyclical: "Unto the Churches of Christ Everywhere"' (1920). In *Orthodox Visions of Ecumenism: Statements, Messages and Reports on the Ecumenical Movement, 1902–1992*, ed. Gennadios Limouris (Geneva: WCC Publications, 1994): 9–11.

Georges Florovsky, 'Confessional Loyalty in the Ecumenical Movement' (1951) and 'The Ecumenical Dialogue'. In *The Patristic Witness of Georges Florovsky: Essential Theological Writings*, eds. Brandon Gallaher and Paul Ladouceur (London: T&T Clark, 2019): 279–88; 303–7.

Peter Heers, 'The Mystery of Baptism and the Unity of the Church: The Idea of "Baptismal Unity" and Its Acceptance by Orthodox Ecumenists' (2004). <www.pravoslavie.ru/english/80888.htm> (15 July 2018).

Holy and Great Council of the Orthodox Church, 'Relations of the Orthodox Church with the Rest of the Christian World' (2016). <www.holycouncil.org/-/rest-of-christian-world> (15 July 2018).

Georges Khodr, 'Christianity in a Pluralistic World: The Economy of the Holy Spirit'. *The Ecumenical Review* 23, no. 2 (1971): 118–28.

Paul Ladouceur, 'On Ecumenoclasm: Anti-Ecumenism in Orthodox Theology'. *St Vladimir's Theological Quarterly* 61, no. 3 (2017): 323–56.

Justin Popovich (Saint), 'Humanistic Ecumenism'. In *The Orthodox Church and Ecumenism* (1974) (Birmingham: Lazarica Press, 2000): 153–76.

Seraphim Rose, 'Introduction'. In *Orthodoxy and the Religion of the Future* (Platina, CA: St. Herman of Alaska Brotherhood, 1975): xxiii–xxxv.

Vitaly Ustinov (Archbishop), 'Report to the Sobor of Bishops of the Russian Orthodox Church Outside of Russia' (1967–1968).<orthodoxinfo.com/ecumenism/vitaly.aspx> (15.07.2018).

Anastasios Yannoulatos, 'A Theological Approach to Understanding Other Religions' and 'Globalization and Religious Experience'. In *Facing the World: Orthodox Christian Essays on Global Concerns* (Crestwood, NY: WCC/St Vladimir's Seminary Press, 2003): 127–53; 179–99.

13. The Christification of Life

Paul Evdokimov, 'Ecclesia Domestica' (Paper Presented at the Paris Consultation, July 1962). In *A Voice for Women*, ed. Suzannah Herzel (Geneva: World Council of Churches, 1981): 174–83.

Paul Evdokimov, 'Interiorized Monasticism'. In *The Ages of the Spiritual Life* (1964) (Crestwood, NY: St Vladimir's Seminary Press, 1985): 135–54.

Paul Evdokimov, 'Love and the Sacrament of Love'. In *The Sacrament of Love: The Nuptial Mystery in the Light of the Orthodox Tradition* (1944) (Crestwood, NY: St Vladimir's Seminary Press, 1985): 105–28.

A Monk of the Eastern Church [Lev Gillet], 'Appendix: Thirty Years Have Elapsed'. In *Orthodox Spirituality: An Outline of the Orthodox Ascetical and Mystical Tradition* (Crestwood, NY: St Vladimir's Seminary Press, 1987): 105–11.

Vasileios Gondidakis (Archimandrite), 'The Divine Liturgy as a Theological Rite'. In *Hymn of Entry: Liturgy and Life in the Orthodox Church* (1974) (Crestwood, NY: St Vladimir's Seminary Press, 1984): 57–79.

Paul Ladouceur, 'In My Father's House There Are Many Mansions (Jn 14:2): New Institutions in Modern Orthodox Spirituality'. *St Vladimir's Theological Quarterly* 55, no. 4 (2011): 439–83.

Alexander Schmemann, 'The Life of the World', and 'Worship in a Secular Age'. In *For the Life of the World: Sacraments and Orthodoxy* (1966) (Crestwood, NY: St Vladimir's Seminary Press, 1973): 11–22; 117–34.

Vera Shevzov, 'Letting the People into Church: Reflections on Orthodoxy and Community in Late Imperial Russia'. In *Orthodox Russia: Belief and Practice under the Tsars*, eds. Valerie Kivelson and Robert Greene (University Park, PE: Pennsylvania State University Press, 2003): 59–77.

Mother Maria Skobtsova, 'Types of Religious Life'. In *Mother Maria, Essential Writings* (Maryknoll, NY: Orbis Books, 2003): 140–86.

14. Social and Political Theology

Sergius Bulgakov, 'An Urgent Task' (1905). In *A Revolution of the Spirit: Crisis of Value in Russia, 1890–1924*, eds. Bernice Glatzer Rosenthal and Martha Bohachevsky-Chomiak (New York: Fordham University Press, 1990): 137–59.

Sergius Bulgakov, 'Social Teaching in Modern Russian Orthodox Theology' (1934). In *Sergii Bulgakov: Towards a Russian Political Theology*, ed. Rowan Williams (Edinburgh: T&T Clark, 1999): 269–92.

Georges Florovsky, 'The Social Problem in the Eastern Orthodox Church' (1950). In *Christianity and Culture*, Vol. 2 of *The Collected Works of Georges Florovsky* (Belmont, MA: Nordland, 1974): 131–42.

Holy and Great Council of the Orthodox Church, 'The Mission of the Orthodox Church in Today's World' and 'Encyclical of the Holy and Great Council of the Orthodox Church' (Crete GR, 2016). <https://www.holycouncil.org/home> (16 July 2018).

Pantelis Kalaitzidis, 'Why Has Orthodoxy Not Developed a Political or Liberation Theology?' *Orthodoxy and Political Theology* (Geneva: WCC Publications, 2012): 65–80.

Aristotle Papanikolaou, 'The Politics of Divine-Human Communion'. In *The Mystical as Political: Democracy and Non-Radical Orthodoxy* (Notre Dame, IN: University of Notre Dame Press, 2012): 193–200.

Russian Orthodox Church, 'Basis of the Social Concept of the Russian Orthodox Church' (2001). <www.mospat.ru/en/documents/social-concept> (16 July 2018).

Maria Skobtsova (Saint Maria of Paris), 'The Second Gospel Commandment' and 'The Mysticism of Human Communion'. In *Mother Maria Skobtsova: Essential Writings* (Maryknoll, NY: Orbis Books, 2003): 45–60; 75–83.

Vladimir Soloviev, 'A Preliminary Conception of the Moral Meaning of Life' and 'Pity and Altruism'. In *The Justification of the Good: An Essay on Moral Philosophy* (1897), ed. Thomas Nemeth (Cham, CH: Springer International Publishing, 2015): xv–xxxiii; 59–76.

Kristina Stoeckl, Ingeborg Gabriel and Aristotle Papanikolaou, 'Introduction'. *Political Theologies in Orthodox Christianity: Common Challenges and Divergent Positions* (London: T&T Clark, 2017): 1–11.

Kristina Stoeckl, 'Modernity and Political Theologies'. In *Political Theologies in Orthodox Christianity: Common Challenges and Divergent Positions*, eds. Kristina Stoeckl, Ingeborg Gabriel and Aristotle Papanikolaou (London: T&T Clark, 2017): 15–24.

Paul Valliere, 'Introduction to the Modern Orthodox Tradition'. In *The Teachings of Modern Orthodox Christianity on Law, Politics, and Human Nature*, eds. John Witte, Jr. and Frank S. Alexander (New York: Columbia University Press, 2007): 1–32.

15. Onomatodoxy: The Name-of-God Conflict

Virtually none of the Russian primary material concerning the onomatodoxy quarrel is available in English translation. Hieromonk Hilarion Domratchev's book *On the Mountains of the Caucasus* (1907), which triggered the quarrel, and also the most important study of the quarrel, that of Metropolitan Hilarion Alfeyev, have been published in French (see the Selected Bibliography above for full references.) Of the major theologians who have addressed onomatodoxy, only the relevant writings of Archimandrite Sophrony (Sakharov) and some by Sergius Bulgakov are translated into English. For this reason, the recommended readings here consist mostly of secondary sources in English.

Sergius Bulgakov, 'The Name of God'. In *Icons and the Name of God* (1931; 1953). (Grand Rapids, MI: Eerdmans, 2012): 115–66.

Tom E. Dykstra, 'Name as Sacrament' and 'Epilogue'. 'Heresy on Mt. Athos: Conflict over the Name of God among Russian Monks and Hierarchs, 1912–1914' (M.Div. thesis, St Vladimir's Orthodox Theological Seminary, 1988). <http://www.pravoslav.de/imiaslavie/english/dykstra/dikstra.htm> (16 July 2018): 133–49.

Helena Gourko, 'Divine Onomatology of Imyaslavie'. In *Divine Onomatology: Name of God in Imyaslavie, Symbolism, and Deconstruction* (Ph.D. thesis, Boston University, 2005) (UMI Microform 3157373): 154–290.

Scott Kenworthy, 'Debating the Theology of the Name in Post-Soviet Russia: Metropolitan Ilarion Alfeev and Sergei Khoruzhii'. In *Orthodox Paradoxes: Heterogeneities and Complexities in Contemporary Russian Orthodoxy*, ed. Katya Tolstaya (Leiden and Boston: Brill, 2014): 250–64.

Paul Ladouceur, 'The Name-of-God Conflict in Orthodox Theology'. *St Vladimir's Theological Quarterly* 56, no. 4 (2012): 415–36.

Vladimir Moss, 'On the Name of God: Against the Name-Worshipping Heresy of Fr A. Bulatovich and Fr G. Louri' (2007). <www.orthodoxchristianbooks.com/books/> (16 July 2018).

Sophrony (Sakharov) (Archimandrite), 'The Jesus Prayer', and 'The Jesus Prayer: Method'. In *His Life Is Mine* (Crestwood, NY: St Vladimir's Seminary Press, 1977): 99–120.
Sophrony (Sakharov) (Archimandrite), 'Prayer: The Way to Knowledge'. In *On Prayer* (Crestwood, NY: St Vladimir's Seminary Press, 1998): 33–60.

16. The Ordination of Women

Elisabeth Behr-Sigel, 'The Otherness of Men and Women in the Context of a Christian Civilization' and 'Woman Is Also Made in the Image of God'. In *The Ministry of Women in the Church* (1987) (Crestwood, NY: St Vladimir's Seminary Press, 1991): 25–80; 81–92.
Elisabeth Behr-Sigel, 'The Ordination of Women: Also a Question for the Orthodox Churches'. In *The Ordination of Women in the Orthodox Church*, eds. Elisabeth Behr-Sigel and Kallistos Ware (Geneva: WCC Publications, 2000): 11–48.
Elisabeth Behr-Sigel, 'Jesus and Women'. In *Discerning the Signs of the Times: The Vision of Elisabeth Behr-Sigel* (1987) (Crestwood, NY: St Vladimir's Seminary Press, 2001): 95–100.
Nicolae Chitescu, 'The Ordination of Women: A Comment on the Attitude of the Orthodox Church'. In *Concerning the Ordination of Women* (Geneva: World Council of Churches, 1964): 57–60.
Ecumenical Patriarchate, 'Conclusions of the Consultation'. In *The Place of Woman in the Orthodox Church and the Question of the Ordination of Women. Inter-Orthodox Symposium, Rhodos, Greece, 30 October–7* November 1988, ed. Gennadios Limouris (Katerini, GR: Ecumenical Patriarchate and Tertios Publications, 1992): 21–34.
Paul Evdokimov, 'Feminism: Its Truths and Lies' and 'The Theotokos: Archetype of the Feminine'. In *Woman and the Salvation of the World: A Christian Anthropology on the Charisms of Women* (1958) (Crestwood, NY: St Vladimir's Seminary Press, 1994): 177–86; 211–25.
Lawrence Farley, 'The Leadership of Men'. In *Feminism and Tradition: Quiet Reflections on Ordination and Communion* (Crestwood, NY: St Vladimir's Seminary Press, 2012): 85–136.
Thomas Hopko, 'Presbyter/Bishop: A Masculine Ministry'. In *Women and the Priesthood* (1983), ed. Thomas Hopko (Crestwood, NY: St Vladimir's Seminary Press, 1999): 139–63.
Georges Khodre, 'The Ordination of Women: A Comment'. In *Concerning the Ordination of Women* (Geneva: World Council of Churches, 1964): 61–4.
Paul Ladouceur, 'Review: Lawrence Farley, *Feminism and Tradition: Quiet Reflections on Ordination and Communion*'. *St Vladimir's Theological Quarterly* 60, no. 3 (2016): 415–21.
Paul Ladouceur, 'Christ, the Fathers and Feminism: Dialogue with Fr. Lawrence Farley'. *St Vladimir's Theological Quarterly* 62, no. 3 (2018): 287–95.
Alexander Schmemann, 'Concerning Women's Ordination: Letter to an Episcopal Friend'. *St Vladimir's Theological Quarterly* 17, no. 3 (1973): 239–43.
Constance J. Tarasar and Irina Kirillova, eds., *Orthodox Women: Their Role and Participation in the Orthodox Church. Report on the Consultation of Orthodox Women September 11-17, 1976, Agapia, Romania* (Geneva: World Council of Churches, 1977). Elisabeth Behr-Sigel, 'The Meaning of the Participation of Women in the Life of the Church', and Evangelos Theodorou, 'The Ministry of Deaconesses in the Greek Orthodox Church': 17–29; 37–43.
Kallistos Ware, 'Man, Woman and the Priesthood of Christ'. In *Women and the Priesthood*, ed. Thomas Hopko (Crestwood, NY: St Vladimir's Seminary Press, 1999): 5–53.

PART III ASSESSMENTS AND CONCLUSIONS

17. Light and Shadows in Modern Orthodox Theology

and

18. The Living Tradition of Orthodox Theology

Matthew Baker, 'Neopatristic Synthesis and Ecumenism: Towards the "Reintegration" of Christian Tradition'. In *Eastern Orthodox Encounters of Identity and Otherness: Values, Self-Reflection, Dialogue*, eds. Andrii Krawchuk and Thomas Bremer (New York: Palgrave-MacMillan, 2014): 235–60.

John Behr, 'Passing Beyond the Neo-Patristic Synthesis'; Pantelis Kalaitzidis' 'Toward a "Post-Patristic" Theology?"; Andrew Louth, 'The Authority of the Fathers in Post-Patristic Orthodox Theology'; and Aristotle Papanikolaou, 'Orthodox Liberalism: Political Theology after the Empires'. In *Neopaterikí sýnthesi í metapaterikí theología? To aítima tis theologías tis synáfeias* (Neopatristic Synthesis or Postpatristic Theology: Can Orthodox Theology Be Contextual) [Proceedings of a conference held at the Volos Academy of Theological Studies, 3–6 June 2010], eds. Pantelis Kalaitzidis and Nikolaos Asproulis (Volos, GR: Ekdotike Demetriados, 2018). (English version forthcoming.)

George Demacopoulos and Aristotle Papanikolaou, 'Orthodox Naming of the Other: A Postcolonial Approach'; and Pantelis Kalaitzidis, 'The Image of the West in Contemporary Greek Theology'. In *Orthodox Constructions of the West*, eds George Demacopoulos and Aristotle Papanikolaou (New York: Fordham University Press, 2013): 1–22; 142–60.

Brandon Gallaher, '"Waiting for the Barbarians": Identity and Polemicism in the Neo-Patristic Synthesis of Georges Florovsky'. *Modern Theology* 27, no. 4 (2011): 659–91.

Hierotheos Vlachos (Metropolitan), 'Post-Patristic Theology from a Church Perspective'. In *Patristic Theology and Post-Patristic Heresy: Symposium of the Holy Metropolis of Piraeus* [ed. Metropolis of Piraeus] (Piraeus, GR: 2012): 92–146. <https://fr.scribd.com/document/305700579/Patristic-Theology> (17 July 2018).

Paul Ladouceur, 'Treasures New and Old: Landmarks of Orthodox Neopatristic Theology'. *St Vladimir's Theological Quarterly* 56, no. 2 (2012): 191–228.

Michael Plekon, 'The Russian Religious Renaissance and Its Theological Legacy'. In *The Cambridge Companion to Orthodox Christian Theology*, eds. Mary B. Cunningham and Elizabeth Theokritoff (Cambridge University Press, 2008): 203–17.

Index